S0-APN-188

MAINCURRENTS IN MASS COMMUNICATIONS

SECOND EDITION

MAINCURRENTS IN MASS COMMUNICATIONS

WARREN K. AGEE
University of Georgia

PHILLIP H. AULT
South Bend Tribune

EDWIN EMERY
University of Minnesota

1817

HARPER & ROW, PUBLISHERS, New York
Cambridge, Philadelphia, San Francisco,
London, Mexico City, São Paulo, Singapore, Sydney

Illustration Credits

p. 1: Orban/Robert, Sygma; pp. 39, 75, 83, 201, 303, 307: AP/Wide World; p. 94: Lopez, NYT Pictures; p. 133: Paul H. Brockmann; p. 169: Maloney, San Francisco Chronicle; p. 186; Kagan, Monkmeyer Press Photo; p. 226; Leinwand, Monkmeyer Press Photo; p. 257: Taylor/Sygma; p. 337: © McNally, Wheeler Pictures; p. 362: Forsyth, Monkmeyer Press Photo.

Sponsoring Editor: Barbara Cinquegrani
Project Editor: Jo-Ann Goldfarb
Text Design: Lucy Krikorian
Cover Design: Edward Smith Design, Inc.
Photo Research: Mira Schachne
Production Manager: Jeanie Berke
Production Assistant: Paula Roppolo
Compositor: ComCom Division of Haddon Craftsmen, Inc.
Printer and Binder: R. R. Donnelley & Sons Company
Cover Printer: Lynn Art

MAINCURRENTS IN MASS COMMUNICATIONS, Second Edition

Library of Congress Cataloging in Publication Data

Maincurrents in mass communications/[compiled by] Warren K. Agee, Phillip H. Ault, Edwin Emery. —2nd ed.
p. cm.
Includes index.
ISBN 0-06-040185-0
1. Mass media—United States. 2. Mass media—Moral and ethical aspects. 3. Mass media—United States—Technological innovations. I. Agee, Warren Kendall. II. Ault, Phillip H. III. Emery, Edwin.
P92.U5M274 1989
001.51'0973—dc19 88-28239
CIP

89 90 91 9 8 7 6 5 4 3 2

CONTENTS

PREFACE

Much as a navigator's map records the shallows, depths, and dangerous eddies of the sea, this second edition of *Maincurrents in Mass Communications* charts the ever-changing trends in mass communications. Growing concerns about ethics, spectacular developments in technology, and debates on pornography, mass ownership, and the media's impact on personal privacy—all these and many other issues come under scrutiny in its pages.

Particular attention is focused on the ethical problems the media face. Part Two, "Ethical and Legal Challenges," has been expanded substantially to include provocative and sometimes conflicting points of view on numerous aspects of the subject.

The commentaries in this book come from both inside and outside the media.

Articles and speeches by prominent media personalities—among them Charles Kuralt, Katharine Graham, Garry Trudeau, Katherine W. Fanning, and Christie Hefner—discuss contemporary issues from the professional's point of view. Question-and-answer interviews with Rupert Murdoch, Howard Cosell, and Jim Lehrer of the MacNeill-Lehrer television news program provide further opinions by insiders.

Commenting on the media from outside, as expert observers unburdened by the heavy responsibility and sometimes unavoidable short-range vision of daily media operations, are contributors from the academic world and critics from the business and political spheres.

If the contributors are an eclectic group, so are the selections. They reflect the complex nature and universal reach of today's mass media. Larry Speakes gives a report card on the White House reporters with whom he jousted as President Reagan's spokesman. Michael J. O'Neill provides a profound examination of the power of the press. Jim Ottaway Jr., publisher of a newspaper group, condemns excessive profit making by some other publishers. The excesses of television evangelists come under examination for their impact on religion as a whole. Stevie Wonder records by satellite, and a weekend is lost to music videos.

Never has the public been deluged with information as it is today. Computers, satellite transmission of words and images, videotape in a multitude of uses—these three techniques alone have brought an enormous expansion of information delivery, and their potential is still only partially realized.

How can one make sense of all this? How can a student sort the mass of words, pictures, and impressions into coherent patterns and recognize the social and ethical problems created, or aggravated, by these physical developments?

We hope that the essays, interviews, surveys, commentaries, speeches, and descriptions in this book—more than 70 in all—will clarify much of what is happening in mass communications. *Maincurrents in Mass Communications* is organized to achieve that goal. It is divided into six parts, each with an introductory essay, as follows:

Part One	The Media's Role in Society
Part Two	Ethical and Legal Challenges
Part Three	The Technology Revolution
Part Four	The Communicators
Part Five	Media Trends and Techniques
Part Six	Living in the Information Society

To understand contemporary mass communications, a student first needs a realization that the diverse elements cannot be packaged into neatly divided compartments. Newspapers, radio and television, magazines and books, and motion pictures do not operate in isolation. They are interrelated financially, technically, legally, and ethically. Second, one must realize that as new methods of mass communications develop, earlier ones do not vanish. The process is supplementary, not restrictive. Financial restrictions, habit, and uncertainty are delaying factors. Leaders of the old forms slowly overcome their fears of the new and adapt their craft to meet the changing circumstances.

When commercial radio came on the American scene after World War I, gloom dispensers predicted that its quick, easy way of delivering news and entertainment would doom newspapers. When television arrived after World War II, another generation of observers said radio was doomed, that it could not compete with pictures on a screen. Yet today newspapers, radio, and television all thrive.

From a vantage point 40 years later, it is difficult to realize that when television first entered American homes, many newspapers refused to publish TV logs because they feared they would be helping a competitor. Motion picture studios forbade their film stars to appear on television shows for the same reason.

American media operate to make a profit, however, and money has a way of breaking down barriers. Publishers added TV logs when they found that the listings helped to sell newspapers. Many newspapers ran their own television and radio stations. After a while, the film studios found that they could make millions of dollars by selling their old movies to television; now the motion picture and television industries are irretrievably intertwined. The melding continues. During the past decade, the expanding cable television industry cut sharply into the audience and profits of the three major television networks. The networks responded by obtaining a financial share in cable operations. Then, when the spectacular growth of videocassettes in the early 1980s took a share of the cable TV audience, cable and motion picture companies entered the field of home videocassette distribution.

The point is obvious: The mass communications industries are so interrelated that they must be examined together. Although their operating methods differ in detail, the media share problems of public perception, ethical standards, good taste, legal rights, and technology. The powerful group of conglomerate corporations that own newspapers, magazines, book publishing houses, and radio and television stations—along with manufacturing companies, insurance firms, and other unrelated commercial operations—reflects this fact. Concentration of ownership in the media is one of the problems this book examines.

Part One explores an issue basic to the entire field of mass communications: Precisely what is the role of the media in contemporary society? Are the media too powerful, arrogant, and insensitive to the rights and feelings of individuals, as critics contend? The part opens with thoughtful examinations of criticisms by two prominent editors, Michael O'Neill, former president of the American Society of Newspaper Editors, and Katherine Fanning, editor of the *Christian Science Monitor,* discussing newspapers, and Mark S. Fowler, former chairman of the Federal Communications Commission, chiding television.

The impact of television on society is scrutinized in a scholarly manner by David Marc and in caustic tones by Norman Corwin, a longtime TV writer and producer.

The following section, "Media and Democracy," focuses on how mass communication systems function as transmission belts in the democratic process. The selections include a research study explaining how the media set the agenda for national political debate, as well as a look at media attitudes toward President Reagan before and during the Iranscam scandal that shook his administration.

Finally, the role of the media in time of war, in the expression of dissent, and international communication comes under examination.

Part Two, "Ethical and Legal Challenges," addresses another critical aspect of media conduct, invasion of privacy. The accusation of trampling on the privacy of others often is leveled against newspapers and television in particular. What are the boundaries of privacy in the balancing act between the public's right to know and the individual's right to keep personal affairs private? How are the decisions made? Two reports from the American Society of Newspaper Editors, a survey by Philip Meyer and case studies by editors describing difficult ethical decisions, provide some answers to these questions. Another selection addresses the question "Should the names of AIDS victims be published?"

The problem of pornography, which received fresh attention with publication of the Meese commission's controversial report, is discussed pro and con. Key excerpts from the commission's report are followed by a rebuttal by Christie Hefner, president of Playboy Enterprises, Inc.

Part Three examines the upheaval caused by technology. Selections describe the video revolution and the rapid expansion in the use of personal computers, including computer networking, sometimes called interactive journalism. Jay Black points out ethical problems created by these new techniques. A description of a transcontinental recording session employing satellite transmission and fiber optics illustrates the use of those methods.

Part Four, "The Communicators," is concerned with people—the individuals who use the technology. A survey examines the poor record of newsrooms in minority employment, and a selection by Félix Gutiérrez describes the marketing of news to minorities in America.

Although women play a large and growing role on media staffs, relatively few hold high positions. Katharine Graham, chairman of the board of the Washington Post Company, talks frankly about the problem in a speech titled "The 'Glass Ceiling.' "

The section of Part Four titled "Provocative People" contains personality profiles of several prominent media figures, among them Rupert Murdoch; Allen H. Neuharth, creator of *USA Today;* and Oprah Winfrey.

Part Five, "Media Trends and Techniques," moves from medium to medium, exploring what is happening in each. A sampling of selections points up the diversity and immediacy of the material covered: "TV News: Life in the Fast Lane"; "Comedy Is Big Hit on Video"; "Howard Cosell Says Sports Writers 'Not Prepared' "; and "Musings of a Newsmagazine Editor."

The cumulative impact of the developments discussed here has created what is popularly called the "information society." To close the book, Part Six, "Living in the Information Society," examines how media methods and electronic technologies affect individuals and families. It explains how computers have stripped away many aspects of personal privacy, how violence on television affects young viewers, and how life in many families has been changed by television.

New to this edition are review questions and suggested essay topics at the end of each part.

The authors thank their professional colleagues for helpful suggestions of areas to be covered and selections to be included. We are grateful in particular to the following professors who prepared articles especially for this book: Dennis L. Wilcox of San Jose State University and L. John Martin of the University of Maryland, whose article, "Developments in Political Communication Theory on Mass Media Potential," was updated and expanded from an earlier work.

We also express appreciation to the authors and publishers who permitted use of reprint material.

On the second edition we particularly want to acknowledge the following reviewers: Val Limburg, Washington State University; Hank Sennott, Dean Junior College; and John Stevens, University of Michigan.

Warren K. Agee
Phillip H. Ault
Edwin Emery

MAINCURRENTS IN MASS COMMUNICATIONS

A strong case can be made that news organizations pulled their punches in covering Reagan—whose popularity, Elizabeth Drew observed in a recent *New Yorker* article, had cowed much of Washington—for fear of irritating the public.

— William Boot
in "Iranscam: When the Cheering Stopped"

No longer do we merely cover the news. Thanks mainly to television, we are partners now in the creation of news—unwilling and unwitting partners perhaps, but partners nevertheless in producing what Daniel Boorstin has deplored as pseudoevents, pseudoprotests, pseudocrises and controversies.

— Michael J. O'Neill
in "The Power of the Press"

Let government pledge to tell the story on the record, and let the press corps pledge to report it on the record.

— Larry Speakes
in "White House Spokesman Rates the Press"

What's needed is responsibility by broadcasters, attention to detail, getting it right. . . . Ride herd on news directors when their programs look less like Huntley and Brinkley and more like Barnum and Bailey.

— Mark S. Fowler
Former FCC chairman

And many rejoice over the internecine strife among religious superstars, who have parlayed computer mailing lists and television satellites into multimillion-dollar empires.

— James M. Wall
in "Preacher Bashing and the Public Life"

PART ONE

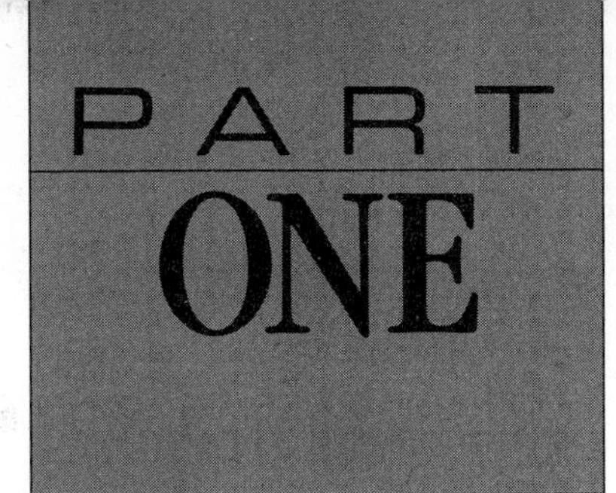

THE MEDIA'S ROLE IN SOCIETY

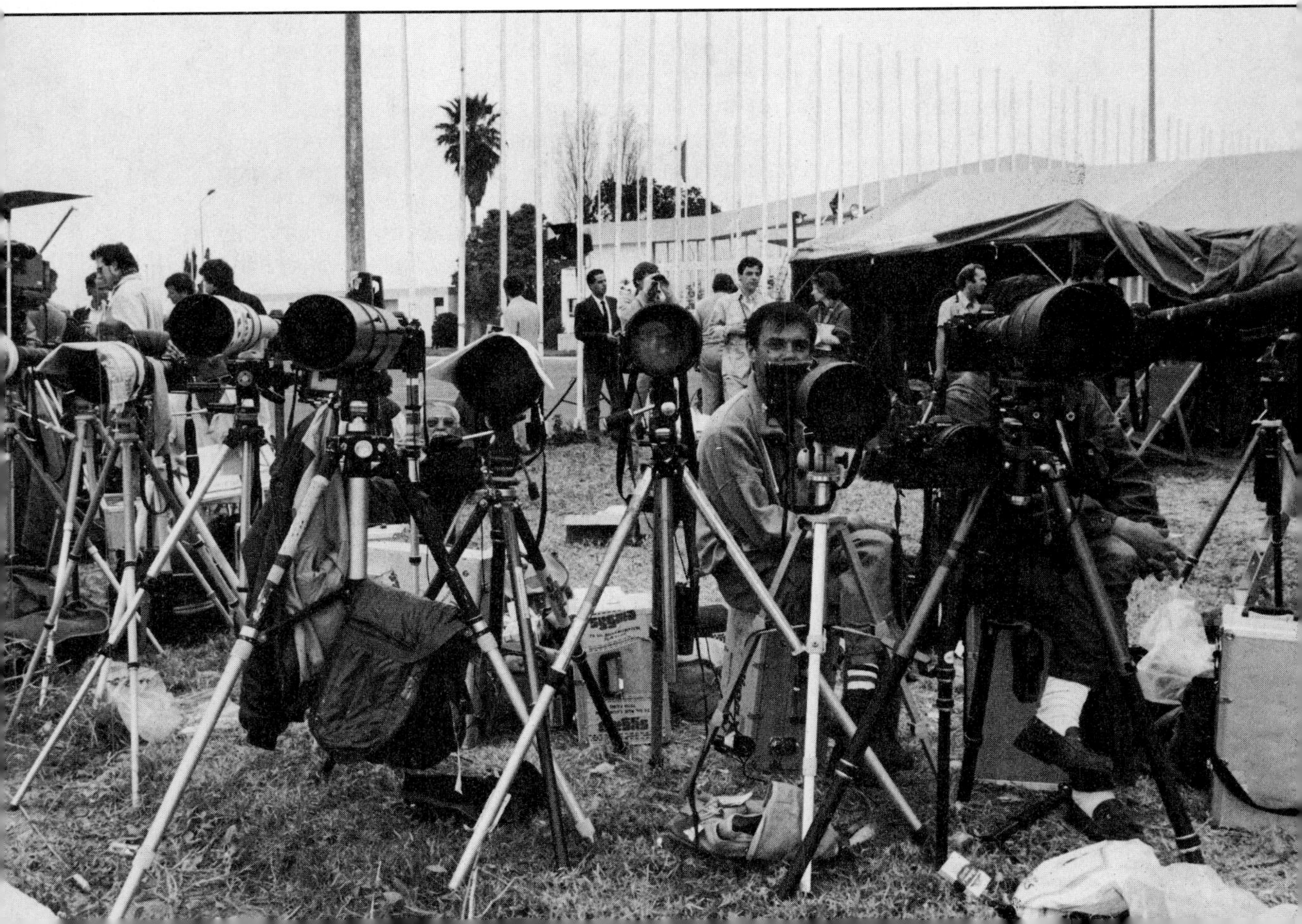

INTRODUCTION

EDWIN EMERY

The historical concept of media rights has been under heavier fire in the United States during the 1980s than at any other time in the twentieth century. Widespread public distrust of both press and government had been spawned in the 1960s by the turmoil of racial unrest, a revolt of youth, and antiwar protests and violence. Distrust of the press had been replaced by grudging admiration in the post-Watergate 1970s, but a turn of the wheel reflecting the Reagan era's political and social conservatism accentuated the dilemmas faced by the media in defending traditional concepts of their rights.

These are the right to publish news and opinion freely, to criticize without fear of reprisal, and to have access to news of public concern. In none of these areas are the rights of the American mass media absolute; rather, nuances of custom and degrees of privilege operate to provide freedom. At times the media have jeopardized their rights by failing to maintain a high degree of credibility with the public.

A newspaper ombudsman, Donald D. (Casey) Jones of the Kansas City *Star and Times,* summed up the eight most common complaints against the press, which, while primarily aimed at newspapers, also fit broadcast news. The list:

1. *Inaccuracies.* "Plain old errors of fact" do more to undermine the trust and confidence of readers than any other media sin ("Accuracy! Accuracy!! Accuracy!!!" Joseph Pulitzer pleaded more than a century ago). Errors open the door to public acceptance of smear attacks on the press by demagogues who sneer at the reliability of investigative reporting by skilled journalists working in the public interest.
2. *Arrogance.* The public's identification of media arrogance begins with refusals by reporters and editors to admit errors, the ombudsman said. It widens to a widespread public disbelief in the need for First Amendment protections of media rights to print, criticize, and report; such insistence on "special protection" is viewed as a form of arrogance.

   By the mid-1980s many Americans cheered the bringing of gigantic libel suits against CBS and *Time* by controversial public figures. Even a child of the media, columnist William Safire, chided "the damnably arrogant and all-powerful Big Media" while defending their legal positions. The 1984 election isolated the traditionally liberal newspapers and commentators, who saw their serious arguments and news stories swept aside by the jests of a triumphant president who labeled their opposition to him as an arrogant rejection of the public will.

3. *Unfairness.* The public perceives traditional expression of opinion by the media as "unfair" when it runs counter to prevailing public acceptance of a popular political or social belief. The investigative reporting of the 1970s that reached a climax with the exposure of felonies in the White House, which forced a president from office, lost favor in the 1980s. They could by then be dubbed "hatchet jobs" by those being investigated. At lower levels, attacks by aggressive writers upon hapless football coaches, mayors, and entertainers have long been construed by many readers as unfair and arrogant.
4. *Disregard of privacy.* This is more an emotional than a legal problem. Most people rather relish forays into the privacy of the rich, well-born, and prominent. But many empathize with individuals like themselves who are thrust into the news by photos that show grief-stricken families or accident victims, or by stories involving ridicule.
5. *Insensitivity.* Despite widespread media efforts to demonstrate sensitivity in matters of race, color, sex, and religion, the problem continues—as it does elsewhere in society.
6. *Contempt for the community.* When "outsiders" take over a local newspaper or station, importing editors, reporters, or anchorpersons, readers and listeners are quick to find the newcomers contemptuous where they are perhaps merely unaware of local mores. More serious is the dropping of locally focused material for bland content from a conglomerate media mix.
7. *Glorification of the unusual.* A demonstration by a handful gets page one play alongside news of a sex assault, the public complains, while the constructive activities of average citizens go unrecorded. This complaint is one of the oldest in journalism and runs counter to studies of reader interest.
8. *Bad writing and editing.* For this complaint, when true, there is no defense.

These media problems, as well as others that follow in our discussion, are analyzed by Michael J. O'Neill, at that time editor of the New York *Daily News,* in his presidential address to the American Society of Newspaper Editors (ASNE), one that stirred his journalistic peers; by Katherine Fanning, editor of the *Christian Science Monitor,* who urges greater compassion by the media; and by Mark S. Fowler, former chairman of the Federal Communications Commission.

Scientific public opinion studies made in 1986 for the Times Mirror Corporation and the ASNE challenged some of the conventional wisdom concerning public opinion and the nation's news media but confirmed there were problems. The Times Mirror study, conducted by Gallup, showed a wide range of public support, but not a deep reservoir. The public appreciates the watchdog role of the press against government and supports the media in any showdown. But it gives the media only good, not excellent, marks for believability. The ASNE study showed that three-fourths of adults have some problem with media credibility; one-sixth expressed frustration with the media.

OPINION ROLE

How necessary to democratic freedoms is the maintenance of a press free to print, criticize, and report? Has such a press played an influential role in the shaping of political and social progress?

Mass communications scholars, using social science techniques, have posed these questions for the past half century: How effective are the mass media in shaping thought (the cognitive aspect of mass communication)? In changing attitudes (the affective aspect)? In moving people to action (the behavioral aspect)?

Historians and journalists have found many convincing examples of media effects involving the cognitive aspects. People do learn from a mass medium (Lincoln's Gettysburg Address became known only through the print media) and then sometimes change their attitudes and opinions (a positive image of John F. Kennedy in the first televised presidential debate gave him the edge for victory). These examples of the conventional wisdom of media power and influence needed scientific proof, however.

Walter Lippmann's 1921 book, *Public Opinion,* contained the provocative thesis that "the pictures in our heads" of the world beyond us collectively constitute public opinion. Harold Lasswell argued that mass communications could change these pictures, posing the query: "Who, says what, in which channel, to whom, with what effect?" The social scientists who pursued that avenue arrived at an answer of "minimal effects" in changing attitudes and moving people to action. This so clearly contradicted conventional wisdom—commonsense observation—that new avenues were sought. Professor L. John Martin points out that the Lasswellian paradigm became switched around. Rather than "who says what to whom?" the question for researchers was "Who needs to receive the message from whom?" This led to studies of the gatekeeping function of the press and the media's power of agenda-setting.

People in authority in the 1600s were quick to see that the printing press had to be controlled, if they were to continue to exercise power. Gatekeeping of information is still vital in an authoritarian society. It involves message selection, shaping, display, timing, withholding, and/or repetition. Agenda-setting is one of the outcomes.

AGENDA-SETTING POWER

The basic idea of agenda-setting—the ability of the media to influence the salience of events in the public mind—was contained in Lippmann's description of "the pictures in our heads." Political scientist Bernard C. Cohen put the thesis clearly in 1963: "The press may not be successful much of the time in telling people what to think, but it is stunningly successful in telling readers what to think *about.*"

A decade later, two mass communications professors, Maxwell E. McCombs and Donald L. Shaw, published a landmark study indicating that media emphasis on an event influences the audience also to view the event as important. Subsequent studies have reinforced the role of agenda-setting. Professor Martin reviews this theory, and others.

The agenda-setting power of the media was never more forcefully demonstrated than by television in the 1984 presidential election. Walter Mondale's mournful lament, "As you know, I never warmed up to television, and television never warmed up to me," summed up the medium's impact when used by a skilled actor-politician who reached the electorate with ease and warmth. Reagan was aided, of course, by favorable economic and political conditions that foreshadowed an incumbent's reelection. But it was still clear that national politics would be forced to readjust to the television medium.

Washington's powerful press corps found itself overshadowed by this "television election." The "boys on the bus" of the 1972 campaign were still influential in their coverage for newspapers, news services, news magazines, and broadcasting (some of them had given up their seats to women by 1984). But they were hustled back and forth across the country in airplanes, meeting deadlines of the candidates for television news "live shows" rather than their own personal ones. They also found themselves outmaneuvered by a skillful White House press office that successfully set the agenda for media coverage on many a day.

This, of course, was not a strategy invented by the Reagan team. Theodore Roosevelt learned to release his news on quiet Sundays; Woodrow Wilson developed a press office; Franklin Roosevelt used radio for "fireside chats" directly to his audience and held frequent intimate conferences in the Oval Office with correspondents who did not always realize the extent of his news management. Dwight Eisenhower's press secretary, James Hagerty, held near-presidential powers; his successors did not fare so well.

An aggressive press corps challenged the White House almost continuously, led by such infighters as Dan Rather and Lesley Stahl of CBS, Sam Donaldson of ABC, Jack Nelson of the Los Angeles *Times,* and Helen Thomas of UPI. They did not fare well with Reagan and his press secretary, Larry Speakes, who sums up his tenure in one of the readings. But then in late 1986 came the Iran-*contra* scandal and a devastating collapse of credibility for the President and his associates. William Boot tells the story in "Iranscam."

Those who despaired of the conventional press during periods of stress produced new forms of alternative journalism. One was the underground press, which flowered during the 1960s and 1970s in protest against social and political conservatism. All through history there has been an alternative press espousing radical political dissent; an example with a life extending from the 1930s to the 1980s is Dorothy Day's *Catholic Worker* magazine, a leader in pacifism and social justice activism. Two selections examine these journalistic movements.

INFLUENCE OF TELEVISION

Television has many other social and cultural impacts, both in programming and in commercials. The effect of violence on the TV screen on viewers, especially children, has been examined extensively; most studies show that excessive exposure to violence does have a damaging effect on the behavior and attitudes of susceptible persons.

Much criticism of television centers on what the critics perceive as management's excessive emphasis on profits, to the detriment of substance, intelligent programming, public service, and at times good taste. In one of the selections that follows, Norman Corwin, a veteran producer and writer of TV shows, bitterly condemns the industry for "trivializing a whole culture." Like some other observers, he laments that television's presentation of news pays more attention to "show biz" glitter than to depth of content.

Even in religion, television's influence is strongly felt. A group of electronic evangelists whose televised programs mix emotional religious appeals with clever money-raising practices have developed a large following; they have used their adherents to form a political power base through such devices as the Moral Majority. A selection on "preacher-bashing" from the *Christian Century* reviews their problems.

INTERNATIONAL NEWS FLOW

The flow of news among nations became an increasingly sensitive concern during the 1970s as Third World spokesmen made urgent proposals to reorder the international communication system. By the mid-1980s the Western countries had a better grasp of Third World concerns, if not a willingness to adopt what was being called the new world information order.

It was clear that the call for some readjustment was in order. The four Western transnational news agencies—the Associated Press, United Press International, Reuters, and Agence France-Presse—along with TASS of the Soviet Union, provided more than 90 percent of the daily international news fare. The Western powers also controlled much of the use of telecommunication channels, including satellites. Developing nations in 1982 had only 5 percent of television transmitters and 12 percent of television receivers.

To the developing nations, this situation smacked of the bygone era of colonialism, inhibiting them culturally, economically, and politically. Without a new information order, they said, there was little chance of a new international economic order striking a better north-south balance.

There had been studies and surveys of world news flow by the International Press Institute in 1953 and UNESCO in 1960. The IPI and other Western groups offered technical assistance in Africa and Asia. In 1970 UNESCO voted to make a study of the free flow of the news one of its major concerns. Nonaligned countries, meeting in Algiers in 1973, called for a reorganization of international communications. By 1975 they had created the Pool of News Agencies of Nonaligned Countries. At its peak the pool exchanged information among some 50 countries with the assistance of Tanjug, the Yugoslav news agency. But the pool failed to achieve operational stability.

The phrase "free and balanced flow" of the news was introduced into the debate during a 1976 meeting in San José, Costa Rica. Western spokespeople said the two terms were incompatible and charged that Third World concepts were endangering freedom of the press in its traditional sense. At the UNESCO General Assembly later that year the confrontation was even more clearly defined, as Soviet-sponsored proposals for limiting access to news and licensing journalists "for their protection" were advanced, to the dismay of Western delegates. A total breakdown was avoided by the appointment of a 16-person International Commission for the Study of Communication Problems, headed by Ireland's Sean MacBride, recipient of both the Lenin and Nobel peace prizes.

At the 1980 UNESCO General Assembly in Belgrade, the phrase "free flow and wider and better balanced distribution of news" was advanced, and the issue of licensing was muted. But Western complaints continued that UNESCO was tilted toward state-run news agencies and media and against private enterprise.

This dissatisfaction reached a climax when, after a year's warning, the United States withdrew from membership in UNESCO at the end of 1984. The American announcement charged UNESCO with mismanagement, politicization, and "endemic hostility" toward a free press, free markets, and individual human rights. Since the United States contributed about 25 percent of the UNESCO budget, the activities of the international organization had to be cut back. Great Britain also withdrew its membership effective a year later. In announcing the American withdrawal, the State Department pledged that the United States would continue to support educational, scientific, cultural, and communications activities through other global agencies. Precisely what would happen to plans for reshaping international communications was unclear even in 1988.

RESPONSIBILITY AND DISTRUST

THE POWER OF THE PRESS

Michael J. O'Neill

Michael J. O'Neill, then editor of the New York *Daily News,* used his presidential address to the American Society of Newspaper Editors to question the power of the press and challenge editors to use it wisely. His analysis of what he terms "a problem for the Republic" has been widely discussed.

While there has been an astonishing growth in the power of the media over the last decade or so, I am by no means sure we are using it wisely. The tendency has been to revel in the power and wield it freely rather than to accept any corresponding increase in responsibility.

In fact, the very processes we use to inform the public have been badly distorted by television and, to a lesser degree, by a whole range of other phenomena from investigative excesses to our enthrallment with adversary journalism. So not only have we failed to match new responsibility to new power, we have also yielded to trends that are hurting the cause of a well-informed citizenry.

The extraordinary powers of the media, most convincingly displayed by network television and the national press, have been mobilized to influence major public issues and national elections, to help diffuse the authority of Congress and to disassemble the political parties—even to make Presidents or to break them. Indeed, the media now weigh so heavily on the scales of power that some political scientists claim we are upsetting the historic checks and balances invented by our forefathers. Samuel P. Huntington of Harvard has observed that "during the '60's and '70's, the media were the institution whose power expanded most significantly and that posed the most serious challenges to governmental authority." Max M. Kampelman has similarly warned that "the relatively unrestrained power of the media may well represent an even greater challenge to democracy than the much publicized abuses of power by the Executive and the Congress." And Sen. Daniel P. Moynihan, who concedes the press already has the upper hand in Washington, says that if the balance should tip too far in its direction "our capacity for effective democratic government will be seriously and dangerously weakened."

This is flattering, of course, because all newspapermen dream of being movers and shakers and the thought that we may actually be threatening the national government is inspirational. In several respects, it is also true. The Communications Revolution, which is profoundly reshaping all of Western society, has also altered the basic terms of reference between the press and American democracy.

No longer are we just the messengers, observers on the sidelines, witch's mirrors faithfully telling society how it looks. Now we are deeply imbedded in the democratic process itself, as principal actors rather than bit players or mere audience.

No longer do we merely cover the news. Thanks mainly to television, we are often partners now in the creation of news—unwilling and unwitting partners, perhaps, but partners nonetheless in pro-

Source: Reprinted with permission from the *Proceedings* of the American Society of Newspaper Editors, 1982.

ducing what Daniel Boorstin has deplored as pseudoevents, pseudoprotests, pseudocrises and controversies.

No longer do we look on government only with the healthy skepticism required by professional tradition. Now we have a hard, intensely adversarial attitude. We treat the government as the enemy—and government officials as convenient targets for attack-and-destroy missions.

No longer do we submit automatically to the rigors of old-fashioned impartiality. Now, not always but too often, we surrender to the impulse of advocacy, in the name of reform but forgetful of balance, fairness and—if it isn't too unfashionable to say so—what is good for the country.

These trends, however, are more symptom than cause. Much deeper processes are at work. The mass media, especially television, are not only changing the way government is covered but the way it functions. The crucial relationship between the people and their elected representatives—the very core of our political system—has been altered fundamentally.

In ways that Jefferson and Hamilton never intended nor could even imagine, Americans now have the whole world delivered to them every day, in pulsating, living color—all of life swept inside their personal horizon. Distant events—Selma, Alabama . . . the riot-torn Democratic convention in Chicago . . . the hostages in Iran—are instant experiences, neither insulated by a reporter's translation nor muted by what Theodore H. White has called the consoling "filter of time."

The flashing images mobilize popular emotions on a truly massive scale and with stunning speed, quickly generating and shaping public opinion. The televised battle scenes from Vietnam, as we know, aroused a whole nation against the war, helped reverse our national policy and ultimately destroyed the presidency of Lyndon Johnson.

"The introduction of modern mass communications," said the sociologist Daniel Bell, "allows us, in many cases forces us, to respond directly and immediately to social issues." Television has thus played a decisive role in the so-called revolution of rising expectations. It has strongly stimulated the consumption culture. It has dramatized the gap between haves and have nots, helping to create a runaway demand for more and more government services and for equality of result as well as of opportunity.

Time and time again, Presidents discover that the public has already made up its mind about issues before they have even had time to consider them. Their hand is forced. The deliberative process that representative government was designed to assure is frustrated.

Television has also indelibly changed the democratic process by establishing a direct communication link between political leaders and their constituents. Now, as never before, these politicians are able to bypass the print media and the troublesome business of depending on reporters to represent them to the public.

More significant, but for the same reason, they are also able to bypass their parties so that the whole system of party government, built up over nearly two centuries, is now breaking down. This, in turn, is contributing to the crisis of government that Lloyd Cutler and others find so threatening to the American system.

In presidential elections, that most central of democratic functions, media appeal has replaced party screening in the primary selection process. National conventions are no longer relevant. Most of the subtle bonds of political power, whether the ritual dispensing of favors or dependence on party for advancement, have been snapped. From the district clubhouse to Washington—especially Washington—political discipline has almost disappeared.

The President no longer has much leverage over the members of Congress, even those in his own party. Congress itself is in a disheveled state with power so diluted that neither floor leaders nor committee chairmen are able to act with the authority, for example, of a Sam Rayburn.

As a consequence, power has been badly fractured. Our capacity for achieving consensus on national issues has been damaged. George F. Kennan cites fragmented authority as one of the chief causes of the disarray in U.S. foreign policy, and he mainly blames Washington's overreaction to popular emotions whipped up by the media.

Where power is frayed, as Douglass Cater has pointed out, "public opinion is called on more regularly than elsewhere to act as arbiter among competing policies and politicians." So we have the paradox of the mass media tearing down power on the one hand, and then gaining power themselves at the expense of the institutions they have diminished.

One of the victims of this process is the presidency itself. Although many complex forces have conspired to undermine its authority, television and the national press have played a major role. For one thing, they have focused tremendous attention on the President, as the personal symbol of the nation and its ideals, as the principal instrument of action and the first resort of complaint or redress. They also rely on him for the drama, the glamour and excitement that television forever craves and must have to survive. Indeed, he happily conspires in the creation of media events and makes all sorts of other concessions in order to present his deeds in a way that TV finds congenial. A skilled communicator like Ronald Reagan is a master of television. He exploits it with great effect to project himself and his policies directly to millions of people, going over the heads of Congress and, incidentally, making an end run around newspapers.

But television can also be cruel. It raises public expectations far beyond the President's reach and then, when he cannot satisfy them, it magnifies the perception of failure. By massive overexposure, the media also strip away the protective mystery of the Oval Office, inviting the same kind of premature disenchantment that destroys so many TV stars.

A more serious concern is how the media merry-go-round is distorting the news, the information base, if you will, that people need to make sound decisions in a democracy. The capacity to mobilize public opinion is now so great that issues and events are often shaped as much to serve the media's demands as to promote the general welfare.

The result is a blurring of the line between the medium and the message, between substance and shadow, like the shadow on Plato's cave. "In the beginning," as Huntington has commented, "television covered the news; soon, news was produced for television." Boorstin has made the same point, but less politely.

Unfortunately, television is an impressionistic medium that marshals images and emotions rather than words and reasons. Its lenses are distorting. They focus on the dramatic and the visible, on action and conflict. News decisions are influenced by what film is available, what events "project" well, what can be explained easily in quickie bursts of audio headlines.

Newsmakers modify their behavior to fit, creating controversy on demand, turning away from debate and petition in favor of protest and demonstration. As the former Tammany Hall chief, Edward N. Costikyan, put it in a manual for political candidates: "Television reporting is not news; it is spectacle. To capture coverage, you must create a spectacle. . . ." Some issues, artificial or real, are churned up to the point that they command national attention and affect national policy. Other issues which may be far more valid and important—lagging investment in basic research, for example—are ignored because they cannot be seen by television's beady red eye.

The raw materials of public deliberation thus become a confusing mixture of the real and unreal, important and irrelevant—a jumble of impressions that confound even the historians. Arthur M. Schlesinger Jr. said that after being involved in the making of history during his White House days, he could never again rely on the testimony of the press.

So we all spin around in a vicious circle. Television first changes the nature of mass communication, including communication between the people and their government. In response, political leaders, single-issue groups and all other players on the public stage change their media behavior. Then the media, including the national press, react and interact. Masses of people become involved, contributing to the surge of participatory democracy that students of government have decried. Public agendas and priorities are distorted. The thrust of the news, the pace and even the content of the news, become captive to the process.

Adding to the general turmoil are two other phenomena: the press' harshly adversarial posture toward government and its infatuation with investigative reporting. These attitudes, which have always lurked in the psyche of American journalists, were enormously intensified by Vietnam, Watergate and the general attack on authority in the 1960's and 1970's. Both news coverage and the conduct of government have been duly affected—but not improved.

It may be foolhardy to say anything uncharitable about investigative reporting; it is in such vogue now. We have all basked in the glory of exposés and gloated while public officials have turned slowly on the spit of newspaper disclosures. I remember the triumph we felt at the *Daily News* when we reported that a congressman had lied about pleading the Fifth Amendment and then saw him destroyed as a candidate for mayor. On balance, investigative reporting has probably done more good than harm, although a wise member of *The New York Times* editorial board, Roger Starr, would dispute the point. He once suggested wistfully that journalism schools should ban Lincoln Steffens' famous book, *The Shame of the Cities.* He said that muckraking did so much damage to the cities that he hated to think what havoc modern investigative reporters might commit.

Muckraking has been overemphasized, tending to crowd out other more significant kinds of reporting. If we had not been so busy chasing corrupt officials, for instance, we might not be guilty of having missed some of the biggest stories of the last half century:

- The great migration of blacks from the South to the industrial cities of the North, something we didn't discover until there were riots in the streets of Detroit.
- The first mincing steps toward war in Vietnam, which we did not begin reporting seriously until our troops were involved.
- The women's liberation movement and the massive migration of women into the job market, a social revolution that we originally dismissed as an outbreak of bra burnings.

In some cases, investigative reporting has also run off the ethical tracks. Individuals and institutions have been needlessly hurt when the lure of sensational headlines has prevailed over fairness, balance and a valid public purpose. Those uninspiring scenes of reporters and cameramen trampling over Richard Allen's front lawn to hound his wife and children raise questions.

Is our duty to inform so stern that we must exile ourselves from our own humanity? Are we like policemen who have become inured to violence? Have we become so cynical, so hardened by our experiences with sham, that we can no longer feel what an official feels, what his wife and children feel, when he is being ripped and torn on TV and in the press? Have we become so arrogant with our power, so competitive, that we cannot decide that the public crime is often not worth the private punishment? The First Amendment is often abused rather than served by those who would defend it.

"Is it not true," Kampelman asked, "that no man is free if he can be terrorized by his neighbor? And, is it not possible for words as well as swords to terrorize?"

Similar questions need to be asked about our intensely adversarial coverage of government, because this, too, is falsely coloring the information flowing to the public.

We are probably the most adversarial people in the world—"the most anti-American," to quote the British poet Stephen Spender—and we are getting worse all the time. The reasons lie deep in the past—in the Enlightenment's victory over authority, in the romantic concept so eloquently expressed by Milton that truth will triumph in any struggle between reason and falsehood, in the Industrial Age's emphasis on competition to sort out good products from bad, in the checks and balances built into our own federal system and in the egalitarian movement that has recently reached such a crescendo in the United States.

In our profession, there are more immediate causes. There are the natural tensions between a President who paints a rosy view of all he does and the messengers who deliver bad news. There is the understandable resentment of officials who feel the media always emphasize the exceptional and negative over the positive, conflict and failure over success. And on the other side, there are the endless official lies and deceits and masquerades that gnaw at the moral intent of reporters.

Within the American context, these tendencies are normal. But they have become much more destructive in the last few years. With Vietnam and Watergate, with new waves of young, committed reporters moving into the profession, with older editors feeling guilty about having been "too soft" in the past, the media's relations with government have taken a sharp turn for the worse. The government has become the enemy.

A regretful Vermont Royster has said that the great difference between the Washington press corps of his day and the one now is that then "we did not think of ourselves and the government as enemies."

"We were cynical about much in government, yes," he said. "We were skeptical about many government programs, yes. We thought of ourselves the watchdogs of government, yes. We delighted in exposés of bungling and corruption, yes. But enemies of government, no."

By the time Jimmy Carter was elected, the critic Anthony Smith has observed, the American press had come "to think of itself as an opposition, almost in the European sense, as a counterpower, part of whose *raison d'être* consisted in the constant search for ways to dethrone the incumbent in office."

Smith may have overstated his point, but the adversarial pendulum has in fact swung too far and this is not good for the press, the government or society. Contrary to 18th-century myth and our own litigious tradition, the adversarial method does not necessarily produce truth. As often as not, it misses the truth and distorts reality. And knee-jerk opposition to government by a free press is only a mirror image of the undeviating governmental support that we criticize in the totalitarian media.

In its more extreme forms, the adversarial attitude creates barriers to the clear observation and analysis necessary for objectivity. It encourages emotional involvement with individual personalities and issues. It invites arrogance. It tempts reporters to harass officials. Ultimately, it undermines credibility, because people intuitively sense when the press is being unfair. They are quick to detect a belligerent tone in a story and then discount it in their own mental ledger. And they become deeply skeptical, in Ben J. Wattenberg's view, when all they get from the press is an endless rat-a-tat-tat of failure.

"Is it so absurd to suggest," he asks, "that if all one reads and all one sees is cast under the rubric of crisis and chaos that Americans will either (a) believe the press and think America is on the wrong track or (b) believe their own senses and think the press and the crisis-mongers they headline are elite, arrogant and so far out of touch as to be noncredible and, even worse, irrelevant?"

If the credibility of news coverage has been hurt, the functioning of government has been damaged even more. Not only are public issues and priorities strongly influenced by the media, every policy initiative, every action, has to run a gauntlet of criticism that is often generated—and always amplified—by the press. In the searing glare of daily coverage, an official's every personal flaw, every act, every mistake, every slip of the tongue, every display of temper is recorded, magnified and ground into the public consciousness.

The protests of special-interest groups, the charges of publicity-hungry congressmen, are rock-and-rolled through the halls of power. Controversy and conflict are sought out wherever they can be found, sapping energies and usually diverting attention from more urgent public business.

In this whirling centrifuge of criticism and controversy, authority is dissipated. Officials are undermined and demoralized. The capacity to govern, already drastically reduced by the fragmentation of power, is weakened still further.

The media have, in short, made a considerable contribution to the disarray in government and therefore have an obligation to help set matters straight. Or at least to improve them. The corollary of increased power is increased responsibility. The press cannot stand apart, as if it were not an interested party, not to say participant, in the democratic process.

We should begin with an editorial philosophy that is more positive, more tolerant of the frailties of human institutions and their leaders, more sensitive to the rights and feelings of individuals—public officials as well as private citizens.

We should be less arrogant, recognizing our own impressive shortcomings and accepting Walter Lippmann's lament that we can never claim to be the merchants of truth when we so rarely know what the truth is.

We should make peace with the government; we should not be its enemy. No code of chivalry requires us to challenge every official action, out of Pavlovian distrust of authority or on the false premise that attack is the best way to flush out truth. Our assignment is to report and explain issues, not decide them. We are supposed to be the observers, not the participants—the neutral party, not the permanent political opposition.

We should cure ourselves of our adversarial mindset. The adversarial culture is a disease attacking the nation's vital organs. The lawyers will never escape it, but we must. We should retain a healthy skepticism, yes. Provide socially responsible criticism, yes. But relentless hostility? No.

Reporters and editors are much more attracted to failure than to success. An expression of sympathy, perhaps, because failure is always an orphan while success has many fathers. Yet, if we are truly to provide a balanced view of the world, we must tame our negative nature; we need to celebrate success and progress, not just wallow in mankind's woes.

For if we are always downbeat—if we exaggerate and dramatize only the negatives in our society—we attack the optimism that has always been a wellspring of American progress. We undermine public confidence and, without intending it, become a cause rather than just a reporter of national decline.

We should also develop a more sensitive value system to be sure we do not needlessly hurt public figures while exaggerating the public's right to know. Rights do not have to be exercised just because they exist or because there is a story to be told. The claim of editorial duty should not be a coverup for titillation. Legitimate public need should be weighed against personal harm because, among other things, the fear of media harassment is already seriously affecting recruitment for public service.

Editors also need to be ruthless in ferreting out the subtle biases—cultural, visceral and ideological—that still slip into copy, into political stories, mostly, but also into the coverage of emotional issues like nuclear power and abortion. Lingering traces of advocacy are less obvious than Janet Cooke's fiction but, for that reason, are more worrisome. Editors—myself included—have simply not exercised enough control over subeditors and reporters reared in the age of the New Journalism.

The problem of television is formidable. Its baleful effect on both government and journalism is beyond repeal. The expanding network news shows and the proliferation of cable promise even more change, confusion and competition for the attention of busy Americans. And there are no solutions that I can think of, only the possibility of limited damage control. The key to this is to emphasize the basics, the things newspapers have always been able to do better than television, services that will become even more important as the electronic networks continue swarming over the mass market and, in the process, define a more specialized role for newspapers.

We should be more resistant than ever to media hype—the pseudoevent, the phoney charges, the staged protest, the packaged candidate, the prime-time announcement and televised interview. Indeed, we should expose these as vigorously as we expose official corruption. For it is our job to cut through the superficial to identify the substantive—to explain and clarify the news, as most newspapers already do, in a reasoned way that television cannot. Although we should be interesting, we should not try to be an entertainment like television, because this would be both futile and out of keeping with our special purpose.

Another issue is accountability. A brooding Ray Price, formerly of the New York *Herald Tribune* and the White House, complained that the press had acquired power "out of all proportion" to its ability or inclination to use it responsibly. Walter Wriston, a banker speaking for many in public life, warned that the media should remember that "the effective functioning of a democracy requires the most difficult of all disciplines, self-discipline."

"The freedom of us all," he said, "rides with the freedom of the press. Nevertheless, its continued freedom and ours will ultimately depend upon the media not exploiting to the fullest their unlimited power."

All sorts of remedies have been proposed, from ombudsmen to news councils, even antitrust legislation. Many critics think it would be wonderful if we were just professionals so there could be the kind of self-policing that doctors and lawyers have—an uninspiring idea, though, when you consider how few doctors or lawyers are ever disciplined.

The fact is that no grievance committees or councils or laws will really work if the general attitude of the profession is not supportive. If the attitude is right, however, all the clanking machinery is probably unnecessary. Our best defense against opponents, our best bet for strengthening reader credibility, is an openness of mind that encourages both self-examination and outside criticism.

With this psychic base, we can expect editors—miracle of miracles—to respond more constructively to complaints, reporters to be more accepting of direction and correction. We can expect a more aggressive pursuit of fairness and a willingness to provide a more effective right of reply than letters to the editor or an occasional op-ed piece.

In the final analysis, what we need most of all in our profession is a generous spirit, infused with human warmth, as ready to see good as to suspect wrong, to find hope as well as cynicism, to have a clear but uncrabbed view of the world. We need to seek conciliation, not just conflict—consensus, not just disagreement—so that society has a chance to solve its problems. So that we as a nation can find again the common trust and unity—so that we can rekindle the faith in ourselves and in our democracy—that we so urgently need to overcome the great challenges we face in the 1980's.

NEW PERSPECTIVES ON THE NEWS

Katherine W. Fanning

Citing extensive public distrust of the news media, Katherine W. Fanning, editor of the *Christian Science Monitor,* urges editors and reporters to develop better perspective and exercise greater compassion in covering stories. She delivered this address at the national convention of the Society of Professional Journalists, Sigma Delta Chi, in Indianapolis in November 1984. She was president of the American Society of Newspaper Editors in 1987–1988.

We in the news world have been shaken by news about ourselves—the news that the public out there doesn't understand or trust us.

It's been a growing perception for several years now. Credibility. Thousands of words have been written or spoken about it. ASNE [the American Society of Newspaper Editors] is doing a massive research study on the extent and the causes of the loss of reader trust. Some of the most thoughtful examinations of the problem within our business have come from Mike O'Neill, former editor of the New York *Daily News,* who posed penetrating questions a couple of years ago about the intensity of the adversary relationship between press and

---

Source: Reprinted by permission of Katherine W. Fanning.

government; and Lou Boccardi, new president of the AP, who last spring said:

> Is it time now for us to examine some of the basic assumptions we make about what we do? . . . have we reached a point where we must recognize an obligation *not* to do some of the things the First Amendment gives us every right to do?

Provocative stuff! Many journalists object to such talk. It's simple, they contend—just keep reporting the news as we see it. But it's not so simple. Nothing is, in our present world. Of course we must continue to fearlessly report the news as *we see it.* It's this *seeing* I'm concerned about. *How* do we see? With wide ranging vision or narrowly through a tunnel? With compassion or with ruthlessness? Most of us long to find a simple set of rules—ethics codes, do's and don't's—and there can be a place for those. But the point is, we journalists must be *thinkers,* unafraid to tackle the increasingly difficult questions facing us. We can moan over the new challenges: declining readership, evaporating trust, increasingly costly libel judgments, or we can see them as opportunities to think more deeply about what we do and how we perceive a troubled world.

During my years at the Anchorage *Daily News* and over this past year at the *Christian Science Monitor,* I've noticed that the talented young—and some less than young—journalists that I've encountered tend to be concerned by the malaise infecting our profession.

If it can be done better, they want to do it better. The press in the U.S. is certainly the freest in the world and probably the best. But it would be sheer arrogance to claim that it can't be much better.

There are some needed improvements that are obvious—although they can't be emphasized too often—greater accuracy, sounder professional ethics, clearer writing.

We've also been hearing from many sources that the press must make itself better *understood* by readers. But what about turning that last point around and considering the need of journalists to better *understand* our world and the significance (or lack of significance) of the news we report?

To better understand and to transmit that understanding calls for clearer vision, better perspective and, I submit, more compassion.

It must have been twenty years ago that I read the novel by Harper Lee, *To Kill a Mocking Bird,* but one passage has stayed with me. You may remember that the novel is the story of a single father, Atticus, and his two children who tell the story of a small town in the deep South. The children are terrified by, and consequently torment, a man they have never seen, Boo Radley, a mysterious recluse, who lives down the street and never emerges from his house. At the climax of the novel the children come face to face with the much-feared Boo only to discover that he has been their friend and protector all the while. This moment of changed perspective strikes when the children actually stand for the first time on Boo Radley's porch and view their own neighborhood from his viewpoint. Scout, the little girl, says, "Atticus was right . . . you never really know a man until you stand in his shoes and walk around in them."

I felt a little like I was on Boo Radley's porch recently, standing at Piskarevskoe Cemetery in Leningrad during an ASNE exchange trip to the Soviet Union. We laid flowers at the base of a monument to over a million victims of the siege of Leningrad in World War II and viewed the mounds of earth under which hundreds of thousands of Russians were buried. It was a moment when I better understood the Soviet's massive fear that hostile troops might again sweep across Europe to the outskirts of Leningrad as the Nazis did in 1940. That perception is, of course, only a tiny piece of the total puzzle of Russia, but perhaps we do need to test our viewpoint occasionally by walking around in Soviet shoes.

Or the shoes of a rape victim when we debate whether to use her name, or to walk around in Geraldine Ferraro's shoes when we reveal that her parents were indicted when she was eight years old—something she herself had never known.

Walking around for just a moment in the shoes of those we write about may make little difference in most cases how we cover a story, but while we walk in them we can ask ourselves, "*Why* am I writing this the way I am—and is it the right way?"

If I had been writing some of the stories about Ms. Ferraro I think I would still have seen the need to reveal her husband's business dealings, her questionable claim of exemption on the House disclosure form, and probably the family's association with Mafia figures. But if I had asked myself the relevance of her parents' indictment when she was eight to how she would perform as Vice President, I would have drawn the line.

When you come to think of it, much of what we report, especially about people, is just plain irrelevant.

Or if I had walked for just a moment in the shoes of the Kennedy family, I would have published many of the details of David Kennedy's tragic death. I would have printed some aspects of the investigation, but would I have savoured every tragic detail with as much relish as some papers did?

If I had been walking in the shoes of disaster victims who have just lost their home and family, would I have confronted them with a microphone, TV camera, or a pad and pencil and asked them how they felt about it?

"What's going on here?" the public is saying. "Aren't journalists human?" And of course most of us are. But we need to think more deeply about when and how compassion relates to our business.

Newspaper people are tightrope walkers. There is always a fine line to tread and we shouldn't shrink from walking it. My daughter was once asked by a magazine writer to describe her mother, back in the financially perilous days of the Anchorage *Daily News*. "My mother is like someone on a balance beam," she said. "If she were to look down, she'd fall—but she never looks down." That was probably true in those days. But we do need to look down, and up and to both sides—and still stay on the balance beam. I am convinced that more compassion, restraint and judgment are needed in our business and that if the line is properly walked, this should in no way impair the fullest, most hard-hitting account of significant news.

Now I'm going to talk about tunnels for a moment.

There's a fable I know that goes something like this: The student of an oriental mystic is in the final stages of his instruction when his guru submits him to a test of his understanding. He is told that he must find his way through a long dark tunnel with only a miner's lamp to light his way. The guru explains that he will see many sights, some ghastly, some threatening, some lovely, but that he mustn't believe any of them for they are all illusions produced by hypnosis. The student starts down the tunnel. He passes a gorgeous mermaid basking in a pool but he never pauses. He encounters a hideous dragon breathing fire and continues on his way. He is chased by lions and surrounded by serpents but he is unfazed. And then he is stopped dead. He has come to a stone wall. There is no way to go forward. He turns back only to find another wall. There is no way out—he is walled in. Then he remembers the guru's final words: "Don't believe anything you see." And he walks through the wall out into the light.

I'm not suggesting we go around walking into walls. But I do think we can examine whether we are creating our own walls as journalists and whether as a society we are walling ourselves into untenable positions. Isn't it up to journalists to open their eyes, look at things in a new way, find out if the walls are real?

I'd submit, for instance, that candidates and the press shared a tunnel syndrome during this past [1984] campaign. . . . Why does the press so often seem to travel in a mental herd all asking the same questions, accepting the same answers? . . .

Is it because the news business is becoming show business? Of course this syndrome is not entirely the fault of the press. The politicians and public are culpable too. But if reporters could overcome the herd effect, do some independent thinking, approach the large issues confronting our society from a new angle, they could positively affect the public agenda.

Here is a small example: This fall the editors of

the *Christian Science Monitor* were striving for some method to bring readers a new perspective. We decided to ask them to look at the question of war and peace in a different way. We launched a contest—the Peace 2010 contest—that calls for an essay written from the perspective of the year 2010 on how a peaceful world was achieved—not just the absence of fighting—but real peace. The entries are not journalism of course—they're fiction. But the point is to lead people to think that peace *could* be achieved instead of accepting the inevitability of a world threatened by nuclear extinction and to search for some feasible building blocks that might lead to a peaceful earth.

A provocative recent book, *Weapons and Hope,* by Professor Freeman Dyson of Princeton University, achieves the kind of breaking out of the tunnel I'm talking about.

In the final chapter, titled "Tragedy Is Not Our Business," he challenges the acceptance of a world of nuclear weapons and ultimate tragedy.

"Morally, we must arouse the consciousness of mankind against weapons of mass murder as we roused mankind against the institution of slavery a hundred and fifty years ago." Dyson says, "We behave like the characters in a Samuel Beckett play, sitting helpless in our garbage cans while the endgame of history is played out."

In the final chapter of *Weapons and Hope,* Dyson addresses another topic that is drawing considerable comment these days—the question of good news and bad news. He expands on the ideas of comedy and tragedy expressed by another author, Clara Park, who says that the fundamental malaise of our time is a loss of the ancient art of comedy. She is not talking about the stand-up comic, but the ancient sense of comedy as serious drama ending in a mood of joy rather than sorrow. In the Park view, we tend to reject happy endings. Even though happy endings still exist, she says, our literature has no major artistic mode to affirm the experience of comedy: healing, restoration, winning through.

How often do we play an acquittal in the same place on page one as we played an indictment? Do we give the same prominence to the result of a probe into wrongdoing that we bannered when the charge turns out to be groundless? Sometimes, but not always.

According to Clara Park, "The essential feature of comedy is not the happy ending but the quality of the characters which enables them to *earn* a happy ending." How often do we treat a question like that in our people profiles?

Is tragedy *our* business?

Is the way we dramatize people's sorrow, seldom balancing it with news about triumph, contributing to the sense of meaninglessness?

These are all questions, not answers. The people in this room are the ones who can think their way through to answers and can make a difference.

I am not proposing that journalists become preachers—or even crusaders. But I am suggesting that we push out the walls of our tunnels, try standing in Boo Radley's shoes, try some new perspectives.

The mandate for relentless pursuit of an important story, fearless exposure of wrongdoing, and absolute devotion to press freedom must always be media priorities.

But if newspeople expand their vision, exercise more compassion, achieve better balance and more often report happy endings, the gulf between reader and media will narrow, trust return and, just possibly, we might have a better society.

BROADCASTERS TOLD: BE MORE RESPONSIBLE

Mark S. Fowler

A convention of the National Association of Broadcasters heard Mark S. Fowler, at that time chairman of the Federal Communications Commission, condemn errors and overaggressive reporting by broadcast journalists. He asked the industry to show a greater sense of responsibility in news coverage and program content.

Source: Courtesy, Mark S. Fowler. No copyright is held in this work.

In my last two visits to your convention, I've expressed my general philosophical approach to broadcast regulation in the United States. My approach is summarized by the term "unregulation." It means getting rid of unnecessary rules that inhibit your ability to serve the public as you best see fit. *Your* reading of what *your* market wants has got to be better than an FCC-based program schedule. . . . We've managed to cut away a lot of program underbrush and other rules, rules that punished broadcasters who promoted their stations too much, or who played one song too much, that said we could just split up your AM/FM combination some day or that you had to wait three years before selling a station. It's as if people sat around the FCC cooking up rules for rules' sake. Police cops shouldn't have a daily quota on handing out speeding tickets. And FCC regulators shouldn't have a quota to dream up rules that aren't necessary.

Those days of schoolroom finger-wagging are over at the FCC. And there's no going back. . . . But . . . with the new freedom of today's broadcast marketplace come new responsibilities.

The government will no longer be the primary source of this sense of responsibility, nor should it be. It's up to you to find your professional goals and stick to them. Let me give a couple of examples of where I see this new responsibility fitting in.

Take news. Not very long ago, a famous network anchor was the "most trusted man in America." Now public confidence in journalism is at a perilous low. According to *Time* magazine, in 1983 less than 14 percent of the public had a great confidence in the media. Witness the public's positive reactions to both the news blackout in Grenada and the call to regulate exit polling at election time.

The timing of this dissatisfaction is ironic. For your profession enjoys greater freedom and a greater understanding of the importance of that freedom. Your reporters and writers, especially at the top, are paid better than ever. More talented young people want into your business. Your technological news-gathering arsenal is awesome.

To me, it all comes down to three words: Get it right. Too often, broadcast journalists are obsessed with getting it first, with confrontation, not coverage. "They won't get one over on me"—that's the attitude of too many broadcast reporters. In his recent book Jody Powell, President Carter's press secretary, noted the Washington press corps' "absolute refusal to ever admit error." The result sometimes is over-aggressive reporting and a reckless disregard for whether facts being reported happen to be true.

Does the profession do itself any good to conduct a virtual stake-out in front of a public official's house and fling complicated questions as he leaves for work?

Or consider the situation when a jetliner is shot down by Russia and hundreds of innocent passengers die. The President issues a statement deploring the act. In order to add pictures to go with the published response, a television news crew arms itself with a telephoto lens and the President is shown that night on horseback at his Santa Barbara ranch over a voice description of the tragedy. What story is a reporter telling by this juxtaposition of picture and word?

Is it political reporting worthy of Edward R. Murrow to ask a presidential contender, during the first serious public scrutiny of his candidacy, to do a comedy impression of Ted Kennedy during a live, election night interview?

Add to that TV reporting techniques bordering on the gruesome. Oakland *Tribune* editor Robert Maynard put it well: "When people see a TV person shoving a mike in front of a grieving relative, all the press appear to be boorish and ghoulish." The broadcast media must remind themselves, again and again, that there's a difference between being shrewd—and being rude.

What's needed is not a bunch of government munchkins in the newsroom. What's needed is responsibility by broadcasters, attention to detail, getting it right. Pat reporters on the back when they do a story accurately. Ride herd on news directors when their programs look less like Huntley and Brinkley and more like Barnum and Bailey. Be willing to retract mistakes. Be willing to stand by reporters when they're right. And insist, always, that they get it right.

And this new responsibility applies to other program areas. Take children's television. Last year the Commission issued its final report in this area. We declined to impose a mandatory requirement on broadcasters and made it clear that we weren't going to use a raised eyebrow instead of direct regulation.

But broadcasters as citizens have an obligation to our youth, a duty apart from what the government can or should impose. We're told that childhood is disappearing, and as parents we see it every day—our kids are expected to be, and eventually wind up acting as, young adults before their minds and bodies are ready. Society is unnecessarily robbing children of their childhood. Television is part of that society.

Do you as fellow citizens not share in that responsibility and in the search for a remedy? And can you truly meet your responsibility between breakfast and lunch on a Saturday morning? I say this as a parent, as a citizen, and as one who cares about both kids and broadcaster freedom. I know the solution isn't government, but we as a people can do better.

The new broadcasting environment also calls for a look at how you're retooling and reinvesting in your operations. As you sow, the Bible tells us, so shall you reap. That's as true for begonias as for broadcast facilities.

I know that not all broadcasters are wildly profitable. But those of you in the larger markets, especially in television, continue to see handsome profits; if you don't, you might consider another line of work. Now, you have every right in the world to take profits from broadcasting and put them wherever you like. The FCC encourages entry by broadcasters into new technologies, and I've made it my business to see that you have every right to participate in them.

But let's not forget about the old technologies. Tend to your knitting. Those who learn to live with reasonable profit margins and pump more revenues into better programs, better transmitters, better environments for your workers—you're planting the seeds for a strong future in your mainline business of broadcasting. As you sow, so shall you reap.

Let's face it—no government agency can improve communication unless the people who communicate sincerely want to do a better job. I've tried to chart a new course for government. It's a course away from being "big brother" to something more like being an older brother. We can step in to settle interference squabbles. But we can't tell you how to be good broadcasters. You're too old for that. It never was the responsibility of an older brother, anyway.

Some of you have seen the new freedom for what it is—a chance to be entrepreneurs, to take advantage of our free enterprise system. To this new freedom must be appended a corresponding responsibility. As a founding father said, "Liberty exists in proportion to wholesome restraint." And some of you have hitched to your rising star this sense of responsibility. You've put the time and money into quality local programs; you understand that the have-nots in this country, and particularly this industry, ought to be dealt into the game.

As an example, I know the NAB takes great pride in BROADCAP—your minority broadcaster capital fund. It's a commitment in hard dollars to let newcomers in. I salute those who have special minority training programs; and those national advertisers who look for ways to support minority broadcaster and minority formats.

Then, too, responsibility is reflected in countless hours of community service by broadcasters—from telethons to emergency food drives, from helping find lost children to warning about contaminated water supplies—these are moments of pure public service for broadcasters, and for broadcasting.

Why do you do this? Why, indeed? Not because the FCC orders you; never has, never will. It's because you know your responsibility to the communities you serve, to the industry you're in.

The future of broadcasting lies with those with strong local service. Let us hear the voices of this industry who demand quality and are willing to pony up for it. For those are the voices of leadership. They'll be around to see the unregulated days, the more exciting days of broadcasting ahead. . . .

IMPACT OF TELEVISION

UNDERSTANDING TELEVISION

David Marc

Television is "the most effective purveyor of language, image, and narrative in American culture," according to David Marc, yet he finds it to be more reviled and laughed at than seriously examined. Marc is a professor of American Civilization at Brown University.

In one of the few famous speeches given on the subject of television, Federal Communications Commission chairman Newton N. Minow shocked the 1961 convention of the National Association of Broadcasters by summarily categorizing the membership's handiwork as "a vast wasteland." The degree to which Minow's metaphor has been accepted is outstripped only by the appeal of television itself. Americans look askance at television, but look at it nonetheless. Owners of thousand-dollar sets think nothing of calling them "idiot boxes." The home stereo system, regardless of what plays on it, is by comparison holy. Even as millions of dollars change hands daily on the assumption that 98 percent of American homes are equipped with sets and that these sets play an average of more than six and a half hours each day, a well-pronounced distaste for TV has become a prerequisite for claims of intellectual and even of ethical legitimacy. "Value-free" social scientists, perhaps less concerned with these matters than others are, have rushed to fill the critical gap left by status-conscious literati. Denying the mysteries of teller, tale, and told, they have reduced the significance of this American storytelling medium to clinical studies of the effects of stimuli on the millions, producing volumes of data that in turn justify each season's network schedules. Jerry Mander, a disillusioned advertising executive, his fortune presumably socked away, has even written a book titled *Four Arguments for the Elimination of Television.* Hans Magnus Enzensberger anticipated such criticism as early as 1962, when he wrote,

> The process is irreversible. Therefore, all criticism of the mind industry which is abolitionist in its essence is inept and beside the point, since the idea of arresting and liquidating industrialization itself (which such criticism implies) is suicidal. There is a macabre irony to any such proposal, for it is indeed no longer a technical problem for our civilization to abolish itself.

Though Mander, the abolitionist critic, dutifully listed Enzensberger's *The Consciousness Industry* in his bibliography, his zealous piety—the piety of the convert—could not be restrained. Television viewers (who else would read such a book?) scooped up copies at $6.95 each (paperback). As Enzensberger pointed out, everyone works for the consciousness industry.

Despite the efforts of a few television historians and critics, like Erik Barnouw and Horace Newcomb, the fact is that the most effective purveyor of language, image, and narrative in American cul-

Source: Reprinted with permission from *Demographic Vistas: Television in American Culture* (Philadelphia: University of Pennsylvania Press, 1984).

ture has failed to become a subject of lively humanistic discourse. It is laughed at, reviled, feared, and generally treated as persona non grata by university humanities departments and the "serious" journals they patronize. Whether this is the cause or merely a symptom of the precipitous decline of the influence of the humanities during recent years is difficult to say. In either case, it is unfortunate that the scholars and teachers of *The Waste Land* have found "the vast wasteland" unworthy of their attention. . . .

As the transcontinental industrial plant built since the Civil War was furiously at work meeting the new production quotas encouraged by modern advertising techniques, President Calvin Coolidge observed that "the business of America is business." Since that time television has become the art of business. The intensive specialization of skills called for by collaborative production technologies has forced most Americans into the marketplace to consume an exceptional range of goods and services. "Do-it-yourself" is itself something to buy. Necessities and trifles blur to indistinction. Everything is for sale to everybody. As James M. Cain wrote, the "whole goddamn country lives selling hot dogs to each other." Choice, however, is greatly restricted. Mass-marketing theory has formalized taste into a multiple-choice question. Like the menu at McDonald's and the suits on the racks, the choices on the dial—and, thus far, the cable converter—are limited and guided. Yet even if the material in each TV show single-mindedly aims at increasing consumption of its sponsors' products, the medium leaves behind a body of dreams that is, to a large extent, the culture we live in. If, as Enzensberger claimed, we are stuck with television and nothing short of nuclear Armageddon will deliver us, then there is little choice but increased consciousness of how television is shaping our environment. Scripts are written. Sets, costumes, and camera angles are imagined and designed. Performances are rendered. No drama, not even melodrama, can be born of a void. Myths are recuperated, legends conjured. These acts are not yet carried out by computers, although network executives might prefer a system in which they were.

Beneath the reams of audience-research reports stockpiled during decades of agency billings is the living work of scores of TV-makers who accepted the marketable formats, found ways to satisfy both censors and the popular id, hawked the Alka-Seltzer beyond the limits of indigestion, and still managed to leave behind images that demand a place in collective memory. The life of this work in American culture is dependent upon public taste, not market research. A fantastic, wavy, glowing procession of images hovers over the American antennascape, filling the air and millions of screens and minds with endless reruns. To accept a long-term relationship with a television program is to allow a vision to enter one's life. That vision is peopled with characters who speak a familiar idiosyncratic language, dress to purpose, worship God, fall in love, show élan and naiveté, become neurotic and psychotic, revenge themselves, and take it easy. While individual episodes—their plots and climaxes—are rarely memorable (though often remembered), cosmologies cannot fail to be rich for those viewers who have shared so many hours in their construction. The salient impact of television comes not from "special events," like the coverage of the Kennedy assassinations or of men on the moon playing golf, but from day-to-day exposure. Show and viewer may share the same living room for years before developing a relationship. If a show is a hit, if the Nielsen families go for it, it is likely to become a Monday-through-Friday "strip." The weekly series in strip syndication is television's most potent oracle. Because of a sitcom's half-hour format, two or even three of its episodes may be aired in a day by local stations. Months become weeks, and years become months. Mary accelerates through hairdos and hem lengths; Phyllis and Rhoda disappear as Mary moves to her high-rise swinging-singles apartment. Mere plot suspense or identification with characters yields to the subtler nuances of cohabitation. The threshold of expectation becomes fixed, as daily viewing becomes an established procedure or ritual. The ultimate suspension of disbelief occurs when the drama—the realm of heightened artifice—becomes normal.

The aim of television is to be normal. The industry is obsessed with the problem of norms, and this manifests itself in both process and product. Whole new logics, usually accepted under the general classification "demographics," have been imagined, to create models that explain the perimeters of objectionability and attraction. A network sales executive would not dare ask hundreds of thousands of dollars for a prime-time ad on the basis of his high opinion of the show that surrounds it. The sponsor is paying for "heads" (that is, viewers). What guarantees, he demands, can be given for delivery? Personal assurances—opinions—are not enough. The network must show scientific evidence in the form of results of demographic experiments. Each pilot episode is prescreened for test audiences who then fill out multiple-choice questionnaires to describe their reactions. Data are processed by age, income, race, religion, or whatever cultural determinants the tester deems relevant. Thus the dull annual autumn dialogue of popular-television criticism:

Why the same old junk every year? ask the smug, ironic television critics after running down their witty lists of the season's "winners and losers."

We know nothing of junk, cry the "value-free" social scientists of the industry research factories. The people have voted with their number 2 pencils and black boxes. We are merely the board of elections in a modern cultural democracy.

But no one ever asked me what I thought, mumbles the viewer in a random burst from stupefaction.

Not to worry, the chart-and-graph crowd replies. We have taken a biopsy from the body politic, and as you would know if this were your job, if you've seen one cell—or 1,200—you've seen them all.

But is demography democracy?

Fortunately, TV is capable of inspiring at least as much cynicism as docility. The viewer who can transform that cynicism into critical energy can declare the war with television over and instead savor the oracular quality of the medium. As Roland Barthes, Jean-Luc Godard, and the French devotees of Jerry Lewis have realized for years, television is American Dada, Charles Dickens on LSD, the greatest parody of European culture since *The Dunciad.* Yahoos and Houyhnhnms battling it out nightly with submachine guns. Sex objects stored in a box. Art or not art? This is largely a lexicographical quibble for the culturally insecure. Interesting? Only the hopelessly genteel could find such a phantasmagoria flat. Yesterday's trashy Hollywood movies have become recognized as the unheralded work of auteurs; they are screened at the ritziest art houses for connoisseurs of *le cinéma.* Shall we need the French once again to tell us what we have?

Though network executives reserve public pride for the achievements of their news divisions and their dramatic specials, comedy has always been an essential, even the dominant, ingredient of American commercial-television programming. As Gilbert Seldes wrote, in *The Public Arts,* "Comedy is the axis on which broadcasting revolves." The little box, with its oblong screen egregiously set in a piece of overpriced wood-grained furniture or cheap industrial plastic, has provoked a share of titters in its own right from a viewing public that casually calls it the "boob tube." Television is America's jester. It has assumed the guise of an idiot while actually accruing power and authority behind the smoke screen of its self-degradation. The Fool, of course, gets a kind word from no one : "Knee-jerk liberalism," cry the offended conservatives. "Corporate mass manipulation," scream the resentful liberals. Neo-Comstockians are aghast, righteously indignant at the orgiastic decay of morality invading their split-level homes. The avant-garde strikes a pose of smug terror before the empty, sterile images. Like the abused jester in Edgar Allan Poe's "Hop-Frog," however, the moguls of Television Row make monkeys out of their tormentors. Profits are their only consolation; the show must go on.

In 1927 Philo T. Farnsworth, one of TV's many inventors, presented a dollar sign on a television screen in the first demonstration of his television system. By the late 1940s baggy-pants vaudevillians, stand-up comedians, sketch comics, and game-show hosts had all become familiar video images. No television genre has ever been without what Robert Warshow called "the euphoria [that] spreads over the culture like the broad smile of an idiot." Police shows, family dramas, adventure series, and made-for-TV movies all rely heavily on humor to mitigate their bathos. Even the news is not immune, as evidenced by the spread of "happy-talk" formats in TV journalism in recent years. While the industry experiments with new ways to package humor, television's most hilarious moments are often unintentional, or at least incidental. Reruns of ancient dramatic series display plot devices, dialogue, and camera techniques that are obviously dated. Styles materialize and vanish with astonishing speed. Series like *Dragnet, The Mod Squad,* and *Ironside* surrender their credibility as "serious" police mysteries after only a few years in syndication. They self-destruct into ridiculous stereotypes and clichés, betraying their slick production values and affording heights of comic ecstasy that dwarf their "original" intentions. . . .

The situation comedy has proved to be the most durable of all commercial-television genres. Other types of programming that were staples of prime-time fare at various junctures in TV history (the western, the comedy-variety show, and the big-money quiz show among them) have seen their heyday and faded. The sitcom, however, has remained a ubiquitous feature of prime-time network schedules since the premiere of *Mary Kay and Johnny,* on DuMont, in 1947. The TV sitcom obviously derives from its radio predecessor. Radio hits like *The George Burns and Gracie Allen Show* and *Amos 'n' Andy* made the transition to television overnight. Then, as now, familiarity was a prized commodity in the industry. The sitcom bears a certain resemblance to the British comedy of manners, especially on account of its parlor setting. A more direct ancestor may be the serialized family-comedy adventures that were popular in nineteenth-century American newspapers. Perhaps because of the nature of its serial continuity, the sitcom had no substantial presence in the movies. . . .

Urgent continuity rarely exists between episodes. Instead, climaxes occur within episodes (though these are not satisfying in any traditional sense). In the movie serial (or in a modern television soap opera) the rescue of characters from torture, death, or even seemingly hopeless anxiety is used to call attention to serialization. The sitcom differs in that its central tensions—embarrassment and guilt—are almost always alleviated before the end of an episode. Each episode may appear to resemble a short, self-contained play; its rigid confinement to an electronic approximation of a proscenium-arch theater, complete with laughter and applause, emphasizes this link. Unlike a stage play, however, a single episode of a sitcom tends to be of dubious interest; it may not even be intelligible. The attraction of an episode is the strength of its contribution to the broader cosmology of the series. The claustrophobia of the miniature proscenium, especially for an audience that has grown casual toward Cinemascope, can be relieved only by the exquisiteness of its minutiae.

Trivia is the most salient form of sitcom appreciation, perhaps the richest form of appreciation that any television series can stimulate. Though television is at the center of American culture—it is the stage upon which our national drama/history is enacted—its texts are still not available upon demand. The audience must share reminiscences to conjure up the ever-fleeting text. Giving this exchange of details the format of a game, players try not so much to stump as to overpower one another with increasingly minute, banal bits of information that bring the emotional satisfaction of experience recovered through memory. The increased availability of reruns that cable service is bringing about can only serve to deepen and broaden this form of grass-roots TV appreciation. Plot resolutions, which so often come in the form of trite, didactic "morals" in the sitcom, are not very evocative. . . . From about the time a viewer reaches puberty, a sitcom's plot is painfully predictable. . . .

The sitcom dramatizes American culture: its

subject is national styles, types, customs, issues, and language. Because sitcoms are and always have been under the censorship of corporate patronage, the genre has yielded a conservative body of drama that is diachronically retarded by the precautions of mass-marketing procedure. For example, *All in the Family* can appropriately be thought of as a sixties sitcom, though the show did not appear on television until 1971. CBS waited until some neat red, white, and blue ribbons could be tied around the turmoil of that extraordinarily self-conscious decade before presenting it as a comedy. When the dust cleared and the radical ideas that were being proposed during that era could be represented as stylistic changes, the sixties could be absorbed into a model of acceptability, which is a basic necessity of mass-marketing procedure. During the sixties, while network news programs were offering footage of Vietnam, student riots, civil-rights demonstrations, police riots, and militant revolutionaries advocating radical changes in the American status quo, the networks were airing such sitcoms as *The Andy Griffith Show, Petticoat Junction, Here's Lucy,* and *I Dream of Jeannie.* The political issues polarizing communities and families were almost completely avoided in a genre of representational comedy that had always focused on American family and community. Hippies would occasionally appear as guest characters on sitcoms, but they were universally portrayed as harmless buffoons possessing neither worthwhile ideas nor the power to act, which might make them dangerous. After radical sentiment crested and began to recede (and especially after the first steps were taken toward the repeal of universal male conscription, in late 1969), the challenge of incorporating changes into the sitcom model was finally met. The dialogue that took place in the Bunker home had been unthinkable during the American Celebration that had lingered so long on the sitcom. But if the sitcom was to retain its credibility as a chronicler and salesman of American family life, these new styles, types, customs, manners, issues, and linguistic constructions had to be added to its mimetic agenda.

The dynamics of this challenge can be explained in marketing terms. Five age categories are generally used in demographic analysis: (1) 2–11; (2) 12–17; (3) 18–34; (4) 35–55; (5) 55+. Prime-time programmers pay little attention to groups 1 and 5; viewing is so prevalent among the very young and the old that, as the joke goes on Madison Avenue, these groups will watch the test pattern. Prime-time television programs are created primarily to assemble members of groups 3 and 4 for commercials. Although members of group 4 tend to have the most disposable income, those in group 3 spend more money. Younger adults, presumably building their households, make more purchases of expensive "hard goods" (refrigerators, microwave ovens, automobiles, and so on). The coming of age of the baby-boom generation, in the late sixties and early seventies, created a profound marketing crisis. The top-rated sitcoms of the 1969–1970 season included *Mayberry R.F.D., Family Affair, Here's Lucy,* and *The Doris Day Show.* Though all four of these programs were in Nielsen's top ten that season, their audience was concentrated outside of group 3. How could the networks deliver the new primary consumer group to the ad agencies and their clients? Norman Lear provided the networks with a new model that realistically addressed itself to this problem. In *Tube of Plenty* Erik Barnouw shows how the timidity of television narrative can be traced directly to the medium's birth during the McCarthy Era. If the sixties accomplished nothing else, it ended the McCarthy scare. The consensus imagery that had dominated the sitcom since the birth of TV simply could not deliver the new audience on the scale that the new consensus imagery that Norman Lear developed for the seventies could. Lear's break from the twenty-year-old style of the genre seemed self-consciously "hip." The age of life-style was upon us. . . .

In *Democratic Vistas* Walt Whitman called for a new homegrown American literary art whose subject would be "the average, the bodily, the concrete, the democratic, the popular." The sitcom is an ironic twentieth-century fulfillment of this dream. The "average" has been computed and dramatized as archetype; the consumer world has been made "concrete"; the "bodily" has been fetishized as the object of unabashed envy and voyeurism—all of this is nothing if not "popular." The procession of images that was Whitman's own art, and that he hoped would become the nation's, is lacking in the sitcom in but one respect: the technique of television art is not democratic but demographic. The producers, directors, writers, camera operators, set designers, and other artists of the medium are not, as Whitman had hoped, "breathing into it a new breath of life." Instead, for the sake of increased consumption they have contractually agreed to create the hallucinations of what Allen Ginsberg has called "the narcotic . . . haze of capitalism." The drug indeed is on the air and in the air. Fortunately, the integrity of the individual resides in the autonomy of the imagination, and is not curtailed by this system. The television set plays on and on in the mental hospital; the patient can sit in his chair, spaced-out and hopeless, or rise to the occasion of consciousness. . . .

Thus far, I have limited my discussion to traditional ways of looking at television. However, the television industry has made a commitment to relentless technological innovation of the medium. The cable converter has already made the traditional tuner obsolete. From a comfortable vantage point anywhere in the room the viewer can scan dozens of channels with a fingertip. From the decadent splendor of a divan the viewer is less committed to the inertia of program choice. It is possible to watch half a dozen shows more or less simultaneously, fixing on an image for the duration of its allure, dismissing it as its force disintegrates, and returning to the scan mode. Unscheduled programming emerges as the viewer assumes control of montage. It is also clear that program choice is expanding. The grass-roots public-access movement is still in its infancy, but the network *mise en scène* has been somewhat augmented by new corporate players such as the superstations and the premium services. Cheap home recording and editing equipment may turn the television receiver into a bottomless pit of "footage" for any artist who dares use it. . . .

Whatever the so-called blue-sky technologies bring, there can be no doubt that the enormous body of video text generated during the decades of the network era will make itself felt in what will follow. The shows and commercials and systems of signs and gestures that the networks have presented for the past thirty-five years constitute the television we know how to watch. There won't be a future without a past.

In *Popular Culture and High Culture* Herbert Gans took the position that all human beings have aesthetic urges and are receptive to symbolic expressions of their wishes and fears. As simple and obvious as Gans's assertion seems, it is the wild card in the otherwise stacked deck of demographic culture. . . .

The networks and ad agencies care little about these particulars of culture and criticism. The networks promise to deliver heads in front of sets and no more. But, as we will find in any hierarchical or "downstream" system, there is a personal stance that will at least allow the subject of institutional power to maintain personal dignity. In the television demography this stance gains its power from the act of recontextualization. If there is no exit from the demographic theater, each viewer will have to pull down the rafters from within. What will remote-control "SOUND: OFF" buttons mean to the future of marketing? What images are filling the imaginations of people as they "listen" to television on the TV bands of transistor radios, wearing headphones while walking the streets of the cities? Why are silent TV screens playing at social gatherings? When will the average "Household Using TV" (HUT) be equipped with split-screen, multichannel capability? What is interesting about a game show? The suspense as to who will win, or the spectacle of people brought frothing to the point of hysteria at the prospect of a new microwave oven? What is interesting about a cop show? The "catharsis" of witnessing the punishment of the criminal for his misdeeds, or the attitude of the cop toward evil? What is interesting about a sitcom? The funniness of the jokes, or the underlining of the jokes on the laugh track? The plausibility of the plot, or the portrayal of a particular style of living as "normal"? What is interesting about Suzanne Somers and Erik Estrada? Their acting, or their bodies? Television is made to sell products but is used for quite different purposes by lonely, alienated people, families, marijuana smokers, born-again Christians, alcoholics, Hasidic Jews, destitute people, millionaires, jocks, shut-ins, illiterates, hang-gliding enthusiasts, intellectuals, and the vast, heterogeneous procession that continues to be American culture in spite of all demographic odds. If demography is an attack on the individual, then the resilience of the human spirit must welcome the test.

"To be a voter with the rest is not so much," Whitman warned in his *Democratic Vistas* of 1871. The shopper/citizen of the demography ought to know this only too well. Whitman recognized that no political system could ever summarily grant its citizens freedom. Government is a system of power; freedom is a function of personality. "What have we here [in America]," he asked, "if not, towering above all talk and argument, the plentifully-supplied, last-needed proof of democracy, in its personalities?" Television is the Rorschach test of the American personality. I hope the social psychologists will not find our responses lacking.

"GIVE US 22 MINUTES . . ."

Norman Corwin

Having himself had an illustrious career in broadcasting, Norman Corwin chastises television, in his book *Trivializing America,* for resorting to "cosmetic packaging" of news and feeding audiences "cultural junk food" for entertainment. He complains that television often discourages originality.

The one medium of entertainment that we and we alone have developed to a technical gloss and commercial clout unrivalled anywhere is commercial television. Much has already been written on the subject—indeed it is a favorite target for criticism—but the worst that can be said about it is not that it is a slave to ratings, which it is; or an assembly line for dramatized violence, which is bad enough; or an attic of old movies; but that it is trivializing a whole culture. It does this both directly and indirectly, acting first upon its own audiences, and secondarily, through its influence among other media, on a widening public.

Take the "least worst"[1] of TV's chronic banes—its handling of news. The average local newscast, almost everywhere in the country, is a kind of succotash served in dollops and seasoned by bantering between anchorpersons, sportspersons, weatherpersons and person-persons. And these people had better be good-looking, sparkling or cute—weathermen with party charm, anchorladies with good teeth and smart coiffures, sportcasters with macho charisma. It doesn't matter if they have a news background or not. One of the highest paid anchorwomen in the business was described by the *Los Angeles Times* as "a leading figure in the ranks of those who know next to nothing about news but can expect to make a quarter of a million dollars annually for dispensing it." Walter Cronkite called the cosmetic approach, "the work of packagers who care more about a hairdo than about the news itself." Not long after he said this, a TV station in Missouri proved he was not exaggerating. An anchorwoman named Christine Craft was dismissed by KMBC-TV, the ABC outlet in Kansas City, because the station's "research" showed that too many viewers thought her "too old, too unattractive and not deferential to men." (She was 37, and was later described in a newspaper account as having "wholesome, outdoorsy good looks . . . it's hard to see how anyone could think her unattractive.")

A "news consultant" retained by the station contended that the clothes newscasters wear have more bearing on their credibility than the style and content of their reporting.[2] Over a sample ten-day period, Craft's on-camera wardrobe chart called for 33 specific items, including pearls, a gold chain, a magenta St. Tropez geometric blouse and cream shirt, a light beige Liz Claiborne linen blazer, a madras plaid J.G. Hook blazer with a yellow Clubhouse silk blouse, and a bright red vertical-light-sleeve Evan Picone creation.

It was not Craft's first experience with image management. Earlier, while employed as a reporter for *CBS Sports Spectacular* in New York, she was required by the producers to dye her brown hair platinum and her brows black.

The cosmetic packaging of which Cronkite complained may make a profit center of the news room, but when a doll is assigned to purvey news, it is not always of high service to broadcast journalism. Beauty may be truth and truth beauty, but today even Keats would agree that it is not all we need to know.

There is something distracting about a phantom of delight who radiates sexuality, filling us in on murder, rape, inflation, corruption, terror, bigotry, turpitude and sports. Newscasting is not a beauty contest. Ghastly tidings delivered by Aphrodite, or dispatches of grave import from an anchorman with a Barrymore profile and the magnetism of a Valentino, tend to lose something in translation; they become an *effect.* When pulchritude and sex-appeal rate as prime ingredients in the dissemination of news, journalism yields to showmanship.

It could be argued that to deny a footing in TV news to anyone on grounds of excess comeliness is to penalize good looks. Actually it works the other way around: plain-lookers are the ones who get passed up, notwithstanding proven competence. Their features just don't come together well enough to satisfy the packager.

Any time broadcast news is twisted or accented by emphasis on personality, "image," bloom, novelty, sensation, or on being first, it is trivialized. The best of the newspeople have always been of earnest purport; none looks upon news as showbiz, as a profit center, but rather as a trust, an obligation to treat with integrity both what is reported and the audience to which it is addressed.

"The only thing that counts," Edward R. Murrow once told his associates at CBS, "is what comes out of the loudspeaker—and what we're trying to make come out is an honest, coherent account of events. It is not part of our job to please or entertain."

That credo has had tough going. Not only are newscasters recruited increasingly out of casting directories, fashion magazines, model agencies and beauty parlors, but the news itself has been minified, often by stations which specialize in news and might therefore be expected to expand rather than compress their formats. Cronkite resented "the hypercompression we are forced to exert to fit 100 pounds of news into the one-pound sack that we are given to fill every night," and was concerned lest the public, persistently being under-informed, will suffer from the effects of distortion and in this way be "led to disaster."

George Schlatter, producer of the television program *Real People* (eccentrics, octogenarian charmers, a violinist who practices daily in a public restroom, a group whose speciality is rummaging through the garbage of celebrities, etc.) believes news programs strain to entertain: "Eight minutes of news, interspersed with chit-chat, banter, and a real-people story. It's show biz."[3]

The all-news Westinghouse radio stations have a slogan which for years has been repeated on the air several times daily: "Give us 22 minutes and we'll give you the world." It's true the world has shrunk—but *that* much? When a marketing survey showed that people who normally listened to their Los Angeles station for an average of 50 consecutive minutes started taking Westinghouse at its word and tuning out after 22, the boast of wrapping-up-the-world in the time it takes to play an inning of baseball was quickly dropped by that station.

But at least Westinghouse's 22 minutes of news, the equivalent in print of two columns in *The New*

York Times, were straightforward and banter-free. The same cannot be said for much of television's formula. Critic Howard Rosenberg, after watching the 11 o'clock news on KABC-TV Channel 7 on a night in July, 1981, wrote:

> What excitement there was on Channel 7's late night loose-marblecast! Sober, respectable, credible Warren Olney, having lately been transplanted to the land of the sillies, [is] swiftly learning the program.

Olney had announced during a prime-time newsbreak that Christine Lund, anchorwoman then on maternity leave, would be paying a visit on an upcoming news program to talk about her new baby.

> Just before 11 p.m., Olney gave it another shot: "Coming up, a terrific surprise from a new mother." Sure enough the 11 p.m. news program included tape of Lund describing her baby's "fat little cheeks."
>
> "Oh, my goodness," said weathercaster Johnny Mountain. . . .
>
> Viewers barely had time to catch their breath before it was revealed that Mountain's wife that very morning had given birth to a son. Later in the newscast Mountain did jokes about his wife and showed pictures of a monkey, which he said was his new son. . . .
>
> If nothing else, this should once and for all settle the hash of critics who contend that TV news is sometimes shallow and emphasizes anchor personalities more than news.

Are Olney, Lund, Mountain and the others chargeable with perpetrating piffle? Certainly they are guilty in part, even if the klatsch may have been the idea of the news director, or an imperative from the station manager. Persiflage has a home on programs expressly made for it; the news need never stay that way. Murrow would have refused, and so would Chancellor, Reynolds, Cronkite, Kuralt, Collingwood, Trout, Sevareid, Clete Roberts, Joseph Benti. The last, a superb reporter in Los Angeles, was released by Channel 2 News in one of those periodic shuffles usually involving beautification, competition, and the *idée fixe* of some executive rating-watcher, that in order for a newscast to get anywhere in the marketplace, its cast on camera must be chummy, good kidders, "human," and altogether hale and well met. Benti's case was a local outrage, but he stands for scores of excellent practitioners who have been shunted aside to make way for darlings.

Of course the audience contributes its share to the syndrome. And the contribution is reciprocal. Consumers of entertainment, if fed cultural junk food long enough, come to expect it. And they get it.

Dr. Rodney Gorney, in *The Human Agenda,* worries that "a satiated public might lose its capacity and will to discriminate [between a] cultural triumph and a cultural travesty." In much the same way, a public fed on prattle may suffer diminished capacity to weigh the news. If the judgment of an electorate is numbed by trivia, there is no guarantee that sooner or later a candidate unfitted to rise higher than senior salesman in a sharp used-car operation will not become president. It has happened.

J. B. Priestley, novelist, playwright and commentator, wrote, "There is now a vast crowd, a permanent audience, waiting to be amused. They look on more and more, and join in less and less." If indeed this vast crowd wants its reporters to be amusing, sociable, pretty and cozy, then trivialization has done its work.

Naturally, decisions affecting such matters are not made in the newsroom but higher up. They reflect the philosophy of the board room, of dividend-warders whose first loyalty is to the ratings. David Sarnoff, head of RCA in the era of greatest glory for its subsidiary NBC, once put it bluntly: "We're in the same position as a plumber laying pipe—we're not responsible for what goes through the pipe." The fact that this statement was made at all is revealing, since responsibility is never shrugged off for something of which one is proud. Sarnoff was wrong in his choice of preposition, if nothing else: The networks *are* responsible for what goes through the pipe, but they are not always responsible *about* it.

It does not take a philosopher to recognize that responsibility, as a social obligation, increases in direct proportion to capacity and power. But in the instance of the presidential election of 1980, broadcasters showed not the slightest interest in making concessions to western voters by delaying their projected victory for Reagan until the polls closed in California. On the other hand, these same broadcasters are generally willing to impose occasional blackouts at the request of government spokesmen or agencies. Notable exceptions have been *The New York Times* and Daniel Schorr, who in separate actions made history in the Vietnam epoch by refusing to suppress information they felt important for the public to know. Later Schorr reported that one Jerry Nachman, news director of San Francisco's radio station KCBS, proposed to black out a network newscast "so that the audience would not learn, before the delayed airing of a climactic *Dallas* episode, who had shot J.R."[4]

But then CBS, of which Nachman's KCBS is a member, set a standard of a kind when its then president, John A. Schneider, decided to cut away from live coverage of a vital senatorial debate on Vietnam policy to broadcast a fifth rerun of *I Love Lucy,* followed by an eighth rerun of *The Real McCoys.* (NBC meanwhile carried the hearing.) Schneider's decision triggered the resignation, in protest, of CBS News President Fred Friendly. It was one of the least proud hours of a network that had glittered in the Golden Age of Radio, the shortest golden age in history. . . .

Sports are only one of the voltaic piles that generate teletrivia. Others, just as tireless, are the *non*-athletic games—tune-guessing, price-matching, blind-dating and all the rest. Innocent enough fun, and enjoyed by enough people to warrant their existence—but so many games? Played so persistently? At the time of this writing, *Family Feud* was being broadcast on the NBC channel in Los Angeles not once a week, but five times a week.

Giveaway programs in general are like sweet-flavored gelatinous cultures on which greed and hysteria colonize like bacteria. The hysteria is visible to the viewer, but the greed is not so obvious. Not lightly to be forgotten are the quiz scandals of the late 50's, which ended in grand jury indictments. There have been no frauds since then (at least none has been disclosed), but big money, princely prizes, paroxysms of delight at winning, childlike dismay at guessing wrong answers to fribbling questions, tears, shrieks, kisses, ringing bells, rasping buzzers, hours of production and transmission, all come together to fill the public's time with pablum.

Then there are the formula melodramas, exercises in brawn, conspicuous consumption of ammo, auto chases, beatings, knifings, corpses. To the extent that all this is repetitious and predictable, that subtlety is rarer than chateaubriand on a poor man's table, that any useful significance or relation to our lives is nil, these programs, too, classify as trivia.

Even many of the so-called "specials," whose specialness implies relief from run-of-the-milieu programming, tend to follow well-worn paths, and in doing so become as predictable in their way as *Laverne and Shirley* and *Charlie's Angels.* They keep coming almost interchangeably over the seasons: *Bob Hope in China, Perry Como's Hawaiian Holiday, Tennessee Ernie Ford in Moscow, Steve Edwards and Melody Rogers in Dublin, Dean Martin's California Christmas.* The *déja vu* of commercial television accumulates very quickly, because the industry relies on safely repeatable formulas. Responsibility for content is passed on to viewers with the familiar shrug, "That's what they want to watch." Naturally cliché programming flourishes in this environment and is in no danger of reform, since television is the most insensitive of the media to criticism, the most intractable when it comes to numbers-versus-quality, and the most assiduous in applying Gresham's law, by which the bad drives out the good.

Critic Cecil Smith, deploring the resignation from a particular network series of three gifted people (a writer, a director and a producer) because of interference from memoranda-dispatchers who pressed them for higher ratings, fired a broadside at the chancellery:

> When network executives, mostly lawyers and computer experts and advertising salesmen who couldn't create a fire with a mountain of matches, drive out the creative people whose work occasionally flickers on the tube, we shouldn't wonder that we have so low a level of bland and lifeless television.

Conscionable TV critics of Smith's outlook have a trickier task than their colleagues in other media, for they are the only members of their genus who find themselves often having to criticize on two levels simultaneously—the artistic and the cultural. Judges of music, painting, literature, the legitimate stage, the dance, even of cinema, are much less frequently obliged to speak of the sociological ramifications of the works they review, of the ambience in which these works are conceived, or of the processes by which they are produced and exhibited.

For years critics like Smith tried to help raise a reluctant dinosaur from its flounderings in a self-perpetuating swamp by speaking out for the kind of television that Edward R. Murrow had in mind when he warned, "The instrument can teach, it can illuminate; yes, and it can even inspire. But it can do so only to the extent that humans are determined to use it to these ends. Otherwise it is merely lights and wires in a box."

Since Murrow voiced that caution a generation ago, the concern of critics has been that the instrument not only did not teach, illuminate and inspire, but that it has too often done nearly the opposite: lowered cultural tastes, promoted numbing escapism and discouraged originality.

Max Beerbohm, successor to George Bernard Shaw on the drama desk of the London *Saturday Review,* believed that not every art can hope to acquire good critics:

> An art sunk in the slough of incompetence, will cry in vain to good critics to rescue it.

However, this was written just after the turn of the century, when television was not yet in Vladimir Zworykin's thoughts. Were Beerbohm around today, he would no doubt acknowledge that the art of television, as manipulated by the lawyers, accountants, computer experts and advertising men of Smith's notice, cries out for good critics *not* to rescue it, but to leave it alone. They don't *want* to be rescued: they like it the way it is. Good critics are anathema in such circles. The industry prefers reviewers who will go along with the herds and the ratings. Smith's administrators (there are good ones, too, who are not included in his sweep, but they form a minority) are impatient with challenges to the numbers derby and they are unmoved by critical lamentations when a superb program like *Love Among the Ruins* ends up in Siberia. They are deaf to shouts of anger because the powerful rating system, that much controverted and often suspect rat race of percentages, remains the chief agency by which mediocrity addicts are made and reared and sustained.

Broadcasters are invariably miffed by criticism of their product and practices, and they protest just as invariably that they are only giving people what they want. But the people have been conditioned to want what they want mainly by years of having gotten what they have gotten.

NOTES

1. British critic Max Shulman's phrase for the television of his country.
2. Not only a Kansas City consultant. According to Ron Rosenbaum in *Esquire* (November 1982), Dan Rather was told by Van Gordon Sauter, president of CBS News, that it was not just important to *be* what you are on a newscast, you have to be *perceived* as what you are. " 'When we talk about the look of the broadcast and bringing it up to date,' Van said, 'I'm not talking about changing your soul, I'm talking about changing your suit!' "
3. Richard L. Strout, for 61 years a journalist in Washington, told a reporter in an interview in 1982, "Television trivializes the news in a disgusting fashion. It's awfully hard to find out the meaning of anything."
4. In *Channels,* August-September 1981.

IMPACT OF TV NEWS OVERRATED

Jeanmarie Kalter

According to this study of media researchers' findings made by *TV Guide,* the often-stated claim that two-thirds of the American people receive their news from television is a myth. Viewers understand only about a third of network news stories and are frequently distracted.

Once upon a time, there was a new invention—television. It became so popular, so quickly, that more American homes now have a TV set (98 per cent) than an indoor toilet (97 per cent). Around this new invention, then, an industry rapidly grew, and around this industry, a whole mythology. It has become a virtual truism, often heard and often repeated, that TV—and TV news, in particular—has an unparalleled influence on our lives.

Over the past 20 years, however, communications scholars have been quietly examining such truisms and have discovered, sometimes to their surprise, that many are not so true at all. *TV Guide* asked more than a dozen leading researchers for their findings and found an eye-opening collection of mythbusters. Indeed, they suggest that an entire body of political strategy and debate has been built upon false premises. . . .

Myth No. 1

Two-thirds of the American people receive most of their news from TV. This little canard is at the heart of our story. It can be traced to the now-famous Roper polls, in which Americans are queried: "I'd like to ask you where you usually get most of your news about what's going on in the world today. . . ." In 1959, when the poll was first conducted, 51 per cent answered "television," with a steady increase ever since. The latest results show that 66 per cent say they get most of their news from TV; only about a third credit newspapers.

Trouble is, that innocent poll question is downright impossible to answer. Just consider: it asks you to sort through the issues in your mind, pinpoint what and where you learned about each, tag it, and come up with a final score. Not too many of us can do it, especially since we get our news from a variety of sources. Even pollster Burns Roper concedes, "Memories do get fuzzy."

Scholars have found, however, that when they ask a less general, more specific question—Did you read a newspaper *yesterday?* Did you watch a TV news show *yesterday?*—the results are quite different. Dr. John Robinson, professor of sociology at the University of Maryland, found that on a typical day 67 per cent read a newspaper, while 52 per cent see a local or national TV newscast. Dr. Robert Stevenson, professor of journalism at the University of North Carolina, analyzed detailed diaries of TV use, and further found that only 18 per cent watch *network* news on an average day, and only 13 per cent pay full attention to it. Says Robinson, "TV is part of our overall mix, but *in no way* is it our number one source of news."

Yet it's a myth with disturbing consequences. Indeed, it is so widespread, says Dr. Mark Levy, associate professor of journalism at the University of Maryland, that it shapes—or misshapes—our political process. In the words of Michael Deaver, White House deputy chief of staff during President Reagan's first term, "The majority of the people get their news from television, so . . . we construct events and craft photos that are designed for 30 seconds to a minute so that it can fit into that 'bite' on the evening news." And thus the myth, says Levy, "distorts the very dialogue of democracy, which cannot be responsibly conducted in 30-second bites."

Myth No. 2

TV news sets the public agenda. It was first said succinctly in 1963, and has long been accepted: while the mass media may not tell us what to think,

Source: "TV Doesn't Affect You as Much as You Think," *TV Guide,* August 31, 1987. Reprinted with permission from *TV Guide* Magazine.

they definitely tell us what to think *about.* And on some issues, the impact of TV is indisputable: the Ethiopian famine, the Challenger explosion. Yet for the more routine story, new research has challenged that myth, suggesting TV's influence may be surprisingly more limited.

For one thing, TV news most often reacts to newspapers in framing issues of public concern. Dr. David Weaver, professor of journalism at Indiana University, found that newspapers led TV through the 1976 campaign. Given the brevity of broadcasts, of course, that's understandable. "TV has no page 36," explains Dr. Maxwell McCombs, professor of communications at the University of Texas. "So TV journalists have to wait until an issue has already achieved substantial public interest." TV, then, does not so much set the public agenda as spotlight it.

Even among those issues spotlighted, viewers do make independent judgments. It seems the old "hypodermic" notions no longer hold, says Dr. Doris Graber, political science professor at the University of Illinois. "We're not sponges for this stuff, and while TV may provide the raw material, people do select."

Indeed, even TV entertainment is less influential than once was thought. According to Robinson, studies found *no* difference in racial attitudes among those who saw *Roots* and those who didn't. Ditto "The Day After" on nuclear war, and *Amerika* on the Soviets. As for news, Graber notes that the public took a long time to share the media's concern about Watergate, and even now are lagging the media on Iran-Contragate. And finally, there are many issues on which the press must belatedly catch up with the public. Which brings us to . . .

Myth No. 3

TV news changed public opinion about the war in Vietnam. Contrary to this most common of beliefs, research shows just the opposite. Lawrence Lichty, professor of radio/television/film at Northwestern University, analyzed network war coverage and found that it did not become relatively critical until 1967. By then, however, a majority of Americans *already* thought U.S. involvement in Vietnam was a mistake. And they thought so not because of TV coverage, but because of the number of young Americans dying.

Yet this fable about the "living room war" is so accepted it has become "fact": that gory TV pictures of bloody battles undermined public support for the war; that, in a 1968 TV-news special, Walter Cronkite mistakenly presented the Tet offensive as a defeat for the U.S.; and that, because President Johnson so believed in the power of TV, he concluded then that his war effort was lost.

In fact, Lichty found few "gory" pictures. "TV presented a distant view," he says, with less than five per cent of TV's war reports showing heavy combat. Nor, as we now know, was a rapt audience watching at home in their living rooms. As for Cronkite's report on the Tet offensive, the CBS anchor said on the evening news, "First and simplest, the Vietcong suffered a military defeat." And, in his now-famous TV special, Cronkite concluded, "we are mired in a stalemate," and should "negotiate." By that time, Lichty says, "public opinion had been on a downward trend for a year and a half. A majority of Americans agreed." And so Johnson's concern, it seems, was not that Cronkite would influence public opinion, but rather that he reflected it.

Indeed, Prof. John Mueller of the University of Rochester has compared the curve of public opinion on the war in Vietnam, covered by TV, with that of the war in Korea, hardly covered. He found the two curves strikingly similar: in both cases, public support dropped as the number of American deaths rose.

Disturbingly, the misconception about TV's influence in Vietnam has had broad consequences, for it has framed an important debate ever since. Can a democratic society, with a free flow of dramatic TV footage, retain the public will to fight a war? Many argue no. And this has been the rationale more recently for censoring the Western press in the Falklands and Grenada. Yet it is, says Lichty, a policy based on a myth.

Myth No. 4

TV today is the most effective medium in communicating news. Most of us think of TV fare as simple, direct, easy to understand—with the combination of words *and* pictures making it all the more powerful. But recent research shows that TV news, as distinct from entertainment, is often very confusing. In study after study, Robinson and Levy have found that viewers understand only about *a third* of network news stories.

Why is TV news so tough to understand? Dr. Dan Drew, professor of journalism at Indiana University, suggests that the verbal and visual often conflict. Unlike TV entertainment, in which the two are composed together, TV-news footage is gathered first, and the story it illustrates often diverges. We may see fighting across the Green Line in Beirut—for a story about peace talks. We may see "file footage" of Anglican envoy Terry Waite walking down the street—for a story on his disappearance. As viewers try to make sense of the visual, they lose the gist of the verbal. "The myth," says Levy, "is that since we are a visual medium, we must always have pictures. . . . But that's a disaster, a recipe for poor communication."

Journalists also are much more familiar with the world of public affairs, says Levy, and rely on its technical jargon: from "leading economic indicators" to "the Druse militia." Their stories, say researchers, are overillustrated, with most pictures on the screen for less than 20 seconds. They assume, mistakenly, that viewers pay complete attention, and so they often do not repeat the main theme. Yet while understanding TV news takes concentration, watching TV is full of distractions. In one study, researchers mounted cameras on top of sets and recorded the amount of time viewers also read, talked, walked in and out of the room. They concluded that viewers actually *watch* only 55 per cent of what's on.

The audience does recall the extraordinary, such as a man on the moon, and better comprehends human-interest stories. But since most news is not covered night after night, tomorrow's broadcast tends to wash away today's. "People don't remember much from TV news," says Graber. "It's like the ocean washing over traces that have been very faintly formed."

Today's TV news is carefully watched by politicians, who keep a sharp eye on how they're covered. But while it may provide theater for a handful, this research increasingly shows it's lost on the American public. And sadly, then, hard-working TV journalists may be missing an opportunity to inform.

Yet TV remains a medium with great potential. And studies show that it does extend the awareness of the poor and ill-educated, who cannot afford additional sources. What's more, research suggests that the clarity of TV news *can* be improved—without compromising journalistic standards. "We have been glitzed by the glamour of TV, all these gee-whiz gimmicks," says Robinson. "And we have lost sight of one of the oldest and most durable findings of communications research. . . . The most important element is the writer, who sits at a typewriter and tries to tell the story in a simple and organized way. That's the crucial link."

Research also shows that viewers *want* a broadcast they can understand. The success of *60 Minutes* proves there's an audience still hungry for sophisticated factual information. "When someone does this for news, they'll grab the ratings," says Levy. "Nobody loses!" Ironically, no corporation would launch an ad campaign without extensive testing on how best to reach its audience. But many broadcast journalists, working under intense pressure, remain unaware of the problems. "There's a lot we have to learn about how people comprehend," says William Rubens, NBC research vice-president. "But no, it hasn't been the thrust of our research." According to Robinson and Levy, this requires the attention of those in charge, a collective corporate will. With the networks under a financial squeeze, their news audiences having recently declined some 15 per cent, "This may be the time for them to rethink their broadcasts," says Levy.

And if they do, they may just live . . . happily ever after.

MEDIA AND DEMOCRACY

IRANSCAM: WHEN THE CHEERING STOPPED

William Boot

President Reagan's popularity fell precipitously after disclosure of the secret U.S. sale of arms to Iran and diversion of profits to the Nicaraguan *contras.* The media adopted a much harder attitude toward the President than previously. William Boot, Washington columnist for the *Columbia Journalism Review,* charges the press with treating Reagan too gently before the scandal broke.

The hot tip from the fashion capital of American journalism for the 1986–87 winter season was as follows: major takeouts on crack were now passé; articles that paid homage to "the Reagan magic" were hopelessly out of style; and the Watergate look was back, along with all the trappings of White House adversarial journalism circa 1973—the high-level investigative targets, the tenacious follow-up questioning at White House briefings, the snarling television exchanges with our chief executive, and his subsequent retreat into growing isolation. Whether it's all a passing craze or a longer-term trend remains to be seen. But for now everyone's doing it. Everyone's dancing the Iran-contra shuffle.

Those who have been longing for tougher press scrutiny of this administration are saying: better late than never. They're right. Still, there are aspects of this sea change to more aggressive reporting that should give one pause. Far from being bold and courageous in the Woodstein tradition, today's Watergate look comes across more as a herd-like exploitation of Ronald Reagan's sudden weakness.

Consider the arduous November 19 press conference at which White House reporters asked Reagan a total of forty questions about the just-exposed arms sales to Iran, hammering away at weak spots such as his denial that the sales were part of an arms-for-hostages deal. Sam Donaldson actually accused the president of "duplicity." Only a few months before, this sort of press corps attack would simply not have washed. Reagan was still very much an "in" person then, with a 68 percent Gallup approval rating, and questioners often took the safe, warm-and-friendly route. They should have been tougher.

But at that November 19 press conference, the reporters, superficially tough, really seemed more like bullies kicking a man who was down. (Iran, after all, was perhaps the most hated country in America and selling arms even to allegedly moderate factions in Teheran had not exactly gone down well with the public.) Only when he was extremely vulnerable did he get the sort of grilling he, like any other president, should have been subjected to consistently.

When the controversy heated up with the revelation that U.S. officials had diverted profits from the Iran sale to Nicaraguan contra rebels, defying a temporary congressional ban on contra military aid, the Reagan presidency went into a free fall. His popularity plummeted some twenty points in a

Source: Reprinted with permission from the *Columbia Journalism Review,* March-April 1987.

month, the fastest recorded plunge since Gallup began polling, and the press was emboldened to kick Reagan around even harder.

To be fair, there is much to admire in the zeal of many Iranscam reporters, some of whom, such as Bob Woodward himself, have been probing dark corners of the administration for years. The scandal appears at least temporarily to have reversed a general trend away from investigative reporting, and the revelations were exciting to watch: CIA AIDING IRAQ IN GULF WAR (*Washington Post,* December 15), U.S. DISINFORMATION REPORTEDLY SENT TO IRAN AND IRAQ, INTELLIGENCE 'DOCTORED' (*New York Times,* January 12), OLLIE'S MAN IN ON PLOT TO SNUFF 'ZERO' (New York *Daily News,* December 12), etc., etc.

As the scandal roared on into February, with a Reagan recovery nowhere in sight, one looked back in amazement to the heights from which he had fallen. In October he was still being lauded in many quarters as a competent, vigorous leader who had restored U.S. pride, daring, and determination after the shame of Watergate and the humiliations of Jimmy Carter's Iran hostage crisis; he brandished the big stick with aplomb, took a never-negotiate line against terrorism, and made America feel good about itself again. But by December, columnists Rowland Evans and Robert Novak were declaring flatly, "The Reagan presidency is dead."

Reagan's long stint at the top, his sudden dive, and the role of the press in his varying fortunes all bring to mind the tale of "The Emperor's New Clothes." Now that Reagan's imperial apparel has been shown to be little more than invisible weaving, some press commentators are saying that the embarrassments of November were an inevitable result of his chronic lax management. "For many close observers of Reagan," *Time* reported on December 8, "the surprise is not that his passive approach has got him into trouble, but that such a fiasco did not happen sooner."

But the press itself (including *Time,* as we shall see) has much to answer for in not having made the naked truth about Emperor Reagan more widely known. If my research (which included Nexis computer library searches of nine newspapers) is any guide, facts about the naked Reagan were generally reported in dribs and drabs—a misstatement noted here, a bungle mentioned there—with relatively muted emphasis.

Press conference gaffes, for instance, were often relegated to the lower paragraphs of a story, as in *The New York Times*'s account of Reagan's August 12, 1986, press conference, in which he incorrectly asserted that South Africa, unlike Nicaragua, had never tried to stifle the opposition press or religious dissidents or to "impose [its] government on other surrounding countries." These misstatements were alluded to without comment in the twenty-first paragraph of an August 13 *Times* report that stressed Reagan's call for a Western parley on South Africa in response to an invitation from Pretoria. (That call was withdrawn the next day by the State Department because Reagan, it turned out, had misunderstood Pretoria's terms, which were unacceptable.)

"It's as if to say, 'He's blind, but here's what he seems to think the trees look like,' " says Duke University's James David Barber, author of *The Presidential Character,* speaking of the way papers such as the *Times* covered Reagan gaffes.

Certainly much more should have been made of the president's shortcomings, which, taken together, constitute an alarming portrait. Reagan, after all, was the man who dozed off in cabinet meetings; who had to consult three-by-five cards for basic facts during meetings with foreign leaders; who called Liberian leader Samuel Doe "Chairman Moe" and said he was happy to be in Bolivia when he was really in Brazil. He was the man who said SS troopers were victims of Nazism, that the Russian people subsisted on a "starvation diet of sawdust," that trees cause air pollution, and that the shah of Iran had been a progressive leader. Reagan's gaffes, by and large, continued to draw a nonchalant response from the news media. *Time,* in a laudatory pre-revisionist essay on Reagan last summer, noted his penchant for misstatements but complacently dismissed it: "Who cared? The results seemed to come out all right."

But did they? In 1983 Reagan had been hard pressed to explain why the 240 U.S. Marines who died in a terror bomb attack in Beirut had been sent there in the first place. After ordering the surviving Americans to pull out, he declared the Lebanon policy a triumph. In terms of the human cost, Beirut was a much greater fiasco than Iranscam, but the press did not treat it as such.

Former Reagan budget director David Stockman, in his book *The Triumph of Politics,* described Reagan as fiscally uninformed, unwilling or unable to understand that he was responsible for building up a larger federal debt than all past presidents combined. The debt problem was covered heavily but it was not treated as a White House catastrophe on the Iranscam scale. If Stockman is correct, it should have been. "The American economy and government," he wrote in a postscript for the paperback edition, "have literally been taken hostage by the awesome stubbornness of the nation's fortieth president." He added that "much of the press" was too intimidated by Reagan's popularity to make the "grand indictment" of his economic policies that was required. Strangely, much of the press commentary when the book originally came out in May 1986 focused more on Stockman and his supposedly disrespectful tone toward his former boss than on Reagan's policies.

After last October's Reykjavik summit, Reagan seemed unable to explain just what arms control proposals he and the Soviets had made. This shortcoming, and the collapse of the summit, elicited a brief spate of critical coverage, but White House Chief of Staff Donald Regan later told *The New York Times* he was well satisfied with his p.r. "shovel brigade," which had used the press to turn a sour outcome into a sweet one.

Perhaps most fundamentally, Reagan was highly disengaged from the substance of his job, delegated his authority heavily, and, in what may have been a sign of things to come, was regularly betrayed by subordinates running amok—as witness the indictments of at least three high Reagan administration officials and the resignations under pressure of a number of others. The departures of these worthies were reported, but little was made of the implications for Reagan's management style.

Some veteran Washington correspondents and columnists weighed in from time to time with acid comments on Reagan's intellect and managerial skills, among them David Broder (who wrote of "the arid desert between Reagan's ears"), and Jack Germond and Jules Witcover (who quoted a conservative Republican congressman after Reagan had undergone cancer surgery in 1985 as saying, "The president is even more disengaged than he was before the operation").

Washington Post White House correspondent Lou Cannon returned often to the theme of Reagan's disengagement. In a January 6, 1986, column, he warned with some prescience: "Increasingly, the Reagan administration functions reflexively, with most of the work done by mid-level aides. . . . [Reagan's] government often runs on automatic pilot, and he seems too distant from his subordinates' deliberations or the outside world's concerns to notice. Eventually, isolation is likely to extract a price."

Cannon described for me the rather disappointing reaction to this column: "As far as I could see, there was no public resonance. It was kind of like spitting into the wind.

"Some people reported on this [Reagan's weaknesses] fairly consistently," he went on, citing the work of *Time* magazine's Laurence Barrett and Gannett's Ann Devroy, as well as his own. "But Ronald Reagan was so enormously popular that people did not give a damn, including some media organizations. . . . There was a kind of 'so-whatness' about it. What was not conveyed was how important the stuff was. . . . There was a national euphoria about Reagan—he was so popular, so apparently successful after a string of presidents perceived as failures."

A strong case can be made that news organizations pulled their punches in covering Reagan—whose popularity, Elizabeth Drew observed in a recent *New Yorker* article, had cowed much of Washington—for fear of irritating the public. As Barber, the Duke professor, says, "Any outfit that sells its goods to the public gives a certain credence to public opinion." Thus, David Broder has confessed that "even those of us who were not so bemused generally decided not to make pests of ourselves by harping on our concerns about Reagan's limited intellectual energy."

(Interestingly, a Gallup-Times Mirror poll issued in January showed that the Iran-contra affair had hurt the credibility of American journalism. Respondents gave the news media a believability rating of only 66 percent, down from 83 percent in 1985. Many felt the story was being overreported. On the other hand, 68 percent rated the coverage as excellent or good. Poll-conscious editors must be wondering, "Do they want us to lay off, or don't they?")

To return to "The Emperor's New Clothes," one might say that reporters like Cannon were trying to play the part of the little boy in the story who pointed out that the leader wasn't wearing any. But, for various reasons, they did not shout loudly enough to be heard.

Many other journalists got caught up in the Reagan euphoria and came across more like the obsequious courtiers who praised the emperor's "garments." The president's appearance at the four-day extravaganza marking the opening of a refurbished Statue of Liberty occasioned the latest of the periodic eruptions of sycophantic coverage of Reagan for his supposed reassertion of vigorous, competent leadership. The networks, which devoted much time to scenes of Reagan in patriotic settings, were particularly gushy. Thus, CBS's Lesley Stahl proclaimed on July 4, 1986: "Like his leading lady, the Statue of Liberty, the president, after six years in office, has himself become a symbol of pride in America; he has devoted himself to reviving the spirit of patriotism across the country."

Time, in a July 7 cover story on Reagan titled "Yankee Doodle Magic," proclaimed: "He is a Prospero of American memories, a magician who carries a bright, ideal America like a holograph in his mind and projects its image in the air. . . . It was Reagan who, in the aftermath of Jimmy Carter's 'malaise' and all that had come before, revived some exuberance of purpose, of entrepreneurship, patriotism, self-pride. . . . He has restored the authority of the American presidency. . . ."

The assertion about restoring presidential authority, which now seems a mite premature, had earlier been made by a number of journalists including the late Joseph Kraft ("Reagan has revived a great office") and Broder ("It is no exaggeration to say [he] has rescued the office"). But *Time* went these worthy columnists one further: "He has shown himself to be one of the strongest leaders of the 20th century. . . . Leadership is a mysterious business, of course, but Reagan seems to derive his strength from the fact that he does exactly what he says he will do." Like never negotiate with terrorists.

Fortune magazine committed a series of retrospectively even more awesome howlers, if that is possible, in its September 15, 1986, cover story: "What Managers Can Learn from Manager Reagan." The piece argued that he had delegated authority more effectively than most presidents and handled disasters well, threw in some perfunctory qualifications, and concluded: "One extraordinarily important if little-noted element of the Reagan legacy is already established: he has proved once again that the presidency is manageable." To misquote Oscar Wilde, I don't wish I'd said that.

To sum up, certain reporters and columnists served to bolster Emperor Reagan's delusions and others could not make their misgivings about him heard. The public now has opened its eyes, if only fleetingly. So who was the little boy of the story, the one who drew the president's nudity to their attention? The answer is Ronald Reagan.

Reagan, of course, has blamed the press for blowing the whistle on his secret operations and, to be sure, it was a magazine—Beirut's *al Shiraa*—to which Iranian sources leaked the first public report of the arms deal. This is almost beside the point. It is often said that the president, not the press corps, dominates the news agenda in Washington.

The Iranscam controversy shows that this domination is so great that the president even certifies which of his snafus are to be elevated by the press into full-fledged scandals.

It was Reagan and his attorney general, Edwin Meese, after all, who—apparently fearing that the press might break the story—let the contra-fund-diversion cat out of the bag in a televised November 25 press conference. And it was Reagan who said repeatedly, then and later, that he had not had the ghost of an idea what his subordinates were up to in diverting that money—the so-called incompetence defense. It's better to appear incompetent than evil, I suppose, and while reporters probed for evidence that Reagan (and his immediate underlings) had been aware of the "contradeception," news organizations also seemed to give him the benefit of the doubt, trumpeting the evidence that he had little control over his own administration. This long-known fact at last had become a major part of a running front-page story.

Reagan's onetime aura of vigorous leadership came in for special debunking. *Newsweek* faulted his "dreamy detachment." In a January 14 piece headlined AN INATTENTION TO DETAIL IS GETTING MORE ATTENTION, Martin Tolchin of *The New York Times* quoted congressional leaders who spilled the beans on a muddled Reagan who had spouted non-sequitur anecdotes and consistently missed the point at a White House meeting. *The Washington Post*'s Lou Cannon reported that, at seventy-five, Reagan was tiring more easily, that his hearing was declining, and that some insiders believed he was "slipping."

Time, which had puffed Reagan's "Yankee Doodle Magic," was perhaps harshest of all. Declaring that "Reagan was out of touch," it decried as "absurd" his tendency "to delegate disproportionate authority to subordinates who took a can-do approach and then to let them operate with little supervision. . . . This disaster throws a pitiless light on the way the president does his job, confirming the worst fears of both his friends and his critics. . . ."

Time echoed many other publications in declaring, after the Reagan-Meese contra revelation, that the Iran affair "had turned into an outright scandal"—largely because "there was every indication that laws had been broken." In fact, there had been strong indications long before that press conference that laws had been broken and the will of Congress defied in pursuit of the contra cause. Evidence of such transgressions—including alleged contra drug smuggling and administration-backed gunrunning—received some news coverage. Yet, prior to the White House contra announcement, the underside of U.S. policy toward the rebels had not been treated as a running, front-page scandal. In my Nexis newspaper search, the word "scandal" did not appear in the headline of an article on the contras prior to November 25.

After that, with the press pack taking its cue from Reagan and Meese, stories on contra shenanigans were suddenly very much in fashion. It looks as though they will remain so, at least through the spring season. But styles are hard to predict, so grab this story now, in case it suddenly goes the way of the miniskirt and the sack dress, the twist and the frug.

WHITE HOUSE SPOKESMAN RATES THE PRESS

Larry Speakes

Serving as President Reagan's chief spokesman for nearly six years, from 1981 to 1987, Larry Speakes conducted 2,000 news briefings. When he resigned to take a Wall Street job, he interviewed himself at his final news conference, posing questions and giving answers about relations between the press and the White House. This is the text of his "interview." In his memoirs published later, Speakes admitted fabricating quotations from Reagan while acting as spokesman. Media reaction to this disclosure was so severe that he resigned from the Wall Street job.

Source: White House press conference, January 30, 1987.

Is the press fair?
Yes. By and large they've given the Reagan administration a fair shake. They've reported the thrust of our goals in depth and generally with a balanced viewpoint. They've called us on the carpet when we needed to be called on the carpet, and they probably gave us a longer honeymoon than we deserved.

My main complaint with the press is they are saddled by a fault that's not necessarily of their own making. White House press are by necessity generalists. They're forced to cover stories day in and day out that run from budget to arms control to economy to politics, and, therefore, they tend to sometimes ignore the broad policy questions and focus on the stumbles and the bumbles and gaffes—and there have been a few—and they ignore the broad policy.

They often can't see the forest through the trees. Take the federal budget—that blueprint of all of the billions of dollars spent on government programs where policy is set. It really isn't a story in Washington until you get a fight going between Weinberger and Stockman over the defense budget.

When I began in this business, the way an editor chose the lead story—he asked himself questions: How many people does this affect? What's the impact on the community or the nation?

Today it seems the number one factor in determining what's news is conflict—better still, if it's personality conflict. I've often thought that if a hundred congressmen came in to see the President and one by one marched on the front lawn and said, "The President's proposal is just great," there'd be no news. But if 99 walked out and said,

Larry Speakes reads a statement to reporters at a White House briefing. Speakes served as chief presidential spokesman during most of Ronald Reagan's two terms.

"The President's program stinks," then you've got news. It takes conflict these days to make news.

How has the press corps changed?
In a word: television. We've been inundated by cameras and microphones, and cables and producers and correspondents. And not too many years ago, when I first came to the White House, the ratio of print media to electronic media was 75%/25% in favor of the print journalists. Today the ratio is reversed.

When you take 200 newsmen on a presidential trip, 150 are representatives of radio and television. When I left the White House at the end of the Ford administration, we had three networks covering the President. Today there are seven. And on a day when there are visiting governors and mayors from across the country, we may have as many as 20 cameras in the Oval Office. Ten minutes of a 30-minute meeting is set aside for photographs.

But more than sheer numbers, the influence of television on the shape of the news is fast becoming the only thing to be reckoned with.

In the Ford days, a spokesman would prepare for eight or ten different issues to be raised in his daily press briefing. Today, more often than not, a single issue will dominate the White House news for the day. This is brought on by television, which generally airs only one story a day from the White House beat. This is having an impact on how everyone, not just television but radio, newspapers, magazines and trade journals cover the news. It is also having an impact on the message the public receives—nearly two-thirds of whom say they receive the majority of their news from television.

What's the toughest part of your job?
Answering questions when you don't have the answers. My job is like a reporter's job. I have to go for the facts just as a reporter does. I have to interview one, or two, or a dozen different people to find out what's going on. Then I weigh the facts. I evaluate news sources, and I decide who's telling the truth and who's not.

We have a saying in the press office, and sometimes it's only half in jest, "When all else fails, resort to the truth." We learned to ask the right questions though, like: "Are you invading Grenada today?" Answer comes back: "No, preposterous." You soon have to learn the follow-up: "Then are you invading Grenada tomorrow?" You live and learn in this business.

Well, what's so tough about this job?
Well, there are a lot of people looking over your shoulder. As Andy said, that book is going to be titled, "Everybody wants to be a press secretary, but nobody wants to go to the briefing room." The screw-up potential in this job is greater than perhaps any other job in the world. Every briefing is like pitching the seventh game of the World Series: you're only one bad pitch away from oblivion.

It's ironic my going to Wall Street. One of my biggest goofs came concerning Wall Street. We were flying down to New Orleans on Air Force One—we always have that pool of reporters with us—and I went back to brief 'em as I always do. A question came up, the Federal Reserve Board is meeting tomorrow, what about interest rates? Well, I didn't think I said anything. Got off the plane in New Orleans, went to my room and the phone's ringing. It's Pete Roussel. He says, "What have you said?" I said, "I don't think I said anything." He says, "Well, the stock market's gone up ten points in the last ten minutes."

And so I beat a quick run down to the pressroom and found out the pool report had said that I had predicted interest rates would go down. And so I quickly changed it; the stock market went down eight points, but yet we made two points on the rally.

You know, there's one thing I want to do when I get to Wall Street—I want to find that person that starts rumors about every six weeks that the President has had a heart attack. There's not a morning that we don't get up—about once a month—that somebody comes in that the President's had a heart attack in the night and trying to make a buck on the stock market somewhere.

The Reagan Presidency is run for television. What have you got to say about that?
To quote Speakes' law, you don't tell us how to stage the news, and we don't tell you how to cover it. We are mindful of the needs of television, and hopefully all of the media. But there's more. We're between the devil and the deep blue sea when we get ready to make arrangements for the press. If we fail to provide everything that the press needs to do its job, then the whole White House is in disarray. Or if we provide everything from fact sheets on complex budget matters to helicopters at the DMZ to fly the film in for network deadlines, then we're accused of running the White House just to suit the press corps.

The press complained so much to me about the President's visit to Normandy a couple of years ago. I told them that Eisenhower's job in planning the original D-Day was nothing compared to getting them ashore to cover the 40th anniversary.

The toughest job I have in the White House is to educate the powers that be that communications planners must be on the ground floor for all policy planning. Presidents have failed, and they have failed miserably, because they were unable to communicate and, thereby, mold and mobilize public opinion. Leadership without communications is a ship of state without power.

Why doesn't the President have more press conferences?
He has more than you think, but not enough, in my opinion. To date, in six years, he's held 39 press conferences; but there have been 497 other meetings with the press, ranging from one-on-one interviews to group sessions to mini-press conferences to brief question-and-answer sessions on the way to the helicopter.

The press has a unique way of keeping tally, though. If it's not in the East Room, if it's not prime time, if it's not a television extravaganza, then it's not a press conference. But the press conference has an important role in the relationship between the President and the press. It presents the President often in a tough give-and-take environment, answering questions about his policies. It gives the public a chance through television to see how the President reacts, how he performs.

But the press conference in its present form may have outlived its usefulness—its usefulness to the Presidency, its usefulness to the press and to the public. And, I might add, the White House and the press must together take steps to save this important institution of the democratic process.

What's wrong?
Press conferences are theater. They're scripted. Reporters ask written questions to which a President gives a rehearsed answer. The spontaneity is lost. The press is not looking for information. They're out to make news. An "I gotcha" syndrome prevails. There's an attempt to entrap a President. "How can we get him to say what he doesn't want to say?"

There was a time when Presidents could, on a weekly basis, call reporters into the Oval Office, and there, with the press assembled around the desk, would follow an honest, thorough, well-mannered, profitable give-and-take on the issues of the day. That's the way FDR did it. That's the way a governor of California named Ronald Reagan did it.

Let us seek ways to recreate the Oval Office atmosphere in a setting suitable to television. Let the press and the White House join hands to save the press conference.

The Reagan White House caters to television and ignored newspapers. Is that fair?
We do give prominence to television in our communications planning. This is essential because most all Americans get their news from television. That's a fact of life that we have to deal with.

On the other hand, we do not and we cannot afford to overlook radio or newspapers. You will often find the lead story on the evening news had its origin in the morning headline of the *New York Times* or the *Washington Post.* Just ask one of our

White House correspondents how hard it is to convince a New York producer that a story isn't evening-news material just because he read it in the paper as he whipped down his cornflakes in the morning.

But let me be very serious for a moment. The time has come when television must not only recognize its prominence and predominance in America today, but even more, it must recognize its responsibility. The impact of television on our society is pervasive. We've got to recognize our responsibilities. And on the part of the government, too much government policy is decided on how it will play on the evening news.

Clearly the news media—mainly television—is the authoritative voice of the nation. And with that authority comes an important responsibility to tell the story and to tell it accurately. The influence of television on American opinion—indeed, on the democratic system—is too great to ever take responsibility except in the most serious of terms.

The time has come for television to examine the way it covers the news, the way it goes about presenting it to the American people, and the impact it is having on our nation.

Competitive spirit, that fundamental drive that made America great, is leading to the distortion of the news. It begins with competition between reporters for the networks who cover the same beat; the morning-show reporters trying to get something that the evening-news counterpart doesn't have. It's a fact of life. There is not a morning-news reporter out there who doesn't wish to have a piece on the evening news. So there's competition between the reporters that work the same beat.

There's also competition between reporters for the same network who cover different beats. The White House reporter is trying to get the story on the air that night, while his colleagues at State, or Defense or Capitol Hill are tugging at the producer's shirtsleeves to say, "We ought to have the story on this end of the street."

And that's just the competition between reporters for the same network, look what happens when ABC and CBS and NBC go at the story, each trying to one-up the other. And mix into that the impact of CNN's around-the-clock news. Few realize the impact is great of the "let's go live with everything" syndrome in today's news coverage. The news is suffering from overexposure.

There was a time when a live broadcast was reserved for a declaration of war, or at a minimum, a presidential address to the nation. Now live coverage is the rule, not the exception. The live broadcast too often elevates the unimportant to the all-too-important. Everything today is trumpeted as bulletin material. We're elevating to new highs public perception of the news that may not necessarily be the news. We may lull a public into a ho-hum response to news that's really important to their well-being.

Competition is driving the networks to a hair-trigger mentality. "We'd better carry this live or our competition will beat our socks off." We're in danger of creating a modern-day equivalent to the boy who cried wolf. Suppose you went live and no one cared?

You've leveled a lot of criticism at the media, Mr. Speakes. After six years, what should be done?
This is a serious question for the Presidency and the press. It is a difficult one to come up with answers to because of the legitimate wall of separation between these two great institutions, the President and the reporter. But it is an integral part of our system that cannot be ignored. It is too important a question to shunt aside. Far too much is at stake because in this day we have a world that is linked by instant communication. Together, we must seek solutions. And here are some recommendations:

- For starters, remember Lincoln. "You cannot fool all of the people all of the time, or even some of the people some of the time." This applies equally to the Presidency and to the press. Let government rededicate itself to the truth first, last and always. And let the press rededicate itself to accuracy and fairness, first, last and always.
- Let's send that well-quoted administration official off to a long-overdue retirement. Let government pledge to tell the story on the record, and

let the press corps pledge to report it on the record. In the post-Reykjavik media blitz, which gained so much notoriety, we told the story on the record—the President, the Secretary of State and the press secretary. We pledged: For our part, we will say everything on the record; public statements and private interviews. And if you report anonymous sources, you may run the risk of getting it wrong. For me, this was a great step, so logical and so simple and it provided a great sense of relief.

Too often, an administration official speaks from behind a cloak of anonymity, making news by sabotaging those with whom he disagrees, by conducting character assassinations on his colleagues in government, and most seriously, leaking top-secret information that may be damaging to our country. This official, hidden by this cloak, is a phantom. Reporting him as a senior administration official makes the press and public unable to evaluate his credibility.

- Let's take a long, hard look at television news. With all the clout you hold in forming public opinion, let's never forget the responsibility. Let's seek new and better ways to present the news. Tell fewer stories and tell them better.
- Let's dust off that old proposal to take the news-shows out of the ratings games. I know that's the way you earn your advertising dollars and ads are essential to foot the bills for the news department. Let's take the news business out of entertainment and put it back where it belongs, in the news department.
- Let us re-examine the question of live television. "Are we putting this on the air because the public needs to know now? Or are we putting it on the air because we are afraid our competition will go live?"

And now let's turn to what the Presidency can do to improve this relationship.

- Let's make good on that age-old promise of less secrecy in government, not more. Sure, there are times when you have to keep a few things quiet. But let's examine every policy initiative in the light of day. Let a little light under the tent of secrecy and the result will surely be better policy.
- Let the press secretary in. Tell him everything. Believe him when he says, "It ain't good policy if the public won't buy it."

- Let's reinstitute the dialogue between the President and the press. Let's open the doors to the Oval Office once a week and say, "Walk right in, and I'll be glad to answer your questions."
- Let's make news when there's news to be made. Let's not write a tv script and then create an event designed for the evening news.
- Let government decide policy on the basis of what's good for the people, not what's good for television. If it's good, television will cover it.

MAKING JOURNALISM SAFE FOR DEMOCRACY

Michael Schudson

In this provocative essay, Professor Michael Schudson of the University of California, San Diego, contends: "A large problem with the press is not that it fails democracy but that democracy is already in trouble and the media mirror its weaknesses and are entrapped in them."

With a Presidential election upon us, it is again time for social critics (I count myself one) to sharpen their knives, ready to carve up the press for its various sins against electoral democracy. Well, I will join in the carving, but reluctantly, because I am convinced that the news media have long been the unheralded patrons of the political process, giving most citizens more political information than they want and better information than they know what to do with. A large problem with the press is not that it fails democracy but that democracy is already in trouble and the media mirror its weaknesses and are entrapped in them.

And yet (the niceties dispensed with, the carving begins), journalists bear some of the responsibility for the fading of the democratic light. Jour-

Source: Reprinted from *The Quill,* November 1984, by permission of *The Quill* and the author.

nalists, like people in other professions, get lazy, fall into ruts, and too often forget what they are here for in the first place. And what they are here for (apart from putting out entertaining and profitable cultural products), what they receive special license for (in favorable postal rates, for instance) and special privilege (the First Amendment) is that they contribute to a more democratic society. The job of the press is to help produce a more informed electorate. A more informed citizenry will create a better and fuller democracy. So goes the litany one can hear at any journalism school, convention, or awards banquet.

This simple and noble vision is, of course, not always kept in view, let alone realized. Moreover, the concept of democracy it incorporates is one that most social scientists have long since abandoned. This leaves conscientious journalists rallying their colleagues to a banner that has long been little but rags and threads.

Reporters and editors oscillate between a misty-eyed, nostalgia-tinged vision of town meetings and a sour, behind-the-scenes ("I have the inside dope") cynicism about how politics *really* works. Neither the vision nor the cynicism helps very much toward a serious evaluation of what rôle the media can play in a democracy. But it's possible to think the problem through more carefully and to arrive at some practical suggestions for making the press a more active instrument of democracy. This will require a brief excursion into theory.

There are, in broadest terms, two ways of understanding democracy. The "classical" view of democracy takes democracy to be an assembly of rational, participating citizens who discuss their public concerns with like-minded people in neighborhoods, private associations, and political parties. Citizens articulate their interests through electoral work and voting for candidates who serve them as representatives in legislative bodies. This model presupposes an interested and informed citizenry. A second view, however, holds that contemporary politics bears no resemblance to the Continental Congress of 1776 or a New England town meeting. If we are looking for a model to serve as a practical goal and not as a fantasy, then it is necessary to define more narrowly what democracy means—what democracy can possibly mean. Walter Lippmann was an eloquent spokesman for this "realist" view of democracy. He held that elites rule in a democracy, that we cannot expect otherwise, and that journalism cannot change matters. . . . Lippmann writes:

"We must abandon the notion that the people govern. Instead we must adopt the theory that, by their occasional mobilization as a majority, people support or oppose the individuals who actually govern. We must say that the popular will does not direct continuously but that it intervenes occasionally."

Lippmann held out no hope that the public could be educated to fuller participation. He did not believe the role of the press was to inform citizens to make rational and informed judgments. The best that could be done would be to provide simple, clear signs to serve as "guides to reasonable action for the use of uninformed people." . . .

To Lippmann's dour assessment, contemporary political science has added two more grim points, which I will briefly capsule:

The party's over. Political parties are an index of viable democracy. Parties stand between the governors and the citizens, enable the coherent aggregation and articulation of popular views, and insist on responsiveness by the governing officials to those views. But today, as one political scientist has argued, "The American political party is little more than one of the many groups, not greatly disparate in their influence, which participate in elections. . . . Specifically, the party has lost its power in Presidential recruitment—personal organizations backing individual candidates have become rivals to party organization. Primary elections have replaced party caucuses. The mass media have stepped into the void, too, with national political reporters acting as a kind of "screening committee" for Presidential aspirants. . . .

The unelected governors: the corporations. In market-oriented societies like the United States, there are *two* rival forms of control over political authority. There is, obviously, the electoral system. But there is also a separate system of privileged business controls. Businessmen perform functions in market societies that are governmental functions in other systems, making decisions about what is to be produced, who is to be employed, how products are to be allocated. In market societies, corporate executives have considerable discretion on these matters. Government delegates these decisions to business. Business then exercises public functions. . . .

Presidents, recognizing the public service that business provides, will sometimes try to shield business from the uncertainties of the mainstream political process. Both Johnson and Nixon suppressed reports of their own committees on antitrust so as to keep a "business" matter out of the normal political arena. This is not to say business exercises its power badly; it is simply to recognize that a vast number of decisions which in democracies like Sweden or Britain are government decisions subject to popular control are, in the United States, delegated more or less permanently to private authorities. The result is that a large portion of public policy lies beyond the purview of popular judgment.

Where do these discouraging assessments of American democracy leave the news media that, hypothetically, would like to devote themselves body and soul to improving the democratic process?

I want to propose that the news media should be self-consciously schizophrenic in their efforts to perform a democratic political function. They should both champion the kind of classical democracy that the realists say we cannot achieve and, at the same time, they should sagely and imaginatively respond to the phenomena of contemporary politics that the realists have observed. . . .

Suppose that citizens are rational, interested in public affairs, and have access for effective participation in politics. Then the job of the news media is to help them achieve an adequate understanding of political issues. What does this entail? Two things. The media can help citizens to "discover" their own preferences and the media can help them act intelligently on their preferences. The first point is often overlooked. People's preferences are not built-in; we do not necessarily know what our preferences are. Political education is not simply a task of making the political scene clear enough for people to match their own pre-determined preferences with the appropriate political actors who share those preferences. It is also a task in shaping the citizens' political tastes and preferences.

It is odd how often political observers forget this. We tend to assume that the wealthy will oppose taxes on high incomes, that blacks will vote for Democrats, and that the pinched middle class will prefer policies aimed at curbing inflation to policies aimed at reducing unemployment. These assumptions are largely—but not entirely—correct. And politics enters at the margin; politics—the art of building coalitions, making compromises, persuading people that their own interests may be redefined—exists only where the powers of determinism stop. . . .

This is the faith upon which a democratic polity rests. Its foe is a determinism that insists that people have identifiable interests, know those interests, and vote them, period. One of determinism's most reliable allies has been public-opinion polling. Not that there is anything wrong in public-opinion polling in itself. But it invariably takes on a permanence and authority it does not deserve. This has dangerous consequences. The press should take special care not to stunt political education by providing poll data carelessly.

The news media, intentionally or unintentionally, serve as political educators. This does not mean slogans or sermons or even editorials. It means that the media, by their reporting, promote an image of the political process. They necessarily incorporate into their work a certain view of politics and they will either do so intelligently and self-consciously or routinely and unconsciously. For instance, the media strengthen determinism when they report on the activities of the myriad single-interest constituencies that so trouble observers of both left and right. They generate a sense of a growing anarchy in American politics, a war of all against all, with dozens of dogmatic groups taking on new power and showing no willingness to compromise in the political arena. . . .

There is much the press can do to improve its conventional function of providing citizens with the information that will enable them to gain an adequate understanding of politics, including their own preferences, and to participate effectively in political life. Take, for instance, the especially crucial problem of covering elections. How well does the press cover elections? How might election coverage be improved?

A recent study of Congressional elections by Peter Clarke and Susan Evans finds that incumbents receive far more press coverage than challengers. Incumbents are almost all reelected; since 1968, over ninety percent of incumbent Congressmen running for reelection have been successful, and their margin of victory keeps growing. There are any number of explanations for this "incumbency" phenomenon. Congressmen have more resources than challengers, typically. Further, with party identification growing weaker among voters, the recognition that the incumbent gains by two years or more in office is an increasingly significant advantage. But another factor is that newspapers provide incumbents much more election coverage than they do challengers. . . .

There is much the press could do to improve this performance. Simply to recognize it might, in itself, galvanize the press to better work. Some simple changes could help. Where in the paper, for instance, is a citizen to find news about the candidates in his or her district? In large metropolitan areas, citizens are at something of a loss. It is not easy to know where in the paper to look—or whether it will be worth looking—since coverage of the different races tends to be episodic. A simpler, cleaner format might make a big difference. In many ways, newspapers help readers to monitor their worlds—the sports scores, the stock market quotations. There will be a big story about the home team's game and then, very often, boxed together, brief reports on all the other games in the league. Why should the newspapers do less for politics? . . .

There is much that can be done if news institutions assume that there is a rational, intelligent, interested citizenry eager to inform itself if information about politics is made available. But what if the democratic doubters and skeptics are right? If the citizens inevitably lie far from the center of activity? If political parties are practically moribund? If business has a disproportionate influence in American politics?

If the press cannot effectively communicate about government to the people at large, it can nonetheless hold the governors accountable to the relatively small number of informed and powerful people. The press can serve as a stand-in for the public, holding the governors accountable—not to the public (which is not terribly interested) but to the ideals and rules of the democratic polity itself.

What I mean is not complicated. One investigative reporter, David Burnham of *The New York Times,* has said that his strategy as an investigative reporter is to hold government agencies and other groups he covers to their own stated goals. The question is not, are they doing right or are they doing wrong? It is, are they living up to what they have committed themselves to do? That is a question one may approach in traditional journalistic ways, holding to the rules of objectivity. At the same time, it is a question the asking of which asserts the responsibility of the press as an institution for public accountability. . . .

What might the press do regarding the privileged position of big business? There are no ready answers to this question. The news media are big businesses themselves, increasingly, and they enjoy some of the special access to government policy-making available to other large corporations. Also, they are financially supported by businesses—local businesses of modest size in the case of the print media and large national corporations in the case of television. One cannot expect the news media to go after big business with a hatchet.

But the job of the press is not to assert that business has too much or too little or just the right amount of power; the job of the news media is to cover the news of political life. The job in this instance is to recognize and report on the ways in which business is a partner in government.

Consider, for a moment, the reporting of Congressional legislation—a measure for environmental protection, a bill for a tax increase or decrease. The way this is now reported, the main "scene" is one in which five hundred-odd representatives make up their minds about how to vote. There may be some attention in feature articles or in news analyses about what happens "behind the scenes"—how active lobbyists are, who they are, what their views are. Though this is a part of the career of any legislation, it receives little notice in hard news. Why? Not, I think, because reporters want to protect lobbyists from public scrutiny. But simply because, ultimately, the story is about how the legislators vote. Their decisions, in the final analysis, will determine whether a tax proposal, say, becomes law.

This is reasonable, but it leaves a major part of the legislative process in shadows.

There may be some simple remedies. Newspapers might identify a certain number of key bills in each session of Congress or of a state legislature and keep a running tab on them. . . .

Obviously, this is not going to be possible or worthwhile on every piece of legislation. But on key legislative matters, it would be an important way to keep the electorate informed and to make lobbyists to some degree responsible to the public. . . .

Would everyone read such dull stuff? Of course not. But remember, now, this is the schizophrenic news media that I am proposing. In this part of my recommendations, it is not required that the media audience be entirely intelligent, rational, and active in the political process. There need only be a small, interested body of readers that pays attention to such news. And the group can be very small indeed. In theory, it could be just the reporters and their editors themselves. For if we abandon the classical notion of rational and interested citizens, then the news media can be viewed not as communicators to the public but as guardians of the public, unelected but conscientious stand-ins for public scrutiny, gatekeepers who monitor the political process on behalf of the public to keep it honest and to some extent accountable. . . .

Too often, journalists—like people in every other field—set no goals. They just want to get through the day, just meet the deadline. But from that perspective they sometime shift to the other extreme and think that their goal should be to educate the people to be shrewd observers of politics and enthusiastic participants in the political process, that they should create the world in which a classical notion of democracy would make sense.

I have tried to argue that this lofty goal, while unreachable, is still in many ways an excellent guide for journalistic practice. At the same time, journalistic practice also should accommodate itself to the reality that not all readers are, or ever will be, rational, intelligent, active, and constant participants in the political process. In cases where an informed and involved electorate does not exist, the news media have available to them alternate models of their democratic obligations. They can act as stand-ins for the public, holding authority (constituted—in the case of government—and unconstituted—in the case of business, lobbies, and interest groups) responsible to its own stated aims and other publicly agreed-upon goals.

As I have said, this may call for a kind of schizophrenia on the part of the news media—to act as if classical democracy were possible, and simultaneously to work as if a large, informed, and involved electorate were not possible. The virtue of schizophrenia is that *both* things are true under different circumstances. Journalists would do well to be of two minds because the world is of two (or more) possibilities. And in this fact, I think, lies not only complication but opportunity.

DEVELOPMENTS IN POLITICAL COMMUNICATION THEORY ON MASS MEDIA POTENTIAL

L. John Martin

This review of communication theory trends since Lasswell develops the thesis that the mass media play an agenda-setting role in politics and thus influence election campaigns. Professor L. John Martin of the University of Maryland updated and expanded an earlier essay especially for this book.

The power of the pen and of the press is conventional wisdom that goes back hundreds of years. Rosencrantz in *Hamlet* says that "many wearing rapiers are afraid of goosequills." But when this purported axiom was subjected to scientific investigation, doubts began to be expressed about its accuracy. Frank Luther Mott, the journalism historian, determined that, in the 35 presidential election campaigns from 1796 to 1940, the American press gave its majority support to the winning candidate 18 times and to the losing candidate 17 times.[1] Chance could not have played a more even-handed role.

HYPODERMIC THEORY

Yet no one to the present day believes that the press is powerless. In fact, the power of the press is implicit in the idea of harnessing the mass media to perform important social, economic, military, and political tasks—a thought that occurred to the U.S. government in World War II, when it had to train a huge citizen army in a hurry. The Army's Education and Information Division needed to know which of the various available communication techniques were most effective in isolation, in sequence, and in combination. To answer these questions, an experimental section was organized under Yale psychologist Carl I. Hovland within the research branch of the division to study, among other things, the differential effects and effectiveness of the mass media.

Hovland and his staff conducted their empirical research in the context of a paradigm suggested by political scientist Harold D. Lasswell to describe the communication process: "Who says what to whom with what effect?" The studies dealt with the persuasiveness of the different media, but were later continued by the same group of psychologists at Yale University to include the effectiveness of various types of messages and communicators. The Yale Communication Research Program, as it was designated, had for its underpinnings Lasswell's "hypodermic model" of the communication process which, at least implicitly, suggests that communication is something someone does to someone else. The only question that the researcher must answer in this approach is: How does one vary the types of communicator (who) or the kinds of messages (what) or audiences (whom) to maximize the effectiveness of the process (what effect)? And that is what many communication researchers addressed themselves to for another 15 years or so.

The conclusion many scholars arrived at was that, all other things being equal, the more personal a medium, the more efficiently persuasive it is. Thus, face-to-face communication is more effective than television, which is more effective than film, radio, and print—in that order.

But quite apart from the fact that this was not always the outcome of their research, all other things are seldom equal except, possibly, in the laboratory. The difference between people in their natural habitats and people in a laboratory experiment was recognized by Hovland himself, who more than anyone was responsible for mass communication experiments in the laboratory. The reason, he said, you can prove so much more in the laboratory than in a survey of people in a real-life situation is that in the latter case people who have exposed themselves to a message did so voluntarily and many of them were on the persuader's side to begin with. In an experiment, opinion change is often measured minutes after the exposure, when the impact is greatest. Experiments are frequently

Source: Printed by permission of the author.

carried out in classrooms where student-subjects are more receptive to the messages, which in any case are selected for their likelihood to show change.[2]

Gerhard D. Wiebe, a research psychologist for CBS and later dean of the School of Public Communication at Boston University, developed deductively a rationale for the greater effectiveness of more personal media; then he tested his theory empirically. He pointed out that the reason television is more vivid, more suggestive of "immediate reality" than radio, which in turn is more real than print, is that radio is one symbol system removed from reality (the spoken word), while print is two symbol systems—two levels of abstraction—removed. This is because the printed word is a symbol for the spoken word, which itself is a symbol for reality. He said that television is experienced in an intimate frame of reference, while newspaper accounts are perceived in a distant frame of reference.[3] What led to the undoing of Senator Joseph R. McCarthy, in Wiebe's opinion, was that he was brought into an intimate frame of reference through the televising of the Army–McCarthy hearings. Wiebe contrasted this to the war in Indochina which, in 1954, was still being experienced in a distant frame of reference. Vietnam had not yet been brought into every American's living room by massive television coverage.

Then, in 1960, Joseph T. Klapper reviewed the research findings (mainly of the previous two decades) and came to the conclusion that "mass communication *ordinarily* does not serve as a necessary and sufficient cause of audience effects, but rather functions among and through a nexus of mediating factors and influences."[4] This was not a new idea. It had been noted by Hovland in a 1954 article referring to Mott's 1944 study and to a 1926 paper by George A. Lundberg. Hovland had to admit that "press support of presidential candidates seems to bear no relationship to their success at the polls."[5] It was just that the hope lingered that somehow a researcher might hit on the right formula—one that would guarantee a gambler's chance to those who are willing to invest their money in mass media time and space to cajole their fellow human beings into taking a desired line of action. But the best that Klapper could offer was the statement that "the efficacy of mass communication in creating opinion . . . can be gauged only in reference to issues on which, at the time of exposure, people are *known to have no opinion at all.*"[6]

INFORMATION-SEEKING THEORIES

What put researchers on a new track was a series of consistency or balance theories developed by social psychologists in the 1950s. Questions had been asked about the effectiveness of mass media in changing people's attitudes. Paul Lazarsfeld and his associates at Columbia University had been doing some panel studies that involved reinterviewing the same group of voters a number of times during the course of an election campaign. They found to their surprise that the mass media played a minor role in influencing people in their voting, especially when compared with the influence of friends and neighbors.[7] But these researchers were still looking for mass media effects and were operating under the hypodermic model. Consistency theorists, such as Fritz Heider, Theodore Newcomb and Leon Festinger, were saying that people like their beliefs and judgments about things and other people to be consistent with one another. To reduce what Festinger called dissonance, a stressful feeling that is created by inconsistencies, people expose themselves to facts, events, and judgments through communication or selectively shut out such communication to avoid dissonance. They might even selectively perceive, or misperceive, and selectively retain information to the same end.[8]

Consistency theories switched the Lasswellian paradigm around. No longer were communication specialists concerned about who says what to whom, since this is immaterial if the "whom" in the paradigm is unable or unwilling to receive the message. The question they now asked was: Who needs to receive what messages from whom? The emphasis was on the seeking and avoiding of information rather than on the transmission of instruction or urging of opinion change. Furthermore, a distinction began to be made between informational communication and persuasive communication. The mass media had been weighed in the balance and found clearly wanting in persuasiveness—at least in the short run. People don't do things or change their attitudes or even opinions simply because they are asked to or told to by an individual, directly or through the mass media.

The change in perspective on the communication process also led to a rethinking of the findings of the relative effectiveness of the different mass media. Pollster Elmo Roper had for years been asking people questions about the medium they consider most informative and the one they believe to be the most credible. He found television to be the medium more than half the audience would want to keep if they had to give up all other media. Television also was the most credible medium in the Roper poll. Over the years, television has consistently been rated the major source of information about national candidates by 60 to 65 percent of the public, with newspapers being rated first by only a fourth to a third of the public. For information about state candidates, television has a much narrower edge over newspapers, while on local candidates, newspapers are considered a better source than television by more people. Friends and relatives are an important source of information only on local candidates (the major source for around one in five). Radio and magazines are rated a major source of information about political candidates—national, state, or local—by fewer than 10 percent of the population.[9]

In the light of information-seeking theories, communication specialist Alex S. Edelstein studied audiences in both the United States and Yugoslavia and concluded that sources of information were evaluated not in terms of their credibility, but in terms of their content, breadth of perception, and availability. Television provided the greatest breadth of perception, and if seeing was important to the audience, television was the preferred medium. Newspapers provided the greatest breadth of content and the most time to think, while radio was the most available medium.[10]

Clearly, this approach is inconsistent with a hypodermic theory and is closer to what Jay G. Blumler and Elihu Katz have called a "uses and gratifications" perspective—one in which the user of information is the person who determines what medium to use.[11] He also makes the judgment about its believability, depending on whether it gratifies his needs. In other words, it is not the communicator who manipulates his medium or his message and its environment to create a desired effect. This new way of looking at the communication process has influenced communication research in one way or another for the past ten years.[12]

AGENDA-SETTING FUNCTION

One bothersome problem with an audience-initiated and controlled communication model is that it appears to leave the man with a message—a political candidate, for instance—in an impotent, supplicant role. His target will attend to his message only if it does not upset the target's existing beliefs and judgments. This means that the politician would tend to be preaching to the already converted; and, in fact, one of the rules of thumb of persuasive communication (such as political campaigning and propaganda) is that "The people you may want most in your audience are often least likely to be there."[13] This follows logically from the selective exposure syndrome mentioned above and supports consistency theories.

While this maxim is not difficult to rationalize, it leaves one dissatisfied. Don't tell us, we feel like saying, that the mass media have absolutely no power beyond merely agreeing with their audience—since, after all, people by this postulate expose themselves only to those parts of the press with which they already agree. Intuitively—since each of us can think of occasions when the mass media have influenced us or when we think we were influenced—we tend to reject this conclusion.[14] Communication researchers have pointed out that to suggest that the media have only a limited effect ignores the universality of the media, and especially the pervasiveness of television.[15] Nowadays, many people are involuntarily exposed to messages on television, sandwiched between entertainment programs that they happen to be watching.[16] Often, the entertainment itself carries a political message.[17] Furthermore, the media have many more effects than merely to influence attitudes. Thus, Jay Blumler and Jack McLeod[18] speak of the effect of the media on voter turnout, the increased use of other media as the result of being exposed to one of them, greater interest in politics and in political activity, which might lead to more discussion of political issues with one's friends.[19]

It is here that communication theorists came up with a new role for the mass media. It involved once and for all separating persuasive from informational communication. Their underlying assumption was that gaining new knowledge has little to do with how that knowledge will be used. It might result in an interpretation that is favorable to the thrust of the message or one that is unfavorable. The focus should be on information gained, not on attitudes changed.

The text is taken from political scientist Bernard C. Cohen, who pointed out that "the press may not be successful much of the time in telling people what to think, but it is stunningly successful in telling its readers what to think about."[20] Picking up this theme, two communication specialists, Maxwell E. McCombs and Donald L. Shaw, in a landmark study published in 1972, showed that undecided voters in the 1968 presidential election tended to give the same priorities to issues in the campaign as were given to the issues by the news media.[21] They concluded that the reason for this was that the press sets the agenda for its audiences. It provides the facts, for the most part, that make up the cognitive world of each individual. This agenda-setting power of the press is directive rather than reactive. The press actually picks certain issues to play up at times that do not necessarily parallel the significance of those events. In other words, it is creating significance in situations that lack intrinsic importance at the time.

G. Ray Funkhouser showed that this is so by doing a content analysis of three weekly newsmagazines for the 1960s. The number of articles on such issues as the Vietnam War, race relations, student unrest, and inflation peaked in years when the events themselves were not at their highest point of importance or activity. What is especially noteworthy and supportive of the agenda-setting role of the press is that the peaks in news coverage coincided with peaks in the proportion of people who picked these issues as the "most important problem facing America" in Gallup Polls. On the other hand, they were not the issues that people felt the government should devote most of its attention to. Funkhouser concluded that "the average person takes the media's word for what the 'issues' are, whether or not he personally has any involvement or interest in them."[22] And, one might add, he rates them as important whether or not they have the salience in reality that the press gives them.

All this agrees very well with what information-seeking and agenda-setting theorists had been saying for some time. The mass media tend to inform rather than to change attitudes. And yet, doubts have begun to be expressed even about that. "'Stunningly successful' overstates the evidence considerably," according to a group of researchers.[23] The public just doesn't pay that much attention to media content and even those things that are picked up from the media—whether informational or attitudinal—are rapidly lost if they are not reinforced. The memory of them is wiped nearly clean within six weeks, according to Doris Graber.[24] It is interesting to note that one remembers those things longest that require the greatest effort to learn. Craik and Lockhart, and Glover, Plake and Zimmer found that highly abstract and difficult material that requires much thought and analysis to absorb is stored at a deeper level of one's memory and is retained longer. Thus, printed information requires more effort to learn than televised information and also has more lasting impact.[25] There may be particular events, such as the assassination of President Kennedy, that almost everyone has heard about. But the members of the public who are interested in public issues, who are knowledgeable about them, and who follow them *on a regular basis* are a small minority. Fewer than 20 percent of the population are in what Gabriel Almond called the "attentive public" on any topic involving public affairs—be it political, military, agricultural, educational, or any other topic of general concern.[26] Philip E. Converse, of the Survey Research Center at the University of Michigan, has found similarly that only about 20 percent of the public have genuine opinions on public issues—opinions that are based on knowledge. While only 10 percent of the public will answer "Don't Know" to an opinion question, it is easily determined that the responses of another 70 percent are totally random.[27] This means that the media are not getting through to major segments of the population—some 80 or 90 percent on any given issue—either to influence their attitudes or to provide them with information.

NEED FOR ORIENTATION

Non-attendance to any side of a political issue discussed in the media is a far more important deterrent to media impact than the previously feared factor of selective exposure. That is, people generally expose themselves only to those views with which they already agree and avoid information that challenges their opinions. Social psychologists Jonathan L. Freedman and David O. Sears, in a paper that upset this neat, intuitive theory, concluded after reviewing most of the literature on the subject that there is no firm evidence that people prefer to be exposed to supportive information or to information that will reduce their unease at being bombarded by contradictory facts and opinions.[28] They did add, however, that "people are disproportionately exposed to supportive information, but for reasons other than its supportiveness."[29]

Agenda-setting by the media, however, may apparently occur without direct exposure to the media. If a person can name any issue, event, or candidate at all, the chances are pretty good that he learned about it through the mass media or through someone who was exposed to the mass media, since few of us are direct witnesses to the news of the day. In fact, it is the media that decide what is the "news of the day."

Does this mean that the media also determine the relative importance of issues? That is exactly what agenda-setting studies have shown they do. Through the sheer frequency with which a story is told, length of the story, headline size, and positioning, the media suggest to the general public how important an event, issue, or candidate is. "Salience of an item is one of the key attributes acquired from the mass media," according to McCombs and Shaw.[30] Not only is this true of media impact on the public, but the news agencies have a similar impact on newspaper wire editors, as several studies both in the United States and abroad have shown.[31] The editor tends to use more of a story, news category, or issue on which he receives more items and longer items from the wire services.

To what extent does this also determine the side people will take on an issue? Probably very little, although as McCombs and Shaw point out, "issues sometimes clearly work to the advantage of one political party or candidate."[32] All it takes is for the press to play up the issue. But coupled with the emphasis given it by the press, the issue must also find a responsive chord in the audience. Each of us has a need to relate to his environment, and if a given issue satisfies that need or stimulates it, we would turn to the mass media (or to our friends who are primed by the mass media) for orientation.[33] The theory is that the "need for orientation" leads to media use, which leads to agenda-setting by the mass media. But the theory says nothing about the side people will take on the issue. In fact, several studies have indicated that people will expose themselves to information that they need and that is relevant to them, regardless of whether the information conforms to their view of the issue or not. At the same time, they will avoid irrelevant information. This is in keeping with the refutation by Freedman and Sears of the selective exposure theory.

Applying these principles to political campaigns, if a voter finds a need for orientation to a particular issue, he will listen to all candidates, regardless of political party. This emerged in the McCombs and Shaw landmark study of the 1968 presidential elections. Even though the three presidential contenders that year placed very different emphases on the issues of the day, voters seemed to expose themselves to all three candidates. The researchers found that their respondents' issue agendas (or priorities) agreed less with the agendas of their preferred candidate than they did with a composite agenda based on the priorities of all three candidates.[34]

Recent research has reemphasized Klapper's statement that mass communication functions among and through a number of other factors and influences. The media, it appears, are an important influence in setting one's personal agenda only when they are dealing with what David Weaver calls "unobtrusive" issues. These are issues that have minimal impact on an individual's daily life. "Obtrusive" issues, such as unemployment, inflation and taxes, are immune to media agenda-setting. Personal experience is far more potent in determining the salience of an issue.[35] It is only when nothing is competing from one's own past experience that media experience becomes real and media values are adopted as one's own. This, however, happens very infrequently in our multimedia society.

The media also are less successful in setting a person's issue agenda when the individual discusses the issue with others. Numerous studies have found that interpersonal discussion reduces the agenda-setting power of mass media.[36] At the same time, discussion leads to more media use.[37] And now this may seem like a vicious circle, but discussion stems from—or follows—interest,[38] which itself is often stimulated by the mass media, although, of course, it may be stimulated by conversation.

All this raises the question of the true role of mass media. Is their principal impact cognitive or affective—that is, informational or persuasive? Some communication researchers are beginning to say that, in fact, attitudes and information are closely related. They seem to be returning to where communication research began in the 1930s and 1940s, and hint that "as a latent consequence of telling us what to think *about*, the agenda-setting effect can sometimes influence what we think."[39] The power of the press, therefore, lies in large measure in the prerogative it has to select the news of the day.

Another insight into the power of mass media has been provided by German public opinion scholar and pollster Elisabeth Noelle-Neumann. She found in the process of doing opinion surveys in West Germany that people were reluctant to take stands on issues on which they believed they were in a minority. For this, Noelle-Neumann blames the mass media, which serve most people as a source of reference for information about the distribution of opinion in the public and, hence, the degree of support or non-support for their views. Noelle-Neumann believes that the media distort the climate of opinion and present a biased, leftist view. As a result, many people—even if they happen to be in a majority, albeit a silent one—refrain from expressing their opinions, which in turn speeds their decline in numbers and leads to a self-fulfilling spiral of silence.[40]

A similar phenomenon is known to develop in small, cohesive, deliberative groups. When most members of a group appear to have reached a consensus, or when the leader, inadvertently or by design, hints at a consensus, members are prevented from fully exercising their critical powers and from openly expressing negative views. They are "anxious to preserve friendly intragroup relations and these become part of the hidden agenda at their meetings," according to Yale psychologist Irving Janis.[41]

Hebrew University sociologist Elihu Katz suggests that revolutionary changes, such as the status of homosexuals following the publication of the Kinsey Report, may result from a changed perception of the distribution of opinion rather than a change in values. Communication may be considered a liberating influence here. The Emperor's New Clothes would be a classic example.[42]

IMPORTANCE OF TV

Until just after World War II, according to political campaign consultant Walter DeVries, political party affiliation was the major determinant of voting decisions, followed by group affiliations (e.g., church or union), the candidate's personality and background, and, finally, the issues of the day. By the 1970s, largely because of television, the candidate's ability to handle the job was rated first, followed by issue-oriented responses; party affiliation was placed third and group affiliations last.[43] It is evident that mass media, especially electronic media, play a more important role today than they did in the past, since it takes candidate exposure to make a candidate's characteristics salient. At the same time, since the press has the power to give some candidates and certain of their traits more exposure than others, its agenda-setting powers have been enhanced. This aspect of agenda-setting, Weaver believes, probably has more influence on voters than issue agenda-setting.[44] Voters referred to the presidential image three or four times as often as they did to issues, Weaver found in a 1976 study, and the less education they had the more likely they were to mention emotional factors rather than intellectual capabilities.[45] To carry this one step further, by focusing on certain issues and not on others, media can set the standards by which people evaluate government. This is referred to as "priming."[46] Party affiliation still plays an important role among the 30 percent who decide on how they will vote before a presidential campaign begins, and another 30 percent who are last-minute deciders. Not having paid much attention to the campaign rhetoric, the latter fall back on their partisan predispositions.[47]

What of the differential effects of the mass media? Do communication specialists still believe that it is futile to talk of one medium being more efficient and effective than another? Given that it is the voter rather than the communicator who decides which medium will be attended to, researchers have found that certain things can be said about differences in mass media effects. DeVries showed that in the 1970 Michigan gubernatorial race different types of television programs (such as newscasts, documentaries, editorials) were rated higher as important factors in influencing voting decisions than any other medium. Of 36 factors that play a role in political campaigning, 12 were rated 5.0 or better on an 11-point scale as influencing voting decisions. Significantly, the only one of these over which the candidate himself had any control was "contacts with candidates"—that is, personal campaigning. None of the purchasable types of advertising—for example, television or newspaper ads, political mailings, or telephone campaigns—was rated higher than 4.9.[48]

McCombs, however, has found that television, unlike newspapers, does not have an agenda-setting effect across time. Furthermore, when different agendas are set by newspapers and television stations, newspaper priorities have a higher correlation with voter agendas.[49] Others have shown that if agendas are studied in terms of issues, sub-issues, and specifics (such as individuals involved or solutions proposed), television tends to set the overall issue agendas, but not the agenda of details. Even among TV-oriented respondents—that is, those who said television was their major source of news—newspapers tended to set their agendas on sub-issues and specifics.[50]

In the face of the great emphasis that is placed by political candidates and their campaign managers on television appearances, and in view of the fact that the candidates who spend the most on television advertising appear to win, it may be rash to downgrade television. Yet there is growing evidence that, although large proportions of voters are exposed to the airing of political campaign messages on television, as for instance in television debates between contending presidential and vice-presidential candidates, it is the newspapers that tend to determine the salience of issues. Conceivably, newspaper editors and reporters are themselves influenced in their judgment by the volume of television exposure. Furthermore, voting is a short-term activity that requires no long-term attitudinal buildup, much as we would like to think of the vote as a considered judgment on the part of the electorate. Television may have a powerful short-term effect, ideally suited to the quick action requirements in politics. It may, therefore, be a useful medium immediately before an election. But for long-range effects, newspapers still are most instrumental in determining saliences.

NOTES

1. Frank Luther Mott, "Newspapers in Presidential Campaigns," *Public Opinion Quarterly,* vol. 8 (Fall 1944), p. 362. There were no campaigns in President Washington's two elections in 1789 and 1793, Jefferson's 1804 election, and Monroe's 1820 election.
2. Carl I. Hovland, "Reconciling Conflicting Results Derived from Experimental and Survey Studies of Attitude Change," *American Psychologist,* vol. 14 (1959), pp. 8–17.
3. Gerhart D. Wiebe, "A New Dimension in Journalism," *Journalism Quarterly,* vol. 31 (Fall 1954), pp. 411–420. Ten years later, Marshall McLuhan was to say: "The 'content' of any medium is always another medium. The content of writing is speech, just as the written word is the content of print." Marshall McLuhan, *Understanding Media: The Extensions of Man* (New York: McGraw-Hill, 1964, 1965), p. 8. He also distinguished between hot media like radio, books and the movies, which are low in audience participation, and cool media like television and telephones. *Ibid.,* pp. 22–23.
4. Joseph T. Klapper, *The Effects of Mass Communication* (Glencoe, Ill.: Free Press, 1960), p. 8. Emphasis in original.
5. Quoted in *ibid.,* p. 54.
6. *Ibid.,* p. 55. Emphasis in original.
7. Paul F. Lazarsfeld, Bernard Berelson and Hazel Gaudet, *The People's Choice: How the Voter Makes Up His Mind in a Presidential Campaign* (New York: Columbia University Press, 1944); Bernard R. Berelson, Paul F. Lazarsfeld and William N. McPhee, *Voting: A Study of Opinion Formation in a Presidential Campaign* (Chicago: University of Chicago Press, 1954).
8. For a good discussion of the various consistency theories, see Charles A. Kiesler, Barry E. Collins and Norman Miller, *Attitude Change: A Critical Analysis of Theoretical Approaches* (New York: Wiley, 1969).
9. Burns W. Roper, *An Extended View of Public Attitudes Toward Television and Other Mass Media, 1959–1971* (New York: Television Information Office, 1971), pp. 8–9.
10. Alex S. Edelstein, "Media Credibility and the Believability of Watergate," *News Research Bulletin No. 1* (Washington, D.C.: American Newspaper Publishers Association, 1974), p. 5.
11. See Jay G. Blumler and Elihu Katz, *The Uses of Mass Communications: Current Perspectives on Gratifications Research* (Beverly Hills: Sage Publications, 1974).
12. See Jay G. Blumler, Michael Gurevitch and Elihu Katz, "Onward and Outward: A Future for Gratifications Research." Unpublished paper, 1984. See also Michael W. Mansfield and Ruth Ann Weaver, "Political Communication Theory and Research: An Overview," in Michael Burgoon, ed., *Communication Yearbook 5* (New Brunswick: Transaction Books, 1982), p. 615.
13. Marvin Karlins and Herbert I. Abelson, *Persuasion* (New York: Springer, 1970), 2nd ed., p. 84.
14. The question, of course, is were we really influenced or were we merely delighted to find some "facts" or views expressed in the press that happened to agree with our own prior conceptions?
15. T. E. Patterson and R. D. McClure, *The Unseeing Eye* (New York: Putnam, 1976).
16. Steven H. Chaffee and Sun Yuel Choe, "Time of Decision and Media Use During the Ford-Carter Campaign," in D. Charles Whitney and Ellen Wartella, eds., *Mass Communication Review Yearbook,* Vol. 3 (Beverly Hills: Sage Publications, 1982), p. 567.
17. See Blumler, Gurevitch, and Katz, *op. cit.*
18. J. G. Blumler and J. M. McLeod, "Communication and Voter Turnout in Britain," in T. Legatt, ed., *Sociological Theory and Survey Research* (Beverly Hills: Sage Publications, 1974.)
19. J. M. McLeod, J. A. Durall, D. A. Ziemke and C. R. Bybee, "Reactions of Young and Older Voters: Expanding the Context of Effects," in Sidney Kraus, ed., *The Great Debates: Carter v. Ford, 1976* (Bloomington: Indiana University Press, 1979); Lee Becker, "The Mass Media and Citizen Assessment of Issue Importance: A Reflection on Agenda-setting Research," in Whitney and Wartella, *op. cit.,* pp. 521–536.

20. Bernard C. Cohen, *The Press and Foreign Policy* (Princeton: Princeton University Press, 1963), p. 13.
21. Maxwell E. McCombs and Donald L. Shaw, "The Agenda-setting Function of Mass Media," *Public Opinion Quarterly,* vol. 36 (Summer 1972), pp. 176–187.
22. G. Ray Funkhouser, "Trends in Media Coverage of the Issues of the '60s," *Journalism Quarterly,* vol. 50 (Autumn 1973), pp. 533–538.
23. Shanto Iyengar, Mark D. Peters and Donald R. Kinder, "Experimental Demonstrations of the 'Not-So-Minimal' Consequences of Television News Programs," in Ellen Wartella and D. Charles Whitney, eds., *Mass Communication Review Yearbook,* Vol. 4 (Beverly Hills: Sage Publications, 1983), p. 78.
24. Doris A. Graber, "The Impact of Media Research on Public Opinion Studies," in Whitney and Wartella, *op. cit.,* p. 560.
25. Cited by Yuko Miyo, "The Knowledge-Gap Hypothesis and Media Dependency," in Robert N. Bostrom, ed., *Communication Yearbook 7* (Beverly Hills: Sage Publications, 1983), p. 630.
26. L. John Martin, "Public Attitudes Toward Science and Technology," in *Science Indicators, 1980.* Report of the National Science Board, 1981, p. 349, Appendix Table 6-20.
27. Philip E. Converse, "New Dimensions of Meaning for Cross-section Sample Surveys in Politics," *International Social Science Journal,* vol. 16 (1964), pp. 25–26.
28. Jonathan L. Freedman and David O. Sears, "Selective Exposure," *Advances in Experimental Social Psychology,* vol. 2 (1965), pp. 58–97.
29. *Ibid.,* p. 90.
30. Maxwell E. McCombs and Donald L. Shaw, "A Progress Report on Agenda-setting Research." Paper presented at the Association for Education in Journalism Convention at San Diego, August 18–21, 1974, p. 30.
31. L. John Martin, *Analysis of Newspaper Coverage of the U.S. in the Near East, North Africa and South Asia* (Washington, D.C.: U.S. Information Agency Research Report R-2-76, 1976).
32. McCombs and Shaw, "A Progress Report," p. 40.
33. See Maxwell McCombs and David Weaver, "Voter's Need for Orientation and Use of Mass Communication." Paper presented at the International Communication Association Convention in Montreal, Canada, April 25–28, 1973.
34. Maxwell McCombs, "Agenda-setting Research: A Bibliographic Essay," prepared for *Political Communication Review,* February 1976, ms. p. 2.
35. David Weaver, "Media Agenda-setting and Media Manipulation," in Whitney and Wartella, *op. cit.,* p. 541.
36. Weaver, *op. cit.,* pp. 541, 550; Becker, *op. cit.,* pp. 523–524; Graber, *op. cit.,* p. 560.
37. Mansfield and Weaver, *op. cit.,* p. 615.
38. Blumler and McLeod, *op. cit.*
39. See Weaver, *op. cit.,* p. 546; Elihu Katz, "On Conceptualizing Media Effects," in E. Katz, ed., *Studies in Communications* (Greenwood, Conn.: JAI Press, 1980), pp. 119–141.
40. Elisabeth Noelle-Neumann, *The Spiral of Silence: Public Opinion—Our Social Skin* (Chicago: University of Chicago Press, 1984.)
41. Irving L. Janis, *Groupthink* (Boston: Houghton Mifflin, 1982), p. 7.
42. Elihu Katz, "Publicity and Pluralistic Ignorance: Notes on 'The Spiral of Silence,' " in Wartella and Whitney, *op. cit.,* pp. 89–99.
43. Walter DeVries, "Taking the Voter's Pulse," in Ray Hiebert et al., *The Political Image Merchants: Strategies in the New Politics* (Washington, D.C.: Acropolis Books, 1971), pp. 65–67.
44. Weaver, *op. cit.,* p. 543.
45. *Ibid.,* pp. 544, 545.
46. Iyengar, Peters, and Kinder, *op. cit.,* pp. 78, 84.
47. Chaffee and Choe, *op. cit.*
48. DeVries, *op. cit.,* pp. 68–69.
49. McCombs, "Agenda-setting Research," pp. 6–7.
50. Marc Benton and P. Jean Frazier, "The Agenda-setting Function of the Mass Media at Three Levels of 'Information Holding.' " Paper presented at the Association for Education in Journalism convention in Ottawa, Canada, August 1975.

IN TIME OF WAR

WHITE SMOKE IN THE PERSIAN GULF

Tim Ahern

U.S. Navy escort warships, protecting oil tankers in the Persian Gulf from Iranian attacks, carried small groups of reporters representing all news media. The Defense Department established this pool system in response to the angry outcry after reporters were forbidden to cover the U.S. invasion of Grenada. An Associated Press reporter tells how the pool operated. It was disbanded in 1988.

It was shortly before 7 A.M. last July 24, hot, hazy, and humid. I was standing on the bridge of the destroyer Kidd, a mug of Navy coffee in my hand, talking with Lieutenant Norm Farley, the officer of the deck. A half-mile ahead and to the right, we could see the huge bulk of the supertanker Bridgeton sliding through the murky gray-green waters of the Persian Gulf. It was the biggest of the two reflagged Kuwaiti tankers that the Kidd and two other Navy warships were leading in a convoy 550 miles up the gulf to Kuwait, in the first test of President Reagan's controversial policy.

As Farley and I were telling each other, the trip had gone quietly up to now, despite threats of attack from Iran, and Farsi Island marked the end of the danger zone. The Kidd had been at "general quarters," the highest state of alert, since nearing the island at 4:30 A.M., with the alert scheduled to end at 7 A.M., by now only moments away.

Source: Reprinted from *Washington Journalism Review,* October 1987, by permission of *Washington Journalism Review.*

I had briefly stepped out on the small outside deck to the right of the bridge—the starboard weather bridge, as the Navy calls it—when it happened. First a loud boom, rolling through the haze ahead, then a big puff of white smoke from the Bridgeton's smokestack. That was all I could see.

"Did you hear that?" I asked Farley.

"Hear what?" Farley said.

The walkie-talkie in his right hand cut my answer short. "Juliet, Juliet, this is Rhine, we've been hit, we've been hit," came the excited voice from the tanker's bridge. Moments later, still using the classified code names for both ships, the voice added that the Bridgeton had probably hit a mine.

Commander Daniel J. Murphy, Jr., captain of the Kidd, rushed to the bridge and ordered a sharp turn to port, and I walked over to ask him why.

Mines are seldom planted alone, he explained. If the Bridgeton hit one, there could be more, and "I don't want to drive the ship through a minefield."

Newsmen dream of a scene like this. A front-row view of the action; straight talk from the man at the top; filing facilities a few steps away; coffee on demand. For me and the nine other newsmen aboard the Navy ships, Operation Earnest Will, as the convoy was dubbed, had turned from a summer non-event into the first live test of the Pentagon's "national media pool."

The good news is that our access to information and ships' personnel was terrific. But we paid a price: the Navy read our copy before it was sent. This trip there were only minor disputes, but the potential exists for worse.

Ironically, the biggest gulf pool hurdle turned

out to be technical. There were delays getting copy to the wires in Washington; problems getting still photos and broadcast material off the ships.

The pool was an outcome of the howls of media protest after the Pentagon barred the press from Grenada for the first 48 hours after the October 25, 1983, invasion. In time-honored style, the Pentagon appointed a commission to study press-military relations, chaired by Winant Sidle, a retired major general who had been top Pentagon spokesman in Vietnam during part of the war.

The panel recommended creating a "pool" to cover military operations consistent with security requirements, an undefined phrase, with pool members sharing their information with the rest of the press, a frequent Washington practice, especially at the White House.

Before the gulf trip, there had been six trial runs of the media pool. I'd participated in an August 1986 weekend trip to the Mojave desert in California, where other pool members and I spent a hot day watching a series of live-fire drills and wound up filing a story about the pool being called up.

More drills had occurred since then. But last July, as the debate intensified over the Persian Gulf reflagging policy, there was speculation that the next pool might be for real. I'd covered the reflagging debate on Capitol Hill and when my bureau chief, Charles Lewis, asked me early in July to be the AP's prime pool person, he and I both agreed that the gulf convoys might be the occasion for the first real-life use of the pool.

That meant I had to get my shot card updated. Members of the pool need valid passports and a card showing they're currently inoculated against a wide variety of awful-sounding diseases. That's the paperwork. They're also supposed to have a bag packed at home that includes, among other things, a pair of hiking boots, some clothes, a towel, toilet kit, and any prescription drugs, and to carry a beeper around like a doctor. The idea is to be ready to go anywhere on very short notice.

Saturday night, July 18, my beeper went off about 9 P.M., but it turned out to be a mis-beep—a false alarm. When it went off later, I thought it might be another false alarm. But when I called Lewis shortly after 11 P.M., he told me that it was real, that the pool had been called, and that I had to get to Andrews Air Force Base by 12:15 A.M. He said he didn't know if it was a drill or the real thing, but we both figured that since the first convoy was supposed to go in a few days, this one was quite likely real.

I grabbed a cab to Andrews, where I met the other pool members: James Dorsey of the *Washington Times,* Mark Thompson of Knight-Ridder Newspapers, Michael Duffy of *Time* magazine, photographer Dennis Brack of *Time,* UPI photographer Doug Mills, ABC Radio reporter Jon Bascom, and Carl Rochelle, the Pentagon reporter for Cable News Network, along with a two-man sound and camera crew from CNN, Ray DeFrehn and Peter Morris.

We all agreed that we were likely headed to the gulf. None of the three military escorts would tell us. Nor were we allowed to use any telephones. It wasn't until after we boarded a VC-135—the military's version of a Boeing 707—that the military escorts confirmed our suspicions. It was a long flight—18 hours—despite the relatively comfortable plane, which was configured to include beds. The military escorts got the beds.

We refueled at Frankfurt, West Germany, and then flew on to the gulf, where even our landing was a lesson in regional sensitivities. Our military escorts asked—and we agreed—that we not reveal where we landed, because that regional confederation of states on the west side of the Gulf of Oman was willing to help the United States, but wanted no official, public confirmation of that fact. And no datelines from the nation.

We landed at an airport so new it didn't even have a ramp for the plane, forcing us to get off by climbing down a ladder near the nose wheel. All the cameras had to be covered with black trash bags, lest anyone on the ground see them. But there was little chance of that. It was 3 A.M. Monday local time, the airport wasn't even open, and anyway, it was ringed by lots of armed Arab guards. Our passports were taken, and later returned without ever having been stamped. We were put aboard a tug, the "Wadi-Ham," for the ride out to the cruiser Fox. That and the Kidd were the two ships picked to host the pool for the week.

After a few hours aboard the Fox—time filled with detailed tours of the ship—five of us boarded a small launch for a trip to the nearby Kidd, and more tours.

By the end of Monday, I'd filed two stories from aboard the Kidd, using Fox datelines since they were mostly based on information gathered there. One was a set-up for the reflagging, the other was a feature about the heavily armed ships. The three print reporters on the Fox also filed a pair of stories.

It wasn't until days later that we found out that those reports had been held back at the Pentagon, supposedly because they breached operational security by reporting about future military events. I didn't think that was so, nor did any of the other reporters, but we didn't have much avenue of appeal aboard the ships.

Tuesday morning, both groups covered the reflagging of the two tankers and filed print stories, which were released by the Pentagon shortly after Robert Sims, the Pentagon's chief spokesman, announced the pool had been activated.

Writing stories was easy. The ship's office had a Wang computer that I used during the week, writing copy and then running it off on a nearby printer—just like at the AP office in D.C.

But then things took a different tack. I turned my copy in to Navy Captain Steve Taylor, the sole military escort aboard the Kidd and the man who had done much to set up the pool system over the past couple of years. Taylor read through my copy and then turned it over to Captain David Yonkers, the commander of the flotilla. After Yonkers read and cleared it, another copy was run off the printer and through a tape machine that turned the story into a piece of buff-colored, perforated tape similar to the kind used by the wires in the pre-computer days. From there, it went to the Kidd's radio room, where it was sent to the Pentagon and released. The copy went out from the ship coded "secret."

There were two instances where Yonkers changed the copy, one where I disagreed and the second where I thought it was debatable.

The first concerned a reference to beer drinking, which Yonkers eliminated because he said it wouldn't look good to readers back in the United States if they knew Navy officers had been drinking during such an important mission. The incident involved a conference July 20 aboard the Bridgeton in which all the top Navy officers and civilian tanker officials met to make sure everyone understood the convoy's rules, procedures, and other details. At the end, according to Yonkers, there were a few beers passed around, something that's permissible on a civilian ship although it's banned on a Navy vessel.

The second occasion came on July 23, when I wrote a piece about the upcoming last day of the convoy. I detailed how and when we were going to pass Farsi Island, the final place where any trouble was expected. Yonkers objected to putting specifics into the story, so we fudged the details and then sent the story.

It felt strange having my copy checked by Navy officers before it was sent out. In future pools, perhaps the copy needs to carry some sort of flag pointing out that it has been cleared by Navy officials, or something to that effect. It's information I think the readers ought to have.

In terms of access, the situation was about as good as a journalist could want. The only exception was the radio room, where I wasn't permitted to go because of all the highly classified and coded material. Otherwise, I had unrestricted, unescorted, 24-hour-a-day access to the entire ship. That included the bridge and the Combat Information Center, the electronic brains of the vessel, located one deck below and a few feet back of the bridge. I got into the habit of often going into "combat," as it's called, sitting down with various officers and asking them what their sensors showed. With only a few exceptions, they told me. I found the men there quite willing to explain what their equipment was, how it worked, and the capabilities of the various electronic sensor systems. That access continued even during "general quarters," the highest state of alert and a time when everyone is supposed to remain in one spot because a lot of the watertight doors are shut. The press was exempted from that rule and we were allowed to wander wherever we pleased.

Although all of us roomed with officers—I had a cot at the foot of a pair of bunk beds—and though we were invited to eat with the officers, I spent a fair amount of time with the enlisted men because I wanted to see how they lived. I ate with them and spent hours sitting in their quarters, talking about how they felt about things.

On one occasion, one of the enlisted men told me that it was his job to man one of the Stinger stations, where the shoulder-fired missiles were ready to be launched against would-be terrorist attacks by small planes. While the existence of Stingers aboard ships had long been rumored, the Navy had never confirmed it. But when the sailor invited me topside to see how the Stinger worked, I took him up on the offer and received a detailed lesson on how to fire it. I mentioned the Stingers in my copy detailing the ship's defenses.

Although it was relatively easy to file my copy from a technical standpoint, the broadcast and photo people had it much rougher. They put together a lot of stuff in the first three days, but none of it got to the outside world until Thursday, when a helicopter from the LaSalle, the command ship of the Mideast Force, flew out as the convoy went by Bahrain and ferried the material back to land. On Friday, as we neared Kuwait, a second file of photo and broadcast material was picked up by a Kuwaiti naval vessel.

I thought—sadly—about that Thursday helicopter flight a week later when I read the story out of the Pentagon about the crash of a chopper that was ferrying material to the LaSalle. It was the same chopper—the "Desert Duck," as it's known there. Only a week before, I'd met Lieutenant William Ramsburg, the pilot and one of the four men killed in the crash.

The Navy made such an effort to get the broadcast and photo material back to shore that one of its ships was delayed for a time Wednesday when the convoy began. While the other two warships and the two tankers headed north from the Gulf of Oman toward the Strait of Hormuz, the Kidd steamed in circles, waiting for a launch that Taylor said had been chartered by the State Department to ferry the material to shore. After the Kidd waited a half-hour and the launch failed to show, Yonkers said he couldn't wait any more because he wanted to catch up with the flotilla before the ships entered the area in the strait where they would be vulnerable to Iran's Silkworm missiles. Yonkers pushed the Kidd hard to catch up, steaming at 28 knots, almost twice the convoy's speed, until the rest of the ships came into view.

As far as I'm concerned, the pool's chief test came Friday, after the Bridgeton hit the mine. The story I filed was the first word released at the Pentagon. Reporters on the Kidd and the Fox filed a lot of material back to Washington with plenty of detail. Marlin Fitzwater referred to the pool reports at his White House briefings.

For me, the reality of the mine danger was brought home when I headed to the ship's office to file. Since the press was exempted from having to wear any of the cumbersome battle gear, I was dressed only in a pair of shorts and a short-sleeved shirt. But as I left the bridge, Farley said, "You should be aware that the office is below the waterline. It might be a good idea to wear a life vest." That sounded like a pretty good idea to me, and I quickly complied.

ONCE AGAIN—DID THE PRESS LOSE VIETNAM?

Charles Mohr

The media have been accused of undercutting the American military effort in Vietnam with bad reporting. Charles Mohr, who, for four years, covered the war for the New York *Times,* replies that, in a broad

Source: Reprinted with permission from the *Columbia Journalism Review,* November–December 1983.

sense, the coverage seems sound in retrospect. This article appeared in the *Columbia Journalism Review.*

At about 3 A.M., January 31, 1968, reporters sleeping in hotels and apartments near Saigon's Lam Son square were awakened by the sound of multiple explosions and heavy small arms fire. Such sounds were not especially unusual, but the volume was. I dressed and left my hotel, but was waved back by a jeepload of nearly hysterical American military police shouting, "Get off the streets, we're under attack." After going up to the hotel roof for a few minutes and watching tracer fire over large areas of the city, I again left the hotel and trotted a couple of blocks to the Associated Press office, which was manned twenty-four hours a day. There I learned that fighting was reportedly taking place in many areas of the city, including near the gates of the Vietnamese Presidential Palace. (Reports of attacks on South Vietnamese provincial and district capitals also began to come in. In an apparent misunderstanding of their orders, the Viet Cong had attacked seven towns the night before.) Even more startling was word that the United States embassy was under attack; my friend Peter Arnett of the AP was checking it out. The Tet, or lunar new year, truce proclaimed by the South Vietnamese government had come to a noisy end.

At first light a small group of reporters and cameramen was huddled with military police at the corner of Hai Ba Trung and Thong Nhat streets near the entrance of the walled United States embassy. A Viet Cong sapper squad had gotten onto the embassy grounds, and some were still alive and holding out. One of the M.P. sergeants told us that the V.C. were also in the chancery building. We heard M.P. radio traffic making the same statement. As it turned out, the report was not true.

As U.S. Army helicopters landed one at a time on the embassy roof and discharged a platoon of riflemen from the 101st Airborne division, another friend, Mert Perry of *Newsweek,* said, "Do you realize we are watching American troops assault our own embassy?"

By about 9 A.M. the embassy compound had been retaken; a talk with the U.S. Mission Coordinator, George Jacobson, who had been trapped in a villa in the compound, had provided a vivid, partly eyewitness, story; and I was at a typewriter banging it out. I was also already slightly behind normal deadline.

In a mixture of journalistic conservatism and sloppiness I waited until the sixteenth paragraph of the story before writing that some of the attackers were "said" to have held lower floors of the chancery building for several hours.

Six hours had elapsed.

THE TEST OF TET

I hope to make several points with the above narrative.

In early 1982, another journalist wrote: "It is charged the American press turned an enemy defeat into a political victory for North Vietnam by concentrating on one brief and unsuccessful Communist action, the attack on the United States embassy." He added that this "emphasis, it is argued, reinforced pressure at home for a negotiated settlement." A number of neoconservative essayists, New Right polemicists, and other Vietnam revisionists, to whom I shall return, have made similar arguments, as part of a larger framework of complaint about Vietnam War journalism.

As I hope to make clear in this article, I believe the performance of the news media during the Tet offensive—and, indeed, throughout the entire course of the Vietnam War—is open to legitimate criticism. It is also worthy of some praise. But let the criticism be legitimate. Some of the criticism of Vietnam war correspondents, it appears, has not been based on a careful re-examination of the journalistic product.

At 9 A.M. on January 31 the Vietnam press corps was in no position to declare a result, victory or otherwise, in the Tet offensive (we were not even calling it that yet), a complex event that was to continue for many weeks of intense combat. We had not yet had breakfast on the first day of what was to be a prolonged adventure; we had not yet even had a formal news briefing by Military Assistance Command Vietnam on the situation in Saigon and in South Vietnam as a whole. But by then we knew that much of Saigon was overrun by Viet Cong, and that many towns had also been overrun, although most government and U.S. military compounds in the towns were holding out.

No professional, serious journalist could have ignored the embassy attack. Not many overplayed it; there was no significant overemphasis on it. My own story was a sidebar to the main war roundup which another *New York Times* reporter, because of the time difference between Saigon and New York, had written the night before, and which he was updating on deadline that morning.

By 9 A.M. of the first day of the offensive the reporters were essentially finished with the embassy story. The next day I corrected in *The New York Times* the deplorable error about the Viet Cong having been in the chancery (an error made by all news organizations, as far as I know, but unfortunately not corrected by all). And I subsequently wrote a couple of other stories about embassy security when facts on that subject that were embarrassing to the U.S. Mission came to light. But I and other reporters did not give the embassy attack prolonged, obsessive coverage while ignoring the subsequent course of battle. If some failed to report Viet Cong losses adequately in subsequent weeks, this was not a consequence of their having reported a six-hour attack by a nineteen-man sapper squad. The thesis that there was such a connection is only one of scores of myths about Vietnam journalism that, together, constitute a larger and pernicious myth.

More is at stake in this debate than wounded journalistic egos.

Almost twenty-two years have elapsed since the administration of John F. Kennedy involved the United States in what was called "combat support" in South Vietnam, a concept that brought thousands of military advisers and hundreds of helicopters to assist in the prosecution of a proxy war. Less than four years later it had become a real war for United States combat troops.

The ultimate failure (I have chosen that word with care—United States troops were never defeated militarily and, until very late in the war, no sizable South Vietnamese unit ever broke, was overrun, or defected) of that enterprise became undeniable by April 1975, when Saigon fell to North Vietnamese troops. So painful was the Vietnam experience that both the U.S. Army and civilians seemed to want to put Vietnam out of memory.

In the last few years, however, there has been a resurgence of interest in the war. A number of historical treatments and analytical discussions of the conflict have been published. Even a controversy about the design of the emotionally moving Vietnam memorial in Washington aroused controversy about the way the war was fought, the way it was supported or obstructed by Congress and the public—and the way it was reported by American journalists. The ambitious public television series *Vietnam: A Television History,* which is being broadcast this autumn, will almost certainly increase the interest of adults who had tended to expunge Vietnam from their memories and to interest people too young to have experienced or understood the war.

Unfortunately, much of the discussion of the war has involved a kind of revisionist "history" which, in fact, comes from people who are not historians and who are not using historical methods.

This does not apply to such careful work as *Vietnam: A History,* Stanley Karnow's recently published history of the war (he was also chief correspondent of *A Television History.*) Nor does it apply to Peter Braestrup's *Big Story,* a lengthy study of how journalism covered the Tet offensive. Braestrup, who himself was an able Vietnam correspondent and a witness to Tet, may have annoyed some of his colleagues with his thesis that Tet was such an "extreme" event and reportorial challenge that it simply overwhelmed the Vietnam press corps. But Braestrup first carefully reread the journalistic record: the product. He then reprinted most of it. If his thesis is thought debatable, or only disagreeable, by some, it at least rests on a foundation of evidence. Being reminded of what we said, and did not say, proves in some cases to be embarrassing. It is less troubling, however, than the surly critiques of the polemicists.

Notable among the critics, writing and speaking with varying degrees of bitterness and coherence, have been the editorial page of *The Wall Street Journal,* Robert S. Elegant (a former *Los Angeles Times* reporter), William F. Buckley, John P. Roche, Walt W. Rostow, William C. Westmoreland, Richard M. Nixon, and Henry A. Kissinger. This is not meant to be a full list, nor do I intend to focus my rebuttal specifically on those I have named. Certain of these critics have also constructed a pontoon bridge from the Vietnam quagmire to Central America by contending that reporters now covering Central America are falling into the same bad habits the critics attribute to the reporters who covered Vietnam.

Some of these critics have drawn conclusions that bear little relation to the actual conduct of mainstream journalists for major news organizations in the years 1961 to 1975. Some of their conclusions also reflect an astonishing misrepresentation, or at least misunderstanding, of the nature of the war. This can be especially disturbing when it comes from former civilian officials who helped to manage and prosecute the war. There is also confusion about the manner in which events actually unfolded, the problems of Vietnam war correspondence, and what the journalists *actually* said and wrote.

THE MAKING OF A MYTH

Although I like to argue that wars are not lost in the newspapers (or in television broadcasts), the revisionist argument goes far toward making that claim. In some cases it is flatly made. The core of the complaint is complicated, and not always quite coherent. Although to answer the critics it is necessary to discuss the entire course of the war, it is also convenient to focus on Tet.

One element of the revisionist argument is that Tet was not only a "victory" for the U.S.-South Vietnamese coalition, but that this was clearly and unmistakably true, and that willful misrepresentation by reporters caused a collapse of United States domestic morale in the first days of the offensive.

Certainly, massive erosion both of domestic American public support for the war, and of public confidence in the country's policymakers, did eventually follow the Tet offensive.[1] Such erosion was already well advanced among the members of the antiwar movement. But, in its magnitude, the loss of support among the general public to some extent genuinely surprised me and a number of other "veteran" Vietnam war correspondents. The revisionists ascribe the erosion to hysterical reporting from Vietnam; my own belief is that it was the result of strong public shock following the highly optimistic public claims of progress by American officials in the fall of 1967. A few journalists lost their composure, but most Vietnam correspondents did not. I and most others, even in the earliest hours of the offensive, did not believe that the enemy was going to "win" a military victory, capture the Saigon post office, and bayonet us and the allied high command in our beds. No fair reading of the body of news stories produced in early 1968 will sustain that myth.

I did not share the sentiments of Senator John Stennis, who said a few days after the Tet kickoff that it was "embarrassing" and "humiliating" to the United States. But I could sympathize with him. Like Arthur Krock of *The New York Times* in 1963 at the time of the battle of Ap Bac, Stennis had tended to support—and for all I know, believe—the official optimism, and now felt betrayed.

In *Big Story,* Braestrup wrote that the press "emphasized the political and psychological effects" of the enemy attacks. (So poisonous was domestic feeling at that time that the mere use of the word "enemy" to describe men who were killing American troops usually drew angry letters. And when, at the end of the three-week battle for the ancient imperial capital of Hue, I wrote of the "liberation" of Hue, one reader angrily denounced me for doing so.) Braestrup's argument, it seems to me, was far more true of stories written in the United States than of those filed by relatively objective reporters in Vietnam, who did not believe it was their job to assess political effects in the United States, but who did speculate about the V.C.'s desire for a psychological victory.

Like many other journalists in Vietnam, I assumed and wrote, early in the offensive, that it was logical to believe that North Vietnam and the Viet Cong were seeking a psychological victory, since it was difficult to believe that they seriously thought they could achieve an actual military victory by pitting a nationwide assault force estimated at about 35,000 men against a force of more than one million regular United States and South Vietnamese troops.[2] This was not a political or ideological notion, but the conclusion of a reporter who had begun to gain some military sophistication.

There followed an irony, or perhaps a paradox. Senior officials of the U.S. Mission Vietnam came to dislike it that a reporter for an influential paper was writing that the enemy had probably not sought a military victory, even though the reporter did so because he believed that the possibility of success had been so inherently remote. Subjectively, the argument that the V.C. had sought, but had been denied, a purely military victory became very attractive to the officials. And objectively, captured documents indicated that the communist leadership had really believed in the concept of a "general uprising" by the South Vietnamese civilian population that could bring about both the collapse of the Saigon government and the forced evacuation of American troops. Some American officials, whose intellectual honesty was respected by the reporters, then met at length with some of us to argue the thesis that the Vietnamese communists had indeed believed in the general uprising and had sought not "merely" the destruction of an already frayed domestic American support for the war, but a clear-cut military victory. The relationship between the journalists and these unquestionably honest members of the official mission was never as hostile or adversarial as some revisionists have painted it. Most of the reporters, including me, came to accept the general-uprising theory and to describe it in news stories.

WERE OFFICIAL VIEWS MUFFLED?

This suggests several other significant elements in the discussion of the role and performance of journalists over the long haul in Vietnam. As early as late 1961, when the great Homer Bigart arrived in Vietnam for *The New York Times,* a degree of tension developed between some officials and most of the then tiny press corps. These differences, however, were not over the "morality" of the war or the desirability of winning (a concept not easy to define, then or later). Essentially, the dispute involved optimism versus pessimism, growing out of conflicting views about the way the war was being prosecuted and about the viability of the South Vietnamese government in a revolutionary conflict.

This debate was not essentially, as some seem to believe, a quarrel between the press and U.S. officials in Vietnam. It was, rather, a quarrel between factions within the U.S. Mission. For the most part, field advisers closest to the action and to the Vietnamese took the pessimistic view. Some of the more senior officials in Saigon, who were reporting to Washington on the progress of the programs they were themselves administering, were publicly and persistently optimistic. The reporters quickly became aware of this dispute because brilliant younger field officials and officers, as exemplified by the late John Paul Vann, increasingly turned to the journalists. The reporters did not invent the somber information that sometimes appeared in their stories. Nor did they relentlessly emphasize it.

One of the persistent myths about Vietnam journalism is that the copy was deeply colored by ideology, that it was loaded with strong advocacy, and that it muffled the voice and views of officialdom. Again, this misrepresents the actual news product. Much of it was cautious and bland—probably, in retrospect, too bland. For practical reasons, journalists always reported the claims, appraisals, and statements of the senior officials who asserted that "progress" was being made. These stories almost always got prominent play. At many points in the war, progress *was* being made and many journalists could see and agree that this was taking place. Less often, and seldom in shrill tones, correspondents also reported the countervailing views of Americans who were eager to place greater pressure on the South Vietnamese for better management of their war. It is mostly the latter stories that the revisionists and embittered officials, now retired, seem to remember today.

There is also the persistent argument that, because of television, Vietnam "was the first war that came into people's living rooms" and that TV coverage caused a fatal revulsion for the war. Several aspects of this argument fascinate me. It is often advanced by prowar people who suggest that "seeing" the war did not bother them, but that other Americans could not be expected to withstand such a shock to the emotions. It also seems to reflect how isolated and safe America has been for most of its history. Most wars literally, not merely photographically, go through people's living rooms. The awesome casualty lists of World War I, the London Blitz, the stark still photography of World War II have never seemed to me to be less psychologically important than Vietnam TV coverage.

Rereading the Tet coverage, I am struck by how much space and emphasis were given to claims of "victory" when they were made. But, as we shall see, officials spent much of that period not claiming victory, but warning of harder fighting ahead and ominous enemy threats.

A VICTORY CONCEALED?

The most serious charge made by the revisionists, and one of the most frequently repeated, is that the Vietnam press corps failed to report an allied victory at Tet and, indeed, concealed its existence. There were, unquestionably, flaws in the purely military coverage; and not all of them were sins of omission. But in its raw form the charge does not seem to hold up.

I believe that Tet represented a serious *tactical* defeat for the Viet Cong and their North Vietnamese superiors. But this did not ultimately constitute a strategic victory for South Vietnam. That should be obvious. It is also argued that Tet shattered, nearly destroyed, the indigenous guerrillas and forced North Vietnam to continue the war with its own regular army troops. This was to a large extent true; but it was also what almost all serious journalists reported (though anyone who was around at the time of the 1973 "truce" quickly learned that there were still many Viet Cong in the countryside five years later).

In early January of 1969, I wrote a story, which was printed on the front page of the *Times,* that began: "After days of overoptimism, false starts, half-completed programs and lost opportunities, the allied forces in Vietnam appear to be making major progress against the enemy." The story also said that officials with reputations for intellectual honesty and skepticism "believe they see a drastic decline in the fighting quality and political abilities of the Viet Cong guerrillas and modest improvements in South Vietnamese and American prosecution of the war. Taken together, these may have broken the stalemate of previous years." (The story also contained plenty of qualifications and warnings that great problems persisted.)

Did the story come too late, as I suspect some revisionists would argue? Perhaps. But, although I was proud of my willingness to follow my reporting to any conclusions to which that reporting led, the real point today is that the story turned out to be essentially wrong. It appeared in print just before Nixon and Kissinger took office. They adopted a policy of "Vietnamization" of the war. And although the pace of American withdrawal seemed too slow to many people in this country, it seemed fatally rapid to some journalists in Vietnam. Then, in 1973, Kissinger signed a peace treaty that left some 140,000 regular North Vietnamese troops on South Vietnamese soil. Together, these steps guaranteed ultimate collapse. The stalemate of previous years was broken, but in an entirely different way.

As for the argument that the reporters were much too slow to accept the concept of at least a purely military victory at Tet, re-examination of the record is again revealing. Claims of victory were faithfully reported, often on the front page; apparently, Congress and the public were no longer so willing to believe. In the meantime, officers and officials in Vietnam kept warning that "second wave" attacks were likely, that the enemy was still full of fight. I and some other reporters tended journalistically to declare the battle for Saigon over within a few days—and we kept being fooled. Space will permit only a small sample of hundreds of incidents. On February 21, 123 troops were killed in heavy fighting at the city line. On March 4, forty-eight Americans were killed in an ambush near the airport. On March 12, General Westmoreland predicted "very heavy fighting" in the northern provinces. On May 5, the "second wave" struck and the notorious police chief, General Loan, was seriously wounded on a downtown bridge. Casualties soared. (Shortly thereafter several journalists were killed in the Cholon section, an American armed helicopter accidentally killed the mayor of Saigon in an airstrike against Communist troops not far from downtown, and, during a spooky jeep reconnaissance of the city, Arnett and I discovered the bodies of several Korean reporters executed by V.C. at a gasoline service station.) In one two-week period in May, more than 1,100 American troops were killed in action, the worst losses in any such a period in the entire war.

The revisionists often suggest that the journalists failed to take into account the heavy enemy losses; in fact, the reporters in Vietnam did report that the Viet Cong were suffering staggering casualties. In any case, I doubt that the journalists can be accused of concealing a transparently clear allied victory—one which did not seem so clear until autumn, even to officials. Only in the post-war era have they tried to rehabilitate their reputations with such assertions.

OF TRUST AND DISTRUST

As both its practitioners and critics should recognize, journalism is an imperfect instrument. The Vietnam reporters were far from blameless. Some stateside editors and executives also failed, both early and late, to assign enough staffers, or any staffers, to the story. The Vietnam press corps was woefully short on language skills (the reporters now covering Central America seem to me better equipped, both linguistically and intellectually, for their assignment). Many were not sophisticated militarily, and too many posed as ordnance experts, ready to pronounce on the caliber of an incoming shell.

Before and after Tet, the story did often tend to overwhelm the essentially conventional journalistic methods we employed. Much went unreported, although this may have been unavoidable in a sprawling nation of forty-four provinces and scores of allied divisions and brigades.

Granted that much went unreported, that factual errors were not rare, that sometimes we were too argumentative and skeptical (although much of the time we were far too gullible), that we spent too much time covering American troops and too little with the South Vietnamese. Still, in a broad sense, the coverage seems sound in retrospect. Not only ultimately, but also at each major milestone of the war, the weight of serious reporting corresponds quite closely to the historical record. Revisionists seem to fault correspondents for distrusting the version of events propounded by the most optimistic senior officials in Vietnam. But what if the correspondents had believed that version and had been guided by it in carrying out their assignment? In that case, the reporters' reputations, which are not unblemished, would be irredeemably tarnished.

NOTES

1. In the latest edition of his book, Braestrup cites poll data which casts strong doubt on the assertion that early Tet reports from Vietnam caused a significant loss of support for the war among the general public.
2. It subsequently also seemed absurd when MACV in the first few days claimed that more than 30,000 V.C. had been killed in action.

IN TIME OF DISSENT

UP THE CREEK WITHOUT A PADDLE

Lauren Kessler

Lauren Kessler, associate professor of journalism at the University of Oregon, is the author of *The Dissident Press: Alternative Journalism in American History,* examining the journalistic traditions of "other voices" over two centuries, including radicals, feminists, immigrants, and war resisters.

They are the forgotten men and women of journalism. No schools or prizes are named for them. They founded no dynasties or empires. In conventional history books, they appear as footnotes, if they appear at all. Yet they are as vital to our appreciation of the richness of American journalism as are Greeley, Hearst, Pulitzer, Ochs, Luce, and all the other giants.

They are the men and women of America's dissident press—journalists who produced the alternative newspapers and magazines that are an essential part of this country's journalistic heritage. In issue after issue, from pre-Revolutionary War days to the 1980s, these dissident publications—tens of thousands of them—chronicled the ideas and actions of those at odds with the norms of their day. Existing alongside the well-established, conventional media of the time, they served as public forums for unpopular political, social, cultural, and religious beliefs.

Source: The Quill, November 1984. A summary of various chapters of the author's *Dissident Press: Alternative Journalism in American History* (Beverly Hills, Calif.: Sage, 1984). Reprinted by permission of *The Quill* and the author.

While the penny press was offering colorful stories about crime, conflagrations, and the vicissitudes of urban life, black Americans were fighting for basic human rights in the pages of their own newspapers. While Hearst was assembling his empire, feminists were insisting on their political rights in the pages of their own journals, and millions of immigrants were learning self-sufficiency and self-respect through their own publications. While *The New York Times* was achieving major stature in the first decades of the twentieth century, socialists and communists were reaching legions of discontented Americans through their newspapers, newsletters, and journals. While the conventional press was calling for and supporting war throughout the twentieth century, war resisters were spreading their philosophy in the pages of their own publications.

History may have forgotten them, but their efforts are too impressive and too numerous to remain obscure. From 1827, when two freemen began publishing *Freedom's Journal,* to the 1980s, when slick magazines reached millions of readers, blacks have published more than 2,700 newspapers and periodicals. During its 140 active years, the American feminist movement has spawned countless publications from pre-Civil War journals that reached only a few hundred readers to today's sophisticated magazines that reach millions. In a single year, 1970, feminists started seventy-three different publications. During the heyday of European immigration, from the 1880s to the 1920s, America's newest arrivals started and supported nearly 3,500 foreign-language publications. Populists—discontented farmers in the South and

West—published more than nine hundred newspapers in the late nineteenth and twentieth centuries. Anarchists, socialists, communists, and their dizzying array of splinter groups published more than six hundred newspapers and periodicals in the early 1900s.

Most dissident journalists worked in obscurity for little or no salary. Their papers were shoestring operations reaching small audiences who were already supporters of whatever cause was being advanced. The efforts of some dissident journalists were deemed so innocuous that the papers—and the ideas they put forward—were simply ignored. In other cases the threat was thought to be minor, and local communities and governmental agencies merely ridiculed and ostracized the journalists. But those papers that were large or loud or angry enough to attract attention suffered worse fates. Townspeople burned their print shops to the ground; government officials raided their offices; federal agents threw editors in jail.

In the face of either obscurity or persecution, why have generations of American men and women persisted in publishing alternative newspapers? The answer is more complicated than it seems: They so strongly believed in their cause that they were willing to risk anything to get their ideas out to the people. But most of these dissident journalists were neither politically nor journalistically naive. They knew that the way to affect public policy—to win freedom for blacks, enfranchisement for women, respect for immigrants—was to reach the largest number of people with the most convincing message. Many stated publicly that they would much rather write for large-circulation, mainstream newspapers than toil away at their own relatively invisible little publications. Yet they felt they had no choice. They founded and maintained their own alternative journals not just because they believed in a cause, but because the mainstream press of their day ignored or ridiculed that cause.

Traditionally, the mainstream press has spoken to and for the homogeneous middle. Generally united by belief in the current political, social, and cultural ideas of their day, the audience of the conventional media receives a rather narrow spectrum of thought that reinforces these beliefs. Although the conventional media certainly report on controversy within a narrow spectrum—Democratic policies versus Republican policies, for example—the "fringe" ideas of dissidents are rarely covered.

Sometimes the conventional press purposefully excludes ideas at odds with contemporary society because it finds those ideas threatening, distasteful, or downright abhorrent. When, in the 1840s, a black wrote a reply to a pro-slavery editorial in the New York *Sun,* the popular penny-press newspaper refused to print it. "The Sun Shines for All" was the paper's motto, but, one of the editors explained to the black writer, that meant: "The Sun shines for all *white* men and not for colored men." The late-nineteenth-century conventional press ignored women's fight for enfranchisement, and instead resorted to name-calling. Feminists were dubbed "hyenas, cats, crowing hens, unsexed females, and dangerous homewreckers." In the early twentieth century, muckraking journalist and socialist Upton Sinclair complained that news channels became "concrete walls" when he attempted to publish exposés of the horrors of industrial capitalism in the major newspapers of his day. History overflows with examples of dissidents representing major national causes who were, in no uncertain terms, denied access to the mainstream media of their day.

In other cases, the press seems to ignore dissident groups because either they or their actions do not fit into current definitions of what is news. Groups of people experimenting with new lifestyles in utopian communities like Brook Farm, Oneida, or New Harmony were simply not considered newsworthy. (Horace Greeley's interest was idiosyncratic, and his newspaper's attention unique.) The concerns of urban immigrants did not deserve coverage in the cities' large newspapers, thought most editors. Dissident groups were not part of any established beat. Often they didn't plan the kind of public acts—speeches, conventions, press conferences—that the press routinely covered. The conventional media's event rather than issue orientation has meant, in general, that people with ideas get short shrift. This turns out to be particularly detrimental to dissidents who need to define and communicate their ideas to a larger public as the first step toward meeting their goals.

It was this need to communicate currently unacceptable ideas, coupled with lack of access to the conventional press, that led to the development of separate news channels for dissident groups. In many cases, it is clear that dissidents would rather have used the conventional press than start their own publications. Not only did the conventional press reach vast audiences that the dissidents wished to communicate with, it involved no extra expense. Most dissident groups were poor and poorly funded. Establishing and maintaining publications of their own was a major financial drain. They did so because they had to. And as long as the conventional press continues to limit its scope to currently acceptable ideas and groups, as long as it defines news as action rather than thought, dissident groups will continue to need their own alternative media.

The men and women who devoted their time and energy to publishing dissident journals were people convinced of both the righteousness of their cause and the power of the press. They were malcontents who wanted change and idealists who believed change was possible. Many were simultaneously leaders and chroniclers of their cause.

Members of every racial, ethnic, and religious group represented in America, coming from both urban centers and rural outposts, they lived and worked in every state of the union. Some were native-born; others were immigrants. A few were wealthy—like magazine publisher Gaylord Wilshire, the "millionaire socialist"; others were poor—like the famous black editor and writer Frederick Douglass, who had to borrow money to buy his freedom. They were young, middle-aged, old. Demographically, they were as varied a group as one could imagine, yet they had in common their devotion to a cause.

For the majority, journalism was not a separate calling or a profession for its own sake. It was a means to reach people with ideas, a way to organize and propagandize for what they believed. Publishing a newspaper or magazine was not the path to wealth; it was the path to a better world.

Some dissident journalists were harassed or ostracized by their communities. Some were harassed by the government. Some were jailed for their writings. But one problem all dissident journalists shared for all or most of their careers was how to continue financing their journalistic efforts. Most publications were started on a shoestring and remained financially unstable throughout their troubled lifetimes.

Publishers had three potential sources of revenue: support from a group or individual, subscriptions and single-copy sales, and advertising income. Those able to rely on the financial support of a group were fortunate. *Woman's Journal,* a leader in the fight for women's enfranchisement for almost half a century, was funded by various suffrage clubs. *National Economist,* a one-hundred-thousand-circulation Populist paper, was underwritten by the powerful Texas Farmers' Alliance. *The Daily Worker,* this country's major English-language communist newspaper, received seed money from the Soviet Communist Party and was financially supported by the American party throughout its life.

On extremely rare occasions, an outside "angel"—such as the wealthy eccentric who for two years supported Elizabeth Cady Stanton's and Susan B. Anthony's *The Revolution*—might step in. But publications receiving financial support from dissident groups or outsiders were the exception. Most groups were resource-poor. Their members, often the poor, the powerless, and the disenfranchised, could not be counted on to contribute significant donations. What little money groups had, they generally spent on organizing efforts, conventions, and lecture tours.

Because in many cases those who would support a dissident publication were themselves impoverished, reliance on subscription and single-copy sales was generally not a successful way for journals to stay afloat. Women without an independent source of income, farmers who mortgaged their crops and land to stay in business one more year, utopians who gave up all personal assets when they joined a colony, underpaid or unemployed workers—many of these people could not afford the price of the newspaper or magazine that supported their cause. The dissident press was full of pleas from editors facing creditors. Pay for your subscription now or this journal will be forced to stop publishing, wrote the editors. We need one hundred (five hundred, one thousand) more subscribers or we won't be able to stay in business, wrote others. Of course there were notable exceptions. A handful of dissident publications had healthy circulations, and a few of the larger newspapers and magazines located in major urban areas could count on single-copy sales for some income.

Most of the conventional press depends on advertising revenue to sustain itself, but this wasn't an option for many dissident journals. Some flatly refused to carry advertising, claiming it would compromise their position. Many would have been glad to carry at least some kind of advertising, but they didn't present an inviting audience to potential advertisers. Not only was the audience usually small, but it was often composed of readers who couldn't afford the goods and services advertisers had to sell. In most cases, advertising was limited to newspapers, magazines, and books that fell within the readers' field of interest.

With negligible financial support from groups and scant income from subscriptions and advertising, publishers of most dissident journals supported their efforts by dipping into whatever personal savings they had, borrowing from friends, using their printing facilities to do outside work, or holding down second jobs. Publishing a dissident journal was not a way to get rich. In fact, for many it was a slow road to poverty.

Most dissident publications attempted to communicate both internally to a group of believers and externally to those not converted to the cause. Intra-group communication gave those involved in the cause a sense of unity and purpose. Before national transportation and communication networks were developed, dissidents separated by geography but united by ideology established and maintained essential links through the pages of their publications. Here they could argue and discuss ideas, ask questions, receive advice, and read about the activities of fellow dissidents. They could learn about and participate in organizational matters. When it appeared they were in the midst of a losing battle, when they were harassed, ridiculed, or ostracized by their own communities, they could look to the pages of their journals for inspiration and comfort. Their publications showed them they were not alone.

In their role as external communicators, dissident journals attempted to both educate and persuade the "unconverted" public by presenting a forum for ideas generally ignored by the conventional press. Here the dissident press encountered its greatest obstacle, for it was generally read by those who were already supporters, not by those it wanted to convert. Successful, large-circulation dissident journals—several of the socialist and populist publications, for example—were read by supporters and those most likely to become sympathetic (not yet "converted" urban workers or impoverished farmers). But both large- and small-circulation dissident publications were rarely read by those in power or those who had the power to effect change. Partially this was because, as communications theory tells us, people tend to seek out those messages they already believe in, through the process of selective exposure. Partially it was because most dissident journals were shoestring operations that couldn't mount the circulation and promotion campaigns necessary to make themselves known to those outside their circle.

Despite those obstacles, some dissident publications were able, over time, to help groups "go public" with their ideas. These were groups whose ideas were ahead of, but not in the long run inimical to, the society in which they lived. Blacks and women fighting for enfranchisement and equality, immigrants fighting for acceptance and respect, workers fighting for the right to unionize, anti-war activists speaking out against Vietnam—the ideas of all these groups, first articulated in the dissident press, eventually found their way into both conventional media and mainstream society. For these dissidents, a press of their own was a starting point. Early on, it helped them delineate their ideas and set up effective organizational structures. It provided at least a limited forum for ideas most Americans were not yet willing to accept. Without a voice of their own, these groups might not have been able to grow strong enough to effect change. Their ideas might have taken even longer to find their way into mainstream thought.

But other dissident groups encountered an even greater obstacle: Their ideas were truly antithetical to the American way of life. Even if a publication were able to make itself known in wider circles, even if unsympathetic nonbelievers occasionally encountered dissident messages, some ideas did not and would never appeal to more than a small segment of the population. Utopianism, populism, socialism, anarchism, communism, and pacifism (during the two world wars) attacked the basic American beliefs of private ownership, consumerism, competition, the role of the government, and the mission of the United States. These dissidents could—and did—publish thousands of journals explaining their beliefs and attempting to convert others, but their causes would never become popular.

Regardless of what they had to say or whether Americans wanted to hear it, dissident groups have had the Constitutional right to speak and publish. When they were harassed and their publications repressed, the First Amendment rights of all Americans were in danger. When dissident ideas were routinely excluded from the mainstream press and relegated to the pages of poorly-funded, small-circulation journals, freedom of speech lost some of its meaning. For when the framers of the Constitution talked of freedom of speech, they did not mean the freedom to talk to oneself. They meant both the freedom to speak *and* the opportunity to be heard.

THE *CATHOLIC WORKER:* 50 YEARS OF FORTITUDE

Nancy L. Roberts

Nancy Roberts, associate professor of journalism at the University of Minnesota, is the author of *Dorothy Day and the Catholic Worker* (Albany: University of New York Press, 1984); editor Day's concern for pacifism and social justice over half a century ranks her with I. F. Stone and other great dissenting journalists.

Fifty years ago this May Day, democracy seemed doomed as crowds around the world surged in ominous political rallies. In Moscow, 1 million soldiers and workers marched through Red Square, flanked by a fearsome array of weaponry. In Berlin, bands played unceasingly while endless paraders sang Nazi songs to honor their new chancellor, Adolf Hitler. While the clouds of totalitarianism darkened the European sky, most Americans, reeling from economic disaster, paid scant attention—except in New York City's Union Square, where 50,000 leftists gathered to hear speeches denouncing Hitler and advocating radical social change.

Into this tumultuous May Day crowd, Dorothy Day and three young men sent by a priest to help her ventured nervously to peddle the first edition of the *Catholic Worker* at a penny a copy. Doubtless some of the demonstrators recognized Day, for she had belonged to the 1920s Greenwich Village avant-garde, and had long associated with communists, socialists, Wobblies and other social reformers.

"Religion in Union Square! It was preposterous!" Day later said, describing the *Catholic Worker's* hostile reception on that historic day. For it was generally assumed that Catholics' focus on the hereafter thwarted the development of their social consciences. But this humble tabloid departed from the rest of the religious press, advocating something revolutionary for 1933 America: the union of Catholicism with a passionate concern for social justice, and with personal activism.

"It's time there was a Catholic paper printed for the unemployed," the *Catholic Worker* boldly proclaimed. "Is it not possible to protest, to expose, to complain, to point out abuses and demand reforms without desiring the overthrow of religion?"

Today the *Catholic Worker* is still a monthly with some 100,000 subscribers; it is still prodding consciences and expressing its simultaneous concern with the everyday and the ultimate. For 50 years it has held to one price and hewed to one editorial line: the communitarian Christianity, voluntary poverty, pacifism, social justice and personal activism that characterize the Catholic Worker Movement, cofounded in 1933 by Dorothy Day and Peter Maurin. The *Catholic Worker* appeals to workers and scholars alike, with contributors including both everyday citizens and the eminent (in prose, Jacques Maritain, Thomas Merton, Martin Buber, Lewis Mumford and Michael Harrington; in art, Fritz Eichenberg and Ade Bethune).

A remarkable achievement in advocacy journalism, the *Catholic Worker*'s ideological commitments have never overshadowed its goal of presenting a professional product. Substance has never been stressed at the expense of style—a hallmark of Dorothy Day's singular devotion to her craft as well as to her ideals. To the end of her life in 1980, she was the final authority at the *Worker,* guiding its content and tone. Her determined leadership as chief writer, editor and publisher gave the paper consistency and continuity through even those periods in American history most hostile to its message. From the start of the paper during the Great Depression, when circulation peaked at 190,000, through the Spanish Civil War and World War II, when subscriptions plummeted to 50,500 and Catholic workers selling the pacifist-oriented paper were sometimes beaten in the streets, and then during the McCarthy era, the Korean War and Vietnam, Day maintained the *Catholic Worker*'s commitment to peace and social justice activism.

Although a radical in many secular matters, Day was a fervent Catholic traditionalist who never criticized the church's teachings, only its failure to live up to them. Her absolute obedience to Catholic authority won her the hierarchy's eventual support, allowing her to continue publication uninterrupted. And the wheel has turned. Today the Catholic bishops' pending pastoral letter promises to break significantly with their church's tradition of unqualified support for the military. Repeatedly, the bishops, clergy and religious have acknowledged their debt to Day and the newspaper she founded.

The *Catholic Worker* overshadows other small, ideological publications run by faith, hope and charity—such as Julius A. Wayland's *Appeal to Reason,* the early socialist sheet for which Eugene Debs was chief editorial writer; Max Eastman's brilliant *The Masses;* and the muckraking *I. F. Stone's Weekly*—in its comparatively much greater impact. While it has never spoken for a mass movement, nor enjoyed a circulation larger than that of a metropolitan daily newspaper, the *Catholic Worker*'s message has reached profoundly influential channels. Nearly everyone in today's Catholic left and in such offshoot organizations as the Association of Catholic Trade Unionists, Pax Christi, the Association of Catholic Conscientious Objectors and the Catholic Peace Fellowship has transmitted Catholic Worker ideals he or she absorbed from the paper. The *Catholic Worker*'s influence on Catholics, non-Catholics and activists both religious and secular cannot be fathomed; but whenever the roots of contemporary concern for peace and social justice are traced, the *Worker* looms large for having kept such ideals alive during complacent times.

Can the *Catholic Worker* again achieve the glorious, vigorous quality it knew under Dorothy Day's exacting editorship? Doubtless only if someone of Day's stature and temperament emerges—someone who can contribute excellent journalism herself and inspire others to do so; someone who, while spiritually part of the Catholic Worker Movement, can yet embrace the most professional values of journalism, thus creating a double appeal. Such a combination has rarely appeared among advocacy journalists, and we may not see its like again for some time.

More important, the stellar achievements of the tenacious little tabloid over half a century underscore the wisdom of Dorothy Day's favorite quotation from William James:

> I am done with great things and big things, great institutions and big success, and I am for those tiny invisible molecular moral forces that work from individual to individual, creeping through the crannies of the world like so many rootlets, or like the capillary oozing of water, yet which, if you give them time, will rend the hardest monuments of man's pride.

PREACHER BASHING AND THE PUBLIC LIFE

James M. Wall

Television evangelists, who have built multimillion-dollar operations, became the focus of public derision in 1987 and 1988 with disclosure of sex scandals involving Jim Bakker and Jimmy Swaggart, and reports of excesses and feuding by some others. James M. Wall, editor of *The Christian Century,* discusses how this bad publicity affects the cause of religion as a whole.

To paraphrase Jerry Lee Lewis's rock'n'roll number, "There's a whole lot of preacher-bashin' goin' on" these days. Lewis, whose frenetic style and emotional intensity made him a popular performer with songs like "Whole Lot of Shakin' Goin' On," just happens to be a first cousin of Jimmy Swaggart, one of the principals in the current struggle for power in the world of the televangelists.

Swaggart, who shares his cousin's intensity and style, and who has been known to combine his preaching with a few numbers on the piano, is the Louisiana-based Assemblies of God minister who, some say, initially went to his church superiors with the tale of Jim Bakker's sexual episode with a young church secretary. Bakker, who says he had already confessed his indiscretion to his wife, now says he headed off a "hostile take-over" of his PTL (Praise the Lord, or People That Love) ministry by turning PTL over to Jerry Falwell, another prominent televangelist.

[After this commentary was published, Swaggart confessed publicly that he too had sinned, apparently with a prostitute; he then resigned from the Assemblies of God church and left the air temporarily.]

Newsweek, in the opening sentence of its April 6 cover story, "Holy Wars: Money, Sex and Power," summed up the attitude of many who have been reporting this series of events: "There was glee among the unbelievers." ABC's *Nightline,* with Sam Donaldson and Ted Koppel taking turns, devoted several programs to what the secular press has, with a certain amount of delectation, labeled "Heavengate," "Gospelgate," and even "Pearlygate." NBC's *Saturday Night Live* turned its satirical "church talk" segment into a devastating attack on the mannerisms and emotional posturing of Jim and Tammy Bakker.

The glee being expressed over this story is not confined to "unbelievers"; it is shared by all who enjoy seeing the mighty brought down, especially from the heights of alleged moral purity. And many rejoice over the internecine strife among religious superstars, who have parlayed computer mailing lists and television satellites into multimillion-dollar empires.

All the big names are feeling the exposure. Pat Robertson is on the campaign trail trying to keep a low profile, hoping nothing will detract from his quest for the presidency. Oral Roberts, who got his $8 million in time to avoid being "taken" by God, has defended the Bakkers, setting himself up for

Television evangelists Jim and Tammy Bakker hired prominent attorney Melvin Belli (right) to represent them after a sexual and financial scandal forced the Bakkers to quit their PTL (Praise the Lord) TV ministry. They are shown at a news conference.

more ridicule of his fund-raising tactics. Even Robert Schuller, whose "positive thinking" California ministry resembles that of the other players in this drama only in that he, too, is an effective user of television, was drawn briefly into the fray.

Certainly there is much to be deplored in the situation: exploitative methods of raising enough money to stay on the air; extravagant lifestyles; the us-against-them mode of proclamation; and what seems to many to be a serious distortion of the Christian message.

But granting the vulnerability of the televangelists to the kind of attacks they are now undergoing, we must still confront the fact that the media overkill is more than an excessive rendering of a sensational story. It smacks of nothing less than a gleeful attack on "holy rollers."

This whole affair has been so messy and so open to ridicule that one subtle result could be a reduction of the religious community's role in public policymaking. How can this be so when Bakker and the others represent such a minority segment of the Christian community? The answer may be found in the relish with which the events have been received. George Will, appearing with David Brinkley on an ABC Sunday morning discussion, argued in his cryptic manner that part of the problem of the televangelists is that they lack the dignity that ought to be associated with "true" religion. Being "civil" is important to Will. He seems to imply that these wild and crazy fundamentalists are too far off the reservation—where religionists ought to reside instead of entering the real world. Religious folk who confine their worship to sedate liturgical centers know their place. But these preachers who invade our homes via satellite have become what Indian-fighters of the Old West called "hostiles."

Hostile or not, religion has a role to play, whether by television or through other methods, in shaping public policy. In *Habits of the Heart,* Robert Bellah and his associates remind us of Alexis de Tocqueville's insight that the mores of our people do not spring from the soil; they are shaped by the influence of families, voluntary groups and, yes, religious communities. Plato's *Republic* describes the important connection between "the moral character of a people and the nature of its political community, the way it organizes and governs itself." Too often in recent decades this connection has been broken and the self-centered individualism that motivates us has gone almost untempered by the sometimes gentle, sometimes harsh reminder that there is a transcendent dimension to human existence.

As much as he rejoiced at the "habits of the heart" he found in the new democracy, Tocqueville nonetheless recognized, as John Diggins has noted, "that the citizen had little of the inner strength needed to discipline his desires and to lead a virtuous life of simplicity and austerity" *(The Lost Soul of American Politics).* The churches and religious communities in our midst are not always up to the task of providing that inner strength that citizens need. At times some segments of the community fail us, as in this present episode involving Jim Bakker. Nevertheless, the mandate of religious communities is to continue to affect public life, in the conviction that the message they have heard is one the entire society should also hear.

Pentecostals and fundamentalists may not speak that word in the accents the rest of us find agreeable. But they do at least begin with a Word related to redemption. And when they are bashed, we are all bashed.

INTERNATIONAL PERSPECTIVE

UNESCO AND THE NEW WORLD INFORMATION ORDER

Leonard R. Sussman

A contention by Third World countries that they are not treated fairly in international news coverage has caused extensive discussion in recent years, much of it centered in UNESCO. Leonard R. Sussman, executive director of Freedom House, examined the issue during International Day at the University of Missouri School of Journalism, April 1984.

Nowhere is the complexity of the journalist's role more apparent than in international newsreporting. Not surprisingly, therefore, the issues and controversies are often bitterly debated. For the flow of news and information across national borders has been a life and death matter for peoples, industries, and, indeed, countries. Communications is that vital—and daily, becoming more so, as new technologies provide ways to store, retrieve and process information over great distances in a moment's time. Why would any country want to be left out of that communications revolution? Put differently, why would any country want to be overwhelmed by the viewpoints, cultural forms, and even news reports that enter the country from abroad, and generally from only three or four centers in the United States and Western Europe?

Why, indeed, would any country that has recently achieved national independence choose now to have its citizens read press reports and watch television programs that feature the events and concerns of an industrialized, market society, when one's own nation is struggling to create a viable economic system, and must devote all its energies to bootstrap development programs?

If you were the leader of such a developing country, wouldn't you want to build speedily a communications infrastructure of your own . . . gain computerized access to the knowledge already available around the world . . . link your broadcast and press agencies to those of other developing countries whose interests parallel yours . . . and, finally, join with them in urging the worldwide news media—especially the big four—the AP, UPI, Reuters, Agence France-Presse—to do a better job of reporting the development news of three-quarters of the world?

If you were in that majority of poor developing countries, I repeat, wouldn't you formulate some plan or objective to give the southern tier a better crack at the vast global flow of news and information than it now receives?

Might you not call that objective a new world information order?

I would not!

I would avoid the implicit challenge to all established systems in the term "new order." That term recalls all too readily the Nazi-Fascist use of "order" over which World War II was fought. It smacks of a dogmatic reordering of society by governments and intergovernmental organizations. And it was bound to frighten even the most friendly representative of the established systems.

So the chief forum in which the new world

information order has been debated for nearly ten years is now under assault by the United States. This country, supplier of 25 percent of UNESCO's annual budget, announced last December it will withdraw this New Year's Eve from the United Nations Educational, Scientific and Cultural Organization.

(The American withdrawal became effective December 31, 1984. The United States said it acted because UNESCO had failed to improve its management and to rid itself of "endemic hostility" toward a free press, free markets, and individual human rights.)

Why?

I believe the principal reason is the struggle over a new order in communications. Several other reasons are cited: the politicizing of human rights as well as information issues, mismanagement of programs and personnel, and runaway budgetary practices. All of these complaints can be supported. UNESCO does need to be reformed. Its administration is particularly in need of restructuring, with power restored to the executive board of the member states. Duplicated programs should be eliminated. Personnel should be selected and advanced on merit, and not mainly with regard to geopolitical considerations. These complaints are increasingly heard in Washington and UNESCO/Paris, particularly as the U.S. General Accounting Office begins a review of UNESCO finances.

But that is not my primary interest. I focus on the communications issues—the new world information [and communication] order, if you will—because the NWICO first attracted the attention of American critics. It attracted them because the NWICO aroused the ire of the American press. The press regarded the NWICO as a distinct threat to press freedom. And the name of UNESCO was repeatedly linked to plans that were perceived in the West as ultimately restrictive and censorious.

If you were a Third World leader, would you have taken that road? Given your need to secure domestic communications facilities, and your own news flow, and have that move on the global nets—would you have chosen the road of restricting foreign journalists' access to your news, and insisted that global wire services employ only your nationals to cover your country? Would you have licensed all domestic and foreign journalists, the better to monitor and control their output; and even penalize those who breached a code of journalistic ethics you had devised; a code that stipulated the content of press and broadcast coverage?

Would you have done these things?

Some representatives of governments who spoke out at UNESCO would, indeed, do all or some of these things. In fact, more than a majority of the countries of the world already control or influence their press and radio in such ways. Many Third World countries, including the democracies, do not engage in these activities. Yet they, too, spoke out at UNESCO for a new world information order.

How does one reconcile that?

By the not-so-simple understanding:

a. that the NWICO has never been defined
b. that UNESCO has never approved a single resolution calling for the licensing or censoring or harming of journalists . . . and
c. that all kinds of proposals are heard at UNESCO communications debates, whether or not these ideas are approved.

The dangers in such discussions are varied:

First, those nations already inclined to control their journalists use UNESCO debates as a pretext. Indeed, the leftist military junta of Peru nationalized all newspapers in the seventies by stating that UNESCO had provided a "mandate." Seven Latin American countries now license journalists—and three more are considering it—after licensing was widely discussed at UNESCO. And South Africa threatened to impose a complex press council on independent newspapers, with monitoring and penalties for breaking a code.

It should not be said that UNESCO proposed any of this: But UNESCO did provide the settings—repeatedly—in which such alternatives were discussed. And the danger lies in creating an impression that some new universal code of practice is being created.

The American press rebounded in utter fright in the initial stages, and was little receptive to the serious, valid criticism of its own coverage of Third World development issues, or of the need to assist the creation of communications infrastructures in the developing countries themselves.

The developed countries, recently, have relented on this last score. They are increasingly training Third World journalists and trying to secure for them modern communications equipment. But the stigma on UNESCO has not been lifted.

The coverage of UNESCO continues to be heavily biased. The Belgrade general conference in 1980 was reported in 448 articles published in U.S. newspapers. Not a single one of these stories reported the work of UNESCO in science, education, monument and heritage preservation, combating illiteracy. Every last piece concerned the communications debates! Similarly, the hundred or more editorials all focused on that issue, and overwhelmingly negatively. Yet communications account for less than 8 percent of UNESCO's budget.

When the State Department last fall asked other arms of the U.S. government for an assessment of UNESCO's value to Americans, the science and education offices found no negative aspects to American participation, but warned of significant losses to America in science if the U.S. withdrew. Indeed, finding alternatives to UNESCO-supplied information and opportunities for influence and sales would be very costly, said the chief American science respondent. This government spokesman for American science—citing physicists, environmentalists, engineers, brain surgeons, geologists, informatics, oceanographers, statisticians and others—concluded: "The withdrawal of United States from UNESCO science activities would lead to a significant reduction in the direct access the U.S. scientific community now enjoys to important data bases, localities, and scientific resources throughout the world. Withdrawal from UNESCO membership would result in a general decline in the leadership position the U.S. now holds in international science and also contribute to the further politicization of UNESCO in ways detrimental to U.S. national interests."

Just last February, the same State Department reported to Congress that nothing done at UNESCO warranted America's withdrawal. That was last February! Indeed, the department added that fully 40 percent of the U.S. expenditure at UNESCO comes back to America in fellowships to Americans, "procurement of U.S. equipment, and consultation fees and payments to American staff."

What, specifically, about the NWICO and its present status?

I speak now in very personal terms.

This past year, I have visited Third World journalists in their own countries: China, Nigeria, El Salvador. I have participated in conferences where Third World journalists gathered from Africa, Asia, and Latin America. Last November I negotiated many of the communications issues at UNESCO's general conference in Paris.

One comes home, then, frustrated by simplistic observations of the information debates; and, more so, by the suggestion that remaining outside UNESCO is either a policy for meeting the legitimate demands of developing countries for communications assistance, or an effective stance for defending American journalism from political attacks abroad.

It is essential, I believe, for America to understand what has motivated the Third World demands for better infrastructure and improved coverage in the developed world. Some demands, to be sure, are authoritarian in motivation; and these are generally exploited by the Soviet bloc. We can discount those. But there is a broad bond of support among moderate Third World countries for the improvements I have mentioned. They deserve our help. It is a pity that the UNESCO debates were muddied by those with ulterior political motives. It is a pity that America had neither the acumen, ten years ago, to separate the valid complaints from others, nor the will to assist appropriately. We did not, and the polarization proceeded. We came to believe our own distorted view of the situation. And, I must add, UNESCO did not help to sort it out. The secretariat, for many years, reflected some of the harsher views of those countries bent primarily on clobbering the independent journalist—whether he resided in New York or New Delhi.

America's repeated promises of assistance were made with great flourishes: $25 million pledged in 1976 for communications development; $25 million promised again in 1978; $100,000 and then $250,000 and then $800,000 pledged when the International Program for the Development of Communications was created three years ago. A fraction of the total is beginning to flow. Yet we are told that if America leaves UNESCO this country will find alternative ways to continue our participation in such programs.

I recall my meetings in Nigeria a few weeks ago at an African conference on communications and education. Some 40 teachers and deans of journalism schools read papers or critiqued them. These were highly qualified scholars, many educated in the United States, who were striving against great odds to raise the level of journalism in their respective countries. Their scholarly papers analyzed African as well as Western journalism, including such sensitive matters as domestic press coverage in times when martial law is invoked.

They do not have your advantages. They must combat a restrictive political system every working day. They must face students without your background and with little encouragement from their societies. For African journalists are low men on the totem pole. Yet, together, students and teachers try to improve the quality and, above all, the integrity of their newsreporting and analyses. The quality of the writing of several newspapers in Nigeria—even after the January military coup that replaced a democratic government—deserves our admiration and assistance.

That, too, is a new world information order!

So is the small print press recently provided the *Grenadian Voice* by American publishers. That brave paper was banned after its first edition several years ago and sprang from the ashes, reborn, after the recent American intervention.

And encouraging, too, was the negotiation at Paris last November. Of 49 communications resolutions introduced, 33 were unobjectionable to press-freedom advocates. Of the remaining 16, the worst—introduced by the Soviet Union and East Germany—were withdrawn before they reached the floor.

More positively, for the first time in a decade, that general conference approved programs that advanced press freedom: studies of the "watchdog" role of the press, and of the harm done by censorship and self-censorship. But perhaps most important, the conference agreed that a new world information order is an "evolving process," not an imposed set of regulations to constrict the free flow of information.

All of that is a new world information order—still undefined; I believe, undefinable beyond this simple, almost mundane statement:

We recognize that the continuing revolution in communications affects everyone on this planet, and makes possible still unsurmised opportunities for personal and national development. Many new interacting systems for transmitting news and information affecting human and national development will be devised. Information is that rare commodity that does not diminish as it is shared. How important, then, for developing countries to share it. That process, by another name, is a new world information order.

UNESCO, however, is paying a high price for not clarifying much earlier that this was its primary goal and that it did not seek to establish either a universal standard of journalism or, worse still, a censorious one.

QUESTIONS FOR REVIEW AND DISCUSSION

1. How many of the "eight common complaints" against the press fit the local newspaper you read?
2. Do you agree with the criticism of the broadcast media by the former chairman of the Federal Communication Commission?
3. Larry Speakes and William Boot present differing perceptions of the confrontation between the press and the White House. Evaluate their arguments.
4. Do you agree that the press has an agenda-setting power in shaping public opinion?
5. Why did the major media organizations all protest vigorously when reporters and photographers were banned from the Grenada invasion?
6. Estimate in terms of your own experience Norman Corwin's criticism of television.
7. Discuss the problems of creating and financing an alternative or protest press.
8. Dorothy Day has won fame as a journalist as well as a social worker. What were the key characteristics of her *Catholic Worker* that made it influential for half a century?
9. Explain the Third World's argument that a new world information order is needed if their new economic order is to gain strength.
10. Why did Western media leaders object to the phrase "free and balanced flow" of the world news?

ESSAY TOPIC

Contrast and compare the roles of the print and electronic media in presenting information and opinion about political issues.

One of the critical flaws of the Meese commission report is that it applies the term *pornography*—which is a very derogatory term—to everything having to do with sexual expression, whether it is obscene, not obscene, violent, romantic, or even if it's mere nudity.

— Christie Hefner
in "The Meese Commission: Sex, Violence, and Censorship"

The most damaging trend, I think, is the predominance of the profit motive over the search for truth, editorial quality and public service in more and more newspaper owners, publishers and managers. . . .

— Jim Ottaway Jr.
in "Publisher Decries Profit over Public Service"

Journalists should be free of obligation to any interest other than the public's right to know the truth.

— Society of Professional Journalists,
Sigma Delta Chi, Code of Ethics

Use of the unregulated mass media to convey the health risks of smoking is severely limited by the tobacco industry's power, via advertising dollars, to minimize the coverage of the negative health aspects of smoking in the editorial content of these media.

— William L. Weis and Chauncey Burke
in "Media Content and Tobacco Advertising: An Unhealthy Addiction"

TV journalists edit film, and when content must be chopped into 25-second bites, the latitude of error and distortion is great.

— Herbert Schmertz
in "Turned Off: Why Executives Distrust TV Reporters"

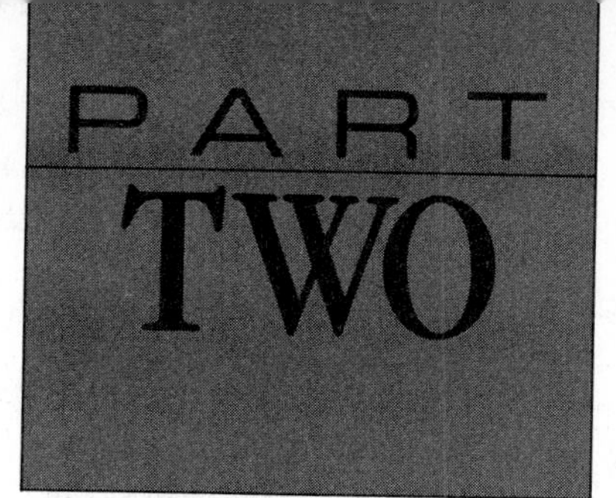

PART TWO

ETHICAL AND LEGAL CHALLENGES

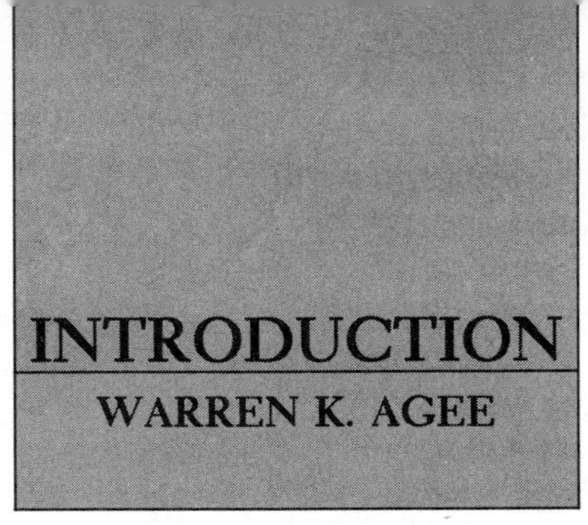

INTRODUCTION

WARREN K. AGEE

Ever since they gained widespread public attention as a powerful force not only reporting but also helping to shape the social and political upheavals of the 1960s and 1970s, the American mass media have come under increasing attack for their perceived lapses in ethical and professional conduct. A series of vexing Supreme Court decisions was followed by a barrage of libel suits resulting in huge money awards by unfriendly jurors. As pointed out in the introduction to Part One, public opinion polls continue to reflect the comparative low standing of the media among many other institutions in terms of public trust.

Much of this ill will can be attributed to a general feeling among the public that the press is too powerful, too liberal in a conservative era, and too much out of touch with its readers, viewers, and listeners—a feeling fueled by the repeated criticisms of powerful political and business leaders.

A greater source of discontent, however, appears to spring from deep-seated public perceptions that the media:

- Invade personal privacy
- Smear the reputations of people in the news, often through unbalanced reporting and use of unnamed sources
- Constantly commit errors through sloppy reporting and fail to correct them promptly and conspicuously
- Engage in confrontational and deceptive reporting
- Put words into a source's mouth
- Develop conflicts of interest that color reporting and editing, or raise suspicions that they do so

The litany of complaints seemingly is endless—when the subject arises, everyone, it appears, is eager to attest to some media failing.

Although most newspeople defend themselves against charges of ethical and professional misconduct when their own actions are involved, journalists are generally well aware of the need to improve their work and have made solid gains in this respect during recent decades. As David Shaw, media critic of the Los Angeles *Times,* has pointed out:

> By virtually any standard of measurement, the press today is more ethical—more responsible—than at any time in history. Most journalists are now well-educated and (at big-city papers) well-paid; they're respectable men and

women working in a true "profession," and they generally demand far more of themselves and their peers in terms of ethical behavior than their predecessors ever did.

ETHICAL ISSUES

Early Press Criticisms Criticisms of the press have been endemic since Benjamin Harris, in the very first, ill-fated newspaper published in the American colonies in 1690—*Publick Occurrences, Both Foreign and Domestic*—scandalized the clergy by reporting that the French king had taken immoral liberties with a married woman. Later, the scurrility of much of the new republic's press caused some historians to label the period as the "Dark Ages of Journalism." Declared Thomas Jefferson: "A suppression of the press could not more completely deprive the nation of its benefits, than is done by the abandoned prostitution to falsehood. Nothing can now be believed which is seen in a newspaper." (And yet Jefferson wrote that, given the choice of whether the nation should have a government without newspapers, or newspapers without a government, "I should not hesitate a moment to prefer the latter.") John Ward Fenno, editor of the *Gazette of the United States,* was even more emphatic when he wrote in 1799:

> The American newspapers are the most base, false, servile and venal publications, that ever polluted the foundations of society—their editors the most ignorant, mercenary, and vulgar automatons that ever were moved by the continually rusting wires of sordid mercantile avarice.

Improvements in journalistic practice were steady, but Charles Dickens, during a visit to the United States in the mid-nineteenth century, characterized much of the penny press in New York City as "sewers." The sensational treatment of news stories, features, and graphics known as "yellow journalism" marked much of the Hearst-Pulitzer newspaper era at the end of the century. Dismayed by the bitterness of attacks on social problems by early twentieth-century magazines, President Theodore Roosevelt called their work "muckraking," comparing the more sensational writers to the Man with the Muckrake in *Pilgrim's Progress,* who did not look up to see the celestial crown but continued to rake the filth. Critic Silas Bent excoriated the tabloid press of the 1920s as "collectors of filth from the divorce courts, and as exhibitors of sex in crime."

Developing a Sense of Responsibility These historical examples of press criticism should help to place in perspective many of the complaints made against today's media. Early in the twentieth century, newspaper, advertising, and journalism education leaders moved to eliminate many gross press abuses. During the 1910s, for example, government and industry leaders began to regulate advertising. About that same time, various state press associations started to formulate the principles presumed to cover the behavior of their members.

In 1923 the American Society of Newspaper Editors (ASNE) adopted a code of ethical standards whose canons called for responsibility, press freedom, independence, sincerity, truthfulness, accuracy, impartiality, fair play, and decency. The following excerpt reveals much of the thrust of the code, which has never been changed:

> A newspaper should not publish unofficial charges affecting reputation or moral character without opportunity given to the accused to be heard. . . . A newspaper should not invade private rights or feeling without sure warrant of public right as distinguished from public curiosity. . . . It is the privilege, as it is the duty, of a newspaper to make prompt and complete correction of its own serious mistakes of fact or opinion, whatever their origin.

Thus the press established its own *nongovernmental* standards, against which it is still measured today. Nevertheless, critic H. L. Mencken later reflected widespread public cynicism with his remark that "no American newspaper, so far as I am aware, has ever made any serious attempt to carry out the terms of any such code."

Journalistic adherence to the ASNE code of ethics was severely questioned when in 1947 the report of the prestigious Commission on the Freedom of the Press, headed by Robert Maynard Hutchins, at that time chancellor of the University of Chicago, found fault with many newspaper practices. The commission deplored a continued reliance by many newspapers on sensational treatment of crime and sex. Most notable, however, was the commission's list of the five requirements that society places on the news media:

1. To provide a truthful, comprehensive, and intelligent account of the day's events in a context that gives them meaning
2. To serve as a forum for the exchange of comment and criticism
3. To project a representative picture of the constituent groups in the society
4. To present the goals and values of the society
5. To provide full access to the day's intelligence

These requirements, considered the heart of the *social responsibility* theory of the press, remain the standard by which many of the public and the media leaders themselves judge the press today.

A number of media leaders criticized the five-volume report on the grounds that the members of the commission failed to include a newspaper editor or publisher and that the overall assessment of the press was unduly critical. Nevertheless, with some notable exceptions, the American press has gradually assimilated the practices recommended by the body. Newspapers that depend on sensationalism for their circulation have for the most part been replaced by those such as the Washington *Post* and the Louisville *Courier-Journal.* The *Wall Street Journal* has surpassed the often-sensationalist New York *Daily News* as the largest-circulating newspaper in the country. A better-educated public has demanded, and is receiving, major newspapers that provide intense scrutiny of the social, political, and economic environment.

A large majority of the 120 or more news organizations in the United States have adopted codes of ethics, many during the last decade. The Society of Professional Journalists, Sigma Delta Chi (SPJ,SDX) established its code in 1926 and revised it in 1972. The code is reprinted in this section.

During its 1984 convention the society added plagiarism to its list of ethical offenses, declaring the practice to be dishonest and unacceptable. Plagiarism is defined as "copying or imitating the language, ideas, and thoughts of another author and passing them off as one's original work." Surveys of print and broadcast newspeople as well as journalism educators, conducted on behalf of SPJ,SDX in 1984, revealed wide-ranging views of what constitutes plagiarism. The most blatant cases involve the appropriation, without credit to the source, of entire passages in columns and news and feature stories; there is no disagreement about such dishonesty.

The writing of stories or the taking of photographs favorable to a commercial (or even a noncommercial) operation in order to win cash awards in the innumerable contests open to journalists has also come under scrutiny. Delegates to the 1984 SPJ,SDX convention voted unanimously that henceforth cash awards would be acceptable only in contests wholly sponsored or controlled by journalism entities.

On still another ethical front, the board of the Society of Professional Journalists in 1985 rejected a proposal that the society enforce its code of ethics by disciplining members, as had been proposed. Instead, the board voted to review and then reissue a policy adopted in the mid-1970s that called for active chapter involvement in efforts to raise the ethical consciousness of journalists through seminars and other types of programs. Soon after adoption of its code of ethics in 1923, the American Society of Newspaper Editors considered expelling, suspending, or censuring its members for ethical violations. After years of debate, the society in 1932 amended its canons to permit such a practice, but the amendment has never been used. However, the Public Relations Society of America has suspended some of its members for violation of its code of ethics, as discussed by Dennis L. Wilcox in an article in this section.

Most newspapers, magazines, and broadcast networks and stations have adopted rules of their own barring gratuities, junkets, and other conflicts of interest by their employees. Recent surveys have indicated that these rules are being rigorously applied.

Because the news media are, of course, produced by people with human frailties, largely in response to reader demands for titillating news and features along with serious matter and at a fast pace subject to errors in judgment, the masses, in the words of historian John Tebbel, have a press today that is "more truly a reflection of themselves than they are willing to believe."

The Problem of Pornography The Attorney General's Commission on Pornography issued a report in 1986 calling for a massive assault on the pornography industry through a combination of more vigorous law enforcement and increased vigilance by citizens' groups. The commission concluded that exposure to most pornography "bears some causal relationship to the level of sexual violence, sexual coercion or unwanted sexual aggression."

Critics contended that this conclusion was not based on firm scientific evidence, pointing out that social scientists are divided on whether most pornography is harmful. The conclusion was in sharp contrast to that of the 1970 Commission on Obscenity and Pornography, established by Congress. That commission declared:

> The conclusion is that, for America, the relationship between the availability of erotica and changes in sex-crime rates neither proves nor disproves the possibility that availability of erotica leads to crime, but the massive overall increases in sex crimes that have been alleged do not seem to have occurred. . . . In sum, empirical research designed to clarify the question has found no evidence to date that exposure to explicit sexual materials is a factor in the causation of sex crimes or sex delinquency.

Attorney General Edwin Meese III, in releasing the 1986 report, said it would not be used for censorship. Instead, he took a number of steps designed to enforce existing state and federal laws against obscenity, especially those involving child pornography.

Excerpts from the Meese commission report are followed in this section by a rebuttal article by Christie Hefner, president of *Playboy.* The magazine is one of several removed from chain convenience stores after pressure by citizen groups and the receipt of a letter from the commission, labeled censorship by civil libertarians and publishers, suggesting that they might be cited in the commission's report for distributing pornography.

LEGAL CHALLENGES TO THE MEDIA

Legal restraints also have a strong if not always easily visible role in shaping the performance of the contemporary media.

Libel A wave of libel suits filed against newspapers, broadcast networks and stations, and news magazines during recent years has caused grave concern that the concepts of free speech and the free flow of information may become seriously eroded. From 1980 to 1984 jury awards averaged more than $2 million each. During the latter two years of that period, the figure climbed to an astonishing $3 million in cases in which punitive awards were made.

Fortunately for the media, appeals courts either reversed these decisions or reduced the amount of damages substantially in well over 7 of 10 cases during that four-year period. According to the Libel Defense Resource Center, established in 1981 by more than 50 news organizations, media payments averaged less than $100,000. Even so, the cost of defending against these suits has been heavy both financially (with attorney fees ranging to $1 million or more in some cases) and in terms of the paralytic effect on scores of newsrooms. By 1987 many insurance companies were refusing to sell policies covering the costs of libel suits against newspapers.

Problems were intensified in the case of *Herbert* v. *Lando* in 1979, when the Supreme Court ruled that plaintiffs' attorneys, in order to establish the presence of actual malice, may inquire into a journalist's state of mind at the time the offending stories or broadcast materials were prepared. This has prolonged trials; in *Lando* alone, a CBS newsman was deposed in 28 sessions, resulting in 3,000 pages of transcript and 240 exhibits. It has also shifted attention from what actually appeared in the stories to the editing process itself, confusing juries and impinging on time-honored First Amendment rights of the press.

Critics contend that press performance will be enhanced by these penalties—that reporters and editors will exercise greater responsibility in their stories and broadcasts. A contrary effect is in prospect, however: Newsroom memoranda questioning aspects of developing stories, as well as internal investigations after publication, may cease. Most serious of all is the chilling effect on the press, almost certain in such circumstances to become more timid in the performance of its First Amendment role.

That role had been reinforced strongly by the Supreme Court's decision in the case of *New York Times* v. *Sullivan* in 1964. The Court held that a public official cannot recover damages for a defamatory falsehood relating to his or her official conduct without proving that the statement was made with actual malice. The Court later extended this relative protection against adverse libel decisions to include public figures, although the protection was narrowed in subsequent cases.

Juries, however, awarded more than $1 million each to plaintiffs in 26 libel cases between 1976 and 1984, according to a Center survey. When more than 70 percent of these decisions were reversed by federal appeals courts, media owners expressed concern that the Burger Court—which had ruled against the press in every case brought before it during the preceding decade—would move to force appeals judges to accept the factual findings of the lower courts and juries.

It was with a great sense of relief and some surprise, therefore, that the press greeted the 1984 decision of the Supreme Court, in *Bose* v. *Consumers Union,* reaffirming the Sullivan standards in ringing terms and endorsing the critical role of appeals courts in reviewing libel judgments made by lower court judges and jurors. The decision ended a 14-year dispute between the Bose Corporation, a Massachusetts stereo speaker manufacturer, and Consumers Union of Mount Vernon, New York, which had published a critical review of a Bose product in *Consumer Reports* magazine. A federal district court had found the report libelous and awarded Bose $210,905 in damages. But a federal appeals court conducted a full review of the facts in the case, finding that the report was not published with "reckless disregard" for its truth or falsity. The Supreme Court upheld that decision.

Three 1986 Supreme Court decisions gave new support to the *Sullivan* doctrine. In *Anderson* v. *Liberty Lobby* the court upheld the granting of summary judgments by trial courts in favor of media defendants. It did so by ruling that a public-figure libel plaintiff must demonstrate actual malice by clear and convincing evidence to defeat a summary judgment motion. In *Hepps* v. *Philadelphia Newspapers Inc.* Justice Sandra Day O'Connor reversed common law tradition in her 5–4 decision, saying that states may not place the burden on media libel defendants to prove the truth in suits brought by private figures if they involve coverage of issues of public concern. And a U.S. court of appeals let stand a summary judgment for CBS dismissing the libel claim by Lt. Col. Anthony Herbert that had occasioned the 1979 ruling permitting the probing of journalists' minds.

In another prolonged contest, the U.S. Court of Appeals for the District of Columbia reversed a $2 million judgment against the Washington *Post* won by the president of the Mobil Oil Corporation, William P. Tavoulareas, on charges of libel in a 1979 investigative reporting article. The court said: "The First Amendment forbids penalizing the press for encouraging its reporters to expose wrongdoing by public corporations and public figures."

Nevertheless, corporations, media watchdogs, litigious groups, and public officials are making increased use of libel suits. The American Legal Foundation opened the Libel Prosecution Resource Center in Washington, D.C., in 1984 to provide legal backing to plaintiffs similar to that available to journalists. The most publicized of the suits filed by public officials were those of General William Westmoreland, seeking $120 million in damages from CBS on charges that the network libeled him in a Vietnam War documentary, and Ariel Sharon, former defense minister of Israel, who sought $50 million in damages from Time Inc. on charges that *Time* magazine erroneously linked him with the massacre of about 700 Arabs in a refugee camp in Lebanon. CBS and Time Inc. spent millions of dollars in their defenses against the actions.

The *New York Times* v. *Sullivan* ruling enabled *Time* to defend itself successfully against Sharon. Early in 1985, a federal jury in New York decided that the key paragraph in *Time*'s article about Sharon's conversation with Lebanese Christian leaders was both defamatory and erroneous. The jury, however, found insufficient evidence to prove that *Time* had acted with malice in publishing the material. As a public figure, Sharon was required to prove that the magazine knew the story to be false or had serious doubts as to its truth. Because he failed to do so, he lost his $50 million suit. He claimed a political victory, nevertheless, because the jury had found the *Time* statement to be incorrect. Although deciding in *Time*'s favor, the six-member jury issued a statement criticizing the magazine's conduct, in which it found that the magazine "acted negligently and carelessly in reporting and verifying" the information it published.

After 18 weeks of trial, and a week before the case was to go to the jury, Westmoreland withdrew his suit against CBS. Under an agreement between the parties, CBS made no apology or retraction for the contents of the program, "The Uncounted Enemy: A Vietnam Deception," and each side paid its own legal expenses. Testimony by fellow military officers shortly before Westmoreland's withdrawal had hurt his cause; he claimed nevertheless that wording of the joint agreement was equivalent to an apology from the network. CBS strongly denied any implication of apology and said it was free to rebroadcast the program if it desired.

The outcomes of these two cases, in which neither prominent plaintiff achieved a legal victory, strengthened the ability of the news media to investigate public issues without excessive fear of retaliatory libel suits. Libel authority Floyd Abrams reviews the problems in one of this section's readings.

Protection for Advertising In another article, two scholars examine how the tobacco industry's advertising dollars may affect the media's willingness to convey the health hazards of smoking. Although adult smoking rates have decreased from 42 percent to 25 percent since a government public education campaign began in 1978, the authors suggest that a federal ban on tobacco advertising in print media may be necessary to win media cooperation. This would raise a firestorm of protest insisting that the First Amendment protects commercial advertising.

Problems with Plagiarism Another selection discusses both the ethical and legal consequences of indulging in plagiarism. Ethically, the infraction is false representation of the source of a work; legally, it is violation of copyright or property right.

The Freedom of Information Crusade Of equal concern to journalists is the continuing battle to obtain public and press access to federal records and files. The documents may be classified as top secret, secret, or confidential or may bear no stamp at all. The crusade, begun more than three decades ago, won passage by Congress in 1966 of the Freedom of Information Act (FOIA). The law states basically that any person may go to court to gain access to public records if they are not provided upon request, and the burden of proof that secrecy is necessary is on the government.

Over President Gerald Ford's veto, Congress strengthened the act in 1974 by enacting amendments narrowing the scope of exemptions that protect certain categories of government files from public disclosure, such as secrets that affect national security. Congress also required agencies to answer information requests within 10 days of receipt, broadened avenues of appeal and court authority to declassify disputed documents, and established penalty guidelines for wrongful withholding of documents. As a result, thousands of documents have been released by such agencies as the FBI and the CIA.

The CIA, however, complained that foreign agents were using the FOIA to attempt to gain information, and the FBI maintained that organized crime has attempted to discover FBI information sources. There were complaints also that law firms and commercial competitors were seeking to gain trade secrets and business advantages by access to documents held by the Federal Trade Commission (FTC) and business-related cabinet departments.

In 1980 Congress exempted most consumer information from being disclosed by the FTC. Bills were introduced in 1981 providing substantial or total exemptions from the act to the CIA and FBI, as well as protecting information from nuclear power plant archives and about offshore power plants. In 1984 Congress passed a bill largely exempting CIA operational files from disclosure. Congressional wrangling and determined media opposition, however, stalled other proposed restrictions until 1986, when agencies won more leeway.

The Reagan administration's efforts to restrict the release of government information have been intense. Since 1984 the Freedom of Information Committee of the Society of Professional Journalists, Sigma Delta Chi has graded the Reagan administration on its relations with the news media. Among the actions given *failing* grades by the committee were these:

1. The Reagan administration gained passage of a bill that provides harsh criminal penalties for people who disclose the names of present or former CIA operatives, regardless of the source of that information or its value to the public.

2. The administration, breaking longstanding wartime traditions, excluded all civilian reporters and photographers from coverage of the early days of the invasion of Grenada.
3. The Justice Department issued guidelines to encourage all federal agencies to be more restrictive in their release of information under the FOIA and to deny FOI fee waivers to journalists, scholars, and others who seek information for public dissemination.
4. President Reagan signed an executive order that makes it easier for federal agencies to classify information (and thus withhold it from the public) and much harder to get information declassified.
5. The President issued a directive, later partly withdrawn under congressional pressure, requiring all federal employees with access to sensitive government information to sign away their First Amendment rights for life and agree to obtain prior government approval for any books, articles, or speeches they might write.
6. The Justice Department sought to restrict the flow of ideas across U.S. borders by labeling as propaganda three Canadian films dealing with nuclear war and acid rain and by denying unconditional visas to a number of writers and political figures with antiadministration views.
7. CIA Director William Casey threatened to prosecute major news organizations for publishing alleged classified information.
8. The FBI created a special squad to investigate the sources of government leaks to the news media.
9. National Security Adviser John Poindexter approved a campaign of "disinformation" to make media believe Moammar Gadhafi was planning new terrorist attacks by Libya.
10. A series of instances involving misstatements, false statements, and concealments of facts marred presidential and administration news conferences during the Iran-*contra* affair. Presidential news conferences came to a virtual halt.

With a $250,000 grant from Central Newspapers, Inc., the Society of Professional Journalists, Sigma Delta Chi opened an FOI Center in Washington, D.C., in 1985 to coordinate its FOI activities in cooperation with other news organizations. FOI hotline networks were planned for every state to help news media keep information channels open. The society also began a national campaign it called Project Watchdog to convey the message to the public that the First Amendment belongs to all citizens and is the cornerstone of a free society. FOI Service Center director Elaine English reviews the accomplishments in her article.

In their efforts to gain the right to report, the news media, among other things, also are continuing their efforts to obtain access to public meetings, to protect the confidentiality rights of reporters, to protect the media from search and seizure, and to broaden access of broadcast reporters and cameras to the courtroom. The media's struggle for "the public's right to know" is never-ending.

PORNOGRAPHY

PORNOGRAPHY AND VIOLENCE

Attorney General's Commission on Pornography

Attorney General Edwin Meese III appointed an 11-member commission to investigate pornography in the United States. The report it released in 1986 is long, intricate, and verbose. Here we publish excerpts covering key points.

DEFINING PORNOGRAPHY

Much controversy has arisen concerning the Meese commission's report, particularly its finding that certain sexually explicit material promotes violence. Its recommendations for citizen protest against sellers of such material also have drawn some criticism.

The commission defines hard-core pornography thus:

> If we were forced to define the term "hard core pornography," we would probably note that it refers to the extreme form of what we defined as pornography, and thus would describe material that is sexually explicit to the extreme, intended virtually exclusively to arouse, and devoid of any other apparent content or purpose.

Source: Final report of the U.S. Attorney General's Commission on Pornography, (Washington, D.C.: U.S. Government Printing Office, 1986).

Citing the wide range of sexually explicit materials available in the United States, the commission divides these materials into four categories and describes the degree of harm it believes each category causes. It states its belief that harm may result from material even though it is protected by the First Amendment to the Constitution.

Sexually Violent Material

> The category of material featuring actual or unmistakably simulated or unmistakably threatened violence presented in sexually explicit fashion with a predominant focus on the sexually explicit violence. . . .
>
> In both clinical and experimental settings, exposure to sexually violent materials has indicated an increase in the likelihood of aggression. More specifically, the research . . . shows a causal relationship between exposure of this type and aggressive behavior towards women. . . .
>
> We have reached the conclusion, unanimously and confidently, that the available evidence strongly supports the hypothesis that substantial exposure to sexually violent materials as described here bears a causal relationship to antisocial acts of sexual violence and, for some subgroups, possibly to unlawful acts of sexual violence. . . .
>
> We . . . thus conclude that the class of such materials, although not necessarily every member of the class, is on the whole harmful to society.

Attorney General Edwin Meese III speaks at a news conference in Washington after accepting report from his commission on pornography.

Nonviolent Materials Depicting Degradation, Domination, Subordination, or Humiliation

We conclude that substantial exposure to materials of this type bears some causal relationship to the level of sexual violence, sexual coercion, or unwanted sexual aggression in the population so exposed.

Nonviolent and Nondegrading Materials

Our most controversial category has been the category of sexually explicit materials that are nonviolent and are not degrading, as we have used that term. They are materials in which the participants appear to be fully willing participants occupying substantially equal roles in a setting devoid of actual or apparent violence or pain. . . .

We are dealing in this category with "pure" sex, as to which there are widely divergent views in this society. . . .

The fairest conclusion from the social science evidence is that there is no persuasive evidence to date supporting the connection between nonviolent and nondegrading materials and acts of sexual violence, and that there is some, but very limited evidence, indicating that the connection does not exist.

Nudity

None of us, of course, finds harmful the use of nudity in art, and for plainly educational purposes. Similarly, we all believe that in some circumstances the portrayal of nudity may be undesirable. It is therefore impossible to draw universal conclusions about depictions of nudity under all conditions. But by and large we do not find the nudity that does not fit within any of the previous categories to be much cause for concern.

CHILD PORNOGRAPHY

The report begins its examination of this topic with the heading "The Special Horror of Child Pornography." It concludes the discussion thus:

> None of us doubt that child pornography is extraordinarily harmful both to the children involved and to society, that dealing with child pornography in all of its forms ought to be treated as a governmental priority of the greatest urgency, and that an aggressive law enforcement effort is an essential part of this urgent governmental priority.

METHODS OF PROTEST

In a long section titled "The Role of Private Action," the report discusses ways in which citizens can protest against pornography as they understand it.

> It should be apparent from the foregoing that citizens need not feel hesitant in condemning that which they feel is worthy of condemnation. Moreover, they need feel no hesitation in taking advantage of the rights they have under the First Amendment to protest in more visible or organized form.
>
> They may, of course, form or join organizations designed expressly for the purposes of articulating a particular point of view. They may protest or picket or march or demonstrate in places where they are likely to attract attention, and where they will have the opportunity to persuade others of their views. . . .
>
> Of some special relevance in this context is the practice of protesting near the premises of establishments offering material that some citizens may find dangerous or offensive or immoral.
>
> We recognize that such forms of protest may at times discourage patrons who would otherwise enter such establishments from proceeding, but that, we believe, is part of the way in which free speech operates in the United States. . . .
>
> Somewhat related to on-site or near-site protesting, in terms of coercive force, is the boycott, in which a group of citizens may refuse to patronize an establishment offering certain kinds of magazines, or tapes, or other material, and may also urge others to take similar action. At times the boycott may take the form of action against an advertiser, where people may express their views about corporate responsibility by refusing to buy certain products as long as the producer of these products advertises in certain magazines, or on certain television shows.

The commission follows these statements with a warning against excesses by protestors and concludes:

> We believe it is fully appropriate for citizens to protest against material they find objectionable, and we know that at times this protest activity will go too far, to the detriment of all of us. . . . We encourage people to object to the objectionable, but we think it is even more important that they tolerate the tolerable.

RECOMMENDATIONS FOR LEGAL ACTION

The commission lists 92 recommendations for new federal and state laws, actions for prosecutors, and steps by social service agencies. One of the most controversial of these is number 5:

> Congress should amend Title 18 of the United States code to specifically proscribe obscene cable television programming.

THE MEESE COMMISSION: SEX, VIOLENCE, AND CENSORSHIP

Christie Hefner

As president of Playboy Enterprises, Inc., Christie Hefner vigorously rebuts the Meese commission report in this article published in *The Humanist.* She contends that the report poses a more serious threat to the First Amendment than to pornography.

When the Meese commission issued its report on pornography in July 1986, the New York *Daily News* wrote:

> The Attorney General's Commission on Pornography has all the trappings of a high-powered fact finding panel, lots of press coverage, lots of critics, and lots of reaction. In its final report, the commission claimed there is a link between pornography and sex crimes. The commission's official status gives that finding some weight, but the public should not be fooled by the veneer of authority. The fact of the matter is that the commission has not proven any such link between pornography and sex crimes, nor has it demonstrated that pornography presents a threat to society. Government censorship, however, presents a very real danger to a society that allows free expression and respects the right of privacy.

Dr. Morris Lipton, who was on the 1970 President's Commission on Pornography, put it even more succinctly: "As a scientific document, the Meese Commission's report is somewhere between a farce and a disgrace."

I want to address the report itself and what I see as the serious problems of it. But, also, I want to state why I think censorship is a dangerous red herring when we are trying to have a serious and realistic discussion about how to create a happier, healthier, safer society. I don't think the issue here is a debate between unbridled hedonism and total suppression. I think the people who are genuinely concerned about those social issues are those people who are having the most difficulty getting their voices heard, not to mention getting government support.

One of the critical flaws with the Meese commission report is that it applies the term *pornography*—which is a very derogatory term—to everything having to do with sexual expression, whether it is obscene, not obscene, violent, romantic, or even if it's mere nudity. So, from the beginning, everything that has anything to do with sexuality is labeled as something inherently bad.

Beyond that, the commission members focus much of their effort on those parts of sexual imagery that are the most violent and hateful, which gives you an impression that, in fact, what's out there is very different from, in fact, what is *really* out there. This problem of faulty methodology was attacked by the two commissioners who filed a dissenting report, Dr. Judith Becker of Columbia University, who has worked with sex offenders, and Ellen Levin, editor of *Woman's Day* magazine. One of the things they wrote in the dissenting opinion was "that the evidence brought to the panel was skewed to the very violent and extremely degrading."

Worse than that, the commission ignored the evidence that points to just the *opposite* conclusion. For example, one of the very few pieces of original research that the commission did was to look not just at *Playboy* and *Penthouse* but at the thirteen best-selling men's magazines to find what percentage of their material was violent. Now, if our society had the serious problem of violent sexual imagery that the commission says it has, one would think it would show up in their analysis. But the actual amount proved to be *less than one percent.* However, this statistic is amazingly missing from the final report, as is the conclusion of the Kinsey Institute, which tracks hardcore, X-rated video cassettes, that *less than 10 percent* of X-rated video cassettes are violent.

Source: The Humanist, January–February 1987. Reprinted by permission of the author.

Also missing from the report is information from Joseph Scott of Ohio University, who tracked not just X-rated material but all categories of the Motion Picture Association of America rating system. Do you know what he found? He discovered that the least violent category of all—again, less than 10 percent—was X-rated films and that much more violent were R-rated, PG-13, and PG-rated films. That isn't consistent with, I think, the perspective the commission wanted to take. At the same time as they were exaggerating the amount of sexually violent material, I believe for political effect, the Senate issued a report based upon a two-year study of child pornography. The Senate report said that child pornography is not increasing and that it basically involves a very few pedophiles who exchange the pictures they have taken. It does not involve organized crime. It is very difficult to buy child pornography today in the United States because the Child Protection Act of 1984 has made it a federal crime. The report concluded, "No child pornography is produced in the United States because the penalties are so severe, and there's not much profit in it."

That's a very different picture than you might get from reading the Meese commission's report. When you read the headlines from the report, you may not see what's behind them: not only the problems in definition of the word *pornography* but the problems in definition of the word *harm,* as in "pornography causes harm." If we're trying to discuss whether or not to censor materials, I think we would all like to know that the basis for censorship is that the material is harmful and that the harm is both real and serious. What does the commission have to say about this? Well, according to Commissioner Becker in the dissenting opinion, "The commission began with the ultra-conservative premise that a majority considered masturbation, oral/genital sex, premarital sex, to be harmful and anti-social behavior." Just think about this: an official government body is telling us that we need to censor material because it might provoke sex between unmarried people. This doesn't give me a lot of confidence in the balance between a safer society and a free society. I'm not going to embarrass you by asking for a poll of your personal sexual behavior, but I would venture to say that, if the above mentioned activities are all crimes, I may not be the only criminal in today's society.

But what about violent crimes—something we're all concerned about? What does the commission do to prove the assertion that some pornography is linked to violent crime? I don't think the Meese commission proved there *is* a link. The *Los Angeles Times* put it even more strongly than I might have when it wrote:

> The kindest thing that can be said about the two thousand page report of the Attorney General's Commission on Pornography is that it's a joke, not funny, but a joke. The commission's scholarship is ludicrous, its conclusions unsupported, its methodology zany.

It didn't have to be this way. Scientific data exist in a variety of arenas that, if it had been looked at, could have pointed to a very different conclusion. First of all, there's evidence from other countries which has been conveniently ignored by the commission. I mentioned Denmark, but take a look at Japan. In Japan, themes of bondage and rape in their printed material are much more prevalent than in this country, but the incidence of rape in Japan is one-sixteenth that in the United States. There's scientific research that has been done on the potential causes of violence and sexual abuse against women and children, and there isn't a single study that suggests that pornography is a cause, let alone a substantial cause, of this violence.

Dr. Becker herself, the member of the commission most experienced in dealing with sex offenders, says, "No serious body of evidence of a causal connection between pornography and crime exists. I believe some of the commissioners are simply attempting to legislate their own personal morality." Dr. Edward Donnerstein, who is one of the experts called in front of the commission, says,

"The problem is, if we are talking about sexually explicit material, we have to conclude there is no evidence for any harm related effects." Murray Strauss, who was also a witness in front of the commission, says, "The fundamental problem is there's a wide consensus about the issue of violence, but the commission's concern was sex, and as a means of getting at sex, they said sex promotes violence, but that's crazy." There's an important perspective that Strauss adds that is especially meaningful to me, as a woman, which is to restate something that the women's movement fought very hard for over a decade ago: "Rape is not so much a sexual act as it is a violent one. Rape is the use of sex to express aggression." Remember when it was perfectly okay to cross-examine the victim in a rape trial about how many boyfriends she had, what kind of birth control she used, and what she was wearing that night? I think it's very close to that to allow people to say, "Sexy pictures made me do it," just like one used to be able to say, "The way she walked made me do it." And, in fact, there's already been reported a case of a man on trial for a sex crime who is using the Meese report to substantiate his claim that "pornography made him do it."

The report fails to focus on violence as distinct from sexuality, even though all the scientific evidence indicates that when you're talking about sexually violent material, it's the violent component—not the sexual component—that has an adverse effect on people's attitudes. When you show people hardcore sexual material without a violent context, you see a neutral effect. When you show them violent material without a sexual context, you see negative results. But the commission is disregarding this distinction at the same time it's disregarding the critical distinction between attitude and action.

In addition to the scientific data and the experience of other countries, part of the problem with the commission's report is that it simply runs counter to the experience of millions of Americans. More X-rated video cassettes were rented during 1985 than there were people who voted for Ronald Reagan. Millions of people have seen sexual material in magazines and films, and they have not become violent. Moreover, if one examines countries that have serious problems of violence and abuse against women—such as South Africa, Iran, or the Soviet Union—you discover that these are countries that are not only politically repressive but sexually repressive in their approach to materials as well.

I would like to turn to the politics of the Meese commission report, because I think that this report is not only wrong in its conclusion but is fundamentally at odds with the very mandate given to the Reagan administration—the mandate to get the government out of people's lives. I cannot think of a more intrusive area for the government to be involved in than in what people read or see or believe or practice in the privacy of their own homes. As *Publishers Weekly* wrote:

> The commission seems to think it speaks for a vast majority of Americans, when it suggests that some sort of citizen action is required to curb excesses for which the law is inadequate. It certainly speaks for a large number of generally right-wing fundamentalist groups and their supporters, who in turn have been supporters of the current administration. But, for the people as a whole?

Every time the matter of censoring constitutionally protected but sexually explicit material has been put to the voters, they have resoundingly defeated it. The voters of Maine, by a margin of three to one, defeated a referendum much like the recommendations of the Meese report. And the same results have occurred in South Dakota, in Cambridge, Massachusetts, and in other parts of the country. Protesters always talk about community values; yet, is it really the *community*'s values or *their* values? When the Lawson's chain in the Midwest was under heavy pressure from groups, such as the National Federation for Decency, which take credit for pressuring 7-Eleven into removing *Playboy* from its shelves, what Lawson's did was say, "We're not going to necessarily rely on who can dump the most mail on our desks; we're going to poll our customers." And, for two weeks, they did just that. Lo and behold, the majority of their customers said that they had no objection at all to the availability of magazines such as *Playboy,* regardless of whether or not they bought them.

If I'm beginning to sound like some sort of libertine who is not offended by anything, let me state that nothing is farther from the truth. The fact is that I deeply resent people being manipulated by others who disapprove of sexually explicit material, *because* I care about the quality of life in this society and because I think a part of that quality comes from tolerating a variety of life-styles and mindsets.

All of us are offended by some choices some people make, but it is the very same pluralism that allows each of us to make our own choices that requires us to tolerate others. If we urge people to picket and boycott stores because of material they find objectionable, where will it stop? When they drive out *The Nation?* When they drive out *Ms.?* When a group of Christians organize to drive a synagogue out of town? With regard to First Amendment protected material, isn't there a fundamental difference between your right not to participate and your preventing other people from participating? I think there is.

Syndicated columnist Mike Royko said:

> Personally, I don't like pornography, but it's not because I think it will turn me into a raging fiend; it's because I find it tasteless, embarrassing and boring. But that's no reason to ban it, because if being tasteless, embarrassing, or boring was a crime, we'd have to get rid of 90 percent of the television shows, hit records, close down most of the franchised fast food joints, muzzle the politicians, and prohibit any preacher from talking more than ninety seconds.

That's the real point: we all find certain things objectionable, but not the *same* things. . . .

What can we do about this material we find objectionable? Obviously, we can avoid it. In my case, I can choose not to publish it. Commissioner Park Dietz of the Meese commission indicated publicly that he believes *Playboy* is the kind of positive, nonviolent sexual imagery that is needed, and even Chairman Hudson has indicated that *Playboy* was neither the focus of nor condemned in the report. But that isn't enough, because all of us are concerned about the serious social problems of violence and abuse.

There are real solutions to these issues to be pursued, and this, I think, is the final public policy danger and tragedy of the Meese report: *it misdirects sincere people's attention away from thinking about the real causes of violence and abuse.* People are led into thinking that, by looking to censorship as an answer, they can divert attention away from the complicated origins of sex abuse or teenage pregnancy or child abuse. Such an attempt can never work because it fails to come to grips with the tensions and complexities of modern society. The report does a disservice because it recommends that scarce resources be directed in the wrong direction. . . .

Lastly, I think there is an important issue here of individual responsibility. I think part of the strength of this nation is its dedication to the rights and responsibilities of individuals. We base our laws on the idea that people are responsible for their actions. When the murderer of Harvey Milk and Mayor George Moscone says that Twinkies made him do it, we don't let him off. When a psychopath pulls a sword on the Staten Island Ferry and kills two people and says, "God made me do it," that isn't an alibi. Why is it so different when we deal with areas of sexuality and sexual imagery? We don't let someone blame alcohol for drunk driving. We say *you* are responsible if you become abusive.

We need to take charge of our own lives—not to look to the government to do it. We need to recapture our confidence in our ability to shape the morals of our families, and, I think, as the commission in 1970 wrote, that values are instilled in the home, in education, in religious training, and through individual resolutions of personal confrontations with human experience. Governmental regulation of moral choice can deprive the individual of the responsibility for personal decisions which is essential to the formation of genuine moral standards. We need to have faith that those basic values will not be easily eradicated by an image here or an idea there. I wish some of the crusaders had a little more faith in people and their ability to make the right choices.

ETHICAL PROBLEMS IN NEWSPAPERS

THE RANGE OF ETHICAL PROBLEMS

Philip Meyer

A study made by Philip Meyer for the American Society of Newspaper Editors titled *Editors, Publishers and Newspaper Ethics* has been published as a paperback book. In this excerpt, Meyer examines the ethical problems newspaper people face. He cites the areas of fairness, balance, and objectivity as the most troublesome.

Ethical issues in the newspaper business can range from the trivial to the profound. Some questions are encountered frequently and others hardly at all. In order to size up the current state of ethical concerns, we needed an objective measure that would tap both the seriousness of different kinds of problems and the frequency with which they are encountered. The study's interviewers used the initial telephone contact with editors to take a rough count of ethical problems.

It was reasoned that an ethical problem was relatively trivial if it could be solved on the spot without discussion. By "trivial," we do not mean that the consequences for those involved were necessarily unimportant, but simply that reaching a solution did not require any mental anguish. And so our objective indicator for defining a problem as nontrivial was simply that solving it required some discussion in the newsroom. A problem whose solution is so obvious that it can be reached without discussion is really no problem at all. Accordingly, editors were read a list of 12 kinds of ethical problems, and asked how frequently cases of each type were discussed at their newspapers. The list came from a survey of recent literature on newspaper ethics. The works relied on most heavily were John L. Hulteng's review of the ASNE ethical code, *Playing It Straight,* Bruce M. Swain's anecdote-rich *Reporters' Ethics,* and a work sponsored by the Hastings Center, *Teaching Ethics in Journalism Education,* by Clifford G. Christians and Catherine L. Covert.

By far the most troublesome area for newspapers—with troublesome thus defined—is the general area of fairness, balance, and objectivity, including the allocation of space to opposing interest groups or political candidates and providing the right of reply to criticism. Editors representing 64 percent of the nation's daily circulation said such problems were discussed at their newspapers at least once a month. No other class of problems came close.

This response should come as no surprise to experienced news people. An editor must mediate among a rich array of competing interests and viewpoints, and perceptions of unfairness by any of them are likely to be met with vocal objection. Ironically, the harder a newspaper tries to cover the news, the more difficult it is to satisfy the conflicting claims for attention. For a newspaper with an aggressive news staff, concerns of fairness and balance can become a continuing preoccupation.

After this primary grouping of ethical problems comes a cluster of secondary concerns which

Source: Excerpted from *Editors, Publishers and Newspaper Ethics,* a report to the American Society of Newspaper Editors by Philip Meyer, April 1983. Reprinted by permission of the American Society of Newspaper Editors.

are encountered at least once a month by editors representing from a fourth to a third of total circulation. For these concerns, fairness to individuals, rather than groups, is more likely to be involved. Thirty-nine percent (circulation-adjusted) said they had discussions involving invasion of privacy—defined as news that causes injury to feelings or discloses embarrassing private facts—at least once a month.

Encountered at nearly the same rate, 36 percent, is the set of problems relating to granting and preserving confidentiality—including situations where a pledge of confidentiality involves potential harm to the reader as well as the source by withholding relevant information about that source.

Problems involving photos which might depict violence or obscenity or lead to hurt feelings are also in this secondary group, with a 29 percent rating. Then, at 26 percent, there is the whole set of problems relating to pressure from advertisers: blurbs, business office musts, keeping things out of the paper to please advertisers—or putting them in.

The problems on the list remaining proved to be relatively rare, with editors representing less than 20 percent of total circulation encountering them monthly or more often. In order of their frequency ratings, they are:

- Government secrecy: grand jury leaks, national security problems, including military secrets and diplomatic leaks—18 percent.
- Economic temptations: accepting trips, meals, favors, loans, or gifts from sources or suppliers—15 percent.
- Suppression of news to protect the community, as in the case of factory relocations, school closings, highway expansion and the like—11 percent.
- Questionable news gathering methods, such as using false identity, stolen documents, concealed recordings, or eavesdropping—8 percent.
- Civil disorder: publicizing rioters, terrorists, bomb threats at the risk of encouraging imitators—7 percent.
- Use of reporters for non-news tasks, e.g., writing advertising supplements, gathering data for the company's financial decisions or labor relations objectives—2 percent.

So far in this survey of the ethical landscape, there are few surprises. But when we get down to cases, some unexpected patterns emerge. The 12-category classification scheme for ethical issues used in the interviews with editors has a certain intellectual neatness to it, but a prudent investigator will wonder whether the real world is really that neat.

If it were, attitudes toward specific ethical situations would fit into the same neatly ordered bins. A person sensitive to one kind of fairness and balance problem would be sensitive to others, assuming that newspaper people, in reaching their real-world ethical positions, are as consistent as we who only theorize expect them to be.

To find the threads of consistency, the mail survey of editors, publishers, and staff members asked for preferred decisions on a list of hypothetical, but reality-inspired, ethical situations. By finding the clusters of consistency in these responses, we can get a better idea of how ethical problems are resolved and see how realistic our original classification scheme was. The statistical technique is complex, but the interpretation is not. Some answers will tend to predict others. For example, if an editor who leans over backward to be fair in a specific case involving balance and objectivity is likely to also do the same on others in the same general area, then it seems reasonable to conclude that there is an underlying dimension, a general concern for fairness and balance, that different news people can be measured against. But if responses to such a question prove to be linked to those of one on some different subject, then some other underlying force is at work. The trick is to find the patterns of correlation and guess at their underlying influences.

What was found is, at first glance, surprising. Questions in the same substantive areas were not always linked in the predicted fashion. There were unexpected underlying influences. Indeed, a search for those influences leads to a conclusion that newspaper ethical positions tend to be arrived at, not so much on the basis of substantive consistency as reflected in our initial questioning of editors, as on the basis of more visceral criteria. Certain situations invoke certain journalistic reflexes, and it may be these reflexes, rather than more complicated codes, explicit or implicit, which determine the ethical outcome.

The analysis of specific situations asked about in this survey produced five broad groupings, and this categorization scheme appears to be more realistic than the original one because it does contain threads of consistency.

It also reveals some inconsistencies. For example, the original questions put to editors assumed that all matters involving reporters' methods could be lumped together. In the mail survey, several specific cases involving different sorts of questionable reporting methods were asked about. The responses were uncorrelated, i.e., a concern for questionable methods in one situation did not mean a better-than-random chance that a similar concern would be expressed in another.

Among the consistencies that were found, some were expected and some were surprising. Among the expected: news people who worry about reporters getting too close to their sources in one situation are likely to be worried in a parallel, but different situation. The two situations are linked by an underlying standard.

This standard was forthrightly expressed by the late Edwin A. Lahey, Washington Bureau chief for the Knight Newspapers in the late 1950s and 1960s before the Knight-Ridder group was formed. Lahey was beloved for his wit and compassion and knew many powerful decision makers socially. Nevertheless, he advised reporters to "pee on your source's leg at least once a week." Maintaining a distance, he believed, preserved honesty in reporting.

One of the survey questions tapping this dimension described a Washington situation: . . .

> Your Washington correspondent has spent years developing friendships with the key people now in power, and it is paying off. He knows the town well, and they are relative newcomers, so he is frequently consulted by the White House staff and the President's political operatives before key decisions are made. Should the editor:
>
> 1. Fire the Washington correspondent?
> 2. Move the correspondent to another city?
> 3. Admonish the Washington correspondent to maintain a reasonable distance from his sources?
> 4. Reward the Washington correspondent for developing such a good knowledge of his subject and such loyal sources?

Editors were more reluctant than either publishers or staff members to take the extreme actions of firing or transferring the correspondent. Across all three groups, those representing 11 percent of the readers would take one of those strong steps.

When the scene was shifted from Washington to city hall, however, the ethical sensitivity of all three groups increased dramatically. Editors were still more reluctant to take strong action than were publishers or staff, but the consensus for such action rose to nearly 31 percent.

Most importantly, the two items did correlate. A person favoring strong action in one case had a better-than-random chance of favoring it in the other case. In fact, they formed a cumulative index. Nearly everyone who wanted stern treatment for the Washington correspondent also wanted it for the city hall reporter. The news people in the study can therefore be divided into three categories: those who want to fire or transfer both reporters for getting too close to their sources (11 percent), those who want to fire or transfer only one of them—in nearly all cases, the city hall reporter—(19 percent), while the majority preferred mild action—or even a reward for the reporter—in both cases.

Some interesting hypotheses about newspaper ethics are supported here. One is that ethical standards are higher closer to home. Priests and psychologists have known this for some time, and we all know how some people behave at conventions. Wanderlust, suggests psychiatrist Allen Wheelis (*The Quest for Identity*, 1958), is based more on wandering for lust than lust for wandering. Most editors are somewhat insulated from the daily ethical shocks and traumas of Washington coverage. . . .

What kinds of newspaper people express the most sensitivity to the problem of closeness to sources? Conventional wisdom suggests at least one possibility. Young people might be expected to be the most sensitive to this issue. They are less likely to have strong community ties or closeness to sources themselves. Youth is generally believed to be more idealistic; young people have not yet been exposed to the world's harsh realities that justify for older persons a greater flexibility. The hypothesis [was] easily tested. . . .

Questioning showed that the hypothesis has very strong support, where staff members are concerned. Among editors, age also makes a difference, although not nearly as much. . . . Among publishers, age makes no difference at all. . . .

The staff members most likely to favor firing or transferring a reporter for being too cozy with sources are those who, in addition to being young, work for medium or large papers and have some postgraduate education. Neither education nor size of paper predicted this attitude among editors and publishers.

Does this mean that an elite corps of young, idealistic newspaper staff people is leading the industry toward increased sensitivity toward the need for reporter-source independence? No. It seems more likely that the staff is a conservative force resisting leadership coming from other sources and moving in another direction. Michael J. O'Neill, former editor of the New York *Daily News*, said in his farewell speech to the American Society of Newspaper Editors that the adversary model of reporter-source relationships has been pushed too far. His concern has been echoed by other industry leaders who sense a loss of public confidence and are reacting to it. The young hard-liners for news-source separation are arguing for keeping conventional news-gathering values. The possibility of a generation gap—with youth, not age, occupying the conservative position—keeps appearing in these data.

The next cluster of attitudes defines another traditional ethical standard in the newspaper business: that financial conflict of interest should be avoided. Financial conflict was asked about in three quite different kinds of situations, and the responses, despite this variety, were intercorrelated—meaning that a person who opposed financial conflict in one case was likely to do so in the others as well. This consistency confirms the belief with which we began that financial conflict is one of the tests by which news people evaluate conduct. The fact that it affects . . . diverse cases suggests that it is a very strong standard. One of the three questionnaire items was:

> The chief photographer moonlights as a wedding photographer. The father of a bride calls the editor and says the photographer has made a sales pitch to his daughter and included a sly hint that if he is hired for the job, her picture has a better chance of making the society page. The editor investigates and confirms that this is the photographer's regular practice. Should the editor:
>
> 1. Fire the photographer?
> 2. Impose lesser discipline and order the photographer to stop moonlighting?
> 3. Allow the photographer to continue moonlighting, but order him not to use—or pretend to use—his position to gain favored treatment for clients?
> 4. Ask the photographer to be more discreet?

Close to half said they would fire the photographer. Editors, publishers and staff were in close agreement. . . .

Who are the news people who are most sensitive to financial conflict?

They are overwhelmingly young, and, this time, the age difference was visible in all three groups, most clearly where publishers were concerned. Nearly half of the youngest group of publishers (circulation-adjusted), but less than 30 percent of the oldest group ranked as highly sensitive on this issue. The oldest editors were less sensitive than younger ones, and the youngest staffers were twice as likely to be in the highly-sensitive group as older ones.

Staff members and editors were more sensitive on this issue if they came from large papers, and all three groups indicated greater sensitivity if their papers were owned by publicly-held corporations—yet another hint of a new variable that may affect the formation of ethical standards. There was also a suggestion of regional difference, with greater sensitivity in the east than in the west. Finally, editors were somewhat less likely to be in the high-sensitivity group if they had a high level of civic activity.

Here, as with the index on closeness to sources, we have wide support for traditional values, with young newspaper people the least compromising. As newspaper people grow older, gain in responsibility, come in increasing contact with the community, they appear to take less of a hard line on financial conflict of interest. . . . The third . . . dimension involves what at first glance seem like three separate ethical issues: invasion of privacy, harassment of innocent sources, and protection of government secrets. Yet, their responses are clustered. Knowing how a news person responds to one issue gives a measurable advantage in guessing where he or she will come down on the other two. An underlying thread connects them.

One of these indicators involves the publication of embarrassing private facts: a wire service story reporting a fire in a Key West hotel frequented by affluent gays lists a hometown citizen among those who escaped uninjured. The citizen says he will commit suicide if you publish his name. The four choices are:

1. Publish the story in full.
2. Publish the story, but without mentioning the gay angle.
3. Publish the story, but without mentioning the local citizen.
4. Kill the story.

Publishers, editors, and staff members alike were closely divided between the first two alternatives, with a modest consensus for the second. There was only scattered support for the third alternative and virtually none for the fourth.

The next deals with harassment of innocent but newsworthy persons:

> The first refugees from the Falkland Islands come to stay with relatives in your town. You know from the Iranian hostage experience that they are likely to be harassed and intimidated by competing news people striving for the last detail. Already, reporters and camera persons are setting up camp in the front yard. Should the editor:
>
> 1. Organize pool coverage to reduce the burden on the family?
> 2. Make a public plea for all media to use restraint?
> 3. Avoid public pronouncements, but order his own staff to use restraint?
> 4. Do nothing, on the theory that competitive news coverage is best for society in the long run?

The consensus response was the third, although staff members were far more willing than either editors or publishers to do nothing and enjoy the benefits of competitive news coverage. This was the second most popular course overall, with only scattered support for the first two alternatives.

The third item in the series deals with the frequently encountered problem of what to do with a grand jury leak:

> Under which of the following circumstances should a newspaper publish material from leaked grand jury transcripts?
>
> 1. Whenever the material is newsworthy.
> 2. Whenever the importance of the material revealed outweighs the damage to the system from the breaching of its security.

3. Only if the material exposes flaws in the workings of the grand jury system itself, e.g., it shows the prosecutor to be acting improperly.
4. Never.

The second response is the most frequent in all three groups, although staff members are far more likely than editors or publishers to let newsworthiness be the only consideration.

Now the nature of the unifying thread begins to appear. Each of these items measures an underlying tendency to want to publish, regardless of the cost. . . . Staff people prefer to err on the side of publishing more often than do their editors or publishers. Now it becomes clear that many different kinds of problems, among all three groups, are resolved on this level. The consistency suggests that the news person's urge to get the story into print can override a great variety of other considerations. Where the urge is strong—and it usually is—it can keep problems from being considered on an ethical plane at all. The decision rule that publishing is better than not publishing is simple, easy to apply, and can become almost a reflex, like a knee jerk.

As in all the other issues examined in this study, newspaper people vary. Some are possessed more than others of this urge to forge into print regardless of cost. And, as with many of the issues, it is not easy to say that one position or the other is the more ethical. There is virtue in publishing, and sometimes there is virtue in not publishing. The point here is that if an issue is resolved on the basis of an inner urge to publish or refrain from publishing, its ethical content may never reach the agenda. . . .

Further questions in the survey sought to find out what kinds of news people tend to decide things one way or the other—to measure the tendency toward self-restraint in publishing among publishers, editors, and staff members.

From the responses we have enough data to venture a broad conclusion or two. News people, in the formation and execution of ethical standards, are subject to two opposing forces, one external and one internal. The internal force consists of the body of journalistic lore, tradition, almost a tribal memory, whose primary values are honesty and independence. It provides the proverbial touch of starch in the backbone of the young reporter who goes out to question the high and the mighty. It places accuracy at the top of the list of objectives and demands that the journalist stand far enough apart from what he observes so that his view remains untainted by special interest or subjective judgment. The inner-directed journalist, like the inner-directed forebear of modern man cited by David Riesman, Reuel Denny and Nathan Glazer (*The Lonely Crowd,* 1950), learns these standards so thoroughly that he or she can act on them instantly and intuitively without conscious analytical effort. The standards are learned from role models in the newsroom, from journalism teachers, and even from textbooks. If there is rigidity in the standards and their application, it is at least partly because the daily pressures and temptations for relaxing the standards are so great that only a rigid and automatic response can deal with them efficiently.

The external force comes from the community which the newspaper serves. This community has standards and values of its own, and it is interested more in substantive outcomes than in processes. Cooperation for civic betterment is high on its list of objectives, and it expects the newspaper to be part of the cooperative effort and not a perpetual or reflexive antagonist. These civic values clash with journalistic values, not when journalists behave unethically by traditional standards of the profession, but when the traditional standards are applied rigidly and unthinkingly.

These standards . . . tend to be observed most consistently by young news people who work for large papers and whose civic activity is low. Those who are older, who work for smaller papers, and who have high involvement in civic activity, are more flexible.

If this conflict between inner and other-directed ethical systems indeed defines the problem, is there a solution? Can the rigid application of traditional journalistic standards be relaxed without inviting the very evils they were formed to ward off? Can a new ethic, which calls for more thoughtful analysis of individual cases and fewer knee-jerk responses, be formed? Is it needed?

Many news people believe that current problems could be bypassed if only the public understood the underlying need for journalists to behave the way they do. Indeed, it is a majority view. Two-thirds of the reading public is served by news people who agree with the statement "Public concern over newspaper ethics is caused less by the things newspapers do than by their failure to explain what they do." Taken literally, this view holds that newspaper ethics is more of a problem of public relations than one of substance, and it denotes a certain smugness. Who is likely to hold this view—the young, big-city, inner-directed news people or the older, less insular people? The answer is not completely clear, but the latter group appears to have the edge on smugness. Newspaper size was a consistent predictor among editors, publishers, and staff.

Age made a difference for publishers, but not for staff members. The older, more experienced publishers were more likely to hold that explaining newspaper behavior was more important than changing it. Civic involvement was also a strong predictor of this attitude, with newspaper people who are high in civic activity the most likely to see ethics as a communication problem.

Positions on substantive ethical issues have very little to do with this attitude, with one exception. News people who are more ready than others to favor self-restraint in publishing are more likely to hold the ethics-as-PR view. This profile lends itself to an encouraging interpretation. Those news people who are most likely to ride the traditional ethic to an adversarial extreme are also the least comfortable with the current behavior of their newspapers. They are at least more likely to believe that the industry's ethical problems are real ones and not just a matter of being misunderstood. The potential for self-criticism and thoughtful evaluation appears to exist where it is most needed.

READERS SERVED BY NEWS PEOPLE WHO VIEW ETHICS AS A PR PROBLEM

	Newspaper size		
	Small	Medium	Large
Publishers	75%	73%	62%
Editors	81	69	69
Staff	64	62	56
Everybody	73	68	63

CODE OF ETHICS

Society of Professional Journalists, Sigma Delta Chi

The Society of Professional Journalists, Sigma Delta Chi, believes the duty of journalists is to serve the truth.

We believe the agencies of mass communication are carriers of public discussion and information, acting on their Constitutional mandate and freedom to learn and report the facts.

We believe in public enlightenment as the forerunner of justice, and in our Constitutional role to seek the truth as part of the public's right to know the truth.

We believe those responsibilities carry obligations that require journalists to perform with intelligence, objectivity, accuracy and fairness.

To these ends, we declare acceptance of the standards of practice here set forth:

RESPONSIBILITY

The public's right to know of events of public importance and interest is the overriding mission of the mass media. The purpose of distributing news and enlightened opinion is to serve the general welfare. Journalists who use their professional status as representatives of the public for selfish or other unworthy motives violate a high trust.

Adopted in 1926 and revised in 1973. Item 6, under "Ethics," was added in 1984.

Source: Courtesy of the Society of Professional Journalists, Sigma Delta Chi.

FREEDOM OF THE PRESS

Freedom of the press is to be guarded as an inalienable right of people in a free society. It carries with it the freedom and the responsibility to discuss, question and challenge actions and utterances of our government and of our public and private institutions. Journalists uphold the right to speak unpopular opinions and the privilege to agree with the majority.

ETHICS

Journalists must be free of obligation to any interest other than the public's right to know the truth.

1. Gifts, favors, free travel, special treatment or privileges can compromise the integrity of journalists and their employers. Nothing of value should be accepted.
2. Secondary employment, political involvement, holding public office and service in community organizations should be avoided if it compromises the integrity of journalists and their employers. Journalists and their employers should conduct their personal lives in a manner which protects them from conflict of interest, real or apparent. Their responsibilities to the public are paramount. That is the nature of their profession.
3. So-called news communications from private sources should not be published or broadcast without substantiation of their claims to news value.
4. Journalists will seek news that serves the public interest, despite the obstacles. They will make constant efforts to assure that the public's business is conducted in public and that public records are open to public inspection.
5. Journalists acknowledge the newsman's ethic of protecting confidential sources of information.
6. Plagiarism is dishonest and is unacceptable.

ACCURACY AND OBJECTIVITY

Good faith with the public is the foundation of all worthy journalism.

1. Truth is our ultimate goal.
2. Objectivity in reporting the news is another goal, which serves as the mark of an experienced professional. It is a standard of performance toward which we strive. We honor those who achieve it.
3. There is no excuse for inaccuracies or lack of thoroughness.
4. Newspaper headlines should be fully warranted by the contents of the articles they accompany. Photographs and telecasts should give an accurate picture of an event and not highlight a minor incident out of context.
5. Sound practice makes clear distinction between news reports and expressions of opinion. News reports should be free of opinion or bias and represent all sides of an issue.
6. Partisanship in editorial comment which knowingly departs from the truth violates the spirit of American journalism.
7. Journalists recognize their responsibility for offering informed analysis, comment and editorial opinion on public events and issues. They accept the obligation to present such material by individuals whose competence, experience and judgment qualify them for it.
8. Special articles or presentations devoted to advocacy or the writer's own conclusions and interpretations should be labeled as such.

FAIR PLAY

Journalists at all times will show respect for the dignity, privacy, rights and well-being of people encountered in the course of gathering and presenting the news.

1. The news media should not communicate unofficial charges affecting reputation or moral character without giving the accused a chance to reply.
2. The news media must guard against invading a person's right to privacy.
3. The media should not pander to morbid curiosity about details of vice and crime.

4. It is the duty of news media to make prompt and complete correction of their errors.
5. Journalists should be accountable to the public for their reports and the public should be encouraged to voice its grievances against the media. Open dialogue with our readers, viewers and listeners should be fostered.

PLEDGE

Journalists should actively censure and try to prevent violations of these standards, and they should encourage their observance by all newspeople. Adherence to this code of ethics is intended to preserve the bond of mutual trust and respect between American journalists and the American people.

VALUES

Norman Isaacs

Long a combative figure in journalism as editor, critic, and educator, Norman Isaacs was chairman of the now-dissolved National News Council. He sees a lack of underlying values as being the root danger to journalism today. This leads, he claims, to the arrogance that refuses to see faults and to make conscientious corrections.

Not long ago, I was in Washington, where hundreds of editors gathered for their annual series of discussions and debates over the state of journalism. Underlying all that they examined was the core issue never mentioned out loud—not because anyone is trying to hide it, but simply because nobody really knows how to get a handle on it.

That core issue is journalism's values.

There are a number of risks involved in tackling the subject of professional values. One risk is that what I may consider a violation of a decent ethical code, another may regard as a professional duty.

Also, one risks tarring everyone with the same sweeping brush strokes. I think there is an ethical code that all journalists ought to abide by and any number of good professionals follow. Unhappily, there are more who find excuses not to follow a code. So I don't mean to besmirch the good while trying to pillory those who deserve it.

There are all kinds of journalists. They represent a vast range of views about life. There are intellectual giants among them and a lot of pygmies. There are the dedicated and industrious. There are the sloths, who don't even merit rank under the "Peter Principle." There is journalism that touches on near-greatness. But there are many more evidences of a mindless, tunnel-visioned journalism that torments all of us who see communications as the most vital of all callings.

In years past, I conducted guerrilla war against publishers, separating good guys and bad guys in a broad Jehovah-like manner. Subsequently, I came to realize that while many of my rockets were well-intended, there was also lack of decent understanding on my part.

Now approaching what Fred Friendly quips as being the springtime of senility, I recognize that the main troubles with most of the journalistic enterprise are weak leadership from managers, and what so many editorial writers so love to denounce—a resistant bureaucracy in newsrooms.

There are, of course, among publishers and editors, the types one editor I knew loved to brand as "JOURNALISTIC STINKERS." But I also know publishers and editors of conscience and integrity who are often frustrated by the bureaucracies that operate on news, copy and city desks, in other departments, and among reporters.

A number of intelligent approaches were advanced at the Washington meeting. Many editors left, intending to put some of the new concepts into practice. The track record suggests, however, that they will struggle to get the messages across, but that these messages will be tortured out of rational purpose in the substrata of enterprises. And finally weary of the endless stonewalling and alibiing, the key executives will grudgingly accept a few minor and really meaningless compromises.

Source: Sigma Delta Chi Foundation Lecture, University of Minnesota, 1978. Reprinted with permission.

R. Peter Straus, director of Voice of America, has been telling an amusing story about Henry Kissinger.

Kissinger's brother Walter, one year younger than Henry, is a highly successful business executive in New York. They came to the United States together, refugees from Germany. Their American educations were strikingly similar. Yet, while Henry's speech has a notably Germanic accent, there is not the faintest trace in Walter's speech. Asked about it, Walter laughed and said, "Well, you know, Henry was never a very good listener."

I relay the story because it seems to me to relate to many of this country's journalists, young and old. It is relevant to ask whether enough of them listen to new ideas, whether they read adequately about the society. To ask how many of them stop once in a while to ponder about journalism's function, or, at the least, to weigh whether any of the many criticisms have any merit.

This is an important part of the equation because there is no escaping the fact that journalism is held in low esteem by many Americans. In a recent issue of *Atlantic* magazine there is an article by Louis Banks, a former editor at *Fortune* and now a professor at MIT. It is headlined: "Memo to the Press: They Hate You Out There." Banks writes about the attitudes of businessmen, but he could just as well have broadened it to include most segments of the society.

There are many in the press who argue that the journalist has no business hoping to be liked, that the only needed response is respect. I agree. But it poses another question: Isn't there something wrong, terribly wrong, when there isn't even respect?

Now mind you, some news organizations and some journalists do command respect. But it is far from general.

In the spring issue of *Nieman Reports,* Professor Chris Argyris, the Harvard scholar who is expert in organizational behavior, has written about what he considers journalism's astonishing predilection for self-destruction.

Both the Banks and Argyris articles, in my opinion, are thoroughly accurate. But Banks does not tap a new vein. For years now, the polls have been reporting deep resentment on the part of many people toward the press.

This is where the lack of respect comes in. It is not basic news judgments people quarrel with. The main criticisms are about inaccuracy, about stories perceived as biased, about defensive and arrogant behavior.

Out of a lifetime of experience in journalism, I see these charges are largely true. Argyris expresses astonishment over the defensiveness. He has studied all kinds of enterprises and professions and he hasn't found one that matches the journalist's defense mechanisms, which the good professor concedes are amazingly skilled.

Here is where my arguments about values enter. I hold that all these things of which we are charged, and of which I say we are too often guilty, stem from the fact that the majority of those in journalism refuse to accept any concept of enduring values, and, therefore, override as inconsequential any and all criticism.

This may stem from the fact that for almost all its history, our press has been reactive, operating by instinct. In moments of crisis—the accident of fate or of major confrontation between antagonists—coverage can be superbly efficient. There is nothing like a visible emergency to galvanize the journalist to skilled, factual coverage of an event, with remarkable ingenuity and sense of pursuit.

But absent emergency, our press has too often lapsed into being habit-prone in coverage patterns, obtuse about complex issues and always exhibiting the standard resistances to self-examination.

Those news organizations and journalists who have been thoughtfully self-conscious about the public's low rating of the press have changed course. There is today more and better examination of important issues than ever before. But the best in American journalism is, unhappily, atypical.

I know editors who say, "What others do is not my business. I run my newspaper for my readers. If somebody wants to be a stinker, that's his business." I can't swallow that. It seems to me both capricious and condescending in reasoning. All of us owe it to ourselves to try to move the society forward all the time. We need better doctors, better lawyers, teachers, engineers, businessmen, politicians, public servants, and, vitally, better journalists, because we are the ones who feed the minds of people.

From square one there are automatic, immense responsibilities that fall on the journalist. What is selected for coverage, how it is written and presented, can alter the course of life, in tiny ways and in giant ones. A wrong diagnosis by a journalist does not affect just a single patient, it can run like a contagion through an entire city. If any calling demands a sense of values, this is the one.

Earlier, I mentioned managerial weakness as one reason for some of the softness about newsroom values. There has been, and there is, too much reliance on the "learning-by-doing" pattern. It might be acceptable at a cub level, but it is crippling when applied to supervisors, the heart of newsroom bureaucracy—a bureaucracy that in too many places crushes initiative, imagination and enterprise.

Reporters operate their own bureaucracy, one fed by what I see as ever-present peer-group pressure. I concede that often it is not pressure as such at work, but the desire of people to be popular. Heaven knows how many young journalists with sound potentials will never rise much above pedestrian levels because of this curious urge to be well-thought of by colleagues. I am not suggesting that the way to the top is by being tough and abrasive. I am saying that the desire to be popular all too often becomes a form of self-suppression of talent.

One good, young reporter was recounting recently how things operate at his paper. He was aghast at the prevailing mind-set that treats every complainant as a kook. There may be a call about a mistake in a city hall story, or in an obit, or anything else, and the desk person taking the call will cup a hand over the phone mouthpiece and announce, "I've got a crazy on the line." Everybody's crazy, you see, except us.

Not until publishers and top editors recognize the vital importance of investing in training people for supervisory responsibility and advancing an honest and valid value system will the evil be cured.

A rational value system need begin with only four goals:

- To do all possible to be accurate.
- When we fail in that, to correct our errors promptly.
- To recognize the responsibilities we carry.
- To abandon all arrogance about what it is we do.

Given the speed at which journalists have to work, error is bound to occur. The fault may lie with a news source, or it may be thoughtlessness or weariness, or some odd electronic error. Whatever the cause, isn't it simple virtue to correct the record—clearly, cleanly and without trace of embarrassment?

Yet the record is that wherever an ombudsman—or people's editor or advocate—is named to deal with these sins of commission or omission, battle lines are drawn immediately by desk editors and reporters.

This fault of refusing to correct error is arrogance of the worst kind. There would never be a need for ombudsmen or press councils if only this elemental principle of fairness were to be accepted by newspeople as a given.

Arthur Miller, the brilliant Harvard law professor, spoke at the editors' meeting in Washington on the subject of privacy. He was stunned by the quotes attributed to him in the subsequent press coverage. For the first time in his career, he read absolutely the reverse of what he had told the editors.

He expostulated immediately. Correction? None.

I suppose Miller goes down on the chart as a "crazy." That, my friend, is journalistic arrogance and it's precisely what led Louis Banks to write "Memo to the Press: They Hate You Out There."

One reason the people Banks talked with hate the press is the fault James Reston of the New York *Times* put his finger on years ago: "The American newspaperman would rather break a story than understand it."

I don't know where in the list of many arrogances this fits, but it ranks very high. One such episode that comes to mind still galls me.

In the 1960s, the late Sen. Everett Dirksen (R-Ill.) mounted a national campaign to try to overturn the Supreme Court's one-man/one-vote decision. Dirksen wanted, finally, the ultimate: a constitutional convention.

I'm still not sure many newspaper people really tried to understand that fight. If they didn't, I'll never know why. The only such convention we ever had was the one called in 1787 under the Articles of Confederation. It was summoned to propose amendments to the Articles, but it proceeded to write an entirely new Constitution. And, given the torments and stresses of our present time, can you not imagine the mischief that a constitutional convention could bring this republic?

There was no obligation for news people to build any emotional campaign. All that was required was reporting the news. But there was no such reporting. Dirksen's drive took on the appearance of a soundless avalanche.

The number of state legislatures that adopted resolutions for a constitutional convention grew to 31. But coverage came in bits and snippets—a couple of graphs now, a couple in a week or two. Not even the American Bar Association, which had become deeply concerned, could determine how many states had passed resolutions, and some key members of the Bar began to set up an informational network to find out.

Chief Justice Earl Warren made some speeches, trying to highlight the importance of what was going on. He said that if the Bill of Rights were to come to a popular vote, it probably would fail, given the public's perceived temper. Those speeches were reported, but customarily minus any broad view of what Warren's purpose was in using such strong terms.

As I say, either the journalists around the country didn't understand, or they didn't care.

Because of my involvement in press/bar matters, I was asked if I felt it proper to try to capture the attention of some leading editors. Feeling that it was, I wrote urgent letters, enclosing detailed information. You can perhaps understand how embarrassed I was to receive only the most casual of responses. I had about as much effect as a gnat on an elephant's behind.

The country was saved the trauma because the bar associations went to work. They had the muscle to lobby enough legislatures to retract their calls, but even that series of recalls drew less attention in the press than a row within some mayoral office or zoning board.

We've improved some. At least, the conflict over the Equal Rights Amendment draws adequate regular attention. It is of far less consequence than a full constitutional convention, but it does have some sex to it and, I suppose, for some troglodytes in journalism, it makes a big difference, even if they don't understand this one either.

And yes, there is a good deal of excellent investigative journalism going on. But how many in the craft have paused to assess whether there is a consistent thread of true-value purpose in all the investigating? Some of it is certainly in order, vitally necessary. About some others, there is room for question, if not doubt; and I say this as the chairman of the jury that passed the investigative category of the Pulitzer Prizes this year.

Might there be some merit to the charge that surfaces here and there that journalism in some aspects is serving as one of the prime destroyers of values—that it is so gripped by the passion to expose that it is on the way to tearing down everything in the society?

All of it rests on values. And the values for journalism are there if only we build equal passion for responsibility. Out of this will come devotion to accuracy. That devotion will see to it that what errors we make are quickly corrected. And in the doing, we cannot help but lose some of the arrogance.

If journalism is going to come to general acceptance of higher ethical standards, the change is not likely to come from within the existing ranks. The good organizations already hold those standards. The resisters are not able to shake off the built-in habits of looking on everyone outside as "crazies."

The changes nationwide are going to have to come from the new generation of journalists and, if we have the time, the generation next.

There are publishers and editors hoping for the emergence of young people with a sense of conviction about journalism—who are determined to try to get the facts straight, who welcome having error corrected, who believe that news and opinion belong in properly labeled separate compartments, who scorn the freebies, who aspire to be thoroughly responsible professionals.

If that kind of partnership can come—a partnership of the new, committed, young journalists with the editors of conscience—then we can have journalism with the touch of greatness upon it.

At the heart of it, this is the kind of value system the true journalist needs: To be aware of the pressures and the temptations, but know that this is a calling demanding men and women ever conscious of the power within their hands to do good or evil—who choose to use that power serving a citizenry that to survive needs the most faithful picture of life and its problems—to the end that the decisions made are based upon rounded knowledge and not sullied by narrow internal or external pressures.

ETHICAL PROBLEMS IN TELEVISION

MAXI BUCKS, MINI ETHICS

Jerry Jacobs

The practice by television stations of showing dubious mini-documentaries to increase their audiences during the rating services' "sweep" periods is explained by Jerry Jacobs, associate professor at California State University, Northridge. These "mini-docs" often are shallow and titillating.

You say you're worried about breast cancer? You say you want to be titillated by half-naked women in bikinis? You say you don't know what to do when the big quake hits? You say you want a peek at the stars' homes?

Tell you what I'm gonna do. I'm gonna satisfy all those needs, desires, lusts, curiosities and fears . . . and it won't cost you a dime. Just tune into my TV newscast for one short week, during any of the three big "sweep" periods. As for the other 51 weeks in the year . . . just hold on to that colon cancer, those symptoms of menopause, that curiosity you have about incest, or that advice you need on sleeping better, slimming down for the summer or buying anything from a car to a house.

Some TV stations call these so-called news stories special reports or in-depth features, but they're most commonly referred to as "mini-docs," basically half-hour documentaries divided into five daily segments and played into the same newscast at about the same time each evening . . . just like those oldtime Saturday morning serials.

Source: Reprinted from the 1984–1985 Journalism Ethics Report of the Society of Professional Journalists, Sigma Delta Chi.

There's no problem figuring out when they're coming. Count on February, May and November, because those are the "sweep" months during which the rating services, A. C. Nielsen and Arbitron, closely monitor which programs viewers watch. The result is like the Olympics—the stations' programs are ranked in descending numerical order—and the "gold" is just as impressive. In the larger markets, a one-point rating increase can mean a million more dollars in advertising revenue for the year. The sponsor pays for commercial time on the basis of how many viewers the station can deliver.

The other harbinger of the mini-doc onslaught is more blatant. The television viewer is inundated with slick, ad agency-engineered on-the-air promotional plugs tailored after TV commercials, complete with actors, mood film and appropriate music. Newspaper and magazine readers are recruited with equally polished print ads, sporting clever ad agency copy and illustrated with models and/or news talent. Nor do radio listeners escape. They are bombarded with "spots" delivered by professional announcers, newscasters and/or actors.

And, just in case anybody has forgotten, the hyping and huckstering push a news product prepared by professional news producers, reporters, writers and technicians, to be aired on a newscast and to be delivered by people employed as newsmen and women.

The question is whether these rating-point-motivated mini-docs are news. If they are, at the very least, people shouldn't have to wait until one of those three magical months comes along. If they're not news, mini-docs have no place on newscasts.

With summer, a weak selling period, coming up, the May sweep is not the most important. However, in Los Angeles, competition for number one is fierce, and the mini-docs this past May illustrate the overall problem.

KABC-TV's "Eyewitness News" advertised two specials on its 4 P.M. newscast aimed at roping in older viewers. One was on how to "dine in style with 'early bird' discount tips." The print ad featured a sketch of an elderly couple with two glasses of water in front of them—just to make sure the reader knows this couple can't afford expensive places—under a quote: "Imagine, eating in a fancy place like this for so little." The subject of the other 4 P.M. series was menopause, with Friday's installment billboarded as hyping "sex after 50."

The print ad for KABC-TV's 6 P.M. mini-doc on mental health problems featured a model made up as a bag lady, sitting on a bench and talking to herself, with a young couple keeping their distance in the background. For 11 P.M., when the kids aren't supposed to be around, KABC-TV took off the gloves and advertised, "What do your TV heartthrobs do in their prime time?" One heartthrob must be into exercise because the print ad showed the legs of a person on a stationary bike in a bedroom, while another unisex character seems to be in bed watching a couple kissing on TV.

KNBC-TV reached for the senior citizen audience for its 4 P.M. newscast by plugging "No Place to Call Home," about people who can't afford housing: "A few years ago they bought a new car. Today they live in it." KNBC-TV filled out its mini-doc schedule with a series on auto care, an "exclusive report" on entertainers—like John Belushi and Natalie Wood—who have died tragically and, to out-titillate KABC-TV, a series called "Beach Body Ratings." Despite the bikini clad model and her Ken-doll boyfriend, this one simply rated the latest in diet and exercise trends.

KCBS-TV, insisting on selling itself as the only real news organization in Los Angeles, modestly plugged a series on inexpensive seafood restaurants and a mini-doc on the impact of defense spending on the local economy.

KABC-TV came on a lot stronger in the previous sweep, February, with mini-docs on the Beatles, fantasy getaways to avoid job burnout, sleeping problems, the best in chocolate, breast cancer and paramedics. The last one raised a few eyebrows in Los Angeles. The ad featured a sketch of anchor Jerry Dunphy talking into a mike while reclining on a paramedic's stretcher. The copy challenges the reader on what to do in a life-threatening emergency, then promises, "You will [know what to do] by the end of the week as Jerry Dunphy talks to lifesavers throughout Southern California . . . including his own."

The mini-doc was not the only time Dunphy involved himself in his own story, dating back to last October when he and another employee were ambushed and wounded by gunfire en route to the studio. Dunphy has reported on his own shooting on several occasions, including one in which he referred to the suspects as really not caring about human life at all. As L.A. *Times* reporter Lee Margulies put it, "Where was KABC's journalistic commitment to fairness? True, what happened to Dunphy was horrible, but the fact remains that the law presumes these men innocent until proven otherwise."

The other two stations scheduled mini-docs ranging from the ridiculous—"what radio personalities are really like" and "baldness"—to the reasonably serious—earthquake-proofing your home, the "dismal" future of social security, the "inside story" on Cuba and adopted people who find their real parents.

From the time mini-docs first hit the airwaves, in the early 1970s, taste, ethics, news judgment and other journalism fundamentals have not been priorities. Subjects covered over and over again include a grocery list of titillating sexual experiences—prostitution, rape, wife swapping, swinging singles, homosexuality and incest; the ghastliest of crimes from child abuse to mass murder; a full menu of nutrition subjects, emphasizing the composition of a multitude of foods from hamburger to ice cream; everything you want to know about physical fitness; and, of course, the disease of the week, featuring the cancer of your choice, herpes, AIDS and heart disease. The result—hot copy for the TV, radio and print ads, more viewers, more commercial revenue.

There is, indeed, a sprinkling of serious subjects during the sweep periods, but there also is a serious ethical question as to why the viewer has to wait several months to be enlightened. And there are stations that refuse to play the game . . . managers and news directors with the courage to maintain that their news product is immediate, accurate, meaningful, attractively packaged and, when necessary, reported in depth, all year.

But the geek-like syndrome, peppered with promises of sex, gore, gossip and how-to-cope problem-solving on every conceivable subject, is the more prevalent news programming on local TV stations.

Unfortunately, it is merely a symptom of a disease that has rampaged through local TV newsrooms for the last 15 years. That's when station management realized that news can be a profitable business and when consultants realized that it's a business that can be packaged and sold.

The result was inevitable. Most local TV journalists stopped reporting news they thought the public ought to have . . . but, rather, a pseudo-news product tailored to and catering to the desires of the public. The tragic turning point was the decision to give them what they want, not what the journalist thinks they should have.

In this environment of show biz and entertainment values, bizarre and journalistically questionable events occur, like a former Miss America, Tawny Schneider, becoming a KABC-TV news anchor in Los Angeles. In addition, Schneider's management saw no conflict in letting her and another news anchor, Chuck Henry, host a network daytime series called "The Love Report." The show, geared to the soap opera audience, died a quick, merciful death.

In 1977, Ron Powers opened his book, *The Newscasters*, with, "The biggest heist of the 1970s was the five o'clock news. The salesmen took it. They took it away from the journalists, slowly, patiently, gradually, and with such finesse that nobody noticed until it was too late."

Powers went on to elaborate on the influence of the professional news consultants and the almighty rating point—factors that changed the face of local news and, today, endanger the integrity of network news as well.

It was my privilege to be part of a network news operation (NBC News during the 1950s and 1960s) that pointedly instructed us, the producers, not to be concerned about ratings, commercial sponsorship or any other factors that might stand in the way of a professional news product. It would be a news decision to pre-empt the hottest nighttime entertainment shows on the air and stay on with continuing coverage until the story was over. That policy started with the cancellation of the Eisenhower-Khrushchev summit meeting in 1960 and continued through a decade of major news events, including the civil rights demonstrations, the astronaut flights, the Cuba crisis, the assassinations and the Vietnam War.

The pleasant surprise was that viewers tuned in and stayed glued to their seats during these continuing coverages, resulting in especially high "numbers." Equally gratifying were the response of the people and being part of the birth and maturation of network television news.

As former NBC anchor John Chancellor told the Radio and Television News Directors Association in September, 1983, "If some of the programs we worked on made a profit, we were not told about it. And many of them made no profit at all. News, documentaries and special events were regarded as necessary, useful and worthwhile things to put on the air and, if they were sponsored, so much the better."

In the early 1970s, I returned to TV news after being away for seven years. This time it was on the other coast, in Los Angeles, and the outlet was local, ABC's owned and operated KABC-TV.

It was a rude awakening. The message to us executives was clear and repetitive—ratings are far more important than journalistic integrity. Engineered by two consulting companies, the slick Eyewitness News machine zoomed forward and up to the tune of ratings, anchor cosmetics, performing reporters, fast-moving stories, "how to cope" features and a barrage of print, TV and radio promotion. Politics and any subject difficult to illustrate with fast moving visuals were out.

We were not only instructed on, preached about and threatened by ratings, but the overnight Nielsen and Arbitron "numbers" were posted in the newsroom each morning as a guide for that day's behavior.

And for the sweep periods, the mini-doc was the ultimate weapon. Because of lead time for print ads and media promotionals, ideas for the docs were collected months before production. The decision on which to produce was not made until the ideas went through a culling process in the station general manager's office. Prior to serious research, checking or production, the chosen ideas would be passed on to the promotional, advertising and sales departments.

Once the station management decided on a subject, the news department had to deliver.

You didn't need an MBA from Harvard to figure out who's boss. Take the case of the "Million Dollar Martini." Actor Jim Stacey was crippled—he lost an arm and a leg—and the passenger on his motorcycle was killed in an accident with a drunk driver. The court ruled that the bar serving the driver was also culpable, which could mean that any bar, restaurant or private host could be sued in drunk driving cases. I thought that would make a meaningful and interesting mini-doc, got the go-ahead and supervised production. The advertising copy hit my desk just a few days before the series was to air. It included the title, a sketch of a martini with a dollar sign on it and a picture of Stacey, whose participation was limited to one short statement on film.

The worst aspect was the print copy blatantly threatening that the martini "could cost you an arm and a leg."

Embarrassed for both Stacey and the news department, I tried to get the advertising department to change the copy. I was turned down by the department as well as the general manager.

Ann Salisbury, in the Feb. 11, 1984, *TV Guide,* tells the story about the CBS-owned station that produced a documentary on the premise that motorists' blood pressure shot up during rush hour traffic. The ads, heralding "The drive that kills," went out, but the station's "tests" showed that rush hour traffic actually calmed their subject. Their solution, Salisbury reported, was to suggest that heavy traffic could cause health problems in the first segment, then contradict it in the second.

The problem is how far TV stations will go in the race for ratings and dash for dollars. CBS' owned and operated station in Los Angeles, KCBS-TV (formerly KNXT), had a close call in 1982. Alan Parachini, a Los Angeles *Times* staff writer, reported that the U.S. Food and Drug Administration was investigating the Los Angeles affiliate as well as CBS outlets in Chicago, WBBM-TV, and New York City, WCBS-TV. The three stations in a series on colon cancer offered viewers a cancer test, for a price. The stations sold viewers the kit for $1 each. According to Parachini, the stations distributed some 221,000 kits. The idea was to determine hidden blood present in a person's feces, so viewers were instructed to dab small amounts of stool on a test slide and send the completed kit to a laboratory.

The *Times* reported that several cancer experts dismissed the tests as "useless" and the FDA's concern was possible illegal "misbranding" of the tests. According to Parachini, competition for ratings was pushing the medium to a "greater and greater role in what amounts to health care delivery." Parachini reported that TV stations, though sometimes well meaning, "could panic their viewers" or "lull them into a false sense of good health."

The issue for journalists is whether this type of news broadcasting and promotion is responsible, accurate, objective or meets any of the standards outlined in the Code of Ethics.

In other words, if it's not journalism, say so. If it is journalism, clean it up.

And, yes, there are beacons and voices out

there . . . a stronger and stronger noncommercial public broadcasting product . . . the many TV stations, independents for the most part, that refuse to "play the game" and have enough confidence in their day to day news programming not to change it three times a year. . . . And the John Chancellors who have the courage to keep reminding us what dedication is all about.

Chancellor, when he received the Paul White Award at the RTNDA, talked of news costs and news profits, which have changed the dynamics of the business, creating "news programs which have little news but lots of glitter. It has emphasized competition, which is probably good, and performance instead of content, which is unquestionably bad."

Lou Cioffi, formerly with ABC and later Washington bureau chief and commentator for the Satellite News Channel, told the Los Angeles *Herald Examiner* in September, 1983, there's nothing wrong with packaging the news . . . "as long as there's a line drawn. There's no reason why you can't inform and amuse at the same time."

There are those of us who feel news, mini-docs included, can be presented attractively, excitingly, even entertainingly and informatively. Unless people watch TV—news or entertainment—the programs will not succeed. But that does not mean any standards have to be sacrificed.

The challenge is to create the talent capable of taking on the responsibility. That takes creative researching, thoughtful assigning, innovative reporting, clever writing and cohesive producing. With those tools, broadcast journalists can, again, pick up the mantle passed on by their print predecessors.

That means reporting as well as interpreting, explaining as well as educating on the countless vital and not so vital subjects that surround us in both obvious and subtle ways.

It's a tricky procedure, taking back that responsibility from the non-news people who try to run news and the audience itself, but it can be done if journalists are good at what they were originally meant to do.

TURNED OFF: WHY EXECUTIVES DISTRUST TV REPORTERS

Herbert Schmertz

As vice-president for public affairs of the Mobil Corporation, Herbert Schmertz was known as a caustic critic of media practices. Here he contends that television editing often presents unbalanced and unfriendly views of executives. Schmertz now heads his own public relations firm.

It is the corporate executive's nightmare. An "investigative reporter" calls. He wants an "in-depth" interview. The executive immediately imagines Geraldo Rivera proclaiming on prime-time TV: "I have no power to prosecute. I have only the power to embarrass, humiliate, to expose."

Contemplating the situation, the executive is likely to think, *No thanks, I'll sit this one out.* He may think that, but what he will probably do—after his heartbeat returns to normal—is grant the interview because he feels that to do otherwise will only make it appear he has "something to hide."

Why is the journalist viewed as the bum of the ball? Maybe because when the executive turns on the 7 o'clock news, he sees that the two-hour interview he taped earlier that day has been boiled down to 20 seconds. Worse, the editing has turned him into a blunt, crude, stereotype of a business executive, something akin to the money-grubbing, cardboard figures on "Quincy."

An exaggeration? Sadly, no. Many executives have been burned this way after granting interviews to television reporters. The problem lies partly with the medium, which both massages and mangles. By contrast, the print media on occasion mislead, even distort the news through the word-editing process, but these are mostly errors of omis-

Source: Reprinted with permission from the *Washington Journalism Review,* July-August 1984.

sion. Print reporters usually have the space to develop complex stories and to produce substantive in-depth interviews. TV journalists edit film, a process that by its very nature is highly subjective, and when content must be chopped into 25-second bites, the latitude of error and distortion is great.

There is another, even more important difference: Newspapers and newsmagazines do not edit to transmit viewpoint. That is left, as it should be, to the editorial pages. Network television news all too often seems to edit, by inclusion or omission, for point of view, and it has no electronic counterpart to the editorial page. So, if the corporate executive has been harmfully misquoted, or edited in such a way that his or her reputation is damaged, the only recourse is to sue.

These negatives are central to business executives' reluctance to talk to the electronic press, which is seen, more often than not, as a glittering creature of hype, frenetic "graphics" and larger-than-life "personalities" with a clear anti-business bias. This colors executives' perceptions of video journalists, just as interviewers have their own negative picture of business people.

Of course, those who read the news on TV can't take all the blame for being looked at askance by executives, since the show-biz tail wags the news content dog. But if the TV news effort sometimes resembles a journalistic Chihuahua, the medium itself is massive: Television is the most potent communications tool the world has ever known. Thus, when Mike Wallace speaks on "60 Minutes," his words are magnified a million times. So, too, is any harm that might be caused to the person who is the target of an "exposé."

Despite all this, a common complaint voiced by television newspersons is that business executives are hostile to them. These journalists protest too much. Look at what they have on their side when they interview a business executive: complete control of the confrontation; instant access to scores of publicity-hungry critics of business, and to armies of "unusually reliable sources," "leading spokesmen," "top-ranking officials" and others of that anonymous ilk who can "balance" executives' assertions with charges they neither have to prove nor defend; the power to shape the agenda, edit the story and place it prominently before the public. And their equipment—obtrusive cameras and cameramen, lights and lighting crews—is intimidating, to say the least.

Now, there is nothing intrinsically wrong with this kind of power, so long as it is not abused. But more and more frequently, corporate executives hear that press power *is* abused. They hear about instances of reporters secretly recording telephone conversations; increasingly using unnamed sources; receiving—and using—stolen documents; coaching witnesses off-camera; launching "ambush interviews" that make the startled businessman look like a cornered burglar; and editing film so that Mother Teresa turns out looking (and sounding) like Mommie Dearest.

Worst of all, TV news editors increasingly seem loath to play the role of responsible watchdog; actually to inquire how their minions got the story, how reliable their sources are, whether their proposals make sense, whether they have deleted or ignored important materials that might diffuse a point.

The pandering to the all-important Nielsen rating is probably the major culprit. But this knowledge hardly makes the corporate executive more willing to grant an interview, especially when the executive has suffered before at the hands of irresponsible journalists.

Here are some specific examples of alleged television press abuse:

- Kaiser Aluminum & Chemical Corp. said a report on ABC's "20/20" accused the company of intentionally marketing dangerous electrical wire. This "trial by television" so infuriated Kaiser executives that they threatened a slander suit. They also asked the Federal Communications Commission to order ABC to give it time to respond to the charge on prime-time TV. ABC did do that—more than a year later, and the response was not on "20/20."
- In 1979, "60 Minutes" broadcast a negative segment on the Illinois Power Co. The company

retaliated by producing its own tape to point out the network's distortions. Called "60 Minutes/ Our Reply," the program included footage not shown in the original segment that effectively answered the "60 Minutes" thesis. While the utility's program has been shown to various groups around the country, it has not been aired on television. In fact, according to the utility, CBS has ignored requests that it air the power company's reply.

- A Mobil Oil representative granted an interview for a "60 Minutes" segment on contaminated drinking water in the community of Canob Park, Rhode Island. The Mobil spokesperson pointed out, on camera, that the state EPA agreed with Mobil that the water would not be fit to drink even if all the hydrocarbons had been removed. *That important statement never got on the air.*

There are numerous other examples, but you get the picture.

What is astonishing, in light of all this, is that so many TV newspersons see crime in the suites. This is not hyperbole. Morley Safer of "60 Minutes" said that, "No businessman who has made a success for himself is entirely clean, probably." And, according to the nonprofit Media Institute, "almost half of all work activities performed by businessmen" on prime-time TV series "involve illegal acts." The report added that "Television almost never portrays business as a socially useful or economically productive activity."

Is it any wonder that corporate executives are less than ecstatic when approached by video journalists for interviews?

These are some of the problems, as many corporate executives see them. What are the solutions? How *can* television journalists "get to" their subjects in the business world for meaningful information?

It would help, first, if journalists dispense with the notion that there is just no way they can interview important corporate executives. That fiction is repeated so many times that journalists have actually convinced themselves it is true. I recall an example of this attitude when I was a guest on a television special that examined the relationship between business and the press. In a hypothetical interview situation, Dan Rather asserted: "If you think Mr. Schmertz is going to let Mike Wallace get Mr. Agee [William Agee, who at the time was chairman of Bendix] on the story, you will believe that thunder curdles milk."

That got a lot of laughs from the audience. But the attitude behind it is hardly funny. It is another bit of baggage TV journalists carry around with them that ought to be discarded. Most executives will make time available, provided they have heard of the interviewers or their publications before. It is simply good public relations. Of course, they cannot be expected to welcome with open arms a reporter who has a reputation for rudeness, regardless of how well he is known. For instance, Roger Mudd's asking presidential candidate Gary Hart on NBC News if Hart would "do your Teddy Kennedy imitation for me now" was hardly calculated to raise executives' estimation of television journalism.

As for television newspersons, they needn't love or even like their subjects; obviously, not all businesspersons are saints. But neither are all corporate executives villains who want to see news that reflects company handouts. Indeed, most would feel extremely uncomfortable in a society where reporters are upbeat clones.

What executives do insist on is that they be treated objectively, and politely. In other words, the way to get a foot in the door is not to try to kick it open. If that sounds like a bit of obvious advice, you would be surprised how often TV journalists do try the overtly hostile approach. That can result in some pretty ludicrous scenes—like Dan Rather, when he was a host on "60 Minutes," pursuing around a parking lot a reluctant subject who turned out to be the wrong man!

Most business executives don't like to answer questions "cold" over the telephone. Say the executive is asked a tough question: "How many tons of quail eggs were sent to Lower Slobovia over the past 13 years and to what dollar-extent did this affect trade relations between the two nations?" The executive may not have that answer on the tip of his tongue. So he might say, "I'll have to have someone get back to you with those numbers." That should not be taken as stonewalling; the executive simply wants to disseminate correct information.

What reporters should do is give the executive time to get a proper answer. Or, better yet, when possible, let the executive know, by letter and sufficiently in advance of air time, what kinds of questions will be asked so he can formulate cogent answers. A corollary to this is to give the corporate executive some notion of who else will be on the show, so he will get a better feel of the context in which he will be presented. The old argument that this ruins spontaneity simply won't wash. At any rate, increasing numbers of executives are saying, in effect, "No letter, no interview."

Too often, TV newspersons apply a pointillist technique to interviews: a dot here, another dot there, yet another dot over there somewhere—and only they know where, when and how all these separate dots will be connected to make a coherent picture. As a result, the person being interviewed is nervous, maybe upset, because he doesn't have a clue where all the questions are leading.

To help alleviate this problem, the interviewer should determine beforehand with his editor and producer the direction of the interview, so the 25-second bit that gets on the air might actually contain something nourishing for the television audience. This information should be passed on to the subject of the interview.

If time permits, it won't hurt to drop by the executive's office, without cameras or lights, sit down, chat about what you plan to do, and then come back with all the gee-whiz electronic gear that, after all, intimidates most people.

There is the unfortunate perception in some journalistic circles that corporate executives are Neanderthals, and fairly stupid ones at that. Mr. X didn't become chief executive officer of the world's largest producer of gidgets by winning a lottery, so if a journalist poses overly simplistic questions, the executive will become incensed and probably won't give the reporter what he wants.

At any rate, perception is a two-way street: The executive may emotionally dismiss the journalist who has not done his homework and therefore is ignorant of how the executive's company works and of issues pertinent to that company.

Journalists should not expect executives to give them whatever they want. Put bluntly, some information is proprietary and is none of their business. A corporation has a responsibility to its shareholders to protect information that can help the competition. In fact, executives know they should (and maybe would) be fired if they gave reporters such information.

It is disingenuous to say, on the one hand, that "I want to interview you so the American people can get a better picture of your corporation," and then, once the interview is granted, ask totally negative questions that make your subject look foolish. This approach may gain a "neat" interview, but it will be the last one with that particular executive.

Shortchanging an interview subject on a powerful medium like television can boomerang. Perceptive members of the TV audience know that corporate executives are not as dumb or venal as they are made out to be on the tube. One recent Harris survey, in fact, showed that only 24 percent of the public had a great deal of confidence in television news—a big drop from 1973.

Journalists should also know that their corporate subjects have not been napping. Many corporate executives have promulgated policies that will enable them to grant interviews while protecting themselves and their businesses. They might write and request a second interview, if they feel the first is less than satisfactory. They might ask to review the "finished product," even see outtakes, before their segment is aired. Some top executives refuse to be interviewed at all, unless it is live. That way, "creative" editing cannot distort what they say.

Journalists, understandably, do not like to be fettered. But given the sometimes tumultuous relationship between business and the press, and the distorted reportage that too often has flowed from this relationship, corporate executives feel they have a right to make such requests.

Rather than retreat in pique, the successful interviewer calmly explains the complexities involved in television reportage—and the special demands the medium makes on the person being interviewed. That way, a compromise might be worked out so that each side is happy.

Is there light at the end of the tube? Yes, indeed. Some television journalists have given thoughtful time—on the air—to the problematical business-press relationship. And that means their bosses, the editors and producers, are making a significant, albeit slow, shift away from the old techniques of confrontation and harassment.

To be sure, some of the self-criticism resembles an exercise in navel inspection, like Dan Rather's assertion that it is virtually impossible to get an interview with a corporate executive. But other commentary is truly open-minded and is welcome by those of us in the business world.

For instance, Walter Cronkite has pointed out that television inadvertently distorts "when we all are forced to fit 100 pounds of news into the one-pound sack we are given to fill each night." Other network television journalists have advocated a kind of op-ed forum of the air where citizens can voice differing opinions.

Ted Koppel acknowledged on a "Nightline" show that "the evidence indicates that there is growing public hostility toward the press and the way it does its job." Koppel also said that some of his "Nightline" guests, who included myself and Labor Secretary Raymond Donovan, had been "mangled by the press."

Robert MacNeil, of the PBS "MacNeil/Lehrer NewsHour," said, "More and more people have had the experience of being interviewed or being at an event that has been covered, and they know what they see on the screen is not the way it was."

Business executives are increasingly being asked to speak on the subject of business and the press before groups of journalists. The feedback has generally been productive.

This does not mean there isn't still room for reform. Talk, as they say, is cheap. Many corporate executives, to say nothing of the general TV audience, would like to see a code of press ethics enforced by the journalists themselves. Newspersons could, for example, do more to protect the civil rights of people they cover as news. At a minimum, this should include giving subjects the right to know who has made damaging remarks about them, and the right to see the full context of interviews.

Some television journalists will doubtless claim that doing this will "paralyze" news-gathering. I disagree. What it should do is make the news better, because a wider spectrum of opinion, fostered by a constructive dialogue between those who provide jobs and those who generate news, will inevitably make television news what it should have been all along: an electronic marketplace for the free exchange of ideas, a forum that engages, educates and enlightens.

INVASION OF PRIVACY

A PUBLISHER FINDS HIMSELF ON PAGE ONE

Walter Jaehnig

A successful newspaper publisher became news himself when another newspaper revealed that 20 years earlier, under another name, he had shot to death his mother, father, and sister. Should the story have been published? Walter Jaehnig is director of the School of Journalism, Southern Illinois University, Carbondale.

By any measure, H. Harrison Cochran has been a journalism success story.

He broke in as a reporter for the weekly *Broomfield Enterprise* in suburban Denver, Colo., in 1976. In 90 days he was in the editor's chair, then general manager of the paper.

He bought into the paper—a prescient move, for it was then purchased by the Cowles Media Company of Minneapolis for its Sentinel group. Cochran joined Sentinel Publishing as a publisher and in 1982—at age 36—was named president of the profitable 13-paper group, which by 1986 had a combined circulation of more than 200,000 and more than 200 employees.

But Cochran became a journalistic story of another sort last January when *Westword,* a Denver alternative weekly, reported that 21 years earlier—as an 18-year-old college freshman—he had fatally shot his father, mother and sister in their Wilmette, Ill., home.

Source: Reprinted with permission from the 1986–1987 Journalism Ethics Report of the Society of Professional Journalists, Sigma Delta Chi.

"I have been trying to prepare myself to be strong enough to handle this when it arose," Cochran told a reporter for the Associated Press the day after the story broke.

The burst of publicity provided a substantial test. Denver's *Rocky Mountain News* ran a long feature. The AP story made the national wire and reportedly was published by 100 dailies. The New York *Times* gave it 14 inches and two photographs—one of a youthful Cochran being bundled from his home in 1965 by two police officers. Cochran's own Sentinel papers printed a 17-inch story, and the *Columbia Journalism Review* and *Editor & Publisher* both produced lengthy articles.

The news coverage not only retold Cochran's painful story. It also raised ethical questions regarding the news media's handling of the story. Was the story sufficiently newsworthy to justify reopening old wounds? Was Cochran given special treatment by the newspaper industry because of his membership in the fraternity of publishers? Why were news organizations unwilling to publish the story initially, but ready to give it a full ride once a giveaway weekly had taken the lead?

Cochran himself is saying very little. He declined to be interviewed for this article, saying he has an agreement with his family and the company not to provide any further publicity on the issue. Not that the opportunities are not there—Cochran said he is still being asked to appear on television talk shows, produce articles on his life or participate in panel discussions, but is declining all such invitations.

Cochran, then Harrison Crouse, was on Christmas break from the University of Illinois at Champaign-Urbana when he shot his family with his mother's .22 caliber rifle. He was found to be mentally incapable of standing trial and admitted to an Illinois mental hospital. "Through endless hours of individual and group therapy they gave me back the ability to feel love and hate and guilt and remorse," Cochran said in the article published by the Sentinel newspapers. "Only after being brought back through all the feeling about what I had done was it possible to begin rebuilding toward a normal life."

Seven years later, Cochran was tried and acquitted on the grounds he was insane at the time of the shootings. After release from the hospital, he completed a bachelor's degree in two years at Southern Illinois at Carbondale. He met his first wife, took her surname after their marriage, and kept it after their divorce in 1977. "It was not to hide anything so much, but my wife was strong in the women's movement. She wanted to keep her name going. I didn't care one way or the other. So it was easier to be a Cochran than a Crouse. It wasn't particularly a subterfuge," he said in an interview with the *Rocky Mountain News.*

By then his journalistic career in Denver was well under way. Rumors about Cochran's background began to surface late in 1985—the *CJR* piece was written by a former Denver *Post* reporter who wrote that one of Cochran's police reporters heard the story from a man in a Denver-area bar in August. Eventually, the tale began leaking out of the Sentinel organization. Patricia Calhoun, editor-publisher of *Westword*—who broke the story in January—says his background was common knowledge in Denver media circles by then:

"I had heard who was working on it at the [Denver] *Post* and who was working on it at the [*Rocky Mountain*] *News* . . . and I said, forget it; one of *Westword*'s basic principles is don't go do a story that someone else is going to do in the same way. Why bother? There are so many stories out there that aren't getting covered."

Calhoun said she rejected several queries from freelancers as more journalists heard the Cochran story. She talked with Cochran and found that the Sentinel newspapers had already prepared a story to be used when someone else broke the story. Calhoun looked further into the story when she returned to Chicago's North Shore for the Christmas holidays—ironically, she and Cochran came from adjacent Chicago suburbs.

But still no one published the story. "It was bizarre; sooner or later someone would do it—it was like a game of chicken, almost."

Why did *Westword* and Calhoun eventually do the story? "Because no one else had done it. Maybe this was a story we should break, because no one else was going to. It always struck me as being a fascinating and absolutely newsworthy story . . . it just didn't seem like a story for *Westword,*" she said.

Much of the debate over Calhoun's decision has been concerned with the newsworthiness of the story—was it worth the intrusion into Cochran's privacy?

David Hall is editor of the Denver *Post,* a paper that has never run a word on Cochran's background. "It's not a story," Hall told the Associated Press. "There was no reason and purpose to run it." Hall had a reporter investigating the rumors last year, but after confirming the truth of the rumors, he and the reporter agreed it was not newsworthy. "There are lots of things people know that they don't put in the newspaper," he said in the *Editor & Publisher* article on Cochran.

Ralph Looney, editor of the *Rocky Mountain News,* was quoted in the *CJR* account as saying, "This is the kind of thing that gives our whole industry a bad name. If you have someone who has led an exemplary life, it gets to the point of sleaze and sensationalism [to print the story]." However, on the Sunday following publication of the *Westword* piece, the *News* ran a long feature on Cochran by the paper's suburban editor.

In the article, the reporter explained the *News'* ethical reversal by Cochran's willingness to be interviewed: "The *News* learned of Cochran's past last fall, but editors decided it was a private matter with nothing new to justify a story unless Cochran was willing to talk. He wasn't. When the story broke last week he agreed to an interview." However, Calhoun of *Westword* said that while Cochran told her he preferred that she not do the story, he consented to the interview and talked fairly openly.

Westword is a nine-year-old free circulation tabloid that distributes 90,000 copies weekly in the Denver area. Its splashy graphics and irreverent tone make it difficult to ignore, even for those in mainline journalism.

"Alternative," to *Westword,* means that the paper tries to present other viewpoints, as alternatives to daily journalism. "That doesn't mean necessarily that it's leftist or radical or underground, or rightist or whatever. It means that it's an alternative way to look at the news," said Calhoun, a Cornell graduate and one of the paper's founders.

Westword's "Cochran issue" carried the front page headline: "Is homicide a dead issue? Only if the killer is publishing." One of Calhoun's themes was that the Denver newspapers had not touched the story because Cochran was a publisher. "I think how the media deals with it is a media story," she told the Associated Press. "I do think, in covering the media, the media does use a different set of standards."

In her article, Calhoun pointed out that in 1982 and 1983, the *Post, News* and Sentinel newspapers all published stories about a man who had killed his parents while on a camping trip, but earned a parole, a college degree, and medical license and is practicing medicine in Colorado—even though he declined to be interviewed.

Hall of the Denver *Post* argued in an interview with Thomas Collins, media critic of *Newsday,* that Cochran's occupation had nothing to do with his paper's non-response to the story: "I think that I have to be able to say that there was something more to be gained [in printing it] than simply bringing out the details of a man's life." On the other hand, Hall conceded, if Cochran "were going to run for city council or mayor, that would be a different story—but he wasn't."

Perhaps the lasting lesson from the Cochran episode was the mainline news media's willingness to let an alternative publication—with patently different ethical approaches to the news—define their ethics. Once *Westword* made the decision to publish, other print organizations fell in line.

Bill Hosokawa, a long-time *Post* editor and now readers' representative of the *Rocky Mountain News,* reviewed the *News'* handling of the story in a February column. The paper's initial reluctance to publish, he wrote, was not suppression of the news: "The editors simply decided, as they do in passing judgment on the newsworthiness of dozens of stories every day, not to use the story. As they explained later when the story was published, they considered it 'a private matter with nothing new to justify a story unless the man was willing to talk.' " But once *Westword* ran the story, Hosokawa wrote that "there was an obligation to share the *News'* findings with its readers."

Similarly, Tom Marshall, United Press International bureau chief in Denver, said in an interview that once "a story's been in the major newspapers, you have a responsibility to report on the news."

And Joe McGowan, AP Denver bureau chief, admits to doubts as to whether the story should have been published in the first place. "My feelings on that day haven't changed. . . . I'm not sure that the story should have been published. How did it pertain today? He had paid his debt, done what society required. There was no impropriety, he was not in a sensitive government position."

Nonetheless, when *Westword* broke the story, McGowan felt the AP had to respond: "It has sufficient circulation. . . . We could not ignore it." McGowan assigned one of his staffers to do a new story, arranged a taped interview with Cochran, and had the story sent to New York City on the AP's internal wire for examination by senior editors before it went on the national wire.

To Calhoun, the national media attention accorded her decision to run the story was the most interesting element of the whole episode. She regards Cochran's story as a local story. "I think the fact that it was picked up by as many people as it was—I think there's something more hypocritical than 'is it newsworthy?'—and that is using that as an excuse for a paper with no connection with Denver to run a story about a local publisher who had killed his family 20 years before. . . ."

THE BOUNDARIES OF PRIVACY

Edited by Frank McCulloch

Journalists frequently face the vexing problem of deciding where the boundaries of privacy lie. In these case studies from *Drawing the Line,* edited by Frank McCulloch for the American Society of Newspaper Editors, a group of editors describes difficult decisions they had to make.

McCulloch writes:

> The most difficult ethical decisions for journalists involve not the conflict between good and evil but the resolution of conflicting goods. It is good to publish information that readers may find useful or interesting. It is also good to protect the privacy of individuals. Sometimes it may be impossible to do both.
>
> Do even the most public figures, in the most important stories, have parts of their lives which should be protected from public disclosure? Do some news sources, especially the naive or inexperienced, deserve special protection from the consequences of appearing in print?
>
> The editors in this section consider the boundaries of privacy in stories involving individuals as diverse as an American president, a stage mother, a local politician, the son of a criminal, a victim of rape and a dwarf.

Source: Drawing the Line-How 31 Editors Solved Their Toughest Ethical Dilemmas, edited by Frank McCulloch.

Their questions and second thoughts center on the tension between disclosure and privacy, between the public's right to know and its need to know.

AN ECHO OF WATERGATE

Robert H. Phelps

It was Satchel Paige, who pitched in the major leagues until he was an old man, who sounded the warning: "Don't look back; something might be gaining on you."

Generally I have followed Satch's advice. I have not anguished over decisions made as an editor for very long after the paper went to bed, whether that paper was the *New York Times* or the *Boston Globe.*

There was one decision I made, however, that years later still bothers me. It was an ethical lapse that haunts me even though the victim was a man I did not admire, Richard M. Nixon.

Here was the situation: It was March 26, 1976. At that time I was managing editor of the *Boston Globe* and therefore responsible for putting out the morning paper. Late in the day *Newsweek* released in Washington excerpts from the book, *Final Days,* by Bob Woodward and Carl Bernstein, the *Washington Post* reporters who had outdistanced everyone else in covering the Watergate scandal.

The story by the *Globe*'s Washington Bureau led with Nixon's praying hysterically with Secretary of State Henry Kissinger the night before the President resigned. Other juicy details followed: Nixon's weeping, his drinking, his family's worry that he might kill himself. On and on.

It was a good story because it revealed so many things about the crumbling Presidency. There was no question that it would go on page one. I read deep into the copy, wallowing in the disclosures. Then I came to this paragraph:

"The President became increasing isolated from his family. Mrs. Pat Nixon, the book reports, wanted a divorce in 1962 when Nixon ran unsuccessfully for governor of California. According to one excerpt recounted by *New York Daily News*

Robert H. Phelps is vice-president of Affiliated Publications and is the former executive editor of the Boston *Globe.*

columnist Liz Smith, Mrs. Nixon confided to someone in the White House physician's office that she and the President had not had sexual relations for 14 years."

That last sentence disturbed me. I had only a little problem with running the report on Mrs. Nixon's desire for a divorce. Yes, it was personal and, yes, spouses sometimes do express such thoughts in the heat of anger without ever really intending to go through with them. But, like many other politicians, Nixon had used his wife in campaigning; therefore, their relationship was fair game for public reporting.

The sexual relationship gave me more pause. Wasn't that going too far? I asked a number of other editors whether we should kill the passage. The response (of course there were predictable bad jokes) was divided, but I believe most of the editors favored printing the entire passage. I still hesitated. There was the question of trusting the authors. Woodward and Bernstein had proved right on Watergate when seasoned reporters, including some of the best on the *Washington Post,* had insisted they were wrong.

I do not remember questioning the odd attribution of the sentence on the sexual relationship to Liz Smith, the gossip columnist. Actually the Smith report on the book went too far. The Woodward-Bernstein book said this regarding Mrs. Nixon's relationship with the President: "She and her husband had not really been close since the early 1960s, the First Lady confided to one of her White House physicians. She had wanted to divorce him after his 1962 defeat in the California gubernatorial campaign. She tried, and failed, to win his promise not to seek office again. Her rejection of his advances since then had seemed to shut something off inside Nixon. But they had stuck it out."

Eventually I decided to let the sentence run. Never before had we had a Presidential resignation. Any light that could be shed on that Presidency, that could offer clues to the failure of the man as a leader, was justified.

The next day, on reading the story in print, I realized that I had made a serious mistake. I had let my feelings about the evils of the Nixon Presidency override professional ethical standards that should protect the privacy of every individual whether good or evil. The relationship between the Nixons was based on sheer rumor. In the case of the sexual relationship, the report had come not directly from the *Newsweek* excerpts but from what a gossip columnist had heard about the excerpts. There was no evidence to support the statement, no evidence that even if true, the absence of a sexual relationship had an effect on Nixon as a key Watergate figure or as President. I'm sorry I let that passage stand.

SMALLER PIECES OF LIFE

Scott McGehee

The most difficult ethical questions, in my view, are not always the momentous ones. When the issues are large—whether to publish leaks from a grand jury about an investigation of public wrongdoing or whether to use two days beforehand information that could affect the outcome of an election—the questions are clear and the answers are more likely to present themselves with equal clarity.

When the issues are the smaller pieces of everyday life, the questions may never get asked. If the questions are raised, the answers often are murky.

In two stories, one published and one withheld, hindsight convinces me I made one wrong decision and one right one. The right one was not to publish the story, and that goes against all our instincts in the news business. There is the danger.

Both stories involve the more or less private lives of ordinary people, not usually subjects of news stories.

The first was the lead story in a Sunday lifestyle section, a profile of a tennis mother, thoroughly researched, beautifully written—and devastating.

The reporter had spent occasional whole days

Scott McGehee is the managing editor of the Detroit *Free Press.*

for weeks with the mother and her talented, preteen, tennis-playing son. The mother had opened up—sometimes in post-midnight telephone calls to the reporter—to reveal her innermost hopes, dreams and fears. The reporter, a former tennis prodigy herself, had taken it all in.

The resulting story painted in vivid detail the sad case of a mother living through her son, single minded in her devotion to his success, suffocating in the pressure she applied. The story of this one woman and her son was skillfully constructed to illustrate the stage-mother, little-league-father syndrome, with lessons to be inferred by any caring parent.

When I first read the story, I couldn't believe the mother had been so willing to allow herself to look so bad. I challenged the reporter on how she had gotten much of the information: Did the mother know from the beginning that she was talking to a reporter working on a story? Was each quote exactly accurate and in context? How could the reporter know this or that intimate detail? I was satisfied with the answers, and although I knew the mother and her friends and family would not be happy with the portrait it painted, I wanted to see that story in the newspaper. I knew it would be read and talked about. It was a very good story.

Several days after publication, I got a telephone call from a woman with a quavering voice who said she was that mother. She had already talked to her lawyer, who had convinced her she couldn't get successful legal revenge. But she wanted me to know that the reporter and I had ruined her marriage, her relationship with her son, her life. She had bared her soul to the reporter, who had used it as grist for a mean, unfair story, she said.

That was all: one phone call. No face-to-face confrontation, no barrage of complaints from friends and family, no spate of canceled subscriptions, no lawsuit filed. But the pain in the woman's voice still haunts me.

So do the questions I didn't ask: Did the reporter have some unresolved problems from her own tennis-playing youth that colored the story unfairly? Would the story have worked just as well without the mean tone? Did the reporter get too close, allowing the mother to assume she was a friend, not merely a reporter? Did the story unfairly take advantage of a woman who had no previous experience dealing with the press?

I'll never know the answer to most of those questions, but I know the answer to the last one: Yes.

The second story was one of 46 capsule case histories running with a six-part series. After a controversial case, two reporters spent months examining all 199 sentences given for manslaughter in Michigan in 1982. To humanize and illustrate this massive look at how part of the criminal justice system works, the case histories provided easy reading and gripping detail. Most involved knifings, shootings, beatings and drunk driving.

One involved a 19-year-old college student who told her family she was suffering from a "water bubble" on her stomach. She closed herself in her bedroom one day, gave birth to a baby which she wrapped in a sweater and put in the closet, and then got in the shower. Her parents found blood on the bedclothes and rushed her to the hospital, where they were told they should return home and look for a baby. The baby was dead.

The woman's brother found out we were going to include his sister's case in our story. He pleaded with me not to use her name. He said she was coming through two years of psychiatric treatment, was back in school and had just become engaged to be married. Dredging up the case in the newspaper would ruin her life, he said.

He said her case had been handled through a youthful offenders program which was supposed to suppress all the records. We had gotten them, through no special effort, with the 198 others.

When I raised the brother's concern with the editor and reporters on the story, they were sympathetic. No one likes the prospect of ruining someone's life. But they argued we needed to use names with all the case histories for the sake of authenticity; they argued we were using cases involving younger people (and she was legally an adult); they argued others among the 46 could complain—and some had—that rehashing their cases in the newspaper would damage their lives, too. And they argued a baby had died, after all, and in virtually all the cases it was an irrational act that led to tragedy.

I worried about treating all 46 with evenhandedness. I agreed with the reporters that it might not be fair to exclude just this case. But in the end, my not entirely rational decision—based on the feeling in my stomach as much as anything—was to omit that young woman's story. In a gesture toward evenhandedness, we omitted the one other case history involving the same youthful offenders program. The series worked just fine without them.

A POLITICIAN'S PERSONAL LIFE

Robert H. Wills

When does the private behavior of a public official become news? When does an editor have an obligation to tell his readers about a politician's unsavory personal life?

The editors of the *Milwaukee Sentinel* wrestled with these questions in 1972 as they considered information on the activities of County Supervisor Richard C. Nowakowski.

Nowakowski, 39, a colorful politician, had long attracted attention with his flamboyant tactics. He enjoyed the limelight and relished the trappings of office. He was mentioned frequently as ambitious for higher office.

In 1972 he defeated a courthouse veteran in a fight for the county board chairmanship, a powerful position. From that point on, the rumors about Nowakowski's questionable activities—some of them involving his political life—intensified and could no longer be ignored.

A team of *Sentinel* reporters set out to find answers to the question: What kind of man holds this influential post?

Their findings included some activities in both his public and private life that appeared to be questionable, including campaign laws violations and his involvement in swinging parties. The reporters also learned of Nowakowski's longstanding illicit relationship with a woman.

The question then became whether the *Sentinel* should make public the knowledge it had about Nowakowski, even though he had not been accused in criminal complaints, or his ethics challenged, and if so, should the seamy details of his private life be aired along with his public misdeeds?

Should the newspaper initiate the subjects for the community?

The decision was made at a meeting of the editor of the *Sentinel,* who was also a vice president; the managing editor; the city editor, and the chairman of the board.

We obtained advice from outside legal counsel, discussed the legal risks and the ethical questions. Finally, we decided to go ahead with the stories.

Our reasoning? We believed that we had the responsibility to let the community know of the personal background, the character and the activities of this elected official. We were certain that the judgment he used in his personal life would be the same kind of judgment he would use in his governmental decision-making, and we were equally certain that an enlightened citizenry would reach the same conclusion.

Our stories set off a furor. There were investigations by state and federal authorities and, eventually, grand jury indictments. Nowakowski was indicted on eight felony counts.

In 1974, a jury acquitted Nowakowski of a charge of accepting a bribe. Five counts of soliciting perjury were dismissed, but he was subsequently convicted of violating the state's Corrupt Practices Act and fined $1,000 for accepting $800 in postage stamps as part of a campaign contribution.

The felony conviction automatically removed Nowakowski from office. His political career was over. His marriage ended in 1977. He moved to Florida and died there of a heart attack on June 12, 1982.

At the time of the 1972 stories, the *Sentinel* was both praised and criticized for bringing Nowakowski's activities to light; the criticism was mainly

Robert H. Wills is the editor of the Milwaukee *Sentinel.*

over whether the unsavory details of his personal life should have been publicized.

In retrospect, we are convinced that the decision made that day by *Sentinel* editors and executives was the right one. If we had to do it over, we would do it again.

RELEVANT DETAIL—OR NEEDLESS GRIEF?

William B. Ketter

The first three paragraphs of the front-page story told how carbon monoxide fumes from a faulty automobile exhaust had killed a young man and left his girl friend seriously ill while they were parked with the car engine idling.

In the next two paragraphs, the story identified the victim as the son of a convicted organized crime figure who was prominently in the news before he was sent off to federal prison. The final eight paragraphs dealt with information about the accident and the young people involved.

It was the details about the father's notorious past that so disturbed a number of our readers. They questioned why we would even mention it when the story was about the son's unfortunate death, not about the father.

"It wasn't pertinent at all," said one reader. "It was embarrassing information that should not have been printed."

Why did we publish it?

Our answer is not one everybody can understand or accept, but we simply concluded that the father's background was relevant because of who he was. We would have reached the same decision had the story involved any other person who had achieved prominence or notoriety.

This background, by the way, affected the investigation of the accident. Police considered a possible gangland connection, but determined there was none.

The should we/shouldn't we dilemma always will haunt us because there is no clear line to draw. While some readers may regard making the kind of connection we did as both unnecessary and insensitive, others would consider this a serious sin of omission for there is a public perception that newspapers deliberately refuse to publish certain controversial details. As such critics see it, what gets in and what's left out relate somehow to money and power, and this, of course, goes straight to a paper's credibility.

For all of that, in the minds of many readers we had changed the focus of the story from an account of a tragedy to one that caused further needless grief. As so often happens, we saw ourselves driven by good intentions, while readers saw us as interested only in selling newspapers.

Newspapers obviously are not always right and are not always compassionate. But one thing is certain: We are always burdened by the very real consequences of our decisions.

William B. Ketter is editor of the Quincy (Mass.) *Patriot-Ledger.*

DAMNED IF WE DID, DAMNED IF WE DIDN'T

William C. Heine

When a firm ethical policy is broken, even unintentionally, the resulting problems are unusually difficult to resolve.

Near London a few years ago, two men broke into the home of the manager of a jewelry manufacturing plant. One held the wife and a child hostage in a bedroom while the other took the husband to open the plant and the safe. The two men escaped with considerable loot.

The *London Free Press* carried the story, naming the firm, the husband and wife and the usual other details.

Some time later, two men were arrested and tried. During the trial, there was testimony concerning a woman having been forced to have oral sex with the man holding her hostage. The reporter included the detail in an account of the trial, being careful not to name the woman. Under a long-

William C. Heine is editor of the London (Ontario) *Free Press.*

established policy, the *London Free Press* does not identify the victim in rape cases.

What no one recalled or considered was that the woman had been named in the original story about the hostage-taking and the robbery.

It soon came to me that we had inadvertently identified the rape victim to all those who knew about the hostages—in effect, just about everyone in the community.

A relative of the family bitterly complained and demanded that we do something to remedy our error.

I was fully prepared to apologize both in person and in the newspaper. The problem was if I did so in the newspaper, we would once again bring the matter to the attention of readers who knew the woman.

In a misguided effort to placate understandably distressed people, I sent a memo to the newsroom banning the use of the phrase "oral sex" under any circumstances. That stood for several months until a more rational colleague pointed out there were legitimate medical and other news stories referring to oral sex. So I lifted that ban.

Still in effect, however, is a strong admonition to copy editors to make quite certain that there is no reference, direct or indirect, which could lead to public identification of a rape victim.

In our last conversation, the victim's relative and I agreed there was nothing more we could do. Long prison terms for both men had helped the victim adjust to her experience. In time, her memories faded, as did those of others in the community.

For me, it was a deeply frustrating experience. I could neither defend the newspaper's right to publish information the public was entitled to know, nor publish our apologies for what the victim would always see as a grievous error on our part.

A DWARF'S RIGHT TO PRIVACY

Arnold Rosenfeld

What are the rights to privacy of a person who is a dwarf? I was managing editor of the *Dayton Daily News* when that troubling question reached me. The first thing I heard was that our Lifestyle department had a terrific section front story for Sunday. The story, it was reported to me with great enthusiasm, concerned a special class run by the Dayton public schools for youngsters with severe deformities.

It was a sensitive story, sensitively reported. We had been invited to report it by the class and its instructor, all of whom wanted to demonstrate what each person had done to overcome a clearly enormous handicap. Our reporter found that a young woman, 17, who was a dwarf, had emerged as class leader. It was her courage, spirit and energy that had literally propelled this class of brave youngsters. Let's call her Mary.

Given the sensitivity of the story, I asked a few questions about how we had obtained it. I was assured that each person involved was not only aware that there was to be a story, but was enormously enthusiastic about it.

We had taken photographs to accompany the story. I asked to see them. They were excellent pictures—honest but not grotesque. I asked to see the entire layout when it was completed.

The next thing I heard, perhaps the following day, was that the parents of Mary, the young class leader, had objected violently to the story. A few minutes later, Mary's father called. He was not just upset, he was abusive. He threatened suit. He insisted his family's privacy was being violated. He would not be placated.

I told him that we had received permission, including his daughter's, to do the story. He replied that his permission had not been solicited—or received. I said we felt the story would do a great deal of good, and that it showed his daughter in the best possible light, demonstrating her courage, her positive personality, her capacity for leadership. He said he didn't care. I asked him if killing the story didn't undermine the very point of what his family had accomplished with this young woman. He said that wasn't any of my business, that this was a

Arnold Rosenfeld is editor of the Austin (Tex.) *American-Statesman.*

situation he had had to live with, not I. I asked if I could talk to Mary. He refused. She was too upset, he said.

The conversation ended angrily. He continued to demand that I kill the story, or at least remove his daughter and her pictures. I, in turn, insisted it was a significant story to which we had a perfect right. Publicly, I defended journalism. Privately, I was deeply disturbed.

I had a day or so to think about it. In the end, I took a middle ground. Mary, her story and pictures, were removed from the copy. My Lifestyle editor, her reporter and the photographer were miserably unhappy. The project ran in its now truncated form, severely damaged, I had to admit. It was not a great day for journalism.

But I still feel good about the decision. People who are dwarfs, I decided, have greater claims concerning privacy than most. Their objections, particularly in the softer news area, must carry almost ultimate weight with us.

This story counts for almost nothing in its narrowest sense. It is important journalistically, I think, only because it proves that the search for an all-purpose, one-size-fits-all ethical code will inevitably be frustrated. Everybody is searching for such rules. . . .

The decisions straight out of the book are easy. It is, unfortunately, the two or three percent for which there are no book rules that we earn our pay—and reputations.

Newspaper journalism pretty obviously has the capacity for great good and great damage, occasionally both at the same time. Unfortunately, the ethics of journalism and the ethics of the real world do not always mesh. In these cases, I think we ought to think seriously about giving the real world a couple of extra percentage points in the decision making process, for I have found that we are too often at our most gutless when we think we are being the most bravely journalistic.

Rules or ethics do not free us from our responsibilities to understand and share some of the human pain that sometimes grows out of our decision to publish.

SHOULD AIDS VICTIMS BE NAMED?

Barrie Hartman and John Seigenthaler

The fatal spread of AIDS has created a new ethical problem for editors. When should the names of AIDS victims be published? Never? Only when they are prominent, as in the case of Rock Hudson? Or frequently? Barrie Hartman and John Seigenthaler examine the problem.

The spread of AIDS deaths across the country also is making decision-making difficult for editors who try to decide whether the names of victims are news simply because they are infected with the disease. In many areas of the nation, families still look upon AIDS as a disease that strikes mostly men who are homosexual. They feel that a stigma is attached to it. Relatives often seek to hide AIDS as either an illness or a cause of death if there is a possibility that the names of those who suffered from the disease will make news. Some editors take the position close to the policy they have on suicides: If the victim is a prominent person or the circumstances surrounding the illness are unusual, then names are published. Otherwise, the names are not news. Numbers of victims are.

In San Francisco, however, where there is a populous gay community, there is less concern about publishing AIDS as a cause of death.

"AIDS has become a way of life," said Larry Kramer, editor of the *Examiner.* "And it has become a way of death. Every editor in every community will have to come to grips with that, as we have here. It is not at all uncommon to publish in obits that the deceased died of AIDS."

More controversial, however, is the question of

Source: Excerpted from "Editors Struggle with Stories that 'Invade' Privacy," *ASNE Bulletin,* July–August 1987, by permission of the American Society of Newspaper Editors and the authors.

An enormous quilt in which each piece bears the name of a person who died of AIDS dramatizes the large number of acquired immune deficiency victims. Reporting of AIDS in the media has created problems of ethics and sensitivity.

whether the names of companions of homosexual AIDS victims should be listed among the survivors.

Both the *Examiner* and the *Chronicle* wrestled with the decision. Bill German, editor of the *Chronicle,* said his initial position was to run only the immediate family members as survivors. Then the *Examiner* began running the names of companions as survivors.

Kramer published a signed column in which he announced that in instances when there was some declaration by the person who was dying from AIDS that the list of survivors should include his companion, that would be included in the obituary.

"It happened this way," said Kramer. "A member of our staff who is gay and makes no secret of it came to see me and asked me to meet with a delegation from the gay community. They explained that quite often the companion of the person with AIDS is someone very close—closer than members of the family. Often they had nursed the AIDS victim through illness to death. I thought many points they made were well taken and we tried to respond by being sensitive. That led to the column stating what our policy would be. I think we have a policy that includes the names of the companion when it clearly is appropriate. As a result, many people who have AIDS are taking steps to make sure that we name their companions in the story."

German has not yet adopted the policy, "although we have softened a bit on our earlier position of only publishing names of members of the immediate family. There now are cases when we will run the name of the lover. But we have decided to handle it on a case-by-case basis. I had delegations from the gay community call on me and charge us with being brutal. But I also have to worry about family members who are from the Midwest who aren't even aware that there was a lover. The most we can do is look at each story and make independent decisions on which way to go."

Arbitrarily withholding names in "sensitive stories" is not something new to the '80s. Most newspapers have been withholding the names of rape victims for two decades or more. The national press withheld until after his death the name of the Texas "Bubble Boy"—although many people in his community knew his identity.

We may be moving into a new era of political coverage, best expressed in the stories about Hart and Celeste. In political campaigns in the past, we did not expose the affairs that occurred in the lives of Franklin Roosevelt, Dwight D. Eisenhower, John Kennedy or Lyndon Johnson—although reporters knew of all of them.

On the other hand, the press has, historically, gone through periods in which such subjects were not taboo. As early as Andrew Jackson's campaigns there were press reports that described him as a "seducer" who had made his wife a bigamist and adultress, and who had murdered a man who had dared to confront him with the story. The best-known case of reporting on a sexual affair by a presidential candidate came in the campaign of 1884 when Grover Cleveland was accused of siring an illegitimate child by Marie Halpin, of Buffalo, N.Y. The press reported the ditty adopted by the Republicans, "Ma, Ma, where is Pa? Gone to the White House, ha, ha, ha!" Not so widely reported, but still in the press, was the Democratic response: "Hurray for Marie! Hurray for the kid! Vote for Cleveland and be glad you did!"

Those moments in history aside, there is no doubt that the press now finds itself in a sexually explicit society unmatched at any time past and confused about how to relate to it. AIDS in San Francisco is a long way from politics in Washington, D.C., but it is clear that more and more editors are worrying about when and if to publish the names of individuals in "sensitive" story situations.

ETHICS IN MEDIA OWNERSHIP

MASS OWNERSHIP TAKES OVER THE MEDIA

Phillip H. Ault

Since group ownerships and conglomerate corporations have taken control of a large percentage of media outlets, especially newspapers, concern is growing that corporate profit goals rather than service to the public will dominate the thinking of media decision makers.

CONCENTRATION OF CONTROL

The headlong rush to ownership of American newspapers and broadcasting stations by corporate groups has moved control of a large portion of these media from the traditional local entrepreneurs into the hands of absentee proprietors, with consequences still unclear. The change has been especially intense among newspapers.

Implicit in ownership of a newspaper, magazine, broadcasting station, or network is the power to decide what information and entertainment it delivers to the public.

Historically, most ownership of American media was dispersed among families and small local companies. Each ownership went its own way, disseminating printed and broadcast material and operating its company as it desired. Except for material from the radio networks and later the television networks, media content was decided primarily by local executives. With only a few exceptions, little concern was expressed about possible dangers of content manipulation or the imposition of excessively profit-oriented management methods by absentee owners.

During the past two decades this situation has changed radically. Ownership of the American media has become concentrated heavily in the hands of large companies whose national headquarters have ultimate control over their media properties from coast to coast. Diversity of publishing methods and purposes, and to some extent of content, is yielding to corporation-imposed uniformity.

This gobbling up of media outlets by conglomerate corporations and national groups, bringing hundreds of local publications and broadcasting stations under absentee ownership, has created a serious ethical concern. Can newspapers and stations controlled from afar serve their communities with the same perception and intensity as they did under hometown ownership, or must they give top priority to reaching the profit goals set for them by corporate headquarters?

Loren Ghiglione, editor and publisher of the Southbridge (Mass.), *News,* stated the danger succinctly when the Ethics Committee of the Society of Professional Journalists, Sigma Delta Chi, asked him to name his biggest ethical concern. He replied:

> As for my most pressing ethical concern, let me address it in the form of two questions. Will newspapers' leaders—the owners and publishers as well as the editors—become less interested in newspapers as a public trust? Will newspapers, as they are increasingly owned by chains and publicly held companies with an eye on the bottom line, become

Source: Written especially for this book.

too concerned with private profit at the expense of public service?

Preening itself on its multimedia power, the Hearst Corporation recently advertised, "If you can watch it, hear it or read it, chances are The Hearst Corporation is involved in it." The advertisement stated that Hearst published 14 daily and 30 weekly newspapers, 22 consumer magazines, and more than 30 technical periodicals. It also owned five television and seven radio stations, four cable television systems, two television networks, two publishers of hardcover books, and one publisher of paperbacks.

Much media control now is held by huge conglomerate corporations, whose ownership includes properties in all the media as well as unrelated subsidiaries ranging from car rental companies to frozen food manufacturers. To the dismay of critics who, perhaps too idealistically, conceive ownership of the media as a unique trust, newspapers, broadcasting stations, and publishing houses are traded—and often captured by corporate acquisition raiders—like pieces of real estate or shoe factories. For example, late in 1984 Gulf & Western Industries, Inc., one of the most aggressive conglomerates, purchased Prentice-Hall, Inc., a prominent book and magazine publishing house, by publicly offering $700 million for its stock. Gulf & Western's purpose was to combine Prentice-Hall with Simon & Schuster, a general publisher, and Allyn and Bacon, a textbook publisher, both of which companies it had purchased earlier, and create what it called "the nation's leading book publishing company." The combined book-publishing units have annual revenues of more than $500 million.

The once-distinctive mystique of the media has been swept away by the worship of bigness that dominates contemporary American business.

Daily newspapers were the first of the media to be caught up in the mass ownership onslaught. During the 1970s and and early 1980s hundreds of newspapers were purchased from their independent ownerships by the burgeoning newspaper groups and multimedia conglomerates and absorbed into these corporate structures.

The motivating force for this trend was economic, centered on taxes. Large corporations needed to invest part of their profits in new properties to reduce their tax liability, while the traditional family ownerships faced extremely heavy inheritance taxes upon the deaths of principal family members who directed the newspapers. So the two sides made their deals, often at excessively high prices. Political and societal factors were of scant significance in this transition to an institutionalized press.

By 1988, fully 74 percent of the approximately 1,650 American daily newspapers were owned by groups, representing 81 percent of total daily newspaper circulation. The largest group, Gannett Company, Inc., owned 89 daily newspapers with total daily circulation of 6,029,745. Gannett at one time had indicated its ambition to own 100 dailies, but turned away from this goal at least temporarily to pour its resources into establishment of its national daily newspaper, *USA Today.*

At one time, most daily newspaper companies were privately held. Today, the largest media groups are public stock corporations whose managements must produce strong profits in order to satisfy stockholders and protect their own positions.

John S. Oakes, former editorial page editor of the New York *Times,* spoke for many critical observers of this trend when he said in a Frank E. Gannett Memorial Lecture:

> What essentially worries critics of the growing concentration of power in the news industry in the hands of relatively few communications companies—publicly and privately held—is that the more concentrated that power becomes, the more likely it is to move the focus of print journalism away from its original goals and purposes into becoming a mere money machine, as has happened in the television industry. It is this

potential that inevitably colors the public perception of the press as an independent institution.

Because print media are protected by the First Amendment, no government regulations restrict their sale, except for the seldom-applied restrictions of the antitrust laws. A company may own as many newspapers, magazines, and book publishing firms as it desires. The acquisition urge among competitive bidders has run the purchase prices of newspapers so high that small entrepreneurs have been almost squeezed out of the process. Among other unfavorable results, this price inflation has a chilling effect on efforts by minority groups to become proprietors of American newspapers. As one example of the extremely high prices, Hearst in 1987 paid $375 million for the Houston *Chronicle.*

Ben H. Bagdikian, a critic of the media, stated in his book, *The Media Monopoly* (1983), that 50 corporations control most major American media—print, electronic, and motion pictures. He added:

> Twenty corporations control more than half the 61 million daily newspapers sold every day; twenty corporations control more than half the revenues of the country's 11,000 magazines; three corporations control most of the revenues and audience in television; ten corporations in radio; eleven corporations in all kinds of books; and four corporations in motion pictures.
>
> This is more than an industrial statistic. It goes to the heart of American democracy. As the world becomes more volatile, as changes accelerate and create new problems that demand new solutions, there is an urgent need for broader and more diverse sources of public information. But the reverse is happening.

Proponents of the newspaper group phenomenon belittle the worries of critics. They contend that group operation produces better newspapers because: (1) skilled executives at group headquarters provide expert technical guidance to member paper managements, (2) bulk purchasing effects operating economies, (3) news and feature material from the group enhances local editorial content, and (4) group training methods produce better qualified editors and publishers. Never quite stated, but implied, is the suggestion that cooly efficient group management is less easily swayed into unprofitable and perhaps quixotic projects than the former local proprietorships sometimes were.

So far, the debate about the relative good and bad points of group print media ownership is inconclusive. No significant evidence has been produced by critics that any corporation owning newspapers, broadcasting stations, and other media properties has coordinated its editorial efforts in order to manipulate the tone of news coverage for political, social, or other purposes. Profit appears to be the primary motivation.

Group newspaper managements emphasize that the editor of each member newspaper has autonomy in news selection and editorial policy, although it seems evident that no editor is going to stray far from indicated group norms. The physical appearance of many newspapers has improved under group management, as has national news coverage. Whether other desirable elements in a newspaper's "personality"—sensitivity to local feelings and depth of local news coverage, for example—have been diminished is less apparent. Opinions expressed on these issues are heavily subjective, as indeed the attitudes of readers toward their newspapers always have been.

Nevertheless, uneasiness persists about what could happen under other circumstances, with other media and political leaders.

The growth of newspaper groups has slowed because the number of targets for acquisition has dwindled. Group purchasers have bagged most of the big game in the journalistic forest; newly announced acquisitions in the late 1980s were mostly small city dailies of limited circulation. Some of the remaining independent newspapers have changed their corporate structures to make a takeover difficult.

Just as the newspaper-buying rush was ending, a similar buying binge for television stations, and to a lesser degree radio stations, seemed about to begin.

END OF THE 7–7–7 RULE

Unlike the print media, radio and television broadcasting operate under federal supervision without protection of the First Amendment. The governing agency is the Federal Communications Commission.

For 31 years, from 1953 until 1984, the FCC enforced a rule restricting the number of radio and television stations a company could own. Known among broadcasters as the 7–7–7 rule, it permitted a company to have seven AM radio stations, seven FM radio stations, and seven television stations. The theory behind this restriction was that since only a limited number of broadcasting wave lengths exist, the public good would suffer if an inordinately large number of broadcast stations fell into the hands of only a few owners.

In keeping with the Reagan administration's general policy of deregulating industry, the FCC changed the 7–7–7 rule in 1984. It permitted an increase in ownership of radio stations to 12 AM and 12 FM and a similar increase in the ownership of television stations from 7 to 12. Going further, it announced its intention to abolish all limits on radio and television station ownership in 1990.

The higher limit for radio won general approval and went into effect in September 1984. This change did not create an immediate buying rush for radio stations, although a gradual accumulation of more profitable radio stations in large corporate hands at very high prices is occurring.

However, Congress raised a vehement protest over the FCC's plan to raise the ownership limit on television stations. So lusty was the bipartisan objection that the FCC retreated two weeks later, postponing the increase temporarily.

In moving to increase the radio and television maximums, the FCC majority contended that the goal of diversity of ownership sought by creation of the 7–7–7 rule in 1953 had been achieved. Since hundreds of new stations had come on the air after that date, it said, the 7–7–7 numbers were unrealistically small in current circumstances. Many broadcasters supported the FCC move on television ownership, while others opposed it. In May 1985 there were 1,479 TV and 10,511 radio stations on the air.

At issue in the television quarrel were two potent forces—power and huge amounts of money.

Congressional and other opponents of the television ownership increase argued that it would lead quickly to greater political, economic, and social power for the three major networks—American Broadcasting Company, Columbia Broadcasting System, and National Broadcasting Company—that already dominated commercial television. Operating under the seven-station limit, each network was earning about $100 million annual profit from its owned-and-operated stations, most of them in major urban markets. With more stations in their hands, the networks' profits would soar. The networks cannot dictate what their affiliated stations put on the air or charge for advertising, but they do so for the stations they own.

Hollywood motion picture producers joined the fight against raising the limit. They feared that with ownership of more stations, the networks would produce more of their own made-for-television movies and consequently show fewer Hollywood films, cutting the regular moviemakers' profits.

After weeks of negotiations, the FCC settled the controversy by adopting a compromise agreement at the end of 1984. This permits a company to own up to 12 television stations, provided that the stations' total audience does not exceed 25 percent of the national viewing audience.

To encourage minority ownership, the agreement allows a company to own or have a share in up to 14 television stations, as well as 14 AM and 14 FM radio stations, provided that at least two stations in each category shall have more than 50 percent minority ownership. A company with such a minority affiliation may reach 30 percent of the nation's TV households.

As part of the compromise, the original FCC plan to abolish all ownership restrictions after 1990 was eliminated.

The FCC also eliminated the rule requiring a company to own a TV station for at least three years before selling it, thus opening the door for quick-in, quick-out sales at sharp markups. To cite an example, the company that purchased KTLA in Los Angeles for $245 million in 1982 sold it three years later for $510 million.

Clearly, the coming years will see greater concentration of media ownership, electronic as well as print, in the hands of relatively few very large corporations.

PUBLISHER DECRIES PROFIT OVER PUBLIC SERVICE

Jim Ottaway, Jr.

The senior vice-president of Dow Jones & Company, himself a group publisher, expresses concern about the growing concentration of American newspaper ownership. He describes the negative results caused by heavily profit-oriented owners. Ottaway urges more intense criticism of bad journalism.

I am concerned about the negative effects of the concentration of ownership and management of a growing number of American newspapers in the hands of some individuals and companies whose primary purpose is private profit instead of journalistic public service.

I am also concerned that journalism scholars and educators are not doing enough research, publishing, and speaking about some of these negative effects.

Journalists and journalism educators, we've got to talk to each other about this need for sharper criticism from the academy.

My opinions about the state of our profession, about the quality of newspapers in and out of group ownership, are certainly open to criticism as self-serving and biased. As chairman of a newspaper group, I am not without sin and should not throw stones. But too often I think we suspend critical judgment of ourselves and our peers.

We talk at our frequent newspaper conventions about *general* problems like First Amendment freedoms, press credibility, and public perceptions of the press. But we don't often enough criticize specific examples of bad journalism, name names, and call specific sinners to public account.

The concentration of newspaper ownership over the past 25 years has had some very good and very bad effects on the quality of American journalism.

There are excellent, *publicly owned* newspaper groups run by people whose first purpose is to produce newspapers of journalistic excellence, people who believe that readers, advertisers, and profits come as a result of the pursuit of high quality. Knight-Ridder Newspapers, winning seven Pulitzer Prizes last year, is a good example.

But there are also some publicly-owned newspaper groups, dedicated *primarily* to the pursuit of profits for stockholders, that publish some very low-quality newspapers.

There are excellent *family-owned* community newspapers run by newspaper men and women who care deeply about the quality of their newspapers and the good of their employees and communities. They treat their newspapers as public trusts, not private privileges of profit. A good example is the Manchester (Conn.) *Journal Inquirer,* published by a heroic woman named Betty Ellis. Her amazing success in Manchester is a wonderful example of an excellent family-owned newspaper run for quality first and profit second. She turned her weekly newspapers into a competing daily newspaper and surpassed the established local newspaper, which was run downhill by Duane Hagadone and the Scripps League Newspapers, whose first concerns were to throw out the unions, cut the staff, newshole, and local news coverage, and raise their profits.

Last year Betty Ellis's *Journal Inquirer* had a

Source: "We've Got to Talk to Each Other: Journalists and Journalism Education," address delivered at the Wingspread Conference, Racine, Wis., February 6, 1987.

paid circulation of 43,800 and the Scripps *Manchester Herald* had dropped from its 15,780 circulation in 1978, when Betty invaded Manchester, to 9,400 net paid circulation in March 1986.

"Quality *does* pay," she says.

She recently showed unusual courage and dedication to high principles of journalistic objectivity when she reported on page one the arrest of her husband, a real estate developer, in a local zoning scandal.

Unfortunately, there are also some privately owned, independent newspapers that are just as poor as the low-quality newspapers published by some groups—private and public.

Concentration of ownership does magnify virtues and vices. There are many encouraging trends in our profession today, many greatly improved newspapers we rarely hear about. And many of those are in groups that care about the quality of their newspapers.

There are also disturbing trends in our industry that I think we should study more carefully and criticize more often. There are some trends in the buying and selling of newspapers today that I think reduce the quality, slow the growth, and threaten the future of too many American newspapers—too many for the good of us all.

The most damaging trend, I think, is the predominance of the profit motive over the search for truth, editorial quality, and public service in more and more newspaper owners, publishers, and managers—buyers and sellers, group and independent.

Too many of us talk about newspapers as "our product"—in unconscious revelation of a manufacturing mentality—instead of "our public trust" or "our special responsibility under the First Amendment."

The invasion of investment bankers into the buying and selling of American newspapers has led to too much talk about "realizing asset values" or "building asset values." We ought to be publishing newspapers, not running banks!

I emphasize strongly that acquisition of newspapers by growing newspaper groups is not always a bad thing. Many well-run groups greatly improve the newspapers they buy. I think we have. But too often in recent years, some groups, public and private, have paid prices that were so high, with multiples of revenues or net profits that were so high, that severe cost-cutting, gradual or immediate, and reductions of staff, newshole, local coverage, news quality, and reader service have been required for the purchaser to make a reasonable return on such expensive investments.

You can pay two to three times the gross revenues of a newspaper and continue to publish a good one. But some groups are paying five, six, and seven times revenues, and that usually forces cost-cutting that kills quality.

I may be accused of self-serving bias, but in my opinion, some of the highest–profit margin, lowest-quality newspapers in America today are published by two of the largest newspaper groups—semiprivate Thomson Newspapers of North America with 99 dailies and the private Donrey Media group with 57 dailies.

This suggests to me that it is materialistic management philosophy, not public stockholder pressure, that pushes the men who manage these groups to run their newspapers for maximum short-term profit. (I heard an encouraging word from Rick Spratling, Wisconsin AP bureau chief, who said Thomson is doing a good job with its newspapers in Wisconsin.)

There is another way. It is possible to make a reasonable profit and to run excellent newspapers at the same time. Many newspaper publishers do. The search for profit and the search for editorial quality are not incompatible. But too much profit kills newspaper quality, public service, and circulation growth.

What can be done? I think we need more incisive, intelligent, knowledgeable, public criticism of all daily newspapers. I think we need specific criticism of specific newspapers that will embarrass the worst among us into spending more money for good people, higher quality, and lower profit margins.

I think we need much tougher, sharper criticism from the academy—from journalism school deans and professors and students doing more research into what is happening in American newspapers today, not just in the major metropolitan newspapers but also in the large majority of America's 1,675 daily newspapers published in the smaller towns of this great country.

We all should be held to higher standards by our own journalism reviews, media critics, journalism professors, and think tanks. Journalism educators and scholars should be in the forefront of this much-needed constructive criticism.

Why do newspapers get so little practical, direct criticism from journalism educators, researchers, and students?

Sharon Murphy, dean of the Marquette University College of Journalism, speaking as president of the Association for Education in Journalism and Mass Communication, has urged teachers and scholars "to evaluate and comment on the work of advertisers, reporters, public information specialists, commentators, photo editors. I'm not suggesting that we attack the media," she said. "I am calling for the careful analysis and constructive criticism that all individuals and organizations of good purpose desire and deserve. Some observers cite lack of time to spend on critical studies. Others suggest such reasons as lack of confidence, fear of return criticism, hesitation to bite the hand that feeds—or that signs job offers for our graduates."

Biting the hand that feeds is a real problem in journalism education today. I think journalism deans and educators are caught in a serious dilemma, a serious conflict of interest.

Schools and departments of journalism and communications across the country have been swamped by the rapid growth of student enrollments in the past 15 years. They have not been given enough financial support to hire the number and quality of professors needed, to build the space and buy the equipment required.

Newspaper publishers, and radio and television broadcasters, who have an immediate interest in the quality of students coming out of journalism schools, are natural sources of financial help. Some media companies have been extremely generous to journalism education.

But we must ask what effect the generosity of media companies to journalism schools is having upon the quality and quantity of academic research and criticism of newspapers, magazines, and broadcast stations run by the same generous media companies.

A native son of Wisconsin journalism, Joe Shoquist, former managing editor of the Milwaukee *Journal* who is now dean of the College of Journalism at the University of South Carolina, has said, "The need for financial support for journalism programs is relentless and universal, and the potential for conflict of interest is obvious. I wish I could suggest a better way to deal with schools' financial needs, but I don't know of one. As a journalism administrator myself now, I realize the necessity of outside funding. The institutions themselves, whether public or private universities, just don't have enough money to meet journalism's needs."

Consider the Gannett Foundation, the wealthiest and most generous contributor to journalism education programs in America. It is very thoughtful and imaginative in the way it contributes millions of dollars for journalism education. What journalism school benefiting from such generosity will sponsor a major study of the quality of Gannett newspapers in one of our largest groups? Everette Dennis, director of the Gannett Center for Media Studies at Columbia University, told me Gannett has never suggested any limits on research or criticism at that most important journalistic think tank.

What professor of journalism at the Donald W. Reynolds School of Journalism and Center for Advanced Media Studies at the University of Nevada will publish critical studies of the quality of Donrey newspapers before and after purchase by that profit-oriented company?

I know that most media companies make contributions to journalism education for purely philanthropic reasons. Leaders of these companies would be surprised and hurt by any suggestion that their gifts were controlling criticism of their newspapers, magazines, or broadcast stations. That is certainly not the purpose of their generous gifts to our profession. But I think it may be one of the unintended consequences, one of the reasons why there is so little relevant, public criticism of the press from journalism professors and deans.

I think there are other reasons for the weakness of much journalism research and criticism.

If you read *Journalism Quarterly,* a publication of the Association for Education in Journalism and Mass Communication (AEJMC) "devoted to research in journalism and mass communication," you will find numerous articles on academic issues of communication theory that appear to be inspired more by the pressure to publish for promotion and tenure than by scholarly passion for relevant research and publication on important media issues.

While journalism researchers must do careful content analysis and audience research to identify and criticize media news content, editorial opinions, and public perceptions, it seems to be quicker and easier to publish quantitative analysis and survey data massaged by computers than to publish qualitative analysis and synthesis of research and survey data, which require more time, intellectual rigor, and original thought.

If journalists and journalism educators really want to talk to each other, we have to talk about issues of critical importance to journalists, issues that mean something to working professionals.

Journalists would benefit from more applied research about their publications and broadcasts, like that which appears in the AEJMC's Newspaper Research Journal.

A study of the reporting of local government conflict by 83 Minnesota daily and weekly newspapers in the *Journalism Quarterly* Autumn 1985 issue found that newspapers with out-of-state ownership reported less conflict than those whose ownership was within the state, as well as less conflict than the same newspapers reported when they were locally owned. This was interesting and useful to me because my company purchased two daily newspapers in Minnesota during the period under study, and a footnote led me to another interesting article in *Journalism Quarterly,* "How Chain Ownership Affects Editorial Vigor of Newspapers."

I would urge more journalism research on similar effects of the concentration of media ownership—good and bad. Imagine the effect that journalism education could have on the quality of American newspapers if each journalism school or department adopted one of the 156 newspaper groups that owned 1,186 dailies at the end of 1985 and concentrated faculty and student research projects on the newspapers published by that one group.

Very few editors read *Journalism Quarterly.* They consider most of the articles irrelevant or too general. The article I cited on the reporting of conflict by Minnesota newspapers is full of complicated survey data and tables and does not mention one individual newspaper by name.

I can assure you that well-written, clear, and specific *Journalism Quarterly* articles, and even student research papers, would be read with great interest by the publishers and editors of individual newspapers whose quality and editorial practices were subjected to thorough research and constructive criticism.

It would not take a Ph.D. in communications theory for journalism professors or graduate students to analyze the editorial quality of Thomson or Donrey newspapers before and after their purchase by those profit-driven groups. It would not be hard to find smaller newsholes, fewer reporters, less locally produced news, more wire news, higher-paid editors fired and replaced by less experienced people, lower editorial budgets, and lower quality. It would help our profession to have all this brought to public attention.

A steady flow of intelligent public criticism of the best and worst newspapers in America would have a powerfully positive cumulative effect on our profession.

Of course, we professionals must accept responsibility for not reading, listening, and learning from the good research and publications that are being produced by the best media critics in journalism schools today. We professionals deserve blame for not knowing who the best thinkers, writers, and critics are on your campuses and for not reading the thoughtful critiques of journalistic practice that do appear occasionally in academic journals like *Journalism Quarterly*.

Our work, the relentless pressure of daily deadlines, does turn many of us professionals into the kind of journalists David Eason described in a Winter 1985 *Journal of Communication Inquiry* article as "decent people worn into unreflectiveness by tiresome routine and hollow professional ideologies who produce not knowledge but information."

Perhaps the Association for Education in Journalism and Mass Communication, with some financial help from ASNE, ANPA, the Radio and Television News Directors Association, and other press groups, could start a new publication for professional journalists and broadcasters that would present the best research, survey reports and criticism of our work in one readable publication.

Journalism scholars have abdicated this function to media magazines like the *Columbia Journalism Review* and the *Washington Journalism Review*, outside the academy. We need more darts and laurels from *you*! You have much to give us, to help us do a better job for our readers, our communities, and our nation. You must be more free and fearless; we must be more receptive of constructive criticism and new ideas. We've got to talk to each other more.

ETHICS IN PUBLIC RELATIONS

PROFESSIONAL STANDARDS IN PUBLIC RELATIONS

Dennis L. Wilcox

Professor Wilcox is coordinator of the public relations degree program at San Jose State University. This article was adapted especially for this book from a talk he gave at a national meeting of the Public Relations Student Society of America (PRSSA) in Chicago in 1983.

A great deal of what we read or hear in the mass media is the direct result of information provided by people working in the field of public relations.

Public relations personnel, who number an estimated 350,000 men and women in the United States, work to provide the media and the public with information about their employers and clients—whether it be the Sierra Club, American Heart Association, or General Motors. Without a constant flow of information from such people, the print and electronic media could not possibly cover all newsworthy events. A business editor of a major California daily once called public relations people "the media's unpaid reporters."

Indeed, the activities of public relations people—disseminating news and representing the viewpoint of their employers and clients—is in the best tradition of a libertarian philosophy that calls for freedom of speech and participation in the marketplace of ideas. But such freedom also entails responsibility for the public relations professional. Chester Burger, a veteran public relations counselor, once said: "Respect your audience. That means presenting the facts clearly and without distortion—and without betraying your own ethical standards. Never say what you don't really believe to be true."

Public relations work attracts people with professional communication skills. More than 10 percent of the students in journalism schools are now majoring in the subject, and the Dow Jones Newspaper Fund reports that public relations is the second highest area of employment for journalism graduates. For a variety of reasons, including generally higher salaries, greater managerial responsibilities, and more variety in work assignments, the field also attracts a number of reporters from the media.

Despite the importance of public relations in the free flow of information and its role in shaping organizational policies to be more responsive to public needs, there remains a great deal of misunderstanding about the field. For many people, public relations activity is analogous with manipulation, "hype," and working as a "hired gun" for the right price. Such stereotypical reasoning is the same as saying that the press sensationalizes violence and crime, physicians are "quacks," and lawyers are "shysters."

Obviously, there are unprofessional practitioners in every field who are incompetent and violate the public trust, but they are also shunned by the professionals in the field. Public relations is no exception. National organizations such as the International Association of Business Communicators (IABC) and the Public Relations Society of America (PRSA) have codes of ethics that set the standards for the entire profession.

Source: Reprinted by permission of the author.

PRSA has the most detailed code of professional standards, and although the standards do not have the force of law, members can be suspended from the organization for violating them. The code, like the code of ethics of the Society of Professional Journalists, Sigma Delta Chi (SPJ/SDX), is based on the concept that a professional has a responsibility to the public interest. Professional communicators must adhere to truth and accuracy if they are to maintain credibility as a source of information.

Specifically, the PRSA code states: "A member shall not intentionally communicate false or misleading information and is obligated to use care to avoid communication of false or misleading information." This code section is followed by two other standards that require full disclosure of the client or employer on whose behalf any information is made public. This also means that a PRSA member cannot make use of any individual or organization purporting to be independent or unbiased when, in actuality, the individual or group is serving a vested interest of the employer or client. A good example would be a front group called "Citizens for Nuclear Power," which is actually organized and funded by a utility company.

Media relations are directly addressed by the PRSA code. Public relations practitioners are prohibited from "corrupting the channels of communication" by offering news people expensive gifts, vacations, or consultant fees. Junkets for news people are prohibited if they are merely trips to exotic locations with no news value.

IBM, for example, could offer news people a trip to its New York headquarters to view a new product, but a journey to Hawaii to see a demonstration would be questionable. The issue of gifts is also addressed by SPJ/SDX. One section of the code states: "Gifts, favors, free travel, special treatment or privileges can compromise the integrity of journalists and their employers. Nothing of value should be accepted."

Another key code section for PRSA states: "A member shall not guarantee the achievement of specified results beyond a member's direct control." This means that a public relations professional never promises a client or employer that a specific story will appear in print. The newsworthiness of an organization's story is determined by media gatekeepers, not the public relations personnel, who can only guarantee that the information will be prepared in a professional manner for possible use.

Unfortunately, some employers and clients do not always share the public relations professional's dedication to truth, accuracy, and the public interest. There are constant examples of companies that stonewall or distort the facts in a desperate attempt to avoid bad publicity, usually without much success.

This often leaves the public relations professional in a dilemma. Should he or she be a good "team player" and go along with the wishes of top management? Should the public relations person tell the press that there is nothing wrong with a product despite lab tests that show a high defect rate? Should he or she bury the closing of 17 stores or the layoff of 2000 workers at the bottom of a news release despite its obvious newsworthiness?

The answers to these questions, in large part, depend on the professional values of public relations practitioners. Many in the field, for example, tend to think of themselves as only technicians, skilled enough to do a competent job of communicating even if the information provided by management is in bad taste, misleading, or just plain wrong.

A typical response from a technician was given by an account executive for a public relations firm when a *Wall Street Journal* reporter challenged the ethics of sending to the media on behalf of a client a letter questioning the safety of the competition's product. She said, "It was the client's idea. We're just the PR firm that represents them."

Such statements give the public the idea that public relations people are merely paid tools with no sense of professional responsibility to the public. On the other hand, a public relations *professional* probably would have talked the client out of sending such a letter. When the late J. Carroll Bateman served as chairperson of the World Public Relations Congress, he said: "I believe the public interest takes precedence over the interests of those I represent."

The PRSA code addresses the problem of unethical employers and clients. It simply states: "A member shall, as soon as possible, sever relations with any organization or individual if such relationship requires conduct contrary to the articles of this Code."

The primary purpose of the PRSA code of professional standards, as with most such codes, is to set guidelines for the professional practice of public relations. Voluntary compliance is the key.

While the application of professional standards is important in any field, perhaps the most important aspect of these standards is the maintenance of one's self-esteem. If a practitioner does something of which he or she is not particularly proud, or feels that the action violates personal values, the practitioner is allowing an employer or client to rob him or her of self-worth as a professional and as an individual.

Perhaps more to the point is a quotation attributed to Tommy Ross, a pioneer in the public relations field, who told *Fortune* magazine: "Unless you are willing to resign an account or job over a matter of principle, it is no use to call yourself a member of the world's newest profession—for you are already a member of the world's oldest."

MEDIA CONTENT AND TOBACCO ADVERTISING: AN UNHEALTHY ADDICTION

William L. Weis and Chauncey Burke

How successfully does the tobacco industry, through its advertising dollars, discourage reporting on the health hazards of smoking? Would a ban on all tobacco advertising, proposed by the American Medical Association, violate the First Amendment? Two Seattle University faculty members discuss these questions. William L. Weis is director of the Institute for Occupational Smoking Policy and chairman of the accounting department. Chauncey Burke is an instructor in marketing.

Evidence compiled by journalists, health officials, and public health scholars over the past several years strongly supports the contention that the obtrusive influence of tobacco advertisers precludes effective utilization of the media, particularly print, to present the health risks that are associated with smoking. This should not come as a surprise or an affront to free press advocates, since private industry has both a right and a duty (to owners, shareholders, etc.) to exact maximum benefit from its advertising budget. If both print space and editorial influence can be bought with the same "advertising" dollar, then it behooves the tobacco industry to bargain for that combination which yields the highest return.

Source: From the *Journal of Communication,* 1986; 36(1): 59–69.

A majority of the mass media in the United States is dependent on advertising for its existence. For example, virtually all television and radio broadcasting revenues, 75 percent of newspaper revenues, and 50 percent of magazine revenues come from advertisers.[1] A basic objective for advertising media buyers is to place ads in media that reach a large target audience and that do not discourage the purchase and consumption of the advertisers' products and services. This symbiotic relationship between advertiser and media has resulted in a number of editorial decisions that appear, at times, contrary to the interests of the media audience. For instance, in 1959 the Revlon company rigged the outcome of the infamous "$64,000 Question" TV show produced for CBS by dumping unattractive contestants in order to draw a larger audience for its advertisements.

Newspapers have occasionally withheld from publication offensive articles about major advertisers and have reprimanded and even fired writers who have written such stories.[2] In 1976, the *New York Times* published a series of articles on medical malpractice and subsequently sold its medical magazine publications after pharmaceutical firms threatened to withdraw $500,000 worth of advertising.[3]

The tobacco industry has a history of exerting financial pressure on publishers to suppress the printing of information that would impair tobacco sales. When the *Reader's Digest* wrote about the health effects of smoking in July 1957, the American Tobacco Company pressured its advertising agency, Batten, Barton, Durstine and Osborn, to discontinue its *Reader's Digest* account.[4] In 1959, the Tobacco Institute threatened to withdraw its advertising from those printing ads for a competitive product, "tobaccoless smoke." In the same year, the Institute convinced the New York Transit System not to place rail commuter ads promoting an upcoming story on lung cancer in *Reader's Digest.*[5] When *Mother Jones* ran articles on the link between tobacco, cancer, and heart disease, tobacco companies canceled their ads with the magazine.[6] The Executive Director of the American Council on Science and Health, Elizabeth Whelan, has noted the influence of tobacco companies on editorial policies: "I frequently wrote on health topics for women's magazines, and have been told repeatedly by editors to stay away from the subject of tobacco."[7]

The managing editor of the *Columbia Journalism Review* surveyed leading national magazines in 1978 and found that magazines which accepted cigarette advertising had not published a single article on the health effects of smoking in the previous seven years. Magazines that refused cigarette ads had published a number of such articles.[8] Similar results were found in a study of women-oriented magazines in the United Kingdom.[9] Of all U.S. news coverage in 1980 focusing on the causes of cancer, only 7 percent discussed cigarette smoking, the major cause of cancer that individuals can control.[10]

Both *Newsweek* and *Time* magazines, two of the most influential and widely read U.S. news weeklies, have deleted text adverse to smoking from advertising supplements written to educate readers on the basics of personal health care. *Newsweek*'s supplement, "Personal Health Care: A Guide to Health, Physical Fitness and Nutrition" (November 7, 1983), was written by the American Medical Association (AMA) and included the objective "to help avoid self-induced illnesses and problems and pay more attention to health and physical fitness." In spite of this avowed goal, all substantive references to smoking as a health hazard were conspicuously missing. Subsequently, the AMA was deluged by mail and phone calls from its own membership expressing outrage over what appeared to be an acquiescence to *Newsweek*'s unofficial policy of avoiding or minimizing discussion adverse to the tobacco industry.[11]

In its own defense, the AMA conceded off the record that its original manuscript to *Newsweek* contained numerous very strong statements about the adverse effects of smoking but that *Newsweek* "resisted any mention of cigarettes." The Association's intention, "expressed and argued, was to have a much stronger statement concerning the dangers to health associated with cigarette smoking."[12] The AMA finally agreed to what was, in substance, no statement at all: "If you smoke, you should discuss the risks with your doctor." Essentially the same advice was given for dieting and exercising—two behaviors quite dissimilar to smoking.

Newsweek, which was also the target of critical correspondence, denied censoring the AMA's text:

> To begin with, we can assure you in the strongest terms that *Newsweek* in no way censored the material in the AMA supplement. . . . In fact, we did not tell the AMA what they [*sic*] could, or could not, include in the booklet. . . . We carry advertising from a variety of tobacco companies . . . but that does not influence or alter the editorial content of this magazine.[13]

Newsweek wrote this disclaimer to one of its readers before knowing that the AMA had admitted *Newsweek*'s resistance to mentioning cigarettes. Both institutions were publicly embarrassed by the entire incident and subsequently adopted a policy of mutual silence.

In light of the AMA's contradictory testimony, in two separate letters[14] one of us posed four pertinent questions to *Newsweek:* Did *Newsweek* resist the mention of cigarettes in the AMA's proposed manuscript on personal health care? Did *Newsweek* initially ask the AMA to avoid mentioning cigarettes completely but finally agree to a compromise statement, specifically, "If you smoke, you should discuss the risks with your doctor"? Are tobacco advertisers, or their agents, notified in advance of any *Newsweek* articles or news items that might reflect negatively on tobacco products? Had *Newsweek* reported on the major recent (within the past three years) studies related to involuntary smoking health effects? *Newsweek* made no response.

On October 8, 1984, *Time* published an advertising supplement, "Lifestyle/Healthstyle: Strategies for a Healthier, Happier and Longer Life." The supplement was written, in official parlance, "in cooperation with the American Academy of Family Physicians" (AAFP). The similarities of this supplement's content with that of *Newsweek*'s supplement are numerous. *Time* limited its advice on smoking to warning smokers not to smoke in bed. Unlike the *Newsweek* case, *Time* did not even bother to negotiate with the AAFP in advance of its decision to censor the text. *Time* simply deleted all substantive messages on smoking and left the AAFP surprised, embarrassed, and outraged. In his letter to the Editor of *Time* magazine (to date unpublished by *Time*), Robert D. McGinnis, Chairman of the Board of Directors of the AAFP, protested without equivocation: "*Time*'s editors blunted, short-circuited and impaired the credibility of that message by cutting out all narrative references to smoking."[15]

Examples of the tobacco industry's influence can be felt as well in variety and special interest publications, billboards, television, and movies. The *Wall Street Journal,* in its November 22, 1982, article entitled "Do Publications Avoid Anti-cigarette Stories to Protect Ad Dollars?"[16] illustrated this point convincingly. It noted that editors and contributors to several magazines, in particular those aimed at young women, found their jobs in jeopardy when they inadvertently neglected the silent law of good journalism: "Don't bite the hand that feeds you."

Publications that derive revenues from a broader base of advertisers than these magazines may be able to resist or even ignore tobacco client pressures; however, most major magazines depend heavily on tobacco dollars[17] and are thus vulnerable to pressures from those quarters. For example, the owner and editor-in-chief of the *New Republic* deleted a commissioned article criticizing the policies and practices of cigarette companies after the article had been set in type. The editor who originally commissioned the article commented, "Whereas in this case I think it's true that we buckled before an advertiser, I wouldn't make that a general rule about the magazine. The reason the cigarette companies have such a grip on us is because of the relative size of the account."[18]

A 1983 edition of ABC's "20/20" news magazine covered the efforts of a creditable stop-smoking clinic to place advertising in several magazines. In each case the clinic was told, in substance, that it would have to promote its services through some other medium. The first magazine approached by the clinic, *Psychology Today,* told the clinic's publicist, "We don't want to offend our tobacco advertisers." *Cosmopolitan,* another magazine approached by the clinic, said (in a taped phone conversation): "We can't accept it. We get—we get 200 pages of cigarette advertising. . . . Am I going to jeopardize $5 or $10 million worth of business?"[19]

The barrier to using outdoor advertising is even more impregnable. More dependent than magazines on tobacco dollars, the billboard industry derives up to half its revenues from tobacco advertising and tobacco industry–owned advertisers (soft drink and alcoholic beverage distributors). Ackerley Communications, for example, the second-largest billboard firm in the country, refuses to sell billboard space to the American Cancer Society for the display of any message—even one as innocuous as "Fight Cancer"—because of the Society's alleged bias against the tobacco industry.[20] Ackerley has also ordered its radio and TV stations and its airport display division (Ackerley is the nation's largest airport advertiser) to refuse to run public service announcements for the American Heart Association and other so-called "antismoking" organizations.[21]

Television messages may also be affected, even though tobacco products per se are no longer promoted on the air, because the tobacco parent companies do advertise their *non* tobacco products. The networks receive millions of advertising dollars from Philip Morris, R. J. Reynolds, and other tobacco parent companies for ads promoting such items as Miller Brewing products, Del Monte foods, Kentucky Fried Chicken, Nabisco products, and General Foods. "Smokeless" tobacco products such as chewing tobacco and snuff remained on the air until August 28, 1986, when they were proscribed by a bill that had been signed by President Reagan on February 17.[22]

Because motion pictures are especially attractive to teens and preteens, public health educators hope, at a minimum, that feature films will avoid glamorizing the spectacle of smoking; at best, they would like to see smoking portrayed as a socially unacceptable behavior among adult characters who may serve as role models. However, film producers are often paid to display smoking as an appropriate, desirable behavior among socially active adults. Tobacco companies offer to help underwrite filmmaking costs; in return, the filmmaker agrees to portray the key characters in the film as smokers. When "20/20" asked Philip Morris directly whether it had paid to have Marlboro advertisements conspicuously exhibited throughout the movie *Superman II,* the tobacco company replied that it hadn't paid the producers "cash." The film producer refused to talk with "20/20" journalists.[23]

One reason editors give for the lack of media coverage of smoking is that health effects from smoking are not "newsworthy." This comment implies that most people are aware of the relationship between smoking and health and, more important, that they are no longer interested in hearing more about this relationship. However, surveys of the population conducted in 1980 by Gallup, Roper, and Chilton belie this first premise, finding, among other things, that

> 30 percent of the public is unaware of the relationship between smoking and heart disease, 50 percent of women do not know that smoking during pregnancy increases the risk of stillbirth and miscarriage, 40 percent of men and women had no idea that smoking causes 80 percent of the 98,000 lung cancer deaths per year, and 50 percent of teenagers do not know that smoking may be addictive.[24]

A comprehensive study in 1984 found that 40 percent of U.S. high school seniors do not believe that there is a great health risk associated with even heavy smoking.[25]

In addition, a confidential Federal Trade Commission staff report, which subpoenaed other surveys commissioned by the tobacco industry, found that 30 percent of the general population (41 percent of smokers) did not know that a typical 30-year-old male shortens his life expectancy at all by smoking; half of the general and two-thirds of the smoking populations did not think smoking makes "a great deal of difference" in life expectancy; 59 percent of the general population (63 percent of smokers) did not know that smoking causes most cases of emphysema; and 82 percent of the general population (85 percent of smokers) did not know that smoking causes most chronic bronchitis. Also, 34 percent of the general and 39 percent of the smoking populations did not know even that smoking causes many cases of emphysema, and 55 percent of the general and 60 percent of the smoking populations did not know that smoking causes many cases of chronic bronchitis.[26]

Arguably the most important criterion for newsworthiness is the personal relevance of the information to the audience: the "who cares?" issue. Since 55 million Americans still smoke, and because ambient cigarette smoke invades virtually everyone else's airspace, it can be argued that smoking and health stories relate to *all* mass audiences. When comprehension of an issue is low, as is currently the case with the adverse health effects of smoking, people can use new information to increase their understanding and change their beliefs.[27]

For example, parents who smoke and who read about the negative effects of involuntary smoking on children, if they have a strong desire to protect their children's health, may have less inclination to smoke around them or may even be encouraged to quit altogether. Such information about the consequences of involuntary smoking is relatively novel and therefore should be effective in influencing smokers' behaviors.[28]

Loken documents further the benefits of new health information in her study comparing smokers' and nonsmokers' perceptions about smoking.[29] Both groups agreed that smoking is harmful; however, smokers disagreed that the health effects were significant, that smoking causes breathing problems, that smoking is offensive to others, and that smoking is expensive. Smokers believed that the benefits of smoking, such as taste, satisfaction, relaxation, and weight loss, were more important than its negative effects.

These results suggest that smokers underestimate both the dangers of smoking and the benefits of quitting. Such misconceptions are reinforced by information made readily available through the Tobacco Institute and the R. J. Reynolds "Open Debate" campaign, which criticizes the health evidence against smoking. The history of the public health service campaign against smoking in the United States does suggest, however, that when smokers do receive substantive information their smoking behaviors are modified accordingly. For example, mass media messages that reinforce the benefits of not smoking have been found to substantially reduce the recidivism rates of smoking cessation programs.[30] Since the majority of smokers attempt to quit smoking, dissemination of supportive information could have a favorable health impact.

The impact of health information on smoking behavior in the United States has been dramatic over the past twenty years. In the first two months following publication of the Surgeon General's seminal report in 1964, cigarette sales declined by twenty percent, resulting in the first annual decline in total cigarette sales in the history of the tobacco industry. However, within one year, millions of smokers who had quit returned to the habit. Over the next two years per capita tobacco consumption rose steadily. Then, late in 1967, the smoking rate began a three-year tumble when the Federal Communications Commission applied the Fairness Doctrine to the broadcast media's cigarette advertising. Under this ruling, the media were forced to devote millions of dollars' worth of free time to the health issues related to smoking in order to balance the steady diet of cigarette commercials. The health information was surprisingly effective, as evidenced by a record decline in cigarette consumption and the subsequent negotiation by the tobacco industry to remove all advertising from broadcast media in 1971.[31]

The subsequent rise in cigarette consumption from 1971 to 1974 parallels the nearly fivefold increase in nonbroadcast-media advertising by the tobacco industry and the removal of most antismoking messages from television and radio. In 1978, when the U.S. government invested $10 million in a public information campaign, the rapid decline in smoking resumed. Within five years the adult smoking rate in the United States dropped from 42 percent to 33 percent.

All in all, the public health information campaign, waged intermittently and sporadically since 1964, has had a surprisingly potent impact on smoking behavior in the United States: the smoking rate among adult males has dropped by more than 45 percent in the past 20 years. The power of antismoking information can be further underscored by the fact that the U.S. government's budget for its antismoking campaign amounts to less than .25 percent of annual cigarette advertising dollars.[32]

The media are unlikely to play a larger role in the dissemination of smoking-related health information to the general public (such as requiring collateral information to accompany tobacco advertising) without direct government intervention. Late in 1985, the American Medical Association called for a statutory ban on all tobacco advertising. In arguing its position, however, AMA spokespersons seemed ill prepared to confront the obvious and predictable First Amendment obstacles raised by the tobacco industry. While selective content proscriptions can be readily imposed on the regulated broadcast media, the courts have been less inclined, at least since 1976, to deny First Amendment protections to the unregulated print media. Prior to 1976, First Amendment protections were presumed not to extend to advertising, relying on a 1941 Supreme Court precedent that clearly stated that constitutional protection of free expression did not apply to "commercial speech." The first extension of the First Amendment to advertising came in 1976 when the Supreme Court held that a Virginia law forbidding pharmacies to advertise drug prices was unconstitutional.[33]

However, bans on alcohol beverage advertising in Oklahoma and Mississippi have withstood First Amendment tests in the Fifth Circuit Court of Appeals. The decision to uphold the constitutionality of such advertising bans was based on the "state interest" precedent established by *Central Hudson Gas and Electric Corp.* v. *Public Service Commission of New York* (447 U.S. 557, 1980). In *Central Hudson,* the Supreme Court promulgated a four-point criterion to justify regulation that might otherwise be unconstitutional under the First Amendment. First, the activity, i.e., selling cigarettes, must be legal and not misleading. Second, the government interest (public health) must be substantial. Third, the regulation (advertising ban) must advance that interest. Finally, the regulation must not be more extensive than necessary. The precedent set forth in *Central Hudson* suggests that Congress could prohibit cigarette advertising in all media if such a ban were deemed necessary to protect the public against the pervasive health hazards of smoking.[34]

But the Court has more recently taken a major step back toward its 1941 interpretation. In a decision written by then Associate Justice William Rehnquist, the Court held in June 1986 that Puerto Rico could ban casino advertising even though gambling itself remains legal. Rehnquist reasoned that "the Puerto Rico legislature surely could have prohibited casino gambling . . . altogether" and that therefore "the greater power to completely ban casino gambling necessarily includes the lesser power to ban advertising."[35] The appointment of William Rehnquist as Chief Justice and Antonin Scalia as Associate Justice bodes for a pulling back of First Amendment protection from commercial advertising.

Another notable departure from First Amendment immunity has been the statutory requirement that "warning" labels accompany all cigarette advertising. Late in 1985 that requirement was modified to mandate the display of four new labels, to appear in rotation with repetitions of each advertisement. The new labels read: "Smoking causes lung cancer, heart disease, emphysema, and may complicate pregnancy"; "Cigarette smoke contains carbon monoxide"; "Quitting smoking now greatly reduces serious risks to your health"; and "Smoking by pregnant women may result in fetal injury, premature birth, and low birth weight." It is too early to assess the effectiveness of the new warnings. The tobacco industry acquiesced to the four new warnings through a compromise that deleted a fifth and sixth warning that would have stated that smoking is "addictive" and may cause "death." It is quite likely that the Public Health Service will lobby for the "addictive" and "death" labels in its next round with Congress on warning labels for cigarettes.

Given the recent weakening of First Amendment guarantees to commercial speech and the print media, an outright ban of cigarette advertising, such as proposed by the AMA, may sustain a difficult and lengthy court challenge. It is possible, even probable, that such a ban could be held constitutional based on the decisions cited above. Less likely, however, is the AMA's ability to elicit broad public support for proscriptive legislation, given that print space for a full discussion of the AMA's proposal has yet to be made available.

In summary, use of the unregulated mass media to convey the health risks of smoking is severely limited by the tobacco industry's power, via advertising dollars, to minimize the coverage of the negative health aspects of smoking in the editorial content of these media. The tobacco industry's objective may be as much to maintain influence over possible negative editorial content as to promote specific brands of cigarettes. The public's naiveté about the relationship between smoking and health, as evidenced by the surveys discussed in this article, suggests that such a strategy may be effective.

Because of the free press tradition, only a statutory ban on all tobacco advertising would reopen much of the media to messages that educate the public about the hazards of smoking. Such a ban might be argued on the grounds that it is against public policy to expose minors to advertising that promotes an addictive product which causes serious health damage when used as intended. The case, however, would have to be so compelling as to warrant a selective exception to constitutional guarantees that, up until now, have rendered the print media relatively immune from content regulation. As long as cigarettes are legally distributed, then, the prohibition of advertising might be construed as a departure from the spirit and letter of the First Amendment. But the U.S. government might attempt to negotiate a voluntary halt to all advertising with the tobacco industry in lieu of taking harsher steps toward restricting the sale of a product that is the most ubiquitous hazard to the nation's health.

NOTES

1. S. W. Dunn and A. Barban, *Advertising: Its Role in Modern Marketing,* 6th ed. (Hillsdale, Ill.: Dryden Press, 1986), p. 97; P. M. Sandman, D. M. Rubin, and D. B. Sachsman, *Media: An Introductory Analysis of American Mass Communications* (Englewood Cliff, N.J.: Prentice-Hall, 1976), p. 127.
2. Sandman et al., *Media,* p. 126.
3. B. Bagdikian, *The Media Monopoly* (Boston: Beacon Press, 1983), p. 165.
4. Ibid., p. 173.
5. E. M. Whelan, *A Smoking Gun: How the Tobacco Industry Gets Away with Murder* (Philadelphia: George F. Stickley, 1984), p. 93.
6. Bagdikian, *The Media Monopoly,* p. 174.
7. Whelan, *A Smoking Gun,* p. xviii.
8. R. C. Smith, "The Magazines' Smoking Habit," *Columbia Journalism Review* 16 (1978), pp. 29–31.
9. A. Amos, "British Women's Magazines: A Healthy Read?" *Proceedings of the Second International Conference on Health Education and the Media* (London: Pergamon Press, 1985).
10. V. S. Freimuth, R. H. Greenberg, J. De Witt, and R. M. Romano, "Covering Cancer: Newspapers and the Public Interest," *Journal of Communication* 34 (Winter 1984), pp. 62–73.
11. H. Wolinsky, "AMA Mum on Smoking, but Health Groups Burn," Chicago *Sun Times,* January 22, 1984.
12. J. Stacey, Science News Editor, American Medical Association, letter to George Weis, December 7, 1983.
13. C. Loomis (writing for "the editors"), letter to Marilyn Roy, February 29, 1984.
14. C. Burke, letters to Christine Loomis, *Newsweek,* March 5, 1984, and to Kenneth Auchincloss, Managing Editor, *Newsweek,* August 6, 1984.
15. R. D. McGinnis, Chairman of the Board of Directors, American Academy of Family Physicians, unpublished letter to the Editor of *Time,* October 17, 1984.
16. J. Guyon, p. 1.
17. Whelan, *A Smoking Gun,* p. 130.
18. D. Owen, "The Cigarette Companies: How They Get Away with Murder, Part II," *Washington Monthly,* March 1985, pp. 48–54.
19. A. I. Piper and J. Stossel, interviewed by "ABC News: 20/20," October 20, 1983.
20. P. Johns, Public Information Director, American Cancer Society, Washington Division, letter to Chauncey Burke, October 8, 1985.
21. J. K. Pierce, "The Billboard King Hits the Smoke Alarm," Seattle *Weekly,* December 11, 1985.
22. Michael Kinsley, "A Puff Piece for the Tobacco Companies," *Wall Street Journal,* October 9, 1986, p. 33.
23. Pierce, "The Billboard King."
24. Bagdikian, *The Media Monopoly,* p. 175.
25. Joe B. Tye, "Cigarette Marketing: Ethical Conservatism or Corporate Violence?" *New York State Journal of Medicine,* July 1985, pp. 324–327.
26. Federal Trade Commission, *Staff Report of the Cigarette Advertising Investigation* (Washington, D.C.: FTC, 1981).
27. M. Fishbein and I. Ajzen, *Belief, Attitude, Intention, and Behavior: An Introduction to Theory and Research* (Reading, Mass.: Addison-Wesley, 1975).
28. M. Fishbein, "A Theory of Reasoned Action: Some Applications and Implications," *Nebraska Symposium on Motivation* (Lincoln: University of Nebraska Press, 1980).
29. B. Loken, "Heavy Smokers', Light Smokers', and Nonsmokers' Beliefs about Cigarette Smoking," *Journal of Applied Psychology* 67 (1982), pp. 616–622.

30. S. A. Neslin, P. P. Magielwicki, D. Balestra, J. Dulac, and J. Carson, *Advertising and Smoking Cessation: An Experiment in Social Marketing*, working paper, Dartmouth College, 1983.
31. U.S. Department of Health, Education and Welfare, *Smoking and Health: A Report of the Surgeon General* (Washington, D.C.: U.S. Government Printing Office, 1979).
32. J. A. Quelch and P. W. Farris, *Cases in Advertising and Promotional Management* (Plano, Tex.: Business Publications, 1983), p. 310.
33. W. Kronholm, "U.S. Clears the Air of Smokeless Tobacco Ads," Philadelphia *Inquirer*, August 28, 1986, p. 6E.
34. L. B. Schofield, "First Amendment Implications of Banning Alcoholic Beverage Ads on Radio and TV," *Journalism Quarterly* 62 (Autumn 1985), pp. 533–539.
35. Kinsley, "A Puff Piece."

GIVING PIRACY A WIDE BERTH

Jerry Chaney

Plagiarism—the passing off of another person's creative work as one's own—is ethically wrong and subject to legal action. Jerry Chaney, a longtime professor of journalism at Ball State University, defines plagiarism and gives tips on how to avoid committing it.

That plagiarism is most despicable is an often-expressed point of view. The thought in back of this disdain is that authors/creators deserve their fame, and robbing them of it is a dastardly deed.

"Tis a worse sin," stated 15th century writer Gerald Langbaine, "to steal dead men's writings than their clothes."

A judge, in a 1940 unfair competition case in New York, remarked, "In books and plays such initiative acts are called plagiarism; in commercial art and design it is called piracy; in general it is given the colloquial term, chiseling."

A *Wall Street Journal* reporter, in a terse letter to this writer, summed up his view of a plagiarizer: "He's a skunk."

Strong though these condemnations may be, the fact is that not everyone shares the same idea as to what constitutes plagiarism; that it has been defended almost as much as condemned; and that the law protects against plagiary in some instances but not in others.

The *Encyclopedia Americana* (International Edition) has a fairly long statement as to what plagiarism is. In part, it states, "Plagiarism is the reproduction, in whole or essential part, of a literary, artistic or musical work by one who falsely claims to be its creator." The *Oxford English Dictionary* says it is the wrongful taking and publication, as one's own, "of the ideas or the expression of ideas of another."

Many journalists, we should add, feel that the passing off as one's own the news photo of another is plagiarism. Another widely held view in academe is that when someone submits his old work as new work, that is plagiarism, also.

"The infraction," says the *Encyclopedia Americana*, "is not theft of the work itself, but false representation as to source."

Thus, copying another person's work is not the wrongdoing; it's failing to acknowledge the source. We would caution, however, that even if the borrowing is attributed, it may still be piracy, if the work copied is protected by copyright, consent from the copyright holder was not obtained, and the taking did not amount to a fair use.

The word *plagiarize* comes from the Latin word *plagium,* meaning "to kidnap or capture." Apparently, it was at first applied to those accused of stealing people and selling them into slavery. Martial, the Roman epigrammatist, is generally credited with having been the first person to apply the word to stealing literary work.

Since then, many authors and other creative people, particularly those who became well-known, have suffered the ignominy of being called plagiarists. Even the great bard himself, Shakespeare, did not escape it, perhaps not without some justifica-

Source: Reprinted with permission from the 1986–1987 Journalism Ethics Report of the Society of Professional Journalists, Sigma Delta Chi.

tion. In fairness to his memory, and to the memories of many others who have been so discredited, it must be pointed out that envy often figured into the criticism, and that not everyone agreed that plagiarism was defenseless.

Blanket condemnation of plagiarism is a modern phenomenon, but even today, it is sometimes excused as a form of flattery, although this view is difficult to accept, unless the plagiarizer acknowledged his theft from the originator from the outset.

Defense of plagiarism was stronger in earlier times. According to author H. M. Paull, Milton felt that plagiary was justified if the borrower "beautified" the work borrowed, and Roman philosopher Seneca complained that creative people were misfortunate in not being born soon enough to create for the first time the works that their predecessors had already created.

"The history of plagiarism is indeed the history of literature," said Paull in his book entitled *Literary Ethics.* However, he adds that regardless of how prevalent plagiarism has been in any era, or how vigorously defended in any era, it has always been deplored.

For journalists, who live by the trust that the public puts in their work, acts of plagiarism seem totally inappropriate. When such incidents unfold, confidence in the exposed thieves must surely be shaken, if not demolished. But journalists have a treacherous path to follow in trying to find their way to originality, and neither their bosses, colleagues nor the public should be too quick in casting stones at them for the slightest hint of plagiarism.

One obvious mitigating factor in the case of journalists is that they usually have to work under tight deadlines, and they don't always have time to think up fresh ways of expressing themselves. Also, journalists often work from the same set of facts, or in the case of photojournalists, the same picture situations. They are also trained to write in much the same manner, especially when doing a hard news story. Furthermore, journalists often take their information from a common source, such as a press release.

Therefore, the appearance of their work is likely to be similar to that of another, though imitation was never contemplated.

When similarity, without attribution, becomes striking, and can't be explained away as coincidence, the journalist's head is likely to feel the plagiarism axe. Here are some suggestions as to precautions they might take to avoid such pain:

- Writers, if you do take information from someone else's story, check out the facts and try to discover a few new details. This will probably result in your story being sufficiently different, both in content and structure, to elude the finger of suspicion.
- In case of a press release, either attribute the information to the release or wholly rewrite it, preferably including additional information that you dug up on your own.
- Don't quote a source unless the quote came directly to you from the source, or you qualified the quote with such a phrase as, "Smith reportedly said . . . ," or "according to the *Morning Star,* Smith said . . ."
- Don't worry about using familiar phrases, such as "finger of suspicion," or facts generally known, such as the Mississippi flows to the Gulf of Mexico, because they are commonly conceded to be in the public domain. But don't rely too heavily on this. Word-for-word copying, even of familiar phrases and generally known facts, without attribution, can bring a charge of plagiarism, if the copying is extensive.
- Columnists, your writing is expected to be more distinctive than that of hard news writers. Never copy the material of someone else, unless you attribute to the source.
- Photojournalists, try to discover your own picture angles, rather than shooting from the same angle as a competitor. The same angle can't always be avoided, but if your pictures have an exclusive look, it can save a lot of suspicion, and finger pointing.
- Cartoonists, graphic artists, layout editors, originality is a must for you. You may legitimately borrow from the ideas of others, but put your own

interpretation on them, so what you produce has your hallmark. Don't just imitate.

- Copy editors, when combining information from a number of sources, such as from wire dispatches and staff reports, credit all the sources. For goodness sake, don't credit wire stories to your own staff. Your paper or station may have bought the story, but falsely crediting it is a plagiaristic deception.
- Finally, to journalists in general, respect the ideas of colleagues. For instance, a colleague mentions to you a good story idea. Then you run to the boss and say, "Chief, I've got this great idea for a story," not mentioning where it came from. Whether this type of conduct is plagiarism or not, it doesn't make for very cordial relationships in the office.

What can be done about plagiarism? If the work is protected by copyright, the copyright holder can, of course, sue for infringement. But it is not altogether certain whether court relief is available when the work isn't protected by copyright. Prior to 1978, when a new copyright law went into effect, relief was sometimes available under state unfair competition laws, but the new copyright law may have subsumed that legal remedy.

The moral rights doctrine protects the right of authors/creators to have their names associated with their works, and to prevent their works from being substantially altered after having been sold, but this doctrine has been recognized in only a few cases and it may very well have been subsumed by the new copyright law, too.

Remember, though, that whether copyright protection is available or not, or whether some other legal remedy is possible or not, the passing off of another's work as your own is still plagiarism. Studies have shown that editors and publishers are highly prone to fire flagrant or repeated plagiarizers, and they are likely to impose lesser penalties in less grievous cases.

WHY WE SHOULD CHANGE THE LIBEL LAW

Floyd Abrams

An eminent New York attorney argues that the law of libel should be rewritten because it does little to protect reputations and much to deter free speech. He suggests ways to make the law more equitable.

Lying on a desk in a government laboratory near Washington is an article about serious misconduct in the scientific community. The article was written more than two years ago, but you cannot read it. You cannot learn whether some distinguished scientists listed themselves as co-authors of published articles they neither wrote nor researched or whether they should have known that research published under their names contained false or misleading statements. You can neither see the evidence summarized in the article nor decide for yourself whether any of the scientists acted irresponsibly or unethically. You cannot do any of this, ironically, because of the law of libel.

Since the Supreme Court ruled in favor of *The New York Times* in *New York Times* v. *Sullivan* in 1964, no country in the world has offered more legal protection for those wishing to speak out frankly and fearlessly. Yet today, American libel law manages to achieve the worst of two worlds: It does little to protect reputation. It does much to deter speech.

Until *Times* v. *Sullivan*—in which L. B. Sullivan, a city official in Montgomery, Ala., sued the paper for printing an advertisement critical of the local police's handling of civil-rights demonstrators—the Supreme Court had rarely heard libel cases. Since 1964, it has decided more than 25 such cases, with two more to be heard in the term beginning this week.

For all the attention now being paid libel in the courts—including the publicity that attended Gen. William C. Westmoreland's suit against CBS and former Israeli Defense Minister Ariel Sharon's case

Source: New York Times Magazine, September 29, 1985.

against *Time* magazine—too little has been paid to the mad jumble libel has become. Who wins? It depends when you ask. Of cases tried around the country from 1980 through 1984, according to the Libel Defense Resource Center in New York, 70 percent were won at the trial level by those who sued. On appeal, however, the situation was reversed. In 64 percent of the cases, the courts ordered judgment to be entered in favor of the press or ordered a new trial. Altogether, according to a newly published study by the Iowa Libel Research Project, only about 10 percent of the cases brought in the nation from 1974 through 1984 were won by the plaintiffs; another 15 percent were settled, usually without any payment of money.

How much do victorious plaintiffs receive? More than half of all initial libel awards are over $100,000. Yet what juries try to do and what appellate courts permit them to do have little in common. Before 1980, figures from the libel defense center show, only one judgment in American history amounted to more than $1 million; from 1980 through 1984, 20 such judgments have been awarded by trial judges and juries. But the appellate courts have yet to affirm a single one. So far, the largest judgment affirmed by an appeals court has been for $400,000. (Some cases, however, have been settled for far in excess of $400,000.)

If all this makes libel law sound like an odd sort of board game with plenty of excitement but little predictability, consider some of the conclusions of the Iowa study to a different question: Why do people sue? They do not sue, the study says, because they have suffered financial damage, but because they feel emotionally harmed by what was written about them. They do not sue because they wish to obtain large monetary awards, but because they wish "to restore their reputations or to punish the media." Since it is cheap for plaintiffs to sue (almost all agree on a contingency fee with their lawyers that requires no payment unless they win), they sue even though their chances of victory in court are slight. Randall P. Bezanson, a law professor at the University of Iowa and co-author of the Iowa study, concluded that plaintiffs do not "sue to win; they win by suing."

But neither side wins much from the way libel law works today. The law effectively chills both the press and private citizens who wish to speak out on public issues. It does this by imperiling those who cannot afford to risk the possibility of huge court judgments or the certainty of ever-increasing defense fees. From the point of view of most plaintiffs, the law provides a bit of psychic gratification in being in court at all, but little more.

The sole purpose of libel law is the restoration of unjustly lost reputation. That intent needs to be brought back into focus. Among the changes that I propose in this article are steps to encourage publishers to print corrections, limits on damages to amounts actually lost by those who sue, and the adoption of a rule providing that the loser in libel cases should generally bear the costs of the case. With changes such as these, we can avoid inhibiting speech while permitting those who should sue to do so.

As things stand today, libel law too often prevents people from having their say at all, a lesson that two scientists, Walter W. Stewart and Dr. Ned Feder of the National Institutes of Health, have regretfully come to learn.

Their idea for an article arose out of a rare occurrence—an indisputable case of skulduggery in scientific scholarship at the highest levels. A 31-year-old scientist, Dr. John Darsee, had been caught forging data at the Harvard Medical School while he worked on a research project on cardiac function in dogs. Three investigating committees were established to review his extensive research done at the Harvard and Emory University medical schools. Most of Dr. Darsee's 109 published articles proved to contain forged data.

Mr. Stewart and Dr. Feder concentrated their efforts not on Dr. Darsee but on the 47 scientists who were listed as co-authors of the articles. The two scientists prepared a searching article addressing questions about Dr. Darsee's collaborators.

To what degree had any of these 47 scientists, including some of the most distinguished in the field of cardiology, failed to examine papers they had signed? Should they have known that articles co-authored by them contained statements that were inaccurate? By focusing on concededly fraudulent scholarship, the N.I.H. scientists hoped to take a giant step toward assuring greater accountability from all scientists for articles published under their names.

Mr. Stewart and Dr. Feder's manuscript has never been published in the two years since it was written. Several dozen distinguished senior scientists were given a preliminary draft. Most praised it. But an avalanche of lawyers' letters, some more than 50 pages long, descended upon Mr. Stewart and Dr. Feder, the N.I.H. and the small scientific journals to which their article had been submitted. Written on behalf of some of Dr. Darsee's co-authors, the letters threatened libel actions if the article was published. Each time Mr. Stewart and Dr. Feder revised the article and advised the lawyers, new letters arrived expressing dissatisfaction with the scope of the changes. One lawyer's letter to the N.I.H. itself warned that "publication of the Stewart and Feder paper by a journal with national circulation would constitute a separate cause of action for libel in all 50 states."

This month, the two scientists received a letter of rejection from *American Scientist* magazine. Michelle Press, an editor, wrote that it had been "sobering to look" at the "clear and convincing report," but that "we see no feasible way to use it" because "both our publisher and our long-time legal adviser believe that the legal costs incurred would be prohibitive."

I learned of the existence of the unpublished manuscript when Mr. Stewart and Dr. Feder wrote to me asking if I could assure the editor of a small scientific journal "that he will be protected against the possibly ruinous costs of a legal defense if he should be sued." It was "our impression," they wrote, "that this is what concerns journal editors, not the possibility (which we have taken great care to minimize) that our report contains false statements which could make a libel suit successful."

I could give them no such assurances. Nor could I allay the fears expressed to me on a regular basis by not only media corporations but also private individuals unable to pay lawyers to defend them. One tenant-shareholder in Queens contacted me because he had written a letter denouncing the president of his co-operative as a "desperate man" who had engaged in "megalomaniacal actions." The co-op president had responded by suing him for libel. A group of citizens from Ocean Beach, N.Y., while supporting one candidate for mayor, had signed a letter accusing the incumbent mayor of official misconduct. The mayor responded by suing them for libel.

Understandably, the fear of being sued for libel has had the greatest impact on small publications, which are less able to defend themselves. Some of them have simply stopped reporting anything that could lead to a lawsuit. Earlier this year, the publisher of one group of Pennsylvania newspapers, Irvin Lieberman, told the *Columbia Journalism Review* that his papers had simply stopped doing "any investigative work."

"Now," he said, "we are concerned only with births, weddings, deaths and stuff like that."

A small Illinois newspaper, the *Alton Telegraph*, lost a $9.2 million libel suit over investigative work on articles it never even published. Its reporters had forwarded a memo to a Department of Justice investigator raising questions about the plaintiff; the memo became the basis of the lawsuit. The case was ultimately settled for $1.4 million—and was paid by the paper's $1 million libel insurance plus $400,000 it borrowed.

The reaction of the *Telegraph* to its encounter with the libel law was predictable. A *Wall Street Journal* article described a change made in one *Telegraph* story about a theft from a local drunken bartender so that it read—less accurately—that the bartender was "diverted by drinks." "I guess," said the reporter, "we were scared a smart libel lawyer would get hold of it and file a libel suit against us."

Book publishers have also reacted to the potential threat of libel litigation. Jonathan Kwitny, author of a book about the Mafia entitled *Vicious Circles,* published by W. W. Norton, observed in a postscript: "This book was turned down by a major publishing house for the frankly acknowledged reason that the house is reluctant to print works that might attract nuisance libel claims. Other houses have shown evidence of similar fears, and other authors have run into similar problems."

Mr. Kwitny wrote that "a terrible chill has been thrown over the free flow of information in this country by libel laws, by the lack of any consistent court standards of what it's permissible to print (even if one concedes that judges should be able to decide what it's permissible to print), and by the power of anyone to threaten a well-intentioned journalist and his publisher with financial ruin."

The threatening effect of libel litigation is not limited to small publications. Although some larger publications such as *The New York Times* have had no increase in the number of libel suits filed against them, the fear of many publications of appearing at a trial in which enormous sums of money are sought—and sometimes won—inevitably has affected their editorial decisions. Then, too, there are the sizable, sometimes immense, legal costs for defendants. Although the amounts paid to lawyers remain confidential, published reports indicate that the defense in the suit brought by General Westmoreland may have cost CBS more than $5 million. Today, an average libel case costs around $150,000 in legal fees.

An increasing number of public officials have recently sought to use the libel law to deal with their critics in the media. Gov. William J. Janklow of South Dakota has pursued a $10 million libel action against *Newsweek* magazine for an article he claims implied that he had caused, for reasons of personal revenge, the state to prosecute Indian leader Dennis Banks for various criminal violations. Governor Janklow is also suing Viking Press, publisher of the 1983 book *In the Spirit of Crazy Horse* by Peter Matthiessen.

Senator Paul Laxalt, Republican of Nevada, has begun a $250 million lawsuit against the McClatchy Newspapers for articles published in 1983 in the company's California papers about his role as owner of a Nevada casino at the time illegal skimming occurred. Former Gov. Edward J. King of Massachusetts and former gubernatorial candidate John R. Lakian have both sued *The Boston Globe,* Mr. King for libel in feature and editorial articles and cartoons—cartoons!—and Mr. Lakian for articles exposing various misstatements he had made about his personal background. (In Mr. Lakian's suit, for $50 million, the jury recently concluded that the gist of the articles was true and that no error in them had harmed Mr. Lakian at all.)

According to Gene Roberts, executive editor of *The Philadelphia Inquirer,* who testified last June before the House Judiciary Subcommittee on Courts, Civil Liberties and Administration of Justice, 15 public officials are now pursuing libel actions in the Philadelphia area alone. They include two former mayors, five judges, three state legislators, one Philadelphia councilman and one member of Congress.

How much does it all matter? Osborn Elliott, dean of the Columbia Graduate School of Journalism, recently asked a roomful of New York editors some hard questions. "How many editors in this room can honestly say," he asked, "that they haven't experienced at least the tiniest shiver at the prospect of pursuing one story or another in recent months, with the threat of libel suits hanging so heavily in the land? How many can say that no hot lead has been blown cool for fear of incurring a lawsuit? . . . How many have bolstered their news staffs with legal eagles charged with adding cotton wool and qualifiers to certain stories, and defanging others altogether?" Mr. Elliott's own response: "Care and caution are giving way to timidity in newsrooms across the land."

It is impossible to know how many stories or how much information has been lost for fear of libel litigation. But it is also difficult to quarrel with the conclusion of Judge Robert H. Bork of the United States Court of Appeals for the District of Columbia Circuit that "in the past few years a remarkable upsurge in libel actions, accompanied by a startling inflation of damage awards, has threatened to impose a self-censorship on the press which can as effectively inhibit debate and criticism as would overt governmental regulation that the First Amendment most certainly would not permit."

Of course, there is the other side of libel law, which, wrote Associate Justice Potter Stewart of the Supreme Court, "reflects no more than our basic concept of the essential dignity and worth of every human being—a concept at the root of any decent system of ordered liberty." Reputation, in short, matters, and libel law exists to protect people from false and defamatory statements.

Sometimes, libel law has done just that. When John Henry Faulk, a prominent radio and television personality of the 1940's and 1950's, was effectively blacklisted as a result of repeatedly false statements by a publication called *Aware* about his supposed (but actually nonexistent) links to Communist-front groups, Mr. Faulk sued for libel and won. As he should have.

When Westbrook Pegler, the extreme right-wing columnist, viciously attacked—and lied about—the journalist and author Quentin Reynolds in 1949, Mr. Reynolds sued for libel and won. As he should have.

When Carol Burnett was falsely accused by *The National Enquirer* of drunken behavior in public, she sued for libel and won. As she should have.

But these stories are exceptions. Some libel plaintiffs wind up far worse off as a result of their legal efforts than had they never gone to court at all. General Westmoreland must wish that he had never heard the word *libel.* His highly publicized legal assault against CBS, culminating in his abject withdrawal of the case on the eve of its being submitted to a jury, only diminished the very reputation the general had sought to restore.

Other libel plaintiffs have found that even a victory renders little satisfaction. When one hunter sued CBS for its documentary that supposedly implied that he had acted in an unsportsmanlike manner by killing a walking goose, he was awarded $1 by the jury. The physicist William Schockley sued *The Atlanta Constitution* for saying that his controversial theories about the supposed genetic inferiority of blacks were Nazi-like. He got $1 from a jury, too. (Both sides are appealing.)

The most important reason why libel plaintiffs fare so poorly is that the law, in order to protect freedom of expression, deliberately makes it difficult for them to win. Libel law permits plaintiffs to recover damages only if what is said about them is both untrue and defamatory. Truth is an absolute defense in libel cases. The expression of opinion—as opposed to the false expression of fact—is totally protected.

Even when a newspaper prints something defamatory and false about public officials and prominent public figures, the publication cannot be held liable unless it did so knowing that what it said was false or printed something that was false with serious doubts about its truth. If the press were obliged to prove the truth of all it wrote about public officials, Associate Justice William J. Brennan Jr. of the Supreme Court wrote in *Times* v. *Sullivan,* "would-be critics of official conduct may be deterred from voicing their criticism, even though it is believed to be true and even though it is in fact true, because of doubt whether it can be proved in court or fear of the expense of having to do so." Even regarding "private" figures, no recovery may be awarded against a newspaper unless it published material that was false, defamatory and printed without taking reasonable care in its preparation.

When libel law is viewed freshly as an effort of the law to permit people to restore their unjustly diminished reputations—something rarely achieved even with a successful suit—certain conclusions follow as to how the law should be changed. Five changes should be considered:

First, and most important, corrections should be encouraged. If a publication or broadcaster is presented with proof that its report was false and it promptly and prominently corrects the error, no suit should be allowed. As Steven Brill, publisher and editor of *The American Lawyer,* has written, "Our goal, it should be remembered, is to restore reputations, not punish publications." There could be some provisions for a modest monetary award, even if a correction was published, if the plaintiff had suffered out-of-pocket losses in the interim. But if a correction was promptly and prominently published, the most that should be allowed by way of damages is the actual amount lost by the plaintiff as a result of the initial publication.

Second, the risk of damages should be limited. Libel suits should not resemble lotteries in which the chance of success is minimal but in which the image of last year's lucky winner leads to the purchase of yet another ticket to possible financial independence. Damages for emotional injury should have a ceiling. In California, for example, awards for pain and suffering in medical malpractice cases have been limited to $250,000. There is no reason not to limit recoveries from emotional injury supposedly caused by libel—the sort of injury the Iowa project found was invariably the only kind sustained—to a fixed figure of, say, $100,000. Actual losses of income should be allowed up to their total amount. Punitive damages should be abolished.

Third, rules about counsel fees should be changed, to add a note of caution to both sides in a libel case. Unlike the British system, in which the losing party always must pay the legal costs of both parties, the American practice has been that each party generally bears its own costs. Our approach has had the salutary effect of opening the courts to more people; the fear of being responsible for costs is one significant factor that deters the less affluent in Britain from suing. In libel cases, courts should be empowered to impose on the losing side the penalty of paying the legal fees of the winning side if a suit was brought or defended without sufficient basis. The rule need not be rigid and could permit judges a good deal of discretion in deciding when costs should be awarded. Still, the rule, not the exception, should be that the loser pays.

Fourth, libel law should be interpreted to permit the harshest commentary on the performance of those in power. This does not mean that the Westmorelands and Sharons of the world should be barred from suing at all. But the concept of what is "opinion" (and thus not subject to a libel suit) should be interpreted most broadly in cases brought by public officials, leaving critics free to attribute evil motives, unworthy purposes and the like to those in power. In South Dakota Governor Janklow's lawsuit against *Newsweek,* for instance, Judge Richard S. Arnold of the United States Court of Appeals for the Eighth Circuit observed that charges against public officials "that one can hear every day wherever government, state or Federal, is discussed" should be protected under the First Amendment even if they are "ill-tempered or ill-considered." Although "good people may shrink from public office" because of the charges, Judge Arnold wrote, the "framers of our Constitution long ago struck the balance in favor of speech." If Judge Arnold's views are not already the law (and I think they are), they should be.

Fifth, a proposal now embodied in a study bill introduced by Representative Charles E. Schumer, Democrat of New York, should be considered. (It is to be discussed in hearings this fall.) The bill, containing variations on ideas first outlined by Marc A. Franklin, a law professor at Stanford University, would permit a public official or public figure who has been the subject of a publication or broadcast to bring an action which does not seek any monetary damages but simply a declaratory judgment that what had been said was false. At the same time, a libel defendant sued for monetary damages by a public person could "convert" the action to one for a declaratory judgment. The principal issue in such cases would be truth; no issues relating to the state of mind of the journalist or the appropriateness of the care taken by the journalist would be considered.

The effect would likely be a major decrease in the cost of and time devoted to individual libel cases as well as the total amount of monetary judgments awarded. At the same time, the proposal might lead to a major increase in the number of libel cases seeking declarations of truth, an increase leading to still more money being spent on libel cases and more time—perhaps too much time—being devoted to them.

Representative Schumer's proposal, thoughtful and innovative as it is, involves a trade-off for both sides in the libel war. Plaintiffs would lose the chance (and defendants, the risk) of monetary damages. Defendants might find themselves, far too often for their comfort, obliged to defend "truth" suits. Although Federal legislation embodying the proposal is now premature, it would be useful for a state or two to enact such legislation to see how the idea works in practice.

Finally, the constitutional rules established in *Times* v. *Sullivan* should be preserved. Too often in recent years, judicial critics of that ruling have carried the day in writing crabbed and grudging interpretations of that case. In the *Times* case itself, the Supreme Court observed that the purpose of the First Amendment was to assure that public debate was "uninhibited, robust and wide open." A reversal of the decision would go a long way toward assuring the opposite result.

HOW TO USE THE FOIA

Elaine English

The Freedom of Information Act provides access to many government records and has been the source of numerous prize-winning news stories. This article, with its sample request letter, explains how to use the act. Elaine English is director of the FOI Service Center, a project of the Reporters' Committee for Freedom of the Press.

Source: Reprinted with permission from the 1986–1987 Freedom of Information Report of the Society of Professional Journalists, Sigma Delta Chi.

Reporters, scholars, and others who use the federal Freedom of Information Act (FOIA) to gain access to government records are finding that the process can be frustrating and time-consuming. During the last five years, agencies have raised the fees for retrieving records, have become reluctant to grant fee waivers even for requests from media and public interest organizations, and have allowed backlogs to develop so that requests take months rather than days to process.

Despite these problems, the 20-year-old Freedom of Information Act continues to play an important role in providing information to the public, and recent changes in the law—especially in the fee area—insure that role will continue. Reporters continue to make frequent use of the act. In 1986, three Pulitzer Prizes for journalism were given to news series developed through information released under the FOIA—*The Dallas Morning News* series on racial discrimination in public housing in the U.S.; *The Pittsburgh Press* series on organ transplants; and the *San Jose Mercury News* series on the transfer of wealth from the Philippines by former president Ferdinand E. Marcos.

Reporters who want to use the act should become familiar with its procedures and exemptions. Informed reporters file better requests. They can anticipate and often head off potential problems. And they generally have fewer difficulties in gaining access to useful information.

The initial problem encountered in using the act is deciding where to send your request. The FOIA applies only to records in the possession and control of federal agencies. It does not cover the courts or Congress, nor does it provide a means of access to the records of those who perform government contracts or receive other kinds of government funds. There is no centralized system for processing FOIA requests, so you must send separate requests to each agency which has the records you seek.

The FOIA helps only a little in determining what kind of records an agency is likely to keep. You can make an FOIA request for blank agency forms routinely used in gathering certain kinds of information, but often the best means of discovering what information an agency has is to ask. Don't ask what information can be released; merely ask

SAMPLE FOI REQUEST LETTER

Tel. No. (business hours)
Return Address
Date

Name of Public Body
Address

To the FOI Officer:

This request is made under the federal Freedom of Information Act, 5 U.S.C. 552.

Please send me copies of (Here, clearly describe what you want. Include identifying material, such as names, places, and the period of time about which you are inquiring. If you wish, attach news clips, reports, and other documents describing the subject of your research.)

As you know, the FOI Act provides that if portions of a document are exempt from release, the remainder must be segregated and disclosed. Therefore, I will expect you to send me all nonexempt portions of the records which I have requested, and ask that you justify any deletions by reference to specific exemptions of the FOI Act. I reserve the right to appeal your decision to withhold any materials.

I promise to pay reasonable search and duplication fees in connection with this request. However, if you estimate that the total fees will exceed $ ^, please notify me so that I may authorize expenditure of a greater amount.

(Optional) I am prepared to pay reasonable search and duplication fees in connection with this request. However, the FOI Act provides for waiver or reduction of fees if disclosure could be considered as ''primarily benefiting the general public."" I am a journalist (researcher, or scholar) employed by (name of news organization, book publishers, etc.), and intend to use the information I am requesting as the basis for a planned article (broadcast, or book). (Add arguments here in support of fee waiver). Therefore, I ask that you waive all search and duplication fees. If you deny this request, however, and the fees will exceed $ ^, please notify me of the charges before you fill my request so that I may decide whether to pay the fees or appeal your denial of my request for a waiver.

As I am making this request in the capacity of a journalist (author, or scholar) and this information is of timely value, I will appreciate your communicating with me by telephone, rather than by mail, if you have any questions regarding this request. Thank you for your assistance, and I will look forward to receiving your reply within 10 business days, as required by law.

Very truly yours,

(Signature)

SUCCESS STORIES BY USERS OF FOIA

Here is a list of some major news stories published in 1986 that were based on material obtained under the Freedom of Information Act.

SPACE SHUTTLE: After several news agencies filed FOIA requests, NASA released documents revealing the space agency and its contractors wasted billions of dollars, tolerated sloppy work and mismanagement, and knew of the faulty O-rings in the booster rockets that caused the crash of the space shuttle Challenger. The shuttle exploded shortly after liftoff on Jan. 28, killing all seven astronaunts.

KURT WALDHEIM: The World Jewish Congress used the FOIA to obtain a 1952 U.S. security check on Kurt Waldheim. The document, compiled when Waldheim led the personnel department at the Austrian foreign office, showed that Waldheim's activities from 1940 to 1944 were omitted. The World Jewish Congress suspects Waldheim, who served in the German army, of involvement in Nazi atrocities against civilians.

AUTO DEALERS: The *Detroit Free Press*, under the FOIA, gained access to pretrial papers that revealed details of the Federal Trade Commission's antitrust charges against Detroit auto dealers. The FTC accused the local dealers of conspiring to limit showroom hours and to fix advertising prices to deter competition. Several dealers canceled ads in the newspaper in protest.

ROCK HUDSON: *Dallas Times Herald* reporter Bill Barrett used the FOIA to gain information on actor Rock Hudson, who died Oct. 2 of AIDS, a disease that primarily strikes homosexual men. The *Times Herald* learned that the FBI gathered data on Hudson—and his sexual activities—as early as 1960.

SAMANTHA SMITH: The FBI refused to release Samantha Smith's file, which was requested by KRON-TV in San Francisco. The file will remain closed for reasons of national defense and foreign policy, the FBI said. Samantha—the Maine schoolgirl who became a celebrity when former Soviet leader Yuri Andropov invited her to the Soviet Union—was killed in a plane crash in August 1985.

ARMS TESTS: Up to 19 secret nuclear weapons tests were conducted by the United States between 1982 and 1984, according to information released by the Natural Resources Defense Council. The NRDC, a lobby group, gained the information under the FOIA. The undetected tests raise questions about the prevention of cheating on a proposed comprehensive test ban treaty.

ALEXANDER HAIG: *The Washington Post* used the FOIA to gain access to summaries of former Secretary of State Alexander Haig's telephone calls and meetings. The request was made in 1982, when a reporter was working on a story about how foreign policy decisions are made. A federal judge ordered the State Department to turn over the records in April 1986, in response to the *Post's* 1983 suit to gain access to the records.

NUCLEAR ACCIDENTS: The U.S. Navy admitted in January that there had been 250 "incidents" involving nuclear weapons since 1965, but officials said the odds of an accidental detonation are one billion to one. The Navy was responding to nuclear accident information sent to the news media by the American Friends Service Committee—a Quaker pacifist group that obtained a list of nuclear accidents under the FOIA.

RADIOACTIVE CLOUD: The *Portland Oregonian* filed FOIA requests for more information about a 1949 military experiment that sent a radioactive cloud drifting over the town of Richland, Wash. The Department of Energy in February released a 1950 document that said the 1949 experiment "related to development of a monitoring methodology for intelligence efforts regarding the emerging Soviet nuclear program," the *Oregonian* reported.

TRUMAN WIRETAPS: Following World War II, President Truman ordered wiretaps on the home and office phones of Thomas G. Corcoran, an ex–New Deal aide for President Roosevelt. The information was released under FOIA requests filed by writers Kal Bird and Max Holland. Corcoran, who died in 1981, left the government in 1940 to form a law firm that represented corporations in dealings with the government.

RAYMOND PATRIARCA: The *Providence* (R.I.) *Journal,* defying a court-imposed gag order, published a story on New England's reputed mob boss. The story was based on illegally taped conversations released by the Justice Department under the FOIA after the 1984 death of Raymond L. S. Patriarca. The 20-year-old tapes contained conversations between Patriarca and his son, Raymond J. "Junior" Patriarca, who officials say took over for his late father as the region's mob chief.

what kinds of records the agency keeps. Pose these questions to sources you have developed within the agency's various programs or to the public affairs office. Once you have discovered what information is collected, then you can formulate your FOIA request to that agency's FOIA office.

Filing an FOIA request is not a formidable task. All that you must do is put your request in writing and send it to the FOIA office of each agency which has records in which you are interested. Your request should include:

1. State that your request is being made pursuant to the federal Freedom of Information Act, 5 U.S.C. Sec. 552.
2. Reasonably describe the information to which you are seeking access. You are not required to give document numbers or dates, but if you have them, the agency will be able to locate the information more quickly. Try to describe the information as completely as you can, keeping in mind that the person receiving your request will be somewhat familiar with the agency's record-keeping system. Also, remember that your request must be made in terms of documents; the FOI act is not a means by which reporters can get answers to specific questions.
3. You should deal with the issue of fees, even though recent changes which take effect next April restrict agency charges to the cost of copying documents. Under the revised law, the first 100 pages of documents cost nothing. But if you anticipate your request will involve more than 100 pages, there will be some duplicating expenses. Basically, you have three options regarding fees:
   a. You can express your willingness to pay any and all reasonable fees which are incurred as a result of your request, even though ultimately you won't likely be charged any. By doing this, you have promised to pay all fees charged you by the agency, so long as they are "reasonable."
   b. You can say that you are willing to pay up to a specified amount but wish to be informed if the agency estimates that the costs of your request will exceed that limit. In this way, the agency will begin to process your request, but you can withdraw or modify the request if the agency estimates the request will cost more than you wish to pay.
   c. As a journalist, scholar, or researcher, you can ask the agency to waive all fees associated with your request. You should make your case for this waiver even though the recent changes make this virtually automatic. Under the language of the new law, the agency must waive fees whenever disclosure of the information you have requested "is in the public interest and is likely to contribute significantly to public understanding of the operations or activities of the government." You should explain in some detail who you are, why you are making the request, and why you believe the public interest will be served by the information you have requested.

   You should know that sometimes asking for a fee waiver can delay your request. Generally, agencies will decide whether to grant or deny your fee waiver before they begin to process your request. If they deny your fee waiver request, you can appeal that decision; but, of course, that also takes time.
4. Despite the fact that most agencies have backlogs of requests which prevent them from processing any new requests within the law's 10-day time period, it is usually a good idea to remind

the agency that you expect a response within that time period. If for some reason you have a special need for prompt review of your request, you should state that in your initial request. For instance, if you are seeking access to information relating to a candidate for political office and the election is coming up within a few months, you should make it clear in your request letter that you need the information in a timely fashion. The agency may not be able to give your request expedited treatment, but if you want to try to get them to release the information quickly, you need to explain why at the earliest opportunity.

Once you have sent your request to the agency and have given it enough time to arrive at the FOIA office, you should follow it up with a personal phone call. Try to talk to the FOIA officer who will be processing your request. This can be invaluable for several reasons:

- If there are any ambiguities in the wording of your request, you can clarify them at this time.
- If your request is too broad, you can narrow it after you have gained a better understanding of how the agency keeps its files.
- You can attempt to find out how long it should take for the agency to process your request. Try one of two approaches here: either ask for an estimate of time, or ask how many requests are ahead of yours.

Either in your request letter or at the time of your phone call, make sure you give the agency your phone number. Agency staff will then be able to call you if there is additional information which they need, and you won't have to wait for them to send you a letter.

Once you have made your request, don't forget about it. In the processing of many requests, it does happen that an agency will lose track of a specific request. If you keep in touch with it, this is less likely to happen. Also, if months or years go by and the agency has not heard from you, it may think you are no longer interested, and stop working on your request.

The act states that you may go into court if the agency does not respond to your request within the 10-day period. However, if you file suit, the agency will generally answer by explaining about its backlog, and the court will dismiss the suit.

The act specifies exemptions under which an agency may withhold information from you. These protect certain governmental or other interests, such as national security, personal privacy, commercially sensitive information, law enforcement investigatory records, and the like. If an agency denies your request, either in whole or in part (by releasing partially blacked-out documents), you should ask the agency to cite specifically the exemptions which they claim justify the withholding.

You can then consider filing an appeal. Your appeal may simply be a letter asking for reconsideration of your request. If you wish, you can include legal or policy arguments explaining why you believe the agency must release the information to you. Your appeal will be reviewed by a higher-level agency official who may decide to release additional information to you. If you are still denied access to the information after your appeal, you have the right to file a lawsuit in federal district court. If you succeed in compelling the agency to release the information to you through your lawsuit, you can collect your costs and attorneys' fees.

To maximize use of the FOI act, reporters need to understand both the act's potential and its limitations. Rarely can the act be relied upon as the sole source for a story. And rarely will the act turn up information useful to daily, deadline reporting. Rather, it is a tool by which information obtained through other sources can be confirmed or background information gathered. FOIA requests can be used to watch for agency trends or to discover new story possibilities. To use it effectively, reporters must continue to aggressively use the FOI act to gain access to government information. The process is not an adversarial one, but reporters should be diligent in pursuing their right to know.

QUESTIONS FOR REVIEW AND DISCUSSION

1. Enumerate the principal complaints of an ethical nature brought against the news media.
2. What steps have the news media taken in response to these complaints?
3. Should editors withhold the names of AIDS victims involved in news stories? What are the pros and cons of doing so?
4. What problems are involved when a mini-documentary is used as part of a television newscast?
5. What criticisms does Herbert Schmertz levy against the news media? In your opinion, are they justified?
6. Review the circumstances under which a Colorado newspaper publisher was exposed as a long-ago killer of three members of his family. Was this exposure justified? Why or why not?
7. In what ways are newspapers often improved or harmed when they become part of large groups?
8. How does the Public Relations Society of America respond to complaints of unethical conduct made by one member against another?
9. In what ways has the tobacco industry affected the content of the various media?
10. Define plagiarism. What guidelines can you legally and morally follow in using the mass media products of other people?
11. Describe the steps that must be taken in using the federal Freedom of Information Act to gain access to government records.

ESSAY TOPICS

1. Discuss your reaction to the report of the Attorney General's Commission on Pornography. Did the report go far enough? Too far?
2. Discuss changes in the libel law that could be considered to permit people to restore their diminished reputations and at the same time lighten the burden of lawsuits brought against the media. In your opinion, which changes are most feasible and fair?

One can obtain "niche" video titles concerning just about any subject imaginable in department stores, supermarkets, convenience stores, bowling alleys, dance studios, and dozens of other outlets.

— Jim Bessman
in "Video Takes Over Main Street"

Several experts interviewed by *presstime* estimate that as many as three-fourths of all daily and nondaily newspapers in the United States and Canada are using at least one personal computer somewhere in their operations.

— Rosalind C. Truitt
in "Use of Personal Computers Soars"

Say you've got a singer and a tape rolling in L.A., and another singer in NY connected by a satellite back to L.A. The signal from L.A. goes to the satellite, about 20,000 miles up, and 20,000 miles down to the NY studio. That takes the radio signal about a quarter of a second at 186,000 miles a second.

— Dr. Buzz Bently
in "Stevie Wonder
Records by Satellite"

A world of instantaneous news militates against careful, rational decision-making. Numerous forces will push journalists to the limits of good sense, good taste and decorum.

— Jay Black
in "Tomorrow's Journalism: New
Technology, New Ethics?"

PART

THREE

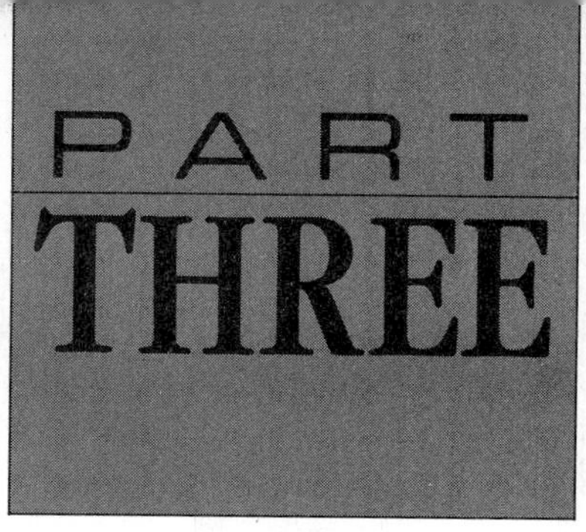

THE TECHNOLOGY REVOLUTION

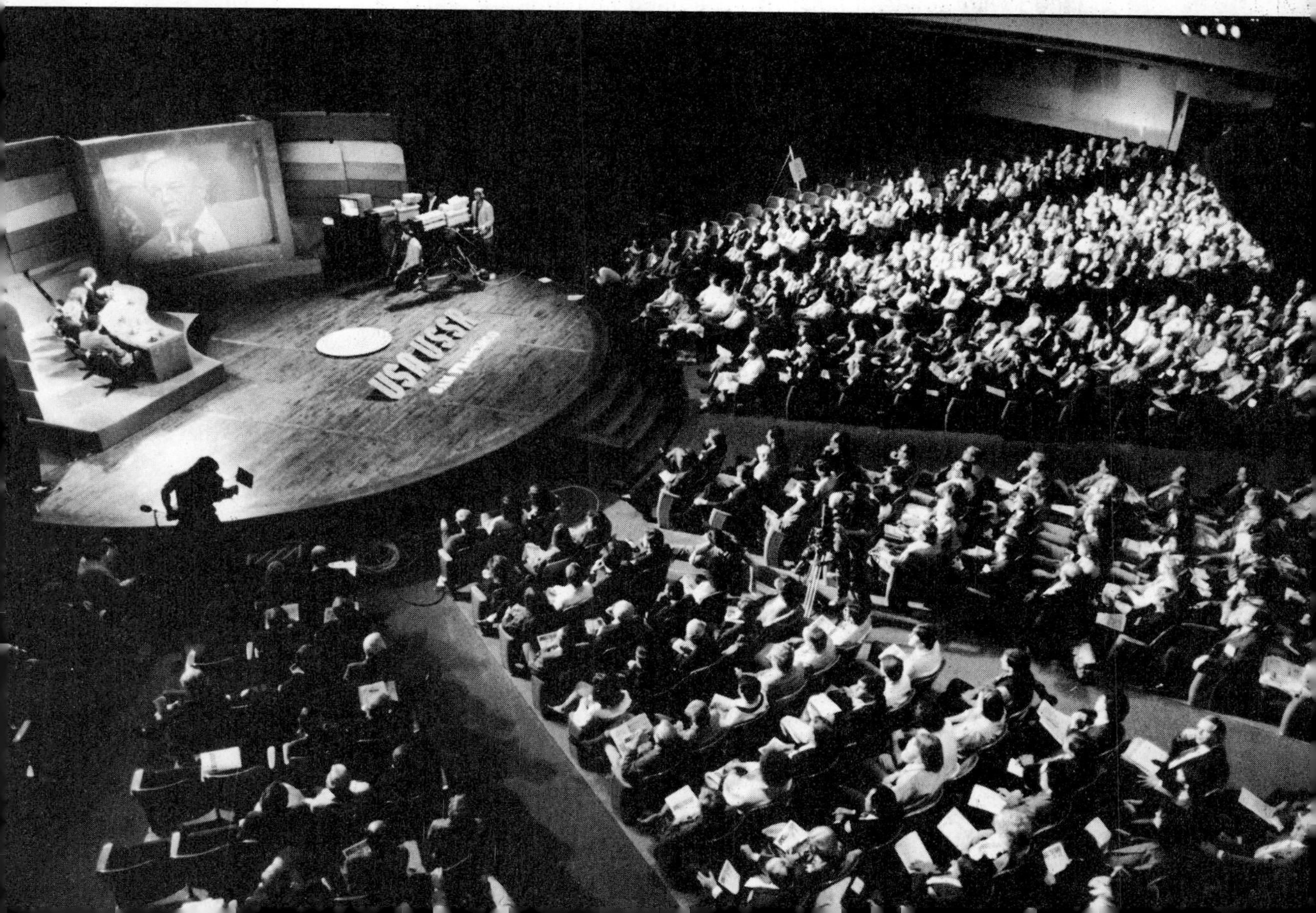

INTRODUCTION

PHILLIP H. AULT

Four American journalists seated onstage in an auditorium atop Nob Hill in San Francisco peer intently at a huge television screen. On the screen, Soviet journalists in Moscow appear, asking questions of the Americans and in turn guardedly answering the Americans' queries. The panelists and the audiences watching them in each country hear the discussions in their own language, through instant translation by skilled interpreters.

The tone of the international interchange is professionally inquisitive, laced with occasional politely phrased nationalistic barbs.

This debate, illustrative of the startling advances in mass communication technology, was possible because of satellite transmission. Only a handful of years ago, the process of bouncing TV signals off an artificial object in space was regarded as a far-out experiment, figuratively and literally. Today it is commonplace.

Within one lifetime—primarily within the last 30 years—our ability to transmit information and entertainment has magnified so enormously that we have become blasé about it. Snatching pictures from satellites hanging in space appears simple when the viewer merely needs to touch a button on a TV.

Beaming a television signal up to a satellite, then down to earth, has important advantages over point-to-point earth transmission. Interference by mountains, large buildings, and similar obstacles is eliminated; the microwave frequencies used make the signals relatively immune to atmospheric distortion. The satellites are placed 22,300 miles above the equator, the height at which a satellite's orbital speed equals the rotational speed of the earth. In effect, the satellite is in a stationary position.

Because of the popularity of satellite transmission, this heavenly parking lot is becoming somewhat crowded. By 1984 there were 16 U.S. and Canadian satellites in orbit for North American transmission, and the Federal Communications Commission authorized 20 more American satellites. As a result, plans were made to reduce the distance between satellites from the original 4°—approximately 1,838 miles—to 2°.

Home satellite reception through backyard receiving dishes is a maverick offshoot of cable television, which in turn developed from the original over-the-air television and took away part of its audience. A more structured form of direct home reception, called *direct broadcast satellite* (DBS), is emerging as a potentially important commercial reception method that may in turn make inroads into the cable television business. This evolution, brought about almost as much by happenstance as by calculation, exemplifies the ever-changing, complex, and often unpredictable nature of the technology revolution to be examined in this portion of the book.

Among the unexpected beneficiaries of satellite transmission is the public television system, which has enlarged its audience and obtained fresh sources of income. The audience has grown because public television programs are carried on local cable systems; the picture cable viewers see is better than the one sent over the air by most public stations. Financially, the benefit has come because in 1978 the Public Broadcasting System built a multichanneled satellite interconnection system to serve its stations. Today, with this system, PBS earns extra money by leasing parts of its excess capacity, transmitting videoconferences for a fee, and selling other profitable transmission services while at the same time distributing its public television programming.

Technology has further altered the way in which people receive broadcast material by wiping out the constraints of time with recording equipment. Thanks to the *videocassette recorder* (VCR), the viewers, not a station program director, decide when they will watch a program. With sales of videocassette recorders skyrocketing, the full commercial and sociological impact of this capability is not yet clear.

Recent technological developments are bringing still another change: a significant reversal in the *control* of information flow. Traditionally, decisions as to what information to transmit to recipients have been made by the sender. The editor of the local newspaper decides which news stories and features to publish; the managements of television and radio stations make similar decisions in broadcasting. Magazine editors and the editors of book-publishing houses select the material that goes into the publications they offer to the public. The recipient has had to accept what is offered by these sources or do without.

These decisions by the gatekeepers are not necessarily arbitrary; the media conduct extensive research to determine what their various audiences desire to receive. Of necessity, however, the decisions are mass decisions. Being engaged in the mass communication process, the gatekeepers cannot isolate and seek to fill the precise needs of each individual.

The new technology is reversing that process for the information-seeking individual. *Information on demand* has come into being, opening an immense new vista. By using new electronic tools, the recipient, having decided what information he or she wishes to obtain, presses a button or two, orders the material, and receives it. The passive recipient has turned into the active decision maker.

THE COMPUTER IS THE KEY

The spectacular developments in communication have been brought about primarily by the digital computer. The computer in its many forms makes possible satellite transmission; high-speed typesetting that has transformed the production of newspapers, magazines, and books; creation of national newspapers in the United States; electronic mail; name selection and personal addressing methods that have created an enormous direct mail selling business; development of on-demand information services, and the linkup of homes by keyboard to the outside world, a capability whose significance is only beginning to be comprehended.

Let us look briefly at what the technology revolution has brought about in the media.

Newspapers Systems of video display terminals (VDTs) connected to a main computer and personal computers have completely altered newsrooms. The stories reporters type appear on screens at their desks; once completed to the writer's satisfaction, a story is put into computer storage until called up on an editor's screen for checking and approval. Reporters in the field—at a football game or a plane crash, for example—can connect their portable computers by telephone to the home office and file stories direct from the scene. The processing of news stories is thus speeded enormously.

Newspapers receive their news from other cities by satellite transmission, from a news service computer directly into a newspaper computer as fast as 9,000 words a minute, ready for instant typesetting. Paper has almost disappeared from the newsroom.

Just coming into commercial use is another form of electronic wizardry called *full pagination.* This enables an editor using a keyboard and screen to lay out an entire newspaper page, placing electronically prepared stories and pictures in their desired positions, then transmit the page to a machine that turns it into a lightweight plate for the printing press. All this is done without a sheet of paper or the hands-on work of a printer in the composing room. The lead type that printers once put together in page form has vanished, and printers themselves may become a dying breed, except for specialized tasks. Control of the type-preparation process has moved into the newsroom.

A combination of computer and satellite has made possible the creation of international daily newspapers as well as national American dailies. The pages of one of these newspapers are prepared in one printing plant, then transmitted by satellite facsimile to widely scattered plants for simultaneous printing and regional distribution. The barrier of distance, which traditionally restricted quick distribution of a daily newspaper to a relatively limited area, has been wiped out.

At *USA Today,* for example, after a page is made up at the home plant, a full-page positive proof is scanned by a laser beam; the contents, thus converted into a digital bit stream, are beamed to a satellite. A transponder on the satellite retransmits the material down to 26 earth receiving stations. These receiving points feed the material into the presses of adjacent printing plants. The *Wall Street Journal,* the New York *Times,* and the *Christian Science Monitor* use similar methods.

In an electronic feat with significant implications for the future, *Corriere della Sera* of Milan and *China Daily* of Beijing exchanged front pages by satellite in late 1984 to focus attention on an international exhibit of communication "hardware" in Beijing.

Going even further, visionaries have predicted that the printed newspaper will eventually disappear. They see it being replaced by the electronic newspaper—that is, electronic delivery of news, advertising, and features into the home to be read on the television or computer screen.

Although the physical capability for such delivery exists, at least in a limited way, the public has shown little interest in having such an electronic newspaper. Research has disclosed that many people prefer to hold a newspaper in their hands, as they have done since childhood. The time and effort required to watch stories unfold on the screen, block by block of words, discourages them. Receiving equipment is expensive, and buying an electronic newspaper would probably cost more per copy than the newsprint variety. The electronic newspaper must still demonstrate its value to the public.

One way of delivering an electronic newspaper would be by *teletext.* This is coded information transmitted over the vertical blanking interval of the normal television broadcast, decoded by the home television set, and shown on the TV screen as words and graphics. Purchasers of teletext service may choose the items they wish to view from a "menu" shown on the screen. The viewer becomes a selective receiver of news, reading only the stories that interest him or her. That, in fact, is precisely what a newspaper reader does normally, skimming the headlines and reading the stories of interest.

To date, teletext may be described as a technique in search of a market. Any significant growth of the audience for teletext will depend on the manufacture of teletext decoders in new television sets and reduction in the cost of decoders.

Broadcasting The great surge of the technology revolution in radio and television *transmission* is virtually completed, at least for the near future. Refinements will occur, but the upheaval of the past two decades is unlikely to be duplicated.

The challenge and uncertainty today can be found at the *receiving* end. How will the material transmitted by satellite be distributed to satisfy best the desires of viewers and earn the profits for purveyors necessary to keep a system operating?

By traditional over-the-air television networks? Network audiences are shrinking because of competition from cable television and other sources.

By cable? Approximately half the homes in the United States received cable television in 1988, but the rate of expansion has slowed; cable operators and networks feel resistance to the prices charged for some services. With at least 20 channels being offered to viewers in most areas, and 50 to 100 in certain cities, reception capacity far outruns the availability of new programming. Cable viewers are seeing reruns of movies and other material that resembles over-the-air station fare. Fortunately, a substantial amount of exclusive cable material, much of it excellent, is being provided to offset this torrent of the routine. Yet many urban areas are still not wired for cable because of high construction costs, and installation has slowed.

A key question remains unanswered: How much cable service will viewers pay for? Once the novelty has worn off in newly wired areas, how willing are viewers to pay the quite large additional monthly fees cable operators charge for the supplemental services they offer beyond a basic cable package?

The newest form of television distribution is called *low-power television.* The Federal Communications Commission authorized creation of hundreds of TV stations operating on such low power that each can serve a radius of only 10 or 15 miles. A few hundred of these stations have begun operation. They do not interfere with the standard very high frequency (VHF) and ultra high frequency (UHF) stations. The types of programming and audiences low-power stations will develop remain uncertain.

For television news operations, the greatest single technical improvement has been the creation of videotape. This magnetic recording method has replaced film in field news reports and in many other uses, providing greater speed and flexibility. Tape can be edited quickly and can be reused, an important economic consideration.

Motion Pictures Videotape has had a lucrative and rather unexpected impact on the marketing of motion pictures. For decades, entertainment films were shown primarily in theaters. With the arrival of television, old movies shown on TV found a new audience and a new source of profit for their makers. Next, cable television provided additional outlets for the standard theater-type films plus films made especially for the TV screen.

The big surprise, however, was the astounding success in the mid-1980s of the videocassette versions of motion pictures. Customers either purchased or rented the cassettes for play at home on their VCRs. No longer did those desiring to see relatively new movies have to go to a theater; they could watch the films at home on videocassettes or cable television. The videocassette market has become about equal to the theater box office as a revenue source for the motion picture industry, a fact that will undoubtedly influence the kinds of films Hollywood will make.

On-Demand Information Another term for this is "computer-based information retrieval." Databases have been developed that store huge amounts of general information, news, and technical material in their computers. Operators of suitably equipped business and personal computers can dial a database by telephone and have their computers plugged into the stored-up mass of information. By using computer commands and certain reference procedures, they can search the database for the specific information they desire. It will appear on the computer screen. The adapter that enables a computer to communicate over telephone lines, calling databases and performing other transactions, is called a *modem.*

To cite one example of the immense amounts of information available for call-up, the Nexis database contains the full text of 25 newspapers and news services, almost 100 magazines, and 60 abstracted periodicals.

Such a cornucopia does not come free, of course. The user of a database pays a monthly membership fee or is charged by the minute for computer time used, or in some cases both. Telephone line charges are additional.

Availability of such information on demand is one reason for the explosive increase in popularity of the personal computer, along with its capability as a word processor, financial calculator, message sender, game player, and teacher. The computer's potential for carrying out personal business transactions is only beginning to be developed.

When a number of computers are tied together so their operators can exchange messages and share information, the activity is called *networking.*

It is evident that an entirely new level of communication has emerged in our society, operating independently of the traditional mass media distribution system but depending on it as the source for much stored-up information.

Fiber optics, a system of transmitting pictures, voices, and data by laser-generated light impulses through fine strands of glass at astonishingly high speed, has become a vital new factor in telecommunications. Fiber optics makes the old system of electrical impulses through copper wire seem slow and limited. Use of fiber optics permits such wonders as transmission of 12,000 telephone conversations simultaneously through a single strand of glass. Researchers predict that within a decade or two, fiber optics will be the fundamental earth transmission system, combining various telephone, television, and personal computer services into a single conduit.

THE "THINKING" COMPUTER

The next giant step in the technology revolution, of untold potential if it can be achieved, is creation of a computer that possesses artificial intelligence (AI) and solves problems by reasoning. Today's computers, marvelous as they are, are limited to storing data and calculating. Those that Japanese and American researchers in particular are trying to create will be able to reason, learn from experience, and inform. Such devices are known as fifth-generation computers.

Some limited applications of artificial intelligence are already in existence, but the computer that will do the things its developers hope to achieve lies tantalizingly in the future. In the words of Patrick A. Winston of the Massachusetts Institute of Technology, "It's like being at Kitty Hawk when the Wright brothers' plane took off."

The selections that follow examine in more detail the accomplishments of the technology revolution and some of the problems it has created.

INTERACTIVE JOURNALISM BY COMPUTER

Mike Greenly

Individuals exchanging news and comment through a link-up of personal computers have created a loosely knit form of communication called interactive electronic journalism. Using his personal experiences, Mike Greenly explains how it works.

I suppose I am living testimony to the dangers of reading a book. Only a few years ago I proudly reigned as a marketing vice president of Avon Products, Inc., the largest beauty company in the world and the most powerful direct seller of any product or service.

Then I discovered Alvin Toffler's *The Third Wave* and careened back from vacation having devoured the book. I put a 16-page memo on the chairs of all Avon's key executives: Read it or sit on it. "The future is coming, the future is coming, and we've got to be there!"

By that time, 1982, I had earned a fair amount of respect at the company. Before I knew it, Avon had bought me a computer, printer, assorted software, and a modem. ("Here, Mike. Learn about the technology and tell us what you think.") What I learned was that I had to be part of this new world. I did the bravest thing I'd ever done as an adult: I quit.

I had seen from the software I was using, with both the products themselves and the documentation, that too many products were created by "techies" for other techies. Instructions weren't clear enough. On-screen usage patterns weren't intuitive enough. I quit Avon to offer my hard-earned marketing and communications skills as a consultant to the world of technology. Ironically, it was in the first week of my new life that I discovered an unexpected passion: interactive electronic journalism.

I had already become a regular user of computer conferencing. Avon had bought me a subscription to The Source, where I began to use the *Participate* conferencing system in electronic global "meetings." The magical speed and ease of my own learning helped seduce me away from corporate life.

A radio executive from Iowa, for example, started a public conference about his medium. From this man, whom I still have never met, I learned about cellular phone technology. It was amazing to ask naive questions and get back full and courteous replies from this man and from other radio experts in other locations. Finally I got up the nerve to host my own meeting. *The New York Times* stimulated my curiosity with a story about the greenhouse effect—before long, scientists and laymen were exchanging ideas, explanations, and grim humor in an electronic salon whose doors I'd personally opened.

ACCIDENTAL JOURNALISM

By the time I left Avon, I had already bought my own small computer for travel. It had become unacceptable to be long out of touch with the

Source: "Interactive Journalism and Computer Networking," *The Futurist,* March–April 1987. Reprinted with permission from *The Futurist,* published by the World Future Society, 4916 St. Elmo Ave., Bethesda, MD 20814.

minds that had become a part of my life. In my first week as Mike Greenly Marketing, I attended "Comdex," the huge Las Vegas computer show. This trade event was a way to study a technological industry up close. With me came my portable computer. Almost by accident, I started sending back reports: what news was hottest, what competitors pushed the hardest, what I overheard through the circus-like din on the floor.

Reader response surprised me. One of the values of computer conferencing, for a journalist reporting to his audience or an organization solving a problem, is the opportunity for fast responses. In the case of my experimental reports from "Comdex," I'd return to my hotel room and find responses to my earlier observations. I found queries for my next trip to the exhibits ("Mike, can you stop by IBM?") and answers by some readers to others' technical questions. I also found enough praise to make me realize I'd tripped over something of interest.

From that week on, I began visiting events, inviting readers to come along via computer. I obtained formal press credentials because, indeed, I had a following to whom I offered my reports. Not just my own attempts at journalism, but *interactive* journalism, since people could write back to me and electronically converse with each other. From Apple's launch of the Macintosh computer to a number of other hardware and software events, I did my best to offer in-depth coverage that would not normally be available via conventional media, including what it really felt like to experience a particular event.

ELECTRONIC JOURNALISM CATCHES ON

One flattering consequence of my work was a conference called "Electronic Journalis." (The software allowed no room for an additional *m* or *t* at the end of the topic name.) A California consultant kicked off the public meeting with his belief that what I was doing had future significance—but what *is* that significance, he wondered. He invited readers to submit their forecasts for how this new form of journalism would evolve.

Before long, we had visions of giant flat screens on living-room walls, with dial-up text to supplement pictures for an extra fee. *Time* magazine or CBS News would create an adjunct computer conferencing channel when computers became more popular. Private individuals and companies would hire Mike Greenly–type observers to attend trade shows or symposiums, answering questions with custom reports.

Meanwhile, it was delightful to observe others experimenting with the medium as well. David Rodale from Emmaus, Pennsylvania, created a series of reports called "Weekend." Rather than report on a formal news event, David invited readers to share a weekend he spent as a house guest. He let us in on meal preparations and the banter with his host and hostess, Frank and Jean. He was a talented writer, and before long he had an avid group of readers sending messages to his friends as they, in turn, discovered computer conferencing through David. Was it "journalism"? Not in the sense we are accustomed to. But there wasn't an existing word to describe experiments in reporting like David's.

Along with many others, I wanted to push the conferencing medium further, especially in the direction of non-tech applications. Successful experiments, many still going on, included self-help group meetings—electronic links among people trying to quit smoking, drinking, or overeating.

Diane Worthington started a group called "Tough Love," based on an organization for parents with difficult adolescents. I attended and wrote about events more populist than computer shows: a major toy fair for retailers, the Academy Awards, and interviews with authors and actors using questions solicited in advance from readers. I placed my interview with Vincent Price, for example, in a continuing series of articles called "Mike Magazine," which now appears on three different conferencing networks.

CONVENTION COVERAGE

One of the more memorable experiments for me was an effort launched by Diane Worthington, Sherwin Levinson, and myself. We decided to become the first people in history ever to officially cover political conventions via computer conferencing. Diane lived in San Francisco, Sherwin in Atlanta, and I was in New York. We threw ourselves into the project only a few months before the Democrats were to meet in July 1984.

The three of us were on totally different schedules, but we created various electronic conference rooms in which to hammer out preparations. We used computer conferencing not only to plan for ourselves, but to help us gain financial contributions from The Source, Participation Systems, Inc., and Apple, who lent us computers.

One of the biggest problems of this venture was getting press credentials. The Democrats had never heard of "Diane, Mike, and Sherwin." So we became the Transcoastal Electronic News Service (TENS). By now, several hundred people knew of our quest to accomplish a news-reporting first. People phoned and wrote to congressmen and senators, asking that TENS be credentialed for the sake of a brand-new medium.

It worked. *The Wall Street Journal, Christian Science Monitor,* and various other media covered the appearance of this new form of journalism at the 1984 conventions.

Especially interesting to us was the reaction of politicians—from precinct worker to senator—as we demonstrated computer conferencing. Several quickly realized the opportunity of the new medium for enhanced productivity of political volunteers. The fund-raising captain of Montana, for example, could hold one set of meetings with local precinct captains around the state while separately sharing ideas and techniques with other captains from other states.

The truth is that computer conferencing, like other communications media from telephones to TV, can be used to share as many kinds of information as the language will permit. It is both limited and blessed by the particular technology it requires—a computer or terminal, a modem, the software—which offers the power to surmount both time and distance.

Because of those high-tech requirements, I became particularly interested in exploring high-touch applications of the process. The most recent example of my efforts has to do with AIDS.

WRITING A BOOK BY COMPUTER CONFERENCE

One night in early 1985, I noticed that my doctor, Ron Grossman, looked tired and drawn. "What's the matter with you?" I asked him. "AIDS," he replied.

At that time, most of what I understood about the disease came from scary 30-second news items on TV, or cursory readings of scientific discussions in *The New York Times.* Grossman explained that caring for AIDS patients is unusually demanding of his time and emotions, because of the horrible consequences of the disease itself and because of the fear and inhumane treatment that people with AIDS must endure. As my doctor spoke, I realized there was an important, hidden story that needed to be told.

I started a conference on *Participate* on The Source called "Chronicle." It was kind of a one-way bulletin board on which I'd post my notes and observations as I had them. I opened a branching conference called "Chronicle Public," which acted as a meeting room among "Chronicle" readers for discussion of the experiences and people I wrote about. Both were available to the general public.

My first note was an interview with Grossman. He drew a chart of the natural progression of epidemics in medical history. I reproduced it with X's and hyphens on my keyboard. Suddenly, I began receiving the most encouraging reader feedback I'd ever experienced.

People were not only grateful for an up-close look at the human side of AIDS, but they began contributing ideas and leads for future interviews to add to the story. A reader in Washington sent me the name of her friend whose lover has AIDS. I would not have made the contact without her. A reader in San Diego suggested I interview a condom manufacturer, which I hadn't considered. A physician helped me interview married bisexuals leading secret lives. I could not have told their stories without the conferencing medium to help me find them.

READER FEEDBACK

In numerous ways, computer conferencing helped me write what eventually was published as *Chronicle: The Human Side of AIDS.* Reader appreciation itself was a powerful motivator for me. It led me to pursue this story with a zeal I would not otherwise have mustered. I traveled to Paris to interview the scientist who first discovered the AIDS virus; to San Francisco to see the doctor who heads the most famous AIDS ward in the world; and to Indiana to see a heterosexual young mother suffering from the disease and an evangelist who says it's God's punishment for "the brutish ways of men." I spent about $10,000 and six months pursuing such stories and was encouraged every step of the way by readers, most of whom I've never met.

Sometimes the material shocked them—male and female prostitutes, heroin addicts, a five-year-old child with AIDS. But what gratified me enormously was participants' willingness, through the conferencing medium, to be open to such material as I discovered it myself. Perhaps the computer offered safety, those on-line being able to read these experiences in privacy or even anonymity. Maybe being able to share reactions with others offered support. I just know that I began to receive inspiring notes from people saying the interviews were of value—which, in turn, made me more determined than ever to press on.

Eventually, I got requests from an additional conferencing system, Unison, to "port" some of the interviews there. A priest in Vancouver asked for permission to print the notes for his parish. A few weeks later, he told of a nurse in his congregation who'd taken the interviews to her hospital. She and other staff members on the ward had originally been against the idea of treating AIDS patients. Once they obtained a more personal view of the real situation, they changed their minds.

A Tennessee doctor on The Source announced that he had just treated his first AIDS patient. He said he knew he had offered more humane care as a result of the interviews. Other readers congratulated him on being able to acknowledge his own growth. He went further, however, in his support of the material. He brought *Chronicle* to the attention of Roche Pharmaceuticals. As a result, Roche purchased 6,100 copies of the hard-cover book for distribution to oncologists and infectious disease specialists—what a wondrous result from electronic networking.

WHAT'S NEXT?

I don't know where I'm personally headed with this "hobby" I've been pursuing. I'm actually beginning to be paid for some of my computer journalism. Networking and World Information (NWI) of East Hartford, Connecticut, asked me to do some exclusive coverage of the World Future Society's 1986 conference, "FutureFocus." I expect to continue earning my living as a consultant rather than a writer, but I'm glad to see a communications system back its vision with money to help stimulate a new medium.

What's particularly interesting about NWI, as a matter of fact, is a potentially key factor in computer conferencing's growth. Through agreement with MCI International, NWI has become the first communications service to link a computer conferencing system *(Participate)* with the more than 2.1 million telex machines around the planet. This link creates an opportunity for truly *global electronic meetings* for any organization that could benefit from the time and money saved by convenient idea exchange and communication without travel. An organization that routinely sends telexes to multiple locations can now save money by sending the communication only once—to the electronic "meeting" that each location has "joined." Replies could be made available to all other (or selected) locations, all accessible via telex in countries where PC development is limited.

NWI's link of PCs and telexes for conferencing is only the start of how computer conferencing capability can be used. NWI recently commissioned Steve Gibson, inventor of the Gibson Light Pen, to develop special software to communicate graphic images via telex. It's going to be interesting to track the evolution of graphics in combination with computer conferencing, both from NWI and other companies in the field.

I'm proud to help move a new communications medium forward. I'm sure that as people and organizations discover the inherent power of the tool—not just for new forms of journalism but for real productivity of an organization—much more growth and innovation is still to follow.

USE OF PERSONAL COMPUTERS SOARS

Rosalind C. Truitt

Personal computers have achieved a prominent place in media technology, and their importance continues to grow. Rosalind C. Truitt, technical writer for *presstime* magazine, describes what these versatile little machines can do and how newspapers use them.

Although their use is growing, personal computers remain a supporting player at most newspapers, with "dumb" video display terminals and central computers still holding center stage.

However, all indications are that PCs will continue their rise to star billing in the newspaper business. As experts are quick to point out, the little machines are versatile, relatively inexpensive, easy to use, capable of storing increasingly large amounts of data, and processing that information faster all the time.

"Personal computer use is more and more common in newspapers, and the use will continue to grow," says George Cashau, ANPA director/technical research.

"I don't think we can turn around at this point and go back to one-use terminals," says William D. McKenzie, systems analyst for the Antelope Valley Press of Palmdale, Calif., a four-days-per-week paper that circulates 53,000 copies in Los Angeles and Kern counties.

"It's too easy to bring in a Macintosh or [other] personal computer and sit it down on the corner of your desk to do computations—and all of the other things a one-use terminal can't," Kern says.

As the trend toward PCs evolves, smaller newspapers are using them in just about every department and for most all computing functions. Larger publications are using them for more individual, specific tasks—graphics, for example—while continuing to rely on big computers for many chores.

However, that may be changing. Experts say the rise in use of PCs is having impact on makers of the big, central systems. John W. Iobst, ANPA manager/computer applications, sees "steady" growth ahead for personal computers at newspapers because many publications believe the stand-alones are a good choice to replace worn-out VDT systems.

The Seybold Report on Publishing Systems assessed the use of personal computers at newspapers earlier this year and concluded: "Surely, everyone must realize by now that PCs are *the* central fact for everyone involved in newspaper systems. You cannot ignore them. They are not going away."

Several experts interviewed by *presstime* estimate that as many as three-fourths of all daily and non-daily newspapers in the United States and Canada are using at least one personal computer somewhere in their operations.

Future Computing Inc., a Dallas market research firm that compiles statistics on computer usage, last year conducted a demographically balanced survey of 100,000 households. It indicated

Source: "PCs," *presstime*, April 1987. Copyright © 1987 by *presstime*, the Journal of the American Newspaper Publishers Association. Reprinted with permission.

that 21 percent of workers in the publishing industry—including newspapers, magazines and books—use personal computers on the job. In addition, another 14 percent predicted they would be using a PC at work within a year.

Future Computing estimates 242,000 personal computers are currently in use in the publishing industry.

Popularity of PCs is reflected in sales of the units, which have soared in the past six years. International Business Machines Corp., which has the largest share of the market, has sold more than 3 million personal computers. Apple Computer Inc., which claims to be selling about 50,000 Macintoshes monthly, sold its one-millionth "Mac" earlier this year. The company estimates 50 percent of U.S. newspapers will have "some type of Macintosh system" by the end of the year.

Sales of personal computers should continue to grow at a rate two to three times that of mainframe systems and minicomputers over the next several years, according to International Data Corp., another research firm that tracks computer sales and use. A mainframe is a large computer that controls the flow of data between a dozen or more "dumb" terminals. A minicomputer performs similar functions but generally is smaller, governing fewer terminals.

There are many reasons personal computers continue to make headway in the newspaper business as well as in other industries. Chief among them is that central-computer systems are known to "crash" from time to time, incapacitating each and every workstation. That can't happen with stand-alone PCs, even if they are linked in a network. When something goes wrong, the bad unit is simply unplugged and a good one is substituted while repairs are made.

Another PC advantage is that they are substantially cheaper per workstation than a mainframe system. A PC usually costs a few thousand dollars at most, while a complete mainframe-based system can average out to $10,000 or more per terminal.

And, of course, there's now a love affair going on between smaller publications and PCs because of what has come to be known as "desktop publishing"—using PCs and a laser printer to produce plain-paper copy at far less expense than phototypesetting systems. While smaller papers are using the technology to produce text and ads for paste-up, larger ones generally have more modest applications. For instance, the *Star-Ledger* in Newark [N.J.] uses Macintoshes to create promotional materials for potential advertisers and others.

In addition, unlike a regular computer workstation, a personal computer offers almost unlimited versatility. It can serve as a text-editing terminal, do complicated spreadsheets, handle mailing lists, calculate bills, process the payroll, keep schedules and perform numerous other tasks.

Features that one newspaper department uses often come to be embraced by others.

For example, accountants find spreadsheets useful in the business office. But investigative reporters like George P. Rodrigue of the *Dallas Morning News* use such software to analyze statistical data for stories. With information gleaned through a computer analysis, Rodrigue and colleague Craig Flournoy won a 1986 Pulitzer Prize for stories showing that public housing tenants were being discriminated against according to race. . . .

The Downside

But as with most new-technology ventures, the world of personal computers is not a perfect one. A number of problem areas have cropped up as PCs are put through their paces in a workaday environment.

Experts say one of the biggest problems is that the rise of PCs came almost too quickly. People began buying them without regard for whether they might be compatible with other PCs being used in the same building. "This new technology grew so fast that before anyone realized it, it was almost too big to manage," says Donald P. Ruthig, circulation systems manager for the *Los Angeles Times*. . . .

Also on users' problem lists are lingering glitches in the networking of multiple PC units. Some newspapers say they have encountered occasional difficulty in sending data from the host computer to another PC.

PCs' champions do not regard any of the problems as insurmountable. . . . And on the networking problem, PC advocates say "protocols"—the rules and formats for conducting communications on a large network—can usually be devised to resolve it. . . .

There is no doubt that the use of personal computers will continue to increase at newspapers and elsewhere for one simple reason: A lot of people say the smaller machines make their jobs a great deal easier.

"Speaking for myself and not for the *Los Angeles Times,* as a user I like personal computers," says Circulation Systems Manager Ruthig. "It simplifies things for me. I can do my own thing when I want."

TOMORROW'S JOURNALISM: NEW TECHNOLOGY, NEW ETHICS?

Jay Black

Does the use of portable computers in the field create ethical questions for reporters? Professor Jay Black, Chairman of the Department of Journalism at the University of Alabama, believes so. He describes problems that may arise in the processing of news when reporters work with high-speed equipment.

One ramification of the communications revolution we rarely hear discussed, but one we would do well to consider, is that the drastic alterations in how we communicate with each other in the future may quite possibly revolutionize the very definition of what it means to be a journalist. At base, some important ethical questions are raised.

VDTs and mini-cams are standard equipment for today's journalists. Satellite dishes adorn nearly every news outlet, print or electronic. Novel and intriguing in their own rights, they are merely the outward signs of a revolutionary system that will soon link almost all of us, everywhere, in a gargantuan electronic and computerized global village.

Buck Rogers telecommunications devices are becoming increasingly commonplace in American and European homes. Satellite and cable-fed messages are now being received on microcomputers interfaced with television screens and printers. Dow Jones, Knight-Ridder, Warner-Amex and other media companies are experimenting with two-way, interactive systems that allow instantaneous and customer-controlled delivery of news, information, entertainment, banking, security, mail delivery and direct marketing of a great many products.

The life of the journalist is already changing as a result of this electronically enhanced neovideo world.

Who knows how many senior journalists are abandoning the frenetic profession, frustrated by a technologically complex craft that some see as dehumanizing the product? Some computer phobics, slow to adapt to sophisticated newsroom technology, have suffered from psychic displacement. Some have retired early, some have changed jobs, some have taken their years of insights and journalistic experience and found themselves out of sorts in a newer, faster-paced news world where mastery of technology may be replacing empathy and communication skills as determiners of success.

Consider the ethical questions that arise in this new world of 24-hour-a-day instant news.

Younger, dexterous reporters, out in the field with mini-cams or portable VDTs, are ever closer to the finished news product, and thus, ever closer to their audiences. Given little time for reflection in this deadline-every-minute business, and given the added pressures of competition from broadcast and print outlets, the reporters will grow increasingly hungry for a "good story," one with graphic

Source: Black revised his article, "New Newsroom Gadgets Bring Ethical Problems," in the 1984–1985 Journalism Ethics Report of the Society of Professional Journalists, Sigma Delta Chi, especially for this book.

impact. Decisions about which stories are newsworthy, which ones can be told objectively and which ones permit inferences or value judgments, will have to be made quickly and decisively by journalists whose decisions affect thousands if not millions of audience members, yet who are cutting their professional teeth in the field, learning while doing. As journalism grows inevitably to be a younger person's career, there will be an increasing number of scenarios in which field reporters will be forced into making the kinds of gatekeeping decisions previously handled only by grizzled veterans. Good intentions of youth notwithstanding, we are reminded of a truism from the literature of psychology and moral development: It is only with years of experience, of routinely working through professional and ethical dilemmas, that one develops an individual sense of social responsibility and empathy.

A world of instantaneous news militates against careful, rational decision-making. Numerous forces will push journalists to the limits of good sense, good taste and decorum—not to mention standards of libel and invasion of privacy—in their eagerness to scoop the competition with instantaneous, live reportage of disasters, accidents, terrorist activities, politicos putting their feet in their mouth, etc.

What's to stop journalists from initiating negotiations with news sources on society's fringes—militants, terrorists, kidnappers, hijackers, drug runners and the like—given journalists' ready access to the action and given that through the reporters, who are wired directly to their news media, the newsmakers are assured of a clear channel to the world's eager audiences?

Because fewer gatekeepers will stand between the newsmakers and the news product, won't there be a tendency for journalists to begin behaving like common carriers? The more like television and radio the newspapers try to be, the greater the likelihood that such a situation will come about even in the traditionally slower print medium. After all, research and development people are already perfecting ink jet laser printing systems that will eliminate the need to stop the presses to update a story; hand-held portable VDTs will soon be linked to miniaturized, perhaps umbrella-sized satellite up-link antennas that are about to permit users to communicate instantaneously, with audio, video and print, with anyone anywhere.

(Of course, the linkage between the field reporter and newspaper readers will be streamlined enormously once the newspapers abandon their antiquarian belief that a newspaper must, by definition, be printed on expensive and nonrenewable paper and delivered through an incredibly cumbersome system that hinges ultimately on the working condition of a 12-year-old's bicycle. But that, as they say, is another story.)

Once the electronically blipped, direct-to-the-home newspaperless medium comes into widespread use, the responsibilities of the copydesk-layout-typesetting-pasteup-proofreading-production gatekeepers will be greatly diminished, meaning the reporters will be drawn inexorably closer to the finished product and thus to their audiences. The cycle will be continued: This again will call for more responsible, mature decision-making on the part of the news gatherer. Indeed, the evidence we muster suggests that the merger of the print and electronic media, and the growth of the information society, will demand more, not fewer, skilled journalists.

Reporters and editors will need ever greater empathy with news sources and news consumers, as the nature of the journalism business changes. When interactive, two-way telecommunications links between home and newsroom become commonplace, special interest consumers will be demanding specialized and in-depth news coverage, and general interest consumers will seek a more broadly based daily news budget. Satisfying the needs of such disparate audiences will be difficult.

At the same time, reporters and editors will have to be more highly skilled at rapidly recognizing and processing news according to the traditional 5Ws and H, but with more attention on the why, on explaining causes and effects of events and issues (even if the majority of news consumers seem quite satisfied to slide along on the surface of events). As indicated above, this will intensify the dilemmas of having to recognize when it is appropriate to not merely report, but also to pass judgment on the news.

A very real danger is the possibility that the sexiness of this new communications environment, of this neovideo age, may mean that people entering the journalism field may be doing so for the wrong reasons. Instead of coming to a career in journalism with an old-fashioned commitment to communicating in depth, they may be attracted to the craft because they have been smitten by the technological marvels, the glamour, the hype, the ego rushes inherent in what is sometimes sarcastically called "The Star Syndrome" of being on television.

We will all lose if some of the tyrannies endemic in television journalism—the golden throat, the bouffant, the orthodontic dazzle—are rewarded at the expense of substance.

Once the local newspaper sees its task as competing for audiences with local and network and cable and direct broadcast satellite television, the reporters might feel pressure to compete physically as well as journalistically with their video colleagues. If this is the case, there may logically emerge a new ethic in journalism, a value on form over substance. (In some strange way, it may already be seen in the case of *USA Today.* The satellite-fed national newspaper resembles the freshman student at a fraternity or sorority rush party, who tries desperately to be something for everyone, and, in the process, becomes very little for anyone. Sadly, too many local papers are indiscriminately imitating *USA Today*'s showmanship and splashy use of color graphics, while forgetting that the Gannett corporation has invested millions in pinpointing its audience's needs and interests.)

The stress on gimmickry, on electronic wizardry, on instantaneous dissemination of news and opinion, may create new priorities in the education, training and employment of journalists.

At a minimum, the new communications environment would appear to call for a back-to-basics movement in the classroom and newsroom, and a greater need for continuing education of mid-career journalists.

From their freshman year, journalism students should be taking a substantial courseload in the arts, humanities and social and physical sciences. Their cries for ever larger doses of journalism skills courses, especially courses in the use of the latest state-of-the-art technology, should not sway educators from insisting that students have come to the university for an education and not for training in technologies that will be changing more rapidly than universities can possibly upgrade their facilities. In short, there should be an emphasis on coping with abstractions, not merely with hardware.

Editors seeking to hire young journalists should continue to stress the values of a general education. Obviously—and recent statistics bear this out—prime jobs should be given to those capable students who have served internships and demonstrated their abilities to put theory into practice, who combine intellectual curiosity with craftsmanship.

Once they have been hired, they should be rewarded for making good judgments, and not solely for meeting deadlines. The "system" should put technology in its proper perspective. A loyalty to readers, listeners and viewers should take precedence over a love affair with equipment.

Likewise, editors and publishers should make it easier for mature journalists to return to the classroom, both as teachers and as students, and media educators should pursue opportunities to return to newsrooms on professional internships. Values and priorities of both groups invariably get a worthwhile adjustment when occupational roles are reversed.

The issues raised here are ethical ones at base, for they ask us to consider what it means to be a fully functioning member of the new information society. The communications revolution means much more than the deployment of new technology. It may very well mean that we have to redefine the place of journalism in society.

VIDEO TAKES OVER MAIN STREET

Jim Bessman

The sale of videotapes has spread far beyond the stock of movies in the neighborhood video shop. Tapes on hundreds of subjects are reaching the public in specialty stores. They tell how to play the guitar, identify birds, enjoy wine, tune a car, and do a great many other things.

It was January in New York, and I could only watch *Golf My Way,* a Christmas present to myself, so many times before running out to the Richard Metz Golf Studio indoor driving range to see whether you really can learn from video. There, amidst the gloves and club covers in a glass case, was not only my recent acquisition but a selection of golf videotapes, most of which I'd never seen in my local video store.

According to co-owner Suzanne Metz, at least one of a dozen or so titles a day have been purchased in the year the store has carried them. She now expects to increase inventory through new golf-tape distributor contacts made at an Orlando trade show. The studio also promotes itself to passers-by, screening Al Geiberger and Patti Sheehan tapes when not using its VCR equipment to tape students' swings.

Video in the pro shop may have been a surprise, but it really shouldn't have. A few blocks over, the Scribner's bookstore on Fifth Avenue had a full window devoted to 25 titles in Home Vision's "Portrait of an Artist" series, along with smocks, paintboxes, and palettes. There were also several videocassettes in the window of Music People, a music-instruction boutique in midtown. Inside were perhaps 70 titles opposite the cash register, ranging from a $29.95 guitar instructional to a series of music business-related titles ($40 per tape) to an $80 exploration of the drum kit.

"A lesson from a good teacher can cost $20 an hour," notes owner Danyale English. "The videos offer four months of lessons, and after three or four repetitions they pay for themselves. It's definitely the way of the future."

Source: Video, May 1987. Reprinted with permission.

Ah, the way of the future. In home video, that future stretches way beyond the bounds of the traditional video specialty store, and as a stroll in any big city will confirm, this future is now. One can obtain "niche" video titles concerning just about any subject imaginable in department stores, supermarkets, convenience stores, bowling alleys, dance studios, and dozens of other outlets. Videos are also available through mail-order catalogues, periodicals, and various TV programs. Tapes are everywhere!

Steve Wolff, president of Stevron, Ltd. in Hazel Crest, Ill., says his *Bowling with Don Johnson* ("not Don Johnson from *Miami Vice,* but the bowler!") reaches alleys through bowling product distributors in addition to mail-order sales via specialty magazines. Sherry Smythe-Green, who produces the Kathy Blake *Let's Learn How to Dance* line of dance instruction tapes in Antrim, N.H., says her 22 titles can be found at Blake's studios, as well as in video catalogues, thus sparing her (mainly male) customers the agony of admitting to video store clerks that they don't know how to waltz.

AUDIENCE HUNTING

"It's like being a detective," states Michael Weiss, manager of tape marketing for Los Angeles' J2 Communications, discussing how he markets such "alternative" non-theatrical video titles as *Chef Paul Prudhomme's Louisiana Kitchen,* Phyllis Diller's *How to Have a Money-making Garage Sale,* and the *Mother Goose Video Treasury* series. "You have to find specific areas of distribution where a specific product works and then get that product into them."

As VCR penetration approaches the 50 percent level, adds Weiss, "a lot of stores that have adopted a wait-and-see attitude are willing to go farther with video than before." Thus, J2 has been able to place *Prudhomme* in gourmet shops as well as food

Video stores carry large selections of entertainment and factual films for rent or purchase, as this picture shows, and titles of specialized interest may also be obtained at such outlets as dance studios and bowling alleys.

and housewares sections of such major department stores as Lechmere, Macy's, and Neiman-Marcus. Weiss hopes to put the Diller tape in hardware stores and the Mother Goose in toy stores, though both are sold in video and book shops and mass merchandise outlets.

As Best Film & Video's Roy Winnick notes, you don't sell carpet in a butcher store. Moreover, today's hit movie tape may be largely forgotten in a matter of weeks. These maxims have formed the basis by which Best has successfully marketed a wide variety of long-lived special interest videocassettes to specially interested consumers. In 1983, when Winnick brought out *John Gnagy's Learn to Draw* in a package containing paper and pencils, he found that traditional video stores weren't interested in his sale-only title. So he went to art supply stores, and later landed it in the drawing-kit section of that year's Sears-Roebuck Christmas catalogue.

More recently, Winnick turned to sports with such titles as Charlie Lau's *The Art of Hitting .300,* which was sold in sporting goods stores and through *Inside Sports* magazine. Benihana cooking cassettes, elaborately packaged with companion cookbooks, have appropriately found their way into bookstores, gourmet shops, elite mail order catalogues, and, of course, the Benihana restaurants. *Play Bridge with Omar Sharif* is available through bridge clubs, supply houses, gift shops, and mail order.

Richard Stadin, president of New York–based MasterVision, is another manufacturer peddling his wares to specific customer bases well outside the bounds of video specialty stores. "With special interest product, water seeks its own level," says Stadin. Case in point: a pair of bird identification tapes, *Audubon Society's VideoGuide to the Birds of North America: 1* and *Ducks Unlimited's VideoGuide to Waterfowl and Game Birds.* "I just got a call from a bird-watching nature shop in Tennessee," reports Stadin. "We're in all kinds of these shops, even governmental ones run by park departments. This applies to every tape I have of special interest, be it karate, biology, language, history—

there's general distribution, catalogue availability, and special environment."

This year, a new "special environment" is Bank of America, which Stadin notes is offering his *Touche Ross Video Tax Guide* to new accounts. Similarly, Al Reuben, Vestron Video's senior vice president of marketing and distribution, says his company is testing the use of videos as premium items. "Tapes can be used to induce someone to purchase another product if the tape subject is related to that product," he says, suggesting that Vestron's *Let's Go Mets* could be given away to New York Mets season ticket buyers. (Incidentally, the video is carried at Shea Stadium concession stands.)

Goodman Enterprises is already marketing *Just for Kicks* soccer instructionals for kids, parents, and coaches as premiums. Regularly priced at $19.98, each tape is available for $11.50 and two boxtops from specially-marked boxes of Kix cereal. The National Soccer Coaches Association of America is promoting the tapes; the equipment manufacturer which co-sponsored the video is also distributing them to sporting goods stores.

NEW VIDEO VENUES

Where else can video be found? Simon & Schuster Software is aiming the *Palm-Aire Spa's Seven-Day Plan to Change Your Life* directly at spas and health clubs, and through health and exercise product distributors. *Fresh Start: 21 Days to Stop Smoking* is sold through local chapters of the American Cancer Society, and offered by the Bureau of Business Practices via direct mail and telemarketing to corporate managers enrolling in "Stop Smoking" efforts. *How to Enjoy Wine* is carried by wine-related equipment and merchandise specialty catalogues.

Karl-Lorimar's *Consumer Reports* home improvement tapes are in hardware store chains, like Ace and True Value, as well as builders' supply houses. Other Karl specialty titles are likewise distributed to appropriate markets. Esther Williams' *Swim Baby Swim* is in swimming pool equipment stores; the Minnesota Fats tape can be found in billiard shops; and Warren Miller's ski tapes are in ski shops. While the company's Jane Fonda exercise tapes are everywhere, Sales V.P. Gary Hunt surprisingly reports their greatest success is in grocery stores, especially Denver's King Super, where they were promoted along with Weight Watcher's food ("Take weight off with Weight Watcher's and keep it off with Jane Fonda") and in a six-week period sold more copies per store than any other outlet in the country.

Over the past year, Hanna-Barbera Productions, the studio that created the Flintstones, has used a network of religious and secular organizations, all outside the usual video store channels, to distribute its animated series. *The Greatest Adventure: Stories from the Bible.* "Distributors are so enthusiastic about it, they're even buying air time after we supply them with commercials and an 800 number," says Sales and Marketing Director Larry Klingman. The cassettes—which have already sold four hundred thousand copies—are just now being offered to video specialty stores for the first time, in response to rising consumer demand. The company's unusual marketing strategy has employed door-to-door salesmen, book chains, religious book stores, direct mail, TV and radio advertising with 800 numbers for ordering, and tape-of-the-month clubs.

Indy ace Rick Mears' *Tune-up America* car care series is already in 150 automotive outlets around the country; executive producer Bill Maloney hopes to crack the big auto part chains, home improvement centers, and sporting goods stores.

Kids, meanwhile, can find video galore in toy stores, with countless low-priced titles doing major business. Adults can buy video for themselves in museums. For example, Kartes sells its six volume art history set, *Museum Without Walls,* to museum gift shops. Another specified marketing area for Kartes is lawn and garden centers, where the new *Yardening* garden and lawn care how-to series will be distributed. It will even be sold to agriculture offices in county government seats, for use as public reference. Meanwhile, the 34-store Flower

Time chain in Long Island, New York is renting arts and crafts tapes and will soon carry gardening videos, including a full line from the Ortho Chemical Company.

CATALOGUING TAPES

"I work from 8 A.M. to 7 P.M. and after I get home and eat dinner I'm too tired to go to the video store," says Bob Jeggers, director of acquisitions and product development for the *Video Schoolhouse* catalogue. "But I can easily order from an 800 number." One hundred thousand copies of the current catalogue have been circulated to stores, schools, and consumers, who learn of it through small ads in newspapers and magazines. Most of the 5,000 titles offered are of the educational and instructional type rarely found in the typical video store.

Steve Troy, whose Norstar catalogue carries major studio movie titles but "specializes in the alternative market because those needs aren't fulfilled by traditional distributors," currently services 15,000 retailers, plus schools and libraries, which take "anything and everything" from classic movies to educational how-to's and, inevitably, popular films. American Express offers its cardholders a video purchase service as well. In addition to catalogues, home video shopping is also now possible through tape-of-the-month clubs like the CBS Video Library and Time-Life Home Video Club.

Another new way to distribute video is vending machines. Mariann Christensen, operator of 24 Chicago-area Video Vendor machines, installs them in large grocery stores and mass merchandisers to generate traffic. One is in a hospital in Des Plaines for employees working the night shift. Video stores section them off in 24-hour access areas to compete with convenience stores.

Even with this seeming glut of videos and access points, there's a whole other subgenre available: tapes made to promote specific products or services. Food Forum, a New York–based advertising/marketing company, distributes an Indian food cooking cassette. The tape, which demonstrates and advertises Sharwood food products, is available at some West Coast supermarkets and gourmet shops, as well as through *Cooks* magazine, where, for $25, readers can order the tape and a bag of samples. (Without the goody bag, the cassette costs $12.95.)

THE FINAL NOTE

According to Lou Berg of Houston's Audio Video Plus store, video merchants are being forced to promote their merchandise better by creating more excitement within their stores. Tim Fry, president of the Congress Video Group, feels video stores must expand the type of merchandise carried. "For the video specialty store to survive, it needs to buy broadbased, family-interested videos and offer a breadth of catalogue in contrast to the 7-Elevens," says Fry, whose company manufactures sports, fitness, fabric, and other specialized titles for marketing primarily to mass merchant accounts. "The major studios' theatrical pricing has gone so high that they can't compete any more with convenience stores when it comes to major movie titles, so they must regain their identity by offering more of our kinds of videos."

WHAT ZAPPED THE ELECTRONIC NEWSPAPER?

Gary Stix

Only a few years ago, some media specialists predicted that the electronic newspaper—news delivered on a screen—would replace the traditional printed newspaper. This revolution failed to materialize in the United States. A senior editor of *Computer and Communications Decisions* explains why.

A turning point for Knight-Ridder in its ill-fated venture as publisher of a home news-and-information service came on Halloween in 1985. A Halloween party was held at which subscribers to the

Source: Reprinted with permission from the *Columbia Journalism Review,* May-June 1987.

service, called Viewtron, sat at home at their computer terminals and typed back and forth, describing to each other their imaginary costumes. There was the Mummy, Frankenstein, even Elvira, Mistress of the Dark. The winners of the best-costume award were a couple, each member masquerading as one side of the split personality of the protagonist of Alfred Hitchcock's *Psycho.* The clear loser was Knight-Ridder.

The eager response from subscribers—Viewtron logged one of its best nights—made Knight-Ridder realize that what people liked to do best with the service had nothing to do with reading up-to-the-minute news on a computer terminal. "We saw that the only way to make it [in this business] was to develop skills we didn't have and develop services to which we couldn't add anything better than the next guy down the block," says Reid Ashe, who was chairman of Viewdata Corporation of America, the Knight-Ridder subsidiary set up to manage Viewtron. It took another five months for Knight-Ridder to announce that it would scrap the service. The total bill: $50 million.

Knight-Ridder was only one of a number of big media companies which, just a few years ago, had hoped to remake the news-and-information business with new technology. Their optimism grew out of research by think tanks and management consultants suggesting that services like Viewtron would transform society. "Individuals may be able to use videotex systems to create their own newspapers, design their own curricula, compile their own consumer guides," predicted a 1982 report prepared for the National Science Foundation by a California organization called the Institute for the Future. A study by management consultants Booz Allen & Hamilton predicted that by the middle of the next decade home-information services would bring in revenues nearly 50 percent greater than the $20 billion raked in by daily newspapers in 1982. Acknowledging the birth of a trend, the cover of *Fortune* magazine's November 14, 1983, issue proclaimed: "Coming Fast: Services Through the TV Set."

It was not so clear that people would take as readily to electronic news as to other services. An AP test of an electronic home news-and-information system found that games, not the eleven newspapers available to participants, were the main draw. But even when publishers had doubts, they were driven to push ahead for defensive reasons: if they didn't start feeding information into homes, capital-rich phone and computer companies would take their place. Electronic Yellow Pages could provide timely information about products or services that could potentially sap vital classified advertising. John A. Scott, chairman of the Gannett Foundation, told a 1981 college commencement audience: "If newspapers lose the advertising base of their publications to the point that they no longer can be profitable, then we will observe an erosion of press freedom because newspapers will have to seek subsidies."

The new electronic services were of two kinds: videotex, which allows a subscriber with a terminal or a personal computer to retrieve information stored on a service provider's computer; and teletext, which, by contrast, sends "pages" of information over a television signal. In most teletext systems, the viewer then selects a news item by pressing a hand-held keypad.

The new business promised a potentially huge new source of revenue. Not only could videotex deliver news and information; it could also permit customers to pay bills, order ballet tickets, and book travel reservations. Says former Viewtron editor John Woolley, "I think we felt we were developing a new medium and that it had the capability of dramatically changing the way people received information, shaped and transacted business, and communicated." Delivering news electronically, instead of on paper, would also be cheaper. "Newspapers were coming out of the nineteen seventies worried about the oil crisis and the price of pulp rising," says Gary Arlen of Arlen Communications. "There was a concern that the physical production of the newspaper could become prohibitive."

In the end, however, nearly every foray into electronic publishing for the home failed—or is in serious financial straits. In 1981, at least 125 newspapers had plans to launch such ventures, according to Arlen Communications, a Bethesda, Maryland, research firm that has tracked the industry since its inception. Today fewer than twenty are left. Many that remain operate with little or no revenues. Besides Knight-Ridder, those that have departed include Time Inc., NBC, Times-Mirror, and The New York Times Company. Knight-Ridder wasn't the only big loser: Time Inc. dropped $25 million and estimates of Times-Mirror's losses reach as high as $30 million. Most other companies were more cautious and registered much smaller losses.

Knight-Ridder's Viewtron was by far the most ambitious venture into electronic publishing, and its history tells a lot about the reasons why, to date, the electronic newspaper has been a failure. Planning began as early as 1976. Field trials in Coral Gables took place in 1980 and 1981 and were carefully evaluated. Knight-Ridder asked again and again about content and costs. "Almost all people in Coral Gables liked it and said they would pay for it," says Knight-Ridder president James Batten. By the time the service came to market, estimates of Knight-Ridder's expenditures ranged from $17 to $26 million.

The service was launched in south-eastern Florida, Knight-Ridder's home base, in October 1983. Using a terminal supplied by AT&T, Viewtron subscribers had access to the full text of *The Miami Herald*'s news section and much of what came across the Associated Press wire, plus selected stories supplied by *The New York Times.*

Stories were updated throughout the day. Freed from the constraints of a fixed news hole, editors would let a long AP story go through with only light editing. A Viewtron subscriber might have to plow through twenty screens of text to get to the end of a story. "It was no more costly to us to put an entire story up than to put part of it on," says Woolley. "In fact, it was less expensive because we didn't have to edit it down."

Viewtron also tried to satisfy an assumed interest in community news, supplying information on events too local to make one of the *Herald*'s eleven zoned editions. The service, called Micronews, allowed subscribers to get police reports on incidents in their own neighborhoods. Terminals set up in schools allowed pupils to create their own stories and school administrators to post the week's lunch menus. Other sections offered the type of articles found in the back of a newspaper—tips on restaurants, lawn care, and stain removal. An experts' forum that included everyone from municipal officials to horticulturists could help answer questions as esoteric as how to rid ficus trees of aphids. Subscribers could also bank, do their Christmas shopping, or check on a plane schedule.

Despite such a carefully crafted strategy, subscribers reacted to videotex as if it were a new toy or appliance rather than a replacement for a daily newspaper. "We found usage dropped off dramatically after the first couple of weeks," Woolley recalls. "There was a sizable amount of novelty in the service. But there was no component that we could find that was addictive." The attrition rate for new subscribers reached 60 percent during an early phase.

In sum, the expectation that subscribers would want an up-to-the-minute service with all the detail of a daily newspaper proved erroneous. Few, except editors and other news junkies, wanted a home wire service. Subscribers used it primarily for a quick fix. "They might come to it for ball scores or stock prices or if they wanted to know whether something happened in the news," Woolley says.

Reading text on a computer terminal, moreover, took work. The Viewtron subscriber often had to wade through a hierarchy of indexes and sub-indexes to get to a desired story. The process was considerably less intuitive than just throwing the front section on the floor to get to the sports section. "My eyes can move through a section of a paper a lot quicker than they could ever go through a data base," says Charles Carlon, a former Miami subscriber.

Another major challenge was the creation of an affordable service. Viewtron had set itself the daunting task of convincing Miami-area residents, many of whom had never touched a computer, to purchase a $600 terminal made by AT&T. Besides buying the equipment, a subscriber had to pay $12 a month in fees and a $1-an-hour charge to the phone company. The bill for a monthly subscription to *The Miami Herald,* by contrast, is $8.20.

Only 1,000 terminals were sold; even after the service was repackaged to allow customers to lease terminals and subscribe—first for $40 a month, later for $25—interest flagged. Says Viewtron editor Woolley: "Arguably what was going on was that newspapers, radio, and TV had defined the price level for news and this medium was coming in way above that price level with nothing unique. As many of my colleagues at the *Herald* pointed out, the newspaper only costs a quarter."

A year after Viewtron's debut, there were only 2,800 subscribers, a few more than half the number the company had projected. Viewtron management tried a series of promotional gimmicks. "Dutch auctions" were held in which the price of a car or a computer would drop until someone made a bid. "I think at one time we sold a trip to a periodontist," Woolley recalls ruefully. "It wasn't a big seller."

One problem seemed to be that subscribers could not use Viewtron if they happened to own one of the IBM, Apple, and Commodore personal computers that were flooding the market. In the spring of 1985, the company made an attempt to solve this by allowing Miami-area customers to gain access to the service with personal computers equipped with modems. Even that didn't help. Once again, although people expressed intense initial interest, their continuing use of the service was desultory.

Without a subscriber base, the only way to sell the service to advertisers was to argue that they owed it to themselves to get experience with a new medium, a pitch that produced only a trickle of income. "We never got ad revenues above the cost of sales," says Reid Ashe, chairman of the subsidiary set up to manage Viewtron.

For a brief period before it went dark, Viewtron was marketed nationwide to personal-computer owners at the relatively low rate of $5.40 an hour during evenings and weekends. Some 21,000 signed up. But for many of these the chief attraction of the service seemed to be that it enabled them to communicate with other subscribers. The anonymity of the service allowed the shy to appear bold, the old to become young. Inhibitions were quickly set aside and so was Knight-Ridder's role as an objective observer of modern life. Subscribers were offered such real-life dramas as threatened suicides and collapsing marriages. And there was always the gleeful subscriber who avoided the prohibition against obscenities by typing "s**t." Viewtron staffers were posted to monitor the service, an anomalous position for a First Amendment defender. "Our rule was that if you heard it on *Johnny Carson,* you could let it go," explains Christine Leberer, an editor who was occasionally called upon to chase down offenders. This was not the news business. On March 31, 1986, Knight-Ridder turned Viewtron off.

Teletext, the other medium that caught the interest of news providers, seemed a simpler, less expensive enterprise than videotex, and thus more likely to succeed. It makes use of existing broadcast facilities, avoiding big investments in computers and complex telecommunications facilities. For users of the service, there are no monthly fees. They pay nothing beyond the cost of a piece of equipment to receive the teletext signal.

Most teletext brings news and other information into the home over an unused portion of the television frequency—the black bar that can be seen when the set's picture loses vertical control. When a viewer presses a hand-held keypad, an index appears on the screen; it directs the viewer to such items as news headlines, the stock market, weather, and television listings. Pressing another key brings up the item selected.

In most cases, teletext was envisioned as a complement to regular television programming. Detail not used in a television report could be called up by pressing a key. "Dan Rather could tell viewers to turn to page thirty-three on teletext for more information," says Albert H. Crane III, who served as vice-president for Extravision, a CBS teletext service, until he and most of the fifteen-member staff were let go last year. Further, a national advertising campaign could be accompanied by a teletext component indicating where to shop locally for a refrigerator, say, or a washing machine.

CBS and NBC developed national services to be distributed to local affiliates, which could then add information about, say, school closings to news about the latest hostage crisis. Time Inc. undertook a much more ambitious venture, which gave the viewer capabilities more like videotex.

From the start, teletext suppliers were plagued by the absence of affordable decoders to translate the broadcast signal into teletext pages. It was hoped that the devices, which cost $200 or more, would eventually become a standard component of a television set. Manufacturers like RCA and Sony held off to see if a market for such an esoteric option would develop. Panasonic and Zenith did bring decoder-equipped sets to market, but the decoders only work with top-of-the-line sets costing $1,000 and more.

To make things worse, different broadcasters use different forms of teletext requiring different decoders. The FCC sanctioned this confusion by refusing to endorse any one standard for U.S. teletext when it gave its regulatory nod to the fledgling industry in March 1983. As a result, only a few thousand homes are able to receive teletext, according to John Carey, a consultant in Dobbs Ferry, New York.

Time and NBC are gone from the business. CBS is limping along, having farmed out to others the production of its teletext service after laying off most of its own teletext staff last summer. A few other services, notably one operated by Taft Broadcasting, which piggybacks on the signal for Ted Turner's WTBS cable station, have also survived. Taft's Electra service has yet to solicit advertising, however.

Even with affordable decoders, it's uncertain whether interest will soon develop.

A few optimists believe the failure of videotex and teletext is temporary. After all, they reason, it took decades for other new technologies to take off. Phone service, initiated in the late 1870s, was so costly in its early years that it failed to reach half of American homes until after World War II. For interactive media like videotex and teletext, improvements in computers and telecommunications may solve cost and ease-of-use problems.

Greater success with these services has been achieved outside the United States. About 20 percent of households have teletext in Britain, where subscribers use it to get news headlines and other timely information. Fewer competing media, lower decoder costs, and a single form of teletext are contributing factors. Also, many Britons lease their sets, taking teletext for a minimal extra charge.

In France, from 12 to 15 percent of homes have small terminals called Minitels, which can be used to call up an electronic phone directory as well as a host of information services, including updates from most of the country's major newspapers. It was the government-run telephone monopoly that got Minitel under way in 1981 as part of a plan to boost phone traffic. The French *Postes Telephones Telecommunications* (PTT) lends terminals free of charge to customers. Directory usage costs nothing for the first three minutes, but there is a charge of about $7.50 an hour for other services, like news. The PTT does not expect to turn a profit until 1990.

A PTT official, Georges Nahon, says that trying to get the French public to subscribe to a news-oriented service like Viewtron would have proved a futile undertaking. "It would have taken twenty years to get a critical mass of potential subscribers," Nahon says. Allowing phone users to grow accustomed to using a free electronic directory laid a foundation for introducing other services. Minitel's news section, he explains, acts as a supplement to other media, updating stories in the morning paper and enabling viewers to respond to panelists on a television debate show by typing comments into the terminals. [Editor's note: About 16 percent of the traffic on the French system is the exchange of sexually oriented messages, nicknamed the "pink mailboxes."]

In the U.S., home interactive services haven't totally vanished, but media companies are virtually absent from the business. The telephone and computer companies that newspaper publishers so feared are among the few still trying to develop home services. IBM and Sears are proceeding with their estimated $250 million Trintex project, an elaborate videotex undertaking. Trintex creators are trying hard to avoid a newspaper-like format.

Trintex expects to pick up where Viewtron left off by taking better advantage of the personal computer's capabilities and by making news just one of a smorgasbord of services, putting emphasis on shopping, banking, and entertainment.

The phone industry, meanwhile, is anticipating the lifting of restrictions, written into the Bell System divestiture agreement at the behest of the American Newspaper Publishers Association, that bar local phone companies from entering the electronic publishing business. Several of the so-called Baby Bells, which own local phone companies, have expressed interest in offering an electronic version of the Yellow Pages. . . .

While newspapers have floundered badly with home information services, publishers can point to a greater measure of success for business videotex services, such as the Dow Jones News/Retrieval service. In fact, despite Viewtron's demise, Knight-Ridder maintains Vu/Text Information Services, which gives the computer-equipped researcher access to back issues of thirty-five daily newspapers. . . . Vu/Text turned its first profit in late 1986.

These storehouses of information are good research tools, as many journalists know. But they are also expensive: service providers sometimes charge more than $100 an hour.

It's unclear, moreover, whether ordinary consumers will wish to pluck news stories from a computer while sipping their morning coffee. Electronic information services require that the informal user develop the habits of a serious researcher. A subject of inquiry must be pinpointed before the user can move ahead. The task of extracting information from a machine demands precision. The act of browsing through a sports section is, by definition, random—and infinitely more enjoyable. In the hackneyed vernacular of the computer industry, a newspaper is more user friendly.

FIBER OPTICS: A NEW TOOL

Paul Kruglinski

Transmission of information by pulses of light through extremely fine strands of glass is expanding swiftly. A single glass strand can handle as many as 12,000 telephone conversations simultaneously. The mass media are finding numerous uses for this new technology, in which the laser has a critical role.

Newspapers are watching and waiting as fiber optics, the advanced voice- and data-transmission process, is pulsating its way into new communications applications. Although the newspaper industry's use of fiber optics so far has been limited to data transmission between central offices and remote production plants, the high-speed capability and proven reliability of this new technology offer the potential of various applications for newspaper operations.

According to Kathleen Criner, ANPA director/telecommunications affairs, and AT&T engineers, fiber optics can provide quicker, more reliable links to replace cross-country or cross-town microwave systems, or, in the office, to replace existing cable or copper-wire connections between computers, terminals, telephones and other electronic devices. It can modernize existing communications ties by replacing tangles of fat cables while eliminating worries about thunderstorm interference and the possibility of wiretapping. . . .

Source: Reprinted with permission from *presstime,* September 1984.

SEVERAL TECHNOLOGIES

Fiber optics is actually a combination of several technologies, principally lasers, glass fiber, analog conversion and digital transmission. The optical-fiber telecommunications process, in rudimentary form, involves converting analog electronic signals—a voice over a telephone—into a digital format—the ones and zeros of the binary computer code.

Controlled by equipment known as "primary multiplexers" or "channel banks," a laser then converts the ones into minute particles of light and the zeros into non-areas of light that are conveyed through a strand of pliable, gossamer glass.

Enormous volumes of information may be transmitted simultaneously over a single optical fiber and then, at the receiving end, deciphered and relayed to the appropriate destination. In the case of telephone conversations, the digitized light is reconstructed into an analog format. A single strand of optical fiber can handle as many as [12,000] telephone conversations simultaneously.

"Also, optics can carry video signals as well, so you can offer integrated data, voice and broadband video," ANPA's Criner points out. "Pacific Telesis has proposed building a coaxial-fiber system in Palo Alto, Calif., part of which will be used to provide cable services."

The concept behind fiber optics is not new. Nearly 30 years ago, researchers proposed using a glass medium as a conduit to transport light that represented information. During the mid-1960s, research in fiber optics began in earnest. By 1977, the first human voice was publicly transmitted by way of optical fiber.

Since then, the technology has been making quantum leaps as a data-transmission medium. AT&T reports that the amount of optical fiber it shipped to its divisions and to other telecommunications carriers ballooned from less than 4,000 miles in 1980 to about 200,000 miles in 1983.

Several technological advances have allowed fiber optics to make greater inroads into telecommunications.

The material used in the manufacture of the optical-fiber strands is much purer today than that of a few years ago. It has been said that a 12-mile-thick block of the raw material from which the fiber is made would appear as thin as a window pane to someone standing in front of it. This purity means that repeaters—the light amplifiers preventing a signal from dwindling into garble—can now be placed at greater intervals.

Experimentally, AT&T has been able to send data nearly 100 miles before a repeater is needed to amplify it.

The lasers used to create the light/nonlight digital data have undergone substantial improvement, too. Lasers made of gallium arsenide have been miniaturized to widths equal to the diameters of the hair-thin glass fibers. These new lasers are capable of creating light impulses at a rate of 2 billion per second.

Also, improvements in the digital transmission have allowed processing of more information more quickly.

However, fiber optics is still in need of improvements in some areas.

For instance, Criner points out that linking homes with fiber optics is not now considered economical.

"Another major drawback to fiber has been the inability to come up with an effective splicing process," she says.

However, GTE has developed what it calls its elastomeric splice, using a quartz tube, that it says has eliminated many of the problems of fusion splicing.

NEWSPAPER USES

The latest advances will ultimately allow TAT-8 to transmit 280 million bits of data per second between North America and Europe.

"Fiber optics has become looked upon as having practical application in telecommunications," says

Richard G. Atkins, director of communications at the Associated Press. "It's reached maturity." However, Atkins said the wire service has not firmed up any plans as yet to use the transatlantic fiber-optics cable.

But in its current newspaper application of linking downtown offices with remote printing plants, fiber optics is winning rave reviews.

The Edmonton, Alberta, *Journal* was the first newspaper to employ fiber optics in this regard. The system was installed about two years ago and operated successfully for about a year, when management decided to deliver negatives by motor vehicle to the remote plant because of problems with equipment unrelated to the fiber link.

[Another] North American newspaper . . . using fiber optics is the Bakersfield *Californian*. The technology is used to link the downtown office with a new remote printing site seven miles away.

"Fiber optics is more consistent and speedier" than microwave, says Jerry K. Stanners, the paper's chief executive officer. "We're very pleased with its performance."

It allows the paper not only to send completed pages to its News-Scan laser film exposure unit at the remote plant but also to relay telephone calls and computer data between the two buildings. Thus, one telephone and computer system serves two separate sites. The local telephone company installed and maintains the system.

Regarding other media applications, perhaps the most ambitious optical-fiber endeavor to date was AT&T's Olympic Project, the telecommunications optical network that connected the numerous and widely scattered Southern California playing sites for the 1984 Summer Games.

The optical-cable itself consisted of 144 glass strands capable of carrying 240,000 simultaneous conversations, transmitting graphics and allowing more than 2000 "electronic message terminals" to interact with each other. It was the most expansive local-area network using fiber optics yet constructed.

Steven R. Copoloff, district manager for 1984 Olympics/engineering and operations, says analog communications technology served the 1976 Montreal Olympics well. But because of the geographic spread of the events, he says, analog technology would not have been adequate for the telecommunications demands at the Los Angeles Games.

With the optical-fiber system, reporters had "access to instantaneous information on the athletes and the results" through a network of terminals displaying the optically transmitted information, he says. There also were electronic message boards to help editors keep in touch with roving reporters. It was "a paperless environment" in which to gather news, notes Copoloff. . . .

Down the road, fiber optics promises even greater breakthroughs for the newspaper business.

Researchers are investigating the possibility of using faster optical conductors as replacements for the silicon chips. Others say that as newspapers move toward electronic darkroom and remote color separation technologies, they will find fiber optics a natural adjunct to these advances.

Pacific Bell's Copoloff predicts that optical fiber will connect almost every household in the nation by the end of the century, possibly providing a single conduit for telephone, videotex, television, and even shopping and banking services. Nippon Telegraph & Telephone Public Corp. is making similar predictions for linking up Japanese homes with fibers.

Clearly, the telecommunications firms are betting heavily that fiber optics *is* the future for telecommunications. . . .

One very possible result of all this activity is that communication satellites may become obsolete, researchers for the firms say. Some experts are saying that by the late-1990s, no more communications satellites will be placed into orbit because there will be ample ground communications via fiber optics cable. Atkins, Copoloff and others say that fiber optics is so cheap and dependable that using satellites won't be cost effective or practical.

STEVIE WONDER RECORDS BY SATELLITE

Mr. Bonzai

The columnist for *Mix* magazine who signs himself Mr. Bonzai attended a first-time-ever session in which Stevie Wonder and a chorus in Los Angeles recorded via satellite and fiber optics with performers in a New York studio. But the laws of relativity remain a problem.

Mrs. Bonzai and I said the magic word—*Mix*—and the gates of Wonderland opened. The old studio is warmed by the spirit of Nat King Cole and other legends who have worked there since the '30s. Stevie's redecorating has come slowly, maintaining the deco style. The layout is eccentric, unlike modern ergonomic facilities, and it takes a while to figure out where things are. Stevie gets around quite easily while strangers get lost.

Having both braved the fortress a number of times for previous *Mix* stories, we felt at home as the press ranks were herded first into the air hockey room (Mr. Wonder is the reigning champ) for briefing and lunching. In Stevie's adjacent office, we could hear a young chorus going through some run-throughs for his anti-crack song, "Stop, Don't Pass Go." Co-producer Quincy Jones emerged, waved a friendly hello, and rushed off to the studio.

Wishing to find out early where the action would actually take place, I asked to use the bathroom, knowing that it is on the far side of the building. "I know where it is," I assured a guard, and briskly slipped through the TV crews waiting anxiously.

I spotted engineer Bob Harlan warming up a synthesizer—a friendly face in the crowd of strangers. Mick Parish, a bespectacled Englishman who has been tending to technical needs for over a decade, said "Nice to see you, mate," Synth wizard Bob Bralove, looking like a beatnik professor, nodded hello. I had the scene wired, but what was going to happen? . . .

This was to be the historic debut of an actual bi-coastal digital fiber optic satellite studio recording session. We've got Nile Rodgers in New York with his guitar and a teenage chorus. In L.A. we've got Stevie Wonder, Quincy Jones, and another teenage chorus. We've also got news crews and spectators crowding both NY's Master Sound Astoria and Wonderland.

Stevie's engineer, Gary Olazabal, informed me that the original goal was to record both choirs simultaneously, but because of the current laws of physics it is impossible. Overdubbing the choirs in sequence is a cinch, with two machines and a digital delay offset to allow for the half-second it takes to get a signal up to the satellite, down to New York, back up again and down to L.A. Afterwards you just digitally bounce it back to the master tape and you've got it. But actual simultaneous dueting can't work, even if we could put a digital delay in the brains of one coast. Our esteemed editor Indiana Schwartz sums it up, "We can't record in the future." It's all a bit boggling to me, so I will leave the explanation to Dr. Buzz Bently, Professor of Anthropomusicosophy (see sidebar).

When Stevie made his arrival, the word quickly spread through Wonderland. As we waited for the press conference to commence, we had the good fortune to be boxed in a corner with Quincy Jones. When we last met, he was just starting to work on *The Color Purple.* This time we learned he was finishing up the long-awaited sequel to Michael Jackson's *Thriller* and meeting with Robert DiNiro for a film which Quincy will direct next year. Dressed casually in a bulky knit sweater, Levis and boots, and speaking offhandedly about the music and film business, you'd never have guessed he was about to launch a new era of recording.

Stevie and Quincy took their places in the center of the studio as news crews began filming. On a large video monitor we could see Nile Rodgers at the console in New York.

Source: "Bicoastal Overdub" and "Lunching with Mr. Bonzai," *Mix,* May 1987. Reprinted with permission.

DR. BUZZ BENTLY EXPLAINS . . .

No, you can't get both singers singing live together on each coast. Say you've got a singer and a tape rolling in L.A., and another singer in NY, connected by a satellite link back to L.A. The signal from L.A. goes to the satellite, about 20,000 miles up, and 20,000 miles down to the NY studio. That takes the radio signal about a quarter of a second at 186,000 miles a second. The NY singer hears the L.A. singer, and sings his part—as far as he's concerned, there's no delay, and he's in sync. So he sings along, and his signal goes back to L.A., which takes another quarter of a second. By the time you pay the taxi and pick up the luggage, it works out to 520 milliseconds for the round trip. So you put the L.A. singer's vocal on a 520 millisecond delay before it goes to the tape, and it's right in sync with the NY vocal, no problem.

Except there's a problem: the L.A. vocalist gets the NY vocalist's part a half-second later, so there's no way the two parts can sound in sync to *him,* though the tape won't know the difference. So he has to sing alone, without hearing the other singer. No way around that delay. If you tried putting the tape machine in the middle, neither singer would hear the other in real time, because they'd both be a quarter-second off.

But we're working on it. We have two ideas. One is a digital delay in the brain of the first singer, so that he hears himself a half-second after he sings, in sync with the second singer. But he has to sing at one time, and hear himself later, so the interference in the brain has to be bypassed in the thalmus, where the time sense is. Very tough wiring in there, but we have the basic diagrams in the computer.

The other way to go is with a splitter coupled to a time machine, so that the L.A. singer is split in two, one half in real time, one half sitting in a time machine that throws him a half-second into the future. He sings the track in real time but his split hears it a half-second later, along with the signal from NY. But then we need a reverse time feedback to send back to the real time singer, so he can hear himself and the other singer a half-second in the future. That's the part that's giving the guys in the lab fits, trying to make an end run around the Theory of Relativity. Very tough. Talk to me next year.

Quincy remarked, "Technology like this can really pull the world together. There are many musicians we respect around the world, but it can be difficult to schedule the sessions. Now we can have an American rhythm section, Brazilian singers and African drummers all recording from their homelands. Even though the musicians are separated physically, the technology has risen to the occasion and maintained an intimacy like a typical recording situation. It's a huge step forward."

Stevie commented on the anti-drug song to be recorded: "I felt that because this was a very historical moment in time for us technologically, what could be better than to record a message encouraging us to make a move against something that is devastating the society of the world. We should use communication to bring people closer together."

Quincy added, "I've been in the business a long time—starting with 78 RPM, then 45s, LPs, cassettes—and today seems to be a natural extension of what technology is all about."

Stevie concluded, "We talk about communicating with life on other planets—it's only fitting that first of all we communicate with each other to the maximum degree possible. This technology brings into focus what I believe the creator has meant for us to do all along. It's a plus; it's tomorrow; it's us in tomorrow today."

With that, we were all ushered into an observation room to watch the session. It was extremely cramped so I asked Bob Harlan if we could go out to the mobile truck where Gary O was engineering. He obliged and whisked us through the studio during a break, and out to the truck, where things were pretty hectic. When we tried to get back to the press observation room we fortunately got stuck in the main room, with Stevie, Quincy, the teenage choir and their mothers.

Standing quietly in the corner, we were close to

the artists and far from the technology. This was just two old friends coaching a group of kids and joking with Nile on the other coast. Quincy asked Nile for another take, this time with "a little more grease." To warm the kids up in L.A., Stevie sat at the piano while they gathered around and he sang them through the chorus. On the monitor we could see Nile nodding and grooving. While Quincy and Stevie stepped into an adjoining control room for a playback, the mothers pulled out their cameras and began taking snapshots for the family albums.

Technically, the session proceeded smoothly, only slowed by the demands for perfection by the triumvirate of superstars in charge. Quincy joked to Stevie, "You're gonna get in a lot of trouble—I can see you wanting to record with 17 different countries." "Yes," Stevie agreed, "I want those cellos from Europe—gotta have those cellos."

After the two choirs were finished, Stevie played harmonica for Nile's new version of the *Moonlighting* theme and Nile piped guitar back to L.A. for one of Stevie's tracks in progress. Just another day in Wonderland.

In a telephone conversation with Ben Rizzi and Maxine Chrein, co-owners of Master Sound Astoria, I felt their elation and enthusiasm. "We had a dream situation," Ben informed me. "We're directly interfaced to an earth station through a fiber optic network. When we first heard Stevie's harmonica we couldn't believe the quality—even the subtlety of his breathing. Nile said he couldn't believe how easy it all was—that there really wasn't much difference between a TV monitor and looking through the control room window.

"A major advantage of the DASH format is that the control track lockup is incredibly accurate. Our time delay offset was .52 seconds and the Sony machines even allow you to offset for phase problems. They lock down to the byte.

"It's a fairly expensive procedure, but still costs less than flying an artist like Stevie and his crew in from L.A. We also wanted to show the possibilities in the most complicated form: full digital satellite transmission and bi-coastal broadcast quality video. It is affordable and we feel that it's a service that works well and can save money for the record companies. Within a few years, it will become available to more and more studios."

"It's exciting for us to be pioneering something that is a first for the music industry," Maxine added. "A lot of talented people contributed to this project, and how often do you have Quincy Jones, Stevie Wonder and Nile Rodgers collaborating like this?"

QUESTIONS FOR REVIEW AND DISCUSSION

1. Describe how information on demand differs from traditional publishing and broadcasting.
2. How did Mike Greenly use computer conferencing in the coverage of AIDS?
3. List three ways in which newspapers use personal computers.
4. Do you agree or disagree with Jay Black's opinion that the new technologies may bring some people into the journalism field for the wrong reasons? Explain your position.
5. What does Jim Bessman mean by the title of his article, "Video Takes Over Main Street"? Cite four examples he gives to support his point.
6. Why do some researchers believe that no more communications satellites will be placed into orbit by the late 1990s?
7. Why is it impossible for two musicians connected by satellite to sing together in exact synchronization?
8. What is "artificial intelligence"?
9. In newspaper publishing, what is the role of full pagination?

ESSAY TOPICS

1. Computer networking permits groups of individuals, often widely separated, to "converse" by exchanging written messages on their screens. News, opinion, gossip, and rumor can be disseminated in this manner, uncontrolled by professionally trained gatekeepers such as those employed in the mass media. Write an essay examining the uses, values, and possible dangers of this information channel.
2. The techniques for publishing an electronic newspaper are in use, as are those for teletext and videotex systems. The American public, however, has shown little interest in using these electronic systems despite its general enthusiasm for new technologies. Discuss the reasons for this lack of interest.

Women have not yet advanced in satisfactory numbers to the *upper* levels. Women have yet to shatter the so-called glass ceiling—the invisible barrier separating middle management women from the power positions.

— Katharine Graham
in "The 'Glass Ceiling' "

Certainly the television journalists are much more competitive than print journalists. They fight each other for stories. I think there is a tendency to be less responsible for television journalists than with the written word.

— Rupert Murdoch
in *Broadcasting* magazine

The rating point equals 874,000 households, and a one-point rating lead for the evening news time period is worth $19 million in advertising revenue annually. So we need not belabor the fact that this is a very high-stakes game.

— Burton Benjamin
in "Network News at the Crossroads"

Neuharth's hands-on style is as intense as everything else about him. . . . He personally approved every radio and television ad for *USA Today* and in its early days he prowled the composing room and rewrote headlines.

— Barbara Matusow
in "Allen H. Neuharth Today"

PART FOUR

THE COMMUNICATORS

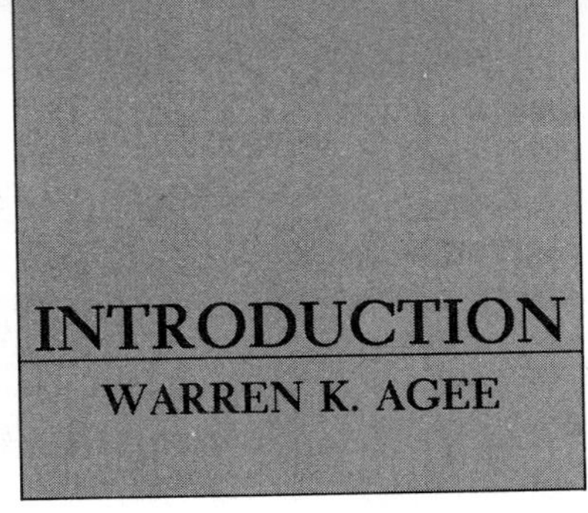

INTRODUCTION

WARREN K. AGEE

The mass communicators are the media *institutions* such as newspapers, broadcast stations and networks, and magazine and book publishers. They inform, entertain, educate, and persuade the public largely with the help of other entities such as news services, public relations firms, advertising agencies, photographic enterprises, and independent television and film production companies.

In this section we look at some of the media mainly to determine the status of their efforts to employ and advance minorities and women. Then we focus primarily on the *individuals* who direct and work in these thousands of American businesses. We consider the careers of television news directors, photographers, and several media leaders who are among the "provocative people" of the media world.

In 1982 and 1983, Market Interviews, a subsidiary of Market Opinion Research of Detroit, Michigan, conducted telephone interviews with a random sample of 1,001 journalists—full-time editorial personnel employed by daily and weekly newspapers, news magazines, news services, and news departments of radio and television stations. The results were analyzed by Professors Richard G. Gray and G. Cleveland Wilhoit of the Indiana University School of Journalism.

The researchers found, not surprisingly, that approximately 66 percent of American journalists are male and 95 percent are white. Fifty-five percent hold bachelor's degrees and, of these, 60 percent either majored, minored, or took courses in journalism. The average age is 32. Approximately 56 percent are married, and three-fourths of these journalists have children. Among other characteristics, the typical journalist:

- Is middle-of-the-road politically (59 percent)
- Thinks the press has considerable influence on public opinion and that its influence should be even greater (percentage not listed)
- Has an equal number of journalist and nonjournalist friends (75 percent)
- Sees "helping people" as a major source of job satisfaction (61 percent)
- Is fairly well satisfied (44 percent) or very well satisfied (45 percent) with his or her job
- Says financial matters (pay and fringe benefits) may cause him or her to seek a job in another field (50 percent)

- Sees investigating government claims and getting information to the public quickly as key journalistic roles (90 percent)
- Disapproves of divulging confidentiality (95 percent) and paying for information (72 percent)
- Says day-to-day newsroom learning (88 percent) and family upbringing (72 percent), a senior editor (61 percent), and co-workers (57 percent) are important influences on his or her journalism ethics

In general, the Gray-Wilhoit research corresponds with the findings of sociology Professor John W. C. Johnstone and associates at the University of Illinois, who in 1976 published a nationwide study, *The News People: A Sociological Portrait of American Journalists and Their Work.* Among other results, the Johnstone study found that most journalists are busy *processors* of the work of others and that they seek the higher salaries afforded by employment with large media institutions but also, frustratingly, seek the prestige and influence found more often in employment with smaller media.

The male dominance of the American newsroom, found in these studies, appears likely to abate considerably. Most newly employed journalists are products of journalism schools, and during the past quarter century the enrollment of women students has steadily increased. In one of his annual surveys of enrollment and career plans, Professor Paul Peterson of the Ohio State University School of Journalism found that about 60 percent of the students enrolled in 1986 were women. This figure compares with only 37.8 percent in 1963.

Peterson also found that the vast majority of the 1986 graduates were not seeking careers in traditional journalism, such as daily newspaper work. Advertising and public relations were the areas of primary interest, followed by radio and television journalism, magazines, "and a host of other fields all related to the basic concepts of writing and editing." Journalism and mass communication educators have reported that newspaper majors now comprise less than 20 percent of total school enrollments.

MINORITIES IN THE MEDIA

Blacks, Hispanics, Asians, and Native Americans account for more than 20 percent of the nation's population, according to 1980 census figures. Only a relatively small number, however, have yet to join the more than 54,700 journalists working for American newspapers.

In 1978 ASNE resolved to hire more minority representatives so that by the year 2000 minority staffing would reach parity with the population. Results thus far have been discouraging. Between that year and 1988, the percentage of minority persons on newspaper staffs moved only from 4 to 7 percent. In fact, 6 out of 10 daily newspapers in America still have no minority members on their editorial staffs.

The situation is only slightly better in the broadcast field. There minorities account for about 9 percent of the more than 14,000 people handling radio news and about 14 percent of the approximately 19,000 engaged in television news operations.

In the wake of inner-city riots during the 1960s, the National Advisory

Commission on Civil Disorders, headed by Governor Otto Kerner of Illinois, indicted the news media for failing to communicate to their predominantly white audiences "a sense of the degradation, misery, and hopelessness of living in the ghetto." During the 1984 presidential campaign, reporters traveled on the candidates' planes but did very little reporting in black communities. Consequently, some media leaders have pointed out, the American press was surprised by the support and emotions generated by the Rev. Jesse Jackson's bid for the Democratic presidential nomination.

The print and broadcast media have continued to develop strategies to increase minority employment. In a speech at the 1984 convention of the Society of Professional Journalists, Sigma Delta Chi, Reginald Stuart, a New York *Times* reporter and chairman of the society's minority affairs committee, said continued white domination of newsrooms has been worsened by a growing tendency to target news to "upper income whites . . . at the expense of others who live in our society." Stuart charged:

> This thrust may have succeeded in restoring and enhancing prosperity in the industry, particularly newspapers. But the good news era and happy talk formats have turned us into a medium for the classes from one that once was for the masses. . . . It is insulting, quite frankly, to hear a manager or hiring personnel say they can't find qualified minorities out of 17 million adult blacks, 6 million adult Hispanics, 600,000 American Indians, and 1.2 million Asian Americans.

A call for blacks to prepare themselves more adequately for careers in television and film production and performance was issued by Dwight M. Ellis, vice president for minority and special services, National Association of Broadcasters, in an article in *Broadcasting* magazine, September 10, 1984. Unless they do so, the windows of opportunity for black and other minority participation in the communications and entertainment industries may be closing, Ellis warned. He pointed out that too many blacks were carried away by the glamour of big-name success. He added:

> The result is that while we are perpetuating generations of star-crazed youngsters reaching for the fame of the Max Robinsons and Billy Dee Williamses, scores of young whites are toiling in the shadows, learning the less glamorous skills of scriptwriting, camera work and lighting.

The formula for minority success in these industries, Ellis wrote, is "preparedness, persistence and professionalism. . . . The objective must be quality over quantity. . . . Only when we are truly ready for prime time can we hope to surge with confidence through the closing windows of opportunity."

In an article titled "Marketing the News in Third World America," in this section, Félix Gutiérrez, a professor at the University of Southern California School of Journalism, discusses the growth of black and Hispanic media and the increased attention paid by advertisers to minority consumers.

THE GROWING ROLE OF WOMEN

Media and women's movement leaders have been pleased with the steady increase in the number of women employed in print and broadcast fields during recent years. They express little pleasure, however, with the relative scarcity of women in high-level positions. After reviewing listings in the 1986 *Editor & Publisher Year Book,* Dorothy Jurney, a retired member of the American Society of Newspaper Editors, reported that women held only 12.4 percent of the directing-editor jobs on U.S. dailies and Sunday newspapers. Gains have been made, Jurney said, but she added that at the present rate, the year 2055 will arrive before women, representing 53 percent of potential readers, share top jobs equally with men. "This is a condition I regard as a calamity for newspapers; a loss for readers, who get only the male viewpoint on what makes news; and a tragedy for women who want to contribute to the profession and fully realize their careers."

In the broadcast field, women are progressing much more rapidly to top positions. The FCC reported that in 1985 women constituted 29.7 percent of broadcast executives, a figure approaching the 32.4 percent of women executives in business and industry reported by the Bureau of Labor Statistics for 1984.

After interviewing nearly 25 news executives, both men and women, Maryl C. Levine, a Washington, D.C., management firm executive, reported in the November 1986 issue of the ASNE *Bulletin* that women face five barriers in seeking promotion beyond the middle management level:

1. Both men and women news executives perceive a "glass ceiling," based on traditional values, subjective factors, psychological hurdles, societal training, and macho role models.
2. There is a strong old-boy network that affects promotion decisions at the highest levels.
3. Some men do not like women as professionals, acknowledging that they are not as comfortable with women as with men.
4. Some men experience fear when they consider appointing women to certain positions, possibly relating to their lack of confidence in women and to a feeling that women are good to talk to and work hard but are really not up to the demands of the top positions.
5. There are conflicts in the newspaper business between work and family.

Katharine Graham, chairman of the board of the Washington Post Company, discusses some of these factors in the article "The 'Glass Ceiling': Women's Barrier to Top Management." An excerpt from the newspaper findings of a massive study on women in the media by Professor Jean Gaddy Wilson of the University of Missouri School of Journalism offers a close-up look at the subject.

THE SHIFTING TELEVISION NEWS SCENE

The communicators of television news to the American public are gradually shifting in influence from those with the national networks to the news directors and staff members of the hundreds of local stations throughout the country.

In his article "Network News at the Crossroads," Burton Benjamin, a former senior vice-president of CBS News, says increasing numbers of people are asking how long network news can survive its declining ratings and increased competition from local stations, syndicators, and cable.

Clint O'Connor, associate editor of the *Washington Journalism Review,* describes in detail the position of assignment editor at a local station, which he calls "The Toughest Job in TV News."

THE REPORTORIAL TRADITION

Sociologist Herbert J. Gans explores the basis and application of the enduring values that shape contemporary journalism. In his article "The Progressive Spirit Today," Gans contends that these values are neither "conservative" nor "liberal" but those of turn-of-the-century Progressivism.

THE PHOTOGRAPHER'S ROLE

As a communicator, a photographer must be as truthful as a reporter: Gone are the days of artificially contrived photos. Ron Mann, director of photography at the *Register* in Orange County, California, emphasizes responsibility in the article "Ethics in Photography: Avoid Preconceived Ideas."

PROVOCATIVE PEOPLE

Part Four ends with profiles of four widely known and influential communicators:

- Rupert Murdoch, controversial newspaper publisher and television entrepreneur, with enormous holdings in America, Great Britain, and his native Australia.
- Ted Turner, freewheeling owner of the Cable News Network, "Superstation" WTBS, and the Atlanta Braves baseball team.
- Oprah Winfrey, whose television program, *The Oprah Winfrey Show,* has captivated millions of viewers.
- Allen H. Neuharth, the guiding genius of the Gannett communications empire and *USA Today.*

MINORITIES IN THE MEDIA

MINORITY HIRING AT A SNAIL'S PACE

Judith G. Clabes

A goal of the American Society of Newspaper Editors is to have minority employment in newsrooms equal to the percentage of minorities in the general population by the year 2000. As chairman of the ASNE minority committee, Judith G. Clabes reports that a 1987 survey shows extremely slow progress toward that goal. She is editor of the Covington *Kentucky Post.*

In March, 1968, the Kerner Commission issued a scathing criticism of daily newspapers in America. It said, in part, "Along with the country as a whole, the press has too long basked in a white world, looking out of it, if at all, with white men's eyes and a white perspective. That is no longer good enough."

Well, that got our attention, though it really shouldn't have taken hell and the Kerner Commission to propel us into doing what we should have been doing anyway.

Since then, however, the newspaper industry has wrestled with the problem of how to improve the ethnic and racial diversity of its newsrooms. I don't have to tell any of you that we haven't set the world afire with our minority hiring practices. But I will tell you that we're working on it—and with some growing energy and commitment.

In 1978, the American Society of Newspaper Editors, unhappy with the snail's pace progress, established a goal of achieving minority representation in the nation's newsrooms equal to that of the general population by the Year 2000. Minorities make up about 20 percent of the general population today and may rise to 25 percent or more by the end of the century.

Today—19 years after the Kerner Commission and 9 years after ASNE's major commitment—there is good news and bad news. The bad news is that the good news isn't so great, but the good news is that the bad news isn't as bad as it used to be.

Frankly, the prospects for success on the Year 2000 goal look bleak—bleak, but not hopeless. In fact, if every daily newspaper hired just two additional minority journalists this year, the number of minorities in our newsrooms would nearly double.

Minority employment in our newsrooms grew from under 4 percent in 1978 to 6.56 percent in 1987, according to ASNE's new survey figures. Still a long way away from the Year 2000 goal and not so far from the Year 2000, but growing slowly.

Too slowly.

- The 1987 survey shows that 56 percent of our newsrooms have no minority staffers at all, and most of these all-white newsrooms are at smaller newspapers, our industry's traditional farm clubs.
- Eighty-four percent of America's newspapers have no minority news executives. And the current data show that only 3.9 percent of the nation's 12,200 daily newspaper supervisors are minorities.

Source: ASNE 1987 minority committee report. Reprinted with permission.

MINORITIES ARE NOW 6.56 PERCENT OF NEWSROOM WORK FORCE

	Total work force	Minorities in work force	% Minorities in work force
1978	43,000	1,700	3.95
1979	45,000	1,900	4.22
1980	47,000	2,300	4.89
1981	45,500	2,400	5.27
1982	49,000	2,700	5.51
1983	50,000	2,800	5.60
1984	50,400	2,900	5.75
1985	53,800	3,100	5.76
1986	54,000	3,400	6.30
1987	54,700	3,600	6.56

The 1987 ASNE employment survey indicates that the percentage of newsroom professional employees who are minorities rose from 6.30 last year to 6.56.

Also, 17 percent of the journalists who are taking their first newsroom job are minorities and 26 percent of the interns hired last year were minorities.

The number of minorities rose from 3,400 to 3,600 while the total newsroom employees reported in the survey grew from 54,000 to 54,700.

More optimistically, among 3,600 minority professionals, the percentage of supervisors jumped from 9 percent in 1985 to 12 percent in 1986 and is up to 13 percent this year.

- The statistics suggest that greater diversity in our newsrooms is on the way. Editors reported that 16 percent of their first-time hires were minorities and that 26 percent of the interns were minorities.
- *All* newspapers over 100,000 circulation employ at least one minority.

Still, there are too many all-white newsrooms, especially at smaller newspapers that lack the resources to recruit and/or attract minority employees. That's why the ASNE sponsored 15 regional conferences and job fairs during 1986–87 that attracted more than 1,500 students. We wanted to make it easier for smaller newspapers to recruit by providing opportunities closer to home and we wanted to provide a willing marketplace for bright, young minority journalists. We think the conferences have been enormously successful. And the reason? Because the excuses become obvious ploys that must go away. No editor can visit a regional conference and continue to proclaim there *are no* minority candidates, or there *are no* qualified minority students looking for jobs in his or her newsroom!

This year's ASNE Minorities Committee put the problems of smaller newspapers at the top of its agenda. We initiated new assaults on two fronts—both aimed at helping smaller newspapers achieve racial parity.

First, we established a Small Newspaper Task Force, headed by John Greenman of the Akron (Ohio) *Beacon-Journal,* to give particular attention to the needs of smaller newspapers. The results are two-fold. One, a consulting program whereby editors of smaller newspapers who have had some success with minority hiring have volunteered to offer their services as consultants, one-on-one, with editors who want help. This is a tremendous commitment of time and energy and an indication of the level of dedication within the profession. Two, recruiting suggestions for smaller newspapers will be included in a recruiting manual to be done by the Publications Subcommittee.

Second, we formed an Education Subcommittee, headed by Bill Barnard of the Cleveland *Plain Dealer.* This subcommittee was charged with establishing a guide to help newspapers develop programs for junior high and high school minority students. By increasing the pool of potential minority journalists and by promoting interest in journalism as a possible career, we expect to increase chances of smaller newspapers being able to hire minority candidates. Another effort of the Education Subcommittee involves a promotional campaign aimed at young minorities.

The committee's new minority scholarship program was a big success this year. The Scholarship Subcommittee, headed by Sanders LaMont, awarded 22 scholarships to minority journalism students, chosen from 200 applicants. Already, the fund drive is under way for next year's scholarship program.

A Program Subcommittee, headed by Larry O'Donnell, is evaluating all of the committee's existing programs and will recommend ways to fill the gaps—as well as ways to improve what we're already doing.

The Publications Subcommittee, headed by Dave Corcoran, is planning an update of our successful recruiting manual, "Minority Challenge—A how-to-do-it list from the American Society of Newspaper Editors."

We believe the efforts of ASNE, through the Minorities Committee, have made a difference—with more to come. We have approached the challenge on many fronts and are always looking for creative, workable ways to do more. The committee itself is a wide-ranging one, and ASNE's largest. As a matter of fact the minorities effort accounts for the largest single commitment of ASNE's resources.

Generally, the Minorities Committee has set these objectives:

- To increase awareness of the importance of hiring, promoting, and retaining minorities in the newsroom
- To increase the flow of minority talent into journalism education and into the nation's newsrooms
- To promote practical help to newspapers in recruiting and training minorities

Why bother?

Simply put, it's the morally right thing to do. And if rightness isn't convincing enough, then consider that it's good business.

A newspaper cannot reflect its total community unless it is represented by its total community. The smart editor is going to look toward an ethnic mix in the newsroom that reflects potential—not existing, but potential—readership.

We must have diversity in our workforce because we have diversity in our readership. We must have diversity because diversity is the stuff of lively, well-read newspapers. We must have diversity because it's the right thing!

I wish we could stop saying this. I wish we could get beyond the *why should we* to the *how do we do it.* But I wish, too, that we were closer to the Year 2000 goal—even that we were beyond it already and could stop talking numbers as well.

Yet we can't stop saying what seems so obvious to so many, because there are still too many who need convincing. And after the convincing, there's still the doing to get done.

Nineteen years from the Kerner Commission and 13 years from 2000, we are—as an industry—in a pretty uncomfortable spot.

MARKETING THE NEWS IN THIRD WORLD AMERICA

Félix Gutiérrez

Hispanic newspapers and broadcasting in the United States have boomed as advertisers try to reach the expanding minority market. Félix Gutiérrez is a professor of journalism at the University of Southern California, a member of the Gannett Center Advisory Committee, and a writer for the Associated Press in Los Angeles.

In late 1986 and early 1987, as major TV networks endured cutbacks and retrenchment, two Spanish-language networks headquartered in Manhattan made plans to beef up their news operations. Univision, formerly Spanish International Network (SIN), hired ex-UPI chief Luis Nogales to head its news division in December; he added late-night and weekend national newscasts to that network's existing schedule of weekday early evening news, and consolidated operations in its new Los Angeles studios. Reliance Capital, owner of four Spanish-language stations, began broadcasts of *Noticiero Telemundo,* produced by former SIN news boss Gustavo Godoy in Miami. This national newscast

Source: Gannett Center Journal, Spring 1987. Reprinted with permission.

went on the air in mid-January and debuted just a week before Univision's new late-night show. It now competes with Univision's evening newscast in Los Angeles, Miami, New York and Chicago.

Hispanic media, especially Hispanic TV, is the big story in minority communications today, and within Hispanic TV news is the big battleground. At first glance, the winner appears to be Spanish-speaking Americans, members of a group that for too long has been cut off from mainstream news organizations because of differences in language or news priorities. And to the extent that other minorities too are sharing in an increased flow of advertising dollars—the driving force behind Univision's and Telemundo's growth—they too have gained.

Overlooked and undervalued by mass audience news outlets in the past, U.S. Latinos and other Third World Americans would appear to be the beneficiaries of the trend toward market segmentation by advertisers. With more news voices to choose from, they have finally been admitted as shoppers to America's "free marketplace of ideas," one of the purported goals of the First Amendment.

"In this situation everybody wins," says advertising executive Mario Lazo. "The viewer wins, the stations win, the advertiser wins, too."

If everyone wins and comes out smiling, the ultimate winner is American democracy, which benefits when all its members are well enough informed to make the key decisions that govern their lives. But all the news is not good. More is going on here than meets the eye.

THE SHIFT FROM MASS TO SPECIAL MARKETS

Third World news media have existed in the United States at least since the founding of New Orleans' bilingual *El Misisipi* in 1808, and have long provided news that was ignored by the mainstream press. Most of them subsisted largely on advertising from ethnic products or from retailers catering to a racial market. This was because mainstream advertisers, both locally and nationally, wanted to reach the largest possible audience. "Mass media" were the best vehicles for that purpose.

In this mass audience system, racial minorities were either ignored or slotted into specific news categories. News was what happened in White America, the mass audience's world, and what happened in Third World America—the world of Black, Native, Asian/Pacific and Latin America—was not news unless it affected or happened to interest White America. Members of racial groups who were part of an unusual problem or success made news. More recently, cultural festivals and events have been added to the news agenda too. But whatever the story, the image of Third World Americans has been packaged in mainstream media to inform or to conform based on the knowledge and attitudes of White America. Racial images in advertising followed the same line.

But in the past 35 years, specialized audience and market segmentation have gradually grown in importance. Advertisers found their messages packed more punch when targeted specifically. The attitude of advertisers toward minorities began to change in the late-1960s, partially as a result of civil rights leaders who called on them to replace racially offensive caricatures with racially integrated portrayals. Part of the new Madison Avenue awareness was the discovery that Blacks, like Whites, are consumers of general market products ranging from diapers to canned foods. Prodded by D. Parke Gibson's 1968 book, *The $30 Billion Negro,* general audience advertisers began to see that Blacks and, later, Latinos were ripe targets for all products. While the creative side of mainstream advertising agencies slimmed down Aunt Jemima and erased the Frito Bandito, media departments began to look for print and broadcast outlets that reached minority consumers.

Today, minorities are more than a sideline interest on Madison Avenue. They are a special category of media consumer meriting special attention, with spending and revenue classifications all their own. The reason for this interest is simple. Black purchasing power in 1986 was estimated at $203 billion, and Hispanic purchasing power in 1987 reached $134 billion.

Black media national advertising expenditures, according to Doug Alligood, vice president for Special Markets at BBDO in New York, increased more than 40 percent between 1982 and 1985, building on a 1982 base of more than $150 million. Hispanic local and national advertising more than doubled in the same period, from $166 million to an estimated $333 million, according to *Hispanic Business* magazine.

Within these overall figures, the breakdowns by media and minority served reveal some interesting patterns. Only ten percent of the total ad dollars spent to reach Black audiences goes to TV, for instance. The reason? There are few Black-formatted TV stations. In this instance, the medium does not lend itself to a minority special market. As David Poltrack, vice president of research for CBS said to *Marketing & Media Decisions* last year, "Even though Blacks represent a significant segment of the total audience [18 percent during prime time], to put on programing that represents viewership less than 30 percent would be foolhardy."

Spanish-language TV, on the other hand, is the darling of the TV industry. Almost 50 percent of the total dollars spent to reach Latino consumers is committed to television. The influx of advertising dollars here is the more important reason why the total amount spent on Hispanic audiences exceeds that spent on Black audiences by more than 25 percent.

The match-up between media and special minority markets clearly has to be looked at on a case-by-case basis. Gains are uneven, and the media most associated with news content are not always those that benefit the most. Between 1982 and 1985, national advertising in Black magazines was up 63 percent. In radio, it was up 20 percent. In newspapers, it was flat. And overall, the prospects for continued growth in Black marketing are dim, according to Alligood. Citing a "slackening of equal opportunity employment and minority business enterprise," Alligood says, "It's very hard to bring to mind Black campaigns that turned products around."

The long-term growth prospects for the Latino market are much more favorable through the end of the century, both because of the anticipated population surge and because of limited competition from English-language media. More than 400 TV and cable outlets now air Spanish-language programs around the United States. The number of full-time Spanish-language radio stations increased from 67 in 1975 to 170 in 1986. And in print, the number of Spanish-language dailies is growing, with competing newspapers in Miami, New York and Los Angeles. The recently formed National Association of Hispanic Publications represents 42 periodicals with an estimated circulation of 1.34 million. Still, Latino print expenditures, where the primary appeal is news and information, lagged far behind television and radio. Hispanic newspapers pick up less than ten percent of national advertising dollars in their special market, and magazines scarcely more than one percent.

Since print is inherently more of a local than a national medium, and draws its advertising from local sources, it is difficult to draw any hard conclusions from national advertising data about quantitative increases in the amount of news content reaching minority audiences. The correlations are indirect, and the flow of advertising dollars, while stronger, is distributed unevenly. The fact to retain here is that Blacks and Hispanics, more than at any time in American history, are recognized by national advertisers as "special markets" worthy of attention. And they are not alone. Asians and Pacific Islanders, who have experienced tremendous growth in newspapers in the past decade, are just beginning to be perceived as a national market. If radio and TV managers are able to convert them into a market for advertisers, a new channel will open, and the dollars will begin to flow here too. Of America's principal minority groups, only Native Americans, in cities or on isolated reservations, have not emerged in some way as a special market for national advertisers. That is one good reason why most successful Native American publications, starting with the *Cherokee Phoenix* in 1828, have been subsidized by tribal leaders.

THE UNDERSIDE OF SPECIAL MARKETS

This growth in special market advertising depends on how well media managers sell their audience as consumers ripe for advertisers, and the boom in minority spending, including spending on news and information programming, serves only those minorities that can be packaged as a consumer market. The media benefiting are those that deliver minority audience segments advertisers want to reach. In this marketplace, it is not ideas that are being sold. It is the attention of minority consumers that advertisers want to exploit. The news content is merely the bait to attract the audience and add credibility to the advertising messages that accompany it.

If a more free and equitable marketplace of ideas results from the expansion of minority news in the United States a better informed public will only be one by-product of that commercial marketplace. For the members of the audience are not the shoppers in the media marketplace. They are the product being bought and sold.

As the historian David Potter wrote more than 30 years ago in *People of Plenty:* "The newspaper feature, the magazine article, the radio program, do not attain the dignity of being ends in themselves. They are rather means to an end. That end, of course, is to catch the reader's attention so that he will then read the advertisement or hear the commercial, and to hold his interest until these essential messages have been delivered."

All American media have functioned this way for all Americans—minority or otherwise—since the beginning of our advertiser-supported media system. But the system cuts differently for Third World Americans than for majority Whites. Circumstances of race, language, culture and socioeconomic standing often mean that minority audiences have less media access, less opportunity to push other levers of social and political power, and greater information needs. And unfortunately, the minority media sometimes play on the special trust they establish through the delivery of news and information to their underserved audiences when they sell that audience to advertisers. In order to win at Madison Avenue's game, minority-formatted media have promoted themselves, and will have to continue promoting themselves, as sales vehicles that exploit their largely low-income audiences as a consumer market.

Just two examples: Los Angeles Spanish-language television station KMEX advertising promotional materials boast of "its ability to deliver powerful demographics in local news," specifically mentioning "the young demographics." In media trade magazine advertisements, *Ebony* has mentioned the trust its Black readers have in its editorial content as a plus for potential advertisers.

Putting advertising in the media driver's seat can lead to controversy in minority-oriented media, particularly when one notices the leading advertisers there. At last year's convention of the predominantly Black National Newspaper Publishers Association, the question of the medium's dependence on tobacco and alcohol advertisers was raised. "There has been criticism in Black communities across the country about the preponderance of liquor and tobacco advertising in the Black press," says Clint Wilson, associate dean of the Howard University School of Communications. "Some publishers are sensitive to this and some are not. Some say, 'We have to get somewhere,' but others, while not turning down the ads, have some concern about it."

While noting that *Ebony* and other Black media have had articles on diseases associated with alcohol and tobacco, Wilson wonders if "this dependence on the tobacco and liquor industries is having an effect on the Black press being able to transmit the message that these products aren't healthful. You'd be biting the hand that feeds you."

"I haven't done a content analysis," he concludes. "But I feel the White press has covered the issue of Black health problems related to tobacco and liquor better than the Black press has."

The same type of advertisers have also targeted Latino consumers. According to *Hispanic Business* magazine's annual survey of Hispanic marketing, three of the top five advertisers to Latinos are primarily identified with beer or tobacco: Philip Morris, $7.5 million; Anheuser-Busch, $6.5 million; and Adolph Coors, $4 million.

THE TWO-EDGED SWORD

Increased advertising dollars, in other words, is a two-edged sword for "special markets" in Third World America. It can lead to a better informed citizenry. It can also lead to increased economic exploitation.

Given the rules of the American media system, just *who* does the exploiting is not the key issue. The increased flow of advertising dollars has made minority media more attractive to Anglo owners. The Gannett Company bought New York's *El Diario–La Prensa* in 1981. A few years later, Black-oriented *Players* magazine was launched by White owners. And in 1986 Hallmark Cards announced plans to buy the ten television stations associated with Spanish International Communications Corporation (SICC) for more than $300 million. This influx of White owners in both Latino and Black media caused concern both among the several Latino groups who had bid for the SICC stations and challenged Hallmark's proposed purchase on the grounds that minority owners should be afforded priorities, and among the national Black-owned broadcasters group, which protested that White-owned stations catering to the Black audience are getting a lion's share of the advertising dollar.

But who is to say that minority owners would run the properties any differently than Hallmark or Gannett. The name of the game for advertisers is to take more money out of a market segment than they invest in advertising to reach that segment. And minority media, whether owned by Latinos, Blacks or Whites, will draw those advertising dollars only as long as they convince advertisers that they are the most cost effective way of reaching the audience and persuading it to use products advertised. It is the system, not the owner, that places minority media in an exploitative relationship with their audience.

Because of language and educational and economic background, many Third World Americans have a greater need and hunger for news and information than Whites. Advertisers often pitch minority audiences with slick, upscale appeals equating social status and acceptance with the consumption of the products advertised. The message is, "You may not have the same education, income or neighborhood as Whites, but you can drink the same beer, smoke the same cigarettes, and drive the same car they do." Minority advertising agencies often stress the effectiveness of immediate gratification in their appeals to their largely low-income consumer. One example was a camera campaign that promised, "Polaroid gives it to you now." The implicit message is that conspicuous consumption, not education and hard work, is the key to the good life.

Other appeals, using food or culture, try to make the products appear to be "at home" with the minority consumer by positioning the product with the meals, activities and celebrations of Third World Americans. Slick promotions, such as the recent Miller Brewing Company exhibit honoring Black journalists, piggyback commercial messages on the recognition of heroes, events and leaders long denied recognition by the White media. Images of persons and events that in their time fought slavery, overcame oppression or advocated human rights are now used to sell products.

The first inside page in February's *Ebony* featured a picture of Sojourner Truth, a leader of the Underground Railway, under the headline "Black History is Alive and Well in America." The sponsor, its logo boldly displayed, was Coors. A few more pages into the magazine, Budweiser, "The King of Beers," offered its latest tribute to its Black counterparts, "The Great Kings of Africa."

Like mining in Third World countries, advertising in Third World America is primarily an extractive enterprise. It enters the barrio and ghetto with a smiling happy face to convince all it reaches that they should purchase the products mentioned and purchase them often. Its true purpose is to stimulate consumption. Like the tailings of any mining operation, the subsidization of minority news media is a by-product for the advertisers. They are buying the audience, not the content that lures them.

But for journalists in Third World America, the content is much more than a by-product. It is the reason they work in the media. They realize their audience needs and wants solid news and information. To them, the advertising may be the unwelcome by-product. And for the audience, the content is the reason they choose one medium over another. Shut off from the main currents of news, Third World Americans look to their own media for news and information.

This is why the advertising and marketing system that is supposed to work for White America cuts across the grain of Third World America. As newcomers and second-class citizens in this society, they have less information and economic resources, and they need more information than their White counterparts to understand how the system functions and how they can improve their lives. Increased news and information sources serve that democratic ideal. But once advertisers and media managers find more profitable bait, any gains from the current advertising surge can easily be lost.

The media in Third World America cannot avoid selling their audiences as consumers on Madison Avenue. That is the unwritten law regulating the marketplace of ideas in an advertiser-supported system. But they can and should make every effort to insure that their listeners, viewers and readers are armed with the information enabling them to make intelligent political and purchasing decisions. To this end the recent developments in Spanish-language TV are encouraging.

America's media system, once a tie binding together people of various backgrounds, no longer lives by mass appeal. Instead, it finds differences in society's members, then exploits those differences through advertising and content that reinforces separate identities. In the future, the nation may be united on product usage, not media usage, and Third World Americans may find themselves alongside Whites in the product marketplace with less information to use in the idea marketplace. If this happens, Third World Americans will have been little more than targets for advertising—integrated as consumers, not as full participants, in the life of the United States.

THE GROWING ROLE OF WOMEN

THE "GLASS CEILING": WOMEN'S BARRIER TO TOP MANAGEMENT

Katharine Graham

Speaking with the authority of one who holds great power in the media, Katharine Graham discusses how subtle prejudice makes it difficult for women to reach the top level in the media and other fields. She is chairman of the Washington Post Company. Her comments were made to the 1986 International Women's Media Project in Washington.

I examined the problems of career women in a speech I gave three years ago. After interviewing many women for that speech—both journalists and those on the business side of media organizations—I came to this conclusion:

Women could not have it all—high-powered careers, marriage, and families, too—at least not in storybook or "superwoman" fashion.

I didn't mean this to discourage women from pursuing careers or families or both. It was more a question of nuance. I believed women could not do *everything* with the *same* degree of perfection. They couldn't spend the 12-hour days at the office that many top jobs require—and still take care of sick children, discuss politics and the economy with their husbands, and have time for themselves. Something had to give.

Women have since told me that they found my views dismaying but realistic. They agreed with at least the broad outlines of what I said.

To prepare for this conference, I wanted to find out what, if anything, is different. So I went back and talked to some of the same women I had interviewed before, as well as to others.

What I learned led me to conclude that the situation for working women has undergone several dramatic and fundamental changes in three short years. Before I describe them, let me set the stage.

For the most part, today's women began their careers with the traditional attitude of the feminist movement: Women can handle anything men can handle. We don't want—or need—special consideration or accommodation. We just want an equal chance, with equal pay for equal work. And by the way, we can manage husbands and children, too.

Armed with these convictions—and with affirmative action laws—women made substantial progress. They entered the work force in great numbers and rapidly climbed into the ranks of middle management. Then, for the most part, they seemed to stall.

Women have not advanced in satisfactory numbers to the *upper* levels. Women have yet to shatter the so-called glass ceiling—the invisible barrier separating middle management women from the power positions.

The reason, it seemed clear to me, had as much to do with age as sex. Women have been pursuing serious careers for only about 15 years. Men are still in charge at the top—a generation of men who feel uncomfortable with women as equal partners. When women remain in the work force long

Source: Address to the International Women's Media Project, Washington, D.C., November 12, 1986. Reprinted with permission.

enough to have paid their dues, I thought, sex will no longer be a barrier to the top jobs.

I now believe the issue has become more complex. That brings me to the first fundamental change I have observed: As overt sexual discrimination has waned, subtle sexual prejudice has come to the fore as a barrier to women's progress.

This subtle prejudice is more insidious and difficult to eradicate for its being less obvious.

Women no longer hear "You don't need a promotion because you have a husband who works" or "We'd like to give you that job but we already have a woman." Sexist language and thought are fading from the office.

But the statistics paint a discouraging picture. Jean Gaddy Wilson has completed a study that . . . reveals that at newspapers, for example, the overwhelming majority of management jobs in papers of every size continue to be held by men. Most women's salaries lag behind men's in almost every job category—even when men and women have the same length of service.

And the communications business—despite its obvious shortcomings—is among the more enlightened when it comes to women's progress. The situation in manufacturing, or banking and finance, must be a lot worse.

What is holding up greater progress? Some of the women I interviewed say they *are* given credit for doing their particular job well. But they are rarely consulted for their views on general issues or a major problem outside their realm of expertise. A man who is competent in one field is usually assumed to be capable of handling others. At least management is willing to take a risk on a man. This leads to advancement. A woman, on the other hand, is judged to be proficient only in narrow, often technical fields. As a result, they're not often considered for jobs beyond their immediate specialty.

In short, women are not "in the loop." Instead, they seem to be developing loops, or networks, of their own. This isn't all good. History has demonstrated that separate is not equal. Women need to be fully integrated into the work force in order to rise to more senior levels. To get in the loop, they need to hold substantive jobs in areas of critical importance to the company's success.

Substantive means operating positions, not just staff positions. Or, in the case of news, it means editing or anchoring responsibilities—particularly in hard news and on the networks.

Seniority, of course, is key. But here we encountered another problem—and another change. Instead of entering the work force and staying there, women are now beginning to depart in alarming numbers—not just any women, but MBAs, professionals, and those once on serious career paths.

Fortune magazine recently reported that fully 30 percent of the more than 1,000 women MBAs from the Class of '76 said they were self-employed, unemployed, or listed no occupation.

Certainly, the slow progress of women has discouraged many from pursuing corporate careers. However, the women with whom I spoke told me that while sexist barriers were *once* more likely to drive them out of the work force, today it is often the personal strain of trying to balance conflicting roles that is making women give up their careers.

The pressures of juggling work and family have not abated in the least. The trials of a couple trying to pursue dual careers are as tough as ever—although it's now the husband who may sacrifice for his wife's advancement. I'm told the new line men use around the singles bar is, "I'm a lawyer. I've got a transferable skill."

Ted Koppel, to cite one famous example, took a year off to become a house-husband so that Grace Anne, his wife, could go to law school. Ted said he leaked the news to the media so that people wouldn't think he had been fired! It didn't seem to hurt his career.

Even if husbands are willing to pitch in and share the load, women, of course, still bear the primary responsibility for child care and household duties. What's more, some women don't want to relinquish that role. It's an issue of control, which they don't want to surrender.

Above all, many women continue to be tortured by the guilt of leaving children at home (or unfinished work at the office)—and by the fear of what may befall children in day-care centers or in the hands of unreliable help. Many women feel they *need* to stay home and be with their children when they are young.

Beyond these conflicts, something else is causing women to think twice about their careers. *Personal* values and goals are replacing *feminist* values and goals for many working women—and indeed they are for many men as well.

Having worked for several years, having confronted frustrations and rewards of careers, many women are now asking themselves: What is more important, what brings me the most satisfaction? Is it my job? Is it my kids? Is it our life together?

Many have decided they do want to stay on the ladder and find it is possible, as long as they have an adequate support system. However, a significant number of women are choosing the traditional role of wife and mother.

How many of *your* friends are thinking about giving up their jobs to stay home, take care of the family, and pursue other interests?

A recent *New York Times Magazine* article even suggested that a regression is taking place, a return to the "we will cook well, we will look well" mentality.

These changing attitudes are having an impact on one of the original tenets of the feminist movement. Women once claimed they were "just like men" and should be treated as such. Today women—and men, too—are beginning to understand that the difference between the sexes must be recognized and accommodated to a certain degree.

I believe women still do everything possible not to require special treatment. But there have been some changes.

Women *do* expect reasonable maternity leaves and a job of equal responsibility when they return. Women *are* splitting jobs, working more at home and making other arrangements that enable them to work fewer or more flexible hours. One husband-and-wife team is going to split a foreign correspondent's assignment for the *Post.* But some women are *not* willing to work the long hours they once did.

One of our top women editors said, "I did anything I was asked to do—worked any hours—in order to get ahead. But women these days are returning from maternity leave and saying, 'I won't work nights any longer.' "

Many companies have been willing to go along, even though these adjustments have caused some real management problems. But I'm afraid there is a limit to what women can expect. Frankly, the higher you get, especially in operating jobs, the less flexibility there is to meet special needs.

Despite this progress, the communications industry—and business in general—has yet to face up to what I believe will be the most important issue in enabling women to combine careers and families. I'm talking about day care.

In order for women to be able to remain on the job long enough to gain the seniority they need to win the top spots, the conflicts of career and child care must be resolved. I believe a new and vastly expanded approach to day care has to be a major part of the solution.

Reliable day care at reasonable cost must become a reality in American life—as common as medical insurance and pensions, which were once thought to be revolutionary, too.

Day care is needed not only for career women who *choose* to work, and may be in the higher income brackets, but even more for the 5 million-plus single mothers in this country who *have* to work and are in lower income brackets.

Day care is needed not only by individual women but by business itself, which must tap *all* the human talent it can find in order to meet the competitive challenges of today. In short, day care is not a feminist issue. It is a societal issue.

Developing adequate day care will be a major challenge. Government must play the leading role. It is too big and costly an undertaking to be left to businesses alone. Yet business can do much more. And parents, too, must take an active part in its development and funding.

Day care will take all of our combined efforts and commitment. We in the media have an essential responsibility to keep the public informed and aware of this issue. We must all work on it together, starting now.

In closing, I am *gratified* by the great progress women have made. I am *concerned* about some of the recent changes I described—the emergence of subtle prejudice, the exclusion of women from the loop of power, the personal strains of conflicting roles, and the departure of women from the work force. But I am *encouraged* by the more realistic view that women have developed about the demands of career and family—as well as by the growing awareness of what business must do to ensure continued progress in the years ahead. Ultimately, I believe we *can* reach the point where women—and men, too—will be able to achieve success in whatever field they choose. We'll know we're there when we no longer have to assess our status in conferences like this!

WOMEN IN THE NEWSPAPER BUSINESS

Jean Gaddy Wilson

Jean Gaddy Wilson's 1986 survey is the most comprehensive study ever of the role of women in the newspaper business. A portion of the extracts reprinted here appeared in *presstime.* Wilson is a faculty member at the University of Missouri School of Journalism.

Source: presstime, October 1987; based on the study *Taking Stock: Women in the Media Before the 21st Century,* published by the Gannett Foundation. Reprinted with permission of *presstime.*

To get a clearer picture of women employed by daily newspapers and other U.S. media, the first national survey on the subject was conducted last year.

Responses from newspaper publishers show that:

- The overwhelming majority of management jobs on the most influential papers continue to be held by men.
- The overwhelming majority of management jobs on mid-size and small newspapers also continue to be held by men.
- Women's salaries lag behind men's in almost every newspaper job in almost every circulation category.
- Even when women and men with the same length of service are compared, women's salaries in a majority of cases lag behind those of their male counterparts in the same job at newspapers of a similar size.
- Although the number of women employed at newspapers is still below the number of men, there appears to have been a steady increase of women in management and professional positions in the past two decades. . . .

According to the U.S. Labor Department's Bureau of Labor Statistics, *for the first time ever,* a historic moment in employment was reached in March [1986] when women became more than half of the "professional" or so-called "white-collar" class of workers.

And 1986 will be remembered as an equally historic year in education—the year when women will have earned half of all college undergraduate and graduate degrees awarded.

CHANGES AT NEWSPAPERS

During the 20-year period in which they reported these fundamental changes in American education and employment, newspapers found themselves being directly affected by the evolution. Women were hired in greater numbers than ever into newsrooms, ad departments, circulation. And sometimes, management.

In a way, it was reminiscent of the years during

World War II, when female reporters kept the papers going. But there was a difference: In the immediate post-war period, a number of female reporters were fired to make room for returning GIs; but in the late 1960s, '70s and '80s, they and women in other newspaper jobs were no longer out of place.

Yes, in the four decades since women were once a majority of employees in a number of newspapers, newspapers have changed . . . and they haven't.

"Women's news" still wraps around the grocery and furniture ads in the back of the paper. "Men's news" still predominates on the front page. Both are sweeping generalizations with exceptions in broad degree. But "hard news" usually means coverage of men, and "soft news" means women.

Women who have reached the top in the business went by one of two routes: by virtue of family ownership, as was the case for Katharine Graham of The Washington Post Co. and Helen K. Copley of The Copley Press Inc.; or by climbing corporate ladders, as was true for *USA Today* Publisher Cathleen Black. Fewer than 60 female publishers run U.S. dailies.

And in a report last January in *The Bulletin* of the American Society of Newspaper Editors, Dorothy Jurney provided results of her ninth annual survey on women in newsroom management. It found that fewer than 10 percent of "directing editors" listed in the 1985 *Editor & Publisher Year-Book* were female.

According to Jurney's survey, at 28 dailies (out of 37) with circulations of 250,000 or more, no women carried the titles of editor, executive editor, managing editor, assistant managing editor, editorial chief, or other high editorial positions.

As an indication of how few women historically have been in newspaper work, the Census Bureau still names jobs for professional news employees that include "newsman" and "legman," even though those jobs may be filled by women. Another indication is that class-action and individual sex-discrimination lawsuits against major newspapers were filed and won by women continuing through the first part of this decade.

Yet there is a sense that the past few years have been a time of unparalleled change for women in newspapers—in newsrooms, business offices, personnel offices, advertising departments and management.

THE NEW SURVEY

The questionnaire titled "The Media in the '80s" was designed, in part, to get a better picture of how the daily newspaper industry in the United States is hiring and promoting women. Publishers were queried on employment, changing news content, business conditions for newspapers, and expectations of where jobs will increase, decrease or remain the same.

Regarding employment, publishers were asked to specify the number of men and women employed in 10 departments and to provide detailed information about 93 jobs including: the exact salary, plus any commissions being earned by the person employed; the number of employees the person supervised; the number of years the employee had been with the company; and whether that person was male or female.

Each job was defined precisely so that a national "snapshot" of employment would emerge. For instance, under the title of "Advertising Director or Manager," the definition was "overall management responsibility for advertising functions. Develops and manages budgets. Supervises sales and/or management employees. Top management position."

When all newspapers' responses are averaged together, women are a majority in areas that traditionally have been "women's jobs"—classified advertising manager, longest-term employee in classified ad sales, feature editor, feature reporter, lifestyle editor and business office manager.

The job with the highest percentage (90 percent) of women employed is, predictably, the lifestyle editor who is responsible for the "women's news" of the paper. Also predictably, the lowest percentages for women are in jobs traditionally held by men—longest-term sports editor (3 percent), sports reporter (5 percent), production manager (3 percent) and pressroom manager (0 percent).

Women represent only 7 percent of top management in the publisher and general manager positions.

Jobs with more than one-third women also include national ad manager, longest-term retail ad sales worker, business manager, copy editor, wire editor, and longest-term general reporter. Women are about one-fourth the employees in the jobs of retail manager, managing editor, news editor and controller. Fewer than 20 percent of the managers of the news, advertising and circulation departments are female.

CIRCULATION BREAKDOWN

The new survey also examines the employment situation by circulation categories:

- **More than 100,000.** At the largest newspapers, women are the majority by a 4 to 1 ratio in one job—lifestyle editor. Women are about half the business office managers, feature reporters and feature editors. They account for about one-quarter of the classified ad managers, longest-term classified ad sales workers, news editors, national ad managers and wire editors.

Women are fewer than one in 10 in these top management positions: publisher, general manager, ad director, editor and production manager. They also account for about one in 10 editorial page editors.

- **25,000–100,000.** Although newspapers of 25,000 circulation are quite different businesses from those of 100,000, they have about the same percentages of women employed in comparable jobs. The employment of women is higher in this circulation category than at the largest papers.

Newspaper publishers reported that the job most likely to be filled by a woman in the ad department of dailies within this range is the longest-term advertising sales rep. In the editorial department, women are a clear majority of lifestyle editors, two-thirds of the feature editors and about half the feature reporters. A higher percentage of women are business office managers than at the largest papers.

Among management positions at newspapers in this circulation category, women are fewer than one in 10 publishers, general managers, ad directors, editors, circulation managers and production managers. They also make up fewer than one in 10 photography directors, editorial page editors, sports editors and sports reporters.

- **Fewer than 25,000.** In general, as newspaper circulation decreases, the percentage of women employed increases, regardless of department.

While women are fewer than one-tenth of the ad directors at dailies of 25,000–100,000 circulation, at the smallest papers they are more than a third.

In editorial jobs, the percentage of women employed increases almost across the board as circulation decreases, whether the position is that of editor, managing editor, city editor, copy editor, general news reporter or sports reporter.

Those jobs filled by a majority of women on the large papers grow to even larger percentages of the papers with less than 25,000 circulation. For instance, while women are about half the feature editors on the largest papers, they have about three-fourths of those jobs at the smallest papers.

THE SALARY GAP

Looking at percentages of women employed in selected positions gives an indication of where women have been hired and promoted. Looking at salaries for men and women in the same positions gives an indication of the salary differences, if any, between the sexes in a given job.

As late as 1980, U.S. Bureau of Labor Statistics figures showed that if all men's and women's salaries were averaged together, a woman made 59 cents for a man's dollar. The figure for women has climbed to 64 cents, reflecting their being hired into jobs outside the purely service sector and into higher-paying jobs.

Although that comparison is used extensively in the United States in talking about the difference between men's and women's salaries, it is misleading to think that standard should be applied to comparable jobs. The expectation would be that the same jobs, in the same size newspapers, would have salaries in the same general range. But that is not the case. . . .

In the "Overall" column, when all men's and women's salaries are combined for a particular job, the figures are shown both as an average and as a median.

For instance, when all publishers' salaries are computed, $65,729 is the average compensation. When all publishers' salaries are computed for the median, half of the salaries are higher than $55,000 and half are lower.

When all male publishers' salaries are averaged, the salary is $66,496. Half of all male publishers' salaries are higher than $56,600 and half are lower. When female publishers' salaries are averaged, the figure is $55,197. When a female publisher median is computed, half the women publishers make more than $45,000 and half make less than that.

On the average in this survey, female publishers make 83 cents for every male publisher's dollar. Women publishers' median salary is 80 percent that of their male counterparts.

As with government statistics, overall figures give a view of the average salary for the entire group of people in a category. Women's overall percentage of men's salaries is lower than in the various circulation categories. Why? Because in most jobs, more men are at the larger newspapers with resulting high salaries.

Women and men are closest to having equitable salaries in the top job (publisher) and in editorial (general news reporter, feature reporter, news editor and wire editor)—all in the 80 percent range.

Positions where salary averages are furthest apart—where women make about 60 percent of men's salaries—include: classified ad manager (many women are in this job at smaller papers with lower salaries); national ad manager (occupied by few women); editor, photography director and sports editor (reflecting a preponderance of men in these positions at the higher-paid, larger newspapers); and general manager, controller, business manager, circulation manager and production manager (also reflecting a dearth of women in these jobs at larger papers). . . .

The most telling factor is that out of the 141 different job comparisions across all newspapers where there were enough men and women to compare, women made equitable salaries in about one-sixth of the cases.

In a number of positions at the bigger newspapers, there were no women at all in the highest-paid jobs such as editor, publisher and general manager.

LENGTH OF SERVICE

It's common perception that women now have a greater role in newspapering than 10 years ago.

In looking at the percentage of females at five-year service increments, it becomes evident that the participation of women in newspaper management has been increasing in recent years.

At each succeeding five-year interval, women become less of the percentage of management people employed.

For instance, in the first five years of employment in management, women are about a third of those hired. At the 6–10-year level, the percentage shrinks to a little less than a third, and it continues to drop with each five-year increment. This may indicate that newly employed women stand a better chance of being promoted into management than women hired some years earlier.

This assumption is bolstered by the statistics on salaries, also. Although women are still paid less than men in management, the gap narrows for the newer employees. For instance, women in newspaper management with 1–5 years of service make $11,000 less than their male counterparts, but the difference generally is much greater for those with longer periods of service.

SUMMING UP

It appears that women have a better chance than ever to be hired in every area of newspaper employment. However, because women have been the majority in journalism education programs for almost a decade, we could expect to see a sharp increase in women's employment and promotion at dailies. As yet, that dramatic increase doesn't seem to be happening. However, the trend seems to be in place.

Before this first-time ever survey, the newspaper industry has had estimates rather than an actual counting of the participation of women at U.S. dailies. This study, made possible through the co-operation of funders, newspaper publishers and interested news people, provides the first national yardstick against which future hiring, promotions and compensation may be measured.

THE SHIFTING TELEVISION NEWS SCENE

NETWORK NEWS AT THE CROSSROADS

Burton Benjamin

The once-dominant TV network news shows have lost part of their audience, face sharp new competition, and are groping for new program formulas to revive their fortunes. Burton Benjamin, a senior fellow at the Gannett Center for Media Studies, is a former executive producer of the *CBS Evening News.*

A decade ago some observers of the press speculated that television news, with its speed, immediacy and huge audience, would make newspapers, as we knew them, obsolete. In 1982, Leo Bogart expressed a more moderate view in the *Wilson Quarterly:* "The real question is not whether newspapers will survive into the 21st century but rather *what kind* of newspapers they will be."

If you take Mr. Bogart's quotation, and substitute network news for newspapers, you have a striking parallel with the situation in television today. Increasing numbers of people are asking how long network news can survive its declining ratings and increased competition from local stations, syndicators and cable.

Will declining ratings affect the way the networks package their news? Is it all a ratings game? Are the networks beholden to the same forces that drive those on the entertainment side of television?

If you asked those kinds of questions a decade ago, in the halcyon days of network-news preeminence, the answer you were likely to get was this: "We're in the *news* business [the emphasis was always there]. Ratings have little or nothing to do with the way we present the news. We have a simple mandate—to present today's news today. We don't let popularity charts dictate what we do."

I heard that view a lot when I was producing the *CBS Evening News with Walter Cronkite,* and it was understandable in a way. We were so far ahead in the ratings that it wasn't too difficult to be a purist. I must say, the view sounds rather innocent today.

THE LESSON IN NEWSPAPERS

Perhaps there is a lesson for network news in how one newspaper responded to rising costs and flat circulation. (It is interesting, by the way, how "circulation" is regarded as an honorable, straightforward business objective while there seems to be something unworthy about its television counterpart, "ratings.") In the 1970s, the *New York Times*'s future was such that, according to one executive, one more rise in the cost of newsprint would have put the paper into the red.

In 1976, the paper added a "Weekend" section, followed by "Living," "Home," "Sports Monday," "Business Day," and "Science Times." Since the introduction of these "theme sections," the *Times*'s daily circulation has risen from 828,000 to more than 1,000,000. The *Times* faced its problem by enhancing its newsproduct in an innovative way.

Not all staffers were pleased. I remember one

Source: Gannett Center Journal, Spring 1987. Reprinted with permission.

saying to me: "The only way to get a piece in the goddamn paper is to hook a menu onto it." He was fortunate he didn't work for one of the networks whose response to falling ratings and rising costs is not to increase productivity but to run a scythe through the newsroom.

The restructuring of news reports already is taking place at the networks. As Tom Brokaw, anchor of the *NBC Nightly News,* said in a recent speech at the Gannett Center for Media Studies: "We are now in the process of redefining our place in the information spectrum. We are now less of a daily news diary and more of a daily news magazine, offering in addition to a capsule of the daily news, a broader and deeper view of some of the big stories. We are slowly conceding the breaking stories to local news stations."

Therein lies the major change. The networks have lost their exclusivity, especially their picture exclusivity. New technology has given the larger local stations and CNN a reach comparable to ABC, CBS and NBC. Local stations, or one of the syndication services to which they subscribe, will bring you the latest satellite pictures from Montana to Mali, just as the networks have done for years. It is this encroachment, along with competition from other program sources (independent stations love to play hardball and program game shows opposite network news; even WABC-TV in New York has followed suit), that [has] cut into the numbers and dictated a new look for network news.

The networks even contributed to the revolution themselves. When I produced the Cronkite News, we held back our best footage from the syndication newsfeed that went to our more than 200 affiliated stations at 5 P.M. each day. We did not want the same stories running on local news before we got on the air. Roone Arledge broke that embargo when he became president of ABC News. He began sending everything down the line to the local stations, and we had to do the same. Our fiercely competitive affiliates no longer would tolerate an embargo. Today, the networks give their affiliates virtually everything they have, and even set up regional news-feeds to sweeten the pot. By the time network news hits the local market (after two hours and more of news in the larger cities), the audience often has seen most of the stories already.

Some former colleagues of mine at CBS News were startled last year when the network news broadcast originated in Los Angeles. They fed to the eastern and central time zones at 3:30 P.M., local time, and then went back to their hotel to watch the Rather News on the air. They watched the local news while waiting. "We never get a chance to see local news when we're in New York," a writer told me, "and it was a revelation to us. By the time we came on the air, we looked so *stale.*"

None of this has come as a surprise to the network news executives. It didn't suddenly happen. The erosion has been slow but steady. In 1980, the three network news broadcasts had a combined audience share of 72 percent (sets in use). Today, that share hovers around 63 percent. In the ratings (percentage of all TV homes), NBC and CBS are in a virtual tie, and ABC is not far behind. One rating point equals 874,000 households, and a one-point rating lead for the evening news time period is worth $19 million in advertising revenue annually. So we need not belabor the fact that this is a very high-stakes game.

All three networks are seeking to come up with a new mix that will bring back the viewers they have lost. Considerable groping is going on. Some nights the network evening news looks like *MacNeil-Lehrer,* other nights like *60 Minutes.* Both Roone Arledge at ABC and Howard Stringer at CBS have used the same words to describe what they're up to. "We are going to start from scratch," they say.

The last time Arledge started from scratch was in 1977, when he became president of ABC News. He went on a talent-raiding spree marked by sharply escalating salaries. Using production techniques he had pioneered at ABC Sports, he gave ABC News a modern and classy look, which the other networks and many local stations have cloned today. He was helped by the network's strong entertainment schedule, and by the switch to ABC of some attractive local affiliates. The journalism improved and the ratings headed north, which is what the game is all about.

No one can expect a "repeat" of that success in network news. Industry circumstances have changed, probably irrevocably, and given the imperatives of the day, the networks will clearly have to change the way they do business. No one has suggested—at least, not lately—that they take the low road and go the *New York Post* route. But it is really quite naive to ask whether ratings-circulation will affect how the network news product is packaged in the future. That would be like asking what yardstick Knight-Ridder or any other responsible news organization uses to determine its success.

It is to be fervently hoped that the networks will succeed, if for no other purpose than to remove the specter of "lean and mean" from the newsrooms. Those Wall Street–inspired buzzwords are making this the worst of times for network journalists. If left alone, they have the imagination and wit to develop a network news for the 1990s. To many of us, the best way for them to go is to lead with strength, with probing, insightful *journalism.* Otherwise, they will be faced with the same lower ratings and reduced advertising revenues that beset them today. They will continue to be savaged by bean-counters and non-journalists, and they might lose the whole ball game.

TOUGHEST JOB IN TV NEWS

Clint O'Connor

Television reporters get their faces on camera, but the assignment editor is the one who gets the news covered. Many assignment editors "burn out" under the pressure. Clint O'Connor, who provides this glimpse of backstage TV, is associate editor of the *Washington Journalism Review.*

At the heart of every television newsroom are its assignment editors. They decide what stories to cover and who will cover them. They're the bleary-eyed, desk-bound people with a telephone wedged in each ear, listening to three or four radios, peering over a mountain of schedules and maps and newspaper clippings. Ostensibly, they deploy crews. But their real job is to irritate people. They wake reporters to send them on mid-winter stakeouts at 5 A.M. They implore photographers to work late on Christmas Eve. They withhold lunch breaks, overtime and time off. Most TV news people acknowledge it's the toughest job in the business, and that assignment editors seldom last long. "They miss one story and they're dead meat," says Bruce Johnson, who has seen eight assignment editors come and go during his 10 years as a reporter for WUSA-TV in Washington, D.C.

Yet many assignment editors thrive on the pressure and responsibility. *WJR* discovered that the good ones are action junkies, capable of absorbing a lot of pressure. "It's the most thankless position in the newsroom," says Judi White, an assignment editor at KDFW-TV in Dallas. "You are put upon by producers, editors, management, photographers, and anybody else who comes through the newsroom. You're kind of at the mercy of everyone else. You kind of get kicked around a lot."

White, a five-year veteran of the KDFW assignment desk, enjoys the challenge of covering the vast terrain of the Dallas-Ft. Worth market. She talks about the "very high burnout rate" and "very stressful" aspects of her job, but it's her word "thankless" that truly echoes the sentiments of most local TV news people.

"It's not the kind of job you would want to do for an extended period of time," says Keith Young, news director at Savannah's WSAV-TV. "Reporters get all of the glory, of course."

According to KUSA-TV's Don Clouston, "You have to be the bad guy all the time . . . if someone has to stay late, you have to break the news to them. You're the buffer, the person they see first thing in the morning and the last thing at night." Clouston was an assignment editor for three years at KTUL-TV in Tulsa before joining the KUSA

Source: *Washington Journalism Review,* April 1987. Reprinted with permission.

desk in Denver. The move took him from trying to placate some 40 personalities in Tulsa to handling more than 100 news staffers in Denver.

"You have to make decisions, and if they don't like it, you have to be the listening board," Clouston says. "You hear all the complaints. . . . You have to be aware of a person's feelings, their personal problems."

"If you give a reporter the best photographer, they complain the story's no good," says George Banks, assignment editor at WTLV in Jacksonville, Florida. "If you put them on the best story, they say the photographer's no good. So you're really between a rock and a hard place."

The rock represents the general manager, the news director, the assistant news director, and maybe an executive producer. The hard place is the producers, reporters, and photographers the assignment editor must coordinate and get to the right place (no easy task) at the right time (even harder) to get the story. Like their brethren in stress, air-traffic controllers, assignment editors are constantly flirting with disaster, making 50, 100, 500 decisions a day under overwhelming pressure. Just trying to get crews out on a breaking story takes a toll on one's digestive tract, especially since the job requires waging psychological warfare with news people who have egos the size of some western states.

Assignment editors do not work alone, of course. There are desk assistants and city editors and managing editors, and story ideas from producers and reporters and photographers, but when the desk blows it, or is perceived to have blown it, when your station is late getting to the overturned school bus, when the competition has tape of the paramedics actually pulling the kids out from the mangled metal, and all you have is a stand-up with a cop in front of where the bus "used to be"—then it's your head.

Bruce Johnson admits that an assignment editor

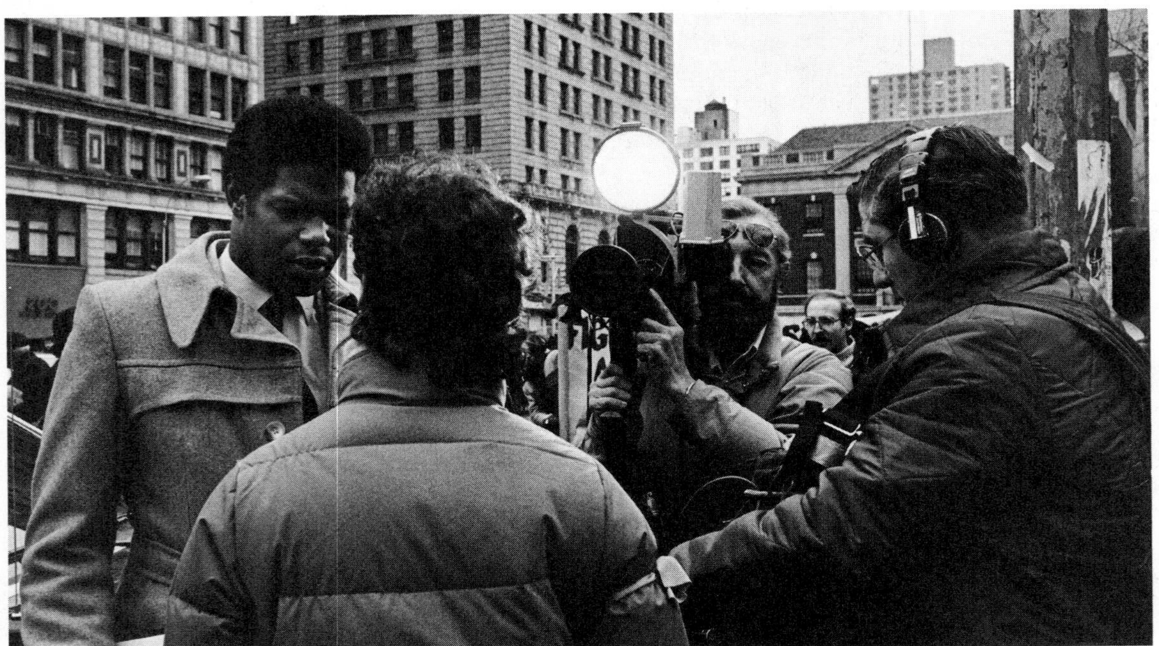

Television news crew conducts an on-the-street interview. The cameraman shoots from close range as the reporter (left) questions man with his back to camera. Such at-the-scene coverage of breaking stories appears frequently on local newscasts.

is "the most important person in the newsroom on a daily basis," but cautions that "a reporter who depends on the desk for stories is in trouble." Johnson says one of the worst aspects of the job is the layout of the typical newsroom, where the assignment editor sits in the center of the action. "When they screw up, they get dumped on in front of the whole newsroom," he says. Johnson passes along a quip from a colleague that typifies the way assignment editors are regarded by many of their coworkers: "If the assignment editor's body was found dead on the station steps, you'd have 200 suspects—everyone in the newsroom."

"It's one of those jobs where you get all of the blame and none of the credit," says John Spiropoulos, a former local and network assignment editor who now reports for Johnson's competitor, WJLA-TV. "People on the desk are like the offensive line [in pro football]; the only time you hear their name called is on a penalty."

Dave Winstrom, assignment editor for WVUE in New Orleans, remembers the night his "name was called." He sat down with the rest of the news staff to watch the city's three 5 o'clock newscasts and saw both competing stations lead with live reports from the U.S. attorney general's office on startling new evidence in the Governor Edwin Edwards racketeering trial. WVUE missed it. "Every mouth in the newsroom dropped," says Winstrom. "I got hell for that one."

Although no concrete statistics exist, most news professionals say the average life expectancy of an assignment editor is two years. And most ex-assignment editors are not exactly retiring to the south of France. According to the 1986 University of Missouri Salary Survey of 273 commercial television stations, assignment editors earn an average of $24,879 annually—less than news directors, assistant news directors, and executive producers, and far less than news anchors make.

So—knowing it's the hardest job in television news without the highest pay, and knowing what anguish awaits those who become assignment editors, why would anyone want the job?

"It's really the most important job in the newsroom," says Dave Winstrom. "The news director is tied up with budgets, and the managing editor is looking ahead, planning stories, but the guy who sits at the desk and starts it off and covers the whole day" is the one in control, he says. "To be perfectly honest, sometimes four or five days out of the week you go home with a feeling that you didn't accomplish anything. But then there's that one day when you really do get it done, and that feels great."

"When that big story hits, that good spot-news story gets everybody going," says KUSA's Clouston. "You've got follow-ups, and trying to explain why things happened that way. . . . It gets your adrenaline going. The whole newsroom is excited and glad to be at work."

"I like being in the thick of things," says Jack Allison, assignment editor for KPNX-TV in Phoenix. "You're responsible, in some ways, for virtually everyone's needs."

Assignment editors must be so many different things to so many different people: hand-holder, scolder, logistics specialist, technology expert, part Joan Rivers, part Joan of Arc. And how do they do that? How, with all the plotting of street routes and soothing of egos, do they keep the news operation in perpetual forward motion?

The best assignment editors "are the ones who are newsroom cheerleaders," says Bruce Johnson, "the ones who don't lie to reporters." Johnson says if you're going to cover a demonstration, "the good assignment editor will tell you, 'Don't take K Street, take Pennsylvania Avenue,' so the crew won't get trampled on."

"They have to be extremely well organized," says news photographer Rob Bennett, who recently moved from New Jersey's WOR-TV to WJLA in Washington. "They have to be good at getting and good at giving directions, or you'll end up in the wrong town, or the wrong state. They have to have a real good listening ability, and trust the judgment of the people in the field."

The trust factor works both ways, according to KUSA-TV News Director Fidel (Butch) Montoya. Montoya, a rare news director who rose from the ranks of cameramen, remembers "a good assign-

A DAY IN THE LIFE OF NANCY VALLE

7:00 A.M. Nancy Valle pushes through the double glass doors leading into WBAL-TV's newsroom. The 28-year-old assignment manager is a five-year veteran of Baltimore's CBS affiliate; she spent the first three years as a producer, the last two as chief of the assignment desk. In the middle of Channel 11's newsroom is a giant glass booth—mission control—where Valle takes the hot seat. In front of her, within arm's length, are eight scanners, a two-way radio, a conventional radio, a TV monitor, several telephones, typewriters, and file drawers stuffed with maps, phone books, newspaper clippings, and story ideas. As her first order of business Valle checks the "Overnight Note," which will bring her up to speed on new stories being developed and the preliminary plans for News Eleven's four daily newscasts: Noon, 5:30, 6:00, and 11:00 P.M. Next she skims the *Baltimore Sun* and *Washington Post.* Today Valle has 10 reporters and nine shooters (cameramen) at the ready. Two reporters are off the street entirely, working on longer features. Except for reporter Marc Mooney, who does the five-minute local cut-ins for the "CBS Morning News," Valle is the only person in the newsroom.

7:36 A.M. Conference call with News Director Frank Graham, Assistant N.D. Betsy Hyle, and Executive Producer Frank "Junior" Traynor to discuss the news lineup. Among today's stories are these: Jon Ausby, a 17-year-old Andover High School student and athlete, died last night during half-time of his basketball game, cause of death unknown. Convict Daniel Allen has escaped from a prison van. There's a beach erosion hearing in Ocean City, and Baltimore residents are up in arms over the possible closing of Pimlico race track and the moving of the Preakness.

7:49 A.M. Valle logs the stories on the chart, a giant erasable-ink board that towers over the middle of the assignment booth, under the headings, "Story," "Rptr/Cam," and "Location." Throughout the day stories will be added, erased, added again, and crews will be reassigned.

8:09 A.M. Mooney tells Valle he has just heard that a woman refusing to vacate her dwelling is being evicted "right now," and thinks it should be covered. The woman's name is Morning Sunday. WBAL has already covered several aspects of the penniless woman's struggle with city officials, and Valle is noticeably sick of the story. She decides not to send a reporter, instead calling a shooter already on the streets to pass by the woman's house (if anything newsworthy happens they will use the footage and do a voice-over later). Valle gives directions to Morning Sunday's house over the two-way radio. She is also on the telephone trying to work around someone's impending schedule change. "I swear," she says shaking her head after hanging up, "I feel like a giant baby-sitter sometimes."

8:14 A.M. Valle dispatches reporter Vicki Mabrey to cover the Jon Ausby story at Andover High School.

8:50 A.M. One of Valle's assistants, assignment editor Lyle Mason, arrives and takes his seat opposite her in the booth. Mason's specialty is dealing with the police. Valle says it's better, when hounding officers for information, to have the same voice calling again and again. Mason will spend a majority of his hours today tracking down leads with police.

9:43 A.M. Three more calls come in about Morning Sunday, but Valle is frying bigger fish. She confers with Betsy Hyle on Daniel Allen's escape. Apparently Allen was out yesterday with a group of convicts collecting roadside trash when he told the driver of the prison van, "I'm getting out," and did. The two women want to know how Allen, convicted of armed robbery and first-degree murder, could just hop out of a van.

9:54 A.M. Valle calls the city jail. She tries to get through to the warden to find out more about recent escapees: "Haven't there been three incidents in the past month?" She wants to know why Allen wasn't handcuffed and how he could get out so easily. The city jail says if Allen was a murderer he does not belong to them. Mason takes over the reporting of the story on his phone. "The wire story was wrong," he says. "Maybe it was a state prisoner?"

10:08 A.M. Valle is working two phones now and, in between answering three questions from a reporter and asking Hyle one of her own, she shouts over to Mason, "I want an interview with [department of corrections spokesman] Bev about the transportation of inmates and how that kind of thing could happen." Valle and Mason are joined by assignment editor Adrienne Walker, who takes the third seat in the crowded booth.

10:23 A.M. Valle comes running down the hallway and charges into the booth to call back a cameraman she sent out minutes before. "Base One to Peter, come back, come back," she commands into the two-way microphone. "We can get Bev, but we have to get her in Annapolis. Come back."

10:53 A.M. Producers meeting. Valle leaves the desk to meet with Graham, Hyle, Traynor, and 5:30 newscast producer Ariane Fenton. Valle updates the Ausby story. "The coach and the parents are at [Ausby's] home. We're trying to figure out where that house is." She runs down her list: Chip is on the insurance story, Edie is doing "Balto Awards," something nice and light to end the 5:30 news. Next, 6:00 producer Helene King replaces Fenton and stories for 6:00 are discussed. Ausby is still the hot topic. "The school does not want us in there," says Valle, "and will not let us interview any students." Hyle suggests the standard "shock and sorrow" coverage.

11:13 A.M. Walker breaks in to report Ausby's cause of death: "hypertensive cardiovascular heart disease." Valle tells Walker to start calling hospitals: "Johns Hopkins or G.B.M.C. [Greater Baltimore Medical Center], to find out what that really means so Vicki can explain at noon some of what that means."

11:47 A.M. After calling three hospitals and trying to track down numerous physicians, Walker finally gets a clearer explanation for Ausby's mysterious collapse: high blood pressure.

11:52 A.M. Valle simultaneously describes the cause of death to Vicki over the two-way radio while talking to her own medical source on the telephone to get a more understandable layman's description.

11:54 A.M. Baltimorean John Wooten, self-proclaimed "Strongest Man in the World," calls Valle to try to get a story on his new Ford commercial in which he lifts up the rear ends of Tempos.

11:59 A.M. Valle calls noon producer Joe DeFeo upstairs in the control room. "Tell [noon anchor] Rudy to ask Vicki what the disease really is. Why high blood pressure?"

12:00 P.M. "News Eleven at Noon" is on the air. Valle says she tries to watch the noon newscasts, as well as the competition's noontime offerings, but it's not always possible. Meanwhile, it's time for some soup, trying not to drip too much on the phone cord as she continues to field calls. Valle says she has developed a sixth sense for distinguishing the nuts from the newsworthy in the hundreds of calls that come through the assignment desk each week, and adds, "the majority of calls turn out to be accurate."

2:00 P.M. Something is beginning to unfold on the streets of Baltimore and Valle turns up the volume on two of her scanners to listen in. Actually, there seem to be three separate incidents involving law-enforcement officials. The first turns out to be a dead end. Through his police sources Mason discovers that the second action involves some kids being chased on foot for stealing a car. Valle is not interested in the kids, but turns up scanner four even louder trying to interpret the static voices.

2:17 P.M. Scanner four reveals that there is indeed a significant surveillance under way. The FBI and the DEA are trailing a "biggie" on North Avenue.

2:21 P.M. A call comes in about a helicopter airlifting a one-year-old burn victim to a hospital. Does WBAL want to cover it? Valle doesn't bite.

2:22 P.M. The surveillance heats up. Valle wants to get one of her street people over to North Avenue. "I'd love to go," she says, "but not in a marked car."

2:25 P.M. Mason is on the phone trying to confirm who the suspect is. "It's going on right now," he says. "No, we don't want to send our people over there, we just want to know what's going on."

2:30 P.M. The scanners tell the story. The chase suspect pulls into a K-mart shopping center. Plainclothes units lie back and wait. Valle calls a shooter on the two-way. She wants somebody ready to move into the area quickly. Hunched over the desk listening to the scanners, Valle intently doodles with her red pen on a giant paper blotter. She anticipates the silence. "They got him . . . they're done," she says before it's actually over. "They just cleared surveillance." Walker and Mason are still on the phones with police and the FBI trying to find out who the "biggie" was.

2:47 P.M. Valle calls her man back into base. Whomever was busted in the K-mart parking lot is still a mystery. No story.

2:50 P.M. Valle relinquishes her seat in the booth and moves to a desk in the newsroom to start organizing her files and schedules for tomorrow. Nightside editor Jill Bloom will be in at 3:00 to cover the desk for the night crews and focus on the 11:00 P.M. newscast.

4:00 P.M. Valle collects her purse and big black bag and heads home, where, with the aid of her remote-control buttons, she will watch news programs (WBAL, her two local competitors, and the three networks) at home from 5:00 to 7:30. The Ausby story leads both the 5:30 and 6:00 newscasts, followed by escaped convict Daniel Allen. Baltimore viewers will learn nothing of the fate of Morning Sunday, the burned baby, or the world's strongest man, at least not from Channel 11. If anything earth-shattering breaks in the city that night, Valle will get a phone call from scanner buff Del Ayler, a retired steel worker who is WBAL's de facto overnight assignment editor. If there are no calls from Ayler, Valle will sleep until her alarm goes off at 5:45.

ment editor was someone I could trust, someone I respected . . . an assignment editor you respected, that made it easy. Because today you might be assigned to a news conference, but maybe tomorrow you'd get the nice feature, the photo essay, that kind of story."

In addition to being honest, trustworthy, inspirational, and a brilliant navigator, a successful assignment editor, Bennett says, must stay a good 19 steps ahead of everyone else.

Paula Polito, chief assignment editor for WBZ-TV in Boston, knows about the 19-step lead time. Polito rises every morning at 5:30 and reads the newspapers while listening to Boston's all-news radio station to catch up on the overnight news and any breaking stories. When she arrives at WBZ at 7:00, Polito scours her folders full of clips and press releases and checks her news calendar. By the time she has her 7:45 conference call with the news director, assistant news director, and executive producer, who are just sipping their first cups of coffee, Polito is ready for anything to pop in greater Boston, or greater anywhere for that matter. The advent of affordable satellite technology has dramatically expanded the reach of local TV stations, and changed the rules of the game for assignment editors. The good assignment editors have adapted to those changes.

"We used to ask, 'Is it worth it, how can we do this?' " says Polito. "Now we just say, 'When can we get there?' . . . The audience is more sophisticated and because of the technology we have, with satellites and Ku trucks, the capability they give us, they have made us do a lot more about news across the country."

Assignment editors also face changes brought on by a less mechanical source: the audience. What viewers want to see on the 6 o'clock news nowadays is less "live from the scene of the accident" and more "here's how the economic crunch affects you."

Tim Culek, assignment manager for WEWS in Cleveland, says his station has evolved from the traditional auto wreck/burning building kind of coverage to more newsroom-generated, civic-oriented features. Culek's big stories these days are on the rejuvenation of downtown Cleveland, the shattered steel industry, transportation, and the farm crisis. Not that Culek has chucked his police and fire radios out the window. The radios are still on, but the news menu has expanded. "The big thing now is work-up stories—look through the *Wall Street Journal* and *New York Times* [to] locate a national story," he says.

"We used to have something like 183 homicides a year in Cleveland," says Culek. "That's 183 bodies coming out of buildings. Now we only do about five or six sensational ones a year. We used to cover any kind of fire. We don't do that anymore."

Polito agrees: "I've seen a real transformation in television news in the past one-and-a-half to two years. . . . I'm not saying we don't cover fires anymore, but they have to *mean* something now." Polito says WBZ looks "for a national story with a local angle—a hostage with relatives in Boston. . . . A two-alarm fire used to take precedent over a national story. That doesn't happen anymore."

Of course, the battle-scarred desk veterans who may lament the demise of "blood and flames" coverage still have one familiar, old standby on hand that supersedes news-diet directives, budgets, and audience-research surveys—the weather. "Weather is still big," says Culek. "Those are the fun days. Then you don't have to think, you just have to get the trucks there." Culek, a former newspaper man, still gets a kick out of the instant news-in-your-face aspect of television. In newspapers, "I could have the greatest story in the world, but if I missed my deadline that was it," he says. "That's what's still exciting about television, the almost instant gratification."

Short of sitting and waiting for a "good" tornado to come swirling through town, here are some tips from desk survivors who know how to beat the odds:

"There are ways to prevent job burnout," says Paula Polito. "By delegating a lot of responsibility. Keep delegating. Get the people around you to participate."

You survive by "telling yourself to leave the job at work," says Beau Fong, an assignment editor at Seattle's KIRO-TV. "When you leave, leave it and don't take the job and its problems home."

Don Clouston recommends "well-timed vacations here and there. Pay attention to vacation schedules. A week off is not necessarily the solution. Maybe just a day off."

"You just can't be excited or off the wall like everybody else," says Tom Read, whose words probably should be etched in stone. He has been directing traffic at the assignment desk at WRTV in Indianapolis since 1972. "I've probably set some kind of record," he says. "I think I've got the best job in the newsroom."

In 31 years in broadcasting, Read, 54, has seen the evolution from black-and-white Speed Graphic stills to Polaroids to black-and-white film to color film ("That was a big deal, and you'd send it to a lab in Kansas City and get it back two weeks later") to videotape, helicopters, mobile trucks, and finally satellites. "We get all of the new stuff in and then we're not quite sure what to do with it . . . all of a sudden you've got all kinds of new problems that you didn't even know existed"—such as the man who demanded reimbursement for the tops of his trees, allegedly sliced off by WRTV's news helicopter; the kid who mooned the camera during a live report from the Indianapolis Speedway, or the exasperated woman who tugged on the arm of a reporter during a live spot to see if he knew anything about her son, who had fallen into the river behind them.

"I could be dead with ulcers," says Read. "It depends on your psychological approach." Read, a desk survivor, is the exception, not the rule. Most assignment editors are destined not to surpass the two-year limit.

"No one is trained to be an assignment editor,"

says WUSA's Bruce Johnson. "No one in their right mind would aspire to be an assignment editor."

So what should local stations do? Keep throwing live production assistants on the fire? Grab an old retiring city editor from the local newspaper?

To combat the high turnover rate, some stations are taking a more active interest in the selection and training of future assignment editors. WLS-TV, Chicago's top-rated news operation, first looks for people who are interested in a stressful position. Then, according to News Director Jim Hattendorf, "We start out training them as desk assistants, then they work weekend nights . . . then weekend days, with some weekdays, then the night shift during the week, then finally the day shift. We ease them into it."

Hattendorf knows about not being eased into it. One day when he was a TV reporter in San Antonio, Hattendorf complained to the news director that "the assignment editor was missing all the good stories." For his frankness, Hattendorf was awarded the assignment desk, where he stayed until moving on to stations in San Diego and Los Angeles. "There are many trash cans and file cabinets at stations with dents from where I kicked them," he says.

In Los Angeles, Hattendorf spent five years as assignment editor for KABC-TV. For two of those five years he worked six-day weeks, but finally had to give it up. "You don't have much of a social life if you're an assignment editor in a major market," he says. "It was like I wasn't living for awhile."

Still, Hattendorf sees the desk as a good career move, an essential stop on the road to becoming a well-rounded news director or general manager, and besides, it's still the hottest seat in broadcast journalism. "I would love to go and run the assignment desk," says Hattendorf. "I miss the excitement, the frantic behavior, the four phones, the radio going, and a big story breaking. I love it. I would still do it tomorrow."

THE REPORTORIAL TRADITION

THE PROGRESSIVE SPIRIT TODAY

Herbert J. Gans

In this essay an eminent sociologist contends that the underlying values of contemporary journalism are neither "conservative" nor "liberal" but those of turn-of-the-century Progressivism. Herbert J. Gans is a professor at Columbia University and the author of numerous books.

The news is not so much conservative or liberal as it is reformist; indeed, the enduring values are very much like the values of the Progressive movement of the early twentieth century. The resemblance is often uncanny, as in the common advocacy of honest, meritocratic, and anti-bureaucratic government, and in the shared antipathy to political machines and demagogues, particularly of populist bent. Altruistic democracy is, in other words, close to the Progressive ideal of government. The notion of responsible capitalism is also to be found in Progressivism, as is the dislike of bigness, the preference for craftsmanship over technology, the defense of nature, and the celebration of anti-urban pastoral society. Journalistic paraideology and Progressivism are further akin in their mutual support of individualism, their uneasiness about collective solutions, other than at the grassroots level, and their opposition to socialism. Moreover, the preservation of an upper-class and upper-middle-class social order, like the need for morally and otherwise competent national leadership, has its equivalents in Progressive thought.

Source: The Quill, November 1984. Reprinted with permission.

The Progressive movement is long dead, but many of its basic values and its reformist impulses have persisted. Why the news is reformist and Progressive I will discuss, but its being so helps explain why the news is not easily fitted into the conventional ideological spectrum. Of course, Progressive thought can be placed on that spectrum, although historians have not yet agreed whether the movement was liberal, conservative, or both. In any case, the news may be marching to a somewhat different drummer; and when journalists are unwilling to describe themselves as liberal or conservative, and prefer to see themselves as independents, they may be sensing, if not with complete awareness, that they are, as a profession, Progressive reformers.

That journalistic news judgment includes values raises the question whether these values are professional correlates of journalistic expertise or lay values that originate from outside the profession. If journalists apply lay values, however, they are selecting stories not only as professionals but also as citizens; in that case, one can ask whether they should do so and whom they are representing when they act as citizens. Furthermore, if professionals are making lay judgments, their claims to autonomy become a matter of debate. These are questions of news policy, but they presuppose a prior and empirical question: Where do the values that journalists apply originate?

The enduring values are part and parcel of news judgment; but even so, they are not, strictly speaking, professional values. They do not reflect technical expertise; rather, they are ingredients in a vision of the good nation and society. As such, they are also lay values, presumably of lay origin.

I have proposed that these values resembled turn-of-the-century Progressivism. A detailed historical study may show that the resemblance is coincidental, but there is at least one good reason to believe otherwise, for journalists were an intrinsic part of the Progressive movement. Whether they or citizen reformers "invented" the movement's values is another question; but in any case, I suggest that the enduring values originated in the Progressive movement.

This is not the place to consider the origins of Progressivism itself, but its heyday was concurrent with the era of the muckrakers; and the principal muckrakers—among them Ida Tarbell, Lincoln Steffens, and their editor, S.S. McClure—had considerable contact with, and were active supporters of, the national leaders of the Progressive movement. Journalists themselves were part of the national leadership; Alfred D. Chandler, Jr.'s study showed that thirty-six of the 260 Progressive leaders he identified were editors. In addition, many local journalists participated in movement activities in their cities and states. But perhaps the best illustration of the tie between the Progressive movement and the journalism of the period is given by the late Richard Hofstadter:

> The fundamental critical achievement of American Progressivism was the business of exposure, and journalism was the chief occupational source of its creative writers. It is hardly an exaggeration to say that the Progressive mind was characteristically a journalistic mind, and that its characteristic contribution was that of the socially responsible reporter-reformer.

Why Progressives allied themselves with journalists is not hard to guess. Political movements need to communicate with actual and potential supporters; and the Progressive movement came into being at about the time that the mass-circulation newspaper and magazine became the dominant news media. Many of the Progressive were small-town Americans of upper-class or upper-middle-class status who sought to control what they viewed as the corrosive influences of the urban-industrial society into which the economic changes and the immigrations from Southern and Eastern Europe had delivered them.

A detailed historical study would be necessary to ascertain why journalists allied themselves with the Progressives; but those who did, and many other leading journalists of the time, came from backgrounds similar to those of the Progressives; and perhaps they, too, were disturbed by the changes taking place in America. Incidentally, many of today's journalists still come from these backgrounds. [A 1976] study of a national sample of journalists by Johnstone and his associates showed that forty-nine percent were children of professionals and managers (and thus presumably from upper-middle-class homes), and almost three-fourths were either "Anglo-Saxon" or descendants of the "old" German, Irish, and Scandinavian immigration. (These data also apply to the news media I studied [*CBS Evening News, NBC Nightly News, Newsweek,* and *Time*], except that many top editors and producers, as well as news executives, are Jewish.)

That modern journalism should invoke values from the turn of the century does not suggest that the profession is operating with old-fashioned ideas, for Progressivism is hardly dead. Although no longer a movement, its ideas remain central to many political, social, and cultural reform efforts. More to the point, these ideas continue to be salient for journalists today. The values signify and maintain a proud chapter in American journalism, for during the Progressive period, journalists achieved a level of power and influence in American life they have not held since, except during the years of the Watergate scandals.

Today these values also serve journalism as a profession, giving it a respected social role. Insofar as journalists are defenders of a set of values, they are more than technicians who transmit information from sources to audiences. Contemporary journalists do not, for the most part, see themselves as reformers; but the ones I studied were proud whenever a story resulted in official investigations and in legislative or administrative reform. Then, too, Progressivism was, among other things, a professional movement that aimed to bring experts into politics and government; and its values enhance the professionalism of journalism, particularly since journalists are not yet certain whether they deserve to be called professionals. Also, Progressive ideology sidesteps or cuts across the partisanship of the political parties; it was, and continues to be, attractive to people who, like journalists, regard themselves as political independents.

In addition, the enduring values are shared by other segments of society, especially those public officials who are the journalists' major sources. In fact, the enduring values coincide almost completely with the major themes of political rhetoric, which is also centered on the nation as a unit, advocates much the same kind of capitalism and democracy, pays allegiance to small-town pastoralism, supports individualism and moderation, and preaches order. Political rhetoric is not political action, but then news is also a kind or rhetoric; and journalistic assumptions about the need for leadership are often expressed in the speeches politicians make during election campaigns and at ceremonial occasions.

The audience may not agree with all the opinions expressed in the news, but it is not likely to find fault with the enduring values. Middle Americans, for example, also favor social order, honest leadership, pastoralism, moderatism, and individualism. Not all may have faith in responsible capitalism, but neither are they happy with government welfare policies that add to their taxes. It appears as if the original upper-class and upper-middle-class Progressive vision of America has by now diffused to a larger portion of the population.

At the same time, the enduring values also serve the business interests associated with journalism, be they sponsors or news firms. Progressivism was (and is) not antagonistic to private enterprise per se, and the journalistic vision of responsible capitalism does not diverge sharply from the notion of corporate responsibility which, as overt ideology, is supported by the large corporations themselves. Moreover, the concept of individualism in the enduring values not only legitimizes the desirability of entrepreneurship but also views the shortcomings of private enterprise as "bad apples." As a result, the enduring values are blind to possible structural faults within the system, which in turn reduces the likelihood of stories that question the legitimacy of the present economic order.

THE PHOTOGRAPHER'S ROLE

ETHICS IN PHOTOGRAPHY: AVOID PRECONCEIVED IDEAS

Ron Mann

Use of setup pictures—shots artificially contrived by the photographer—is a topic of ethical debate in photojournalism as critics equate truthfulness in picture-taking with honesty in reporting. Ron Mann, director of photography at the *Register* in Orange County, California, examines the issue.

A photographer in St. Petersburg, Fla., writes a cute message on the bottom of a baseball fan's feet trying to produce a feature photo he thinks his editors will like. The 17-year veteran is later fired for "submitting a staged photograph for publication."

In Buffalo, a wire service transmits a news picture that actually is a composite. A mandatory kill is issued and the bureau is instructed never to use that photographer again.

An editor in Columbus, Ohio, is upset when a photographer returns without a picture showing excited cheerleaders leaving for the state tournament. The photographer said nothing happened during the early morning departure. The editor, counting on the photo for the p.m. edition, asks why the photographer did not set up a photo of the cheerleaders looking excited.

In Knoxville, Tenn., a news photographer recreates a photo of a story's key moment. The reporter includes a description of the moment in his lead and the news editor wants to use the picture. The photo editor says the setup shot is dishonest and kills it.

Ah, for the good old days when a discussion of photographic ethics simply centered around the issues of dead-body shots, flopped negatives, retouching and setting up pictures.

Setups? Some problems just refuse to die. Or, they are slower to reach a consensus opinion, if not a solution.

As photographers continue to become more valuable members of most papers' news-gathering team, the same standards demanded of reporters are now also expected from those photographers. In most cases, that demand for conformity has come from within the photo department.

But editors share the concern.

"If photographers are entitled to the same professional regard and respect as writers, then they should be held to precisely the same professional standards as writers," said Robert J. Haiman, then-executive editor at the *St. Petersburg Times*, who had the task of dismissing the photographer.

"Taking the setup picture [by the *Times* photographer] was not a firable offense," said Don Black, news editor at the *Oregon Statesman* in Salem. "Turning the picture in as a real photo was the firable offense. He was lying. He was treated the same way a reporter would have been treated."

Black has an unusual perspective on the subject. He's been a photographer, a photo editor and a features editor.

"Would you ask your writer to go to that same

Source: Reprinted with the permission of the American Society of Newspaper Editors from the January 1985 *ASNE Bulletin.*

event, get names of the people going on that trip, then make up quotes?" asked C. Thomas Hardin, director of photography for the Louisville (Ky.) *Courier-Journal and Times,* referring to the Columbus incident. Hardin is president of the National Press Photographers Association.

Another frequent speaker on the subject is Rich Clarkson, assistant director of photography at *National Geographic* magazine and a veteran of more than 20 years in photojournalism.

"Any time you're publishing a photograph there is a degree of acceptance and believability inherent in the fact that it is a photograph," Clarkson said. "You really need to be sure the photographer is one of the strongest links in the equation as you put it together. The photographer has to be as concerned about ethics, propriety, and honesty and truthfulness as you are as an editor."

As assistant managing editor at the *Denver Post,* Clarkson made the decision that all illustrations would only be made by the art department.

"Subjects know about phony situations," says Hardin. "They wonder what else [in the paper] is phony. Can we put trust in the public trust of your paper [they ask]?"

Having seen the dilemma from both sides of the journalistic fence, Black feels preconceived ideas are at the heart of the problem.

"Editors need to assign stories or ideas but not pictures. Assigning photos instead of story coverage is the mistake many editors make," Black said. "Ideas are too often preconceived and forced on other people—not just photographers but also the reporters. Editors are hung up on preconceptions. It is fine to have high standards and expectations but you can't put everyone under the onus of doing things the way they would have done it or the way they wanted it done. They must go with their people in the field to produce a honest picture."

Chicago Tribune director of photography Jack Corn has even more specific advice for photographers and editors.

"Don't direct people. Let people be themselves. Photograph what's there. If it is not there, let the editors have enough guts to say it wasn't there. If you miss it, you miss it. Editors don't have any guts."

Clarkson feels there is no ultimate answer as to when to pose and when you don't, "but don't fool the reader," he said. "What you present to the reader has got to be honest."

"Integrity and believability is all you have to sell," Black said. "If you have nothing to sell you're out of business. It's not just a matter of morality."

Haiman believes "that there is one thing about the journalistic community which is more important in it than in any other community. And that is the obligation to tell the truth, the whole truth and nothing but the truth. There is simply no room for people who don't tell the truth."

While every editor and every paper have an individual opinion on ethical standards and practices, Clarkson has some advice that can be used as a guideline by everyone.

"You have to trust the photographers a lot to come up with situations that are legitimate, that are real, that are honest, that are not misleading and yet still speak to the story that you're really trying to cover that day.

"You are no worse than, no better than the weakest link. Everyone along the whole trail has got to have this in mind, has got to use good judgment. Because no situation has an ultimate answer, we can't have black-and-white rules. The only good rule is to have no ultimate rules. Everyone has to use perfectly good judgment all of the time. And that starts with the photographer on the street."

PROVOCATIVE PEOPLE

RUPERT MURDOCH, INTERNATIONAL MEDIA BARON

Broadcasting Magazine

Rupert Murdoch's spectacular entry into the American media market and the sensationalism displayed by some of his newspapers have raised many questions about his thinking and plans. In a long interview with *Broadcasting* editors, excerpted here, he provides some answers.

Keith Rupert Murdoch is many men to most people. Owner of the flamboyant *New York Post* and the stately *Times* of London. Of the sensationalistic *Star* tabloid and of the prestigious Harper & Row. Almost a billionaire, personally, and proprietor of a $4 billion media empire that now includes seven major market U.S. television stations, a major motion picture company and the first programming entity in years to aspire to fourth networkhood. A force, certainly, in 20th century communications. [Murdoch sold the *Post* after this interview was published.] *Broadcasting* editors met with Murdoch at News Corp. headquarters in New York as his Fox Broadcasting was beginning to roll out a string of new TV series. They found him a professed newsman at heart, if a midas by profession, with a desire to bring broadcasting as close as possible to the real world.

Is your network modeled on a conventional network or does it have a different design in mind?

No, I think it has ambitions to grow into a conventional network, in the sense that it would one day be able to provide programing for its affiliates pretty much around the clock. What we're starting this week is one hour, and next week two hours, so we are building up very slowly.

There is a tremendous need for original programing on independent stations. The average independent station today lives on counterprograming, just as they put in old comedies against the news channels from 5 until 8 o'clock at night. That is where all the revenue is; there is some additional revenue late at night and there's some additional revenue from sort of exploitative animation during the day, in which I must say, I dislike very much.

You're talking about children's animated programing?

Well, that part of it which is simply designed to sell toys, simply to sell particular items to children. There's nothing wrong with advertising to a child audience, but to make your programing that way I think is really a prostitution of the broadcaster's function. If you did that in a newspaper, you'd be run out of town. Or in a magazine.

Do you then forbid that in your company?

We don't, but we're going to try to cut it down. We are moving to become less dependent on that, to be able to shrink it down over the years. You can't just wipe it out overnight.

There's nothing wrong with good animation. There's nothing wrong with a Disney type or Hanna-Barbera traditional cartoon animation, which we can all find amusing.

Source: "The Thinking Man's Media Baron," *Broadcasting*, April 13, 1987. Reprinted with permission.

Considering the various ways you might invest in the American media system, which do you think presents the best opportunity to you now: television stations, television networks, radio, cable TV systems or cable TV networks, VCR software, newspapers, magazines or book publishing? The thrust of the question is to ask you to evaluate the American media system today and put your own relative dollar value on it.

That's a very good question. If I knew the answer to it, life would be a lot easier. If anyone knew the answer to it, it would be good. But I believe that all of those you mentioned present opportunities for professional people with good professional communications skills.

Which is the most profitable of all those things? I have no idea. The safest profit-making thing at the moment, it would seem, would be a traditional local monopoly newspaper. But then again, you have to pay a price to get into that game, which many people would consider exorbitant.

Television stations you buy at what seem like exorbitant prices on the gamble that you can improve their position in the marketplace by bringing your skills and radically changing the situation. A great example of that would be channel 7 [WABC-TV] in New York. I don't know what their ratings are, but by changing their afternoon and early-evening lineup they have dramatically increased their share of the audience and, I'm sure, dramatically increased their revenues at probably no expense. There's always a way of doing things better on television.

You can't do that sort of thing with newspapers. You work on smaller margins and things are really much more predictable. The operation of television is more of a crapshoot; the upside is high, but so is the downside. It's a risky affair. But if you get it right, it can be more rewarding. It's a terribly different sort of business.

I guess the same would be true of radio. Not that I know much about radio at all. Magazines are a terribly different business. Talking as a businessman I would say that the most difficult magazine to have today would be one of the newsweeklies. As a publisher and a journalist, there's nothing that I would enjoy more than that challenge.

But the truth is that the decline of print advertising, and particularly of cigarettes and alcohol, presents those publications that are on fairly small profit margins and are very high-cost operations with terrible difficulties.

Another side to that is that the enormous improvement in television news, and the much greater availability of television news, and the enormous improvement in newspapers in this country, qualitatively, in the last 10 years—all have made the newsweeklies more difficult.

But that's just one type of magazine. There are other types of magazines—monthly magazines, special interest magazines, which have had great success, like our *Elle* and another that's beginning to experience great success, *New Woman*—that permit our applying editorial skills, taking over a moribund magazine and doing something with it, finding what we think is a niche in that market.

We expect to be doing a very up-market automobile magazine, and we're curious to see whether that will succeed or not. But all these things take a lot of seed money, have considerable risk—and the rewards are pretty good.

But there's really no way you can relate or compare the different businesses and say that television is better than magazines and what sort of magazines. What I would say about television is that certainly so long as there are networks, and probably with or without networks, television is going to continue to increase its share of the advertising pie. Now whether the advertising pie is going to increase as well is an open question. We have to have better minds than mine to be applied to that.

But are we beginning to undergo certain changes in our society, which will tend to mean a little less consumption—through conservation, through the improvement of products, buying things that will last longer? Automobiles are an obvious choice. Are we going to have cars now that last the average person four years instead of 18 months? What effect is that going to have on advertising?

Before we get away from the question of media values, I'd like to ask you about cable, which you skipped over in your rundown. You have no cable investments. Are you staying away from it deliberately?
I'd have to say yes. I had in the past always said it was too expensive in relation to the ultimate rewards, and I've been proven quite wrong. But now I feel more than ever that it's too expensive to buy into. You know, when you see people paying $2,000 a sub, I think that's pretty scary.

Clearly it's looking very good for the cable industry for the moment. But I believe that if they are in fact monopolies, you will have an activist Congress looking more and more at cable. No democracy will really tolerate someone standing at the gates of every city, with a toll, and that's really what they're doing. I think we're going to find that unregulated monopolies are not going to stay unregulated forever, particularly if they try to maximize their profits too much, or start to interfere with the competitive broadcasts within those markets.

I was struck by your comment about $2,000-per-subscriber cable systems. That once was an unthinkable figure. But as long as I've been reporting this business, that has always been the attitude about each new record sale. It was thought that no one would ever pay more than $25 million for a television station, and now the record is up to $510 million.
I paid a billion five for six stations. You'd really have to say that I paid more than $500 million for channel 5 in New York. At the time I think it was more like $600 million and I'm sure you can get it now. In my mind, I should have paid less, but I knew that I was paying a premium of $200 million-300 million for the chance to get all those cities together in one hit. It was a unique opportunity to buy them together rather than on a stand-alone basis. Certainly for a New York or a Los Angeles, and probably Chicago and Washington, those prices have probably since been surpassed. We could certainly get all our money back, that's for sure.

If we get a network going, we'll make those stations make a lot more money. That's the secret of what we're doing. If we can make those stations turn over much better profits, if we can increase their value, we increase the value of our company and everything else. Even if the network itself is a fairly long-term loss maker, it's quite possible to conceive losing $50 million on the network, but increasing the earnings of those Fox stations by $100 million.

That's the history of the conventional networks. They never made much money in their network operations until, say, the 60's, and then suddenly they started making great amounts. But their owned stations were making it long before. And I lost sight of that in terms of what you're up to.
What got out of hand was their expenses. It suddenly became easy money for a period there. If you look at these huge network salaries of $2.5 million a year for anchormen—that really started only 10 or 12 years ago. I mean, the sudden big escalation.

Do you share the concern about bottom-line operators taking over American television? It's often phrased as a fear that "stations are being bought and sold like pork bellies." That's led to a great sentiment for a return to the three-year rule that once prohibited the sale of a station until it had been operated by a new owner for three years. How do you come down on that?
Oh, I'm not worried about a free market for the stations. What I would like to see is more stations run by people who graduated out of the news departments and the programing departments than out of sales or business management. Not that I want to downgrade capable people, but broadcasting is about what programs you put on the air, and the people making those judgments are the people who should know more about that, be trained in it more perhaps, and who have a greater sensitivity to the viewer.

Someone who has come out of a news department or program department—not every time, but almost always—is much more likely to have that sensitivity, quite apart from responsibility as well, but also the general sensitivity to the viewer than someone whose sole talent in life has been to sell advertising. I think there's too much station management in this country in the hands of sales people.

That's a magnificent response but it's not quite the question. We were talking about people like you, perhaps, who are conspicuously successful in the financial area or some other activity and then come in and buy a station and then sell it. It might have been you except that you're an operator. But say KKR, for example, which bought KTLA[-TV] Los Angeles for $245 million in 1982 and sold it for $510 million in 1985.

Well, I don't see that any harm has been done there. If they came in and wowed the station up a little bit, even if they didn't do much themselves, but hired someone and got some expensive new programs and got the ratings up, and the Tribune Co. went and paid $510 million for it—if there's any suffering in there, it's strictly the shareholders, and maybe they'll profit a lot from it. But that's just the marketplace.

I really believe that, in the long run, the value of stations can be dictated by their programing. It all flows from that. And the marketplace corrects these things. Now if a bank owns a station for a while, and sells for a profit or loss, I don't know that that's terribly relevant.

You have been quoted as saying about American journalists—talking specifically about the ones who graduate from journalism school and you say get 90% to 95% of the jobs at the big city newspapers—that they don't know how to compete and that they're not in touch with their readership. Will you elaborate on that?

They don't get much of a chance to compete these days because the press is basically so monopolistic anyway. That's not a criticism of the press; it's an accident of history or of economics or whatever. But the great majority of newspapers in this country have a community to themselves. That's one side of it.

As far as the journalism schools go, maybe they serve a purpose, but I haven't seen—I've seen many great journalists who have come out of journalism schools, but not because of the journalism school. And I don't see the skills that are displayed in the daily newspapers or in magazines that ever could have been learned at journalism schools.

And what are the skills that you expect your journalists to have?

The use of the English language, to be able to write well and clearly. An honesty of purpose and an objectivity in reporting. And a high level of energy and inquisitiveness. The great journalists are the ones who are never reluctant to make those extra six or 10 telephone calls. They're the ones who really do the best work.

Now I don't know that any of those qualities are particularly taught at journalism school. One should have a command of the English language before you ever get to a journalism school. I don't really know enough about what they do. I went once to address a group at Columbia, and I didn't find anyone from journalism school who had definitely made up their mind they knew what a newspaper was. It was a sort of soft course they were doing. They hadn't decided whether to go into the theater or the arts or whatever. I don't know that any great discipline is taught at the journalism schools.

Does your criticism of print journalists apply to television journalists?

No, I think my criticism applied to types of journalists. Certainly the television journalists are much more competitive than print journalists, no doubt about that. They fight each other for stories. I think there is a tendency to be less responsible for television journalists than with the written word. And that is perhaps the nature of the beast—you hear about these terrible things, you can be very intrusive with television. And it passes. With the newspaper, the written word has a more lasting effect. And it's still around later when they pick it up and put it in your face and say, "Look what you said."

I think the standards, the ethical standards on television in practice tend to be a bit more slipshod than they are in print. I'm not talking about network news, as I think they are very, very careful—almost to the point of being pretentious a bit—but when you get a really vigorous local city competition, such as in some of the big cities, not just New York.

Then again, there is the lack of responsible journalists running television stations. Too often you get an advertising salesman who arrives as a general manager of a station and hires a couple of pretty faces to run his news, and gets some very energetic people. But they don't actually have anyone there with a history or a sense of media relations or even just the training and experience in the responsibilities of public journalism.

Does one have to exercise more restraint with television and its influence than one does with newspapers?
I think the influence is very different. With a newspaper, one can quite openly and strongly argue a particular political issue. With television, the influence is more pervasive. You probably have more influence on taste and behavior. I think you have influence on issues and how you present the news. I would argue that some of television news today has a much stronger, more consistent bias to it than the news in newspapers.

Whether it be the *Post* or the *New York Times* or whatever, I think there is a consistent bias, a more obvious one. There's more obvious liberal bias on television news today than, say, in the *New York Times.* Or even the *Washington Post.* And it's more blatant; I think the *New York Times* can display bias by choice of stories, by choice of emphasis, and how much it writes about a subject.

In television you have no editorial breaks, but you can have a great influence on the news by how much time you give those sorts of stories and by how they are presented or by what particular twist you give them.

Considering your background and your international vantage, what do you think of broadcasting in your adopted homeland? How does it rank in terms of sophistication and vision, and just in terms of general ability, against the British or the French or the Germans or Japanese?
Let me say that I'm only slightly acquainted with the British; I'm not at all acquainted with the other countries you mentioned. In that case, you can even throw in Australia, too, as it's somewhat a combination of the two.

I don't think there's any doubt that the public is better served by the American system, because they've got a choice. And as far as the scope of what is on the airwaves and what is not, I think it's fair to say that the open competition for programing has not been accompanied by a great lowering of standards. There's a lot of stuff on television that has excellent production qualities, and there is the stuff that appeals to the lower taste, yes—but nothing as low as some of the English programs. There's a difference in taste; it's very interesting to try and explain the difference in soap operas here and in England.

But you ask which is the better system? I think no doubt at all, this is the better system. There is a lot of money spent on some programs in England which are of beautiful quality, but which don't appeal to a large audience—we tend to get those here on PBS. And I think we'd all be a lot poorer if we didn't have PBS channels here and the availability of some of that programing. Not that many of us watch that much of it, but it's a luxury to have it available. A lot of that programing has been made by the British taxpayer and it comes here and is picked up by PBS for nothing or 5% of whatever it cost those taxpayers.

I don't know how you do it. All I know is that the degree of control by an elitist group in Britain, the pseudo public servants known as the Independent Broadcasting Authority, deprived the British public of good choice programing, and it's very wrong. They have their institutional monopoly in private television, which makes an inordinate amount of money, and therefore attracts very special taxes. Just takes it away from them. And the public really gets very little choice.

We would not fulfill our responsibility if we didn't give you a chance to speak to the subject of global media operations.
Well, there aren't much of them. But there are two things that are happening. People are attempting to spread the costs of programing around the world, and as the non-U.S. market gets bigger and bigger and more prosperous, as it will with deregulation, there's going to be a chance to co-produce or lay over some of the costs in Europe or other places. That's one thing.

The other thing that's happening—it's very slow, but is beginning to happen—is the investment in worldwide name brands. McDonald's has become an international institution and so has Coke, and I think you'll find that now with beer. Some day you may be able to take an ad for the whole world.

It is going to lead to opportunities to do certain global things—sponsorship of sporting events would be an obvious example, where an advertiser would buy worldwide sponsorship rights to Wimbledon tennis, for instance, or the Olympic Games. I think that's coming.

At this stage it's certainly not significant at all, but with the ease of communications by satellites or international cables and so forth, I think you will see it. That is not to say that someone is going to own it all. Maybe on down the line there will be some sort of worldwide industry of broadcasters—in fact, CBS already has formal and informal affiliations around the world. NBC has. NBC works very closely with the BBC. And with the network in Australia. They have Japanese affiliations. Now whether those things get stronger because of the pressure of advertisers, I don't know.

As a citizen of the world, and as a person who has media experience internationally, it's interesting to think of you coming to the table in the United States and deciding to play a major role. Would you sit down at the table and say: "I'm going to do it differently than all the others have been doing it because I want to accomplish something that I find lacking in the system as it is"? I'm not inviting you to be critical, but wondering how you might play the game differently.
I would come at it more from what I may have learned on the way through from other countries, and I don't know how applicable it is. But what I'd love to be able to do is to make television a lot more real. And by that I mean a lot more urgent, and by which I mean more live programing, and not just in the daytime, but to be able to do exciting things in prime time. Not just sports events, but entertainment programs.

I think television is an enormous part of all of our lives, and that it's got to be closer to the world and what goes on in it. It can't all be highly polished six-month-old Hollywood entertainment, and not that we don't all enjoy entertainment, but somehow it should be brought closer. That's the journalist in me talking, probably, but I'd like a more journalistic approach to all programing.

Are you then first and foremost a journalist?
I'd like to be; I certainly think that way. I mean, if you haven't got the journalism right, you can call it something else on television, but if you haven't got the words and the images right, the business doesn't run. There is no business. Get that right, and you can have good managers or bad managers to play around with it to make a profit or not to make a profit out of it. But if you haven't, if the product isn't there, then you haven't got a business.

And the product is the programing. And I think all these other issues of should one be allowed to buy a television station and make an inordinate profit overnight and whatnot doesn't really matter—particularly in this era of deregulation, where we're getting more and more alternatives for people to watch. In the old days when there were one or two stations in every community, you might say, well, that was a regulated franchise in the sense that it was one that was given down from people's representatives. Today it's much wider than that. You really can't talk about the lack of diversity in the market; they've got all the diversity they can possibly consume or want. There's no danger of anyone having a monopoly of anything in the media.

TURNER'S WINDLESS SAILS

Bill Powell, Vern E. Smith, and Peter McAlevey

In a media world of calculated deals, flamboyant Ted Turner is famous for his audacity and bravado. But "Captain Outrageous" seems to have over-reached himself, according to this *Newsweek* article.

Somebody asked me about power. I said, "You tell me who's got the power. Doesn't seem to be Reagan. When you find out who's got the power, let me know."

—Ted Turner

There's always been something disarming about Ted Turner. Yes, his ego is substantial, but let's face it: the guy has always done exactly what he pleases. Take an impossible run at CBS? Well, he wanted to own a network. Stage a pseudo-Olympics in Moscow that no one watches? He thinks it promotes world peace. And it's not only what he's done, it's the *way* he's done it. Call it bodacious élan. In 1977 he won the America's Cup, the Super Bowl for the rich and stuffy, and then showed up at a press conference deliriously drunk. Win or lose, it seemed, he played by his rules.

For Captain Outrageous, those days are over. Turner's purchase of M-G-M, the fabled Hollywood movie studio, has all but scuttled Turner Broadcasting, his flagship company. Sinking under $1.2 billion in debt. TBS desperately needed a bailout. Last month it got one, a consortium of 14 cable-television companies allied with Kirk Kerkorian—the same California financier who sold M-G-M at a steep premium to Turner in the first place—injected $550 million into TBS. For now the help guarantees the company's survival, but for Turner it comes at a steep price. The investment group will be able to choose five new board members; more importantly, the corporate bylaws will be amended to permit a "supermajority" of the board to vote approval of "matters out of the ordinary course of business." As one TBS executive puts it, Turner's "play days are over." Turner insists reports of his demise are greatly exaggerated, but even he admits he "won't be able to make any large acquisitions or do any large projects without board approval. My power will be somewhat diminished."

His reputation in Hollywood may already be beyond repair. When Turner bought MGM/UA—soon after Rupert Murdoch had purchased Twentieth Century–Fox—there was talk that a new breed of Hollywood mogul had been born. "They're visionaries, they're showmen," exclaimed one analyst at the time. Since then, Turner's image in Hollywood has gone from the swashbuckling new man in town to the philistine from the South. He recently tried to calm frayed nerves in Hollywood by throwing the First Annual Turner Broadcasting Bowling Party in Studio City. But Turner himself failed to show up, and many Hollywood luminaries made only token appearances.

Turner's business woes are the result of his audacious "nothing's impossible" attitude. After his improbable attempt to acquire CBS in the spring of 1985 failed, he decided that if he couldn't be the next William Paley, he'd be the next Louis B. Mayer. He turned around and bought M-G-M, which in 1981 had merged with United Artists. MGM/UA's majority stockholder at the time was none other than Kirk Kerkorian. In a complicated deal, Turner paid $1.2 billion for M-G-M—financing it all with borrowed money—while Kerkorian retained control of UA.

The deal, perceived as favorable to Kerkorian

Source: From *Newsweek,* February 9, 1987.

then, is now considered a sensational score. In Hollywood Turner is almost unanimously regarded as "a pigeon," as one analyst puts it. "He took a bath," says Art Murphy, a University of Southern California economist and a highly respected Hollywood analyst. "He came to town fully clothed and left in a barrel." Many of the most marketable films in MGM/UA's library were UA properties—"Annie Hall," "Rocky," the entire "James Bond" series; they remained in Kerkorian's hands. Turner got some classics—"The Wizard of Oz" and "Singin' in the Rain" among them. But many of the vintage films he owns have limited appeal in the lucrative TV market.

For Turner the fleecing was doubly disastrous. By the mid-'80s, TBS's rights to many of the television programs on its manifest were expiring. Signing up shows such as "Leave It to Beaver" and "The Beverly Hillbillies" in the late 1970s had been a stroke of genius—Turner at his best. Syndicators thought they were selling to a local TV station—and thus to a small market—so Turner got them cheaply. He then turned WTBS in Atlanta into a satellite-feed "Superstation" and beamed the shows to a national cable audience, reaping a huge windfall in the process.

The syndicators were only going to get taken once. After 1979 Turner got shut out of the syndicated-program market almost completely. In the interim, he had started up his all-news cable network, CNN. But it was slow to realize a profit, and as 1986 approached, TBS still desperately needed programming. That made MGM/UA's 4,600 films look awfully attractive. "Turner saw stars in his eyes and said, 'This is the answer to my dreams'," says Anthony Hoffman, an analyst at Los Angeles's Union Bank, a major lender to the entertainment industry.

The answer to his dreams turned into a nightmare. M-G-M's accumulated problems led Turner to champion "colorization," thus further offending the Hollywood establishment. His campaign to boost interest in his old black-and-white films by injecting them with color has been more than just an esthetic flop. The effort shows no signs of providing the financial relief he hoped for, at least not for awhile. The process is extraordinarily expensive—about $1,800 per minute, or $180,000 for an average film—and very time-consuming. "Even if he had access to the entire colorization industry in the United States today, he'd be able to do only about two films a month," says Hoffman. "That's not going to make a dent in his problems."

The infusion of cash from Kerkorian's group is a lifesaver for Turner. TBS lost $121 million during the first nine months of 1986, and Wall Street began to worry about the company's ability to make payments on its staggering debt load. Analyst Hoffman, among the more pessimistic TBS watchers, figures the new money gives the company at least 12 to 15 months of breathing room. Others in the cable business and on Wall Street acknowledge that the investment group includes some of the most able executives in the industry. John Malone, president of Denver-based Tele-Communications Inc., the nation's largest cable-TV operator, was responsible for putting the group together. "These are smart guys," says one industry executive. "They wouldn't be making their investment if they didn't think they could pull out TBS in the long run."

"Squandering Millions"

The group may immediately rein in Turner on his latest pet project, the so-called "Better World Society." As Turner explains it, the society "raises funding and commissions programming on what we feel are the critical issues of the times: the nuclear arms race, aiming toward peace on earth and controlling the population and preserving the environment." Noble, perhaps, but according to TBS insiders the society is spending a fortune. "He just cannot take the millions of this company and squander them away on an ideology that's out there in the wild somewhere," says one. "It's just not good business." More promising is a bid to acquire rights to NFL football games—a likely prospect now that the 14 cable operators could send the games out over the TBS network. "That's step two in Turner's recovery plan," predicts one industry source.

That Turner needs a recovery plan is beyond doubt. In more ways than one, these are hard times for the man once dubbed "the mouth from the South." His son just recovered from injuries sustained in an automobile accident. He is separated from his wife, Jane. As if that's not enough, when he and the woman he's now seeing (his former pilot) bought Ryan O'Neal's ranch in Big Sur, a Hollywood gossip columnist quoted a neighbor saying, "Nobody here likes him." In the past Turner would probably turn around at a time like this and do something outrageous. But this week they're sailing for the America's Cup without him—and anything else he might try now needs the board's approval.

OPRAH WINFREY: TALK STAR OF DAYTIME TV

Charles Whitaker

Effusive and energetic, Oprah Winfrey is the hot new daytime television talk show star. Her off-the-cuff interviewing manner and enthusiasm have won her a large national following, and she enjoys the luxurious lifestyle her success has made possible. Movie roles have followed, too.

It is 15 minutes to showtime and the Rosemont Horizon, one of the Chicago area's most cavernous arenas, is filled to the brim for a Lionel Richie concert. Suddenly an agitated murmur echoes through the hall. A "star" has been spotted amidst the Richie worshippers. As word of the celebrity sighting spreads, the crowd's murmur swells to a loud, rhythmic chant, "OPRAH! OPRAH! OPRAH!"

Source: Ebony, March 1987. Reprinted by permission of Charles Whitaker and *Ebony* Magazine. © 1987 Johnson Publishing Company, Inc.

Finally, Oprah Winfrey is coaxed into hopping onto a chair. She waves vigorously and the crowd erupts into a minute-long ovation punctuated by cheers, whistles and shouts of "We love you, Oprah!"

Oprah Winfrey has indeed arrived. And it is not just in Chicago, where her morning talk-show has been the dominant force in daytime television for three years, that she is a sensation. Since September, when *The Oprah Winfrey Show* went into national syndication, the entire country seems to have been swept into a video love affair with Oprah. Her effusive, off-the-cuff interview style has given a badly needed transfusion to the anemic talk-show format.

Oprah's show has obliterated the hold that game shows and Phil Donahue had on daytime ratings and regularly trounces her competition in head-to-head matchups.

Some critics, however, have called her approach "fawning." Some Blacks, in particular, charge that Oprah's touchy-feely manner toward the members of her predominantly White audiences is reminiscent of the stereotypical Southern "Mammy."

Oprah is deeply stung by such comments. "I live my life and I do this show to try to raise people's consciousness, to give people a sense of hope in their lives," she says. "So when people write or say negative things like that about me it really upsets me because it means they don't understand me or what my show is about. They've missed it. But I'm convinced that if people who believe that really got to know me, they wouldn't think I was that kind of person."

Still, the dominance of *The Oprah Winfrey Show* in the 138 television markets in which it appears is so complete that local stations on which the show airs clamor to have her promote their news programs in hope that some of the Winfrey magic will rub off on local programming.

Then, there's the lure of Hollywood. Oprah made an auspicious movie debut in *The Color Purple* last year, earning an Academy Award nomination for her performance as Sofia in the screen adaptation of Alice Walker's Pulitzer Prize–winning novel. She followed that triumph with another appearance in a film treatment of a literary work, Richard Wright's *Native Son,* which opened to mixed reviews in December. Still, her portrayal of protagonist Bigger Thomas' mother was hailed as moving and heightened her growing reputation as an actress.

Today, Oprah Winfrey, 33, is a bona fide phenomenon and media darling. She has been featured on magazine covers and profiled on television. Her life story has been retold in so many periodicals that even she is beginning to wonder if it doesn't now sound cliche.

Actually, the Oprah Winfrey story is part Horatio Alger, part Booker T. Washington and part Cinderella. Born in Mississippi, she was reared partly in Milwaukee by her mother and, when she became too precocious to handle, partly in Nashville by her father (a city councilman there) and stepmother. Hers was a typically poor-to-working class childhood that she describes as "not much different from anybody else's who grew up in the Black experience during the time that I grew up."

She excelled in speech and drama in high school and at Tennessee State University. It was during her sophomore year at TSU that she was tapped by a local television station to become a reporter. She has spent virtually all of her adult life in front of the camera. After graduating from college, she moved to Baltimore to become news co-anchor at WJZ-TV, the ABC affiliate there. Then, in 1984, it was on to WLS-TV in Chicago where she transformed the failing *AM-Chicago* show into the giant killer that toppled the venerable Donahue. Some say it was Oprah's success that forced Donahue to pull up stakes in Chicago and head for less heated competition in New York.

Oprah refrains from making such a claim. However, she acknowledges that going solo in Chicago was just what she needed to make her mark. "Part of the reason I've been able to do so well in Chicago is that for the first time in my career, I am alone," she says. "Up until now, I've always been paired with somebody else. The thing about working with a co-anchor or a co-host is that it can be stifling, like a bad marriage. Somebody has always got to surrender to the other person. And usually, the person doing the surrendering was me. But I knew that I would just bide my time and get good at this; so good, that moving to the next place would be easy. That's why I feel very good about where I am right now. I feel I've earned the right to be here."

She rules over the blue and gray set on which the show is played like a combination of Barbara Walters and Joan Rivers. One minute she's all quips and one-liners, the next minute she is eliciting painful and personal testimonies from guests or celebrities. She also confesses her own personal tragedies. In the past, she has recounted her failed relationships, a childhood episode of sexual abuse, and her constant battle to lose weight. These insights have endeared her to America, making her one of the most sought after speakers in the country.

Oprah, however, demurs when she is described as a "star." Never mind the fact that she has a $800,000 apartment on the 57th floor of an exclusive high rise with a glorious view of Lake Michigan and the Chicago skyline, that she tools around town in a chauffeur-driven Mercedes limousine (a luxury she may forego when her new Jaguar convertible arrives), that she cannot walk down any street in America without someone asking for a hug, an autograph, or a picture, Oprah Winfrey says she still has trouble thinking of herself as a celebrity.

"This morning, as I sat in my marble tub," she says, "surrounded by bubbles, with the water pouring from the golden swan faucet, I thought, as I opened my box of apple cinnamon soap, 'Is this it? Is this what being a celebrity is all about?' It's interesting, because I don't feel any different. My ability to acquire things has changed, but *I* don't feel any different. So, I keep saying to myself, 'Well, I guess I'm not a star yet, because I don't feel like one.' "

She does admit that her rapidly escalating income, acquired from her television contract, movie deals and speaking engagement has allowed her to be a rather conspicuous consumer. It is estimated that she will make close to $11 million in 1987. Her personal indulgences include a wardrobe of fur coats, the most eye-catching of which may be the $10,000 dyed-purple fox that she wore to the Academy Awards telecast last year. Her recently decorated, marble-floored apartment is accented with high tech touches like pedestal lamps that resemble fluorescent rocket ships. The custom-designed furniture is swathed in fabrics of either deep purple (her favorite color) or cream.

Yet, she also spends lavishly on others: mink coats for relatives, a condominium for her mother, clothes and cash for members of her staff. "Oprah is generous to a fault," says her cousin Jo Baldwin, vice president of Harpo (*Oprah* spelled backwards), Inc., the development company Oprah started to handle her interests outside of her talk show.

For example, two Christmases ago, when the seven members of her staff were denied raises by station bosses, Oprah gave each staffer $10,000 in cash stuffed inside rolls of toilet paper. "It was great," she says. "Everyone wept and had a wonderful time. It feels good to be able to do things like that with no strings attached, just because I can."

Some worry that news of this generosity will attract toadies who want nothing more than a free ride on Oprah's gravy train. She dismisses the possibility. "I do not have people around me who want anything from me other than my friendship and my emotional support," she says. "I have the most difficult time giving things to people who I think want them. The way to get something from me is to never ask for it. The minute I get asked for anything, my red flag goes up."

Nor is she concerned that her good fortune will abruptly come to an end. In fact, she is adamant that it will not. She maintains that she is "destined to do greater things."

Her confidence is rooted in her belief in God. She says she has undergone a recent spiritual evolution that has enabled her to "press to the mark of the high calling, as Paul said." She declines to call the development of this spiritual consciousness a renaissance. "It's not being born again," she says. "It's an evolution, a realization of how life works—meaning that God is the center of the universe. Once you understand that, it's all really very simple."

She is proud of the fact that she reads the Bible and prays—on her knees—daily. "I remember when I was little and my grandmother first taught me to pray. She said, 'As long as you have the power to bow your head and bend your knees, you do it and God will hear you better.' I have not been able to get that out of my brain."

As successful as she is at present, Oprah admits that the going has not always been smooth, particularly in her personal life. In her less confident days, she says that she relinquished her self respect to men. "The relationships I had were totally detrimental," she says. "I was a doormat. But the thing about it is, you realize that there is a doormat overload out there because everybody's been one. Now, I say 'I will never give up my power to another person.' "

Her current boyfriend is Stedman Graham, a part-time model and executive director of Athletes Against Drugs, a coalition of sports figures who campaign against drug abuse. She is loath to discuss the relationship, but she does allow that Graham is "an overwhelmingly decent man. He has made me realize a lot of the things that were missing in my life like the sharing that goes on between two people."

Unfortunately, even the upswing in her lovelife has not made dieting any easier. Some critics have complained that Oprah's obsession with losing weight occupies too much of her conversation. At approximately 180 pounds on a 5-foot 6-inch frame, Oprah says she talks about her weight no more than any other overweight woman. "It *is* an obsession," she says. "It's all any overweight woman talks about. It just happens that I'm in the public eye so people think I talk about it more."

She does plan to lose weight and has hired a trainer and a cook to help change her eating habits and whip her into shape.

She is also weighing other acting assignments. ABC is negotiating with her production company in an effort to develop a situation comedy to star

Ms. Winfrey. In it, she would play, what else, a single talk show host who lives in Chicago. The show would be filmed in Chicago concurrently with the talk show. Ms. Winfrey says the schedule will be easy to maintain. "I have boundless energy," she says.

Her next film role probably will be an adaptation of novelist Gloria Naylor's *The Women of Brewster Place.* "I want to be a great actress," she says.

As film offers pour in and television negotiations progress, she is enjoying life as it is. "It's a glorious time for me," she says. "I'm doing exactly what I wanted to be doing at age 33. I feel I'm ripening, coming into my own. It's an exciting time, an exciting age."

ALLEN H. NEUHARTH TODAY

Barbara Matusow

Allen H. Neuharth built the Gannett newspaper group into the country's largest and created *USA Today.* This profile shows him as an imperious yet often charming publisher who epitomizes the power that group ownership wields in American publishing. Barbara Matusow is senior editor of the *Washington Journalism Review.*

The annual Gannett shareholders meeting last May was drawing to a close. It had been a celebratory affair, best summed up by stockholder Frank Fantanza of Rochester, who told Gannett's chairman and chief executive officer, Allen H. Neuharth, "Whatever you're doing, just keep on doing it. You're making a rich man out of me."

Before adjourning the meeting, Neuharth ticked off a litany of the company's accomplishments since he took over as CEO in 1973. Then, Gannett owned 51 daily newspapers; now it has 93. Circulation has climbed from 2,224,000 to more than six million. Television stations have grown from one to eight, radio stations from none to 16. Then, Gannett stock was worth $17.55 a share; now it's valued at around $80. Annual earnings have increased from $23 million to $253 million. Neuharth proudly cited the company's record for promoting women and minorities to positions of influence and noted that many of the key players in the company today are in their 30's and 40's.

Neuharth could be excused for sounding pleased with himself. Only the day before, Gannett had emerged as the high bidder for the Louisville *Courier-Journal* and *Times,* a prestigious acquisition that followed close on the heels of another triumph: a joint operating agreement between the *Detroit News*—also recently acquired—and its archrival, the *Free Press.*

Standing there dressed in his signature grey, looking healthy, relaxed and brimming with good humor, the 62-year-old executive cut a commanding, controlled figure. Suddenly, however, his voice began to quaver as he startled the room with an unexpected announcement. "My instincts as an investigative reporter and editorial analyst tell me the time has come to take another step in the planned and orderly transition of Gannett's leadership to the next generation," he said, seemingly on the verge of tears. "Accordingly, . . . I will recommend that President John J. Curley be elected chief executive officer, succeeding me in that role."

Neuharth said he would remain as chairman until March 1989, when he turns 65, after which his 10-year contract calls for him to serve "as a reporter-at-large and an ambassador-at-large."

Anything Allen H. Neuharth, the colorful, imperious chief of the largest newspaper chain in America, does attracts attention. Thus, when he decides to relinquish some of his power earlier than necessary, the question naturally arises: Why? Even more important is the question of his future role in Gannett. Will he really withdraw from the day-to-day running of the company to concentrate on long-range planning, as he has pledged? Where, in effect, does this extraordinary press lord, still at the top of his form, go from here?

Neuharth's looming retirement raises another

Source: Washington Journalism Review, August 1986. Reprinted with permission.

question. What kind of legacy will he leave to journalism? Will he be remembered as a force for good or for ill—or as someone who simply made a lot of money?

Although the announcement of Curley's promotion seemed stunning, it should not have come as a surprise to Neuharth-watchers. "The moves were all in place," says John Quinn, editor of *USA Today* and Neuharth's closest confidant in the company. "It was just a question of timing." In fact, the transition had been put in motion as far back as March 1984, when Curley, then 45, was named president of Gannett.

As anyone in the company and the financial community can attest, Neuharth's cardinal rule as a manager is "No surprises." Thus, insiders say, he wanted to give everyone connected to the company—employees, stockholders and financiers—a blueprint for the future. "I hope [my decision to retire] is another example of the orderly approach to planning and implementing things that we follow at Gannett," Neuharth said in an interview a few weeks before the stockholders' meeting. "I've had some first-hand knowledge and experience of corporate transitions that didn't work very well."

Neuharth was alluding to the time back in the early 1970s when his predecessor at Gannett, Paul Miller, seemed reluctant to step down. Neuharth is known to feel that the uncertainty and press speculation surrounding that episode were bad for the company and he was determined history would not repeat itself. "He has a real love affair with Gannett," says John Seigenthaler, editor of the editorial page of *USA Today* and publisher of the Nashville *Tennessean.* "He was afraid unless the transition was spelled out, he was running the risk of hurting the company that's his life."

It is not likely that Neuharth will disappear into his hot tub in Florida anytime soon, however. "This company is as much his vocation as his avocation," says stock analyst R. Joseph Fuchs, vice president of Kidder, Peabody, and Co. "It's going to be a long time before he withdraws from active participation in Gannett."

Speculation about Neuharth's future role arises because he is no ordinary business executive. Widely regarded as a marketing genius, he has cut a wide swath with his numerous acquisitions and technical and editorial innovations. He is also a high-profile sybarite who has made the most of the trappings and perks he commands; anecdotes stick to this man like barnacles.

Neuharth's temperament is not suited to a life on the sidelines; a more competitive, restless, dominant character could not be imagined. He frequently leaps to his feet in the course of a conversation and strides around the room. If forced to sit still, he cracks his knuckles. Even at a baseball game (Neuharth is a sports nut who will fly his friends halfway around the country to attend a Yankees game with him), he has to liven things up by betting whether the next pitch will be a strike.

Constantly on the move, he logs hundreds of thousands of miles a year on his corporate jet. Yet, this perpetual-motion machine has formidable powers of concentration, and he is a good listener. Charming when he wants to be, he is soft-spoken and attentive to guests, making sure he is briefed about them ahead of time. Afterwards, he makes a point of remembering their names.

Neuharth's hands-on management style is as intense as everything else about him, particularly when he tackles a venture in its formative stage. He personally approved every radio and television ad for *USA Today,* and in its early days he prowled the composing room and rewrote headlines. As Gannett launched *USA Today* in stages across the country, Neuharth stood on the loading docks at midnight in each new city, rejecting copies that did not meet his standards. In San Rafael, California, he consigned nearly 8,000 copies to the dumpster.

The most exacting of employers, Neuharth has no use for those not as hard-working or detail-oriented as he. Paul Flynn, now publisher of the *Pensacola News Journal* and a regional vice president of Gannett, recalls feeling Neuharth's displeasure some years back when he was assistant promotions director at the old company headquarters in Rochester. "We ran an ad showing someone in pajama legs reaching for his paper," Flynn says. "That morning, before our afternoon delivery, I got a call from Neuharth, who said, 'Can you prove you can deliver that paper to every doorstep?' In fact, in outlying areas we couldn't. We tossed them in the driveway or put them in tubes. He made us stop the presses and change the ad."

"If you want to succeed [at Gannett]," says newspaper analyst John Morton, "you have to give up everything. It can easily get to be a six- or seven-day-a-week job. Without much notice, they instruct you to show up at the airport and you do it with a smile on your face. Of course, Neuharth doesn't ask any more of others than he gives himself."

Neuharth usually is very controlled, but when he gives vent to his famous temper, employees run for cover. In one widely circulated anecdote, Neuharth blew up at a limousine driver for showing up late, in his own car. It seems Neuharth's personal limousine had broken down. As the trip progressed, Neuharth continued to berate the driver. Finally, the driver is said to have shot back, "I don't care whether you walk, fly, swim or hitchhike. Just get out." Neuharth ended up hitchhiking.

Even Vice Chairman Douglas McCorkindale, Gannett's chief financial officer, is not immune to the boss's anger. On the way to a meeting in Louisville, Kentucky, this spring to woo the owners of the *Courier-Journal,* Neuharth noticed that McCorkindale was wearing royal-blue socks with his grey pin-striped suit and black shoes. "For Chrissake, Doug," Neuharth said. "You're going to blow the whole deal with those socks."

While many underlings fear Neuharth, he inspires deep loyalty as well, often going to great lengths for company stalwarts. Flynn recalls the time he was planning to fly from Rochester to St. Louis, where his daughter was to undergo major surgery. Before leaving, however, he had to attend a meeting in Rochester. "In the middle of the meeting, [Neuharth's] secretary passed me a note, telling me the boss had arranged a plane for me. I had never even mentioned the operation to him, and remember, this was in the heat of getting *USA Today* up and running. When I got to St. Louis, the president of Gannett Outdoors in St. Louis was waiting to meet me at the airport. Meanwhile, the head of Gannett Radio was on hand at the hospital to make sure my wife was taken care of. Neuharth handled all that himself. He is someone who never forgets what you do for him."

Even as the company has grown, Neuharth has remained fairly accessible. An editor who urgently needs to talk to him usually gets a call back by the end of the day. He also lets people know when they've done something particularly good or bad. In the old days, they used to hear from him personally. Now, they are more likely to get an "orange meanie," Gannett-talk for the notes Neuharth sends on pumpkin-colored note paper.

Neuharth also has made himself readily available to the media and the financial community. "The whole profile of the company is one of openness," says Fuchs. "Media barons historically have been very secretive and non-accessible. [But] Neuharth has led the industry to a higher level of corporate disclosure to both the financial community and the public at large."

A biographer in search of the real Al Neuharth has a problem, because the man operates so differently with different people. John Quinn says he uses the tactics of a good city editor. "He has an ability for histrionics like in the old movies, but he also has the ability to massage people, to handle them in a way to get the best out of them. . . . With some, he uses the intimidating style. We call them the 'Al says' guys. They love to go into a meeting and say, 'Al says.' It shows he has been talking to them. With others, he'll sit down and talk things over. Whichever way he thinks will get results, he'll use."

Neuharth's managerial skills this year won him, for the fourth straight time, the *Wall Street Transcript*'s recognition as Chief Executive of the Year in Newspaper Publishing. Neuharth's services do not come cheap, however; the last stockholders' proxy lists his cash compensation alone at $1,333,333. (His stock is estimated at $5.5 million.) The company also permits him a baronial lifestyle.

Wherever he alights, the local Gannett publisher is on hand to greet him at the airport, limousine at the gate, hotel suite readied to precise instructions. His rustic-looking but luxurious Cocoa Beach house on 500 feet of ocean front sports an indoor fountain, sauna, hot tub, tennis court and screened pool. It's a long way from Eureka, South Dakota, where Neuharth recalls being one of the poorest kids in town.

Neuharth's father died when he was two years old, leaving his mother to raise him and an older brother alone. She worked as a waitress, a seamstress and a housekeeper, and evidently taught her son the value of self-reliance.

Although he started working while still in grade school, he thinks he was fortunate. "Under those circumstances, it became pretty clear that in order to succeed, you had to do it on your own. You weren't going to have anything handed to you."

Neuharth's first ambition was to be a lawyer, but by the time he got out of the army in 1946 at the age of 22, he still faced four years of college and three of law school. Journalism, he decided, might be a quicker route to fame and fortune. After graduating cum laude from the University of South Dakota and putting in two years as a reporter with the Associated Press in Sioux Falls, he made his first big plunge into publishing. But *SoDak Sports,* the weekly tabloid he started with a friend, was a bust. It folded after two years, leaving him $50,000 in debt to family and friends. Again, he says he was lucky. "Getting really bloodied as I did there at the age of 28, 29, was a tremendous stroke of good fortune for me. I thought I was a red-hot journalist then, a sportswriter who thought he ran great prose through the typewriter. And I thought if you did that, you would automatically succeed with a publication. Then I found out without advertising and other revenues, you couldn't pay the rent, no matter how much you and your friends enjoyed what you were writing and publishing. . . . And all I've done since—whether it was starting a new daily in Florida or starting *USA Today*—was to multiply what I did unsuccessfully at *SoDak Sports* in terms of the people necessary, the resources necessary and the effort necessary, and recognize more readily what factors had to be there in order to have a better risk-reward ratio."

After his *SoDak Sports* fiasco, Neuharth headed south and found a job as a $95-a-week reporter on the *Miami Herald,* the start of what was to be a breathtaking ascent in the newspaper world. "He was far and away the best reporter on the staff," says Neuharth's longtime friend Derek Daniels, a copy editor on the *Herald* at that time, who went on to become president of *Playboy* magazine enterprises. "He was a good writer, too, who wrote crisp, clear, clean sentences. He was never dull and deadly serious." Neuharth also is said to have had a talent for ingratiating himself with his superiors. "After they made him executive city editor," Daniels says, "he was on his way like a Fourth-of-July rocket." . . .

In 1960, Neuharth moved on to the *Detroit Free Press,* [a] Knight paper, as assistant executive editor. There he created more controversy, in part because he fired a number of people. "He was not beloved in the newsroom," says a news executive who knew him then. "The impression I encountered when I came in was that he was very ruthless, very much on the move."

In 1963, he left Knight to join Gannett as general manager of the two Rochester papers. Gannett was then a little-known group of 12 newspapers, but it held certain attractions for the ambitious Neuharth. "Gannett did not have a single Gannett in the organization," he later told a reporter for the *Miami Herald.* "There was no family. I figured therefore you could about do what you wanted with it."

Neuharth made his first big move at Gannett in 1966 with the founding of *TODAY,* a Cocoa, Florida, newspaper designed to serve the state's fast-growing space coast. It was a carefully conceived venture, started at a time when many newspapers were folding, and in many ways it served as a prototype for Neuharth's later and much better-known creation, *USA Today.*

Operating in great secrecy, Neuharth bought up a string of suburban papers around Cocoa Beach and set up a task force to study every aspect of the new paper, which was to use the latest and best in printing technology. Like *USA Today,* it would be strictly formatted, with the same features and columns in the same place every day.

TODAY, renamed *Florida Today* in 1985, also taught Neuharth the value of color. All of the best columnists and comic strips already belonged to newspapers in Miami and Orlando, but a syndication expert suggested that the Cocoa paper put color on whatever leftover comics they could acquire. "It helped a lot," says John Quinn.

TODAY had the benefit of Neuharth's fanatical attention to detail as well as his determination to make good on his promises. "One of the big features [we promised] was 'your home town newspaper delivered at your screen door,' " Quinn recalls. "We would have dry runs with phony newspapers. Al would be out at 5 A.M. trailing the delivery guys to see if the papers were in the bushes or on the lawn. Then, a truck would come by to pick them up. He was riding in the car in between, checking to see that each delivery was made properly."

Neuharth rightly saw *TODAY* as a test of his future at Gannett. Happily for him, the paper was successful, and by 1970 he was running the company, even though CEO Paul Miller had not yet stepped down. Around this time too, Neuharth began to cultivate some of the personal idiosyncracies that helped boost his visibility, including his penchant for dressing in black and white. (He says he switched to grey to match his hair on his last birthday.) "When I met him in 1955," recalls Derek Daniels, "from a fashion standpoint you might say he looked like a nondescript country boy. He did not have a style that was memorable. Later on, in Detroit, he wore brown or grey business suits, like most other folks. I think he later made a concerted decision to dress [in black and white] as part of his campaign of image-building." Daniels used to tell him that with his black outfits and his coal-black hair he looked like a left-over bit player from *The Godfather.*

Neuharth's flamboyance became even more marked after his second marriage—to Lori Wilson, a former Florida State Senator—in 1973. They were married in a ceremony at dawn on the beach, both dressed in white. Sometimes the two would show up at publishers' conventions decked out in black, at other times in white. Even the corporate jet, a Grumman-manufactured Gulfstream III, was fitted out entirely in black, white and grey.

Some publishers, watching Neuharth's flashy ways and growing appetite for grandeur, used to sneer at him behind his back. His eccentricities made good copy, however, and they focused attention on the once-unknown company. "It all depends which constituency you're serving," says R. Joseph Fuchs. "Is it the journalism professors, the old-line publishers or your own shareholders and readers and advertisers? His style is to serve the latter and not pander to the publishing establishment."

No one, however, could make fun of Gannett's bottom line, which became more impressive year by year. The basic formula called for acquiring monopoly newspapers in small and medium markets and promoting them heavily. Neuharth's publishers always enjoyed autonomy on editorial matters, but they were expected to keep their editorial budgets lean and their advertising rates high.

To his critics, he became "No Guts Neuharth," a profit-minded publisher who would not risk going into major metropolitan markets. But Neuharth says it made no sense to go after the big-city papers that were becoming available at the time. "I thought there were easier ways to be successful in journalism and the media than to say, 'Well, I must prove I can take a number-two newspaper in a major market and win a battle with it.' " . . .

Neuharth the businessman also made enemies. As Gannett swallowed more and more papers, some in the publishing world began to regard him as a dangerous predator. When Al turned up in his sharkskin suit, they used to say, you couldn't tell where the shark ended and Neuharth began. Neuharth resents such criticism. "All of our growth has been absolutely on invitation only," he says. "We don't show up unless invited. Then we don't pursue possible additions unless, after the invitation to look has been extended, both parties feel it's a good idea."

The one serious blot on Neuharth's record as a businessman stems back to an episode in Salem, Oregon, in the late 1970s. There, an over-zealous Gannett publisher, N. S. (Buddy) Hayden, set out to cripple a rival newspaper, the *Community Press.* The *Press* went out of business after two years and the owners, claiming violation of antitrust laws, sued Gannett for $6 million. Ultimately, the case was settled out of court, and Gannett reportedly paid more than $1 million in damages. Although the records from the proceedings were sealed, the weekly *Santa Fe Reporter* in New Mexico—another Gannett competitor—published accounts of their contents, which accused Gannett of lies, bribery and coercion. Neuharth later conceded that "Buddy Hayden did some things he shouldn't have done. I didn't know about it until after it happened."

By 1980, Gannett owned 80 daily newspapers in 32 states, seven television and 12 radio stations and a growing number of other ventures, including the nation's largest outdoor-advertising company. Neuharth finally was poised to prove that he did indeed have guts. For the first time, satellite technology made it possible to consider launching a general-interest national newspaper and Gannett, with its far-flung printing plants, probably was the ideal company to undertake such an experiment. Still, virtually no one besides Neuharth thought *USA Today* was a good idea. The day the project was announced, Gannett's stock dropped four points.

With the aid of Gannett's formidable research resources, Neuharth had spotted a niche—one that was filled by neither the *Wall Street Journal* nor the *New York Times,* the two other dailies with national readership. His target audience was the hurried business traveler and the media junkie, the generation that had been raised on television and was used to getting its information in a hurry.

USA Today, which burst onto the national scene amidst great promotional fanfare, was greeted coolly by critics. *The New Republic* wrote it off, saying "television fans can now have their tube and eat it too." Others derided the "comic-book colors" and the brevity of the stories. "The newspaper that brought new depth to the meaning of the word shallow," its own editor, John Quinn, joked publicly.

Many journalists were particularly disturbed by the paper's relentlessly upbeat tone—a reflection of Neuharth's philosophy that news is something more than a recital of hurricanes and other calamities. He has a point, but the early *USA Today* sounded mindlessly breezy at times; one headline, following a Minnesota plane crash, proclaimed: "Miracle: 327 survive, 55 die."

[Nowadays] *USA Today* sounds less boosterish, although it consciously pursues a different editorial agenda from other papers', using more feature stories and "news you can use." . . .

Despite the criticism, and long before it showed any sign of becoming profitable, *USA Today* began having a profound impact on newspapers across the country. Many editors decided it was time to put colored weather maps on *their* pages, while others began using shorter stories, more photographs, expanded sports coverage and op-ed-page debates. *USA Today* "is held up as an example in newsrooms," says Harold Lifvendahl, publisher of the *Orlando Sentinel.* "Editors say, 'Here is how they took the NFL's drafts and condensed them into a quick, easy read.' "

While the paper still has detractors, it seems to be winning a grudging acceptance in the journalism community. "*USA Today* fills a niche," says Reese Cleghorn, dean of the journalism school at the University of Maryland. "Although it has a lot of trivial material and does not do a serious job of covering the news, that's not what they set out to do. But what they do, they do extremely well. I don't read it instead of my regular newspaper but as an addition." . . .

For Neuharth, the success of *USA Today* has seemed a make-or-break affair—an assessment his fellow publishers appear to share. "*USA Today,* in the opinion of many," says one publisher who requested anonymity, "was one huge ego trip for

Neuharth. If it turns out to be a wise business decision as well, he'll have put his stamp on the industry. He'll prove that he is top dog."

If *USA Today* does succeed, Gannett stands to become an even stronger company than it is today. . . .

While continuing to shepherd Gannett's expansion, including "trading up" the company's television stations for properties in larger markets, Neuharth will be pursuing another goal—establishing his legacy in the field of communications. Even without the success of *USA Today,* Neuharth has secured his reputation for brilliant marketing. But it's clear that he wants to be remembered for his contributions to journalism as well. "Neuharth wants to close out his career as a fully respected member of the newspaper fraternity," says Thomas Winship, former editor of the *Boston Globe.* "He wants to be taken seriously by the serious newspaper people."

QUESTIONS FOR REVIEW AND DISCUSSION

1. In macro terms, are the mass communicators (a) the media or (b) the people who direct and work for the media? Why do sociologists make this distinction?
2. According to the findings of the Gray-Wilhoit survey, are journalists, in your opinion, different from other Americans? If so, in what ways?
3. One study termed most journalists *processors* of the news. Is this a fair characterization?
4. What are the two primary career fields of journalism and mass communications students today? Why these and not other fields?
5. Describe some of the barriers to the movement of more women into top-level news positions.
6. How is the American Society of Newspaper Editors seeking to attract more minority personnel into journalism?
7. Why are the Hispanic media of growing attractiveness to advertisers?
8. What is causing the decline in the number of people watching news programs on the traditional networks, NBC, CBS, and ABC?
9. To what primary journalistic standard are photographers being held today? Does this standard unduly restrict photographers in their work?
10. Recount five principal beliefs Rupert Murdoch expressed in his interview.
11. What are some of Ted Turner's successes and failures?
12. To what can Oprah Winfrey's phenomenal success be attributed?
13. What publishing formula has led to Allen Neuharth's success in building (a) the Gannett group of newspapers and (b) *USA Today?*

ESSAY TOPICS

1. To what does sociologist Herbert J. Gans attribute what he calls the enduring values of contemporary journalism? Are these values shared by other segments of the society? Discuss.
2. Compare and contrast the apparent operating philosophies of two of the "provocative people" profiled in Part Four.

If the very subject that should have been treated thoughtfully is McJournaled, abbreviated to the trivial, then isn't the editor saying to the reader that it really isn't worth his or her attention?

— Ray Cave
in "Musings of a Newsmagazine Editor"

As the weekend progressed, I began to see that veejays, the fulltimers, come in two denominations: Smug and Cloying.

— Pamela Marin
in "Rock 'n' Roll Video Vibrations"

Reporting must be lodged in an understanding of moral values. Television reporters especially—but newspaper reporters too—give little or no thought to these basic values.

— Howard Cosell
in "Howard Cosell Says Sportswriters 'Not Prepared' "

Yet there is one constant on the Hollywood scene: Eight multinational corporations formed more than 50 years ago still have hegemony over the production and worldwide distribution of feature films.

— Douglas Gomery
in "Hollywood's Business"

I read every good writer all the time, and I'm envious, jealous, of all of them. But to try to imitate them? I think I have too much gray in what's left of my hair to imitate anybody.

— Jules Loh
in "What Writers Think About Writing"

PART
FIVE

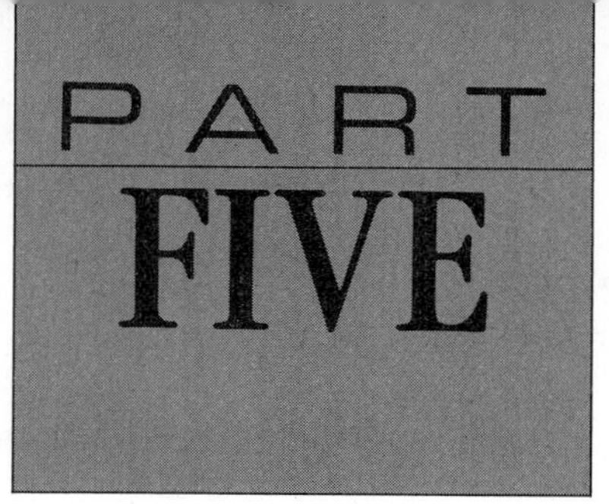

MEDIA TRENDS AND TECHNIQUES

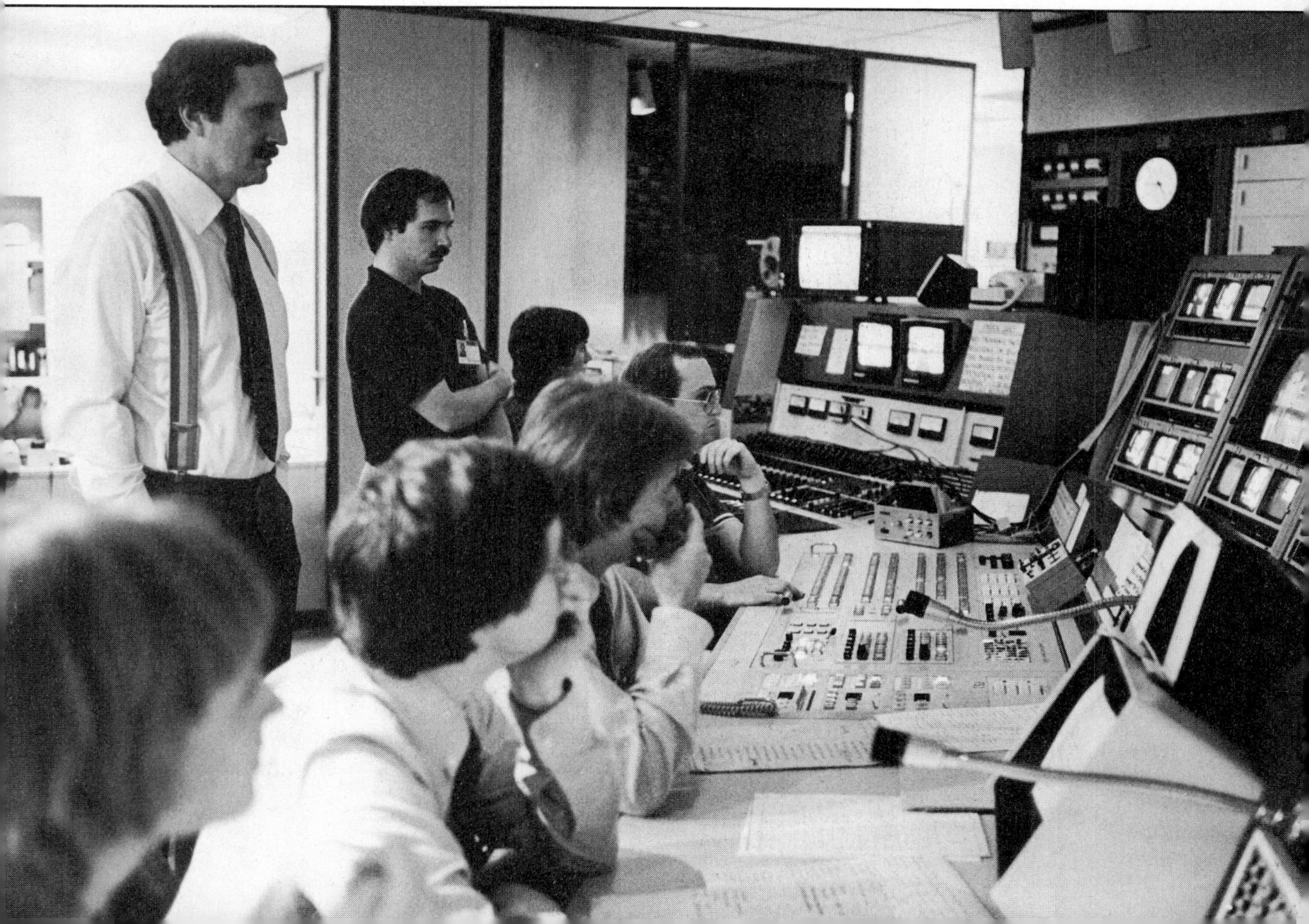

INTRODUCTION

PHILLIP H. AULT

Why did a *Time* magazine issue with Michael Jackson on its cover outsell one depicting the Mount St. Helens eruption? Why has *USA Today* received so much international attention, if not yet financial success? Would a local television news program attract more viewers if it covered fewer fires and protest marches and did investigative reporting instead?

Media editors and managers think about such questions. They use research staffs to dig out facts to help them. If enough of them reach identical conclusions, a trend is born. The audience begins to receive different types of information and entertainment from its favorite newspaper, television station, or magazine.

A trend may cross the line from one medium to another. Or the decision makers in two media may go in opposite directions—more violence in television shows, for example, and less in newspaper stories and photographs.

Those are the types of media trends and techniques we cover in Part Five. Our discussion focuses in turn on each of the media, beginning with television. The selections form a broad picture of the changes taking place and the psychological, technical, and profit-making reasons behind them.

Each of the mass media has undergone a fundamental change since the 1960s. The development of cable television has opened dozens of new channels to viewers and weakened the grip on the television industry of the three primary networks—the American Broadcasting Company, the Columbia Broadcasting System, and the National Broadcasting Company. Many radio stations, especially smaller ones, have become heavily automated, with much of their music and talk supplied in package form by specialist producers. Newspapers have had a revolution in their production processes and, under pressure from competing media, have amended their content to emphasize news that helps readers cope with the problems of daily life.

Magazines have altered their ways, too, as special-interest periodicals have largely replaced the general-readership type. In the book industry, the rise of the mass-market paperback book has placed emphasis on action fiction. These novels stress slam-bang movement and sex rather than character development and interpretation; they must succeed commercially during the brief periods of exposure they receive on sales racks in drugstores and supermarkets. Romantic novels have caught the public fancy too, with large paperback sales, but they began to decline in the mid-1980s. Mass-marketing techniques have shaken up the book industry, once known for its personal touch and leisurely pace.

The growth of television has created a huge stay-at-home audience that receives its entertainment from the TV screen. The recent popularity of videocassette recorders has accentuated the trend. This development, in turn, has brought about a radical change in the type of motion pictures being shown in theaters, away from the family films watched by earlier generations.

Most of the motion picture audience is under 25 years of age, young people who find social satisfaction in "going out." Consequently, few films with appeal to all ages are being produced. In their place are pictures aimed at youthful interests: space adventure, horror, the supernatural, bawdy comedy, and rock music. Many of these are laden with violence, profanity, and sex, and they are not intended for a family audience. Ingenious special effects and shock value often receive more attention from producers than solid story lines.

THE MUSIC VIDEO PHENOMENON

Nothing demonstrates better the manner in which trends develop in the media than the spectacular and unpredicted success of the music video. This marriage of music and visual imagery on videotape that rarely lasts 10 minutes, usually less than 5, came into existence in 1981; however, the elements of which it is constituted—music, visual motion on videotape, and cable television—had existed for years. Within four years, the music video had expanded beyond its original role as a promotion device for selling rock music recordings and taken on a life of its own as a specialized art form.

Aimed straight at the under-25 audience that buys rock recordings, the MTV (Music Television) cable network began broadcasting in 1981. For 24 hours every day it shows a succession of short videos in which rock bands perform a song while strutting and gyrating on the screen or while other performers act out visual fantasies. Sometimes the visual aspect is tied clearly to the message of the song; often the two seem only remotely related. The impressionistic effects of some videos are striking.

MTV became the sensation of cable television, creating a special and enthusiastic audience. Soon, any rock band that made a recording almost automatically had to tape a music video of it and try to place the video on MTV. The recording industry, once largely dependent on radio airplay to introduce new material, smiled at its good fortune and pulled in the money.

So did MTV. By 1984 its program was being carried into the homes of 24 million cable TV subscribers. To assure a constant flow of new videos, MTV signed contracts with five major record companies under which these companies gave rock video clips to MTV for exclusive play for 30 to 60 days before they were released to other TV music programs.

Ted Turner, the energetic entrepreneur who created the successful Cable Network News, tried in 1984 to compete with MTV by establishing the rival

Cable Music Channel. This outlet offered a broader range of music than MTV's rock but failed to catch on with the audience. After only a month of operation, Turner sold his music channel to MTV for $1 million plus $500,000 in advertising expenditure on his other cable systems. Soon programs of rock music made their appearance on traditional over-the-air stations. Suddenly television, which had previously offered its listeners little music, was playing it in abundance.

New applications of the video music form appeared, too. Seeking the youth vote, the conservative Republican governor of Indiana, Robert D. Orr, made a rock music video as a reelection campaign device. Paramount Pictures broke new ground by creating a music video to promote its film *Thief of Hearts,* starring rock singer Melissa Manchester and Steven Bauer. On the 3½-minute video, Manchester sang the movie theme song and Bauer was shown in several brief, sexy scenes, the entire video forming a lure for TV viewers to attend the movie. The motion picture video serves the same purpose as the coming-attraction trailers shown in theaters but reaches an entirely new audience.

Groups of brief rock videos were packaged into longer videotapes and sold in music stores, gaining a form of permanence. Machines appeared in bars and restaurants on which patrons could see and hear videos by dropping coins into a slot. Thus within five years, an entirely new form of mass communication was created, caught the public's fancy, and began to expand into uses unforeseen by its originators. No one can tell what its ultimate boundaries might be.

FINDING THE AUDIENCE

A fundamental trend apparent in all mass media—print, broadcast, and film alike—is to identify the elements that make up the audience and to shape the offerings of the media outlets in ways that will please particular audience segments.

Traditionally, newspaper and magazine managements looked on the public as a nebulous mass from which they drew subscribers on a rather haphazard basis. General-interest magazines aimed for the broad market, with relatively little concern about the interests of particular groups. Most of these magazines, such as *Look* and *Collier's,* once household mainstays, died in the 1960s and 1970s; they were replaced by periodicals designed to reach special audience segments. Nonfiction books similarly aimed at special-interest audiences form a large part of the book publishing industry's annual output. Radio and television stations too originally sought to entertain everyone on an indiscriminate basis, but many have developed formats focused on narrowly defined groups. The term *narrowcasting* has become a part of the broadcasting industry's vocabulary.

Newspapers are still edited for the entire population, as in the past. However, they now make a calculated effort to increase their appeal by devoting special attention to the identified desires of their present and potential readers.

The key factor today in identification of audience makeup and interests and in ability to reach carefully selected target audiences is the computer. Let us examine the role of the computer in pinpointing the various elements of a newspaper audience and in controlling the distribution of printed advertising. In precomputer days, isolating and reaching geographic and special-interest groups within the mass audience was difficult. Today, the computer virtually controls many print media distribution systems.

This control in turn influences the material newspapers and magazines publish. It also heavily affects newspaper advertising. The recent upsurge in preprinted advertising—those colorful sections printed in commercial plants and inserted in newspapers—is tied directly to computer techniques. The appearance of newspapers has been changed by the growth of preprints; today the typical newspaper publishes fewer multipage advertisements by large merchants in its regular sections than in the past, while including an abundance of removable preprinted sections that contain no news or feature material.

Newspapers and magazines place the names and addresses of subscribers in their computers. Once this is done, a newspaper can develop a list of all addresses in its circulation area where the occupants do not subscribe. By matching up these positive and negative lists, a newspaper can create a total marketing concept.

On a certain day each week, for example, it can deliver to nonsubscriber homes by mail or carrier an advertising supplement containing preprinted sections that also appear in the regular newspaper. Or, if a big advertiser desires, blanket coverage by the newspaper and/or its advertising supplement can be made to every address in certain specified zip code areas whose residents the advertiser particularly desires to reach. The same method can be used on days when the newspaper publishes special editorial sections of particular interest in certain zones.

Variations of total market coverage are numerous. In a reverse application, a real estate section promoting the sale of expensive suburban homes would be of scant interest to residents of a low-income inner-city zone. With computerized zoning, it could be omitted from copies of the paper delivered there.

In their distribution of preprinted advertising, newspapers face intense competition from free-distribution publications, sometimes called "shoppers," which may contain a smattering of feature news to fill the chinks around the advertising. Competition comes also through a system called "marriage mail." This consists of several preprinted advertisements grouped together by a sales firm and distributed by mail, sometimes only to certain zip code areas.

Through their use of the computer for circulation and advertising purposes, progressive newspapers and magazines have gathered stacks of information from which their researchers can develop audience profiles of much value to editors. That nebulous mass public of the past is now recognized as a collection of overlapping target audiences, each with distinct characteristics and interests. Demographic and psychographic information such as age, sex, occupation, income level, and known interests can be programmed into the computer. What emerges is a multifaceted audience profile that an editor can use in shaping the publication's content.

Do the computerized studies show strong interest among local residents in boating and sufficient average income in certain circulation areas to afford the purchase of a boat? A monthly advertising-supported section on boating during the summer might be precisely what readers would like. The possibilities are virtually endless.

Magazines go even further in the target audience direction. Hundreds of successful periodicals today are single-theme publications appealing to people who desire to read about that topic—perhaps motorcycles, science, water skiing, computer programming, or wines. Their circulation departments solicit subscriptions by mailing sales literature to addresses rented from list specialists who develop from many sources tabulations of persons with identifiable special interests.

Among the skillful media users of computerized mailings are the television evangelists. Names of contributors who respond to their on-the-air appeals for money are stored and categorized in computer memory for future solicitations and for political purposes. A group of electronic ministers pooled their resources during the 1984 political campaign to conduct voter registration drives among conservative-minded citizens. They combined their best lists of supporters, eliminated duplications, and produced a list of about 100,000 preachers around the United States. Each of these individuals received first a package of literature, then a postcard saying that a telephone call would follow.

Using the elaborate bank of telephones at the Rev. Jerry Falwell's headquarters in Lynchburg, Virginia, the evangelists arranged for automatic taped messages to be phoned to each of the 100,000 persons, urging them to participate in the registration campaign to help conservative candidates. At the end of each call, space was left for the recipient to respond. Six of each 10 recipients of the calls said yes. These 60,000 persons then became a nationwide organization for the voter registration drive, a political force that evolved from televised religious broadcasts. The Rev. Pat Robertson used similar techniques to build support for his unsuccessful attempt to win the 1988 Republican presidential nomination.

As these examples indicate, use of the computer in shaping mass media communication to individuals and groups is having an intense effect on the distribution of information in the United States, an effect that is certain to increase.

MEDIA TECHNIQUES

The techniques used in creating mass media information and entertainment change as new communication devices are developed, but the underlying principles of newsgathering and photography remain unaltered. The same is true in the entertainment media. Each development must be measured against these standards.

In their delivery of news to the public, communicators should be guided by three precepts:

1. Be accurate, balanced, and fair.
2. Illuminate the facts as well as merely relate them—give them meaning by delving beyond the obvious to disclose the reasons why things happen.
3. Deliver the information in written, spoken, or visual form with such clarity that everyone in the intended audience can understand it.

In entertainment, the story, and the message if there is one, should be presented in a form and context that a mass audience or a specialized audience—whichever is the target—can grasp.

TELEVISION

TV NEWS: LIFE IN THE FAST LANE

Philip Weiss and Laurence Zuckerman

Television news has increased in abundance and grown "softer" in recent years, with emphasis on technique and reduced attention to thoughtful investigative discussion. The trend was examined in the *Columbia Journalism Review* by Philip Weiss, a contributing editor, and Laurence Zuckerman, former associate editor.

While the character of newspapers has changed as they have learned to coexist with TV, the nature of television news has been changing, too. But if papers have been reacting to television, television news has had its eye on the all-encompassing environment of television itself: from music videos to sitcoms to cop shows. In adjusting to its own environment, television has slowly escaped its original influence, the print world.

The distinction is clear even in a thirty-three-year-old tape of *See It Now.* One hears the pages rustling as Edward R. Murrow reads an earnest response to a personal attack by Senator Joseph R. McCarthy, saying, "I require no lecture from the junior senator of Wisconsin upon the evils of communism." At last Murrow puts the speech aside and, looking up, says, "We shall hope to deal with matters of more vital interest to the country next week." It's an unscripted line, and twice Murrow's voice catches and he has to repeat words. The emotion he has held in check throughout his speech is suddenly revealed as his eyes meet the camera: wounded, proud, mortified by the necessity of making himself a center of attention. It's a moving moment that makes what came before—to a viewer today, anyway—seem windy by comparison.

Source: Philip Weiss and Laurence Zuckerman, "The Shadow of a Medium." Reprinted with permission from the *Columbia Journalism Review,* March–April 1987.

As technology has improved and a print-trained generation has given way to one raised on TV, television journalism has aimed more and more for the stammer and not for the rustle. *Nightline,* for instance, has found a video idiom for reporting on intellectual and policy clashes. By using satellites and live television, it creates (and of course captures) spontaneous, even emotional arguments in a way no scripted report could ever do.

The object is "to put the camera in settings where things will happen in front of it," explains Tom Yellin, a senior producer at CBS. James Wooten also stresses the need to allow the story's subjects and images to speak for themselves. "One mark of a really good television piece," he says, "is that the track—the reporter's voice, his script—is very short."

There is today more news programming than ever before. A whole network (CNN) is devoted to news, and the big-three networks and public TV program as many as sixty hours a week, from Sunday morning shows with a touchy-feely gloss to MacNeil-Lehrer's often endless hour. As has been widely reported, local TV news operations have expanded and, by transmitting more and more breaking national news, have forced the networks to run stories "where we can explain things that the local guys can't," in the words of NBC health and science correspondent Robert Bazell.

If the programming has increased, so has the amount of soft news. On *60 Minutes* Diane Sawyer flirts with violinist Isaac Stern as he prepares for the reopening of Carnegie Hall, and on *West 57th* the ringletted Bob Sirott nods gravely as another rock star describes her drug problem. Jeff Greenfield, the columnist and ABC correspondent, says that more and more *People*-magazine-style pieces are showing up on the nightly news. Meanwhile, the networks are competing fiercely over the latest trend in news programming: nostalgic hour-long presentations about the country's history.

Journalists have for decades complained about the infiltration of entertainment values in news decisions, a charge reiterated recently by Bill Moyers, who in leaving CBS for public TV charged (in *Newsweek*) that the model for news programming had become *Entertainment Tonight.* Perhaps the biggest change in recent years is that there no longer exists any shame about marketing considerations. Judy Crichton, a longtime documentary producer who left ABC last year to become the executive producer of a documentary series for WGBH in Boston, recalls her former boss at CBS Reports, Perry S. Wolff, blowing up at her twelve years ago when she asked what the overnight ratings had been on the documentary *Caution: Drinking Water May Be Dangerous to Your Health.* Don't even think about such things, she says he told her. She was urged to think of the viewers as her own friends, people who would explore the same issues on their own if only they had the time.

Today such a high-minded attitude seems faintly ridiculous. Ratings are posted prominently around the ABC documentary unit, Crichton says. CBS correspondents get taken out to "21" to celebrate their shows' ratings successes, and network publicity people brag about how well the numbers for magazine shows stack up against adventure series like *Magruder and Loud* and *Remington Steele.*

The most distinct loser has been the documentary, which has all but died on commercial television. "There isn't time to go out with thirty-five-millimeter cameras and record at great length," says *Washington Post* critic Tom Shales, perhaps the prime cheerleader for the new video values. "It's a different age."

The difference is plainly illustrated by CBS's documentary coup of 1986, *48 Hours on Crack Street.* Hailed by Shales as an "instant documentary," *Crack Street* was put together in just six weeks last fall, some say as a sop to a news division demoralized by corporate infighting. It was shot on video rather than film and used an army of correspondents and producers to reveal all the dimensions of the drug problem. The result was great footage that was faintly reminiscent of brash local TV news efforts. A machine-gun-paced opening with a rock-and-roll theme gave way to street types in raw splendor, selling, buying, or under the influence of drugs. Dan Rather was shown accompanying New York City police officers on a drug raid. In the end, however, the two-hour documentary made little effort to probe the depths of an issue that was coming to dominate the election campaign. Its focus on reporters-in-action—Bernard Goldberg tussling with a dealer outside Washington Square Park, medical reporter Dr. Robert Arnot sweating through his shirt as he assisted an overdose victim—perhaps made inevitable the video experiment that so horrified critics later in the fall: Geraldo Rivera's live, on-camera participation in a drug bust, a show that won the highest ratings of the year for a syndicated TV show.

But if the network numbers-crunchers are reluctant to give up time to documentary investigations, they are willing to give the news divisions an opportunity to match the now-legendary success of the *60 Minutes* magazine. Several efforts have come and gone, most recently NBC's *1986* (which didn't become *1987*). The magazine that has caused the greatest stir, because it exemplifies the clash between traditional documentaries and entertainment values, is CBS's *West 57th.* The show's opening minutes have achieved a certain fame, or notoriety: a string of intense, seemingly spontaneous shots of the show's production ("We've got the piece and it works and that's fine"), interlaced with music. The kinetic correspondents are introduced as though they are characters in an adventure series.

When it was first aired a year and a half ago, Howard Stringer, who now heads the CBS News Division, hailed *West 57th* as an "experiment in form and structure and style" that drew from the techniques of TV commercials and filmmakers Steven Spielberg and George Lucas. Others were less enthusiastic. Don Hewitt, executive producer of *60 Minutes,* called it "light summer fare." *New York Times* television critic John Corry said, "Looking and sounding good is all that *West 57th* has on its mind," and Moyers pointed to it as a symbol of what was wrong with network news programming. As for the *Post*'s Tom Shales, he says *West 57th* is the most exciting development in television journalism in the last five to ten years.

FAST FORWARD ON *WEST 57TH*

Tom Yellin's office on the eighth floor at CBS does not seem an outpost of the video age. There are artworks on the wall and novels on the shelves. Yellin is thirty-four and wears a tweed jacket and spends several minutes explaining his "paranoia" about misquotation. He is sore over a statement attributed to him that his viewers are "video fluent," which he says was a reporter's lazy contraction of a complicated thought. And he gets angry when reminded of a line in the *Times* pointing out that people with a background in music video are on his staff. It was misleading, he says, because the *Times* chose not to mention his background as a producer of documentaries, *Nightline,* and ABC's *World News Tonight.* All in all, Yellin seems concerned about the written word.

When Murrow and Fred W. Friendly were producing *See It Now,* Yellin says, the only daily news programming was a fifteen-minute network newscast. *West 57th* exists in a far more competitive news environment. And the shows that fail do so because they don't succeed in storytelling, he says. As for the documentary, its recent decline is not symptomatic of TV's shallowness but of its immediacy. He points to a documentary about terrorism which CBS aired in the middle of the hijacking of TWA Flight 847 in 1985. "Almost everything in the documentary had been seen already, on the *Today* show, on *Nightline,* on the evening news. As a result [it] had a kind of stale feeling."

Yellin says his show looks for stories that are not being done and presents them in a shorthand familiar to a generation of viewers that is—well, video fluent. "The average age of the country is twenty-eight or twenty-nine," he says. "Everyone who is below that age grew up watching television, and most people who are in their seventies have watched TV for thirty or forty years. Therefore, as a maker of television, it's not unrealistic to assume that people are familiar with how it conveys information and are fluent in the language of television."

Commercials, which have shrunk from sixty to thirty to fifteen seconds, are evidence that viewers can "absorb information" at a faster pace. A producer should watch music videos, too. "You can talk faster" to your viewers, Yellin says, by eliminating some of the "traditional television storytelling tools," such as the use of standups (correspondents talking directly into the camera) and stock footage that evokes historical moments.

Yellin also says that *West 57th* is not interested in doing stories about issues. ("I've done many, many of those kinds of things, and to me they're not satisfying.") The criteria a *West 57th* story must meet are, first, "Is it a story rather than a subject?" and second, "Are there compelling characters who can tell the story well?" Compelling, he says, is in ways synonymous with entertaining.

The *West 57th* piece that perhaps most dramatically exemplifies the video values Yellin expounds was the story about a precocious nine-year-old boy living on the North Side of Chicago that led off the April 30, 1986, show. Yellin had described "Little Anthony—Living on the Edge" as a "bold" and "experimental" story, "stripped" of many traditional journalistic techniques.

The story contained little narration, in large part the voice of the boy as he walked the streets, attended school, went to his aunt's home, etc. So many of the shots were intimate, from very nearly the standpoint of the fly on the wall—in fact, that selfsame celebrated fly of the New Journalism in magazines fifteen years ago—that you wondered if the camera was on somebody's tieclip. In part because of the camera's size, in part because the American public is now conditioned to seeing people walking around with video equipment, taping can capture cinema verité scenes impossible in the old days. A drunk comes leering up into the corner of the screen, a tattooed boy taunts correspondent Meredith Vieira about the pointlessness of life, and so on.

As for its message, "Little Anthony" had the open-ended quality of the short fiction that's now in vogue. Its theme was that an attractive, verbal boy might turn out bad because of his awful environment. In the story's slightly sensational climax, Anthony's teacher—and teachers were the only authorities shown in this place that was alleged, with very little evidence, to be rough and lawless—says that she's seen boys like Anthony end up serving time for murder.

"Meredith discovered the kid in Chicago when she was doing an evening news piece about poverty," Yellin had said. "And she just was overwhelmed by him and he kept popping up in her mind and she came in one day and said, 'We should just do a story about him. . . . He's poor and he's really smart and very articulate, he talks just like an adult because he watches so much TV. . . .'

"I said, 'What's the story?'

"She said, 'I'm not really sure, but it would be interesting.'

"I said, 'All right.' "

Yellin says the piece made its points "implicitly" and succeeded—without traditional storytelling tools, without "didacticism," repetition, or interviews with cops and social workers—if at the end you asked the person sitting next to you what the story said about society. But the viewer was very much on his own in such speculation. Had Anthony's family broken up because of the welfare system? The culture of poverty? How much of a problem is delinquency? Is the social support Anthony lacks more prevalent in affluent communities? "Little Anthony" offered little information on these points. This is, of course, a weakness found in a lot of New Journalism in city magazines today; hating didacticism, its practitioners hope to tell engaging stories and often end up making no point at all.

West 57th has done pieces of a highly pointed nature. Last June, for instance, it did a superb story alleging efforts by the National Security Council (and none other than Lieutenant Colonel Oliver North) to arm the Nicaraguan contras, in apparent violation of laws barring lethal aid. This story, too, was a narrative, built around the mystery of a farm in Costa Rica owned by John Hull, an American with alleged ties to the CIA. An earlier piece pointed to continuing American responsibility for repression in Haiti after Duvalier. Both these pieces made points with imagery—say, the uncommented-upon shot of a faded poster of Duvalier on a wall. Silent touches like that one are leagues away from the old documentary, which was so explicatory.

Yellin is no partisan of high-mindedness. "If you are setting out to do something that's boring and that is somehow self-serving in some sort of intellectual construction of what is noble, you're an arrogant asshole," he says. "What you ought to be doing is saying, How can I tell the story well so that people will care about it?"

THE STORYTELLERS—AND WHAT'S MISSING

As TV journalism seeks out a culture of storytelling and immediacy, the loss may be reporting that centers on ideas and issues. In such an environment hard thinking is not especially valued; when it came to making a point, *48 Hours on Crack Street,* for instance, merely reflected the most conventional (and slightly hysterical) position on drug use. ("Crack Street. It could be anybody's street," Dan Rather said portentously.) Murrow's *Harvest of Shame* had its slow moments, but it also had ideas that it articulated and illustrated, and the only thing *implicit* about it was how much the poor guy smoked. At the end of the documentary Murrow made a passionate appeal—about labor conditions, on grounds of social justice—to Thanksgiving Day viewers and expressed the sort of fervor it's difficult to imagine in a self-dramatizing video milieu.

There's an analogy in politics. Just as television, with its direct access to the viewer, has reduced the importance of parties in the political selection process, so, too, it has lessened the importance of journalists as interpreters and commentators. Koppel has said that he must not take a stand on issues or he will lose his influence; indeed, the journalists who speak out on his show are, by and large, print ones. Greenfield notes that he can be much more "whacked out" in print than on TV. Tom Brokaw, who concluded two recent NBC public affairs hours with the mild assertions that teachers should be better compensated and that we had better wake up to the health crisis posed by AIDS, says in an interview, "Obviously, I do have passion. My friends who know me well will tell you that." But in large part TV doesn't encourage its expression. Interestingly, *USA Today,* that most TV-oriented of papers, decided not to endorse a candidate in the [1984] presidential election.

The moderating of point of view and the emphasis on coverage with dramatic potential suggest that in TV journalism the very top end is missing. With notable exceptions, TV has yielded the most thoughtful, investigative discussions to print. Today you are far more likely to *read* a documentary about, say, toxic waste in a big-city paper than to see one on TV, and more likely to *see* tabloid shots of blood and guns on TV than on the front page of a newspaper.

Meanwhile, newspapers that model themselves on television may well be underestimating print's stamina. Truisms about the fast pace and short attention span of American society discount the fact that people continue to seek out in-depth coverage of many issues. Editors who in essence say, let *The New York Times* and *The Washington Post* do it, may end up producing papers that are less serious than the problems confronting their communities. Many of these papers enjoy monopoly status, which theoretically should free them up to offer more penetrating accounts of the sort that television has not generally provided.

Some argue that the differences in orientation between newspapers and television have to do with intrinsic differences between the media. "You can't Xerox a TV show," Ben Bradlee told *American Heritage* a few years ago, meaning that anything you can't pass around has limited influence. "Television, even with the VCR, is a medium where it's thrown at you and either you get it or you don't," Jeff Greenfield says. "The thing that makes print still a powerful medium is, to use the computer idiom, it's randomly accessed. . . . If you're trying to come to grips particularly with an intellectual or a policy argument, it's just much easier to do it when you have the time to sit back to look at an argument two or three times." Pieces on air have to compete with the dog barking and the doorbell ringing, says Robert Bazell, the NBC science correspondent; he finds that his articles in *The New Republic* generate more mail than does his on-air reporting, which he considers just as substantive. Tom Shales celebrates this ephemerality—and even its resulting lack of point.

Surely the different orientations also have to do with the ways the two media are marketed: print and TV have staked out opposite positions on the American class divide. In his book *Press and Public,* newspaper researcher Leo Bogart says that "a long series of studies, academic and commercial," shows that higher-income, better-educated people tend to read papers and lower-income, less-educated people tend to watch television. And so a TV piece on Haiti is produced with the understanding that it must compete with action-packed adventure series, while a newspaper piece on the same subject operates under constraints far more tolerant of complicated analysis. TV journalism's coups have tended to come on the sly, when it doesn't matter—in time slots that are given up for lost or long past prime time. In spite of such limitations, television has done wonders at reinventing forms that were once the province of print: narrative journalism, eyewitness journalism, and a journalism that presents intellectual disputes. Think what else it might reinvent, if it only put its mind to it.

BACKSTAGE AT *THE MACNEIL–LEHRER REPORT*

Edmund Ghareeb

The MacNeil-Lehrer Report and its successor, *The MacNeil/Lehrer NewsHour,* on public television, are widely respected for their news coverage in depth and stimulating discussions with newsmakers. This interview with Jim Lehrer by the editor of *Split Vision: The Portrayal of Arabs in the American Media,* provides an inside look at how the program operates.

Ghareeb: What are some of the key factors that determine what type of people you choose for your program, especially when it comes to discussing foreign affairs?
Lehrer: There are many things. The first criterion is the story, the development that we're going to report on. The next factor is the people; who would the best people be to come on and talk about it. Then, we find out who's available and who will come. We have what we call the Brezhnev-Carter rule. If we do a story about problems between the Soviet Union and the United States, ideally, we would like to get the president of the United States and the president of the Soviet Union to get on and debate it. That's the ultimate; that's where you always start. But you don't always get there.
Ghareeb: Is there a subjective point of view that leads you to determine who the best person is? Is the best person the most knowledgeable, the expert, or the person who can communicate his point of view better on television than somebody else? Is he from a certain geographical area? One of the points that I often notice not only on *MacNeil-Lehrer* but on some of the other programs is that they usually bring people only from Washington or New York. Are these the only people available? Isn't there a certain milieu that influences all of these people and moves them to think in a certain direction?
Lehrer: If you've got a Middle East question, for example, and there's a development that involves a very clear difference of opinion, you want somebody to represent the Arab position and somebody to represent the Israeli position. You've got two problems. You've got the problem of finding the person who has the credentials and holds the position that you decide editorially you want to represent. But because we're doing a live program, you've got another criterion—the question of whether that person can articulate his position. It's a cop out to say, "We had an Arab. The fact that the Arab couldn't get his words out is his problem. The Israeli was ten times more articulate and won the argument, but this Arab was the most qualified guy." That won't work, and that is just one of the problems that you have got when you do our kind of television program. Not many times, but occasionally, one of our reporters or producers will come and say, "Sammy Sue Smith is the most knowledgeable person in a particular area, but he talks with such a heavy accent that our audience would never understand him. So we're going to have to go with the second best, who is Billy Bob Dunn." That's just the way it is. If you could sit down and talk to him and distill it like a newspaper man does, or as you do for a book, that's a different matter.
Ghareeb: It appears that your program is spontaneous, but is it?
Lehrer: It's done live. We plan, obviously, because the way we do it you have to plan. If somebody is supposed to be on there presenting a particular

Source: Excerpted from *Split Vision: The Portrayal of Arabs in the American Media,* edited by Edmund Ghareeb (Washington, DC: American-Arab Affairs Council, 1983). Reprinted by permission.

position, that person better represent that position or we've ended up with an unfair show. That happens to us occasionally. Somebody comes on and doesn't articulate quite as well. We plan the order that we're going to introduce and interview the guests. We certainly work out our questions in advance. However, a lot of times I'll interview my guest and never look at my questions, just because of what the guest says, and carry it on. That sort of thing.

Ghareeb: When you raise questions is there an image, a stereotype, a perception that you want these people to get out, or do you want them to focus on what you're asking them?

Lehrer: Oh, yes, absolutely. In most cases the people we interview are invited on for a specific reason, because they hold a particular opinion. My job is to help them get that opinion across so the audience understands it. I don't care what that opinion is, as long as it fits the way we're trying to structure the program. I'm not there to beat up on anybody. I'm there to help them, and to test them a little bit. Ninety-nine times out of 100 there's somebody sitting next to them who disagrees, so you can test them with the other guest. I don't have to browbeat people or play devil's advocate.

Ghareeb: How do you decide on what questions to ask? Do you usually meet as a group or . . . ?

Lehrer: There's a series of things the producer and the reporter on the story work out, and then they give us a list of recommended questions. After we have read and distilled everything, MacNeil and I then write our own questions. He and I talk about it between us, and then we write them. Right before the program, which is at 7 P.M., the reporter on the story, the producer on the story, and Robin and I get on the telephone and go through every question. At that time people—anybody willing—are open to say, "I don't think that's the right question," and the reporter would say, "You ought to be prepared for this, if you ask that," and so on. So nobody's going to get surprised, at least in terms of our staff. We get surprised when we get out of the studio sometimes.

Ghareeb: How many of the people who appear on your program do you know personally, and how much time do you talk to them? Does that affect the type of questions that you raise?

Lehrer: I would estimate that I know personally less than one percent of the guests. A lot of these people have been on before, so I've met them, but of the people with whom I socialize in my private life, less than one percent appear on the show.

Ghareeb: When you're going to be discussing a certain topic, do you call and talk to people?

Lehrer: Our reporters do, our staff does, but I don't do that. The only time I talk to them is when they're in the studio. They come in about ten minutes before air time, and I go over with them in a general way what we're going to talk about. There are no secrets. I interview them and they leave. . . .

Ghareeb: When it comes to the Middle East, I would say that your focus, and this is not a scientific study, is first on Israel and then on Egypt or Iran. There has been almost nothing on Saudi Arabia, for example, or on the other issues in the area. Why does it happen this way and why is it that you do not focus on some of the other issues in-depth, say the Iraq-Iran War. It seems to be oriented toward the great deal of interest about Israel, and unless there's a crisis in the area, there is no focus on other developments in the area.

Lehrer: We've done a few programs on the Iran-Iraq War. It is very difficult to get information on it and to get people to come on and talk about it. The last program we did on it was excellent because we had the foreign minister of Iran and one of the Iraqi diplomats. They really got into it. But there is no independent information about the Iran-Iraq War. These two men sat one in one studio and one in the other, and you'd never have known they were talking about the same thing. Iran had crossed over into Iraq and said, "We're going all the way, we're going to throw Saddam Hussein out." The Iranian said, "Yes, we've captured this and that, the Iraqis are throwing down their arms, and the war is over." The Iraqi said that the Iranians had been stopped at the border; the war was over, and the Iraqis had won. There was no way to turn, no way to grab some independent force that could bring any kind of order or understanding to the issue. The fact is when you deal with Iran and Iraq and some of the other Mideast countries, the diplomats don't tell the truth. They tell the lie, and they do it in such a way that it is impossible to cut your way through. I had a long talk with a representative from the PLO about this. He comes on our program every once in a while, and will look one straight in the eye and say something that I know, and he knows, is not the truth. He says, "That's our thing." We do the story because we feel that we have to once in a while. But to the average American watching that stuff, it's awful.

But that didn't answer your question. That's no reason not to do the story; it just makes it very difficult for us when we do it. Why haven't we done anything on Saudi Arabia? Why have we done more on Israel? Because Israel is more involved in the news. You can argue with the definition of news, but it is a fact that the United States is the major ally of Israel, and that one-fourth of all U.S. foreign aid goes to Israel. They're using our weapons, they're using our training, etc. We are doing a program for the United States. Our program does not go all over the world. As for the Saudis, you picked a bad example there. We did many, many stories on the Saudis. During the oil . . .

Ghareeb: There was something on OPEC, but on Saudi Arabia alone . . .

Lehrer: But that's where the Saudis most affect the average American for whom we're doing our program. The Saudis will never come on television to discuss foreign policy. We have invited them, but they have yet to send a representative. Not only won't they send a representative, they won't send a substitute and they won't help us find anybody. Their position has never been represented on our program because they won't play. So, when we have a Saudi Arabian story, as a Saudi Arabian angle we get a former U.S. Ambassador to Saudi Arabia or an American who is a lawyer for Saudi Arabia or a Member of Congress. The Saudis will never come on and explain themselves on our program, and I've never seen a Saudi on anybody else's television program.

Ghareeb: There have been a few.

Lehrer: There have been a few, but damn few.

Ghareeb: I think one time you had Sheikh Yamani on.

Lehrer: Sheikh Yamani is in a separate category. I'm talking about foreign policy people. For instance, the Jordanians will come. We've interviewed King Hussein several times, and we interviewed his brother once. . . .

Ghareeb: Your program was among the first to recognize what the story in Iran was all about. You had people like Khomeini interviewed. You also had people like Rouhani and Yazdi, and did a superb job with it. Why is it that you got onto the story before other networks or the newspapers?

Lehrer: Because our contacts are different. One of the strengths of our program is that our reporters don't talk just to government officials, but to people at the universities. They talk to all kinds of people. I'm always stunned when we do a program on Iran, for example, and we invite one of the leading foreign affairs reporters and an expert on Iran, and they've never met before because that person is not in the government. He's at the Georgetown Center for Strategic and International Studies, or at the Johns Hopkins School of Advanced International Studies. Reporters tend to go to government officials to get their information, you see. On Iran our reporters didn't. They were talking to other people who were saying, "I don't know what they're telling you over at the State Department, but the Islamic revolution is real. You ought to talk to Rouhani at Columbia or a guy named Yazdi out at so and so. There's something going on here." They would never have gotten that at the State Department. They talked to him and became convinced this was real, and they did some other checking and so we went with the story. That's a judgment call, as you know. But if you don't talk to the right people, you're never going to get the right information.

Ghareeb: On Iran, I found it a bit strange to see journalists interviewing other journalists about an issue on which they probably had no more expertise. How do you explain this, and do you feel that this is a useful means of trying to get information?

Lehrer: We do it only when we have to, when we can't get the information. We're dependent on having people come on our program. If we cannot get somebody to come on who is a non-reporter, then we'll ask a reporter to come on. I agree with you basically, but it is something that we sometimes have to do in order to get things on the record. For instance, if the State Department won't come on to talk on a sensitive issue, sometimes it fits our purposes to have a State Department reporter come on and reflect on what those people are thinking and talking about. . . .

Ghareeb: How much do you rely on press coverage for your information? I am referring specifically to *The New York Times, The Washington Post* and the weekly magazines.

Lehrer: Sure, we're like everybody else, we read all those things.

Ghareeb: Why is it that you spend so little time trying to get the people to understand the background to the problems in the area? As I said, you do a better job than others but you still wait until a crisis emerges and then focus on a story. How do you expect people to understand an issue without giving some background information beforehand, so that anybody who's not following the area closely would know that there are potential problems there?

Lehrer: We're not in the education business; we're in the news business. If you say "Good evening, there's nothing going on in Saudi Arabia but we're going to talk to you for thirty minutes about Saudi Arabia," nobody's going to watch it. What's the point?

Ghareeb: This raises two questions. First, how much of the news or the material you give is information and how much is entertainment? And secondly, do you create the news or are you responsive to events?

Lehrer: We're in the reporting business. When there are developments we try to find out what happened, report it, and explain why it happened. That's not saying we always do it well or we always do it the right way, but that's what we're here to do.

Ghareeb: I have a question on the Lebanon story. People have often referred to the Lebanese conflict as a Christian-Muslim war, as a conflict between rightist Christians and left-wing Muslims, or as a civil war. There are constant references to Saad Haddad's Christian militia. But these terms are not accurate; they are simplifications, generalizations. Why are they constantly used?

Lehrer: We have done three or four programs in the last three or four years in which we explained in detail all the various factions in Lebanon. There are certain identifications that arise. In American politics, it's like calling a certain Congressman a liberal. How do you define a liberal? These are terms that have grown up over the past several years to identify these various forces. Certainly there are subtleties, but we have explained it time and time again, and then we continue to use what we think are the words that people understand to distinguish these groups from one another.

Ghareeb: But even when they are not accurate?

Lehrer: Obviously they are accurate; we think they are accurate.

Ghareeb: Do you think something could be done to change that image? You put the blame on the Arabs but don't you think that part of the problem is the fact that journalists here do not know the area well?

Lehrer: Edward Said is a Palestinian who is very critical of the American press for the way it has handled the Arabs. In a recent *New York Times* article he made the point that some 300 Palestinians were massacred in Lebanon. And where are the demonstrations about that? In Israel. Not in any Arab country. Life goes on in Lebanon; there's no crisis as a result of that. Nor is there a crisis in the Arab world. But in Israel the people got so upset about it that they forced the government to take some action. His point was that until the Arabs start reacting to massacres the same way the Israeli people do, they're always going to have problems. This has not been lost on the average non-Jewish American. The United States is very upset with Israel but the Israeli people rose up and said, "Hey, government, we want to know what happened."

Nobody in the Arab world even issued press releases. As Edward Said said, this feeds the stereotype that many Americans have of Arabs as bloody people who just go out killing each other all the time. That's an awful thing, and it must be awful for an Arab to see this. I can't think of a more recent example of where the problem is. This is not a public relations image problem, it's a reality problem. The most articulate Arab spokesman who is going to come on and be as straight as an arrow cannot get around that fact.

Ghareeb: Are you saying that the image is a reflection of reality?

Lehrer: I don't know. But those kinds of things contribute to a negative image, if there is one. It's much better now than it has ever been, but those kinds of things contribute to any negative feeling about some of the Arab world.

Ghareeb: To what do you attribute the improvement that has taken place in coverage of the Arab issues in recent years?

Lehrer: I think it's an increased awareness on the part of the Arab nations that if American public opinion is important, than you have to deal with it. You have to be willing to come on television programs to explain yourself. If you want the people in Kansas to understand what your position is, you have got to talk to the people in Kansas. The Israelis do that. The Israelis have always understood the need for that. If you are engaged in a battle with the Israelis for the hearts and minds of the American people, you've got to do it too, particularly when you're dealing with Israel's traditionally close ties to the United States. Israel is a democracy, and its way of life is kindred to the American way. The Arab world does not have those things going for it in the first place, so you have a double burden. In fact, you could argue that the Arabs ought to be more willing, just from a public relations standpoint, to explain the Arab perspective. . . .

The Middle East didn't begin in 1948. You've got to understand cultures; things have to be explained. You say it's the American news media's responsibility to explain that. I will concede that, if you're willing to concede that without the cooperation of the Arab world there's no way we can explain it. We have tried, but we haven't been that successful. It is a very difficult thing and you've come a long way. There's no question about it.

Ghareeb: The recognition that there is a problem and how to deal with it is very important. Can you compare the problems you have had trying to get Arabs or Israeli spokesmen on your program? Have you often had problems trying to get certain spokesmen?

Lehrer: We never have trouble getting Israeli spokesmen; they will always come. We always have trouble getting representatives of Arab governments. Most of the people in Washington who represent the Arab governments will not do anything unless authorized by their home country. My feeling is that there are many Arab diplomats in this country who would love to come on our program and talk. I know a couple of them personally. The problem is by the time it goes through the bureaucracy back home the story is gone, and they've missed the opportunity. They are as upset and frustrated as anybody, but without the authorization of their government they can't come on. Their hands are tied but it's not their fault. They are very open for the most part.

Ghareeb: Have you ever tried to get foreign ministers, ministers of petroleum or prime ministers either when they are here or when they are there?

Lehrer: They usually end up not coming.

Ghareeb: They tell you they are going to come and they end up not coming?

Lehrer: They're always very nice about it. They always say they want to come, but it just doesn't come off. The exceptions to that are the Egyptians, who will play usually. The new Egyptian foreign minister has been on the program once. Usually we can get the Jordanians.

But there's a difference, a subtle difference. The Israelis will come on. It's a very interesting public relations question. When the news is the worst for the Israelis, that's when they will always come on because they feel that's when they need to be there to explain. When some news develops that is negative, or appears to be negative, you'll never get an Arab spokesman to come on. It's not his fault, it really isn't. I think it's a lack of understanding. If you want American public opinion on your side, the people in Amman and Cairo have to tell the people in Washington and at the United Nations, "Do what you think is right. If that means debating Yehudah Bloom on prime time American television, do it, whatever you think. If that means addressing the Kiwanis Club in Wichita, Kansas, do it." That's where the problem is. Am I wrong?

Ghareeb: Absolutely right, I think. This is one of the many problems, although there are others. . . .

ROCK 'N' ROLL VIDEO VIBRATIONS

Pamela Marin

For an entire weekend Pamela Marin watched music videos on television and, she says, emerged "dizzy, strung-out, . . . brain turned to humus." Her report in *University Man* shows what has happened to music videos since the MTV channel first brought rock to TV screens a few years ago.

I should have felt like singing and dancing, or at least getting a perm. I should have mastered the sultry pout, the ingratiating smile, the tentative lip sync. I should have played air guitar.

But when it was over, I was in no condition to emote, much less cavort. I was glommed onto the couch like a leech to a jugular, brain turned to humus.

The assignment had sounded so easy. Watch music video shows, my editor had said. Write about them. Piece of cake, I thought. I'll just attach myself to the old coucheroo, flip the dial, take a few notes, kick back. Perfect assignment for the clinically lethargic, no?

That was Thursday. By Monday I was a wreck—dizzy from jump-cuts and fab graphics, strung-out on veejay babble and certain that, were I forced to witness Suzanne Vega's "Luka" video one more time, I would grab the nearest heavy object and hit the streets searching for small, helpless persons to assault. I like that video. At least I did before The Lost Weekend.

Viscera scarred by vids in heavy rotation, multiple synapses mushed by inane blather, I staggered to the typewriter, mumbling "smash hit" and "hot new group"—veejay argot for "sold at least a hundred" and "nobodies." For days, I sat paralyzed before a blank page, sifting lifelessly through press releases. From them I learned that: 1) Music video shows are beamed to 18 billion homes, give or take a bil; 2) The target age group for music video shows is 12–34, which, I assume, is figured in dog years.

In the beginning, there was MTV. While it seems like music videos have been with us since man discovered Dick Clark, it was actually around the time Bonzo and His Conniving Handlers boogied onto Pennsylvania Avenue that record companies discovered the black hole of cable broadcasting. It was a marriage made in p.r. heaven. Why should you, the spendthrift public, simply listen to music, when you could be watching Jackson siblings gyrate or zoom within flossing distance of Billy Idol's sneer? If your answer is, "Because I'd rather play records and dream up my own pictures than watch lip-sync performance tapes or two-fisted symbolism," turn to the next article. Lip-sync and stupid symbols are the lifeblood of videos, with a few notable exceptions (personal to Robert Palmer: I'm yours).

The masterminds at MTV were both quick and smart, getting there first and doing it up right. MTV still has the slickest, wittiest station i.d.s—an effect aped to some degree by all its video progeny. And it was MTV that cast the hip-but-wholesome mold for a flock of fledgling veejays to come, epitomized in the person of Martha Quinn, now 86'ed from videoland, who was, and will always be, The Girl Next Door Who Has Smoked Dope.

From this marriage of music and pictures have sprung countless promotions. In any given week, MTV viewers can win trips to: Asia with Asia; Saville Row with Robert Palmer; Seymour, Indiana, with John ("Don't call me an animal") Mel-

Source: Pamela Marin, "Video Vibrations," *University Man*, Winter 1987. Reprinted with permission.

lencamp; or Cedars Sinai for rhinoplasty with Michael Jackson. Sensing that even the video devout get more than an eyeful in 24 hours, MTV breaks the pace with some wonderful concert specials, some less-than-wonderful interviews ("So, you've been playing piano since you were three?" "Um, like, y'know, I guess, yeah.") and sitcoms like the BBC-made "The Young Ones." At some point during The Lost Weekend I watched an episode of TYO which consisted, in its entirety, of four Brit punks screaming at each other in a living room, screaming at each other in a backyard, and trying to rob a bank while screaming at each other. Am I collie years past this cutting-edginess? I switched over to VH-1, the MTV folks' bid for yups, newagers, dincs and jabrogroos (Jackson Browne groupies).

I saw mountains, I saw flowers. I saw a stream rushing past grassy fields—that was the station i.d. I managed to stay awake through a set that included videos by dead pop star John Lennon, career-dead pop stars the Bee Gees and 10,000 Maniacs' cover of "Peace Train," by pop-star-turned-Islamic-fundamentalist Cat Stevens. Is VH-1 mellow? Is Huey Lewis square? Surely there is room in the videorama for this kind of visual rest-stop. Hey, I might even tune in again when I wasn't getting paid to watch, if someone in management, who is not yet in a coma, would do something about treacly slop like ABC's "When Smokey Sings." Here we have a group of pale young men, one of whom bears a striking resemblance to the Pillsbury doughboy, who can neither sing nor dance nor do they have big hair (any one of which qualifies you to star in a music video; two combined in the same person guarantees celebrity). And these limpets are cashing in on a Motown legend so they can what? Buy personalities?

I dialed over to NBC's *Friday Night Videos* just in time to catch the end of "Luka." Fade out—Suzanne Vega staring down child abusers everywhere. Fade in—guest veejays Ahmad Rashad, football-player-turned-sportscaster, and Cosby kid Malcolm-Jamal Warner.

Ahmad: "I'm telling you, man, this girl is strong, strong. She can do it, man."

Malcolm-Jamal: "Hot."

And again, several videos later:

Ahmad: "I know this guy that is one of the biggest Dee-troit Lions fans in the world, man, and he's a great songwriter."

Malcolm-Jamal: "Who?"

Ahmad: "Bob Seger, man."

Malcolm-Jamal: "Oh, uh, right."

So I'm thinking: Why does Ahmad Rashad—a man who has worked in front of cameras for years—suddenly sound like David Crosby? Is it possible that veejaying, like amphetamines and pharmacy school, wipes out whole neighborhoods of brain cells?

As the weekend progressed, I began to see that veejays, the full-timers, come in two denominations: Smug and Cloying. The smug tend to squint and sit still; the cloying rock and smile and thrust their eyebrows toward their hairlines. And where does this leave guest veejays—who have had neither the time nor financial incentives to become fully smug or cloying? Many try to talk like rock stars. This is always a mistake, man.

I fled to *Night Flight,* on the USA Network, and was greeted by comedy, sort of. In addition to music videos, *NF* programs a mix of comedy specials, celebrity interviews, concerts and old movies. I turned into a segment called "Assaulted Nuts," which included a bit about a "Galloping Vasectomist," a couple of Benny Hill–type skits, and a talk show sendup featuring a flatulent "government spokesman for the environment." Was I having fun? Nyet. But I stuck around for the oldies concert clips—Elvis jailhouse rocking, Joplin giving another-little-piece-of-her-heart-now, bay-beh. Two thumbs up (mine) for honest sweat.

I scanned past *Nick Rocks,* on Nickelodeon—"Luka" was on—and stopped off at WTBS's *Night Tracks,* an MTV clone sans veejays. Fab graphics they've got. They clump their vids in twos and threes. But the voices of veejays Frazier Smith and Joanne Ehrhart are just that—voices. Off-camera. So when Frazier said, "Hey there you crazy *Night*

Tracks fans!" I didn't have to see him squint or smile or otherwise ingratiate himself (as they all must, it's the essence of veejayness). Which brings up the question: Is the only good veejay an invisible veejay?

There is wheat among the chaff and I found it, at last. Black Entertainment Television's Donnie Simpson, host of *Video Soul,* is a fine example of low-profile hip. He does not flirt, giggle or smarm. He can sit still. He has a sweet smile, but more important, he has the good sense to use it sparingly. I watched him introduce videos by Whitney Houston, Lisa Lisa, The Time and Sting and not once (I swear) did he say "hot smash."

We were doing so well, Donnie and me, until the Herb Alpert incident. Herb was coming to the studio for an interview. "I know a lot of you are familiar with his new album," Donnie said, "but Herb Alpert's musical career dates back 25 years, before I was born. . . ." Oh yeah, right. The Stridex generation.

BET also offers *Video LP,* a half-hour show that focuses on one band a pop. This is a good idea, and not a bad show, if you ignore the seriously cloying Robin Breedon. The show I saw featured Club Nouveau—four of their videos and an enormous amount of insignifica (labeled "Star Stats") about lead singer Samuelle Prater. Thanks to "Star Stats" and veejay Breedon's cue-cards, I now know that Prater is a Scorpio; his favorite colors are turquoise, red, white and black; and he "maintained a B-average throughout his high school years." Is it just me, or do we all really want to know that Samuelle Prater's favorite cities are Atlanta, Denver and Boston? And if so, what about his top ten vegetables?

Okay, it's me. I turned to Nashville Network's *Video Country,* which is hosted by Shelley Mangrum, a former Miss Tennessee and second only to the youthful Donnie Simpson as Most Normal-Seeming Person Functioning As A Veejay. With Shelley leading the way, I sat through video after video packed with smiling children, laughing couples and bearded men playing steel guitars. Bliss 'n grits, I was thinking peacefully—when out comes Dwight Yoakum singing "Little Sister" with go-go dancers in cages and Yoakum himself chasing down and lassoing a li'l sister right there at the end of the song. Yee ha!

Nash Net's got another video show called *Country Clips,* hosted by a puppet named Shotgun Red who dresses like his idol, Willie Nelson. I read that part about his idol in a press release, but I saw the damned puppet myself, one of the very last images I remember before my eyes glazed over like a couple of doughnuts.

I had seen all I could bear to see, heard more than I could possibly remember, and spent the $9.98 my editor fronted for expenses. It was over. A weekend lost to vidiocy.

I drifted into fitful sleep and dreamed the strangest dream: Luka and Janet Jackson joined Motley Crue and Jackson Browne onstage at the Grand Ole Opry. They all looked happy, lip-synching together.

CHILDREN'S TELEVISION "TOO COMMERCIAL"

Broadcasting Magazine

The weekend TV periods known as "children's prime time" were condemned during a congressional hearing as being "strewn with war toys, insipid cartoons, and oversweetened cereals." This report from *Broadcasting* summarizes current complaints about overcommercialization of television shows for children.

Children's television was back on the congressional agenda last week. Lawmakers at a House Telecommunications Subcommittee hearing took a hard line on children's programing and chastised the FCC, broadcasters, toy companies and program producers for contributing to what they called the overcommercialization of children's television.

Source: "Telcomsubcom Holds Hearings on Children's TV," *Broadcasting,* September 21, 1987. Reprinted with permission.

CHILDREN'S TV VIEWING TIME

The extent of television's involvement in the lives of American children is indicated by the Nielsen People Meter survey data for October 1987.

Average weekly television viewing by children aged 2 to 5 years was 22 hours, 58 minutes. Children aged 6 to 11 averaged slightly less viewing time, 19 hours, 47 minutes.

Children in the 2-to-5 age group spent 23 percent of their total weekly viewing time looking at Monday-to-Friday daytime programs and 22 percent watching prime-time shows.

Those in the 6-to-11 age group watched prime-time programs the most (31 percent of their weekly total time) and Monday-to-Friday late afternoon programs, from 4:30 to 7:30 P.M., second (18 percent).

Daily average viewing time was 3 hours, 17 minutes for the younger group and 2 hours, 50 minutes for the older group.

"If I may paraphrase Newton Minow [former FCC chairman], children's television today is not a wasteland, but a waste site, strewn with war toys, insipid cartoons and oversweetened cereals," said Ed Markey (D-Mass.), the subcommittee's chairman.

Markey and Congressman Terry Bruce (D-Ill.) introduced legislation coinciding with the hearing. Their bill would reimpose the FCC's 1974 guidelines limiting advertising to nine-and-a-half minutes per hour during "children's prime time"—Saturday and Sunday mornings—and to 12 minutes per hour on weekdays. The measure would ban so-called "program-length" commercials for toys.

It also would codify current FCC policy to "eliminate host-selling and tie-in practices and other practices that involve the use of program characters to promote products." And it would "assure an adequate separation between program content and commercial messages, by use of an appropriate visual, aural, or other device or separation."

Bruce decried the existence of "a chaotic market which is being polluted by artificiality in the form of commercial tie-ins between toy manufacturers and the cartoon show producers." (Bruce sits on the parent Energy and Commerce Committee.)

Markey convened the hearing in response to a U.S. Appeals Court panel's remand of the FCC's action eliminating its children's programing guidelines in 1984 on the ground that the commission had failed to justify the deregulatory action with either facts or analysis.

There are no immediate plans to move the Markey-Bruce bill, said Larry Irving, senior counsel to the subcommittee. But Irving did not dismiss the possibility of future action, particularly if the FCC "ignores the court's remand and insists the marketplace is working."

The FCC was a primary target of criticism. "This hearing would be unnecessary if the FCC was doing its job," said Representative Al Swift (D-Wash.). "The commission and industry are daring Congress to take action," he warned.

Later Swift lost his temper and lashed out at John Weems, vice president for entertainment at Mattel, the toy manufacturer. Weems told the lawmakers that Mattel was producing children's programs because it "is in the business to entertain children." But Swift didn't buy that: "You're in the business to entertain? That's sophistry," Swift told Weems. "You're in the business to sell toys. . . . I am not a fool. I have a list of 61 programs based upon toy products. At some point our patience will finally break."

Weems came to demonstrate a new "interactive" toy designed for use with a television program. The toy enables viewers to interact with characters in a new half-hour television series, *Captain Power and the Soldiers of the Future,* which is financed by Mattel. . . .

Weems showed the lawmakers how the toy laser gun is fired at targets on the screen, with viewers keeping score of their hits. Weems said the toy costs between $30 and $40. He described the program as "family-oriented" and resisted criticism that it was created to sell toys. "To insure that *Captain Power* stands on its own, each story is entirely independent of the toy line; no mention of the toys is made during the program, and the interactive segments are brief (generally less than four minutes total in each weekly episode)," Weems said.

Few members were convinced.

Dennis Eckhart (D-Ohio) found the concept of interactive television promising, but was disappointed with its current application. "I can't help but feel we've dropped to the lowest common denominator," Eckhart said.

Representative Jim Cooper (D-Tenn.) wanted to know whether Mattel had an agreement with the program's producer to set aside between four and six minutes of the show for "target practice." Weems said there was no specific agreement concerning time set for the program's interactive position.

Despite those grumblings, Weems was commended for appearing before the subcommittee. Other toy manufacturers and program producers had refused, "absent a subpoena" to testify, Markey reported. "It is particularly galling that Hasbro, a company that has profited from program-length commercials and program-toy tie-ins to the tune of tens of millions of dollars, and has over 7,000 employes, could not spare anyone to testify about its practices or to discuss the various policy options that we will consider today," Markey said.

A further condemnation of programs featuring interactive toys came from Action for Children's Television President Peggy Charren. That type of problem, she said, "creates two classes of child viewers, the haves and the have nots." Mattel, she said, "is not in the business of making TV programs, it's in the business of making toys."

As for program-length commercials, Charren felt such toy-based programs are a barrier to the entry of other children's shows. ACT has petitioned the FCC to reinstate its guidelines limiting advertising on children's programs.

The lawmakers were asked to delay action on the children's bill until completion of a study on children's viewing habits. Preston Padden, president of the Association of Independent Television Stations, suggested the delay. The study has been commissioned by INTV to determine why television viewing by children has declined. "We're asking for a chance to conduct the survey. Then you can judge if something needs to be done," he said.

Padden presented a tape of segments from various children's shows airing on independent stations. Padden also took issue with critics of current children's fare on television. "Whatever argument you may have about the social value of *My Little Pony,*" he said, it's "less harmful" than the "depraved" music videos on cable television with "violence, sex and bizarre behavior."

Joining Charren in calling for a legislative remedy were Gerald Lesser, Bigelow professor of Education and Psychology, Harvard University; Dr. Jerome Singer, Yale University department of psychology; Dr. William Dietz, chairman of the task force on children's television, American Academy of Pediatrics, and Dale Kunkel, professor of communications, University of California, Santa Barbara.

"Is this what we should allow?" Lesser asked the congressmen regarding program-length commercials. "To deliberately blur what is program and what is commercial and then leave it to children to somehow sort it all out for themselves? It simply is not fair," he said. Singer told the subcommittee he thought the television industry was failing to provide "appropriate programing" for children and that Congress should step in.

Kunkel, who testified on behalf of the American Psychological Association, is author of a study that maintained that the FCC's deregulatory policy has led to a drop in network and local programing for children. Dietz expressed concern about interactive toys and what he said was "their power to promote violent and aggressive behavior in children, increase the passivity with which children view television and reduce and inhibit imaginative play."

VIDEO

COMEDY IS BIG HIT ON VIDEO

Chris McGowan

Jokes make laughs, and they also carry social messages. Derision in joke form can destroy a politician's ambitions. The impact of a fashion trend is multiplied by jokes about it—the miniskirt, for example. Comedy is a big seller on home video and television currently, as this *Billboard* article explains, and in motion pictures such as Eddie Murphy's *Raw.*

In 1987, the comedy genre was one of the hottest genres in the home video industry. In sell-through *and* rental. We'll throw a few numbers around later, but let us at least note that the top five all-time best-selling non-movie comedy titles (Murphy, Belushi, Cosby, Aykroyd, Nesmith) have, to date, sold a combined total of more than 850,000 units (according to label estimates).

Comedians have been on a roll lately, packing a burgeoning number of comedy clubs around the country. In 1987, according to *Rave* (a comedy performance magazine), there were close to 200 clubs in America featuring comedy as their primary attraction, a 10-fold increase from a decade ago. Eleven comedy clubs now operate in New York alone and nine exist in Los Angeles.

The Catch A Rising Star comedy-club chain—which currently has venues in New York City and Cambridge—has even gone public. Catch A Rising Star Inc. plans to open 29 more clubs in the next two years, in conjunction with St. Louis–based Funny Bone Corp., which runs 12 comedy clubs in the Midwest and South. Television, radio and video projects are also planned. The Comedy Store and The Improvisation are two other growing national comedy-club chains.

A large number of network and cable specials are also devoted to the comedic arts, with performers feeling free to deliver one-liners, act out skits or explore "attitude comedy."

The jokes are freer these days, in no small part because of the '70s success of "Saturday Night Live" (which brought conceptual and fringe comedy into the mainstream), Steve Martin (the first comedian to achieve "rock star" status) and Richard Pryor (whose brilliance and outrageousness [have] also wielded great influence).

Home video has been host to comedy in all its many forms. Funny films and funny hybrids (such as comedy/action and comedy/sci-fi) have done a brisk video business; hot sellers and renters of the last 12 months include: "Beverly Hills Cop," "Crocodile Dundee," "The Golden Child," "Critical Condition" and "Ferris Bueller's Day Off" (Paramount); "Back To School," "The Three Amigos," "Radio Days" and "Hannah And Her Sisters" (HBO); "Raising Arizona" (CBS/Fox); "Burglar" and "Police Academy 4" (Warner); "Blind Date" (RCA/Columbia); and "Down And Out In Beverly Hills," "Ernest Goes To Camp" and "Ruthless People" (Touchstone).

And who can forget the huge recent successes of "Ghostbusters" and "Back To The Future"?

Source: Chris McGowan, "Comedy Video Is Big," *Billboard,* December 26, 1987.

The biggest stand-up/non-theatrical sellers have been "Eddie Murphy Delirious" (Paramount), "The Best Of John Belushi" (Warner) and "Bill Cosby: 49" (Kodak), each of which has sold a respectable 200,000 units or more.

And "The Best Of Dan Aykroyd" (Warner) and Michael Nesmith's "Elephant Parts" (Pacific Arts) have passed 140,000 and 100,000 units, respectively, according to manufacturer estimates. . . .

Sponsorship has also arrived in the genre: one example is Rave Communications' "The Dodge Comedy Showcase," a four-tape series that features new, young stand-up comedians. The first two tapes are on sale nationwide in comedy clubs for $11.95 apiece and each video has a 60-second Dodge spot at the beginning. Comedians are also being used extensively for commercial endorsements, such as George Carlin's TV and radio involvement with Fuji videotape.

But does all this success in the relatively new medium of video please comedian Bobcat Goldthwait, who just put out "An Evening With Bobcat Goldthwait: Share The Warmth" on Vestron . . . ? Does he think that the medium of home video will expand comedic boundaries, offer additional opportunities for rising, up-and-coming talent, even boost creativity in the art?

"Video is definitely a new place to get a check cut," notes Bobcat.

Goldthwait, who has had his biggest exposure to date in the "Police Academy" movies, has developed a unique on-stage persona in which he fluctuates between a wimpering, angst-ridden fool about to have a nervous breakdown and a snarling madman who seems capable of biting your head off. And all the while he is commenting on and attacking politics, religion, drugs, show business, other comedians, even Dr. Seuss. Anything is a potential target during his outlandish shows.

But Goldthwait has a human (or semi-human) side, too. He participated with Whoopi Goldberg, Robin Williams, Billy Crystal and many other comedians in the "Comic Relief" HBO specials (the first, sponsored by Pepsi-Cola, is out on Lorimar Home Video). . . .

Promotion has been key to the success of many comedy videos, especially in the case of J-2 Communications, which has created perhaps the first comedy how-to tape, "Dorf On Golf." The video stars Tim Conway and features his character Derk Dorf, who shows viewers how to putt, drive, dress and cheat on the fairways, and even how to find the 19th hole.

The tape has been a big hit both in traditional video stores, as well as in non-traditional outlets such as live theater concession sales (Conway recently toured the country in the play "The Odd Couple"), professional golf tournaments and men's toy stores. . . .

J-2 also recently released the first two tapes of "Carol Burnett's My Personal Best," and the famed comedienne also promoted her product heavily, appearing on several network TV shows and in publications such as *Los Angeles* magazine during the last two months.

Bobcat, of course, takes more of the "Abbie Hoffman" approach to promotion.

"I did my one and only promotional appearance for the video at the VSDA this summer," recalls Bobcat. "I went there for Vestron and they had me perform at a luncheon and I told everyone, 'Don't buy this video! You can just tape it off HBO.' I was just being honest, and the place freaked."

Vestron will indeed have to be careful with his future in-store appearances!

Jeffrey Peisch, director of non-theatrical programming for that label, has found that comedy both sells and rents well. "The tapes usually go out at a rental price [$59.95] and we do a good number of sales," says Peisch. "Then later we often reduce the price to $29.98 and $19.98 and promote them as sell-through. . . .

"Once the price is down," continues Peisch, "the tapes have a great collectability. They are true evergreens, one of our most profitable genres. They are great party tapes and you can watch them over and over."

Our roving consultant finds this prospect startling. Says Bobcat, "The idea of someone, you know, actually listening to my stuff over and over is kind of frightening. I don't think I'd watch my tape more than once."

Of course, some critics would agree with Goldthwait and would warn that repeated viewing of his videos might cause brain damage or possible unrest in the populace.

"My videos are dangerous only if you play them backwards and turn off the audio," counters Bobcat. "They have hidden messages if you rewind them."

Goldthwait feels that comedy is at a low point in '87, generally "mindless" and informed by an attitude that "ignorance is bliss."

But a recent article written by Tom Shales in *Esquire* magazine points out that today's American comedians are more numerous and in general more insightful, more varied in their performance styles and more successful than in a long, long time.

"In comedy, as in airlines and broadcasting and the telephone company, deregulation appears to have taken hold," writes Shales.

"There must be more comedians per capita in the U.S. now than ever before in history," he also comments. "Comedians are the new troubadours. People don't go to clubs to hear folk singers anymore [perhaps you've noticed]. They go to clubs to hear folk talkers.

"Comedians are now what folk singers were to the '60s. . . ."

One of the most successful of the new breed is Gallagher, who has five Paramount videos, each of which has sold between 20,000 and 45,000 units. He has been criss-crossing the country the past five years honing his act "in the trenches" and describes himself as a visual comedian, one who has made a career in comedy by skipping albums altogether and proceeding straight to video. "A comedy album," he says, "is like a blind man at a nightclub because an album works for music but not comedy. Because if you make a face or pick up something they [audiences] miss it, so you've gotta have video."

Though video is taking over, and new technology is driving comedy into the '90s, he claims to have a great idea for the "old tech," and he's been trying to get a hold of world-connector Ken Kragen about the idea. It's called "Free Rock To Russia."

Explains Gallagher, "Russians have turntables but no albums, and we have old albums and CD players, so let's turn Russians on and catch them up to our heritage by giving them our old records. Russians don't care if it's *old,* it's all rock'n'roll. We couldn't give them our old albums before, but now it's O.K., they're all on CD."

A lot has changed in the short lifespan of comedy on video, not only in terms of better production values but also in acquisition/marketing savvy.

"When we produced our first comedy video ['How To Party' on MPI], we had no idea how to go about it," admits Joy Grdnic of the Stevens & Grdnic syndicated-radio comedy duo, "but the home video business was so young there were still no rules. As amateurish as our video was, three prominent video labels bid for rights to distribute it. We know we'd never get away with that again, because now it would break almost *all* the rules."

These days, the tapes of Gallagher, Conway, Goldthwait and their comedic peers mentioned above are part of a large and very successful section in most video stores. Other hot video comedy acts include Woody Allen, Jim Varney (Ernest), Joe Piscopo, Pee-Wee Herman, Rodney Dangerfield, Guido Sarducci, Joan Rivers, Howie Mandel, Martin Mull, Jay Leno, Carol Burnett and Redd Foxx.

There are also videos available of such venerable stars as W.C. Fields, Laurel & Hardy and the Marx Brothers, as well as TV shows such as "Saturday Night Live," "Candid Camera," "I Love Lucy," "The Honeymooners," "The Carol Burnett Show," and "Your Show Of Shows."

And there are "concept" tapes such as "Truly Tasteless Jokes," "Bloopermania" and "Party Games For Adults," as well as multiple-star concert videos such as the aforementioned "The Best Of Comic Relief" and "The Paramount Comedy Theater."

Indeed, comedy video is in good shape. . . .

"The bottom line is that people love to laugh," concludes J-2's [president, Jim] Jimirro.

RADIO

RADIO LIVES!

Eric Zorn

With 500 million receiving sets and 10,000 stations, radio is thriving. Automated programming and satellite transmission are bringing rapid changes in the medium, with much additional broadcast material available. This *Esquire* article describes the transformation.

When Robert G. Hall, a midmorning disc jockey on the Satellite Music Network's soft-rock station, punches a little red button on his broadcast console in an isolated studio on the flatlands of north-central Illinois, he silently cues tape cartridge machines in some 130 cities across the country. No matter which city you are listening to him in, his prerecorded voice identifies him as your hometown jock, just down the street a-spinnin' records. On one station he's reading a weather report—"We can expect chilly temps in the Lehigh Valley"—taped months earlier and squirreled away by the affiliate for a cool day; on another he's advising residents of an emergency power outage via a special announcement taped a few minutes earlier and sent through a separate satellite channel; on still another he's promising that nobody—but nobody—beats the local Chevy dealer for bargains. Listeners never hear the word *network.* Everywhere everything is customized, sanitized, and synchronized, a charade that has made it possible to start dismantling the old process, which has hundreds of independent owners paying hundreds of different jocks to play hundreds of copies of the latest Culture Club single more or less simultaneously.

Source: Reprinted from the March 1984 issue of *Esquire* by permission of the author.

Call it McRadio, the fast-food enfranchisement of the airwaves, and only one of the many revolutionary changes taking place right now in the radio industry. Some are good, some are bad, but the speed and intensity of these changes make this the most exciting era in the medium since the Top Forty format saved it from death in the jaws of TV thirty years ago.

Not only are small- and medium-market stations hooking up with SMN-type services at a rate of twenty to thirty a month, but satellites have also made possible dramatic movement within the major old-line radio networks; NBC, ABC, CBS, National Public Radio, RKO, and Mutual have all experienced great growth in revenues and services by interconnecting their affiliates. Stations can choose from a huge menu of special programs and regular features produced nationally, a development that also makes life interesting on the local level, where garden-variety stations, now feeling the squeeze from new competition, are being forced to break away from their old formulas and experiment with new formats in order to stay alive.

The instruments necessary to carry such changes are already in place: There are almost 500 million receivers in the United States at this moment, more than the number of cars, telephones, or television sets, not to mention people. The average number per household is 5.5.

Improvements in microelectronics will make radios still smaller and cheaper and give the medium a ubiquitous presence: listeners of the future, instead of having access to just thirty or forty stations (many playing the same music and aimed at the same mainstream audiences), will be able to hook into hundreds of channels—blues stations, business-news stations, Czech-language stations, even full-time stations for the blind, anything you can't hear now because the audience for it is too small and scattered for even the biggest cities to support. Given the variety of tools—the shortwave band, FM subcarriers, cable distribution, a Direct Broadcasting Satellite (DBS) system that will be able to beam cheaply both TV and radio programs straight into your home—the number of potential radio channels is practically unlimited.

Looking way ahead, radio in the twenty-first century may well be an addressable push-button home console from which, for a small monthly fee, the subscriber will be able to program hours of the latest, or the greatest, or the worst in music, making obsolete the distinction between record player, tape player, and tuner. The flip side of the "nationalization" of radio is that by better serving individual tastes, radio will also be the instrument that will break apart the monolithic national visions of art, culture, and news that it helped create. This "demassification," to use the phraseology of Alvin Toffler, practically guarantees that we will never see an artist or a group as popular and influential as Elvis or the Beatles again. Individual tastes will rule, and no longer will the music business be dominated by a small number of anointed supergroups.

What this means is that a sizable number of the stations now broadcasting in this country are dinosaurs. Today you still see stations that tinker with the old music formats looking for a quick fix, but in the long run any format that relies on music and records can be reproduced easily and distributed cheaply by satellite stations. Those myriad stations in particular that now bank on wall-to-wall music, few commercials, and innocuous deejays have written their own epitaphs—creating a market and demand for the ad-free, voice-free cable audio services that will eventually render them obsolete.

But local stations can and will adjust to the changes. If radio has been anything over the past sixty years, it certainly has been resilient. And as the video generation grows up you can be sure that the feisty, indomitable audio medium that kicked off the electronic age will not just roll over and die. The little guy is fighting back. Welcome to the new radio revolution.

FORMAT FEVER

One of the most poignant moments in radio history was May 10, 1982—the day the music died on WABC-AM, once the mightiest rock music station in the nation, as it surrendered to the creeping domination of FM music radio by switching to all-talk. To many in the industry, WABC's chin music sounded like nothing more than a funeral march for AM as we knew and loved it for half a century.

In a sense this was true. AM was in fact on its deathbed, the victim of poor fidelity and a stuffy image, but it has since exhibited encouraging signs of reviving, fighting back with new formats. At the same time, new formats have also been the salvation of FM stations, themselves feeling the pressure of new competition.

The history of radio is the history of formats. With the rise of FM in the mid-Sixties, the six or so standards—rock, adult, classical, beautiful, black, and country—were split into subcategories: rock broke up into adult contemporary, album-oriented-rock, contemporary hit, and oldie; country into hard-core and crossover. Talk stations divvied into news, news-talk, and telephone-talk. Even beautiful music, once just the sweet strains of the Longine Symphonette Society, split into young/old and vocal/instrumental variations in order to find specific new audiences.

These organisms are dividing yet again: The album-oriented-rock format alone is splitting into so many distinct subcategories—techno-pop, modern rock, eclectic, neoprogressive, and so on—that the umbrella term *AOR* is already obsolete. Two beautiful-music stations are playing only love songs; black-oriented stations now specialize in funk, rap, soul, and urban contemporary; and in the crowded area of adult-contemporary music, stations are experimenting with shades of "hard" and "soft" in an effort to capture the ever-elusive forty-year-old pop-music fan.

AM stations, now attracting fewer than 38 percent of all listeners, are converting rapidly to formats that do not necessarily demand high fidelity. That's the reason we're hearing, for instance, so many radio psychologists dispensing chipper advice. Meanwhile, at least two all-comedy stations have already premiered, one AM station in Texas is going with wall-to-wall Beatles, and sports play-by-play is growing impressively on AM stations all over.

Targeting a small segment of the audience is called narrowcasting. Listeners like it because highly specialized radio stations give them more control over what they hear, but the real reason it is so popular is that advertisers *love* it. With narrowcasting, advertising efficiency goes way up as overall costs go down. Diversification is the goal of cable too, but the costs of programs and delivery are comparatively so low in radio broadcasting that the audio medium ought to be able to beat out video by several years. We are approaching the unstated goal of all radio programmers: to create a station aimed so perfectly that the listener will no longer have to wait, ever, for the song that he wants to hear.

STAR POWER

Aft all the big-name stars defected to television in the 1950s, radio had little choice but to localize, and as a result it ceased to be a celebrity-making medium. Radio stars in New York were unknown in Los Angeles, and vice versa—unless, like Gary Owens, Dick Clark, or Wolfman Jack, they also happened to slip into movies or national TV. But today the growth of networks and syndicated programming has revived the phenomenon of the national radio star, with some talents who have been talking for a dozen years finally getting the followings they deserve.

- *Larry King* may have the most ubiquitous voice in America. His all-night five-and-one-half-hour gabfest, syndicated live from Washington by the Mutual Broadcasting System, is heard coast to coast by four million listeners on more than 255 stations. A nimble interrogator who has become radio's equivalent of Phil Donahue, King regularly attracts famous guests; the consistent popularity of his program proved the bellwether that made possible the recent spate of wee-hours network and cable TV news programs. He recently expanded his act and is the star of *Sunday Night Live,* a ninety-minute syndicated TV version of his radio show.
- *Charles Osgood,* the puckish poet and commentator, has become the star of the CBS Radio Network on the strength of his morning *Newsbreak* and *Osgood File* segments, short features of wit and wisdom often rendered in Dr. Seussian doggerel. Though he has published two volumes of collected works, *Nothing Could Be Finer Than a Crisis That Is Minor in the Morning* and *There's Nothing That I Wouldn't Do If You Would Be My POSSLQ,* and is also a member of the CBS television news team, his primary claim to fame and his first love is radio.
- *Garrison Keillor,* a shy, wistful eccentric, became something of a cult figure as the host and sole writer of *A Prairie Home Companion,* on the American Public Radio Associates network. The nostalgic comedy/variety show, featuring a combination of folk music, homespun stories from Keillor's mythical Lake Wobegon, and messages from peculiar (and fictional) sponsors, aired on close to two hundred noncommercial stations until Keillor retired.
- *Casey Kasem* is the creator and star of *American Top 40,* the weekly pop music countdown heard by forty-five million listeners on more than nine hundred stations around the world. Though he is best known as the granddaddy of the weekly chart countdown and the originator of the by now routine technique of holding listeners on the dial by teasing them with trivia questions, Kasem has become a millionaire on the strength of his crackly,

whimsical voice. The "voice of NBC" for three years, he has also been the spokesman for Ford, Hallmark Cards, Maxwell House Coffee, and Kentucky Fried Chicken. Kasem is also a star of children's cartoons—he's Shaggy on *Scooby Doo* and Waldo on *Mr. Magoo*—and the voice behind fifteen different letters and numbers on *Sesame Street.*

• *Susan Stamberg* is the premier personality on the innovative National Public Radio network. As the veteran co-host of the nightly *All Things Considered* news and documentary program, Stamberg is heard via satellite in 281 cities. The thirteen-year-old program, filled with detailed news analysis, offbeat features, penetrating interviews, and other colorful, meaty segments, is often cited as proof that radio news does not have to be just headlines and weather. Stamberg's style, which some have characterized as a kind of "gonzo radio," is also a disarming blend of sophistication and simple curiosity—it sets the tone for the entire program.

• *Paul Harvey,* the peppy, curmudgeonly commentator, reaches more than twenty-one million listeners a week on some 1,175 ABC network affiliates. He has actually been on network radio since 1951 and has since expanded his domain to include record albums, inspirational books, a newspaper column, syndicated TV editorials, and an aggressive schedule of public-speaking engagements for which he is paid twenty thousand dollars a clip. Based in Chicago, Harvey is the only national radio star from the medium's heyday whose popularity and influence have actually grown over the past three decades.

• *Barry Hansen,* better known as Dr. Demento, has made his name as the last of the big-time defenders of zany, deranged, risqué, absurd, and loony songs on the radio. Each week Hansen, cackling ghoulishly in his Demento persona, spins novelty records such as "Dead Puppies," "Pencil Neck Geek," "Another One Rides the Bus," and "Psycho Chicken" during a two-hour program syndicated to more than 125 stations worldwide. Most of his material is drawn from a personal library of more than 150,000 discs stored throughout his home and in cardboard boxes that fill his garage. He created the Demento shtick fourteen years ago when, as a deejay in Los Angeles's first free-form rock station, he pulled out his old Spike Jones, Haywire Mac, and Nervous Norvus tunes. His act proved so popular that in 1974 he signed on with a radio syndicate. His show, heard mostly on album-oriented rock stations by approximately one million listeners a week, is now virtually the only national outlet for musical satirists and comic recording artists.

NEW TOYS

From Fibber McGee to Pac-Man, technology, not necessarily taste, has proven to be the catalyst of cultural change in the twentieth century. Radio first linked the nation in the 1920s and 1930s and then helped lead the way, via FM "underground" stations, for the countercultural movement of the late 1960s. If the wealth of new technology is any indication, radio should continue to have a strong cultural impact. Most of the new communications technology was pioneered and financed with video in mind, but radio has been clever enough to steal it for its own purposes, particularly where satellites are concerned. One reason is that you can fit more than twenty audio signals into the satellite space allocated for a single video signal, and it's easy for multiple audio signals to "piggyback" on television satellite channels.

The Satellite Music Network signal, for example, travels ten miles via microwaves from studios in Mokena, Illinois, to a thirty-three-foot "uplink" antenna in the middle of a huge open field. From there the SMN program (along with Bonneville Broadcasting's generic beautiful-music format and other audio programs, all of them riding on the electronic fringes of superstation WGN-Chicago's TV signal) is beamed . . . up to RCA's Satcom III. The satellite, in stationary orbit over the equator, then blankets the entire Western Hemisphere with a reflected signal that, at under ten watts, has less power than a Christmas-tree light bulb. Anyone who has a ten-foot dish antenna pointed in the right direction and properly tuned can now receive the programming; automated radio stations, equipped with tape cartridge machines that are hooked to a computer that reacts to inaudible signals sent through the satellite, are plugged in so that when SMN cues out, the tape machine cues in with weather, station identification, jingles, commercials—you name it.

The putative new wave in transmission is the Direct Broadcast Satellite (DBS) systems, wherein relatively high-powered signals are beamed directly from outer space into your own private (and inexpensive) receiving dish—a dish that might be as small as a large pizza. The first company to fly with DBS—United Satellite Communications—offered the service in the Midwest. . . .

Cable radio works a variant of the satellite transmission. At the same time as the cable TV systems pick up the audio and deliver it into subscribers' homes along land lines, special programs can be broadcast through locally vacant FM frequencies. It's all a matter of coding, and circuitry is now being engineered that will make it possible—within ten years—to receive such specialty programming not only in the home but also in cars and on portable radios.

AM stations are hoping that the distinction between the AM and FM bands will blur in the future, given AM's reputation for lousy music transmission. Their main hope is AM stereo broadcasting, a technology that has been bollixed up because of four competing patent holders, each of whose system is totally incompatible with the others. Station owners, for the most part, are playing Alphonse and Gaston with the radio manufacturers, who have so far been unable to see a clear choice; and the FCC hasn't helped either, refusing to take a stand on the issue. In any event, consumer polling indicates that the issue may be moot anyway: those polled take to it like they took to quadraphonic hi-fi, forty-channel CB, and Bone Fones.

A more interesting development is the pay-per-listen concept pioneered by Codart of Novato, California, and tested with moderate success at KQED-FM San Francisco. The service is an audio version of ABC Video Enterprises Tele-First, on which special programs are broadcast in the middle of the night; in those homes that have paid for the service, preset remote controls switch a recording device on and off, and the programs are taped. In this way subscribers could "purchase" new releases, or just a few songs off new releases, for about half the retail price. Because royalties are paid to copyright holders, the Codart system creates the possibility for custom home recording, on high-quality tapes, that does not cheat the music industry. . . .

There's no limit to where custom radio will take us, from a programmable home stereo to programmable news: one can easily envision a single station owning six or seven different narrow-band information services—local news, sports, national news, traffic reports, international news, and so on—and transmitting returning information so that a listener will be able to program his own newscasts, in whatever order he wants, from his home. The technology for this and many other presently unimaginable things is almost ready.

BAD BOYS

On July 12, 1979, in the middle of a scheduled twi-night doubleheader between the Chicago White Sox and the Detroit Tigers, thousands of members of the "Insane Coho Lips Antidisco Army" stormed the Comiskey Park diamond, tore up the pitcher's mound, and set a bonfire in center field. When the "Disco Demolition" riot was over, the White Sox had become the first team in history to forfeit a baseball game on account of a disc jockey.

It was not the first or last time that churlish deejay Steve Dahl, engineer of the "promotion" that turned into a disaster, found himself in the midst of civic controversy. By his own count he has been fired from some twenty radio stations during his thirteen-year career. Today he has a healthy $200,000 contract at WLS-FM Chicago, where he has called the general manager "scum" on the air, bemoans his inability to make love to his wife, teases minorities, ridicules the pop-rock he is forced to play, and makes prank phone calls to foreign countries.

Dahl's rise tells a lot about where radio is now. For even those who hate him admit that he is something of a prodigal prophet, a bad boy whose antics have opened new frontiers in radio. Dahl, Howard Stern, formerly of WNBC New York, and Frazer Smith of KLOS Los Angeles have been arguably the three most important, talked-about radio personalities in recent radio. These jocks and their imitators, who are legion, are as much a part of radio's future as the seamless satellite presence of SMN's Robert G. Hall: they provide the local identification and personality to stations striving to survive massification. . . .

Dahl offers what amounts to a talk show for the disenfranchised. "What I do," says Dahl, whose show features a cast of real characters, including his wife and a sidekick, "is observational comedy, and almost all of it is unprepared when I go on the air. I'm a real person first, and the audience responds to me on that level, not necessarily as a comedian. They allow me to have bad days. They allow me to go too far."

Indeed, Dahl and Stern are famous for breaking the taste barrier. Dahl was recently excoriated for urging his listeners to dump Necco wafers in the change basket on the Illinois Tollway—and Stern has found himself the subject of citizens' protests and angry editorials for, among other things, such TV show satires as *Hill Street Jews.* The two are frequently less than amusing, but their sheer, spicy unpredictability has garnered them a solid following, especially among men in the attractive eighteen-to-thirty-four demographic—Stern quadrupled the morning ratings at WWDC when he was in the nation's capital, and Dahl's overall ratings numbers are typically twice the average for his station during the rest of the day.

Frazer Smith also draws a hefty audience and regularly makes the newspapers with his antics, but his show is sheer Los Angeles—elaborately produced and scripted three-hour daily theme-dramas created by his personal staff of comics and writers and featuring movie satires *(Footsie),* television send-ups *(The Lust Boat),* oddball news *(The National Frazequirer),* and just about anything else that is both topical and irreverent. Most of his stunts seem engineered to draw attention to himself in a city filled with people starving for attention: once he did a Valentine's Day show from an ABC yacht during which he had women take off their shirts so he could autograph their breasts; another time he created a "Hate Hotline" for listeners to call and explain why they hated him (supplying the number of an unwitting citizen who subsequently sued him for harassment). He also credits himself with introducing the buzz words *party animal* and *too hip* to southern California parlance.

Perhaps the most interesting thing about Smith is how much his three-hour morning quasi dramas resemble old-time radio. His rapid-fire delivery, use of 125 different voices, and smooth blending of sound effects make Smith's the most ambitious daily entertainment program in the medium. . . .

One can be fairly certain that no matter how radio spreads out and innovates, it will never provide the money or glamour of TV or movies. However, the general opening-up of the medium to new kinds of acts—the progeny of the *Mad* magazine, *National Lampoon,* and *Saturday Night Live* crowd—has created a new interest in radio among emerging creative talents. No matter what one thinks of the current crop of pranksters, that's good news.

BIG MONEY

Radio's bottom line is right down there with everyone else's: the only reason it has survived so many years is that in the face of all the changes and competition from other media it has adapted well enough to continue stuffing the wallets of enough people. This year close to $4.5 billion will circulate in the radio industry, more than ever before.

A future marked by scads of new stations and new programs means not only more money but a wider dispersement of what money there is. As the medium evolves, big money will be invested in, and made by, the superstations and the radio networks, but smaller, more specialized stations ought to be able to tap into whole new sources of ad revenue to keep themselves solvent. That said, however, it is also true that the nuts-and-bolts economics of the business will remain essentially the same.

Here's how it works: The vast majority of radio today is a rather humble business, with an average annual per-station budget of $500,000 and a comparatively minuscule profit margin. The real money makers in radio are those who own clusters of big stations—often corporate groups; for them, annual income approaches $15 million. The featured performers of the industry, the disc jockeys, are for the most part considered dispensable and consequently are underpaid. A large number of jocks work for close to the minimum wage, and even the most well established, popular local radio personalities in the country don't command salaries much higher than $300,000—a pittance next to a Johnny Carson or even an Alan Thicke. Because few radio contracts are public, salaries can only be estimated, but it can be assumed that in the $300,000 range we would find the likes of Don Imus (WNBC New York), Wally Phillips (WGN Chicago), the Al Lohman–Roger Barkley team (KFI Los Angeles), John Gambling (WOR New York), and Dick Purtan (WCZY Detroit). American Federation of Television and Radio Artists (AFTRA) union minimums for air talent at most major market stations range from $15,000 to $55,000, with the larger salaries at the old AM giants.

The bulk of the money comes in, of course, from advertisers. The rate that a station gets for a minute of advertising time relates not just to audience size but also to audience demographics, the product advertised, the time of day, the number of minutes purchased, merchandise trade-offs offered, and the credibility of the program host. A local station offering a program with good ratings and a top personality such as the men listed above can charge up to $600 a minute, close to twice the maximum rate on an all-music station with identical ratings; a teen-oriented rock station will charge a pimple-cream company 25 percent more than it will an airline for the same minute.

Radio advertising all comes down to horse trading—almost everything's negotiable—and rates literally range from a dollar a minute late at night at a small station in the middle of nowhere to $15,000 for a thirty-second spot during the World Series on a three-hundred-station network. Top rates at most of the major market stations run in the $50- to $300-a-minute range. The combination of the relatively low prices (local TV spots can go as high as $5,000 a minute) and the tight demographic group that an advertiser can hit makes radio an attractive, efficient medium for whoever is flogging a product, especially during tough times.

Still, with the growing number of new stations and futuristic entertainment delivery systems, competition for ad dollars is fiercer than ever. Fifteen to twenty years ago the title to a station was virtually equivalent to a license to print money. But now associated costs keep rising; radio is getting more expensive to operate.

Stations require an omnipresent technical engineering staff, to keep the signal clear and constant, for example, and AM/FM combination stations can have more than twenty-five electronic whizzes on the payroll. Powerful FM stations drop around $1,500 each month for antenna space on the tops of large buildings to increase their coverage area, and AM stations pay up to $6,000 each month just for electricity to run their antennae.

Large music stations also dole out up to $100,000 a year or more for three to five full-time music researchers who call unsuspecting citizens on the telephone and play them a few seconds of up to sixty different pop songs and ask them which ones they like.

Promotion budgets, mainly for TV and billboard advertising and giveaways, run well over $500,000 per year for aggressive competitors, and subscriptions to the Arbitron ratings report—the industry bible—can easily top $100,000 a year. Annual royalty payments to the American Society of Composers, Authors, and Publishers (ASCAP) get as high as $175,000, according to the society's New York office.

Because of increased fan interest, caused in part by expanded free and cable television coverage of sports, a lot more money than ever before is now also being spent by radio stations on play-by-play sports coverage. Though the cost of broadcasting a game is only about $500, radio rights packages run up to $1 million a year for top pro football and baseball teams. Top college football teams reportedly can command $750,000 a season, the best college basketball team can draw up to $100,000, and the sweetest NBA package is not much higher than $100,000 a season.

RECORDING

MICHAEL JACKSON'S *BAD* STAGE EXTRAVAGANZA

Bob Doerschuk

When a rock star goes on tour, the behind-the-scenes operations required to make the performance click are intricate, demanding, and costly. This account of Michael Jackson's 1987–1988 world tour, as experienced by the keyboard players who backed up his singing, appeared in *Keyboard* magazine.

Somehow, calling the keyboard rig on the Michael Jackson tour "bad" isn't quite adequate. Try "amazing." "Spectacular" sounds pretty good too. Or, as keyboard tech Ran Ballard puts it, "Biggest one that's ever been on the road." Whatever you want to call it, this massive amount of keyboard power may stretch the imaginations of fans throughout the U.S. and Europe who think they've heard everything that keyboards can do in concert. . . .

Much of the credit for the *Bad* sound goes to the three keyboard players, Chris Currell, Rory Kaplan, and music director Greg Phillinganes. The ace keyboard techs, Ballard, Tim Myer, and Mitch Marcoulier, deserve credit for much of the programming and sampling, and all of the maintenance and repair work. But the buck ultimately stops with Jackson himself, whose ideas dominated every aspect of the tour rehearsal as much as his presence commands the stage at each concert.

Source: "Michael Jackson's *Bad* Stage Extravaganza," by Bob Doerschuk, *Keyboard,* January 1988.

Preparing a Michael Jackson show is one of the toughest assignments any musician can tackle these days. When the tour launched its Japanese and Australian leg last year, the performance lasted about an hour and 35 minutes, during which the complex program changes, MIDI (Musical Instrument Digital Interface) routings, and other technical elements had to flow without glitches. The sound quality had to meet Jackson's demanding standards, even when playing stadium gigs in the middle of a monsoon.

The musicians had to memorize the whole show, go onstage without charts of any kind, and play it perfectly. Every note—every note, in every voicing—had to be right. The sounds had to match those on the albums, so that, as Jackson put it, the band would sound as exactly as if they were playing to everyone in the stadium through headphones. Yet the band had to groove. And no matter how weird the weather or uncomfortable the stage costumes or tricky the choreography, everybody had to look as good as they sounded.

And now, staring at nearly a year of travel ahead of them, they'll have to pull all this off again and again, roughly three nights a week. A year of hotel rooms and unpredictable food. A year of hoping that you don't get the flu. A year of long stretches without family, far from carefully constructed careers back home. Now, *that's* bad!

And, in the beginning, it was almost bad beyond belief. The rehearsal schedule before the first gig in Japan was uncomfortably short. The band came together around July 20 in '87, so late that the personnel couldn't even be listed in the Japanese tour books. The entire show had to be put together in time for the flight to Japan on September 9—not just the musical arrangements, but the programming and sampling, even the keyboard rigs. Contrast this with the three-month rehearsal schedule for the Jackson's *Victory* tour, and you get some idea of the logistics involved. . . .

Kaplan was the first keyboardist recruited for the tour, mainly because he had participated in the Jackson brothers' *Victory* tour several years earlier. "I got called around July 8," he remembers. "Michael wanted me to help get the auditions going, so I decided not to worry about putting the keyboard rigs together yet. We spent the first week videotaping auditions for Michael. At the same time, they rented me some DX7s, a [Roland] Jupiter-8, and a Minimoog, so I could start teaching the songs to the band as it came together."

Currell was the next keyboardist to come aboard. A specialist in the New England Digital Synclavier, he had spent more than a year working closely with Jackson, offering technical help as the singer used his own Synclavier to compose and arrange the *Bad* tunes. . . .

Kaplan had to figure a way of covering all the keyboard sounds that the four *Victory* synthesists covered. That meant getting more gear for the two or, eventually, three *Bad* keyboardists to share. . . . "It was like being in kiddieland, because we could literally get whatever we needed. It was like a running joke: We'd wink and say, 'It's for the tour.' "

What seems like extravagance to some was necessary to achieve Jackson's goal of reproducing the album sounds to near perfection. For example, Kaplan has five MIDI controllers in his setup: a KX76, KX88, D-50, DX711FD, and Fairlight keyboard. "There are songs like 'Heartbreak Hotel,' where I play horns on the KX76, then I play the Akai samplers from the 88, then I go to the Fairlight for something that sounds like a big anvil being hit, and finally I go to the DX for flute sounds. I couldn't possibly use one controller in that song, because some of that stuff happens at the same time." . . .

Throughout this preparatory stage, Jackson made himself available to his musicians, guiding them toward the results he wanted through perceptive criticism and encouragement. "As much as people think that he's out in some other world, he's very tuned into his music," Kaplan says. "If what we came up with didn't sound quite right, he would make a mental note, and afterwards he'd come up to Greg or me and say, 'This didn't sound right. Fix it for tomorrow.' He was pretty specific about what he wanted too. He'd tell us, 'That sound needs a little more attack,' or 'I want these horn sounds to be like [horn arranger] Jerry Hey exploding,' or 'I want these strings to be warmer than warm.' Then Greg and I would work on it until four in the morning, then show up again at ten sharp. I tell you, Michael had the sharpest ear of all."

Ballard agrees. "When he turns around after a song and says, 'Where's the Minimoog in the bass?' you know that the guy knows what he wants. He insisted on having [bassist] Don Boyette play the MIDIed Minimoog from his [Yamaha] KX5 because he wanted a big bass sound. I've worked with a lot of people who are concerned with other things, but Michael insists on going after the sounds he wants until he gets them."

Jackson was just as exacting in hammering the arrangement together. "Every day in rehearsal, Michael would get a different feel of how long a dance cut should be or something like that," Marcoulier says. "Since he and Chris had worked together for so long, Michael knows what the Synclavier can do, so he'd say, 'Chris, go in and chop this out.' Chris and I would get on the terminal, edit, and five minutes later it would be done."

While everyone was polishing their sounds and samples, Phillinganes was in charge of making sure the band had nailed down all the songs. This responsibility, coupled with his own programming chores, quickly took its toll. "When you do a full-out show at least twice, if not three times a day, that makes a difference in your body," he points out. "I would average getting to rehearsal around one in the afternoon, and leaving between two and three the next morning. One morning I stayed up until six. It was so intense that after a while, I started losing weight!" . . .

Though solos are relatively rare in the show, the ones that happen have to work every time. This doesn't mean they have to be reproduced note for note, but the spirit of the solo has to be the same each night. Kaplan remembers how he worked to perfect the Jimmy Smith organ solo on "Bad." "First, I listened to Jimmy's version, then wished I could play like him," he laughs. "I tried it out in rehearsal a few times, until Greg pulled me aside and said, 'Why don't you bone up on that solo a bit? Michael's not really happy with it.' I was trying to improvise it, but I had to get the feel of what was intended behind the solo. So I went home, really listened to it, and pretty much nailed it down. Now, when I play it, I keep Jimmy's first four bars. Then I kick into my own thing and go a little more out with it, to make it more concert-like. I even got the sound I needed from a factory sample on the D-50; it's Bank 1, No. 8."

Work continued up to the last hours before the flight to Japan. Special flight cases had to be designed for some of the gear; Myer and Marcoulier built special cases to protect the Synclavier's Winchester disk drives and Paracom terminals, Ballard and Myer were still putting racks together at seven in the morning the day of departure. Even while setting up for their first concert, they were wrestling with problems related to interfacing the three keyboard stations. "Grey and Rory access the Synclavier through a Cooper MIDI Blender," Myer explains, "and we were having some real strange ground loop problems because we were running an intricate batch of gear on different voltage."

Inevitably, once a band moves on from rehearsing to playing live, bugs will crop up. The Jackson crew anticipated many of the worst. To avoid onstage catastrophes due to irregular electrical systems overseas, for example, they run everything through an uninterruptable offstage power supply, which puts out a steady 120V, 60Hz current, and will keep putting out for ten minutes on batteries if the house electricity dies. And the sound-checks before each show are painstakingly thorough; each keyboard station gets an audio check, followed by a complete MIDI check and a run-through of every program change.

Inevitably, some glitches did crop up. Most weren't too serious. During some of the early shows, weird messages crackled over the sound system until someone traced them to the stage crew's walkie-talkies. At one concert, while Phillinganes was playing 'Heartbreak Hotel,' his keyboards locked, but Ballard came to the rescue by punching the all-notes-off panic button on the Sycologic MIDI switcher. Kaplan also had some tuning drift with his Super Jupiter. But by far the biggest disaster took place in Yokohama, where the band played a stadium gig in the middle of a monsoon.

"A lot of water came down on the equipment," Marcoulier remembers. "One of the Synclaviers was already full of dirt, what with smoke from the smoke machines, and people running saws three feet away and kicking a lot of sawdust in the air. All that gathered in the Synclavier and when the humidity hit it, it all turned to mud. The machine just went nuts. None of the standard trouble-shooting worked, so I had to pull it apart, take out all 135 of the circuit boards and clean them by hand, clean the inside with a vacuum cleaner, use freon spray to clear off the contacts, and put it back together. The thing has worked like a gem ever since."

Aside from the occasional crisis, the tour went smoothly all the way up to the time of our interviews. "There's a lot less tedium on this tour than on some others, because we usually work three days and then have three days off," Ballard says. "Sure, sometimes you find yourself turning the television dial for the fiftieth time and there's nothing but Japanese language shows on. It was really a big deal before the show one day when *Ghostbusters* was on TV in English the night before. That was our main topic of conversation as we were setting things up. But we make sure in every city to find the next joke shop and move up to the next level of craziness."

There are as many ways to blow off road tension as there are members of the company. The crew loosens up at sound checks by jamming while checking the gear. A lot of time is passed on Kaplan's or Myer's Mac, playing Flight Simulator. Currell pores through tech magazines or sets up Synclavier seminars. Phillinganes relies on prayer for his emotional nourishment, and a quick basketball game for his physical release. And everyone is into his own HRS, or hotel room system. These mini-studios were provided by the Jackson organization to allow players to write and record original material, or work out knotty parts of the show, on their free time. "It gives us something to do besides go out and party," Myer says.

Beyond these diversions, the band's camaraderie provides that peculiar kind of strength that live musicians use to combat the tedium of touring. Though everyone is free to do what he wants on days off, they conserve their energy on the morning of a concert, then make their way to the venue around mid-day for sound check, makeup, and wardrobe. Just before going onstage, they gather for a quiet moment together. "We say a prayer," Currell says. "After that, we start screaming bloody murder, then we run onstage and it's boom, bang, and kick ass. It's like going to war."

From opening notes to finale, the group concentrates on providing infallible accompaniment to the star. They don't fade into the background, however. Everyone realizes that they are also part of the show. "I have this idea, however silly it may be, that somebody is always looking at me," Phillinganes says. "Not everybody in the audience is always looking at Michael. Although he's definitely enough to look at, there's too much else going on. My contribution might be small, but I tend to be animated without taking away from Michael's spotlight."

Though the emphasis is on tightness and consistency, there is enough looseness within the arrangements to keep the band from going stale. Sometimes Jackson himself throws in a surprise. One night in Yokohama, he suddenly darted from the stage into the audience. It was a spontaneous move; even the security staff was caught unawares. But the band didn't miss a beat, and simply jammed until his return.

After each show, the group waits for the most opportune time to run for the bus, slip past screaming fans, and cruise back to the hotel. The mood varies on these trips. Sometimes there's a boisterous burn-off of concert energy. The group may hold a serious discussion the next night on fine-tuning parts of the show. Often the mood is quieter, as one or more band members reflect privately on the life they've put on hold back home.

Most of the guys have no second thoughts at this point about devoting more than a year of their lives to this tour. "I did a bit of soul searching in taking the gig," Myer says, "but it got obvious that, if anything, it will help me expand my business, to take in more of the touring services or even work back in L.A., based on what I've learned about being on the road."

For Kaplan, the Jackson tour is a career milestone. "It's made me more of a full-time playing artist instead of a technician," he says. "Even Chick said that this is the greatest thing that could have happened to me. It's like a wild dream come true. In the past, I've built systems for Chick, Joe Sample, Herbie Hancock, and all these great guys. To do as good a job as possible, I always work as if I were building for myself, but still I've always wished I really could play them, and play as well as these guys. I watched Pat Leonard on the *Victory* tour, and he's such a good player that I decided I'd better get my chops much better than they were then. So I practiced my tail off, and got to where I am now. To have it all come together, to have all the keyboards I've always wanted, to be performing with Michael . . . I couldn't have made it any better than this."

NEWSPAPERS

AMERICA'S DAILIES TRY TO CAPTURE LOST READERS

Susan Miller

The U.S. population has grown faster than newspaper circulation. Trying to reverse the trend, editors and managers have made their papers look far different from a decade or two ago and have changed the definition of news. This report on their efforts was written by the director of editorial development for Scripps Howard.

[The 1970s and 1980s] have been a period of tremendous upheaval and transition for America's daily newspapers. There are many reasons, but none more important than this: Editors and publishers have been trying everything they could think of to hold and recapture adult readers, and to turn the younger generation into future readers.

The typical daily newspaper editor of 1970 would have been taken aback if he'd been told that in 15 years he'd be publishing "promo boxes" and informational graphics, or running more business news and fewer weddings; or that the editor next door might be a she.

But that, and much more, has happened.

Both the physical appearance and the content of newspapers has changed dramatically. What readers actually hold in their hands looks different. Almost every daily has experimented with new sections or topics, and new ways of presenting the news. Many have ridden a pendulum from "hard" to "soft" coverage, and back again. The industry as a whole seems only recently to have settled down and concluded that its future truly lies with "news." But even "news" isn't defined quite the same as it once was.

Newspaper editors have been, and continue to be, the people in charge of newspaper content. But while they once dismissed research as hokum and left newsroom budgets to bean counters, they now have embraced a new operating lingo and set of concepts. They are increasingly convinced that a business-oriented approach is necessary to their survival. . . .

THE PROBLEM: DISAPPEARING READERS

Just how bad was—and is—the problem of lost readers?

First the good news: In 1970, America's 1,748 daily newspapers sold over 62 million copies. Fifteen years later, the total number of morning and evening papers had shrunk to 1,674, but the total circulation of those papers had risen slightly, to nearly 63 million copies. As the total number of Sunday papers increased from 586 to 798, total Sunday circulation went from 49 million to nearly 59 million.

The bad news is that the U.S. population grew proportionately faster than newspaper readership. More than 78 percent of all adults said they were daily newspaper readers in 1970. by 1985, it was fewer than 64 percent.

And that's just part of the bad news. Americans

Source: Susan Miller, "America's Dailies and the Drive to Capture Lost Readers," *Gannett Center Journal,* Spring 1987. Reprinted with permission.

used to buy several newspapers per family. In the past 15 years, newspaper executives have watched with dismay as overall industry penetration (newspaper sales per household) fell from around 1 to .74. The growth in new households has far outpaced daily circulation growth.

It wasn't so much that readers *disappeared* (although some did die, of course). It's that new readers, the expected replacements, did not follow the traditional reading and buying patterns. Readership habits have been eroded by a variety of factors: lifestyle changes (resulting in less time to read, especially afternoon papers); competition from television and other media; and even security-conscious high-rise apartments (which make paper delivery more difficult). Increasingly, regular readers are becoming occasional readers. Surveys find that about 85 percent of adults say they read a paper "once a week" or more often, but only about 55 percent read one "every day."

GREATER READABILITY

Even before the industry responded in a concerted way to the problem of "disappearing" readers, two factors helped to "open up" newspapers and brought editors to a more flexible attitude about news content. One was the change in look brought about by modular layout, the anchoring of features, and a more magazine approach to visual presentation.

Modular layout was a key innovation in the way newspapers presented themselves visually. This design style presents the news in rectangular patterns of different sizes and shapes. The fewer the ads, the more modular the page layout can be, but modular design can be used regardless of how many ads are on the page, whether the page contains six or eight columns, or how wide these columns are. Modular layout groups related items, and breaks the page into units that can be more easily browsed. Almost invariably, it makes for a more attractive page. Purely from a presentation point of view, editors grew to prefer this approach to newspaper layout.

But the industry had to overcome an inherited bias before modular layout became widespread on pages with ads. A long-held understanding was that the effectiveness of newspaper ads was linked to their proximity to news stories. Ads with text next to them were more likely to be read, advertisers traditionally assumed. As long as this logic held, newspaper design remained captive to ad placement. When pages were designed, the ads were placed first and then news stories were fit around them. Text tended to wander across the page, looping from column to column in order to abut as much advertising as possible. And readers often literally got lost trying to follow stories.

However, readership studies eventually debunked the widespread belief that ads had to be next to news text in order to be read, and the industry gradually arrived at a new view: A better-looking page was just as important to the effectiveness of an ad as was its proximity to the text. By the mid-1970s, modular layout was increasingly common, along with briefs, better indices, and standardized placement of features. To accomplish this new look, newspapers hired or designated designers, who then put their own stamp on the product with other graphic elements, magazine-type illustrations, large photos and color, and promo boxes on the top of page one that touted the contents inside.

In more or less the same period, cultural and sociological changes caused a re-thinking of the traditional definitions of "news." The civil rights movement had stirred re-thinking of newspapers' coverage of minorities, and editors began to realize that defining "news" in terms of "events" often meant that major sociological trends went unreported. To wit: The exodus of Blacks from the South to northern cities after World War II drew little attention until the race riots of the late 1960s.

The message that news is more than events was reiterated as the women's movement emerged. Women believed that traditional definitions of news were stacked against them. "Bra burnings" got covered, but issues like "equal pay for equal work" or safe, affordable child care were ignored until someone introduced legislation—or until someone sued.

The transition from "society" sections to "people" or "lifestyle" sections was one indication of a re-thinking about news content. Sometimes the shift away from clubs, parties and weddings and toward lifestyle trends and "coping" stories was systematically plotted by top editors. Just as often, it was instigated by the women working in "women's" sections, who recast their sections according to their own sense of priorities. Sometimes they covered "hard news" stories about female political candidates or legislation about women in the workplace not because they thought it belonged there, but because the paper was not covering it elsewhere.

THE NEWSPAPER READERSHIP PROJECT AND RUTH CLARK I

By the mid-1970s, many newspapers had contracted with market research firms for studies of local readership and shopping patterns. And with the birth of the Newspaper Readership Project in 1977, the industry began to address the problem of sagging readership in a systematic way.

The six-year Readership Project, spearheaded by the American Newspaper Publishers Association and the Newspaper Advertising Bureau, brought together representatives from 16 different newspaper associations and organizations. Altogether, the project published more than 70 research reports, several of which were featured at conventions of the American Society of Newspaper Editors (ASNE) and the Associated Press Managing Editors (APME). In 10 regional gatherings between 1980 and 1983, it provided research training for more than 200 editors. The project launched dozens of other training programs, and an ASNE newsletter, "The Editors' Exchange." It also encouraged contact between editors and industry organizations involved in market research.

The sheer scope of the Readership Project indicates how acutely the problem of declining readership was perceived in the late 1970s. The project made it respectable—and ultimately de rigueur—for newspaper editors to concern themselves with business questions like household penetration and market share of advertising. And one of its most enduring contributions was to encourage a pattern of interdepartmental cooperation at many newspapers, as editors, circulation directors and advertising managers learned for the first time to talk to one another about research, training and marketing. The "readership committees" established at some newspapers evolved into ongoing, interdepartmental marketing and management groups.

The study that probably led to more changes at more newspapers than any other single factor in the last 15 years was commissioned by ASNE as part of the Newspaper Readership Project. "Changing Needs of Changing Readers," or "Ruth Clark I," was based on focus group discussions in 12 U.S. cities, and billed as "a qualitative study of the new social contract between newspaper editors and readers." It preached the need for better bonding between journalists and readers, and advocated news content geared to self-fulfillment and helping readers "cope" with their personal lives.

This was a dramatic departure from the traditional emphasis on government coverage and other "hard" news. Ruth Clark, a media vice president at Yankelovich, Skelley and White, was a featured speaker at the 1979 ASNE convention. . . . "Serve us and help us to cope . . . Don't just tell us about the world—help us to understand it . . . Be our surrogate . . . Remember we are hungry for good news, not just bad news"—this was Ruth Clark's message.

But the study instigated far more than a wave of "coping" stories. It also reinforced other emerging trends: correction boxes, op-ed pages, greater accountability and acknowledgment of error, more interpretation and long-term analysis, and more "why you're reading this story" explanations providing perspective or context. It also stressed better organization of news content generally, and time-efficient presentation of stories. It suggested greater use of news summaries and briefs, indices, "anchored" features and standardized placement (the technical term is "booking"), and labeling and graphic aids.

Ruth Clark I, in other words, accelerated and reinforced an ongoing revolution in daily newspaper design and content. . . .

USA TODAY

If Ruth Clark I was a recipe book in nouvelle newspaper cuisine, *USA Today* was a full-course meal. Certainly the most talked-about, maligned and imitated newspaper of the 1980s, the national daily debuted in September 1982. What was the industry's first impression? Color, lots of color. *USA Today* used full-color photos lavishly, and reproduced them brilliantly. It stressed slick, colorful informational graphics, and had an elaborate weather map, a penchant for "we" in headlines, and reams of agate (i.e., small type) in sports. And all those features got copied by other dailies. Next to Ruth Clark's "Changing Needs of Changing Readers," *USA Today* probably has been the second-most influential source of recent industry changes.

The paper was also a lesson in market analysis. It was launched after extensive planning and months of formal product research. Prototypes were distributed in homes, and reactions were studied in markets across the country, especially in large cities with high rates of single-copy sales. Meanwhile, Gannett was analyzing everything from the logistics of satellite transmission to the design and location of sidewalk vending boxes.

Coincidentally, at about the same time Gannett was gearing up to launch *USA Today,* newspaper executives in Minneapolis were struggling to save the afternoon newspaper there. In an effort to reverse readership trends, editor Stephen Isaacs had radically revamped the *Minneapolis Star.* "When I walked in the door, it was losing 6 percent day-to-day from the year previous," he told the APME Changing Newspaper Committee in 1982. "Over half the readers were over 55. People between the ages of 21 and 34 flock to this town, but 90 percent of them, when they subscribed to a paper, subscribed to the *Minneapolis Tribune* [the morning newspaper] and not to the *Minneapolis Star.*"

Isaacs's retargeting relied heavily on local market research. The strategy was to focus on 13 different content areas, and to become "so indispensable in so many different ways to groups of readers . . . [as to] become indispensable generally."

"We did a lot of research indicating that this market had some peculiar characteristics . . . [and] would eagerly accept this kind of paper," Isaacs reported. He termed the redesign "intelligent but risky."

"It was a great idea," associate publisher Christopher Burns said. "It just didn't work . . . We walked away from the audience. We said: 'We're going to glow in the dark. Incandescent newspaper. Young. Hip. With it. Innovative. Emphasis on television. Emphasis on Style . . .' [But] the *Minneapolis Star* just got up and walked out of the room as far as the city was concerned."

The *Minneapolis Star* and *USA Today* may have shared some of the same "brand new" qualities, and a desire to appeal to a youthful, hip and innovative crowd, but there were fundamental differences between their markets. One was an afternoon paper, locked into the demographics of the local community paper and already failing when its overhaul began. The other was able to start fresh in a morning spot and go after a particular market slice all across America. The other main difference is that *USA Today* was backed by deep corporate pockets—owners able and willing to keep the paper going until it could turn a profit. . . .

RUTH CLARK II

Five years after the industry had embraced the notion of "soft" news, Ruth Clark came back with "Relating to Readers in the '80s," a scientifically conducted, quantitative survey that sounded a "back to basics" theme very different from her earlier study.

The first Ruth Clark had never said, "You shouldn't do hard news," but what got editors' attention was its focus on soft news. Meanwhile, those who believed that circulation would rebound if they followed the recipe book had been largely disappointed. At the ASNE convention in 1984, Clark told editors that readers were now saying, "Give us the news, hard news, real news. Tell us the facts about health, science, technology, diet, nutrition, child-rearing, and we will do our own coping." In other words, "less advice, more information."

Clark also presented a highly positive long-term view of the industry in general. "We like you and your newspapers. The majority of us think you're indispensable, though the younger among us are somewhat less sure of this," is how she characterized readers.

"Newspapers are here to stay, regardless of what becomes possible on our TV or computer screens. After all, you're the best bargain in town."

The "rewrite" of Ruth Clark I was a relief to many newspaper editors. Perhaps the chief outcome of "Relating to Readers in the '80s" was that it reinforced a gut feeling many of them already had. They had never felt quite comfortable with the "help me cope" thrust. Their training lay in hard news, and that was where they believed they did their best work.

One can ask whether readers' tastes really changed as much between 1979 and 1984 as the Ruth Clark studies indicated, or whether the methodology was flawed, or whether the studies themselves reflected what the industry needed to hear at two different points in time. In any event, the "back to hard news" trend reflects something more than a pendulum swing. The industry may have come full circle, but it has arrived at a place quite different from where it began. Thanks to lifestyle diversity and the mass entrance of women into the work force, the world has dramatically changed. Thanks to market research—and to the increased hiring and promotion of women—editors realize that women do not require a separate section of the paper filled with anything and everything that might interest the members of their sex. Rather, women in the mid-1980s have a wider range of interests than in 1970—and so do men. . . .

ADVERTISING AND CIRCULATION

Most changes in newspaper design and content over the past 15 years have resulted directly from editors' attempts to attract and keep readers. But several important changes were encouraged by newspaper business executives who, along with some editors, perceived a growing need to meet the interests and demands of advertisers. For example, zoned sections with local community news (distributed either daily or weekly) were introduced in part for readers living in the targeted areas. But perhaps the more significant aim was to provide advertisers vehicles for reaching particular communities and neighborhoods. Daily papers also introduced free total market coverage (TMC) supplements as a way to compensate for low circulation penetration and to give advertisers a guaranteed vehicle for reaching "all" households within a given market. Often, TMCs were launched as a defensive measure too, to stem the growing competition for the suburban advertising dollar from new weekly papers, "shoppers," and direct-mail products.

Increasingly, the community of newspaper advertisers buys space not just for total circulation, but also for reader demographics. The Simmons and Scarborough studies that started in the early 1980s were an entrepreneurial effort by professional market research groups to provide such data in major markets to national advertising representatives. That partnership dissolved in 1986, but advertiser interest in specialized audiences is a major source of editorial change at many local papers. The old-style calendar of "special interest" sections (bridal in the spring, back-to-school in August) now includes all manner of health, fitness, and even child-care supplements. By devoting staff and newshole to stylish, substantive sections with titles like "Living," "Weekend," "Science Times," "Business Day," and "Sports Monday," editors at the *New York Times* helped make it respectable for editors at newspapers around the country to create special sections for which there was not only reader but also advertiser interest.

But the overall financial experience with special sections has been mixed. Some have failed to produce enough incremental advertising revenue to cover their costs, and some have even siphoned off advertising from the rest of the paper. Expanded business and sports sections have tended to draw additional advertising lineage, but health and fitness supplements have generally failed to attract enough advertising.

The rule of thumb at Knight-Ridder papers now is that any new special-interest section must be cost-justified. When the "Business Monday" section of the *Miami Herald* proved a solid moneymaker, it became a model for the company's other papers. A separate fashion section, on the other hand, was ultimately folded back into the paper's more general lifestyle section. But Knight-Ridder (and the industry generally) does make an exception to the cost-justification rule for science sections. These tend to be justified by reader interest alone.

Another important change recently prompted by advertising considerations was the industry's adoption of a Standard Advertising Unit (SAU). This universalized an ongoing switch from eight-column to six-column formats, and also established a standard column width. Studies had established that readers preferred a wider column width, and many editors had already adopted a six-column format on pages without advertising. Now a national advertiser needs to produce just one version of an ad, instead of multiple versions for varying column widths.

TRENDS

. . . The new trend for some papers is a shift away from total readership to a focus on market niche. As newspapers adjust to the reality of lower market penetration, many are making strategic decisions about how best to market themselves both to readers and to advertisers. Some are deliberately narrowing their geographic and demographic sights. This re-thinking may eventually be as profound in its long-term consequences as the efforts of the past 15 years to capture lost readers.

At the 1986 convention of the Associated Press Managing Editors (APME), Steve Star of the Sloan School of Management at MIT outlined two models for newspapers in the future. The first are papers that can maintain penetration levels of 60 percent or above, which as mass media will stay attractive to a broad range of advertisers. The second are papers whose penetration falls well below 60 percent. These must conceive of themselves as segmented media, and seek out advertisers wishing to reach their particular segments.

Star's presentation was noteworthy not because it contained any revolutionary business concepts, but because he was delivering it to APME, the organization that prides itself as being the nuts-and-bolts association of "shirt sleeves" editors. Star, who has taught marketing to editors and other executives through a series of sponsored industry seminars since 1975, effectively was telling APME that the "customer" is not just the reader, but also the advertiser. After spending much of the last 15 years learning to market themselves better to readers, editors seem destined to spend the next 15 becoming equally expert about what they have to offer advertisers. . . .

Thanks to interdepartmental efforts, editors and their colleagues in the circulation and sales departments are moving to address their combined concerns with a teamwork and technical sophistication that would have been unthinkable a decade ago.

"A major challenge is to reduce the costly 'churn' in having to sell the same reader over and over again," said a recent primer, "Readers: How to Gain and Regain Them." It was issued under the umbrella of the industry's Future of Advertising Project, which is carrying on some of the work of the Newspaper Readership Project. . . .

Minimizing churn, building brand and reader loyalty, selling the newspaper as a "value added environment" to advertisers—these are all light years away from newspaper journalism's fiercely proud history of exposing corruption and covering politics. But in the last 15 years, perhaps more than at any time in its history, the industry has learned a harsh and sobering lesson: It cannot do good if it can't pay its bills.

THE VIEW FROM THE ROAD

Charles Kuralt

While delivering the Red Smith Lecture in Journalism at the University of Notre Dame, Charles Kuralt discusses good writing in the homey storytelling style that has made his *On the Road* features so popular on the CBS television network.

We are gathered in memory of a stylish writer, one of the best—Red Smith, whose life and work honored Notre Dame, and honored human beings as a species. So the subject, at least the first subject, is writing. I'll begin with a few random thoughts about writing. I met Elmore Leonard who writes good crime novels. He said he had three rules for writing: Number One—in dialogue, never use the word, "besides." "Besides" is a transition word, he said, used by a speaker to change the subject. It's a lazy device for a writer. Never use "besides" in dialogue. Rule Number Two: Use no more than one exclamation mark per 50,000 words of manuscript. Rule Number Three: As an author on a book promotion tour, never agree to be met at the airport by a limousine, because in this way a writer is captured by the trappings of success. This last rule, Elmore Leonard told me, he had broken, however, once people actually started *offering* to meet him at the airport in a limousine.

I have fallen into all the traps that await the unwary writer. As a young writer at CBS News in the Fifties, I had Douglas Edwards wish everybody a "fulsome" Christmas. And that is how I learned the hard way that "fulsome" is a synonym for "nauseating." I have learned that "livid" does not mean flushed and crimson; it means "black and blue." I discovered, much to my surprise, that a "hail fellow, well met" is actually a h-a-i-l fellow, not "h-a-l-e." He is well-greeted, not hale and hearty. When I read about a car careening down the street, I know the writer meant "careering" down the street, although the car may "careen" or tilt sharply if it goes around a corner.

I treasure all these small distinctions, and I think they are worth preserving—now that *I* have gone to the trouble of learning them. I understand that the language changes by majority vote, by usage, but I agree with Theodore Bernstein, the old *New York Times* man who has written about the language a good deal, that there are some fields of human activity in which a count of noses does not provide the best basis for law and order.

I have served on the usage panel of *The American Heritage Dictionary.* They send us ballots, and ask us to vote whether to accept new usages. I always vote no. The pilot says on the public address system, "We are presently at 32,000 feet over Kansas City." Do you accept this popular usage as a synonym for "at present"? No, I always say. Presently, I may change my mind, but I doubt it.

I don't think the young writer is wasting his time who browses through Fowler or Eric Partridge or Bergen Evans from time to time, or who keeps Otto Jesperson's seven-volume *Modern English Grammar* on a shelf in the bathroom.

Proper usage, of course, is only the foundation of the house the writer is trying to build, however. The risers, beams and rafters are subject matter, and the wallpaper and furniture of the house are all style. I think good writing comes from good reading. I am sure of that, in fact. I think writing is imitative. When I sit down to write, I know that I hear in my head the rhythms of writers I have read and admired. Sometimes, I can even remember *which* writer's rhythm I am hearing. I think all the good writers hear the music of good writing they've read. The *great* writers like Red Smith compose new music for the rest of us to hear when we sit down at the typewriter.

I was surprised to discover that he learned to write the same way I did. He wrote better, but here's what he said about it. I was just reading *The Red Smith Reader* on the airplane coming here. I came here from Moscow, and I took this book with me—so I had plenty of time to read it on the way back. In an interview one time Red Smith said, "In my later years I have sought to become simpler, straighter and purer in my handling of the language. I've had many writing heroes, writers who have influenced me. Of the ones still alive, I can think of E.B. White. I certainly admire the pure, crystal stream of his prose. When I was very young as a sportswriter I knowingly and unashamedly imitated others. I had a series of heroes who would delight me for a while and I'd imitate them. . . . But slowly, by what process I have no idea, your own writing tends to crystallize, to take shape. Yet you've learned some moves from all these guys and they are somehow incorporated into your own style. Pretty soon you're not imitating any longer."

I think it was E. B. White—no longer alive—who taught us all that one could write movingly about small things—the birth of a spider, the death of a pig. Red Smith also wrote about small matters with an insight that gave them importance. And now we have all learned from him. It was E. B. White, his model and mine, who said that good writing elevates people, and bad writing depresses people. I believe the aspiring writer (I assume there are some in this room) has a responsibility to himself to read much, and to learn to recognize the difference between good writing and bad writing.

I believe good writing takes patience. Red Smith said it was the one part of the job he didn't enjoy, sitting at the typewriter. But he knew it was important to sit there until he remembered the right word. Mark Twain said in an inspired moment, "The difference between the right word and the nearly right word is the difference between the lightning and the lightning bug."

Eric Sevareid once said it differently. He was one of the better writers who ever worked around CBS, one I always admired and whose work I used to read. From time to time, he collected his pieces into books, and I found those books in my high school library and I admired Sevareid's essays greatly. But when I got to know him, I found that he was never entirely comfortable with television, the lights, cameras and all the things you have to put up with to do a story in television. He said it was like "being nibbled to death by ducks." Once, when he was feeling particularly grumpy about television, I heard him murmur, "One good word is worth a thousand pictures."

Words matter, even in a picture medium. Not many good words are used in television these days, I think. The characteristic young television journalist is more interested in images, especially his own image, I'm sorry to say. There are so many young men and women who are good at performing, or producing, or shooting pictures, and so few who are good at writing, that whenever a writer shows up at CBS, people treat him with respect and whisper behind him in the halls, "He's a writer, you know." Charles Osgood and Bruce Morton and Andy Rooney are among those who are whispered about as they walk down the hall, and a few others.

But if it's writing in which a young journalist excels, probably, to tell you the truth, he would be well-advised to shun television and enter some other field—newspaper or magazine writing, or writing for the wire services. As things stand today, all of those options offer a better opportunity for the writer to practice his craft. The writer will be frustrated by the abbreviation of his work in television—television news stories are short and getting shorter, as you may have noticed, and the writer will be distracted by the flashing graphics and shifting gears and ringing bells that are characteristic of most television news programs these days.

It might have turned out differently. When I came to work for CBS News 29 years ago next month, there were writers on the premises. Stylists. Eric Sevareid, Winston Burdette, Dick Hottelet, Charles Collingwood and many others. Hottelet was the last to retire, last fall in the same week that Collingwood died. And there was Murrow, who reminded us that a television set is only a box with wires until innovative and thoughtful and resourceful men and women give it substance. Edward R. Murrow, surrounded by powerful egos, deplored the egotism of broadcast journalism. Sometimes at the end of the day he would say, "Well, we've done as much damage as we can do for one day. Let's go have a drink." And that was an invitation all of us who were kids accepted eagerly because we knew we were going to have more than a drink. We were going to have a little seminar, a little discussion about this thing we were doing.

News on the air was being invented in those days and Murrow was its Edison. One thing I heard him say more than once was, "Look. Just because you have a loud voice, just because 16 million people hear you every time you open your mouth, don't think that makes you any smarter than you were when your voice only reached the other end of this bar!" Probably that ought to be engraved and put on the walls of television newsrooms. Murrow recognized that amplification did not confer wisdom.

If he could come back today and walk into our newsroom, I think he would be impressed by many things. I think he would be impressed by the size, by the fact that CBS News has grown so much, from the small collection of talented individualists he assembled to a mighty and far-flung and bureaucratic organization upon which the country has come to rely, together with its competitors. I think he—who spoke of lights and wires—would be impressed by how much more advanced our lights and wires are. I don't know how it works, but I was over in Moscow yesterday and the day before that we put on a program which people saw right away. We didn't have to process the film and put it in a can and give it to some Pan Am passenger to give it to a customs guy in Frankfurt and hope that it would somehow get back to America. It all arrived in America instantaneously. Murrow spoke into an old ribbon microphone and was heard, scratchily, in people's living rooms. We flash pictures in color into those same living rooms across oceans from Moscow or across space from the moon. He would love all that.

I think he would notice other improvements. Because he was fair-minded and humane, I think he would be pleased that not everybody who is on television these days, or working behind the scenes, is white and male. . . .

I think he would deplore the show business aspects that are creeping into our line of work. He would be dismayed that all these years after *See It Now* there is no place in the schedules of any of the networks for documentary treatment of important subjects. He would be surprised by the extent to which good writing has been devalued. By the way, he would notice the same old egos in the newsroom, though in many respects we have less to be egotistical about than did Murrow and his colleagues.

Events sometimes conspire to bring you back to earth. I have told the story about how one day in Fort Myers, Florida, we parked the *On the Road* bus on a residential street. People are forever coming up offering story ideas or praising us for all the sweet little stories we do. A woman came out of her house smiling, and I smiled, and she smiled, and I opened the door to accept the usual pleasant remarks and she said, "I think I would like a couple of loaves of rye today, please." She thought we were the bread truck. We've also been mistaken for the X-ray van and the Bookmobile. That's good for you, you know. The reporters who genuinely begin to think of themselves as important—and you see them, you can almost tell them on the air, the ones who have a greater interest in themselves than in the story—those are reporters who are not doing themselves or their craft any good. And people like the lady in Fort Myers will always help you remember that you're not such a big shot as you may be tempted to think.

It's been nearly 20 years for the three of us *On the Road*—Izzy, Larry and me—and we have learned, if we have learned anything, not to come on like a big-time television news crew. I hope not to be lofty and philosophical in these remarks. I'm really trying to give practical advice to some of you who I suspect are going to enter this field. Most of the people we do stories about have never been on television before, and they are likely to feel a little

Charles Kuralt's "On the Road" reports on CBS television about obscure people and off-beat situations have won acclaim for helping viewers to understand what he calls "the jigsaw puzzle" of America. Kuralt stands alongside the van in which he and crew members crisscross the country.

apprehensive about the experience. So we try to put them at their ease just by being ourselves. It helps, to tell you the truth, if you're in my line of work, if you're fat and bald. That's the truth. Because people look at me and they say, "If that guy can look like that and talk like that, then I can just be myself." Which is what you're hoping for, of course.

We have adopted what we call the "tricycle principle." We watch a lot of local television; everywhere we go we see the local news. Izzy and I were in his motel room someplace watching the local news when a story came on about a children's tricycle race, little kids trying to ride their tricycles fast. Pretty cute story. And Izzy said, "You know what? Before this story is over that reporter is going to ride a tricycle." And I said, "No, he wouldn't because that would ruin it." Sure enough, he signed off—"Joe Doakes, Eyewitness News," and the camera pulled back to watch him peddling down the sidewalk on the tricycle. Then and there we adopted the tricycle principle, which is very simple: "Don't ride the tricycle." Try to keep yourself out of the story if you can. Don't appear on camera at all if you can avoid it. People are not interested in the reporter, or shouldn't be, and if the reporter does his work well, people will be interested in the story he is telling. If they end up thinking about him instead of the story, he has succeeded as a celebrity but failed as a storyteller.

Which brings us back to substance . . . which brings us back to writing. I don't think a journalist can be a very good writer unless he is first a pretty good thinker. I have encountered television journalists who know a lot about television, and even a little bit about journalism, but not much about anything else. I am happy with your arrangement here at Notre Dame; I am glad this talk is sponsored by the Department of American Studies. I think the reporter's mind should be cluttered, and my own is cluttered with American studies—not the systematic sort which might gain me a passing grade in a course at this great university, but a chaotic jumble of facts which nevertheless comes in handy. I know that daffodils bloom in Savannah the last week of February, but they don't bloom till the second week of April in Hartford. I know that there was a member of Custer's Seventh Cavalry in Major Reno's outfit who was there at the Little Big Horn and who didn't die until 1950. I am intrigued by all the things Americans use to hold their mailboxes up—welded chain and wagon wheels and old plows and cream separators. I know that the whistling swans migrate every year from Siberia to the Chesapeake Bay. I know that the weakest coffee in America is served in Brookings, South Dakota; that a barrel is 31 gallons if it's beer, but 31 and-a-half gallons if it's water, and 40 gallons if it's a barrel of whisky; . . . that starting in 1917 if you wanted to immigrate to America, you had to be able to read; . . . and that if you need to stop a cut from bleeding what you do is say the sixth verse of the 16th chapter of Ezekiel while walking towards the sunrise, or so they say in the mountains of North Carolina, where I come from.

Now, most people can get through life perfectly well without knowing all these things, but if you are a reporter you need to know them. And if you are a feature reporter, you can find a way to do a story about every one of them, and as a feature reporter, I have. And I have done stories about musical saw players and swimming pigs. The swimming pig was one of our big ones. The Remarkable Swimming Pig of San Marcos, Texas. We even rented an underwater housing for the camera to get underwater pictures of that little porker paddling along. We made a big thing out of it. Afterwards, a lot of farmers wrote me letters and said, "You idiot! Any pig can swim!" It would have been helpful to have known that before we did the story, but all knowledge is imperfect and incomplete.

Red Smith had a lovely cluttered mind of the perfect sort. It was just an accident, you know, that he got into sportswriting. He could have done anything. He told how it happened. Let me read you another passage from this interview in *The Red Smith Reader.* He was working on the copy desk of a newspaper called the *St. Louis Star.* He said in this interview:

> That fall the managing editor, a man named Frank Taylor, fired two guys in the sports department, and he came over to me on the copy desk and he said, "Did you ever work in sports?"
>
> And I said, "No."
>
> "Do you know anything about sports?"
>
> And I said, "Just what the average fan knows."
>
> "They tell me you're very good on football."
>
> "Well, if you say so."
>
> And he said, "Are you honest? If a fight promoter offered you ten dollars would you take it?"
>
> I said, "Ten dollars is a lot of money."
>
> And he said, "Report to the sports editor Monday."

After that he never was at a loss for something to write about. You have to have something to write about. It's all right with me if Red Smith's mind was cluttered with facts about the Kentucky Derby, which it was; or if the reporter's mind is cluttered with facts about corruption in Chicago, as Mike Royko's mind is; or the political philosophy of William Howard Taft, as George Will's mind seems to be. But I am sure that felicitous writing comes only from felicitous musing on the contents of a kind of jumbled file cabinet or wastebasket of the mind. Good writing comes from consummate curiosity and keen observation. Curiosity, that's the thing, and from an inborn sympathy for human beings and the human condition, and always from broad, even if disorganized, knowledge. If I were hiring a reporter, I would sooner hire one from American Studies here than from a full-fledged School of Journalism someplace else, because the American journalist-to-be who has studied America has his priorities straight. Journalism is not so complicated that you can't learn it on the job, but America is complicated, and deserving of much contemplation.

It is a country full of surprises, you know. After all these years of meandering through it, we have been to every part of every state many times by now. I believe the country to be more neighborly, and more just, and more humane than you would think from reading the papers or watching the evening news.

The country I have found is one that presses upon the visitor cups of coffee and slices of pie and great gobs of local history, and always wants you to stay longer than you have time to stay—and doesn't bear much resemblance to the country that makes it to the front pages, which have room only for wars and politics and calamities—or perhaps I should say politics and other calamities—and not enough room for telling the story of people living and working and trying to be good neighbors. But that country is there, as we all know. Journalism, by its nature, rushes about shouting. The country, by its nature, moves slowly and talks softly.

I don't mean, of course, that we in journalism shouldn't be telling the story of everything that goes wrong. That is why we are doing our work. This kind of country cannot work unless we persist in rushing and shouting and pointing out everything that goes wrong. But I have wondered whether the historians, whose job it's going to be to sift through the refuse we reporters deposit on the pile of history, might not find some articles of value we didn't much notice at the time—impulses of humaneness and decency and the will for justice.

There's such a thing in this country as a national conscience, or so I have come to believe. Things are a lot fairer than they used to be for a lot of people in our country. And besides that we have reached the conclusion that we really shouldn't pave every meadow, or terrace every hillside, or pollute every trout river, that we have to leave a bit of wild America for our children to love as we have loved it. We have faced a lot of problems of our people and our land. The technical problems don't worry me so much. Technical problems, which admit of purely technical solutions—we're just wonderful at solving those in America. I bet we live to see the day of abundant energy from unexpected sources just because that's become identified as a big problem. It's these very much more difficult human problems that we have gone to work on as a people in the last 20 years and actually found a few solutions to. We're not much for congratulating ourselves. We would much rather go galloping off in search of new problems to solve, but I think there are grounds for modest self-congratulation in the history of our country in the last 20 years or so. We cover government but these impulses I'm talking about sprang up outside of government, sometimes even in spite of government. Well, very often in spite of goverment. They didn't originate in Washington. One woman wrote a book, Betty Friedan—the book which Alvin Toffler said "pulled the trigger of history." One woman decided that no, she was tired, she thought she would not move to the back of the bus. And in these ways—these human ways—the country is changed forever.

My first grandchild was born last month. I hope he undertakes American Studies when he gets to college, because he won't understand from the papers and the television news alone how profoundly his country has changed. If American journalism has one great weakness, it is that we lack a sense of history. I advocate a journalism of context. It would take a conscious effort. It would require writers with exquisitely cluttered minds, and editors able to relate today's wire service bulletin to events of the past. It would immeasurably improve our newscasts and newspapers, however, and it would serve the country.

Well, I have been talking as if I know something about journalism, and I am not sure I do. Red Smith said pounding a typewriter is a pretty easy way to make a living—a lot better than lifting things, he said. I have worked myself at the edges of the craft; it's been a long time since I covered anything important. I have tried to keep importance and relevance and significance entirely out of my work, in fact, on the grounds that with everybody else covering the Senate hearings, somebody has to cover the greased pig contests and the guy who has a car that runs on corncobs. And that's been me.

WHAT WRITERS THINK ABOUT WRITING

An Associated Press Panel Discussion

The bylines of Saul Pett and Jules Loh on Associated Press dispatches guarantee warm, bright, well-written stories. In this discussion with Lou Boccardi, president and general manager of the AP, these masters of their craft explain how they work.

BLOCKBUSTERS

Boccardi: How do you cope with writer's block?
Pett: I'm a student of writer's block. I'm a professor of writer's block. I'm a victim of writer's block. As a matter of fact, if I had enough money to buy it, I would change the name of the saloon across the street to The Writer's Block and make a million dollars. I've been a victim of writer's block quite often, and I think that usually it results because you're trying something you shouldn't be trying to write. This is especially true of leads. We've all had trouble with leads. One of the problems, I think, is going through your material and there's this little thing, a perfect anecdote or a funny little thing or something poetic or dramatic, and it's in our heads, even before we put it down or try it at the typewriter. This is the thing we're trying to pursue, and two days later, or however much time, you have finally figured out that this was on the wrong track completely.
Boccardi: When you're having trouble with the lead, do you ever skip it and go on to the rest of the story?
Pett: No, I just can't do it because to write the wrong lead keeps starting you off one way when essentially your material is going the other way. Four pages later, five days later, however longer, you finally discover that. And you feel stupid for having taken so long. Actually, the lead is not the very first thing, whether you have two weeks to write it or two days or two hours. Ask yourself what the hell is the essence of this thing. I realize that sounds pompous. Before the lead, that's what I try to figure out.
Boccardi: Jules, you spent five years writing "Elsewhere in America," which essentially was a shortish feature story. Do you find, when you're working in the 600–700-word range, that you leave the interview with the lead already fairly clear in your mind?
Loh: Of course I had five days to write the two columns. I think all of us in this room have left an event and headed to the telephone and had to dictate the lead. There is no crush on me to get to a phone for this cycle or that cycle but just to write my feature story. I'll leave the interview thinking of the story, but invariably I get to a typewriter and I have a way of outlining a story, whether it's 300 words or 3,000 words, and when I do that often the lead I have in mind, the trick, or the clever trick, doesn't wind up there. It winds up another lead altogether, and it's not a large process, either. It's not any Roman numerals or big *A* or small *a*. It's just a simple little process of outlining. What I do when I come back from any reporting and before I write the story is without reference to my notebook or all of the mound of research I've accumulated. Other people have different techniques, but mine is simply this: I put everything aside, and I write down what I know about the story, what I really know without reference to anything, things that struck me about it or made a large impression or for some reason have made themselves indelible in my mind. I don't even have to look at my notes to know that. I list them and these are going to be the ingredients of my story. And then I go through my notebook and start filling out each one.
Boccardi: That first group comes essentially from your memory, from your impressions.
Loh: From my impressions because that's what really . . . you know, you get involved in a story, the research and the reporting, and certain things just stick out. In my case, these always seem to be the elements of the story that I'm going to expand on.

Source: Reprinted from *AP World,* 2 (1982) by permission of *AP World.*

Two eminent Associated Press writers, Jules Loh (left) and Saul Pett (right) discuss their work methods at a meeting of editors moderated by Lou Boccardi, AP president and general manager (center).

So the lead that struck me after this interview or that one might not wind up being the lead of the story, but it will wind up being high up.

THE MATERIAL

Boccardi: Saul, you have a different technique with handling material.

Pett: On the longer, more complicated features, what I do . . . I may have six or seven of these notebooks, and I have stacks of tearsheets, clips of magazine pieces, books, chapters folded over, and now I'm theoretically done with the reporting and research. What do you do with it? Well, it's just material scattered all over the place and it needs to be put in categories somewhere. It's like moving into a house. The movers move in, and you've got to decide where the furniture has to go. Then I do an outline. It's not an outline of the story; it's an outline of my material. Let's say it's Koch. Okay, Koch, examples of his wit, his spontaneity, his unique kind of political courage. Or it might be something related to his background, his life story or how he got to be. All these things are spread out all over these notebooks and over the clips and magazine pieces, and the first problem is to just organize it in piles. So that's what I do. It's donkey work. It's dull work. I hate it, and it seems like it takes an ungodly long time to do it.

Boccardi: Do you literally rip your notebook up, take pages from it?

Pett: No, I just take long pages like that and say, Koch humor.

Loh: Rip his notebook up? He sends it off to the Pulitzer committee.

Pett: And it just goes on and I have many pages like this. And it's not inspiring work.

Boccardi: There will be a little reverence here.

Pett: Everybody has his version of it, and that is organizing your material first. The disadvantage of it is it's a boring several days. But the advantage of it is you've now put it in sections and you've also learned where that damn material is so that when you get to write you don't have to stop and look over there and look over here. The result is that frequently, when I'm writing, I don't even have to refer to the stuff.

Audience question: What about the end of a story? Do you let something come the same way the lead does, or do you just write until you're done?

Pett: I have read somewhere that John McPhee, for example, thinks of the ending first. Well, I just don't believe in that at all. I try not to think of the ending too soon. The ending, if you're going well, will suggest itself; also there are natural endings that can end quietly and don't have to be home-runs. It's just a way of getting off the stage with some quiet dignity.

Loh: I think it's foolish to write an ending, but in my way of arranging a story, I do have in mind an ending—not words, mind you, but an end, and it's somehow going to tie back to the beginning. And the sonofabitch that cuts it is going to end it, see, so you put that in and it makes him work like hell to get words out of there. I have in mind a beginning, and a middle and an end, and the end will somehow come back to the beginning so that the thing is sealed. That's what I try to do.

Pett: Okay, we all try to do that, but I think that where we go wrong is to try to get this perfect and, I submit, artificial, symmetry when you're really straining to bring it back up to the end and so the poor professor looked out the window as he did in the lead and the snowflakes come down . . . there's that danger.

IN STYLE

Boccardi: Have you ever consciously tried to study other writers and incorporate that into your writing?

Loh: Well, I read every good writer all the time, and I'm envious, jealous of all of them. But to try to imitate them? I think I have too much gray in what's left of my hair to imitate anybody. You know, when I read somebody I really like—Joan Didion—it takes me a long time to read a good writer because I'm seeking to find out how she worked out this problem. It's interesting to me, and I'm sure I learn from it and become a better writer.

Boccardi: Let's stay on that point. Are there authors that you would advise young writers today to look at?

Loh: I mentioned Joan Didion and John McPhee, but you get down to our writing and you have to look at people like Red Smith and Mike Royko. These are people who really cherish the language and make every word tell. That's the fundamental point—they make every word count. What really irritates me about our writers: they don't let me discover, they tell. So an AP writer says that Cardinal Cody was angry; Royko tells me that Cody kicked the wastebasket and slammed the door, and lets me discover. It's better writing and it's better journalism. I've imitated Hemingway, Joyce and everybody . . . Hemingway wasn't worried and neither was Joyce. I tried everybody. But finally style is something that just comes.

Pett: I think you are in deep trouble if you are Saul and trying to write in "Saul's style." You are in worse trouble if you're trying to write in "Jules' style." I don't think I can imagine a respectable writer who would consciously sit down and write in what he thinks his style is. I don't know what the hell my style is. And I'm sure Jules doesn't either. But I'm sure the more intrinsic thing is: what interests me as a reader? What would I like to read? And that may determine the thing you are loosely calling style.

Audience question: You guys discard things because they don't fit your style, isn't that right?

Pett: I don't and I'm sure Jules doesn't. It is discarded because it doesn't serve the story, and the story is the material. I cannot emphasize that enough. It is the material. You are not a much better writer than you are a reporter. If you don't have it in the material, there is no clever way or subtle way of getting around that fact, and it is quickly discovered by the reader. And if you are any kind of writer, you'll discover it.

Audience question: Do you find yourself with much more material than you need? Or before you set out do you decide what you're going to write and how you're going about it and just ask the questions you need?

Pett: You don't know. The beginning of it is a groping. You don't really know which way you're going. You can't know, and that I think is a thing that writers and editors have to be aware of. If it is a large subject, it can't be all that clearly defined. In the bureaucracy story, Jack Cappon came up with an outline and had given it much thought—and it was a guideline. But he couldn't know in advance what are all the things we ought to cover in a big monstrous vague thing like bureaucracy. He had many good notions about it. But it can't be defined in advance. You have to just go this way, and this way, and that way, and then hope it spells mother.

Loh: You always overresearch a story. If you don't you don't have enough. The temptation is to use a fact gathered with great difficulty, that you are very proud of getting, even if it doesn't serve the story.

Pett: It cost four days and $300 of AP's money and you feel obliged to use it, and boy you look at it. . . .

Loh: And so you've got to put that down. After you get all this overresearch—what we have both been saying here—is that you serve the material. But you also make the material serve your story, and that is by weeding this crap out.

Audience question: Saul, when you did the Reagan story, I know you spent some time traveling with him, but you only had half an hour with him in his office. How and when did you draw up a list of questions? Or did you have a list?

Pett: I had a list of questions. If I were interviewing Lou Boccardi tomorrow, I'd have a list of questions. I worked very hard on the questions. You're only going to get a certain amount of time. Oh, I had brilliant questions. I had funny questions. The funny ones he laughed at but it didn't do me any good. I got another minute. But I do work hard at the questions, at the whole shape of the interview, tone of the interview. I try to pace them, I try to start off with something a little funny, and then start off with something that would be interesting to them. I always hope that they will be expansive. I love the important people like presidents to be confident and to talk to me out of a sense of confidence.

Audience question: What kinds of questions get a person to be expansive?

Pett: Well, you ask how they feel. You ask what's surprised you about this job. It worked with Jimmy Carter; it didn't work with President Reagan. A thing I learned to advantage some years ago was even though you prepare your questions, you give them time to answer, and even if the answer is just yes or no, I try if possible to create a pause and let them worry about their short answer. And sometimes that brings something else on; another thought or whatever.

Boccardi: I'd like Jules to get into the technique of interviewing.

Loh: I don't interview presidents, much as they would like me to. I interview people who have never been interviewed. . . .

Pett: Oh, a populist writer!

Loh: And that's important because that's what most of us do. I have a few tricks that I just learned over the years. These people are scared to death when a reporter comes along, so you've got to get over that and get them comfortable with you. The subject has read all this stuff about how reporters pry and they see people on TV asking, "How did you feel when your boy's body with both legs cut off came up from the surf?" And they think that all reporters are going to talk to them like that. Well, you really have to give them confidence in you. The way I do it is talk to these people and tell him why I'm there, what I want to write about. By the way, I never disguise myself. If I'm writing about a coal miner in West Virginia I do not wear overalls and drive a pickup truck. I just go and say, "I'm Jules Loh, a reporter from the Associated Press." Because if you try to pretend, they see through it. Now, how do you get the notebook out? I talk to them and I say—we get to talking about what we're going to talk about—and then comes the time when I say, "When did you say you graduated from high school?" A *fact.* Now that does two things: it gets the notebook out on a subject that is not their opinion or anything controversial. It is just a matter of fact. Now you have it out. The second thing, it tells them that you want to be accurate.

Pett: Despite what Jules says, now and then I've interviewed people who weren't presidents. I remember doing a profile on a baseball umpire named Jocko Conlan. That's years ago. At any rate, there weren't any spontaneous questions. Hell, I had written down my list of questions the night before. I said, "Do you umpires as a regular thing have to have your eyes examined?" He said, "Why? We're not tailors."

VERSUS THE EDITOR

Boccardi: This gives each of you a chance for a wisecrack. What is the role of the editor?

Pett: Completely invisible.

Loh: Stay the hell out of the way.

Boccardi: Be serious.

Loh: Well . . .

Pett: That's enough.

Boccardi: A lot of people here are editors more often than they are writers.

Loh: But nobody in this room got here because he was a bad writer. Everybody here got here because he was a good writer. And the editor ought to have the utmost respect for the writer but save the writer from his own foibles. Any writer who wants to go to the wire unedited has a death wish. The editor has an easier time with writing when it is not on deadline. When we are cranking it out—well, then you just get it out and have an editor who saves you from clichés and redundancies and all of these things. But when you are writing a feature story, and there is some time to think about it, I want the editor to respect the work that the writer has put in on it. And he didn't write this way on a whim, and he has put in a whole hell of a lot of time on this and knows a lot about it, while the editor's got four or five stories that he's working on. I would ask the editor to not have a preconceived notion of how this story ought to be from the assignment, because the material a reporter gets often changes that a little bit.

Pett: I agree with him on one point. I think it's very difficult to be a good editor. I used to think it was more difficult to be a good writer, but without making comparisons, I'll just say it's difficult to be a good editor.

Loh: They're rarer.

Pett: AP once was curious about how I would be as an editor, and I was curious about it, and within six or eight months both of us overcame our curiosity. I was a lousy editor.

Boccardi: Why do you think you were?

Pett: Well, because I was a writer. I tried to really not edit stories but write them, rewrite them. I think that's foolhardy.

Boccardi: A good editor fixes what has to be fixed but not in a way that wipes off the fingerprints of the writer. Especially with feature copy, you want to be careful as an editor not to overedit so that you drive out the writer's style and essentially replace it with your own.

CRITIQUE

Audience question: What bothers you most about the news writing you see?

Loh: It's that notion of the writer telling me instead of showing me about the story. The good reporter will have enough detail to make the reader discover what he's writing about without the writer having to use generalities.

Pett: I say this just as a reader of newspapers. Too often in a large news story I can't tell what the hell happened. This is particularly true of disaster stories. Big hurricane in Texas or a sniper goes wild. Now that, I submit, is a problem for editors and writers. Tell the reader what happened, not just the results of what happened—so many killed, so much property loss—but to picture it from beginning to end. That remains a challenge in our business.

Boccardi: I'd like to ask how your specialized feature writing, which is usually timeless, relates to the work done all day every day in AP bureaus around the world.

Loh: Whatever the story, it has a beginning. Whatever time you have to do it, you have to make the story with a selection of details. That's why I think when you're talking about news writing or feature writing, you're really just talking about writing.

HOWARD COSELL SAYS SPORTSWRITERS NOT PREPARED

John Seigenthaler

Always frank and controversial, Howard Cosell argues that many sportswriters are poorly educated for their jobs and are too heavily influenced by the teams they cover. He expressed his opinions in an interview with John Seigenthaler in the *ASNE Bulletin.* Seigenthaler is editor and publisher of the Nashville *Tennessean.*

Q: You have criticized television sports reporters as superficial and unprofessional. You now are writing a syndicated column for newspapers. Is it your opinion that print sports reporters are not adequately prepared to cover the complex issues that face them on the job?

Howard Cosell: I would say in general that that is true. Print sports reporters are not prepared, in general, either by experience or by education, to deal with the multiple complexities that are involved in covering today's sports.

Q: Why do you say that?

Cosell: Today a sports reporter must be a kind of renaissance man. He must be knowledgeable in all areas of life that touch sports: the law, politics, economics, sociology, academics, the medical health of the society. And, in my view, sports reporters generally are not prepared for that sort of challenge. I know there are exceptions—a handful of sports journalists who are prepared for it.

Q: Is it your view that sports reporters for newspapers aren't interested in stories that might lead them into controversy?

Cosell: For most of them, the whole concern is the game—merely what happens in the arena; the wins and the losses. But now, so much more is involved in covering the world of sports.

Q: Of course, most readers are interested primarily in the game. Fans don't want to read bad news about their college team or the professional franchise.

Cosell: I know that. And it takes courage for a reporter to face the reality of that. So courage is one dimension a reporter must have. Educational background is another dimension. Reporting must be lodged in an understanding of moral values. Television reporters especially—but newspaper reporters too—give little or no thought to these basic values.

Q: But is society interested in sports reporters moralizing?

Cosell: It isn't a question of moralizing. It is a question of honest reporting. Listen, most people are taught from birth that sport is pure. Well, it isn't pure. There is no question about that. Most people are indoctrinated to believe that the game is what is important; that winning the game is everything; that winning, in fact, is the only thing. Win at any cost. Reporters who become indoctrinated with that do themselves and their readers a disservice.

Q: The Lexington *Herald-Leader* in Kentucky won the Pulitzer Prize this year for reporting critically on sports at the University of Kentucky.

Cosell: Yes. And that paper understood the meaning of real values. But the people in Lexington were caught up with the idea of the game as the all-

---

Source: ASNE Bulletin, September–October 1986. Reprinted with permission.

important thing. That is a terrible postulate and it affects too much of our society.

That is the attitude in too many places. And there is too little concern with what should be real values in sports: honesty, decency, morality. When the media fails to address standards then our whole sports world is turned upside down.

Q: Is it your view that sports reporters are too close to those who manage and play the game: coaches, players, managers, athletic directors, league officials, professional owners?

Cosell: Of course they are. In most cases the reporters' employers expect the journalist to get close and stay close. Again, it is more the rule in television. But it is true in print as well. Television is committed to *X* number of hours of sports programming. And so television enters into a partnership with a sports operator. They don't hire people to report on the sports whose criticism would damage the partnership. So you have what I call "jockocracy," which is the jock, or the former jock, filling the role of sports reporter. They aren't journalists. They protect the partnership.

Q: Are you suggesting that print reporters are involved in that sort of partnership?

Cosell: No. But a partnership. If the reporters don't go along, sources dry up. They often become cheerleaders for the team. Or the league. The National Football League is the best example of what I am talking about. The NFL has almost total control over the sports press in this country. The NFL has a director of communications named Joe Brown. He puts out releases and they are copied, almost word-for-word, by some writers who put their by-lines on what Brown gives them. The league intimidates reporters and they get that control. They threaten. A good example: They tried to threaten Brian Burwell of the New York *Daily News,* who did an honest job in covering the recent trial between the NFL and the USFL. Burwell was not a lawyer, but he worked hard, studied hard, consulted with lawyers and wrote things that were critical of the NFL. They let him know in no uncertain terms that he wouldn't get any more stories and that he could forget the National Football League. They called Gil Spencer, the editor, and tried to pressure him. But the *Daily News* supported Burwell. So there are exceptions.

Q: In your view, is professional baseball less offensive than pro football in seeking to compromise sports reporters?

Cosell: Well, the owners, generally speaking, create the same sorts of problems for reporters. But because of the integrity of, first, Bowie Kuhn as commissioner of baseball and now Pete Ueberroth, his successor, there has not been nearly so much of that sort of conduct. Baseball, then, is less preemptive of the reporter's integrity.

But you know, newspaper editors often deal differently with sports reporters and other journalists in other departments of the paper.

Q: How so?

Cosell: Well, for example, television critics in the news and feature sections of the paper criticize the performances they see on television. But not in sports. You get nothing but raves when a sports reporter comments on the performance of the jocks as journalists. For example, a recent column in the New York *Post* praised Frank Gifford for excellent and total preparation. Any knowledgeable person who watched Gifford's performance knew that the rave wasn't justified.

Q: So you say that sports reporting too often gives the readers and the owners what they want?

Cosell: Yes, and the result is that they come to live for "the team." That, too often, is the reporters' mentality. Look at what happened in New York with regard to the problems four Mets players had with the law enforcement authorities in Houston. Why, the reaction was crazed. And the media did nothing to provide sanity. People were wearing T-shirts that read: "Houston Police 4; the Mets 0." The charge was "police brutality" by people who knew nothing about what had occurred in Houston. When players are involved with the police they have to face up to the requirements of the law. The police chief in Houston is a remarkable black man with an outstanding record in Fresno, Calif., then in San Jose, Calif., then in Atlanta. Then he goes into Houston, the fourth largest market in this nation, and his good name is smeared with a charge of police brutality. That's awful. You'd think that somebody would ask what the hell those four Mets players were doing in a bar at 3 A.M. Not that any citizen doesn't have a right to be in a bar anytime it is open to the public. I could have been there. But if the media is going to raise questions about police conduct it ought to raise questions about the players' conduct. And the media ought to help due process take its course in a case like this. But what happened? The Mets writers, some of them, have indicted an entire police department and its chief for police brutality when they weren't there, don't know what happened, didn't see what happened. It just says something about the power and the value of a sports franchise in a city.

Q: Well, sometimes sports journalists are attacked by players who think that the reporting is unfair, intrusive into private lives, critical of errors on the field.

Cosell: Well, generally, that sort of journalistic criticism has to do, once more, with "the game." There are personal vendettas by the sports reporters. For example, in New York they love the New York Mets. But they hate George Steinbrenner. It is always criticism that is leveled at him on a personal basis. And it almost always is criticism that relates to the game, wins and losses. Narrow, one-dimensional reporting produces that sort of coverage of sports.

Q: Any exceptions come to mind? Can you name reporters who you think do an outstanding job?

Cosell: Well, there is a sportswriter in Atlanta, David Kindred, formerly with the Washington *Post,* who is probably doing the best job in the country in dealing with the larger issues that should be addressed by all sports journalists. He is equipped to do the job. Then, in Los Angeles, you have Jim Murray, who is a satirist. He deals with the issues in a different way. And there is an extraordinary writer, now in television, who is perhaps better informed and better able than anybody to address these important issues. His name is Robert Lipsyte. He wrote maybe the best sports-related book ever published, *Sportsworld: An American Dreamland.* It sold all of about 2,000 copies. The public is not attuned to accept it. But there are some journalists who have the talent to do it and who are making the effort.

Q: What about your own book. It was a best-seller. It was critical. People read it.

Cosell: Don't ask me how or why. I'm still befuddled by it.

Q: Let me ask you what you think reporters should be doing in exposing the problems of drugs in sports.

Cosell: Well, in Maryland, reporters should be focusing on the travesty of Lefty Driesell. There was no indictment, but indictment in the Bias case is irrelevant. Lefty should have been ordered to leave that university by the chancellor, who is a man who has become a mockery in education. The student body should have been exhorted by the press to demand Driesell's departure. The university and Driesell must be exposed in the manner I am doing it in my column because decent, honest kids who went to that school deserve a school that isn't tarnished by something like this tragedy. That's the kind of thing that should be written about. Reporters should be on that campus talking to those students; getting their view of it. And reporters in other communities where there are schools with drug problems should not fail to report on the situation.

Q: Do you think your legal education helped you as a sports journalist?

Cosell: It was of tremendous help. And, of course, majoring in journalism was of great value.

Q: If you were advising a young man or woman entering college and interested in pursuing a career in sports journalism, what courses of study would you recommend?

Cosell: A broad-based liberal arts degree, as an undergraduate, and then a graduate degree in journalism. And I would recommend the Medill

School. Or Columbia. There are some outstanding graduate programs in journalism.

Q: Do you look upon your syndicated column as a means to write critically about some of these other issues in sports?

Cosell: Absolutely. It is the best forum I've ever had. I'm proud of the Emmys that my television show, *Sports World,* has won. I am proud that it has just won another Emmy for the program on point-shaving. Digger Phelps, from Notre Dame, told me that he shows it to the members of his team as a means of communicating with them about this evil. But I never had the time on television to do all that I wanted to do. The column is the best vehicle I have ever had to say the things I wanted to say.

A NEW LOOK AT THE NEW JOURNALISM

Sharon M. Murphy and James E. Murphy

Loosened-up writing styles and a more personal approach to reporting characterize the New Journalism. This article from *The Quill* discusses its values and goals. Sharon M. Murphy is journalism dean at Marquette University. James E. Murphy died in 1983.

The reaction to Janet Cooke's infamous "Jimmy's World" hoax found summary in a 180-page book, *After "Jimmy's World": Tightening Up in Editing,* published by the National News Council. NNC chairman Norman Isaacs prefaced the book by decrying journalistic changes over the past two decades and wrote of the wrenching experiences caused by "the so-called 'New Journalism' which was an amalgam of impressions, personal feelings, social biases and imaginative and manipulative uses of fictional techniques, including the broad use of unnamed, and sometimes nonexistent, sources." Isaacs called for an end to the "permissiveness and arrogance" of the New Journalism. The rest of the NNC report was itself an extended analysis and vindication of the system, with veteran viewpoints and traditional conventions invoked to prevent "Jimmy's World" from ever happening again. The key seemed to be reassertion of stronger editorial control, intensive scrutiny of reporters' products, and universal acknowledgment of New Journalism's evils.

But a closer look at this style so vehemently inveighed against could be instructive—and even provocative of valuable reflection on just what it is we say we do, either as journalists or as educators of prospective journalists. As a literary genre, New Journalism can point to some basics of journalism all too infrequently and superficially considered. It raises serious questions about the social roles, functions, and responsibilities of journalists and, by extension, of journalism educators. And in doing so it focuses, perhaps most noticeably, on the conventional ethic we call objectivity. This essay offers two perspectives on the New Journalism as an attempt to balance the objectivity discussion.

One is its literary face. Using dramatic, "fictional" literary techniques in non-fiction, it has offered alternatives to and often improvements of conventional reporting. Magazine and book-length journalism by Talese, Wolfe, Capote, and others in the 1960s promoted a freer, more affective and impressionistic style than did conventional news and feature writing. The more individualized approach and style it represented and the use of techniques ranging from scene construction to dialog, from detailed description to metaphor and image found their way into much non-fiction writing. But the New Journalism probably was less a cause than a symbol of the loosening up in reportorial styles. It might be seen as one response to calls by editors, writers, and critics for humanizing reporting, greater depth of interpretation. It could be seen as a response to increasing reader sophistication and a growing public desire for the dramatic involvement that other media forms (notably television) provide.

Source: Reprinted from the April 1984 issue of *The Quill* with the permission of *The Quill* and the authors.

Writers who rejected formula-bound writing styles and experimented more widely with unique approaches found at least initially positive reinforcement from editors for the interesting copy they were producing. However uneven the quality of their work, they were pioneers in a more "literary" reportorial product. Their "journalit," Seymour Krim's apt albeit cute term, blurred distinctions between fiction and non-fiction. In many ways the blurring reflected a more honest assessment of journalistic insights. Reporters tell what they (think they) see happening. They write the facts (as their perspectives and biases and backgrounds and assignments suggest they write). And they see these facts according to their own interior programming, according to the principles of importance and interest and drama each takes to viewing the world. The difference may be that writers in the New Journalism mode admit their biases and work openly amid them.

One can also reflect on New Journalism from the viewpoint of its epistemology. In that sense, in considering one's world-view or philosophical stance vis-à-vis the "report" in a social context, the phenomenon offers more challenge—and more instruction. Journalistic experiments in the 1960s suggested serious questions about the rationale and the validity of conventional reporting forms. They spotlighted dissatisfaction with such industry conventions as the formalized news lead and the summary "five W's"; the almost cavalier notion of absolutes in news values and news selection; the sometimes incestuous relationships with official sources of information. These and other elements had developed during the past century or more and had come to be viewed as natural means of gathering, conceptualizing, and presenting the "news." The New Journalistic style put the spotlight on some of these sacred conventions, raising questions about just what constituted "truth," "objectivity," "accuracy," and "balance."

The writers not only reported, they wrote about reporting. Reporting became the subject of their work, just as reporting and other aspects of journalism became the subjects of journalism reviews which sprang up in many parts. This "metajournalism" held "regular" journalism up to reflection. It philosophized. It questioned, through various literary tricks, the kind of journalism that did not use such techniques.

In Tom Wolfe's "saturation reporting," intensive reportage replaced extensive. Gay Talese developed "interior monolog" to report on the thoughts of his subjects. Hunter Thompson used anti-journalistic scatology and injected himself into his reports. Joan Didion's first-person mood pieces used story and image to depict the drama of an era. These and other New Journalists reflected their reporting backgrounds as they took unique approaches to non-fiction. Norman Mailer and Truman Capote brought to journalism backgrounds in fiction and belles-lettres. Capote claimed invention of the "non-fiction novel" *(In Cold Blood),* and Mailer subtitled his *Armies of the Night* "The Novel as History; History as the Novel." Regardless of background, they and their colleagues tried to extend the boundaries of journalism (or "non-fiction"), all the while questioning its limits and its formulas.

Joseph Webb called the New Journalists Romantic (as opposed to Rationalist) reporters. Their Romantic orientation was one of diversity, dynamism, holism—in contrast to rationalist reporting, which emphasized uniformity, statism, atomism. John Merrill called the Romantics "existential journalists," and saw them challenging the journalistic establishment by emphasizing individuality, commitment, and personal responsibility. The Romantics looked for interpretation, re-definition, deep-down meaning. They tried to be the eyes and ears and emotions for their audiences who could not read the data nor feel the heat nor see the tears. They tried to convey, as Malcolm MacLean had said reporters ought to, "what it means to be poor among the rich, to be hungry among the well-fed, to be black among the white . . . to be unheard, unheard, unheard . . . in a society noisy with messages."

Their work can be more clearly analyzed

through three key concepts. First is the concept of the journalist as storyteller. But stories, however they are described and however they are dissected, have myth-making characteristics, metaphorical elements. People tell stories to make sense. Journalists are taught to "get the story," to use drama, description, human interest. That's what earns editorial praise, Pulitzers, star status—and readership. So, for example, a war becomes a drama about good and evil, about personal rights, about conflict itself. Reporters, in fact the entire journalistic establishment, become dramaturgists, scripting and allowing the enactment of human dramas before the entire reading and viewing world. The more chaotic and incomprehensible society becomes, the greater the importance of storytelling and myth-making via the media.

A second concept is that of news construction. Scholars have created a large body of literature on the journalistic construction of reality. The somewhat naive perception of news as "natural" ("That's the way it is . . .") has given way to a hesitant recognition of news as a socially constructed and manipulated "reality," a commodity to be sold like any other in the marketplace. And, to paraphrase one prominent anchorman, "News is what I say it is," and what his network sells nightly, in competition with other networks and other media. It is constructed, selected, assessed, and packaged for audience consumption.

The third concept requires a more critical epistemology. In New Journalism, such an epistemology can be framed as follows: The distinction between "fact" and "fiction" is shaky at best and is not useful in distinguishing between literature and journalism. If, indeed, the current practice of journalism (whatever the medium) is storytelling, and news is constructed reality, then it can also be acknowledged that to dichotomize literature as fictional and journalism as factual is an oversimplification.

Sixty years ago Walter Lippmann called the journalistic report a "joint product of the knower and known, in which the role of the observer is always selective and usually creative." Such an attitude, expressed by a renowned journalist and scholar, can be disputed only in relation to a naive world-view that sees "facts" as the same as "truth," and that would define the world outside oneself as the same for everybody, and knowable "as it is." Such a way of conceiving reality also makes little sense of differing versions of the same presidential press conference, or political convention or international event. Whose "story" can readers believe? Or might several stories be believable even if they look different?

In commenting on the Cooke debacle, Ben Bradlee, *The Washington Post*'s executive editor, told the National News Council, "The truth is not something that can be grasped. It is revealed in increments. There may be more truth in the Jimmy story than we are acknowledging." But little attention was paid to his comment. It seems to have gone unheeded. The rest of the report called for retrenchment, a "return to the basics." Yet Bradlee's remark bore similarities to ideals stressed when the Twentieth Century Fund Task Force made its proposal for a national news council. It called the proposal "A Free and Responsive Press." Decades earlier the Hutchins Commission had titled its report "A Free and Responsible Press," and stressed the concept of social responsibility as a commitment for journalists. In both cases, emphasis was on reflective response to issues, events, and ideas.

When cities across the country exploded in racial unrest in the late 1960s, journalists and their critics raised questions of media responsiveness to people's ignorance about the poor and oppressed in America. A great deal of talking and breast-beating went on for a while, and some changes seemed to be taking place: a minor increase in minority representation on news media rosters; questioning of patterns of coverage and treatment of non-majority issues. But it was hard to keep reflecting on ideals while there were deadlines to meet and products to produce and bottom lines to contend with. So the dilemma was one of pointing to social responsibility and the people's need to know while yet risking offense to targeted audiences and endangering efficiency of operation and financial base.

One change that the New Journalism phenomenon suggests is a return to individual journalistic responsibility, in a rediscovery of moral journalism—not in industry-protecting codes of ethics but in personal accountability. And the implication that grows out of that is for more social concern and less "professionalism" in the media, the "resurrection of the journalist and the death of the reporter," as Robert Fortner has argued so well.

We may have to admit that the noble picture of objective journalism painted for students and the consuming public is misleading and self-serving. Demands for objectivity can be thinly disguised abrogations of the roles of social critic, watchdog for the public good, keeper of the flame of truth. Objective reporting is often more aptly defined as conveyance of facts with the pretense of absolute impartiality. Or, as one veteran black journalist, Ed Blackwell, wrote in 1974, it may be the way we make peace with situations with which we do not agree but which we are unwilling to do anything about.

Of course, we cannot tolerate sloppy, lazy, self-centered, "anything goes" journalism, even if it tries to call itself "new journalism." Nor can we accept dishonesty and lack of depth. But we must, in the classroom and the newsroom, go beyond the rigid, monolithic reporting and writing patterns that still pervade the textbooks (many written with or by practicing journalists), the classrooms, and the newsrooms.

Until naive world-views and narrow conceptions of the mass media's social functions and economic imperatives are faced up to and re-defined, there can be little hope of improvement. And technology is not the answer.

The best New Journalism of the past two decades offers some patterns for a needed transformation. They are not the answer. There is no single answer or best approach. But they illustrate approaches to moral responsibility and personal commitment to truth. They offer little comfort and less complacency. But perhaps in the ambiguity and un-ease they promote may be hope for reflection, re-definition, growth, and improvement.

OBJECTIVITY PRECLUDES RESPONSIBILITY

Theodore L. Glasser

Objectivity as the standard for news reporting is criticized by Theodore L. Glasser, who contends, in *The Quill,* "Objective reporting has transformed journalism into something more technical than intellectual." Glasser teaches journalism at the University of Minnesota.

By objectivity I mean a particular view of journalism and the press, a frame of reference used by journalists to orient themselves in the newsroom and in the community. By objectivity I mean, to a degree, ideology; where ideology is defined as a set of beliefs that function as the journalist's "claim to action."

As a set of beliefs, objectivity appears to be rooted in a positivist view of the world, an enduring commitment to the supremacy of observable and retrievable facts. This commitment, in turn, impinges on news organizations' principal commodity—the day's news. Thus my argument, in part, is this: Today's news is indeed biased—as it must inevitably be—and this bias can be best understood by understanding the concept, the conventions, and the ethic of objectivity.

Specifically, objectivity in journalism accounts for—or at least helps us understand—three principal developments in American journalism; each of these developments contributes to the bias or ideology of news. First, objective reporting is biased against what the press typically defines as its role in a democracy—that of a Fourth Estate, the watchdog role, an adversary press. Indeed, objectivity in journalism is biased in favor of the status quo; it is inherently conservative to the extent that it encourages reporters to rely on what sociologist Alvin

Source: Reprinted from the February 1984 issue of *The Quill* with the permission of *The Quill* and the author.

Gouldner so appropriately describes as the "managers of the status quo"—the prominent and the élite. Second, objective reporting is biased against independent thinking; it emasculates the intellect by treating it as a disinterested spectator. Finally, objective reporting is biased against the very idea of responsibility; the day's news is viewed as something journalists are compelled to report, not something they are responsible for creating.

This last point, I think, is most important. Despite a renewed interest in professional ethics, the discussion continues to evade questions of morality and responsibility. Of course, this doesn't mean that journalists are immoral. Rather, it means that journalists today are largely amoral. Objectivity in journalism effectively erodes the very foundation on which rests a responsible press.

By most any of the many accounts of the history of objectivity in journalism, objective reporting began more as a commercial imperative than as a standard of responsible reporting. With the emergence of a truly popular press in the mid-1800s—the penny press—a press tied neither to the political parties nor the business élite, objectivity provided a presumably disinterested view of the world.

But the penny press was only one of many social, economic, political, and technological forces that converged in the mid- and late-1800s to bring about fundamental and lasting changes in American journalism. There was the advent of the telegraph, which for the first time separated communication from transportation. There were radical changes in printing technology, including the steam-powered press and later the rotary press. There was the formation of the Associated Press, an early effort by publishers to monopolize a new technology—in this case the telegraph. There was, finally, the demise of community and the rise of society; there were now cities, "human settlements" where "strangers are likely to meet."

These are some of the many conditions that created the climate for objective reporting, a climate best understood in terms of the emergence of a new mass medium and the need for that medium to operate efficiently in the marketplace.

Efficiency is the key term here, for efficiency is the central meaning of objective reporting. It was efficient for the Associated Press to distribute only the "bare facts," and leave the opportunity for interpretation to individual members of the cooperative. It was efficient for newspapers not to offend readers and advertisers with partisan prose. It was efficient—perhaps expedient—for reporters to distance themselves from the sense and substance of what they reported.

To survive in the marketplace, and to enhance their status as a new and more democratic press, journalists—principally publishers, who were becoming more and more removed from the editing and writing process—began to transform efficiency into a standard of professional competence, a standard later—several decades later—described as objectivity. This transformation was aided by two important developments in the early twentieth century: first, Oliver Wendell Holmes's effort to employ a marketplace metaphor to define the meaning of the First Amendment; and second, the growing popularity of the scientific method as the proper tool with which to discover and understand an increasingly alien reality.

In a dissenting opinion in 1919, Holmes popularized "the marketplace of ideas," a metaphor introduced by John Milton several centuries earlier. Metaphor or not, publishers took it quite literally. They argued—and continue with essentially the same argument today—that their opportunity to compete and ultimately survive in the marketplace is their First Amendment right, a Constitutional privilege. The American Newspaper Publishers Association, organized in 1887, led the cause of a free press. In the name of freedom of the press, the ANPA fought the Pure Food and Drug Act of 1906 on behalf of its advertisers; it fought the Post Office Act of 1912, which compelled sworn statements of ownership and circulation and thus threatened to reveal too much to advertisers; it fought efforts to regulate child labor, which would interfere with the control and exploitation of paper boys; it fought the collective bargaining provisions of the National Recovery Act in the mid-1930s; for similar reasons, it stood opposed to the American Newspaper Guild, the reporters' union; it tried—unsuccessfully—to prevent wire services from selling news to radio stations until after publication in the nearby newspaper.

Beyond using the First Amendment to shield and protect their economic interests in the marketplace, publishers were also able to use the canons of science to justify—indeed, legitimize—the canons of objective reporting. Here publishers were comforted by Walter Lippmann's writings in the early 1920s, particularly his plea for a new scientific journalism, a new realism; a call for journalists to remain "clear and free" of their irrational, their unexamined, their unacknowledged prejudgments.

By the early 1900s objectivity had become the acceptable way of doing reporting—or at least the respectable way. It was respectable because it was reliable, and it was reliable because it was standardized. In practice, this meant a preoccupation with *how* the news was presented, whether its *form* was reliable. And this concern for reliability quickly overshadowed any concern for the validity of the realities the journalists presented.

Thus emerged the conventions of objective reporting, a set of routine procedures journalists use to objectify their news stories. These are the conventions sociologist Gaye Tuchman describes as a kind of strategy journalists use to deflect criticism, the same kind of strategy social scientists use to defend the quality of their work. For the journalist, this means interviews with sources; and it ordinarily means official sources with impeccable credentials. It means juxtaposing conflicting truth-claims, where truth-claims are reported as "fact" regardless of their validity. It means making a judgment about the news value of a truth-claim even if that judgment serves only to lend authority to what is known to be false or misleading.

As early as 1924 objectivity appeared as an ethic, an ideal subordinate only to truth itself. In his study of the *Ethics of Journalism,* Nelson Crawford devoted three full chapters to the principles of objectivity. Thirty years later, in 1954, Louis Lyons, then curator for the Nieman Fellowship program at Harvard, was describing objectivity as a "rock-bottom" imperative. Apparently unfazed by Wisconsin's Senator Joseph McCarthy, Lyons portrayed objectivity as the ultimate discipline of journalism. "It is at the bottom of all sound reporting—indispensable as the core of the writer's capacity." More recently, in 1973, the Society of Professional Journalists, Sigma Delta Chi, formally enshrined the idea of objectivity when it adopted as part of its Code of Ethics a paragraph characterizing objective reporting as an attainable goal and a standard of performance toward which journalists should strive. "We honor those who achieve it," the Society proclaimed.

So well ingrained are the principles of objective reporting that the judiciary is beginning to acknowledge them. In a 1977 federal appellate decision, *Edwards* v. *National Audubon Society,* a case described by media attorney Floyd Abrams as a landmark decision in that it may prove to be the next evolutionary stage in the development of the public law of libel, a new and novel privilege emerged. It was the first time the courts explicitly recognized objective reporting as a standard of journalism worthy of First Amendment protection.

In what appeared to be an inconsequential story published in *The New York Times* in 1972—on page 33—five scientists were accused of being paid liars, men paid by the pesticide industry to lie about the use of DDT and its effect on bird life. True to the form of objective reporting, the accusation was fully attributed—to a fully identified official of the National Audubon Society. The scientists, of course, were given an opportunity to deny the accusation. Only one of the scientists, however, was quoted by name and he described the accusation as "almost libelous." What was newsworthy about the story, obviously, was the accusation; and with the exception of one short paragraph, the reporter more or less provided a forum for the National Audubon Society.

Three of the five scientists filed suit. While denying punitive damages, a jury awarded compensatory damages against the *Times* and one of the Society's officials. The *Times,* in turn, asked a federal District Court to overturn the verdict. The *Times* argued that the "actual malice" standard had not been met; since the scientists were "public figures," they were required to show that the *Times* knowingly published a falsehood or there was, on the part of the *Times,* a reckless disregard for whether the accusation was true or false. The evidence before the court clearly indicated the latter—there was indeed a reckless disregard for whether the accusation was true or false. The reporter made virtually no effort to confirm the validity of the National Audubon Society's accusations. Also the story wasn't the kind of "hot news" (a technical term used by the courts) that required immediate dissemination; in fact, ten days before the story was published the *Times* learned that two of the five scientists were not employed by the pesticide industry and thus could not have been "paid liars."

The *Times* appealed to the Second Circuit Court of Appeals, where the lower court's decision was overturned. In reversing the District Court, the Court of Appeals created a new First Amendment right, a new Constitutional defense in libel law—the privilege of "neutral reportage." "We do not believe," the Court of Appeals ruled, "that the press may be required to suppress newsworthy statements merely because it has serious doubts regarding their truth." The First Amendment, the Court said, "protects the accurate and disinterested reporting" of newsworthy accusations "regardless of the reporter's private views regarding their validity."

I mention the details of the *Edwards* case only because it illustrates so well the consequences of the ethic of objectivity. First, it illustrates a very basic tension between objectivity and responsibility. Objective reporting virtually precludes responsible reporting, if by responsible reporting we mean a willingness on the part of the reporter to be accountable for what is reported. Objectivity requires only that reporters be accountable for *how* they report, not what they report. The *Edwards* Court made this very clear: "The public interest in being fully informed," the Court said, demands that the press be afforded the freedom to report newsworthy accusations "without assuming responsibility for them."

Second, the *Edwards* case illustrates the unfortunate bias of objective reporting—a bias in favor of leaders and officials, the prominent and the élite. It is an unfortunate bias because it runs counter to the important democratic assumption that statements made by ordinary citizens are as valuable as statements made by the prominent and the élite. In a democracy, public debate depends on separating individuals from their powers and privileges in the larger society; otherwise debate itself becomes a source of domination. But *Edwards* reinforces prominence as a news value; it reinforces the use of official sources, official records, official channels. Tom Wicker underscored the bias of the *Edwards* case when he observed recently that "objective journalism almost always favors Establishment positions and exists not least to avoid offense to them."

Objectivity also has unfortunate consequences for the reporter, the individual journalist. Objective reporting has stripped reporters of their creativity and their imagination; it has robbed journalists of their passion and their perspective. Objective reporting has transformed journalism into something more technical than intellectual; it has turned the art of story-telling into the technique of report writing. And most unfortunate of all, objective reporting has denied journalists their citizenship; as disinterested observers, as impartial reporters, journalists are expected to be morally disengaged and politically inactive.

Journalists have become—to borrow James Carey's terminology—"professional communicators," a relatively passive link between sources and audiences. With neither the need nor the opportunity to develop a critical perspective from which to assess the events, the issues, and the personalities he or she is assigned to cover, the objective reporter tends to function as a translator—translating the specialized language of sources into a language intelligible to a lay audience.

In his frequently cited study of Washington correspondents—a study published nearly fifty years ago—Leo Rosten found that a "pronounced majority" of the journalists he interviewed considered themselves inadequate to cope with the bewildering complexities of our nation's policies and politics. As Rosten described it, the Washington press corps was a frustrated and exasperated group of prominent journalists more or less resigned to their role as mediators, translators. "To do the job," one reporter told Rosten, "what you know or understand isn't important. You've got to know whom to ask." Even if you don't understand what's being said, Rosten was told, you just take careful notes and write it up verbatim: "Let my readers figure it out. I'm their reporter, not their teacher."

That was fifty years ago. Today, the story is pretty much the same. Two years ago another study of Washington correspondents was published, a book by Stephen Hess called *The Washington Reporters.* For the most part, Hess found, stories coming out of Washington were little more than a "mosaic of facts and quotations from sources" who were participants in an event or who had knowledge of the event. Incredibly, Hess found that for nearly three-quarters of the stories he studied, reporters relied on no documents—only interviews. And when reporters did use documents, those documents were typically press clippings—stories they had written or stories written by their colleagues.

And so what does objectivity mean? It means that sources supply the sense and substance of the day's news. Sources provide the arguments, the rebuttals, the explanations, the criticism. Sources put forth the ideas while other sources challenge those ideas. Journalists, in their role as professional communicators, merely provide a vehicle for these exchanges.

But if objectivity means that reporters must maintain a healthy distance from the world they report, the same standard does not apply to publishers. According to the SPJ,SDX Code of Ethics, "Journalists and their employers should conduct their personal lives in a manner which protects them from conflict of interest, real or apparent." Many journalists do just that—they avoid even an appearance of a conflict of interest. But certainly not their employers.

If it would be a conflict of interest for a reporter to accept, say, an expensive piano from a source at the Steinway Piano Company, it apparently wasn't a conflict of interest when CBS purchased the Steinway Piano Company.

Publishers and broadcasters today are part of a large and growing and increasingly diversified industry. Not only are many newspapers owned by corporations that own a variety of non-media properties, but their boards of directors read like a *Who's Who* of the powerful and the élite. A recent study of the twenty-five largest newspaper companies found that the directors of these companies tend to be linked with "powerful business organizations, not with public interest groups; with management, not with labor; with well established think tanks and charities, not their grassroots counterparts."

But publishers and broadcasters contend that these connections have no bearing on how the day's news is reported—as though the ownership of a newspaper had no bearing on the newspaper's content; as though business decisions have no effect on editorial decisions; as though it wasn't economic considerations in the first place that brought about the incentives for many of the conventions of contemporary journalism.

No doubt the press has responded to many of the more serious consequences of objective reporting. But what is significant is that the response has been to amend the conventions of objectivity, not to abandon them. The press has merely refined the canons of objective reporting; it has not dislodged them.

What remains fundamentally unchanged is the journalist's naively empirical view of the world, a belief in the separation of facts and values, a belief in the existence of *a* reality—the reality of empirical facts. Nowhere is this belief more evident than when news is defined as something external to—and independent of—the journalist. The very vocabulary used by journalists when they talk about news underscores their belief that news is "out there," presumably waiting to be *exposed* or *uncovered* or at least *gathered.*

This is the essence of objectivity, and this is precisely why it is so very difficult for journalism to consider questions of ethics and morality. Since news exists "out there"—apparently independent of the reporter—journalists can't be held responsible for it. And since they are not responsible for the news being there, how can we expect journalists to be accountable for the consequences of merely reporting it?

What objectivity has brought about, in short, is a disregard for the consequences of newsmaking. A few years ago Walter Cronkite offered this interpretation of journalism: "I don't think it is any of our business what the moral, political, social, or economic effect of our reporting is. I say let's go with the job of reporting—and let the chips fall where they may."

Contrast that to John Dewey's advice: that "our chief moral business is to become acquainted with consequences."

I am inclined to side with Dewey. Only to the extent that journalists are held accountable for the consequences of their actions can there be said to be a responsible press. But we are not going to be able to hold journalists accountable for the consequences of their actions until they acknowledge that news is their creation, a creation for which they are fully responsible. And we are not going to have much success convincing journalists that news is created, not reported, until we can successfully challenge the conventions of objectivity.

The task, then, is to liberate journalism from the burden of objectivity by demonstrating—as convincingly as we can—that objective reporting is more of a custom than a principle, more a habit of mind than a standard of performance. And by showing that objectivity is largely a matter of efficiency—efficiency that serves, as far as I can tell, only the needs and interest of the owners of the press, not the needs and interests of talented writers and certainly not the needs and interests of the larger society.

DOONESBURY VS. PRESIDENT REAGAN

Garry Trudeau

After an extended time-out period, cartoonist Garry Trudeau, creator of the satirical *Doonesbury* comic, returned to newspapers at the height of the 1984 presidential campaign. Many of the strips bitingly criticized President Reagan, bringing complaints from some editors. Trudeau explained his point of view to the Associated Press Managing Editors Association.

The great majority of you seemed to have gritted your teeth through reader protests you had over what has been called my endless pillorying of the Reagan-Bush record. For your forbearance, I thank you. To those of you who sympathized with readers who found my strips unbalanced, a plea for understanding: Satirists are supposed to be unbalanced in their work. They are supposed to be unfair. It's part of the job description. Telling a political satirist he's not fair is like telling a 290-pound NFL noseguard he's too physical.

Moreover, I would hope that a good case could be made for my political independence through the years. George Bush's assertion that I was carrying water for the Democrats would certainly be news to Tip O'Neill, Jimmy Carter and Jerry Brown, among others. Even John Anderson, whose early campaign I tracked in New Hampshire, alternatively embraced and rejected the Doonesbury connection, in apparent confusion over where I stood.

I have always tried to choose my targets strictly

on their individual merits. I would not exactly describe the floundering campaign of a presidential candidate 20 points behind in the polls as a "juicy target." Certainly, the Walter Mondale of the primaries would have made an inviting subject, but for the most part, cartoonists have always gravitated toward those in power, those who affect our lives most immediately.

A satirist by definition must stand in opposition to something. His only obligation, which I have always sought to honor, is to make his values felt through implication, not through naked advocacy. It is for this reason, among others, that I have tried to hold my own counsel through the years, to not project myself as a public personality, and to not submit to interviews that would inevitably allow the public to pigeonhole me, thus reducing my effectiveness. If this sounds a tad self-serious, I would encourage you to refer to some of my early interviews, or to even read the text of my speech before this group 12 years ago. Without the filter of my art, I am an uncontrolled fountain of pontification. Believe me, both *Doonesbury* and its readers are better off for my failure—in George Carlin's memorable words—to develop a lifestyle that actually requires my presence. It is enough of a chore to simply safeguard a reputation without having to worry about fame.

Independence, of course, is in the eye of the beholder, and I'm sure many of your readers felt I was being anything but independent during the weeks preceding the election. If the number of negative letters they chose to publish was any indication, some editors were clearly pleased to find they had readers who were every bit as irritated with me as they were, albeit for different reasons. One editor complained in an editorial that I shouldn't be writing about campaign politics so close to the election. When *else* would one write about campaign politics—*after* the election? Could this editor actually be agreeing with the reader who wrote, "Your comics pages have been politicized. . . . This is a blatant attempt to negatively influence the immature minds of the readers of the comics pages"?

To be honest, I was a little surprised by the vehemence of some reader reaction. After all, I said very little about Ronald Reagan that I hadn't already said, to a far more subdued response, only two years earlier. Moreover, it never occurred to me that I was under any formal obligation to lacerate Mondale simply for the sake of equal time. The FCC, thank God, has not yet begun to regulate satire—if it did, satire would be quickly transformed into simple humor, and humor and satire are not the same thing. Humor is all in good fun. Humor is what allows an Art Buchwald to have lunch with the people he writes about. Satire, on the other hand, is deadly earnest. The cartoonists I know who present "balanced attacks" are the same cartoonists who receive countless requests for original drawings from their victims. It is a ritual that appeals to the vanity of both parties. The cartoonists who make a real impact, on the other hand, tend to be those whose vanities are nurtured by the lack of requests.

The effective political satirist isn't in the business of making friends with the people he writes about. As a form of social control, he simply reacts to the agendas of those in positions of power or prominence. All the tools of his trade—distortion, caricature and ridicule—[militate] against endearment. Certainly, he has a formal obligation to try to entertain people, and to those of you who found the Reagan strips unfunny, I am truly sorry. You may inform your disgruntled readers that I will try harder during the next election, although I somehow doubt this will satisfy them.

Indeed, of the hundreds of letters to the editor that have been sent to me recently, almost all conveyed deep suspicions not only about my sense of humor, but also my lack of patriotism, my disrespect for the presidency, and my general negativism in an age of good feeling. Several threatened not only to switch papers, but also to change their morning news shows. [Trudeau is married to Jane Pauley, co-host of NBC's *Today* program.]

As far as I could tell, it wasn't what I said that infuriated such readers most, it was my impertinence in saying anything in the first place. The mere fact of Reagan's popularity was considered proof that I was out of line. It is true, of course, that the president seems to have fulfilled a deep yearning in this country to feel positively about ourselves as a people. And yet, the Reagan presidency very much reminds me of a remark made by a woman to sportscaster Heywood Broun following Secretariat's victories in the Triple Crown races. After the trauma of Vietnam and Watergate, she told Broun, Secretariat restored her faith in humanity.

I would submit to you that Ronald Reagan is the Secretariat of the '80s. He has restored our faith in ourselves as a people, and for that, we are all in his debt. It does not, however, entitle him to immunity from criticism from concerned citizens who love their country as much as he does.

I need not offer any bromides to this audience about the usefulness or need for alternative voices. It is, presumably, a major reason why you buy features like *Doonesbury* in the first place. For your patience and patronage, I thank you. I have always considered it an enormous privilege to be given a place in the nation's newspapers from which to voice my interests and concerns. I will try in the years ahead not to give you any further reason to regret your valued support.

MAGAZINES

MUSINGS OF A NEWSMAGAZINE EDITOR

Ray Cave

The corporate editor of Time Inc. and former managing editor of *Time* talks candidly about the issue of "what sells" versus "good journalism." He uses the sales record of *Time* covers to make his point. Cave also bemoans trivialization of the news.

There are two quite different subjects I would like to raise, following the old dinner party approach of having at least two topics of conversation ready. With luck one of them will interest your partner; then you end up seated next to an ornithologist from Nepal.

The first is a question I have thought and talked a lot about in recent years: "Is What Sells All That Different from Good Journalism?" Under this heading come Cheryl Tiegs and Madonna, cats and babies, cocaine, and herpes, and other stimulating matters.

The second is a vague idea that is just beginning to interest me—so vague that it is probably wrong. To wit: Are journalists themselves one of the greatest threats to our cherished "freedom of the press?"

"WHAT SELLS" VS. "GOOD JOURNALISM"

The issue of "what sells" vs. "good journalism" is often phrased in exactly this confrontational fashion, and a wise editor would sooner walk through a cow pasture barefoot than try and say something substantive on the subject. The public is convinced that journalists are in business to enrich themselves. This enrages journalists, who are equally convinced their *raison d'être* is the enrichment of the society. The truth, of course, is in between.

One man who got journalism's imperatives right was Harry Luce, when he said early on of *Time*'s efforts to report the news that it was in "the business of making a nickel and interpreting the world." Note that Luce put the nickel first. He appreciated an obvious fact in the argument: If you don't have a nickel, you have no way of reaching an audience at all.

Let me try to sneak three fastballs by you:

One, there is much less difference between "what sells" and "good journalism" than one might think.

Two, it is not what an editor puts on the pages of a publication that matters most. It is what comes off those pages into the minds of the readers.

And three, it is an editor's duty to give readers what they ought to read, not what they want to read. The most difficult task is to make them want to read what they ought to read.

Perhaps the primary responsibility of good journalism is to tell us about us, to illuminate the society in which we live, and to help us with that most difficult of all imperatives: Know thyself. For me, this has long muddied the question of "frivolous" covers on *Time.* I am often asked how a serious newsmagazine could do a cover on Madonna, on cats, on a fashion model. I would ask, How could

Source: Gannett Center Journal, Spring 1987. Reprinted with permission.

a serious newsmagazine not do such covers? News is what is happening in the society in which we live. News is what people are talking about, as well as what people should talk about, and it is a newsmagazine's responsibility to explain the phenomenon of Madonna as much as it is to explain the esoterica of arms control.

True, readers will more readily buy a cover they know they are curious about—Cheryl Tiegs, cocaine, the cats craze—than one they only fear they should be curious about—arms control. Less than five percent of *Time*'s U.S. circulation is newsstand sales, and impulse buying is not, in itself, a significant factor in *Time*'s editorial decision-making. But much can be learned from watching newsstand numbers closely. Here, in order, are the nine best-selling covers in my eight years as editor of *Time*:

12/4/78	The Jonestown Massacre
12/22/80	John Lennon's Murder
3/19/84	Michael Jackson
8/2/82	Herpes
3/6/78	Cheryl Tiegs
11/7/77	Richard Leakey
6/2/80	The Mt. St. Helens Eruption
2/27/78	Muhammed Ali
7/14/80	Aching Backs

. . . Of those nine, only three were news covers. And if one looks at the five best-selling covers year by year for the last ten years, a consistent pattern emerges; on average only one and a half is a news cover. The year 1985 was typical. The best-sellers in order were: *AIDS, Madonna, Dinosaurs, Miami Vice,* and *Hiroshima.* Of these, only AIDS had any element of serious news, and at that time AIDS was more a medicine story than a news story.

Indeed, after years of examining cover sales I came up with Cave's Cover Commandments:

1. Photographs sell better than art. Cartoons sell awful.
2. Girls sell better than boys.
3. Cocaine sells better than Coke.
4. Things that really pain me (my aching back) sell better than things that mentally anguish me (my empty wallet).
5. Things common to my experience (marijuana) sell better than things that will affect my experience (genetic engineering).
6. Politicians sell badly.
7. The economy sells worse.
8. Cities sell terribly.
9. Small towns sell worse. (Yes, I tried them both.)
10. Sports won't sell at all. (Exception: Muhammed Ali will always sell.)
11. Dead popes sell better than live popes sell better than wounded popes.
12. When in doubt, run Cheryl Tiegs. (I did twice, with gratifying results.)

Where does this kind of information lead you? If you are smart, it leads you nowhere. Once a year or so, some Time Inc. executive would fret to me about the magazine's newsstand sales. I always said the same thing: I can double them, and not shock your readers. Their eyes would light up, and then I would add the obvious—"of course, you will be out of business in five years."

In sum, *Time*'s strength is in the covers that don't sell best, ones that deal with significant social problems, geopolitical issues, and such. But at the same time, an editor must not spurn the ones that sell very well indeed. Such covers—by definition—are in a newsweekly's franchise. I contend they are—by definition—news. This dictum probably applies to many magazines. Their franchise dictates what they are, but editors should never get so precious and arrogant about it that they turn their backs on the "popular" and the "frivolous"; these are part of the franchise too.

My second pitch: What matters most is not what the editor puts into a publication, but what the reader takes away. And here, the great concern today is trivialization. We are all running out of time. The 24-hour day is proving not long enough. Our society is swamped with information, news opinion; hundreds of news magazines, thousands of hours of cable television, millions of video cassettes. It all descends on us—dawn to dawn. Only God can save us from circuit overload. We who are in the business of selling all this news and information are rightfully concerned. If our customers have less time, must we not give them what requires less time? Not just McPaper, but McMagazine, McNews? Shorter stories, punchier stuff, the quick hit? Journalistic freebasing? The circuits may be overloading, we argue, but we've got to get our share. So in the process, we trivialize the substantive. We signal to our readers something they, in a way, rather like to hear, namely: "This stuff really isn't important after all." If the very subject that should have been treated thoughtfully is McJournaled, abbreviated to the trivial, then isn't the editor saying to the reader that it really isn't worth his or her attention? The reader looks at what is on the page, and may find it interesting, titillating—but irrelevant. And so the reader, rightfully, takes nothing off the page and eventually—some day, some week—stops paying attention at all.

One way for editors to fight the trivialization trend is to think more about their readers than they do. When is a magazine read? What day? What hour? Under what circumstances? Why is it read? Do readers pay attention when they read it? No, I don't want any surveys about this. I hate reader surveys, and may be the only editor alive who has never attended a focus group. But it is essential to bear in mind that the readers—and only the readers—are the people who matter, not because we want to sell them magazines, but because we want to get something inside their heads. The medium is *not* the message. The message is the message. If I am an artist, I shouldn't care about who might buy my painting or for how much. But I should care desperately about what people think when they look at it. Too often, I fear, journalists perform for other journalists. They want the approval of their peers. What they should care about instead is the attention of their readers. If out of a given weekly issue of *Time* some of its 32 million readers remember one meaningful sentence, or are emotionally moved by one single passage of prose, or fully understand one difficult concept, just one, then the magazine has probably done its job that week.

Fastball number three is also about the difference between sizzle and steak. As editor, I make the choice of subject matter in a magazine, but I still must make the reader want to read it. In this respect the editor is a packager, a con man, a huckster and a whole lot of other things that journalists don't want to think they are.

For example, magazines and newspapers today must be visually appealing. It's that simple. We live in a visual era. Magazine design has improved immensely in the last ten years. At any major newsstand now there are 50, even 100, fine-looking magazines. Not so long ago, that number would have been ten. If a magazine is to survive as an editorial product, it must be thoughtfully designed, elegant, visually stimulating. Does this mean turning it over to the art director? Absolutely, unequivocally, no. Magazines dominated by art directors look as awful as magazines that have no art direction at all.

In a text magazine, the role of the picture is the same as that of a head, subhead or caption. It is there to entice the reader to read. *Time* is a text magazine. It has wonderful prizewinning pictures that often come at great cost to the magazine and sometimes at great personal risk to the photographer. But they are not the story. Conversely, a picture magazine must not be text driven. In it, the pictures are the story. An editor must have a clear vision of these distinctions. Admittedly, some magazines are truly a blend of pictures and text, but there the editor's responsibility is to make plain to the reader which element—text or pictures—is the most important for any given story. An effort to play the two equally will almost always fail.

A newsmagazine is more than the sum of its parts, and pacing is an increasingly significant aspect of magazine making. The reader must think that whoever put it together had a sense of the magazine from beginning to end. Why? Because this creates a subconscious awareness that the editors know what they are doing. And if they know what they are doing, they probably deserve attention.

Just when readers are totally comfortable with a

magazine—and if they are not comfortable, they will not be readers for long—you want to surprise them. Do what you don't do. Get them saying: "I've never seen them try that before." You may never try it again, but you surprise a magazine reader for the same reason you surprise a spouse—it is refreshing. It means "Don't you dare get bored with me." It means "You'd better pay attention." Incidentally, most of the time the journalists who work for the magazine will be firmly against such surprises. So the editor talks them into it.

So that's how readers get covers on cats and babies and Tiegs and Children of War and Madonna on a newsmagazine. We don't make the news at *Time,* but we define it for our readers, and sometimes we surprise them. If it all works, we get readers to want to read what they ought to read. And that is what we are paid for. In the process, we sell some magazines. That is secondary, but also what we are paid for. No nickel, no magazine.

ANOTHER THREAT TO FREEDOM OF THE PRESS

An enticing bit of heresy came to mind recently when I was asked to write a few paragraphs about the 200th anniversary of the Constitution and freedom of the press. Think what a great advantage it is to the press that it will never run out of anniversaries. Since the teaching of modern history virtually has been abandoned, journalists are among the few remaining practitioners of the craft. A *Time* cover on the 25th anniversary of D-Day not only sells very well, it replaces Miss Simpson, who once handled such matters in the seventh grade.

So what about "freedom of the press," a phrase that will be much repeated in this anniversary year? As comforting as those four words may be to journalists, they do not produce the same tranquillity in the public mind. "Freedom to do what?" is the question often asked, in the same tone of voice as the familiar "Who elected you?" Nobody elected us, of course, and "Freedom to do what?" is a fair question from a public seemingly annoyed by what it too often perceives as insensitivity, abuse of power and galling self-righteousness on the part of the press.

But if that is the instinctive reaction of many Americans to their press today, why do they, on reflection, seem so satisfied, and frequently even proud, that their Constitution has provided this sometimes maddening "freedom?"

The answer rests, I suspect, in a fundamental understanding that neither the American press nor the American people much care to state openly: The people are the press.

We journalists like to think we shape the dialogue and that the people then attend to what we say. There is truth in that, of course, but curiously there may be more truth in the opposite notion, that it is the people who set the press agenda. They tell us what is on their minds, what they need to know, what troubles and delights them. We listen, and in the main it is their concerns and their curiosities that we address. The American press today is a responsible and responsive institution, certainly compared with that of most other countries, and most journalists take this responsibility very seriously. Ours is far from the raucous, brawling press of 1787 that the drafters of the Constitution had in mind. But they never could have envisioned a press so much a part of the fabric of the nation that it could be considered, in a manner of speaking, the people themselves.

Which leads to a cautionary footnote. Is it possible, 200 years later, that the greatest threat to the Constitution's "freedom of the press" does not come from outsiders who would try to limit that freedom, but from our own unrecognized willingness to limit it ourselves? In the name of responsibility and responsiveness, we edit—perhaps even censor—ourselves. And we certainly must. But have we, for several reasons, become unwitting co-conspirators with the very institutions—the White House, government, the military, big business—that we are supposed to report upon? I do not think we have, but we get uncomfortably close. So the lesson is clear: Let us never forget that with "freedom of the press" comes a continuing obligation to exercise that freedom vigorously.

MOTION PICTURES

HOLLYWOOD'S BUSINESS

Douglas Gomery

Behind the glamor of Hollywood lies a hard-nosed world of deals and creative gambles—a world in which television and videocassettes have caused great changes. Douglas Gomery, associate professor of communication arts at University of Maryland, tells how the wheels of Hollywood turn in this 1986 inside look.

[A famous artist] is lunching poolside, amid the palm trees and exotic bird-of-paradise flowers. CBS News's Mike Wallace has already dashed off for a taping, but director Robert Benton is still sunning himself on one of the 200 chaise longues. Nearby, a young Paramount Pictures executive is poring over a script. Gossip hounds Susan Mulcahy of the *New York Post* and Barbara Howar of "Entertainment Tonight" are sniffing out stories. In a yellow-and-white striped cabana (rent: $35 per day), executives from Tri-Star Pictures shake hands on a new venture with a group of movie producers.

It is just another day, as the *Wall Street Journal* reported last year, at the Beverly Hills Hotel pool, long "the watering spot where movie stars and moguls meet to make deals." The hotel management even furnishes poolside secretarial service. In Hollywood legend, the Olympic-size pool (for hotel guests only; their visitors pay $10 for admission) rivals Schwab's Pharmacy as the place to go if you want to be "discovered." Even the pool's manager, Svend Peterson, has appeared on the big screen, in bit parts in *The Prize* (1963) and *Torn Curtain* (1966). He keeps his Screen Actors Guild membership current, just in case. Robert Evans, who became the producer of *Chinatown* (1974) and *The Cotton Club* (1984), was a women's clothing manufacturer until destiny plucked him from his Beverly Hills Hotel lounge chair three decades ago.

A mile or two down Sunset Boulevard is the University of California, Los Angeles (UCLA) film school, which emerged during the 1970s, along with the University of Southern California (USC) film school across town, as another launch pad for success. Enroll, Hollywood lore says, and before long the film school "mafia," led by George Lucas (B.A., USC, 1966) and Francis Ford Coppola (M.A., UCLA, 1968), will discover you.

Unfortunately, neither the "by-the-pool" nor the "at-school" method has ever produced a very high individual success rate. For anybody who really wants to make it to the top in Hollywood, who wants to be in a position to hire and fire the movie crowd at the Beverly Hills Hotel pool, there is a much clearer path: Go to law school, land a job with one of the conglomerates that dominate the movie business, and slowly work your way up.

THE $1 BILLION QUESTION

That is how Ted Tanen of Paramount Pictures and Frank G. Wells of Walt Disney Productions did it.

Hollywood's executives preside over an industry whose public profile far exceeds its economic heft. The annual net *profits* of the International Busi-

Source: Wilson Quarterly, Summer 1986.

ness Machines Corporation (IBM) are greater than the domestic box-office revenues ($4.2 billion) of the entire U.S. motion picture industry. Including cameramen, actors, secretaries, and film editors (but not theater personnel), it employs only 220,000 people. Why all the glamor? Some of it comes from the high-stakes character of the business and the enormous earnings of the stars. The difference in gross revenues between an expensive flop like *Heaven's Gate* (1980) and a smash hit like *Star Wars* (1977) can amount over a period of years to nearly $1 billion. Big films, such as *Jaws* (1975), *Out of Africa* (1985), and *The Color Purple* (1985), can leave their mark on fashion, fads, behavior, and, sometimes, public debate. But, above all, Hollywood captures the popular imagination because it is still the nation's (and the world's) "dream machine," projecting private hopes and fantasies and fears onto a big screen for all to see and share.

Despite some considerable changes in the way Hollywood does business, an industry "insider" from the 1930s would still recognize today's dominant companies. Gone are the flamboyantly tyrannical movie moguls like Louis B. Mayer and Darryl F. Zanuck, the paternalistic studio system, and Hollywood's old monopoly on stardom, American-style. Many of the vast and glorious backlots, where the likes of Gary Cooper faced *High Noon* (1952) and Gene Kelly went *Singin' in the Rain* (1952) have disappeared or shrunk, now occupied by office buildings and hotels.

Yet there is one constant on the Hollywood scene: Eight multinational corporations formed more than 50 years ago still have hegemony over the production and worldwide distribution of feature films. Of the old Hollywood film factory giants, only RKO (producer of the 1933 version of *King Kong* and those dazzling Fred Astaire–Ginger Rogers musicals) has gone under, dismantled during the 1950s by its owner, the eccentric billionaire Howard Hughes.

Studio executives still make or break the careers of the Robert Evanses, Jessica Langes, and Richard Geres. They also decide whether to distribute the films of George Lucas, Francis Ford Coppola, and those of every one of Hollywood's legion of aspiring producers and directors. And without a studio distribution contract, few film-makers can raise the $12 million required for the average Hollywood production budget, even if they spend a lifetime at the Beverly Hills Hotel pool. (Distribution and advertising expenses add at least another 50 percent to a movie's costs.) Orson Welles, the brilliant director of *Citizen Kane* (1941) who died last year, never directed another major release after *Touch of Evil* (1957) because the studios viewed him, as his biographer Joseph McBride put it, as a "wastrel, a rebel, a continuing challenge to the Hollywood system."

"The new Hollywood," as Metro-Goldwyn-Mayer (MGM) executive vice-president David Chasman observed in 1981, "is very much like the old Hollywood."

CITADELS OF FANTASY

The Big Eight studios have survived repeated challenges: the breakup of their theater networks, the rise of broadcast television, the advent of cable and "pay" television, and, most recently, the videocassette revolution. They show no signs of weakening. The studios, despite their age, are among the nation's most adaptable, agile corporations.

Today, old-fashioned entrepreneurs own just three of the eight studios—20th Century–Fox, MGM, and United Artists Communications. Yet their economic reach vastly exceeds anything ever dreamed of by the moguls of Hollywood's Golden Age.

The Australian-born press lord Rupert Murdoch, for example, created America's first vertically integrated movie-television company when he bought 20th Century–Fox for $575 million in 1985 and combined it with the chain of six big-city independent TV stations that he recently acquired from Metromedia Television. This means that a Fox-made film such as *The Jewel of the Nile* (1985) can be shown by the new Fox TV stations after it appears in the nation's theaters, keeping all the film's revenues within the corporate family. Ultimately, Murdoch hopes to create a fourth television network to challenge ABC, CBS, and NBC.

Ted Turner of cable television fame agreed to buy MGM in 1985 for similar reasons: MGM's film library will feed his television operations. He made the deal with Kirk Kerkorian, another entrepreneur who still owns United Artists, which he acquired in 1981.

Two of the Big Eight are now subunits of large, diversified conglomerates: Columbia Pictures Industries has been a division of the Coca-Cola Company since 1982. And Paramount Pictures is the corporate stepchild of a billion-dollar giant, Gulf & Western Industries. Hollywood still prides itself on being a liberal, "creative" community—although Orson Welles once lamented the "gray flannel shadow" over Movieland—and not a few of its celebrities are chortling over the tribulations of the buttoned-down corporate types from Coca-Cola, which has not been notably successful in the motion picture business.

In recent years, top honors at the box office have gone to studios owned by two conglomerates that specialize in entertainment: Warner Brothers, owned by Warner Communications, and Universal, a division of MCA. (MCA, following the Murdoch-Turner strategy, recently bought an independent New York television station for $387 million.) The Disney studio, part of the Disney entertainment conglomerate, has not done so well. But with the release of *Down and Out in Beverly Hills* (1986) under its new Touchstone Films banner, it is now pursuing adult audiences, and greater profits.

In Hollywood parlance, the Big Eight corporations are "the majors." Year in, year out, they control almost 80 percent of the movie business in the United States and approximately half the market in Sweden, West Germany, and several other nations in Western Europe, not to mention Asia. (Hollywood derives roughly 50 percent of its revenues from overseas film rentals.) Every few years, a couple of bold pretenders (recently, Orion Pictures and New World Pictures) emerge to challenge the Big Eight at home, and as often as not they succeed in creating a modest hit or two. But no challenger has survived over the long haul.[1]

There is no secret to the majors' success. In essence, their power derives, as it always has, from their ability to distribute films. At considerable expense, they maintain offices in about 25 cities in America (and up to 65 overseas), where their representatives are in constant contact with the heads of regional theater chains. The studios' "hit parade" record at the box office is what impels theater owners (a conservative lot) to rent their products.[2] In the "new" Hollywood, there are dozens of independent producers, but virtually all of them pay the big studios to distribute their films.

In 1945, during the high tide of movie-going in America, the majors owned most of the nation's movie theaters. Downtown "picture palaces"—the Paramount in New York, the Oriental in Chicago, the Mastbaum in Philadelphia—were the showcases of the system. "In Hollywood's heyday," notes *Time* magazine, "the films were only celluloid but the cinemas that showed them were marble citadels of fantasy and opulence . . . some of the most exuberantly romantic architecture ever conceived in the U.S." Marcus Loew, the founder of MGM, once said, "We sell tickets to theaters, not movies."

GUESS WHO'S GOING TO THE MOVIES?

From these Xanadus, with their baroque architectural splendor and acres of seats, came the bulk of any film's revenues, even though smaller neighborhood houses, with about 500 seats, outnumbered the dream palaces by 9 to 1. In the years right after World War II, the theaters sold some 90 million tickets every week.

That all began to change in 1948, when the U.S. Supreme Court declined to hear an appeal of the Paramount antitrust case, forcing the majors to sell their theater holdings. They gradually divested themselves during the next decade—just in the nick of time, as it turned out. As middle-class

Americans migrated to the suburbs, many of the downtown movie houses decayed or closed their doors.

Today, 50 regionally based companies dominate the film exhibition business, led by Cineplex Odeon, General Cinema, and United Artists Communications, each with more than 1,000 screens. (Total screens in the North American market: 20,200.) Many of these new film exhibition giants got their start as operators of drive-in theaters, the "passion pits" of the 1950s. They prospered not only because they offered a trysting place for older adolescents but because they offered a cheap night out for young parents—they could put the kids in the car's backseat, no babysitter needed. (Some families also threw their dirty laundry in the trunk: A few drive-ins offered laundromats for overworked mothers.) Opening a drive-in required only a fence, a macadam parking lot, some speakers for the cars, a projector, and an enormous screen. Best of all, the drive-ins could be built on cheap land at the edge of town.

As the suburbs matured and land became relatively more expensive, "hardtop" cinemas enjoyed a comeback, usually in the form of mini-cinemas with a couple of hundred seats squeezed into a plain box shell in a shopping center. Then, during the 1970s, came the cineplexes, usually with three to 12 screens under one roof.

In a way, the exhibition business has come full circle: The new cineplexes essentially are unadorned, chopped up versions of the glorious Paramounts and Orientals of old. (A few new theaters are even putting on some frills again to lure customers.) The economics, as *Fortune* magazine explained earlier this year, is simple. "A theater with four screens, roughly the national average, is four times more likely than a one-screen house to book a hit picture." A hit movie can be shifted to a big room, a dud to a smaller one.

The cineplexes are far better suited to the film release patterns that developed as the majors sold off their theater holdings. Under the old system, the studios turned out nearly a picture a week to feed their chains: A film would open for a week at downtown picture palaces, return a few months later for a week at the larger neighborhood houses, then appear on successively lower rungs of the distribution ladder. At each step down, the price of admission dropped.

"Once separated from their theater chains," writes film historian Arthur Knight, "the studio heads quickly realized that they no longer had to supply a new movie each week for their own houses. They cut back on their production schedules." The change spelled the end of the already ailing studio system: Why keep stars and directors and screenwriters on costly year-round contracts merely to work on two or three films a year?

Viewing patterns also changed. After 1948, television siphoned off part of the film audience, and moviegoers who once went to the pictures no matter what was showing changed their ways. "Filmgoing used to be part of the social fabric," observes Art Murphy, a USC film professor. "Now it's an impulse purchase."

After dropping from a peak of 4.5 billion during the late 1940s, annual admissions leveled off at about one billion during the 1960s and have remained relatively steady at that number. Considering the growth of the population, this represents about a 25 percent decline in the proportion of the U.S. population going to the movies. At the same time, the composition of the movie-going audience has changed. The new schedule targets today's biggest ticket buyers: teen-agers on school vacations. According to the *1986 International Motion Picture Almanac,* young people aged 12 to 19 make up 40 percent of the typical movie theater audience. They go out to the movies almost three times as often as their parents or grandparents. The over-40 set accounts for a mere 15 percent of ticket sales.

ADAPTING TO TV

In the cineplex world, summer, beginning before Memorial Day and ending on the Labor Day weekend, is the season when the majors unleash their hoped-for hits. Blockbusters such as *Back to the Future* (1985) hang on for months, sometimes even a year. According to *Variety,* the industry's trade newspaper, the summer movie season accounts for nearly 50 percent of the domestic box-office take. The Christmas and Easter vacation periods are also peak periods.

Where have the older folks gone? Literally, nowhere. Most are staying home, parked in front of their television sets. The "tube" serves up not only cop shows and other standard TV fare, but a surprising number of Hollywood productions. A quick survey of *TV Guide* reveals that about one-quarter of the average television broadcast day is devoted to movies, most of them aired by independent stations. Add cable television's film-heavy menu and the movie time vastly increases.

During the late 1940s, the majors had tried to deal with the rise of television in a number of ways: Several attempted (unsuccessfully) to establish their own television networks or to ally themselves with existing ones. Others tried to offer more of what the public could not get from television. They came up with "3D" films, wide-screen pictures, and, in two extremely short-lived experiments, AromaRama and Smell-O-Vision. The big shift began in 1955 when Howard Hughes, then in the process of dismantling RKO, agreed to rent pre-1948 RKO feature films to the fledgling TV networks. One by one the major studios followed suit.

Thereafter, Hollywood became indispensable to television. By the late 1950s, all of the major studios had plunged into the production of TV series. Universal's television division now boasts such prime-time hits as *Miami Vice* and *Murder, She Wrote.* During the 1960s, Hollywood began to rent recent films (usually three to five years old) to the television networks, which, thus provisioned, mounted a "Night at the Movies" for every night of the week.

Unhappy with the ever-increasing rents that they were paying for Hollywood studio features, the networks moved during the 1960s to create their own movie fare—the made-for-TV movie, then the mini-series and novel-for-television. Some critics dismiss these low-budget productions as the "disease of the week," but in reality today's made-for-TV dramas are successors to Hollywood's "B" movies of yore. In any event, these in-house TV products have not eliminated the networks' need to rent Hollywood films.

In 1972, Time Inc. entered the fray with Home Box Office (HBO), which for a modest monthly fee of about $10 offered cable television viewers recent Hollywood motion pictures uncut and uninterrupted by commercials. For the first time in the television age, a way had been found to make viewers pay for what they watched in their living rooms. Thus, the term "pay television." The result was aptly summed up by a headline in *Broadcasting* magazine: "Ten Years That Changed the World of Telecommunications."

Four years after HBO appeared, Sony introduced its revolutionary Betamax half-inch home videocassette recorder (VCR). Originally priced over $1,000 (double that in today's dollars), the cost of Beta machines and their newer rivals, the VHS, dropped to just over $300 by 1986. And the price keeps falling. An enthusiastic American public has snapped up some 25 million machines; the industry expects to sell 10 million more in 1986. Such numbers, notes *Washington Post* critic Tom Shales, give "home video nearly the penetration of cable TV and, thus, virtual 'mass medium' standing."

From the beginning, Hollywood loathed the new machine. In allowing VCR owners to tape movies from their television sets, and to control when and where they would view pre-recorded films, the device seemed designed to rob Hollywood and the movie theaters of patrons. The VCR, declared Jack Valenti, president of the Motion Picture Association of America, "is a *parasitical* instrument."

THE FUTURE AS RERUN

But, characteristically, Hollywood has already found a way to make the most of the VCR.

At first, the studios tried to sell pre-recorded movies to the public. But the $80 price tag on most popular films kept the public away in droves. Then, in 1980, local entrepreneurs began to buy multiple copies of pre-recorded tapes and offer them for rent. By the mid-1980s stores renting video tapes seemed to be popping up on every street corner. Record stores and even grocery stores jumped into the business, including, most recently, the Southland Corporation, with a trial run in some of its 7,250 7-Eleven stores in the United States. These outlets are something like the old neighborhood picture houses—except that today's most popular neighborhood theater is the living room.

The studios have been quick to capitalize on the trend. In 1985, they grossed $1.5 billion at the box office, and between $1.5 billion and $1.8 billion from sales of videocassettes, mostly to the rental clubs. Complaining that there is not enough "product" to satisfy demand, one videocassette manufacturer has announced plans to make its own films.

Videocassettes have created new markets. Some films only become hits when released as videos. For example, director Martin Scorsese's *Scarface* (1984) did reasonably well for Universal at the box office but later commanded the top spot among VCR rentals, thus gaining a fresh new audience.

Citing the 12 percent drop in theater attendance in 1985, the head of one large theater chain remarked recently, "Anyone who doesn't believe videocassettes are devastating competition to theaters is a fool." But Richard Fox, head of the National Association of Theater Owners, thinks that Hollywood "just didn't make the movies people wanted to see this year." The only certain victims of the VCR revolution are pornographic movie houses: As many as 40 percent of them have closed their doors since viewers gained the ability to watch movies of their choice at home.

For better or worse, the VCR is making an impact on everybody who shows motion pictures. Paradoxically, new movie screens are now going up at the fastest pace since the 1920s, mostly in shopping malls in America's outer suburbs and in affluent city neighborhoods. Why? In order to offer movie-lovers ease of access to the latest in first-run Hollywood films. For their part, HBO and other pay television channels are fighting back against the VCR by offering one-time "pay per view" showings of new films after they debut in the theaters but before they appear on videocassettes.

All of this competition guarantees that the TV networks will reduce their reliance on Hollywood's motion pictures. The trend is already well advanced. When CBS aired *Star Wars* in February 1984, that blockbuster looked to be a sure-fire ratings hit. The network doubled its prime-time ad prices. Then *Star Wars* was beaten in the ratings by ABC's *Lace,* a steamy, made-for-TV movie that cost only $3 million to make, less than half what CBS had paid to rent *Star Wars.* Yet, as the networks seek alternatives to Big Eight products, the cable superstations and over-the-air independent TV stations will gladly take up the slack, gradually moving toward round-the-clock showings of the best and worst of Hollywood's past.

All of these changes, from the expansion of cable to the rise of the VCR, add up to one clear trend. More and more people are going to be watching more and more motion pictures. And to filmdom's Big Eight, that is nothing but good news, for they will still be shaping most of what people watch.

NOTES

1. The U.S. film industry is unique: In the nations of Western Europe (including Great Britain) and most other areas of the world, directors and producers must secure the backing of a single national government-owned film production authority. The search for more money and wider film distribution occasionally drives noted foreign directors such as Ingmar Bergman and Kurosawa Akira to Hollywood.
2. The studios and the theaters engage in a never-ending tug-of-war. The studios' revenues come from the rental fee and a share of the box-office receipts; both sums are negotiable. To enlarge "profit centers" in which the studios cannot share, some theater owners now deploy ushers hawking popcorn and soft drinks in the aisles as well as in the lobby. One reason: Three cents worth of popcorn can be sold for $1. Theaters now ring up some $340 million in popcorn sales annually.

QUESTIONS FOR REVIEW AND DISCUSSION

1. Documentary programs have almost disappeared from television. Why has this happened?
2. According to Leo Bogart, a researcher, studies show that higher-income, better-educated people tend to read newspapers and lower-income, less-educated people tend to watch television. Why is this so?
3. *Narrowcasting* is a word frequently heard in discussions of radio. What does it mean?
4. What is meant by the statement "The new trend for some papers is a shift away from total readership to a focus on a market niche?" Why is this done, and how?
5. Charles Kuralt says that if the late Edward R. Murrow could return to the CBS newsroom, he would be impressed by some things and deplore others. Name the good and bad things.
6. Explain why Howard Cosell believes that sportswriters are not prepared to cover the current sports scene. Do you agree?
7. Why does Theodore L. Glasser contend that objectivity precludes responsibility in journalism?
8. The cover of *Time* has featured Madonna, cats, and aching backs. What is Ray Cave's explanation for such choices by a serious newsmagazine?
9. Long-famous mass-circulation magazines such as *Look* and *Collier's* have disappeared, yet hundreds of new magazines flourish. Explain the conditions that have brought this about.
10. One age group covering a span of only seven years provides 40 percent of the typical movie theater audience. What age range is this?

ESSAY TOPICS

1. Newspapers are trying numerous methods to improve readership and build circulation. Discuss in an essay the methods you believe could be most effective in achieving this goal. For background, draw upon Susan Miller's article "America's Dailies Try to Capture Lost Readers" and your own reading of newspapers.
2. Garry Trudeau, who draws the strip *Doonesbury,* says that by definition a satirist must stand in opposition to something. Some subscribing newspapers drop his strip temporarily during episodes they regard as excessively biting attacks on public figures or issues. Are these editors protecting their readers' feelings or merely exercising their own prejudices? Discuss the role of satire in newspapers and broadcasting, citing examples in addition to *Doonesbury.*

Advances in computer technology are making it easy to do what was impossible not long ago: cross-match information almost at the touch of a button to create portraits of individuals—and even to try to predict what they will do.

— *Business Week*
in " 'Big Brother Inc.'
May Be Closer than You Thought"

As a society we are overinformed and underenlightened.

— Henryk J. Skolimowski
in "Freedom, Responsibility, and
the Information Society"

When you tap into these databases, how do you determine the accuracy of the information you're getting? You don't. You usually take it as an article of faith. And that's something a good reporter would never do if he weren't using a computer.

— Charles Marshall
in "The Information Society:
Promises and Perils"

The acid rain of TV images pollutes healthy attitudes towards food, alcohol, and sex, and it promotes violence as the American way of solving problems, and even of having a good time.

— Harry Henderson
in "The Acid Rain of TV Images"

One thing is certain: this family is engaging in a form of behavior that 50 years ago was unthinkable. Even 25 years ago, when Mark and Joan were growing up, it was different. . . .

— Rushworth M. Kidder
in "At Home with the Video
Revolution"

LIVING IN THE INFORMATION SOCIETY

INTRODUCTION

PHILLIP H. AULT

So far this book has examined significant current developments in mass communications, as well as problems and achievements of the communicators. It has shown how the institutions of communication are evolving in a time of remarkable advances in technology.

In this final part, the focus switches from the dispensers of information to its recipients. How are the changes that have been discussed affecting our lives? How can we cope effectively with the torrent of fact, opinion, and entertainment that engulfs us?

The "information society" is more than a popular catchphrase. Studies based on research for the Department of Commerce show that more than half the United States gross national product derives from the creation and distribution of information in some form.

The immensity of this information deluge raises provocative questions.

Do viewers really wish to receive more than 50 channels of cable television programming, as some do? Probably not; studies indicate that after the novelty of such abundance wears off, most viewers confine their watching to about five channels. But which five? The choice varies according to each viewer's interest.

Are we in fact being subjected to information overkill? Much of the material offered to us is mere snippets of fact and scraps of trivia. Numbed by volume at the expense of comprehension, are we in peril of being a less solidly informed society than some previous generations were?

The solution lies in selectivity—the exercise of intelligent choice by the viewer and reader and the willingness to turn off the switch occasionally in order to discuss, to think, and to digest what we have received.

Look for a moment at the choices facing a family as it decides how to spend the evening. Should it watch the news and a drama on television? Play a rented movie on a videocassette recorder? Play video games? Read a newspaper, a magazine, or a book, perhaps with the radio turned on softly for music and news? Connect the personal computer to a database and search through its massive electronic files for information on a desired topic? Go out to the movies?

TELEVISION'S DOMINANT ROLE

Viewer statistics published by the television rating services indicate that the largest proportion of families decide to watch television, either over the air or cable. The A. C. Nielsen Company rating service reports that the average American household television set is turned on more than 7 hours a day.

The rating reports compiled by Nielsen and Arbitron are treated by the television industry as irrefutable statistical evidence. Programs are kept on the air or killed on the basis of these ratings. Nevertheless, one must be cautious about interpreting them when examining the impact of television on the individual and the family. The rating services have not yet developed a satisfactory way to measure the audiences of the cable television networks. Since an increasing number of viewers tune their sets to cable channels, a significant segment of program selection goes inadequately reported. Adoption of a new measuring device called a "people meter" raised questions about the accuracy of the audience measurements. First used by the networks for the 1987–1988 season, people meters showed smaller audiences for some popular shows than previous Nielsen methods did.

Another critical reservation is that the rating reports tell how many sets are turned on and to what programs they are tuned, but they cannot report how carefully those programs are being watched.

Television was created as an information and entertainment delivery system. However, sociological research shows that it also provides uses and gratifications going well beyond and quite afield from that purpose. In many homes, the turned-on television set is a background companion, watched intermittently but serving mainly as a constant reminder of the world outside. Also, it is a regulator of the daily family cycle; meals and domestic duties are planned around the hours at which favorite programs appear. Indeed, the rigid 30- and 60-minute time segments of television network programming form something of a "life clock."

Dr. Charles Winick of the City University of New York recently completed a six-year study of families who had unexpectedly been deprived of their home television viewing because their sets had broken down or been stolen. He interviewed 1,512 people in 560 homes, an especially television-aware body of opinion, to determine why people watch TV.

Dr. Winick asked his subjects to indicate which of six major categories were reasons why they watched television. He found that for the average person interviewed, five of the six reasons applied. Fewer than 10 percent of the interviewees cited a single reason.

The categories and responses:

Information	83%
Entertainment	82
Conversation	72
Social cement	68
Punctuating the day and week	58
Companionship	57

"Social cement" was defined as meaning that the television set provides a focus for other activities: the predictable television schedule provides structure to family life.

Although these findings may not entirely please advertising sales executives of the television industry, who treat the rating reports as gospel and seem to assume that every program is watched intently by its viewers, they emphasize the penetrating impact of television on American life.

One need only look at sports to see television's influence. In earlier days TV cameras were present at scheduled football games to report what happened. Today, because of the huge sums of money its commercials generate and the consequent very large fees it pays the participating schools and teams, television dictates the scheduling and tempo of American spectator sports. Television executives decide when certain games will be played, often at hours inconvenient to the on-the-scene spectators but chosen to fit network programming needs. The directors of TV game broadcasts interrupt the competitive action to broadcast commercials. The role of the TV camera has been reversed. Once present at events as a spectator, it has become a dictator.

This manipulative power affects the lives of families and individual sports enthusiasts, shaping the way they spend their leisure hours. Television has a surfeit of sports broadcasts, even creating pseudoevents such as amateurish competitions between entertainment personalities. To cite one manifestation, it was not so long ago that there were four great New Year's Day football games: the Rose Bowl, the Cotton Bowl, the Sugar Bowl, and the Orange Bowl. At year end 1984–1985, however, television networks broadcast 19 bowl games between December 15 and January 1! Many of these bowl events were created as devices to generate television income for the networks and participating colleges.

At least this pervasive influence of television on contemporary life is measurable to a degree; the impact of the newer forms of electronic communication is more nebulous. It is evident that some are cutting into the amount of traditional information and entertainment the average family receives from TV broadcasts. When children use the screen of the family television set to play a video game, that set cannot receive programs. A set connected to a videotex circuit or used to show home movies filmed with the family's video camera isn't available to receive a network situation comedy. When a videotaped movie rented from a local supermarket is being played through a videocassette recorder onto the TV screen, a network news program cannot enter the home. Collectively, these supplementary uses of the television set are beginning to have a measurable effect on family life.

THE COMPUTER'S IMPACT

Perhaps the greatest imponderable factor of life in the information society is the growth of home computer ownership and the commitment of time its use requires. Some families already lead lives dominated by computer use, the adults at work during the day and the entire family at home in the evening.

The immense resources of information that can be unlocked from databanks by computer commands and the intriguing kinds of calculation that can be done on computers are intellectual challenges. Meeting them becomes an almost compulsive commitment of time and concentration.

Exchanges of electronic messages and creation of personal relationships through interlocking groups of computers, called "networking," open new forms of social relationships. Romances and even marriages have grown from contacts through electronic "bulletin boards." "Conferencing" is a form of electronic mail among linked computers that permits their operators to exchange letters by keyboard.

If the ownership of personal computers, and the extent of their use, grow as enormously as computer promoters predict, the nation may one day possess a new, invisible network for information exchange, less organized and defined than the standard mass media but swift and far-reaching. We may be entering an era in which we will need to expand our definition of mass communication. Technically, a piece of news—or indeed a falsehood—can be spread electronically around the country without being published in a newspaper or magazine or broadcast on radio or television. Fascinating as this sounds, it has an inherent danger. Information or rumor thus exchanged falls outside the control of responsible editors and could give widespread circulation to false impressions, misunderstandings, and dangerous untruths.

Perhaps personal electronic mail and networking will not reach such proportions in the predictable future, although business uses of these techniques, already extensive, will continue to grow. Enthusiasts for new techniques often get carried away with their predictions. One newspaper columnist forecast recently that electronic mail will become so universal that letters as we know them won't exist and the Postal Service eventually might be reduced to a simple parcel delivery service.

A limiting factor on use of electronic delivery methods is cost to the consumer. Videocassette recorders, personal computers, and related equipment are expensive to purchase, and the fees involved in certain operations with computers can become high. In some communities, an enthusiast who purchases all available cable television services must spend $40 a month or more. Tying a personal computer into a database requires telephone charges and in some instances user fees as well.

U.S. News & World Report described how the parents of a 16-year-old girl in Jefferson Valley, New York, canceled her subscription to The Source computer service after discovering that she had run up monthly bills as high as $150, mostly for exchanging electronic mail with boyfriends. Her mother called this behavior "electronic flirting."

On a more disturbing level, sociologists foresee the danger that these methods of electronic information delivery may, because of their cost, be available only to more affluent families. Poorer families, and especially their children in school, may thus be effectively shut out from information that members of better-situated families receive. The cost of electronic equipment should decline under mass-production conditions, but the fees for using it probably will not.

SURVIVAL OF READING

Although the full impact of electronic information delivery to the home is unclear, one assertion by more extreme futurists is already proving to be unfounded. Reading of printed matter in newspaper, magazine, and book form will not disappear from our lives. In fact, the publication of printed reading material is thriving. Nevertheless, the surprisingly high rate of illiteracy in the United States, blocking thousands of citizens from the impact of the printed word, is a distressing national problem.

A few years ago, much was heard about creation of the "electronic newspaper"—that is, delivery of a newspaper's contents into the home on a television screen rather than in traditional paper-and-ink form. So far, the electronic newspaper has failed to develop in the manner its boosters predicted. Some of them said the traditional newspaper of paper and ink was doomed to disappear.

Teletext, the selective one-way system of delivering news on the TV screen, and videotex, the two-way system that lets the recipient order news as desired and transact business as well, were expected to be the delivery systems for the electronic newspaper.

In experiments to date, users of videotex and teletext have indicated quite clearly that they view electronic news delivery as a supplement to the traditional newspaper, not a replacement. The interest of videotex users runs much more heavily to commercial transactions and acquisition of specialized information that newspapers do not usually publish.

When Viewtron, a videotex service operated by Knight-Ridder Newspapers, Inc., cut its staff by 20 percent in 1984 because it had attracted only half the expected number of subscribers, its president, Reid Ashe, said quite candidly, "We are coming to the realization that this is still a research and development project, not a business." Later Viewtron went out of business entirely.

Quite a few newspaper publishing companies are engaged in electronic information delivery in some form in order to have a stake in the developing field, but as a group they are concentrating their efforts on delivery of specialized information and services. As far as can be seen today, the daily newspaper will continue to arrive on the doorstep.

However, that delivery will be made to more and more homes in the morning rather than in the evening. The trend to morning publication results from changes in family living habits, deriving in part from the fact that a large proportion of women now hold jobs outside the home. After their return home from work, these jobholders lack the time for newspaper reading around the dinner hour. In many homes, television viewing fills the evening hours when newspaper reading formerly took place.

DANGER TO PRIVACY

Personal privacy is cherished as a precious right of individuals in a democratic society, to be protected against intrusion by government and private snoops. At the same time, the immense strides made in electronic methods of communication and in our ability to exchange information are generally regarded as socially helpful. It is ironic, then, that the improvement in the machinery of information gathering tends to shatter the barricade of personal privacy that individuals desire.

The computer, purveyor of so many good things, is at the same time a villain that destroys privacy. Enormous amounts of private information about virtually every American are stored in the computers of government, private credit-reference organizations, and the direct-mail companies that stuff our mailboxes with sales literature and fund solicitations.

When the eminent English justice Sir Edward Coke said 400 years ago that "a man's house is his castle," the concept of the computer was of course far beyond his wildest imagining. Even in 1949, when George Orwell wrote his prophetic "Big Brother is watching" novel, *1984,* such an electronic marvel had not become a factor in everyday life. Today, as we edge toward the year 2000, the computer in some of its applications is undercutting Coke's dictum. It threatens to become "Big Brother."

A man's house may still be his castle, but the more he communicates through his home computer with businesses, information sources, and other individuals, the less secure his private fortress becomes. Computer memory banks may hold records of the purchases he has made, his banking transactions, the literature he reads, the home movies he watches, and indiscreet statements he may have made in electronic mail exchanges. Who knows into what hands that computerized information might fall through theft, mishap, or sale for profit? A frightening example of the potential for evil is the experience of a *Newsweek* reporter in San Francisco. After his disclosure of how computer "hackers" penetrate security systems was published, the angry hackers retaliated. They put him on "teletrial" in their computer-to-computer conversations and smeared him with insults on electronic "bulletin boards" for others to read. One message even suggested, "Kill the dude."

Going even further, the hackers illegally broke into a TRW Information Services computer and obtained from it a list of his credit card numbers, home address, wife's name, and social security number. They posted this information on an electronic bulletin board for use by everyone who desired to harass and perhaps cheat the reporter.

Coke, that stiff-backed royalist son of the Elizabethan era, would have been shocked almost beyond belief could he have known that one day a teenage English electronics buff using a personal computer would be able to read the personal electronic mail of Prince Philip, husband of the present Queen Elizabeth. Yet precisely that happened. While a London *Daily Mail* reporter watched, the young hacker broke into a state-owned telephone company's computer files and read the prince's mail. One item was Prince Philip's private message of congratulations to Princess Diana, his daughter-in-law, on her twenty-third birthday.

In the selections that follow, invasion of privacy and other problems of life in the information society are discussed, along with the benefits the electronic age has brought us.

THE BROAD CONCEPT

THE INFORMATION SOCIETY: PROMISES AND PERILS

Charles Marshall

Further spectacular advances in communication technology are coming, and they will intensify the problems of journalists on such questions as privacy, truth, security, and freedom of expression. Charles Marshall, vice-chairman of American Telephone & Telegraph Company, explores the future in a speech he made at the 1986 University of Missouri Journalism Week.

What I'd like to do today is three things: first, share some idea of where the technologies of telecommunications are headed; second, discuss some of the challenges still ahead to assure their fullest and best application; and finally, talk about some of the issues we'll all face as these changes take place as we move into the so-called information age.

I want to put all of this in the context of not just telecommunications but what we call information movement and management (IM&M). That is the new name of the game.

Business today no longer involves just the transmission of information, whether in the form of voice, data, or video. It includes the collection, storage, selection, processing, and integration of that information as well.

It's not just the name of the business that's changed, it's the scope, the mission, the ambitions.

The basic technologies behind all this are relatively few, principally microelectronics, lightwave, and software. These are rapidly growing technologies. They are extremely complex technologies. Yet their goal is essentially to make the complex simple—to allow people to use complex technology, to perform complex tasks, easily.

Microelectronics is at the heart of all this. And here we continue to see remarkable progress. At AT&T, for example, we're manufacturing a million-bit memory chip—one smaller than your fingernail that contains over two million components. It can store one hundred *pages* of typewritten text. Ten years ago we could only store the equivalent of one hundred *words.* The number of components we can put on a chip is still doubling about every eighteen months. And we can expect that pace to continue for a decade.

Similar progress is also taking place in lightwave technology. Ten years ago the lightwave system that AT&T pioneered could carry the equivalent of about 700 simultaneous telephone calls on a single pair of glass fibers. Today's commercial lightwave system can carry more than 24,000!

This technology will be essential for moving large amounts of data and video as well as voice traffic. And the process of fibering the world, so to speak, has already begun. Lightwave systems of great capacity have been planned to span the Atlantic and Pacific oceans. And fiber is now moving across our country, throughout cities, and into many buildings. All this will greatly influence the flow and uses of information in the future.

The third technology I mentioned—software—is progressing more slowly than the others because it's dependent on the productivity of programmers.

Source: Printed by permission of Charles Marshall.

Yet even here we're finding ways to advance significantly, including automating some aspects of programming and [making] improvements in software algorithms.

So as you can see, the basic information technologies are booming.

But in a larger sense—that of creating a real information society—this is only a beginning. The real challenge lies ahead. It is the challenge of weaving these individual technologies into seamless systems. . . .

The future holds a lot more. And actually it's based not as much on some far-out vision as on demands taking place today.

Simply put, the current needs of people are already shaping the future. The needs of businesses trying to be more competitive and profitable—literally trying to survive. The needs of governments trying to operate more efficiently and effectively. Of doctors and hospitals trying to deliver better health care. Of schools trying to deliver better education. All these are driving the information business today. And they're shaping a very challenging tomorrow.

What are some of the things we in the information business have to do to help meet these needs?

As I mentioned before, people want computers that can talk to each other—that can be linked together as systems. But they want the option of being able to buy these computers, and any other information equipment, from the vendor of their choice and have everything fit together and work together.

They also want this equipment to have consistent user interfaces. That's fancy language for being able to use everyone's equipment without having to relearn where things are or how to operate them every time you move to someone else's keyboard, display, or directory.

Meeting such needs requires that you have universal standards. And the industry is hard at work trying to achieve these, nationally and internationally—[though] not without some emotion. . . .

Now, as we're able to distribute more and more intelligence in equipment and the network and as more databanks and other information sources become available to go "on line," the possibilities challenge the imagination.

For example, it's been envisioned that the network of the future would be a remarkable research system, one able to draw from sources anyplace in the world and bring you the information you needed in the right form and the right language. You would not even have to know where the information was located. You would only have to ask the right question. The system would do the rest, including translation from a foreign language if necessary.

In addition, such information could be transformed into action. Businesses could transform the latest market information into input that directly changes factory operations—that affects inventory control, CAD-CAM operations, even packaging and shipping. Medical patients could have complex diagnoses and procedures conducted remotely, with the possibility of having so-called expert systems built into the network to offer second opinions.

And certainly such networks are revolutionizing education. Universities, for example, are becoming global electronic campuses, where students and faculties draw not only on the knowledge in their own libraries and laboratories but on those of other centers of learning and research anywhere in the world. . . .

Assuming we accomplish all that we envision in the way of advancing information movement and management—linking computers and communications equipment, tying them all into vast intelligent networks through which it's possible to access, store, process, and use information in almost any way we can imagine—how might this affect the world of journalism? What possibilities—and what problems—does it raise? What are the promises and the perils?

A great many of the promises are already obvious. Current and emerging technologies have already revolutionized the gathering of news, its editing and publishing. I don't think I have to tell this audience how computers have changed the job of reporters, both in researching and writing their stories.

You also know how dependent large city newspapers and national newspapers and magazines are on the computer, satellites, and other telecommunications technologies to compose, print, and distribute their publications. Such publications as the *Wall Street Journal,* the New York *Times, Time,* and *Newsweek* have, over recent years, had their operations revolutionized by these technologies.

For example, two AT&T services—AT&T SKYNET Digital Service and AT&T ACCUNET T1.5 Service—enable *Time* magazine to transmit a page of text and color to all its presses throughout the country in less than a minute. A full-color page can be done in less than two minutes. These services enable the magazine to conduct its whole process, from closing to distribution, in less than twenty-four hours.

In the years ahead such services will continue to advance, nationally and internationally. So no doubt we will continue to see the growth of publications of such national and worldwide scope and influence.

At the same time, the technologies will increasingly allow such publications to be tailored to regional and local needs and tastes. Computerized systems will carefully monitor these and feed their findings into the publication's computer network.

This and similar information technology could further generate the need for tailored news and dedicated publications. It all seems to be part of a process that has been unfolding for some time now—a process that began in the 1950s, when computer technology spawned the information explosion. By the early 1960s people were speaking of knowledge and information as "growth industries."

This incredible growth continues. Today the world's knowledge is said to be doubling about every eight years. And a recent study in Japan shows that the production of information is growing at a rate of about four times the consumption of information. In other words, we are creating what some people call an "infoglut."

But now we've entered a new phase of this process. It's going to be the job of the same and similar technology to manage all this information better—to allow us to handle it more selectively to meet people's needs.

One of those needs will remain the need for news—news in its broadest sense of the latest happenings, local, national, and international. However, we are also becoming more and more a nation of special information scanners, dealing with the infoglut in very selective ways. That accounts for the explosion of specialized magazines, books, journals, and newsletters that allow both the capsulizing and in-depth reporting of so many subjects.

Last year some 5,000 new book publishers and 230 new magazines were started up in this country. And a good number of these pursued their readers by computer-selected direct mail. You can also bet that the computer played a big role in the preparation of those publications.

Is this the wave of the future? How far can this trend go? In the past technological revolutions have always fostered specialization. That creates ever-greater experts in ever-narrower fields. Then every once in a while we wake up to find we have a desperate need for interdisciplinary people and those who can see and deal with the big picture. In journalism the latter have emerged in the [form] of Walter Lippmann, Edward R. Murrow, James Reston, and Bill Moyers.

But to meet the needs of specialists, and those who want the ability to scan information, there is the concept of the electronic dedicated newspaper. This is the system through which an individual can receive selectively edited news on his home terminal. This dedicated news can even be printed out in hard copy at the terminal.

This kind of service, even when and where it becomes available, will remain quite expensive for some time. And it will probably be attractive only to people with very special, professional needs. So I don't believe that dedicated, electronic news distribution will pose much of a threat to conventional journalism or publishing for the foreseeable future.

In the past there's generally been a tendency to overestimate the amount of information the average person needs or can use. This has been demonstrated somewhat by the past videotex trials in this country, which seemed to show there was not widespread need yet for such home information systems. Videotex must serve a specific need, such as banking. But that's another speech.

Of course, this may change in the future when the technologies are refined, when costs come down, and when the variety of the offerings grows. I won't make any predictions on this.

However, one thing I will predict—and I'm not alone on this—is that it will be a long time before electronic images replace print. Certainly television has not done this, even though it commands so much of our time and has had such an impact. In fact, despite television, more books, magazines, and newspapers than ever are being bought. In short, silicon has not saved trees.

The issues that the information technologies raise for journalists, however, go far beyond how they will work, their media, the tools of their trade. They involve the fundamental issues that have always been at the heart of your profession—such issues as privacy, security, freedom of expression, protection of intellectual property, truth, morality—little things like that.

And all these issues will be magnified many-fold. The reason is that like any powerful technology, the information technologies are not just tools but amplifiers of humanity's force and foibles. In the case of the information technologies—which are basic to so many of our activities, and increasingly powerful—perhaps this is more so than in most cases.

For example, as the New York *Times* recently reported, "Journalists are using powerful newspaper computers to analyze data from computerized public records. The ease of access afforded by these computers produces information about people that the police and other government agencies either cannot match or are barred by law from obtaining."

What does this mean? It means that this technology bestows enormous new power on the Fourth Estate. And the future is bringing even more. How is this going to be managed? By new laws? By new codes of professional ethics?

And who is to determine the accuracy of the databases that will be the sources of so much we depend on in the future? In a sense these are the gold mines, oil wells, and libraries of the future. A major industry is already growing up in information services that produce and distribute electronic information. In 1983 they produced some $2 billion in revenues. . . . They consist of some 700 firms, industrial and professional associations, and government agencies. About 350 of these maintain the 1,500 databases available today, four times as many as just eight years ago.

When you tap into these databases, how do you determine the accuracy of the information you're getting? You don't. You usually take it as an article of faith. And that's something a good reporter would never do if he weren't using a computer. His editor would insist that he cross-check his facts to make sure that any story was accurate. And errors do creep into databases just as software bugs inhabit computer programs.

How do we handle this? You may dispute a computerized department store bill, but how do you discern, no less dispute, errors in databases that you almost have to accept as authoritative sources of information if you want to get any work done?

Let me raise another issue that challenges those of you who will be workers and gatekeepers in this incredible information age we're entering. This also relates to the fact that knowledge is power, and those who have some responsibility for and control over information cannot exercise [this power] lightly.

Perhaps I can illustrate this best by a story. A number of years ago, long before the current terrorism problem but when we were plagued by violence in our own country, a well-known publishing company put out a book that caused some concern. The title of the book was *The Anarchist's Cookbook.* And it was just that—recipes for making in your own basement or garage all kinds of destructive devices. This sort of light reading for revolutionaries raised some eyebrows and some ire at the time, and the publisher eventually withdrew the book from publication.

Why do I raise this point? Is it to advocate censorship? Definitely not. But it is to emphasize responsibility. We talk often—and sometimes rather glibly—of freedom of speech, freedom of expression, freedom of the press. But are these really free? Or are they borrowed with the promise that they are ours to use as long as we treat them as the precious, complex, and fragile things they are?

The information age we are entering will force us to confront this basic question again and again. Because as the new information technologies place at our disposal powerful new information, and the capabilities to use it with widespread impact, our responsibilities in all this will grow.

So like other powerful and pervasive technologies—perhaps even more—the information technologies will put us all to the test. They will demand more human excellence. They will challenge us, professionally and personally, to be the best we can. All of us. Those who develop information systems that must be most reliable and useful, that must meet the important new needs of our society. Those who use such systems to gather and communicate information and develop it into the knowledge that drives and shapes that society.

Journalism will play a major and critical role in that latter task. With the advent and the growth of some of the technologies I've mentioned today, journalists will face that task with new tools, new opportunities, and new responsibilities. It will be challenging. It will be exciting. It will be hard work. It will be rewarding. It may even be fun.

FREEDOM, RESPONSIBILITY, AND THE INFORMATION SOCIETY

Henryk J. Skolimowski

Speaking from a philosopher's point of view, Professor Skolimowski of the University of Michigan asserts that "the more sophisticated technology becomes, the more it disengages us from life." He emphasizes the need for responsibility and wisdom in handling the new tools of communication.

I find myself in a strange position; almost in an embarrassing position. I am supposed to give a lecture in the series on the information society. The information society is a very interesting idea; and the source of my trouble. When I agreed to give a talk in this series, I thought to myself: "If everybody talks about the information society, surely it must be around." In a soft kind of way I remonstrated myself for not noticing its arrival. I thought to myself again: "Philosophers are notorious for locking themselves up in the ivory towers, so I must have been dozing over some obscure philosophical subject while the information society was triumphantly arriving." "Since it is here," I continued to think, "let us take a look and observe its glorious characteristics."

And here lies the source of my embarrassment. I do not see it around. I do not see any Information Society, worthy of the name *society.* Like Diogenes I have searched with my lantern in various nooks and corners for the signs of the existence of the Information Society as a new social form. My search has proved disappointing.

Well, yes I see a lot of computers around. But this does not make a new type of society. I hear a lot of loose talk about the information revolution.

Source: Condensed from "Freedom, Responsibility, and the Information Society," speech delivered March 28, 1984, at Eastern Michigan University and published in *Vital Speeches of the Day.* Reprinted by permission.

But this does not make a new society either. Perhaps I am a bit old fashioned. But perhaps I am a bit stubborn, resisting new verbal gimmicks that try to persuade me of the existence of the phenomenon that may not be here. We can talk about lots of fictitious things. And the fact that we talk about them does not constitute their existence. Let me state my main argument.

If we live in the information society, why are we so poorly informed? The President is not informed. We are not informed—to know how to live our lives. Evidently more is required than tid-bits of information which we can store in computers. All those billions and zillions of tid-bits, stored in computers, can help us but little.

In my humble opinion what is involved and what is required is judgment, wisdom, enlightenment. You don't make your judgment sharper and more mature by acquiring more bits of information. You do not make your judgment wiser by acquiring more tid-bits, of whatever sort. You make your judgment wiser by becoming a wiser person. You do not acquire more enlightenment by acquiring more computer programs. You acquire enlightenment by becoming an enlightened person—not a reservoir of information (for encyclopedias serve this purpose) but a source of light. In all the three instances: of judgment, of wisdom, of enlightenment we deal with new qualities.

The information society deals only with quantity. The information society does not know the meaning of quality; computers don't at any rate. Hence the Information Society (based on computer information) cannot help us to acquire quality: of judgment, of wisdom, of enlightenment.

Let us remind ourselves, also, that every society has been an information society. We therefore want to know in which way our information society differs from other societies. What is *qualitatively* different about our information society as compared with other societies which equally depended for their existence on the flow and exchange of information. The answer to our question is of course—the computer. Because it is such an easy answer, it is so inadequate. Whatever number of computers you take, they cannot make a new society.

To conceive a new social design, or to invent a new society is a task much more difficult than splitting the atom or inventing the steam engine. During the last millennium, especially the last two centuries, western civilization has shown its prowess in technical inventions. We cannot claim the same power of inventiveness in the social realm. Moreover, we may be astonished to realize that major social inventions have eluded us during the last 25 centuries. Democracy was the last large social invention of the western world. All other social forms, which we have continued, were brought to existence before the dawn of the Greek reason.

The social legacy of technological change is something that we should really ponder over. I am talking about those social innovations that came in the wake of technological change, or were induced by it, in recent times. It would appear that the only new social innovation of the technological society is the shopping mall and the suburbia. They were created inadvertently. They happened by default. The shopping mall functions in a way similar to that of the well in traditional societies: it draws people from the entire surrounding area. But there is a difference. While the traditional well was a vital center of exchange of information, of sharpening of wits, and a real social school for living, the shopping mall is a monument to non-communication, it dulls the mind by the appalling uniformity of goods, and is a school of alienation.

The suburbia is like the village in olden times. But while the village taught self-reliance and brought out gregariousness and conviviality from people, the suburbia teaches isolation, dependence on gadgets, and prepares the ground for moroseness to be appeased by drugs. One does not wish to rub in the obvious point. But alienation has become the hallmark of advancing technology. There must be something unholy in the nature of the beast if it continuously creates (if only inadvertently) those undesirable state of affairs. Let us put it plainly, technological change has produced undesirable social mutants: the atomic family and the isolated individual who is in touch with the world by touching buttons but cannot be touched by his neighbors or be in touch with himself. Technological change has required a corresponding social change based on imagination and inventiveness. Instead we have become numb, stupidly waiting for the fruit from the horn of plenty.

It would thus appear that there is a law that governs technological change: *the more sophisticated technology becomes the more it disengages us from life.* I will call it the Skolimowski Law. The question is whether the recent developments in electronics and computers are an exception to this law. Are we closer to life and to *ourselves* as the result of the information revolution? Will we be closer to life if each of us possesses a personal computer? I wonder. And I suppose you wonder too.

Yet those personal computers are multiplying and so many people say that they are wonderful things. I myself could not quite determine why they are so wonderful, and what they actually *do* that makes them so wonderful. Knowing well my limitation, I have looked around in order to learn from knowledgeable people, that is to say from the experts.

I think I have found the answer; at least one answer given by Marcian E. Hoff Jr., a high ranking executive in the prestigious firm called ATARI (what a lovely name). Thus one of the Atari directors informs us that: THE PERSONAL COMPUTER IS A WONDERFUL SOLUTION LOOKING FOR A PROBLEM.

Now, I know. Yet, many people believe, or at least say, that computers in the 1980's will be what the drugs were in the 1960's—an extension of the self. The other day I heard—no one else but a high guru of the 60's, Timothy Leary, expanding this very view. With a great gusto too. And so completely was he sold on the idea that computers are smarter than we are, and that we are entering the phase of complete symbiosis with them, that I was taken aback—until the interviewer asked Leary the question: "We seem to have an abundance of information. But wisdom seems to be in a short supply. Will computers supply us with wisdom?" To which question Leary responded without hesitation: "Yeah, yeah. In five years we shall have wisdom programs. For $39.00 you will buy a wisdom program and will play a wisdom game with the computer." At this point I knew it was all rubbish. If you think that you can buy a wisdom program, you don't know what wisdom is about; and perhaps you never will if you accept it on the computer's term.

Thus there is a great deal of loose talk and often plain rubbish going on about the greatness of the coming age of the computer. When I listen carefully to those exaggerated claims, which really so often are false, I am persuaded (in my soul at least) that if the information society means buying wisdom programs, going underground to live closer to nature (as Isaac Asimov advocates), having everything done for you by computers and robots—then you may have it, but I part company from you. *I want a society that engages me with life, not eliminates me from it.*

The columnist Sydney J. Harris has put it so well when he said: THE REAL DANGER IS NOT THAT COMPUTERS WILL BEGIN TO THINK LIKE MEN, BUT THAT MEN WILL BEGIN TO THINK LIKE COMPUTERS.

Perhaps we have already started doing that. Hence all this loose talk about the coming greatness of the Information Society.

My talk is entitled: Freedom, Responsibility, and the Information Society. Let me now say a few words about freedom and responsibility. In what sense and to what degree can computers make us freer? The possession of information does not make you free. Do we communicate better with each other when we have computers at our disposal? Hardly. The essence of human exchange is the capacity to empathize with the innermost states of other human beings, is an exchange of emotions, visions, things that make us uniquely human; the kind of things that cannot be easily, if at all, translated into objective bits of information.

Our lives had to be adjusted because of the demands of the computer. But have we enlarged our freedom? Computers and the invasion of privacy is a well known story. I shall not dwell on it, for we all know what a menace the information stored in the computer can be if it concerns our intimate habits. We don't want others to know the history of our illnesses, or what are our sexual habits, or what are our emotional predilections and aversions—for this knowledge could lead to manipulation, control and coercion.

Now let us be kind to computers and think in positive terms. Let us assume that each of us possesses a personal computer which helps us with *everything* we do. Would this represent an extension of our freedom? I respectfully submit that it would not. On the contrary it would curtail our freedom. Let me explain.

Freedom is equivalent to the ability of exercising choices not outlined for you but chosen by you. Freedom is the privilege of being at one with your human nature. The more structured the environment the less choices (in the genuine sense) we possess. The computerized environment will be highly structured; one of the most structured in history. So structured will it, in fact, be that from the standpoint of traditional freedom, *a perfectly computerized environment will be a form of electronic prison.* Every exchange will have to be performed according to the rules of the computers; no room for spontaneity, improvisation, quirkiness, the unexpected, the unstructured. As Ivan Illich says: WHATEVER STRUCTURALLY DOES NOT FIT THE LOGIC OF MACHINES IS EFFECTIVELY FILTERED FROM A CULTURE DOMINATED BY THEIR USE. How can you talk about freedom in such circumstances?

Furthermore, you cannot have freedom without exercising responsibility. You cannot exercise responsibility if everything is done for you. Freedom is the capacity to act when your action springs from responsibility. Your responsibility is annihilated when you are an appendage to computers and robots; and so is then your freedom annihilated.

Our life is helped by mechanical and electronic gadgets only to a certain point. Beyond this point, a further mechanization and automation of our life does not contribute to the enlargement of our autonomy and freedom, but on the contrary, to the decrease of our autonomy, dignity and freedom; so that when we live in a totally automated world, in which all our life-functions are automated, we then have no autonomy and no freedom. The computer being totally automated and programmed is not an expression of freedom but of slavery. At the other end of the spectrum is GOD, for whom nothing is done, who is totally free as he takes the responsibility for all. We have been moving in recent times from the God-end of the spectrum to the computer-end of the spectrum.

There is this other argument which holds that the computerized society will make a Participatory Democracy a reality, and in this way our freedom will be increased. When we all have personal computers, we can then vote directly, and through our computers, we can participate in a democratic process *par excellence.* On the surface the argument is attractive and plausible. When we look deeper into it, it is not so plausible. Will the voting through our personal computers be an important step toward Participatory Democracy? Hardly. We, as human beings, will not really be participating; only our computers will. The whole process of this so called Participatory Democracy will be on computers' terms. Thus the process will be reduced to pushing buttons and to punching numbers. Is this a Participatory Democracy in action? When you never will be able to say to other human beings what you feel, and how you think? In short, to have a genuine democracy you have to have wisdom in order to vote wisely, and you have to have wise people to vote for. Otherwise, Participatory Democracy via computers is another game of appearances.

I have said earlier that unless you exercise your responsibility you cannot genuinely exercise your freedom. Let us look at the concept of responsibility in the context of the Information Society, and see whether the Information Society is likely to enhance our responsibility, or on the contrary, muffle it.

Responsibility is one of the most peculiar concepts of our language, and of our moral universe. It is very hard to define; even harder to live without. There is no logical necessity, or even natural necessity, to assume responsibility. Yet we render ourselves less than human when we do not assume it. Responsibility is one of those invisible human forces—like will power—for which there is no logical or natural necessity, but without which human history is inconceivable.

In the consumption society we want to escape from responsibility assuming that without it our lives will be easier and better; whereas in fact our lives become shallower and cheaper. Like faith, responsibility enhances the variety of our existence—when we possess it, or diminishes us when we lack it. What blood is to the body, responsibility is to the spirit.

To be a human being is to live in the state of responsibility. When we are unable to be responsible, or voluntarily give up our responsibility, we are, in a sense, annihilating our status as human beings. . . . You can now clearly see what my arguments are aiming at: to show that insofar as the Information Society (or at least computers) take over and deprive us of responsibility, they dwarf our status as human beings. It is a pity, and indeed a blindness of our times, that the proponents of the computerized age never address themselves to this problem.

In retrospect, we can now see that we made a serious mistake some three centuries ago when we decided to make things easy for ourselves. In making things easy for ourselves we have been cheapening our status as human beings. This mistake has not been a technological mistake but a philosophical one. All serious mistakes are either philosophical or religious.

All society worthy of the name 'society' is human society, is society for us, humans, and not for smooth functioning of efficient computers. It may have dawned on some of you that what I am advocating is not so much the Information Society as WISDOM SOCIETY. Our dilemma has been beautifully summarized by T. S. Eliot who said, some 50 years ago:

> WHERE IS THE LIFE WE HAVE LOST IN LIVING,
> WHERE IS THE WISDOM WE HAVE LOST IN KNOWLEDGE,
> WHERE IS THE KNOWLEDGE WE HAVE LOST IN INFORMATION?

We need wisdom in order to be responsible. We need wisdom to manage our information. At present we have a superabundance of information which we are unable to digest. *As a society we are overinformed and underenlightened.* . . .

Wisdom is the possession of the right knowledge but for a given state of the world, for given conditions of society, for given articulation of the human condition. Insofar as the state of the world changes, insofar as the conditions of society change, insofar as the articulation of knowledge goes on, insofar (therefore) as the articulation of the human being proceeds, insofar as the human mind and human sensitivities become refined, we cannot embrace one structure of wisdom for all times, but we must seek a different structure, a different form of balance for each epoch. You cannot be a student of wisdom and acquire wisdom. *Acquiring wisdom is like sculpting the inner man.*

Wisdom is therefore a historical category, not a set of permanent forms but a set of dynamic structures; always to be re-built, re-structured, re-adjusted, re-articulated. Evolutionary wisdom is the understanding how the human condition changes through centuries, millennia, aeons of time. Only such a conception of wisdom can aid the race in its evolutionary journey. . . .

When we arrive at wisdom society, and one day we shall, we will not need the information society, and those endless mountains of information—for wisdom, by its very nature, creatively transforms information into acts of living.

Yet we must be fair. Without computers and all the sophisticated tools that go with the handling of information, we would be paralyzed in our complex world. But would we, really? We should say that business and particularly big business would be paralyzed, not we, as individuals. I would not be paralyzed, and *you* would not be paralyzed. So computers do make a difference. But let us clearly see *to whom,* and why.

The symbiosis of computers with society has not yet occurred. It is too early to envisage what will become of a society in which the computer is integrated into our lives in a *creative* and *life-enhancing* manner. For the time being, if we are honest, we must observe that those slick slogans "Information Society is here" [are] a slick self-advertising talk promulgating [the] self-interests of the information processing industry.

LOSS OF PRIVACY

"BIG BROTHER INC." MAY BE CLOSER THAN YOU THOUGHT

Business Week

Without realizing it, individual Americans leave an electronic trail of transactions that reveals their private affairs to government and commercial investigators. Cross-matching of information from databases has created deep concern about invasion of privacy.

All Rudine Pettus wanted was a place to live. But as the clerk-typist applied for apartment after apartment in the spring of 1981, no one in the Los Angeles area had room. Not until she was well into her search did one rental agent explain why: A dispute with a previous landlord had gotten Pettus on a computerized list of potentially undesirable tenants sold by a company called UD Registry Inc. A California law requires that people be informed if they're on such a list. But Pettus says she "had no idea such a thing existed."

Pettus is a casualty of the information age, and she's not alone. Computerized data bases are proliferating fast. The top five credit-rating companies have records on more than 150 million individuals. About 85 federal data bases contain some 288 million records on 114 million people. And it's not just the volume of information that's frightening. Advances in computer technology are making it easy to do what was impossible not long ago: cross-match information almost at the touch of a button to create portraits of individuals—and even to try to predict their behavior.

"People are leaving an electronic trail of transactions with various institutions—educational, financial, governmental, professional, criminal justice," says Clement Bezold, co-author of a recent study on the subject commissioned by the Information Industry Assn., a trade group. The result could be an invasion of privacy unparalleled in any democratic society.

BOON OR BANE?

No clear legal definition of privacy exists, but experts agree on a few basics: It means the right to keep personal affairs to yourself and to know how information about you is being used. The issue has big implications for information companies. "I think the industry feels that [individuals must sacrifice] a certain amount of privacy in the information age," says Peter A. Marx, an attorney specializing in computer law. The public disagrees. A 1984 Harris Poll found 75% of respondents "very" or "somewhat concerned" about threats to privacy. Says Bezold: "We have to make sure the information revolution is a boon, not a bane."

It's been a boon to Harvey A. Saltz, the president of UD Registry. Every day he sends a squad of employees to dozens of Southern California courts to gather information involving bankruptcies, evictions, property damage, and other landlord-tenant disputes. The workers type information from current cases into portable personal computers, then enter it into Saltz's main computer via phone lines. Saltz combines this information with credit reports he buys from companies such as TRW Inc. The $9 fee that UD Registry charges for the data doesn't include any advice on how to use it. But landlords get the idea.

Pretending that she was from out of state, Pettus says she eventually lined up an apartment from a landlord who didn't check UD's list. But then she got into a dispute at the new place over leaks—and refused to pay rent until they were fixed. After the landlord tried to evict her, they settled out of court with the understanding that the incident would be kept off of the list, says her attorney. But because UD Registry includes landlord-tenant cases regardless of their outcome, it was listed anyway. It took Pettus months to find a new home—where she has lived now for more than three years.

Government data bases form the most cohesive web of information on individuals: Some 15 agencies mix and match data. Ostensibly, they are restrained by the Privacy Act of 1974, which requires the consent of individuals before an agency collects and uses information on them for a different purpose than the information was originally intended. But there's a big loophole: If the agency wants the data for "routine use," little notice is necessary. Privacy experts say that the few perfunctory checks that are made take a back seat to efficiency.

Computer matching started in the late 1970s as part of an effort to reduce welfare fraud, and the Reagan Administration has expanded its use. The Veterans Administration uses it to keep federal employees from receiving excess benefits. The Education Dept. looks for federal employees who are delinquent on student loans. Although exact figures are hard to come by, the number of matches tripled from 1980 to 1984, with more than 2 billion separate records being exchanged during that period, according to the Office of Technology Assessment (OTA). Now a special Presidential committee is looking into how to expand computer matching.

SPENDING HABITS

The 1984 Deficit Reduction Act already has gone a step further. It requires that states set up verification systems to head off cheaters. These computer systems will use Social Security numbers as the key for linking dozens of government data bases.

The most aggressive agency may be the Internal Revenue Service. Its debtor master file, created in 1986, is used to withhold tax refunds owed to borrowers who default on federal loans. So far it lists about 750,000 people who owe money to the Education Dept., the Housing & Urban Development Dept., the VA, and the Small Business Administration, according to the OTA. The IRS even experimented briefly with buying lists from direct-mail companies—to find out if the spending habits of targeted individuals jibed with their reported income.

That test was dropped. But the upshot of such federal and state projects, says Priscilla M. Regan, an analyst with the OTA, is that the U.S. "is starting to move toward a national data base." A damning report, released last summer by the office, said: "The opportunities for inappropriate, unauthorized, or illegal access to and use of personal information have been expanded."

This leads to big problems. As anyone who has run afoul of a computer knows, incorrect information is hard to fix. Raulinea Howard learned the hard way. In 1982 a Massachusetts computer match uncovered $11,000 in a bank account that she supposedly hadn't reported to welfare officials. Howard insisted that the account wasn't hers, but the department threatened to cut off her aid anyway. Eventually, she traced the account to a woman with a similar Social Security number. Howard was one of many cases inaccurately uncovered by a state program to match welfare lists with state bank records. "The process had glitches," concedes Joseph V. Gallant, associate director of the state's Public Welfare Dept. "But we've ironed them out."

Whether computer matching is worth the trouble is hard to tell. Joseph R. Wright Jr., deputy director of the Office of Management & Budget, says it has saved money, although he doesn't have figures. And the IRS says that in 1985 it recovered $2.5 billion in taxes that would have gone uncollected. But the OTA study and another by the General Accounting Office argue that few agencies have adequately calculated the cost-effectiveness of computer matching.

Of course, government data bases are only half the story: Lots of private companies sell information about individuals. For example, Chicago-based Docket-Search Network Inc. sells a service called Physician's Alert. It consists of information on patients who have filed civil suits; its clients tend to be doctors in high-risk specialties, such as obstetrics and orthopedics. Like most suppliers of data, President Michael G. Eckstein claims that his product does nothing to threaten individual privacy per se. "We are in the information business," he says. "We do not instruct our clients on how to use the data."

Probably the most ubiquitous sellers of private information are credit-reporting companies. Unlike most data base suppliers, these companies, which gather a wide range of information from department stores, banks, and finance companies, are regulated under the Fair Credit Reporting Act of 1970. The act says that all negative records have to be purged after seven years. But companies don't have to let people know when they've been added to a data bank or whether they're being investigated.

That's noteworthy because credit bureaus are expanding their businesses. The federal government uses them to verify applications for loans. And some credit companies sell data for checking out the backgrounds of potential employees. TRW says that while it doesn't do this, it is feeling market pressure to start. With no laws governing the use of this information, job applicants are at the mercy of prospective employers who don't bother to take more than a thumbs-up-or-down reading. "Some customers are very harsh," says one credit bureau executive. "But it's their money. They can do what they want."

TASTE TEST

Few people know this as well as Joseph Miller. In the spring of 1985, Miller, now 26, quit his job at a large retail store in New York to look for a better position. He remained unemployed for months as several potential jobs fell through. Then, in September, he received a notice of his dishonorable discharge from the Army—an odd occurrence, since he'd never been in the service. The truth was out: A former college roommate was using his name. "I realized that my Social Security number was stored in I don't know how many data bases across the country," recalls Miller. "He had jail records, bad credit—all under my name." Unable to persuade credit agencies to change his records, he has applied for a new Social Security number and driver's license.

Most people will never face such problems, of course, but they may be affected in more subtle ways—by experts who use data bases as marketing tools. Dataman Information Services in Atlanta, for example, provides basic data. It compiles real estate and mortgage information from courthouse records in 48 states and sells it to companies as diverse as Citicorp and Neiman-Marcus. It also compiles phone numbers of homeowners for telemarketers. A subsidiary of Metromail Corp., a big direct-mail company, it has access to Metromail data as well. Says William Flaherty, Dataman's chief executive officer: "If you gave me your name and address, I could match that name with Metromail's files and probably tell you how old you are, how many children you have, and how old your house is."

Other market researchers are more sophisticated. They buy census data, which divide the country into 250,000 neighborhoods of about 250 households. Using these figures as a foundation, the marketing companies break the country into 40 or so socioeconomic groups. Combining this with up to 100 other data bases, they guess at an individual's tastes. For example, National Decision Systems in Encinitas, Calif., has determined that an individual who falls into a category dubbed "high-tech frontier" will be five times as likely to buy a Japanese car as one not in the group.

WATCHDOGS

For now, few laws govern the use of data bases. An effort to enact a medical records privacy act, similar to the Fair Credit Reporting Act, failed several years ago. And few states regulate the quality and accuracy of data bases. One bill, just reintroduced in the Senate by Senator William S. Cohen (R-Me.), would set up official boards to oversee computer matching of federal data bases.

Cohen's approach is modeled after those used by countries such as Sweden, West Germany, and France. Most European countries have some form of legislation regulating the use of government data bases—and sometimes private ones. In France, for example, a watchdog commission created in 1979 oversees government, private, and university use of electronic information. It regularly steps in when it thinks cross-matching is getting out of hand. The commission has even required that mail-order companies inform consumers when their names are transferred from one computerized list to another.

Without regulation in the U.S., say proponents of the Cohen bill, privacy may become more threatened as technology advances. A new technique called computer profiling is a case in point. It combines sophisticated software with data bases to create profiles of people who are likely to exhibit certain characteristics. The Secret Service, for one, is reported by privacy analysts to be developing a system to help identify people with the tendencies of assassins. Says one privacy observer: "If [these data bases] are ever all connected, it will be Big Brother Inc."

TELEVISION AND HOME LIFE

THE ACID RAIN OF TV IMAGES

Harry Henderson

The writer analyzes a report on television funded by the National Institute of Health, in which he finds evidence that televised violence has a negative influence on society. Juvenile viewers in particular may become aggressive and disobedient. This article was published in *Sexual Medicine Today* in 1982.

No one would ever guess from media reports of the landmark study, *Television and Behavior: Ten Years of Scientific Progress and Implications for the Eighties,* that physicians were significant in focusing attention on this troubling aspect of American life. Or that this report has value for physicians who are concerned with the healthy development of children, and the impact of countless commercials pushing sugary, fatty, nonnutritious food.

The acid rain of TV images pollutes healthy attitudes towards food, alcohol, and sex, and it promotes violence as the American way of solving problems, and even of having a good time. The *Dukes of Hazzard* (a very popular CBS show) insists recklessly smashing cars is really living.

The NIMH study covered *all* behavior, including snacking, alcohol use, sexual roles, and TV doctors—although these aspects were less widely publicized than the information on television violence. Of the 2,500 studies on which the NIMH report was based, "the great majority . . . demonstrate a positive relationship between televised violence and later aggressive behavior" and show that girls as well as boys are so influenced. Moreover, "the viewer learns more than aggressive behavior from televised violence. The viewer learns to be a victim and to identify with victims. As a result, many heavy viewers may exhibit fear and apprehension, while other heavy viewers may be influenced toward aggressive behavior. Thus, the effects of televised violence may be even more extensive than suggested by earlier studies . . . and exhibited in more subtle forms of behavior than aggression." The report leaves no doubt that, while not all children watching TV heavily will develop aggressive behavior, many may come "to accept violence as normal behavior."

The NIMH study confirms the fears expressed in the 1972 Surgeon General's Report on TV Violence and a 1975 AMA resolution that TV violence has an "imprinting" function that may lead to society's acceptance of violence. "Banging Daffy Duck on the head is *fun!* Hit him again!" This is how the conditioning of children to violence is begun. The Saturday cartoon programs are among the most violent broadcasts.

However, the 1982 NIMH study, which was set up by Julius B. Richmond, M.D., former Assistant Secretary of HEW, is not limited to violence; Beatrix A. Hamburg, M.D., and Chester Pierce, M.D., both of Harvard, were advisors to the study along with communication, education, and other behavioral scientists.

About 50 different TV families are presented weekly—and real family life is definitely influenced by them, first by bringing the real family together at the set. With TV on, conversation fades and interaction ceases, with each family member "iso-

Source: From *Sexual Medicine Today,* September 1982. Reprinted by permission.

lated" in his or her attention. Who decides what to watch? In general, male wins out over female, father over mother and children. But "in a surprisingly large number of instances," parents defer to children, "who often have emerged as arbitrators of what the family will view; they have become family decisionmakers."

MEN STRONG, WOMEN PASSIVE

Sexual roles—that is, how to behave as a man or woman—are rather sharply defined on TV. "The men are mostly physically strong and virile, the women usually passive and feminine, with the women being even more stereotyped than the males." However, "lately there has been more sexual reference, more innuendo, and more seductive actions and dress." The NIMH report also says: "Both parents and behavioral scientists consider television to be an important sex educator not only in depictions specifically related to sex, but in the relationships between men and women throughout all programs."

Watching how TV families solve problems and communicate appears, in some instances, to help real families solve their problems. A show on rebelling teenagers may, for example, reveal how they feel belittled by parental overconcern. Yet there is very little research in this area. One major study of 600 urban fourth, sixth, and eighth graders revealed that *The Waltons* and other idealized family shows led to a belief among the school children that real life families are cooperative and helpful. Shows with broken families and/or with teenagers in them led to the belief that families are antagonistic, verbally aggressive, and punitive.

The research shows that families spend about half their waking hours at home watching TV.

INACCURATE, MISLEADING, OR BOTH

For physicians, some of the most interesting sections of the NIMH report deal with television as a dispenser of health nonsense. In one Detroit study, health-related topics appeared in 7.2% of the total broadcast time in one week, but "only 30% of the health information was rated useful," the remainder being considered "inaccurate, misleading, or both." Messages urging the use of pills and other remedies appeared ten times more often than messages on drug use and abuse. Some of the brief public service messages rated as informative and useful concerned heart disease, smoking, and crisis centers. However, information on most major health problems, such as cancer, stroke, accidents, hepatitis, maternal death, hunger and malnutrition, VD, mental health, sex education, child care, lead poisoning, and family planning, were virtually nonexistent.

Obesity on TV is rarely seen and has a racial character, with 16% of the black characters and 80% of the Asian-American characters portrayed as obese, "which is not realistic," says the study.

Alcohol consumption, shown or mentioned in 80% of prime time programs in 1975 and in 12 of 15 most popular programs in 1980, "rarely results in strained relationships, harm to self or others, hangovers, loss of jobs, or embarrassment. Mostly, drinking is happy, sociable, and fun without indications of possible risks."

Yet the entertainment programs are not wholly ignorant of health hazards. Smoking is no longer common. A recent study found only 11 instances of smoking in 40 hours of top-rated shows.

The NIMH study reports daytime soap operas contain so much health-related material that they require special additional research. Half of their characters are involved in health-related problems—psychiatric disorders, heart attacks, pregnancies, automobile accidents, attempted homicides and suicides, and infectious diseases in that order. "Much of the talk" on these programs "is in the form of medical advice."

61% OF DOCTORS ON HOUSE CALLS

Doctors and nurses are among the most frequently encountered professionals on TV; only law enforcement types outnumber them. A prime time viewer sees about 12 doctors and six nurses a week. The doctors are "good characters, successful, peaceful, fair, sociable, and warm . . . and more personable and smarter than nurses." The study points out that doctors "symbolize power and dominance. They give orders and rarely receive them. They are also ethical, kind, and willing to take risks to help patients." One study noted 61% of the doctor's work is done on house calls or in the field.

Young children who are heavy viewers see real doctors as similar to those on TV. Heavy viewers among adults, and particularly those who follow the "doctor shows," also have more confidence in doctors than do light viewers.

Yet almost no research is concerned with TV's influence on health—although TV is demonstrably a major source of health information. In one study, 31% of the respondents named "TV programs" as the source of their health information; only doctors and dentists outranked programs. In one study of 600 teenagers in two midwestern cities, 24% of the relevant information on family planning they had came from TV, far more than from any other source, and 45% recalled at least one specific family planning message.

Important sections of the NIMH report deal with research into cognitive and emotional functioning in TV viewing. For example, the signaling of content changes by camera cuts, music, and rhythm changes are used to reinforce attention and emotional arousal. An understanding of this is important because people use TV both to "unwind" and for stimulation. Sports usually elevates arousal levels; comedy may soothe, although genuinely hilarious comedy can be highly arousing. "The one kind of content that consistently produced the highest arousal in both men and women is explicit erotica"; nature films actually lower arousal.

By stimulating residual feelings in the viewer, excitation can be transferred from the TV screen to real life. To quote again, "Aggressive behavior has been shown to be the result of, or at least correlated with, violent scenes on TV. These effects conceivably could be the result of arousal or excitatory features of the violent scenes rather than the violence as such." In one investigation, adult males were first provoked, then after seeing a neutral, an aggressive, or an erotic film, they had the opportunity to retaliate against the person who provoked them. As predicted, "The erotic film—the most arousing—produced the most retaliation."

Yet arousal of residual feelings does not necessarily lead to antisocial, hostile, or aggressive acts. Positive behavior is just as likely to occur. After the TV character "Fonzie" in 1980 *Happy Days* episodes took out a library card, the attendance in libraries of 8- to 14-year-olds reportedly increased by 500%.

BEHAVIOR IS CHANGED

The programs children see on TV "change their behavior. If they look at violent or aggressive programs, they tend to become aggressive and disobedient. But if they look at prosocial programs, they will more likely become more generous, friendly, and self-controlled. TV can have beneficial effects; it is a potential force for good," says the NIMH report.

The NIMH report is weak in assessing violence in American life. This is a far more violent country than anyone wants to admit. A comparison of handgun deaths in 1979 shows 48 deaths in Japan, eight in Britain, 52 in Canada, and 10,728 in the United States. In short, it can be argued that American television reflects American violence.

Films made for the box-office and rerun on TV are the leaders in dramatizing violence and sex, the NIMH report points out. But in made-for-TV movies as well, habituation develops—tolerance in pharmacological terms—with strong reactions to violence growing weaker, even vanishing with repeated exposures. "More important," notes the report, "is its potential impact on real life behavior. If people become inured to violence from seeing much of it, they may be less likely to respond to real violence by, for example, helping the victims."

The evening hours after 9 P.M. contain more

violence than other hours, but "over the last ten years there has been more violence on children's weekend programs than on prime-time television. . . . Television remains a form of violent entertainment." So we killed 10,728 people last year with handguns. As physicians know, infectious bacteria grow in a culture that nourishes [them]. We have a violent culture.

"Parents worry about the amount of violence and sex on TV, but not on the amount of time [children] watch," asserts the NIMH report. Its analysis indicates parents underestimate the amount of violence seen and "may not recognize how much children respond to TV content, with the children perceiving more violence than the mothers and the mothers underreporting how frightened their children are after watching scary programs."

In actual fact, parents exert little control over TV viewing; for high schoolers "there is essentially no guidance."

Although TV families help to shape family attitudes, particularly how parents interact with their children, little research concerns the actual content of these TV "messages" or the influence of siblings and peers on what is watched. Unfortunately, notes the NIMH study, research has too often focused on the parental control of viewing instead of asking under what conditions there is an effect and what the effect is. Parental comments on shows watched with children (70%) appear to be limited to "Real life is less simple than TV" or "There are better ways to solve problems than violence."

About half the adult audience consider some TV programs unsuitable for children, especially those with violence. There is also concern about vulgar and profane language, sexual behavior, alcohol consumption, smoking, lying, and the exploitation of children in commercials.

The major hope expressed by the NIMH report is that schools will develop ways to teach children "how to watch and understand television. Much as they are taught to appreciate literature, to read newspapers carefully, . . . they need to be prepared to understand TV as they view it in their homes. The field of critical TV viewing is essentially in its infancy, but it reflects the general trend toward setting the medium of TV in its place as part of the overall system of cognitive and emotional development."

Physicians have much to contribute to the use of TV to convey accurate messages about health and emotional well-being and have already established their concern. Awareness of the influence of TV is simply the beginning.

AT HOME WITH THE VIDEO REVOLUTION

Rushworth M. Kidder

Every evening American families watching television see a world of prime time strikingly at odds with reality. How much does this exposure affect their behavior and thinking? Rushworth M. Kidder, writing in the *Christian Science Monitor,* reports the findings of researchers in communication.

For Joan, it's a typical spring Thursday in this mid-American suburb. Coming home from work about 4:45 P.M. with her fourth-grader son, Josh, she lets the dog out and sets down her groceries. Josh crosses the living room, flicks on the TV, and settles down to a robot cartoon.

It's the beginning of what will become, that evening, nearly a seven-hour stretch for the family television set. Not that it will always be watched—nor, even when watched, will it always be watched attentively. But, like 95 million other Americans this evening, she and her family will be an active part of the nation's video culture—a culture which, in 1984, found an estimated 193 million television sets in use in American homes.

Her husband, Mark, will watch part of the local news at 5:30, interrupting it to chat with their high-school-age daughter, Elaine, when she arrives

Source: Reprinted by permission from the *Christian Science Monitor,* June 14, 1985.

home. Their dinner, beginning with a rerun of "All in the Family," will end during the network news. For the next hour they will be in and out of the room, leaving the set tuned to a magazine program with segments on African wildlife, inner-city auto theft, and a punk fashion-designer-turned-author.

They'll gather again at 8 P.M. for an animated discussion about whether to watch "The Bill Cosby Show" (Elaine's vote), "Magnum, P.I." (Josh's favorite), or a movie Joan saw advertised the night before. As a compromise, they'll switch among the channels during the commercials, picking up bits of each show.

The evening passes; phone calls come and go; Joan sends Josh off to bed, and leaves for 20 minutes to tuck him in; Mark opens his briefcase and pays some bills. Elaine, her homework finished, comes back for a few innings of baseball. She heads for bed as "Hill Street Blues" begins—during which, in and around the action, Mark and Joan finally tell each other about their respective days. As Joan gets ready for bed, Mark gets caught up in a half-hour PBS business show, finally switching off the set at 11:45, midway through "Nightline."

According to the statistics, it's an average evening. But what does it tell us about the impact of television on American society?

Is this family subject to what Jerry Mander, in "Four Arguments for the Elimination of Television," calls the "artificial unusualness" of a medium that has "mesmerized" them?

Are they the "lowest common denominator" of American taste, in the grip of what Todd Gitlin, in "Inside Prime Time," describes as a "trashiness" in programming so debased that "mediocrity would be too kind a word"?

Or are they, as Tony Schwartz suggests in "Media: The Second God," beginning to "use the media in the interests of man" by benefiting from broad new channels of information and a breadth of contact with the world never before available?

And are they practicing what SRI researchers describe as "visiospatial processing"—the capacity for "simultaneously filtering and processing vast amounts of data in a wide variety of forms,"

In the evenings the television set becomes the focal point of family life. Selection of programs to watch influences attitudes of individuals and those of the group as a whole.

markedly different from the "serial processing" needed for absorbing information through print?

One thing is certain: this family is engaging in a form of behavior that 50 years ago was unthinkable. Even 25 years ago, when Mark and Joan were growing up, it was different: Then, the TV had a place of honor, and the family gathered quietly in front of it to watch carefully pre-selected programs.

What are we to make of this change?

One way to understand the change is to see it in its historical context—as the latest development in a train of centuries-old changes in man's patterns of communicating.

The change from an oral to a written language, and then from writing to print and from print to broadcast, may appear to be fairly neutral developments. After all, the important thing is the message, not the delivery system, right?

Wrong, say a number of scholars working in the field of communication theory. To them, changing the means of delivery changes the nature of the messages themselves.

It's a point made popular, if not perfectly understandable, by Marshall McLuhan's famous observation that "the medium is the message." McLuhan's speculations in "Understanding Media," published in 1964, encouraged a new generation of scholars to examine the ways that a particular medium (speech, books, newspapers, the telegraph, the radio, movies, television) shapes the kinds of messages it delivers.

Since then, media theorists have tended to agree on two points: that Gutenberg's 15th-century development of the printing press ushered in the world's first major communications revolution; and that, with the appearance of television, we are in the midst of the second great revolution.

How significant is this movement from an oral culture to a print culture and, finally, to a video culture? Hugely so, say many scholars, who trace the development as follows:

Oral Cultures

Before Gutenberg, the primary means of communication was speech—which, by its very nature, demands certain conditions. It requires an audience (even if only one other person) gathered into the same place and time as the speaker. It demands reserves of memory in both speakers and hearers. And it suggests a sense of participation in an activity, an event.

"Without writing, words as such have no visual presence," writes Walter J. Ong in "Orality and Literacy." "They are occurrences, events." Sound, he notes, "exists only when it is going out of existence."

Most messages in a pre-print culture, then, are shaped by the requirements of a medium that provides no permanence except in memory. So the messages naturally come to depend on verbal formulas and mnemonic devices. They are highly redundant, even repetitive. They are often weighted with clichés. Moreover, they are not usually shaped into long, subtle, analytical arguments with many subordinate points: The memory simply can't organize that kind of information very well.

Print Culture

With the spread of printing comes an entirely different set of demands on the message. No longer does an audience need to gather at one place and time: Reading is a solitary, quiet occupation that can happen miles away and years apart from the writer. No longer is formulaic speech so all-important: Extended logical analysis is finally possible.

The result, paradoxically, is a medium of communication both broader and more restrictive than speech. "The complex, step-by-step nature of print," writes Joshua Meyrowitz in his recently published "No Sense of Place: The Impact of Electronic Media on Social Behavior," "allows for the development of extended and connected descriptions and analyses." But, he adds, it also "tends to create sharp divisions between those who have access to a given information-system and those who are restricted from it."

That "access" is literacy. It is achievable only through the intricate, time-consuming process of learning to read—a process that absorbs much of the energy of childhood education. But in an oral culture, there is no distinction of literate from illiterate—and therefore, as Meyrowitz observes, little to distinguish childhood from adulthood. What adults know, he says, children also know.

Meyrowitz even argues that childhood itself—as a distinct period between infancy and adulthood, in which the child is excluded from the "privacy" of the adult world—is an invention of the print culture. That theme is argued in detail by New York University professor Neil Postman. "A child evolves toward adulthood," writes Postman in "The Disappearance of Childhood," "by acquiring the sort of intellect we expect of a good reader: a vigorous sense of individuality, the capacity to think logically and sequentially, the capacity to distance oneself from symbols, the capacity to manipulate high orders of abstraction, the capacity to defer gratification.

"And, of course, the capacity for extraordinary feats of self-control."

Video Culture

Until the development of television, the electric and electronic media were still word-centered. With television came a wholly new development: The use of the moving image for mass communication. And with that development, as many scholars have noted, came a return to some of the conditions of the oral culture.

Once again, messages were "events" to be absorbed in a group (if only in a living room), rather than concepts to be pondered in silence. Once more, the successful message involved redundancy and formula. Once more, the extended rational argument proved ill-suited to the medium.

Critics of television go a step further. The very qualities that (they say) the video culture tends to destroy—individuality, logical and sequential thought, abstract conceptualizing, deferral of gratification, and self-control—are the very ones Postman attributes largely to a print-oriented education. Postman, in fact, speaks of contemporary society as the "childless age," in which children behave essentially as "miniature adults"—a shift in behavior which he lays at television's door. Meyrowitz notes two other distinctions that have broken down under the impact of video: that between male and female (since women, seeing the man's world in great detail, can no longer so readily be segregated within the home), and that between leaders and followers (since the camera shows us the humanness and the flaws of leaders once placed on pedestals).

How does all this relate to our mid-American family? In nearly every way imaginable.

If young Josh is like 40 percent of his fellow fourth-graders, he watches (according to a recent report from the National Assessment of Educational Progress) five hours or more of television a day. Time spent watching television, note many educators, is time spent not doing something else—for example, practicing reading. By his eighth grade year, he'll come face to face with another fact: Students who watch less than two hours of TV a day read better than those who watch more.

If Elaine is like her friends, she will have logged 16,000 hours of television upon graduation from high school—more time than she will have spent in classes. She will have seen something approaching 500,000 commercials. Her own tastes in music, clothes, habits of behavior, and forms of speech may not have been shaped directly by television—she may have too much built-in skepticism and "sales resistance." But the tastes of her peers will have been influenced—and they, in turn, will contribute largely to shaping her tastes.

If Joan and Mark are like many viewers of television, they may find that, whether they like it or not, they are accepting a certain "heavy viewer" view of the world. Studies by George Gerbner, dean of the Annenberg School of Communications at the University of Pennsylvania, suggest that those who watch more than four hours of television a day begin to fall into the "mean world" trap: They tend to view the world as a "meaner" and more unpleasant place than those who watch less.

Furthermore, despite their ideological and polit-

THE "TAFFIES" JOIN THE "YUPPIES"

Market researchers, who refer to young, upward-bound professionals as "Yuppies," have identified another segment of contemporary American society by the initials TAF, nicknamed "Taffies," for "technically advanced families."

These families possess numerous electronic media instruments in their homes, and their style of living is heavily influenced by use of these instruments.

William R. Oates of the University of Miami, Shailendra Ghorpade of Shearson Lehman Hutton, and Jane D. Brown of the University of North Carolina presented a study of Taffies to the Association for Education in Journalism and Mass Communication convention in 1986. The three researchers offered this stereotype of a TAF family:

> Virtually by definition, Taffies have a home computer, a videocassette recorder, and a source of diversity in television programming either by means of cable or a satellite dish. Taffies are in a higher income and higher education group more often living in an urban setting. They are more likely to be married and to have school-age children. More Taffies take vacations and drink alcoholic beverages than do others.
>
> Taffies seem more willing to exert some effort to obtain and use information sources; besides operating their media technology at home, they go to the library and read news magazines more than others.
>
> Fewer Taffies listen to rock music, on the other hand, while they read newspapers and watch TV news the same as the rest of the population. They also go to church and vote in elections about as frequently as everyone else. Minorities have their share of Taffies; race is not a factor associated with being a technically advanced family.
>
> Among all families, having a home computer is associated with having school-age children. Computers seem to give children new opportunities, and VCRs seem to be used often for entertaining children. These technologies in the home may be the solution some parents have been seeking to the dilemma of inadequate, inappropriate and insufficient programming for children.

ical backgrounds, the attitudes of heavy viewers typically seem to have more in common with the attitudes of other heavy viewers than with the views of whatever party they come from.

Mark and Joan may pride themselves on their individuality. But they are more a part of the ebbs and flows of mass culture than they realize.

Why? What are Mark and Joan seeing in all those hours of television viewing?

"There's a stable cast of about 300 people that the average viewer sees" each week, says Gerbner. "Of these 300 people there are 44 in law enforcement; 12 doctors; about 23 criminals; 6 lawyers; 3 judges. . . . Stars and series come and go, but this cast becomes very stable."

What he calls "the world of prime time" is strikingly at odds with reality. The studies he has conducted over the last 15 years with his Cultural Indicators Group (Larry Gross, Michael Morgan, and Nancy Signorielli), bolstered by other scholars' studies of television content, add up to a curious picture of the world. In that TV world, Gerbner and other researchers have found that:

- Men outnumber women at least 3 to 1.
- On the TV screen there are significantly smaller proportions of young people, old people, blacks, Hispanics, and other minorities than in the U.S. population at large.
- While blue-collar or service work occupies 67 percent of the American work force, it engages only 10 percent of television's characters—since, after all, 70 percent of television's characters are middle class.
- Crime is at least 10 times as prevalent on TV as in the real world (there are an average of five violent acts per prime-time hour), but 90 percent of the crimes are solved.

Meanwhile, prime-time programming has peculiar views of certain groups. Arabs, it seems, are among television's favorite "baddies," while doctors, says Ms. Signorielli, are "the true gods on television [who] can do very little wrong."

Prime time also shows, year by year, an escalating use of innuendo concerning sexual relations—although homosexuality is still largely avoided. As for drinking, a 1983 study published in the *Journal of Drug Education* found that prime time's preferred drink was alcohol, that the incidence of drinking on TV was increasing, that it was generally glamorized, and that heavy drinking was rarely shown to have any detrimental consequences.

Even driving habits pass through a curious warp in prime time. A 1983 study in the *Journal of Communication* found substantial amounts of "irregular driving"—squealing brakes, speeding, screeching tires, and property damage. Death and physical injury were infrequent, however, and legal penalties rare.

As with all research, there are, of course, dissenting views.

"In many ways, we're not so different from those people who put together the Gutenberg Bible," says Syracuse University scholar George Comstock, whose massive "Television and Human Behavior" is one of the most widely cited books in the field.

He admits that television introduced an effect similar to that of the printing press, but on "a slightly lesser scale." What creates changes, he says, is not so much the technology as "human consciousness."

From his office at Massachusetts Institute of Technology, media researcher W. Russell Neuman agrees. Describing himself as part of the "minimal effects school," he says that "the mass media generally don't seem to make much of a difference" in social patterns.

In the scholarly community, he says, "Nobody's looking at a big enough piece" to be able to make broad, sweeping comments about television's effects. Every study of negative effects, he says, can be countered with studies showing something else.

On one point, however, there is widespread concern: the question of whether violence on television promotes violence in society. Professor Comstock, who has followed the research for years, concludes, "I think there's no doubt that the evidence indicates that media violence facilitates or encourages aggressiveness and anti-social behavior in real life."

"Television has never caused a murder," he adds, "but it may have precipitated a particular kind of murder by suggesting how one could be committed."

Mark and Joan are not about to commit murder. But they may be worried about what many Americans see as an increasing thirst for the sensational on television—including violence.

Should violence, they ask themselves, be regulated on entertainment programming? If so, should it also be regulated on news shows? How different are the effects of news and entertainment? What impact does television news have on the political process?

IN CONCLUSION

YESTERDAY, TODAY, AND TOMORROW

Phillip H. Ault

Maincurrents in Mass Communications has provided a wide-ranging examination of what is happening in the mass media. Articles by knowledgeable commentators from the professional media and academic fields have explored problems and clarified issues. This closing commentary identifies important themes that run through the book.

During a tour of a restored nineteenth-century home on the West Coast recently, two women were admiring the intricate patterns of a patchwork quilt sewn by a farm wife in the 1870s. One expressed surprise that anyone could have found enough time to do such tedious work.

"Of course, they didn't have television then," the other observed.

A puzzled look of surprise, almost disbelief, crossed the face of a 9-year-old girl standing nearby. "They didn't have *television*?" she exclaimed.

Such an abysmal gap in daily life is indeed almost incomprehensible to two generations of Americans. No radio existed, either, when that farm woman stitched her quilt. Or movies. Or telephone. Or harnessed electric current that eventually made them possible.

Perhaps the best way to comprehend the role of the mass media today is to visualize as best we can what life's daily round would be like if we didn't have them. What automatically accepted parts of our day would disappear? There would be no football games or soap operas on TV. No television or radio newscasts. No Grateful Dead tapes, no videotaped horror movies to play in the darkened living room at night, no Top Forty rock songs on the car radio.

Little of what we call mass communications existed for our forebears. Of the media we know today, only the printed forms—newspapers, magazines, and books—were in existence 100 years ago. For "fast" communication, people had only the Morse telegraph, transmitting dot-and-dash messages at 30 words a minute. Twelve hundred words a minute by satellite across the country from computer to computer, as is commonplace today? Inconceivable! Even the frenzied imagination of Jules Verne, whose concept of a man going around the world in 80 days drew condescending chuckles, could not conjure up such a vision. Ordinary people rarely received a telegram; in fact, they cringed inwardly at the sight of a Western Union delivery boy at the door because so often he carried a notice of a death in the family.

No wonder women had time to make quilts!

Newspapers were small, and their distribution was slow because transportation away from the railroads moved at a horse's pace. People made their own entertainment at home or went to theaters to see traveling theatrical troupes and, later, silent movies. News reached them only through newspapers; newsboys hawked "extras" on the street when a big story broke. Presidential candidates spoke to voters from the rear platforms of "whistle-stop" campaign trains and rubbed shoulders with them at torchlight processions.

Residents in remote areas of the country were isolated to a degree difficult for us to comprehend.

Barely 75 years ago, mass communication still had a minimal impact on the nation. Social customs and attitudes shifted slowly through word of mouth. The pace of change began to accelerate when radio developed in the 1920s, but not until 1950, when television began to flourish, did the age of mass communication really begin.

FORWARD AGAIN TO TODAY

Now let's put back into our lives all the manifestations of mass communications we arbitrarily pulled out a few paragraphs ago. It becomes obvious immediately how much our existence is filled with, and influenced by, what we see and hear in the media.

In our eyes, our great-grandparents were handicapped by the shortage of information and entertainment, although they may not have realized their lack. We, on the contrary, are overwhelmed with messages in the forms of news, entertainment, interpretation, and advertising. Our need is not to obtain a greater supply of these things but to know how to use what we have. Almost benumbed by the abundance, we resemble a child who loses interest in opening packages of Christmas toys because the stack of gifts is too big.

This abundance has brought us enormous benefits, of course, but simultaneously has created problems our forebears didn't worry about. Three of these are equal availability, selectivity, and passivity.

Equal Availability of Information

The world's astounding supply of information and entertainment is useful to individuals only to the extent that it is available to them.

In an earlier era, virtually everyone could afford the penny or two a newspaper cost. Today, personal reception of such material frequently requires possession of expensive electronic gear: TV sets, videocassette recorders, personal computers, compact disc players. As a selection in Part Six points out, the term *Taffies* is used to describe "technically advanced families" that possess these and other instruments. The term also implies "affluent families."

But what about the non-Taffies, those who can't afford such purchases? True, 98 percent of American homes have television sets; only about half of the sets receive cable TV programs, however, and the percentage of videocassette recorders is about the same. Thus millions of Americans do not have direct access to much valuable material.

A child in a home equipped with a personal computer with a modem attachment can call up enormous amounts of material for school assignments from databases. A child without such access cannot. How much inequality of opportunity does this create in their education?

Selectivity

Consumers of mass communications material, which means all of us, should use care in selecting what they see and hear. We can read and watch only an infinitesimal portion of what is available to us, and we have only so much time in which to do so.

Customers in a supermarket encounter an enticing cornucopia of merchandise, brightly packaged and skillfully positioned to coax impulse buying. Some shoppers wander the aisles indecisively, picking up and putting down items and buying things they don't need. Those who know what they want and shop from a list, with perhaps slight leeway for add-on impulse items, save time and money.

The supermarket analogy can be applied to the mass communications output that flows over and around us constantly. We need to recognize that some of those who produce the material are trying to manipulate us and that others are offering products on which we would only be wasting time. We must focus our information and entertainment shopping on what seems most likely to satisfy our needs. The nightly decisions on which television shows to watch are an obvious example of this process.

Passivity

The products of mass communications often reach us in such easily swallowed, small-bite form that our minds slip into neutral and merely idle while the material inundates us. The average American family has its television set running 7 hours a day, according to an A. C. Nielsen survey. That much television makes the eyes glaze; the good and the bad, the excellent programs and the trash, melt together into a meaningless glob.

Sociologists complain that family members don't talk to each other as much as they once did. Some mathematics teachers contend that while computers have opened spectacular new vistas of knowledge, children who depend on them and calculators excessively to solve problems fail to sharpen their own intellectual powers. We must guard against becoming mental couch potatoes.

In a nation endowed with an almost unbounded fund of knowledge, how can hundreds of thousands of adults be functionally illiterate? These include adults who have gone to school for years and in some cases even have high school diplomas—individuals who have been bombarded by media messages since infancy yet cannot read a timetable or pass a simple quiz in basic geography.

A high school principal, trying to explain this distressing situation, grumbled recently, "They say we don't teach the subjects they need. We do! But some students simply don't care. They turn off their minds. They claim there is too much to learn, and they don't need it, anyway."

These are some of the issues with which we must come to grips in learning to live wisely with the mass communications explosion.

A QUICK REVIEW

Maincurrents in Mass Communications illuminated and interpreted contemporary trends in the media. Part One, "The Media's Role in Society," examined how the media influence, and are influenced by, other elements of society. Among the questions raised in it are: Do the media intrude improperly—even indecently—into private lives? Are they too sensational, oblivious to the feelings of people they cover, too arrogant? Conversely, are they too complacent about exposing greed, illegal behavior, and excesses in politics, business, and other segments of life, including religion?

Where is the middle ground between the mob scenes of reporters and photographers badgering an embattled candidate under an umbrella of extended microphones and a lackadaisical failure to protect the public's right and need to know what is happening in situations that involve its well-being?

In Part Two, the text addressed contemporary concerns about establishing an ethical and legal foundation for mass communications. Perhaps the broad primary conclusion to be drawn from the selections is that ethics cannot be easily legislated and codified. The principles of honesty, fairness, and independence of judgment are easily enough stated, but many traps and cross-pressures face the best-intentioned mass communicators in their daily work.

The examination of the technology revolution in Part Three helped us to understand how the marvels of electronic communication made possible the explosion we have been discussing. Unfortunately we become blasé about these advances and take them for granted. It all seems so smooth and easy to the recipient. When we see pictures of a disaster in India on the evening TV news and realize that they have been beamed 22,300 miles into space, bounced off a satellite, and relayed back in seconds to our television screens, we should retain our sense of wonder.

A word of caution is in order here: Electronic communication methods create the possibility of trickery that makes lies look like the truth. Editing of videotape to remove or insert material can create a false report; "hackers" who penetrate computer files can kill important stored information or enter incorrect material; and tinkering with photographs to remove buildings, alter the sky, or change the positions of persons can manipulate the truth.

In Part Four, *Maincurrents* emphasizes an essential point, that mass communications methods are valuable to society only when human communicators use them well. And in Part Five, "Media Trends and Techniques," the contributors examined ways in which communicators use the tools at their disposal.

A LOOK AT TOMORROW

As the world moves into the 1990s, with still more ingenious electronic communication tools coming into use, the people of the United States and other democratic countries find themselves faced with an apparently unavoidable trade-off: The more efficient the machinery of mass communications becomes, with all the benefits it brings them, the less personal privacy they will enjoy.

The chilling article in Part Six, " 'Big Brother Inc.' May Be Closer than You Thought," shows how far electronic record keeping and information exchange have gone in penetrating our personal walls of privacy. Spy satellites have wiped out secrets of nations just as thoroughly. Despite efforts by lawmakers to put limits on this intrusion into personal privacy, the dark side of the information society will almost inevitably become more worrisome.

Ironically, while the information society exposes the private affairs of individuals to greater scrutiny, the mass communications explosion has in another sense caused a growth in social isolation. This trend, too, may increase. People who spend hours at a time watching a television screen receive a broad yet shallow and frequently unrealistic view of the world. Their personal interaction with others, a basic source of mental stimulation and original thinking, is reduced proportionately.

The computer screen creates isolation even more intensely. Individuals who spend their working days in front of a computer keyboard and screen are interacting with an impersonal screen, obeying its rules and commands. This subservience to the machine increases for some persons who do their office work almost exclusively at home, tied to the outer world only by a computer line. Human companionship dwindles. Indeed, the computer screen can become a refuge from interpersonal relationships, a fact that has opened a new field of practice for psychologists.

In the world of tomorrow, when mass communications will pervade our lives even more intensely than they do today, society must seek ways to solve the problem of cost versus benefits in these matters. Fortunately, the new knowledge that the system generates, if applied intelligently, can help us find answers.

QUESTIONS FOR REVIEW AND DISCUSSION

1. List three reasons, in addition to entertainment and information, why people watch television.
2. Discuss what Henryk J. Skolimowski means by his statement that as a society we are overinformed and underenlightened. Can you think of any specific examples?
3. Charles Marshall describes a danger in the use of databases by reporters. What is it?
4. What is computer matching? Name two ways in which the federal government uses it to track individuals.
5. The Fair Credit Reporting Act of 1970 specifies that all negative records about an individual must be purged after a certain number of years. What is that time period?
6. Is the portrayal of doctors in television programs generally favorable or unfavorable? In TV shows, doctors are second in frequency of portrayal to what other professional group?

7. From your own television viewing, do you agree or disagree with a survey finding that on TV "the men are mostly physically strong and virile, the women usually passive and feminine, with the women being even more stereotyped than the males"?
8. What do SRI researchers mean when they say that television viewers are practicing "visiospatial processing"?
9. Name three ways in which programs on prime-time television are at odds with reality. Why do you think this is so?
10. Do you know any Taffies? How did you identify them?

ESSAY TOPICS

1. In describing a typical family's deep involvement in television viewing, Rushworth M. Kidder states that the family is engaged in behavior unthinkable 50 years ago. Discuss the ways in which television has changed family life, for better or worse, and the possible consequences of these changes.
2. The concept of personal privacy is deeply rooted in the American tradition. Yet computer technology in the hands of government and commercial interests is eroding this privacy. Using information from the *Business Week* article on "Big Brother Inc.," write an essay examining the trade-off of increased information for less privacy as it affects you personally and society as a whole.

INDEX

INDEX